Planning and Organizing Instruction

Planning and Organizing Instruction

G. HAROLD SILVIUS
Professor of Vocational and
Applied Arts Education
Wayne State University

RALPH C. BOHN
Dean of Continuing Education and
Professor of Industrial Studies
San Jose State University

McKnight Publishing Company, Bloomington, Illinois

SECOND EDITION

Lithographed in U.S.A.

MCKNIGHT
MCKNIGHT
MCKNIGHT
MCKNIGHT
MCKNIGHT

Copyright © 1976 by McKnight Publishing Company, Bloomington, Illinois

Ronald E. Dale, Vice President-Editorial, wishes to acknowledge the skills and talents of the following people and organizations in the preparation of this publication.

Wesley D. Stephens
President

Donna M. Faull
Production Editor

Linda Hoerner
Production Coordinator

Willemina Knibbe
Production Assistant

Bettye King
Copy Editor

Elizabeth Purcell
Layout Artist

Shirley Brinton
Proofreader

Eldon Stromberg
University Graphics Incorporated
Carbondale, Illinois
Cover Design

M. R. Typography
Bloomington, Illinois
Composition

McLean County Graphics
Preproduction

Illinois Graphics
Preproduction

William McKnight III
Manufacturing

R. R. Donnelley & Sons
Chicago, Illinois
Printing

All rights reserved. No part of this book may be reproduced or utilized in any form or by any means, electronic or mechanical, including photocopying or recording, or by any information storage or retrieval system without permission in writing from the publisher.

Library of Congress
Card Catalog Number: 75-34984

SBN: 87345-720-X

First Edition Copyright 1961

Preface

This volume has been written to serve as a textbook for a collegiate course where the major purpose is the preparation of teachers for **planning and organizing instruction** in VAE (vocational and applied arts education). Within this context, the book is designed to serve as a textbook to prepare or upgrade personnel with competencies for developing curriculum materials for any of the VAE subject areas, including:

- Industrial Arts.
- Trade and Industrial Occupation.
- Health Occupations.
- Distributive Education.
- Office Occupations.
- Home Economics (including the wage-earning occupations).
- Agriculture.

The book is designed also as a major resource for more advanced VAE graduate students as it focuses on such contemporary considerations as these:

- VAE as an integral part of the career education thrust.
- Professional efforts now being directed toward the unification of separate vocational areas into a broad-based approach to VAE education.
- Seven approaches now used to identify content for VAE programs.
- The various approaches for organizing instruction into occupational clusters.
- The application of the systems approach in the development of curriculum for VAE programs.
- The identification and development of modules of instruction to facilitate individualized development, which, in turn, shifts the role of the teacher from **"presenter"** to **"facilitator"** of instruction.
- The use of "simulation" as an evolving method in VAE programs.
- Criterion- vs. norm-referenced evaluation.
- "Accountability."

A third goal of the authors is to provide a handbook that would be useful as teachers, supervisors, and administrators prepare curriculum guides, courses of study, and instructional materials appropriate for the community, learners, and school systems. It is hoped that this volume may be useful as a major resource for staff now working in area vocational schools on the great array of occupational programs in these centers.

Considerable space in this book is devoted to contemporary concepts in curriculum development that should be of interest to administrators and persons giving leadership to overall curriculum efforts. These promising organizational and administrative strategies include:

- Identification and evaluation of each VAE program in terms of its contribution to the total educational effort.
- Personalized educational programs.
- The development and assessment of behavioral objectives for a competency-based program.
- Contractual vocational programs with individuals and agencies in the community.
- Changing the role of the professional teacher and supporting staff in respect to mediated instruction.
- Flexible modular scheduling and differentiated staffing.
- Planning — Programing — Budgeting — Procedures (PPBS).
- Providing for **input, process,** and **product** evaluation.
- Use of national standards for accountability.

The first four chapters, it will be noted, are devoted to strategies and philosophy that underlie VAE programs. The remaining chapters are devoted to procedures and practices employed by VAE curriculum builders in **planning and organizing instruction** for a specific VAE program. The text is followed by several **Appendices of Curriculum Examples,** chosen from a wide variety of VAE subject areas. These examples illustrate applications of curriculum development discussed in Chapters 5 through 12. Each chapter concludes with (1) issues and questions "For Self-Assessment and Discussion," (2) "Assignments to Demonstrate Competencies," and (3) "References and Resources." The section "For Self-Assessment and Discussion" is designed so that it might be used as a pre- or post-test on the content of the chapter. The assignments for each chapter are structured to culminate in written materials needed by teachers for their own teaching situation, as they gradually come to see their complete responsibility for planning and organizing instructional materials.

The American Psychological Association's system of footnoting is used. Publications cited in each chapter are therefore classified as "References." The "Resources" are the other entries in the bibliographies that are recommended for further study. The appendices are followed by a special index of acronyms used in the book. These acronyms are spelled out the first time they are used in the chapter, with the possible exception of VAE, CVTE, and ERIC used extensively throughout the book.

The genesis of this book dates back to a research project reported in 1946[1] that identified the activities of teachers as they prepare

---

[1] G. Harold Silvius, Instructional Units for Professional Courses in Undergraduate Teachers Education, Doctoral Dissertation (University Park: The Pennsylvania State University).

curriculum materials for industrial education. During the past thirty years these activities have been analyzed, enlarged in scope, and refined as they have been field-tested by the authors as they continue their work in curriculum development at Wayne State University and at San Jose State University. The results of this research were made available to industrial education teachers in syllabi published by Wayne State University in 1951, under the titles **Job, Trade or Activity Analysis** and **Course of Study Construction** (revised in 1954). The authors then undertook the development of manuscript for **Organizing Course Materials,** published by the McKnight Publishing Company in 1961. With the move in recent years toward a more unified VAE program, the authors were encouraged in 1972 to revise **Organizing Course Materials** and broaden its application to all of the VAE curriculum areas. Wayne State University granted a sabbatical leave to one of the authors (1972-1973) so that he might give his undivided attention to such an objective. This book then is the result of this motivation and encouragement. **Planning and Organizing Instruction** is essentially a second edition of **Organizing Course Materials in Industrial Education.** Those curriculum practices included in **Organizing Course Materials,** having stood the test of time, are retained in the new edition. They will be found in Chapters 5 through 12 of **Planning and Organizing Instruction.**

G. Harold Silvius
Ralph C. Bohn

Acknowledgments

The authors of this book are obligated to many persons and organizations that have become involved in its development. As sections of the manuscript were written, they were sent to selected VAE leaders for critical review. Persons invited were those who are recognized for their work in an area covered by a chapter. These leaders were: **Leslie H. Cochran**, Associate Dean, School of Fine and Applied Arts, Central Michigan University, Mt. Pleasant; **William A. Hulle**, Associate Professor, Industrial Education Department, Keene State College, Keene, New Hampshire; **David L. Jelden**, Professor, Department of Industrial Arts, University of Northern Colorado, Greeley; **Jacqueline R. Killam**, Industrial Arts and Career Education Teacher, Beverly Hills Unified School District, California; **John P. Novosad**, Associate Professor, Department of Industrial Education and Technology, Central Michigan University, Mt. Pleasant; **Harold S. Resnick**, Director, Planning and Evaluation, Minuteman Regional Technical School District, Lexington, Massachusetts; **Elizabeth J. Simpson**, Dean of the School of Family Resources and Consumer Sciences, University of Wisconsin-Madison; and **David H. Soule**, Director, Division of Vocational Education, Oakland Schools, Pontiac, Michigan.

The following members of the Wayne State University faculty generously reviewed selected major topics as they were being developed and refined for this book: **Willard M. Bateson**, Professor, Teacher Education Division; **John D. Bies**, Assistant Professor, Teacher Education Division; **John W. Childs**, Professor, Educational Leadership Division; **Robert C. Henderhan**, Associate Professor, Educational Leadership Division; **Bette LaChapelle**, Associate Professor, Teacher Education Division (specialist in home and family living); **Frank W. Lanham**, Professor, Teacher Education Division; **Rita C. Richey**, Assistant Professor, Teacher Education Division; and **Chauncey W. Smith**, Assistant Professor, Teacher Education Division (specialist in educational psychology).

The following faculty members of the Industrial Studies Department, San Jose State University, generously reviewed and contributed to selected materials as they were being developed and refined for this book: **Donald J. Betando**, Professor; **Howard S. Decker**, Professor;

Daniel C. Lopez, Professor; Angus J. MacDonald, Professor; Louie Melo, Professor; Ralph P. Norman, Professor; and Roger A. Smith, Assistant Professor.

Interwoven throughout the text are the names of persons, schools, or other agencies that provided photographs or other materials for illustrations. These acknowledgments are included with the captions for the figures.

The following persons generously responded to the author's request for special resource materials and information needed to develop the manuscript: **J. Maurice Ansolabehere**, Coordinator, Research and Educational Planning Center, University of Nevada, Reno; **Fred Baer**, Supervisor of Industrial Education, and **Joe R. Tijerina**, Assistant Administrative Coordinator—Division of Career and Continuing Education, Los Angeles City Unified School District; **William A. Baranyai**, Consultant, and **James Hannemann**, Consultant—Vocational Education Division, Oakland Schools, Pontiac, Michigan; **James B. Baymler**, Coordinator, Wadena Area Vocational-Technical Institute, Wadena, Minnesota; **Charles H. Buzzell**, Associate Commissioner Occupational Planning, U.S. Office of Education; and **Henry A. Haroian**, Director, Career Education Document Information Service—The Commonwealth of Massachusetts; **Tommy R. Brown**, Assistant Professor, and **Clyde O. Craft**, Chairman and Professor—Industrial Education Department, Eastern Kentucky University, Richmond; **Fred S. Cook**, Professor, Teacher Education Division, Wayne State University, Detroit; **William Gayde**, Director of Vocational Education, Fitzgerald Public Schools, Warren, Michigan; **Donald V. Heales**, Director of Technical-Vocational Education, Cleveland Public Schools, Ohio; **Barbara R. Koscierzynski**, Teacher of Career Education, Isaac E. Crary Junior High School, Pontiac, Michigan; **Leonard E. Kunzman**, State Director of Vocational Education, and **Monty E. Multanen**, Coordinator of Career Education—Oregon Board of Education, Salem; **Stanley G. Lyons**, Teacher of IACP, School District City of Pontiac, Michigan; **Frank Mahon**, Teacher, Technical Arts Department, Beverly Hills High School, California; **Earl S. Mills**, Assistant Professor, Institute for Personal and Career Development, Central Michigan University, Mt. Pleasant; **Derek N. Nunney**, Vice President for Academic Affairs, Oakland Community College, Michigan; **Jerry C. Olson**, Superintendent for System-Wide Programs, Pittsburgh Public Schools; **Stig E. Ralstrom**, Head, Vocational Department Northeastern High School, Detroit; **O. Karl Rose**, Curriculum Analyst, Henry Ford Community College, Dearborn, Michigan; **John P. Takis**, Trade and Industrial Coordinator, Ferndale High School, Michigan; **Eugene J. Simms**, Associate Dean of Instruction, Seattle Central Community College, Washington; and **Robert M. Worthington**, Consultant, Vocational Technical and Manpower Education, Ewing, New Jersey.

As Wayne State University serves as one of the national centers for leadership preparation and research, it provided the authors an opportunity to secure critical reviews for chapters and topics under development. The following persons contributed as they were associated with the University during the period that the manuscript was being prepared: J. Kenneth Cerny, Alvin C. Clark, David H. Curry, Arthur K. Deane, Kathleen M. Herschelmann, Sylvia C. Johnson, Ronald J. Koscierzynski, Welton L. Lawrence, Neil S. Levine, James C. Martini, Kenneth R. McLea, R. Terry Messenger, Thomas M. Pierson, John N. Popovich, James T. Sadlier, Kenneth M. Schultz, Theodore L. Sipes, Ted R. Streit, Edward W. Sturgeon, Karin S. Syzdek, and Susie G. Washington.

Quotations taken from publications other than reported research, professional periodicals, and dictionaries have been used with the courtesy and consent of the publishers and, in some selected cases, the authors. The names of teachers and leaders, with their professional affiliations, are identified with the VAE curriculum materials used in the text as examples or selected for Appendices A through R.

The authors are grateful to those numerous college and university students and practicing teachers who have reacted to sections and parts of the manuscript as it slowly evolved into the first edition and now the second edition of this publication. All professional materials for teachers need to be "road tested" by prospective and in-service teachers.

W. D. Stephens, President of McKnight Publishing Company, made a significant contribution to this book as he worked with the authors in the planning, developing, and editing of this publication.

Table of Contents

	PAGE
Preface	v
Acknowledgments	viii

Chapter 1. The Unified Program 1

The Period of Change	1
Development of Vocational and Applied Arts Education (VAE)	3
Development of Career Education	5
Instructional Emphasis	19
Programs to Meet Special Needs	24
Chapter Summary	26
For Self-Assessment and Discussion	27
Assignments to Demonstrate Competency	28
References and Resources	28

Chapter 2. Identifying and Selecting Content 32

Occupational Surveys Provide General Direction and Scope	32
Eliminate Dichotomy Between "Vocational" and "Academic" Education	34
Content Selected in Relation to Goals, Behavioral Objectives, Methods, Evaluation, and Physical Facilities	35
Approaches for Identifying Content	36
Curriculum Content That Does Not Discriminate Against Minority Groups	74
Use of Advisory Groups to Validate Programs and Content	76
Summary	77
For Self-Assessment and Discussion	78
An Assignment to Demonstrate Competency	79
References and Resources	79

Chapter 3. The Systems Approach 82

    The Systems Approach Defined 82
    The Systems Approach in Education 83
    Behavioral Objectives Are the Heart of the Systems Approach 84
    A Curriculum Development Model 86
    Learning Packets for an Electronics Course 88
    The Systems Approach Employed in the NOBELS Study 96
    Concomitants of the Systems Approach 101
    For Self-Assessment and Discussion 102
    Assignments to Demonstrate Competencies 102
    References and Resources 103

Chapter 4. Organization and Administrative Strategies 107

    A Personalized Approach to Education 107
    The Changing Role of the Professional Teacher and Supporting
        Staff in Mediated Instruction 111
    Organizational Strategies and Curriculum for Implementation of
        Flexible Modular Scheduling 115
    Differentiated Staffing in Occupational and Applied Arts Education 122
    Community Resources Employed to Expand Occupational
        Education 126
    For Self-Assessment and Discussion 138
    Assignments to Demonstrate Competencies 139
    References and Resources 140

Chapter 5. First Considerations in Course or Program Planning 143

    What Is a Course of Study? 144
    An Educational Philosophy Gives Direction to Education 146
    Course Goals Are Formulated for the Unique Contributions of
        Each Course 149
    Behavioral Objectives Determined After Course Goals 151
    Course Goals Give Direction for Behavioral Objectives and
        Content, Methods, and Evaluation Procedures 151
    Course Goals, Behavioral Objectives and Content, and Methods
        Determine Needed Physical Facilities 152
    Systems Approach Provides the Coordinating Agency 154
    For Self-Assessment and Discussion 155
    An Assignment to Demonstrate Competency 155
    References and Resources 156

Chapter 6. Instructional Materials Needed by the Professional Teacher 158

Materials for Preplanning 158
Materials for Content, Methods, and Evaluation 170
Student Study Materials 173
Physical Facilities 174
Needed Instructional Materials Determined by the Teacher 175
Instructional Packages for Individual Development 175
For Self-Assessment and Discussion 176
Assignments to Demonstrate Competencies 176
References and Resources 177

Chapter 7. Organizing Course Materials for a Specific Teaching Situation 180

Review Preplanning Materials 180
Adapt Instruction to Community, School, and Students 181
Relationship of Course to Subject and Subject to Curriculum 186
Student Involvement with Life Learning Skills 187
Why Behavioral Objectives? 188
Identifying Behavioral Objectives with Specific Instruction 189
Three Organizational Patterns 191
For Self-Assessment and Discussion 198
Assignments to Demonstrate Competencies 199
References and Resources 200

Chapter 8. Educational Justification of a Course or Program 201

General and Specialized Education 201
The Function of General Education 203
The Cognitive, Affective, and Psychomotor Domains 205
A Possible Fourth Domain 213
Identify Overall Aims for Education 213
Compare Well-Known and Published Aims for Education 215
Committees Develop Aims for a Program within a School System 222
Develop Specific Goals for a VAE Course 227
Relationship between General Aims for Education, Departmental
  Aims, and Goals for a Course 235
Techniques for Showing How Course Goals Contribute to Fulfillment
  of Department Aims and Overall Aims for Education 236
Stating Behavioral Objectives 241
Summary 244
For Self-Assessment and Discussion 245
Assignments to Demonstrate Competencies 246
References and Resources 247

xiii

Chapter 9. The Instructional Units 250

    The Unit of Instruction 251
    Identifying Administrative Units 252
    Selecting and Placing Unit Titles in an Instructional Order 254
    Scheduling of Instructional Units 266
    Developing the Units of Instruction 271
    Examples of Units of Instruction 275
    Summary 276
    For Self-Assessment and Discussion 277
    Assignments to Demonstrate Competencies 278
    References and Resources 278

Chapter 10. Methods, Aids, and Teaching Techniques (Delivery Systems) 281

    Pertinent Definitions 281
    Identify Appropriate Methods for a Teaching Situation 282
    Feasible Methods and Specific Teaching Aids Identified with
        Titles for Units 300
    Descriptions of Teaching Techniques for Each Unit 305
    Adequate Forms and Records for Administration of a Program 307
    Provisions for Substitute Teachers 307
    For Self-Assessment and Discussion 309
    Assignments to Demonstrate Competencies 309
    References and Resources 310

Chapter 11. Evaluation Procedures 313

    The Emphasis on Accountability 314
    Criterion-Referenced vs. Norm-Referenced Evaluation 324
    Program Evaluation in Terms of Specific Course Goals 328
    Student Evaluation in Terms of Behavioral Objectives 329
    Objective vs. Subjective Evaluation 333
    Teacher-Made Tests and Evaluation Devices 335
    Interpretation and Utilization of Test Results 344
    Student Participation in Evaluation 345
    Cumulative Records 350
    Evaluation of Teacher Competency 353
    Summary 359
    For Self-Assessment and Discussion 359
    Assignments to Demonstrate Competencies 360
    References and Resources 361

Chapter 12. Specifying Equipment and Instructional Supplies 365

Instructional Facilities Needed for a Program 365
Develop Floor Plan Showing Machines Equipment, and Instructional
    Areas 376
Facilities Provided with Mobile Laboratories 386
Maximize the Use of Community Facilities in Development of VAE
    Programs 387
For Self-Assessment and Discussion 388
Assignments to Demonstrate Competencies 389
References and Resources 390

Appendices of Curriculum Examples 393

A. Content and Plan for Organizing IACP Learning Experiences 394
B. Steps in Specifying the Curriculum and Content for the Oregon
    Career Cluster Approach 399
C. Selected Tables Showing Outputs from Computer Programs of
    Task Analyses of Medical Laboratory Specialists for the
    Air Force 407
D. Examples of Operational and Informational Topics Identified
    through the Process of Instructional Analysis 412
E. Curriculum Information for a Two-Year Preparatory Program
    in Radio-Television Service 420
F. Format for a Preface for a Course of Study 426
G. The Common Goals of Michigan Education 427
H. Interrelationship of Course Goals and Aims of Education for
    Henry Ford Community College 430
I. Units of Instruction on Business and Office Machines 434
J. Examples of Laboratory Units 438
K. Examples of Units Concerned with Informational Topics 442
L. Examples of Modules of Instruction Organized Around the
    Development and Construction of a Project 445
M. Modules Designed for Individualized Instruction 452
N. An Example of a Teacher's Plan for a Unit in a Course in Child
    Care and Development 457
O. Individualized Instruction and Problem Solving for Design,
    Drafting, and Model Building 459
P. Examples of Behavioral Objectives with Criteria for Evaluation 469
Q. Examples of Entries for Tests Developed by VAE Teachers 473
R. Examples of Questions from Safety Tests 478

Index of Acronyms 480

Index 482

chapter 1

The Unified Program

The emphasis on integration of instructional content and the thrust for relevancy at all levels of education have produced a strong and interrelated program of Vocational and Applied Arts Education (VAE). This unification of individual programs into a structured and related program of VAE, occurring throughout the nation, contributes to the planning and development of meaningful and well-planned programs of instruction.

This chapter identifies many of the efforts bringing about this unification, and outlines the structure and objectives of instruction in Vocational and Applied Arts Education.

The Period of Change

History will identify the present decade as one of rapid changes in education. The changes which are now occurring are the results of efforts initiated ten to twenty years ago. Fortunately, current changes are directly improving instruction and hold the promise of producing a better educated and informed society. During the past few decades, education has undergone a series of stages which led to the present program and state of change.

The initial stage occurred during the fifties and was primarily **a period of self-examination and criticism.** Educators, representatives of government, and citizens expressed serious concern regarding the educational process, indicating that students were often weak in basic subjects (reading, mathematics, writing); and minimum emphasis was being placed on advancing the educational level of the more competent students in mathematics, science, and languages. Toward the end of this period, strong concern was expressed regarding the need for knowledge and skills which would help high school graduates (and high school dropouts) obtain employment.

The second stage began during the period of self-examination and criticism, and produced numerous innovative programs and ideas. This period, **an era of innovation and individual program development,** was supported by numerous federal and private research and development grants. Many ideas, such as the Industrial Arts Curriculum Project (IACP), were developed into operational programs and the literature is rich with descriptions of programs placed into operation on a pilot or experimental basis.

During these two stages, a revolution in instructional media was taking place. The growing technology, especially in electronics, provided a variety of devices which permitted major improvements in both individual and group instruction. As a result, we now have computer-assisted instruction, various forms of programed instruction, instructional television, closed-loop single-concept films, and a variety of additional devices and systems, many of them discussed in Chapter 10. The use of overhead transparencies is about as common as the use of the chalkboard, and they are usually more effective as well as more efficient.

The third stage represents the present, and includes the late sixties and early seventies. It is **a period of integration, bringing together the individual innovative programs.** The formats emerging from this integration include career education, programs emphasizing individualized instruction, vocational and applied arts education, and plans which integrate the instructional program into a meaningful entity. The developments in instructional technology are permitting this broad-based approach to focus on "individualized instruction" and the recognition of individual differences, learning rates, and attention spans.

This third stage developed its own creative concepts, for the "tools of program integration" had to be invented. These include the systems approach, behavioral objectives, and accountability — all concepts presented in later chapters.

The reader should recognize that even though these three stages are distinct, each represents an emphasis rather than a singular concentration of effort. At the present time, integration and total program development is the principal emphasis. However, innovative program development, self-examination, and professional criticism are the continuous processes leading to the improvement of education.

The coming decade should see the maturation of this process of integrated instruction, with tremendous advances made in using instructional technology to individualize instruction. Education will become more a part of each person's life, rather than a separate and often unrelated entity. Concepts, such as "schools without walls" and "self-paced instruction," will help improve education for groups able to profit from these new concepts.

Another concept studied during this period is the process of producing educational change. The fact that the world's total knowledge is now doubling each seven years has numerous implications for education. New courses to acquaint students with new knowledge cannot be added to the curriculum each year. Instead, this rapid growth of knowledge requires a new focus which teaches students **how to learn** as a process. In addition a **continuous evaluation** must be conducted of the school curriculum to assess the effects of new knowledge on the instructional program, and to determine when identified changes should be implemented. In some cases, this involves content deletions and additions. In others, new instructional formats are needed to provide instructional programs designed to match the new knowledge and its effects on society.

The need for almost continuous change within many programs of the school, including most VAE programs, has developed during the past few decades. With this development has come the need to identify an effective process of producing this change. There are three principal elements necessary to produce educational change. They are:

- **Acceptance of Need to Change.** All of the people involved in implementing a curriculum must be convinced that the change is needed and should be put in effect. While the most important person is the teacher, school administrators, supervisors, parents, students, and the public are nearly as important since they must provide the needed support and financial resources. School administrators and supervisors are responsible for supporting changes on a school and district basis.
- **Teacher Knowledge and Ability.** Even if everyone is convinced that the change should occur, it cannot take place until the teacher has the knowledge and ability to provide the new instruction or use the new method of instruction. In-service education must accompany most plans calling for the implementation of new course content or methods of instruction.
- **Instructional Materials.** Most changes require new textbooks or other study materials and workbooks. In VAE, changes often involve new equipment, teaching aids, transparencies, or filmstrips. The necessary instructional materials must be available if the change is to be presented in an effective manner. Good instructional materials are very important to the introduction of new programs.

These three elements of the educational change process are interrelated. Teachers often attend continuing (in-service) education programs where all three elements are provided: discussion of need, instruction in content, and familiarization with prepared instructional materials. When this is done effectively, new programs are implemented and curricular offerings improved.

Development of Vocational and Applied Arts Education (VAE)

Vocational and Applied Arts Education includes all programs of education which prepare people to enter employment, upgrade them to better positions, and/or assist them in understanding and living in our technological society. Specifically, it includes the applied and general education programs of industrial arts, health, home economics, and business. Also included are all of the programs of occupational education, such as trade and technical education, distributive education, health occupations, occupational programs of home economics and business, cosmetology, agriculture; it includes apprenticeship, formal programs conducted by business and industry, and the large variety of specialized occupational education programs conducted by private and public community colleges, high schools, adult education programs, skill centers, etc. Essentially, **VAE programs provide people with the knowledge and ability to (1) gain employment, (2) progress in their employment, and (3) make productive use of the products of our technology**, as described later in this chapter under "Instructional Emphasis."

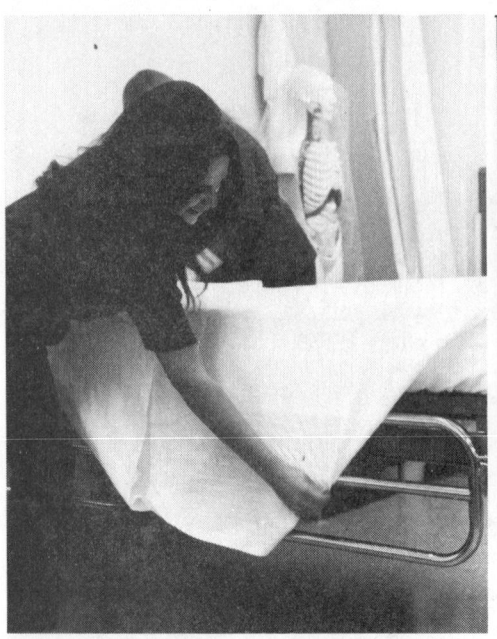

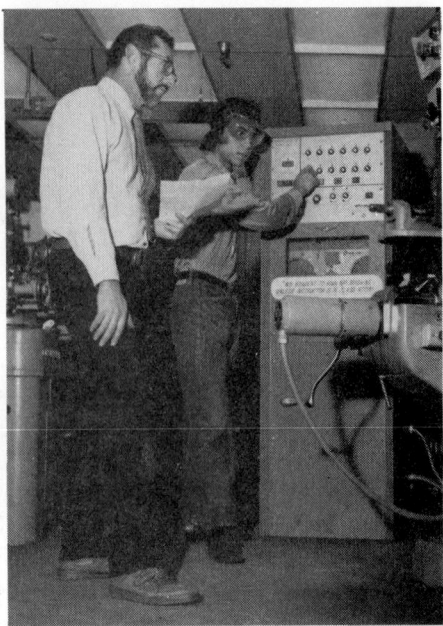

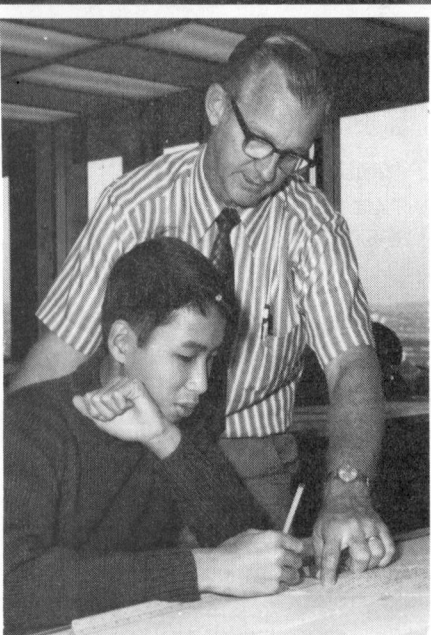

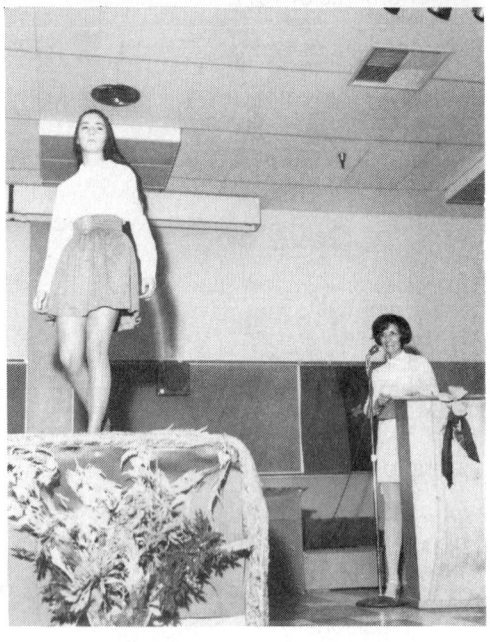

Fig. 1-1. A sample of the diversity of vocational and applied arts education is shown in these photographs. From upper left, clockwise: nurse aide, numerical control, fashion design, and civil engineering drafting. A quick review of the other photographs placed throughout this book will further emphasize the existing diversity of VAE. (Los Angeles Public Schools)

This concept preserves the individual integrity of the numerous disciplines, such as industrial arts. The development of VAE recognizes the commonality of many objectives and instructional procedures of the different disciplines composing VAE. Individuality will continue to be emphasized since the specific instructional programs are provided by the individual disciplines or by division into clusters, and not by a unified VAE concept. However, integration enables the disciplines to combine forces and present interrelated programs which can better meet student needs. For example, the cooperative efforts of elementary industrial arts and trade and technical teachers can develop effective programs and instruction in career awareness and can provide the information needed in the elementary school. Programs in health occupations are the direct outcome of the expanding concept of VAE and are best integrated with existing school programs in health.

While the philosophical concept of a unified program of vocational and applied arts education is quite old, it is now becoming a reality. The Vocational Education Act of 1963, Amendments to the Act in 1968, and the further amendment to include industrial arts through the Educational Amendments of 1972 have been the primary tools for integration. Prior to this time, programs were divided on the basis of whether they received or did not receive federal vocational funds, a division more often political than logical.

The integration of programs under a VAE concept has taken place in many universities, state departments of education, and school districts. The acceptance of this concept should strengthen the individual course offerings of the numerous instructional programs of VAE.

Development of Career Education

Career education is emerging as a major unifying emphasis. Within this framework the school can focus instruction on helping each individual student find a self-fulfilling and productive life within our democratic society. This is an ambitious goal, and requires the combined efforts of all segments of society — the schools, business and industry, and the general public.

The concept of career education will continue to evolve during the years to come. When Sidney Marland, then Commissioner of Education, issued his call for "Career Education Now" to the National Association of Secondary School Principals in January, 1971, he also established the strategy of inviting wide participation in the development of a definition, encouraging as much dialogue and interaction as possible. As a result, the conceptualization of career education has progressed steadily.

Traditionally, **a career has been defined as a person's life-work, occupation, or profession; one's advancement or achievement in a particular vocation.** During the early stages of conceptualization, many labeled this definition as being inadequate since it considers only economic activities, omitting leisure, avocational, social, and personal pursuits. If the focus was to be on the unification of all of education, career education must encompass life's important and significant activities.

Banathy (1971, 27-28), in structuring a career education model utilizing employers as an alternative to the regular school program, defined career education as:

> ... covering the individual's total life: that is, his occupational, social and personal concerns.
>
> Career encompasses the selection of and advancement in a worthwhile vocation within the world of work, the selection and pursuit of fulfilling avocational and leisure activities, and satisfying participation in the social and political processes of society.
>
> Career education is conceived as education for one's progress through life. It is the aggregate of involvements by which an individual acquires and develops knowledge, attitudes, and skills needed to engage in meaningful vocational, avocational, leisure, social and personal pursuits. Career education enables the student to assess and develop realistically his own interests and potential in view of the opportunities offered and constraints imposed by society.

This definition recognizes the broad potential for career education to serve both the economic and self-fulfilling needs of students.

Goldhammer and Taylor (1972, 6) ascribe a similar potential for career education. However, their concept of career education is more oriented towards employment, viewing a person's career as the vehicle for making possible a desired lifestyle.

> Specifically, career education is designed to capacitate individuals for their several life roles: economic, community, home, avocational, religious and aesthetic. It recognizes the centrality of careers in shaping our lives by determining or limiting where we work, where we live, our associates, and other dimensions that are significant in defining our lifestyle. Designed for all students, career education should be viewed as lifelong and pervasive, permeating the entire school program and even extending beyond it.
>
> Career education is a systematic attempt to **increase** the career options available to individuals and to facilitate more rational and valid career planning and preparation. Through a wide range of school- and community-based resources, young people's career horizons should be broadened. Their self-awareness should be enhanced. The framework for accomplishing these goals are the phases in the career education program: career awareness, career exploration, career preparation.

Both of these concepts recognize a need for the school to contribute to the total development of the student; **occupationally, avocationally, socially, and personally.** The first definition, which attributes the total process to a broad and unified program of career education, is a laudable goal towards which education should strive.

The second definition gives more recognition to existing educational programs, permitting a more traditional definition for career education. The concept receiving widest acceptance is presented by Worthington (1973, 58) when he stated:

> Its [career education] main purpose is to prepare all students for successful and rewarding lives by improving their basis for occupational choice, by facilitating their acquisitions of occupational skills, by enhancing their educational achievements, by making education more meaningful and relevant to their aspirations, and by increasing the real choice they have among the many different occupations and training avenues open to them.
>
> It is similar to vocational education, but there is a fundamental distinction. For while vocational education is targeted at producing specific job skills at the high school, post-high school, and adult levels, up to but not including the baccalaureate level, career education embraces all occupations and professions and can include individuals of all ages whether in or out of school.

This definition clearly defines career education as the development of the knowledge and abilities necessary to gain entry into a chosen occupation or profession. It is hoped that the decade ahead will see the education profession build a strong program of career education, progressing from an acceptance of the need to provide for economic welfare to one of providing for all aspects of a person's lifestyle.

While full agreement has not been reached regarding the definition, most educators agree that career education is a **lifelong process**, reaching from pre-school thru adult and continuing education, including both formal and informal education. Most will also agree that the process of choosing and preparing for a career includes developing **career awareness, exploration of career interests,** and **preparation for career entry.**

Elementary Education

The developent of career awareness and exploration must begin in the elementary school, and even in pre-school programs, where the students can start to develop realistic views of the world of work and their future roles in society. Three major aspects of career awareness and exploration must begin in the elementary school. These are:
- Awareness of self.
- Awareness of career options.
- Matching of self and career options.

In order to begin the selection of an occupation or profession, or to identify activities which will provide a lifestyle contributing to self-fulfillment and recognition, a person must understand him- or herself. As with all aspects of career education, **self-awareness is a lifelong process** — having its beginning with life and the first organized development in elementary school.

8   Planning and Organizing Instruction

Fig. 1-2. Career education should begin in early elementary school where students begin to understand themselves and their interests. (Central City Occupational Center, Los Angeles)

Maley (1972, 8) and a broadly representative group of industrial arts people from the state of Maryland identified the following questions which an individual should be able to answer:
- Who am I?
- What are my strengths and weaknesses?
- What are my interests, ambitions, and goals?
- What are the kinds of activities and experiences compatible with my emotional and physiological makeup?
- Do I enjoy working with others?
- What kind of an environment do I enjoy working in?
- What do I want to do with my life?

The answers to these questions are highly individualistic and vital if a person is to make successful career choices as he/she passes through life. Finding answers to these questions is a lifelong process that is begun in elementary school.

The second aspect, awareness of career options, is better understood and already a part of some school programs. It is important that each student become aware of the wide variety of available occupations and professions.

As each child passes through early elementary school, he or she should:
- Develop identification with father, mother, and people with high visibility occupations (teachers, firemen, postmen, etc.).
- Gain knowledge that different careers require special training or special abilities (doctors study many years, teachers like children, basketball players are tall, etc.).
- Develop the realization that people must make choices regarding the occupations they will enter to earn a living, as well as activities they will perform for self-satisfaction and for social and personal reasons.
- Develop an initial understanding of relationships among different careers (carpenters, plumbers, electricians, etc., all work together to build houses).
- Gain knowledge characteristics which will assist in making career choices (geologists work outside and walk many miles each day, accountants and secretaries work indoors at desks, etc.).

In the later elementary grades, each of the above characteristics should be developed to greater depth, with the student gaining more knowledge about available career options. The child's knowledge about different careers, special characteristics and requirements, length of training, salaries, and working conditions should grow rapidly during this period.

In addition, the elementary school program should assist in these ways:
- Provide initial experience in simple motor and mental skills common to the performance of a number of tasks.
- Assist each student in realizing the impact that the choice of a specific occupation or profession will have on his/her future lifestyle and self-fulfillment.
- Provide for the sampling of different activities to determine individual interest and abilities.
- Provide opportunities for each student to gain satisfaction from career activities and learn to work with peers.
- Begin the development of an awareness of the total structure of occupations and professions, and how they relate to the daily lives of everyone.[1]

If the broad definition of career education is used, the study of career options must also include avocational and leisure activities as well as social and personal pursuits. Each student must become aware of the fact that he/she must either make choices of the large variety of activities which will determine his/her lifestyle and own self-appraisal or simply drift into occupations and activities by chance.

As students gain an understanding of self and of career options, they can begin to evaluate their interests in specific careers. This involves matching their awareness and knowledge of self with (awareness of) career options. As they do this, they must evaluate career options in terms of their own interests, abilities, and special talents (or short-

---

[1]An example of a program incorporating many of these characteristics is shown in Chapter 9, p. 268.

comings). Even though this process is not used in elementary school to choose a career, the process can begin by eliminating incompatible careers and spending additional time learning about careers that tend to match interests and abilities.

In addition to the guidance functions of career awareness and exploration, the initial processes of career preparation begin in the elementary school. Students should become aware of the fact that their facility with numerical skills, reading, writing, spelling, mathematics, getting along with others, and their effectiveness in the variety of other elementary school learning experiences are important considerations in many careers. Career preparation at this level should emphasize skills and abilities common to all careers, whether for establishing a lifestyle or entering a specific occupation or profession.

Secondary Education

In the past the major emphasis on career education has been in the junior and senior high schools. In many cases, the prevailing programs are fragmented into a series of subjects, often unrelated to each other or the world in which the students live. Traditional secondary education has provided the student with three tracks: college preparatory, general, and vocational. Career education is proposed as a unifying force for the secondary school program, **focusing education on the world in which the student lives — the societal problems, the world of work, the benefits and pleasures, and the opportunity to plan and develop a chosen lifestyle.** In order to accomplish this unification, the instructional program will have to take on the following characteristics:

- **Career clustering** would focus instruction on the clusters of occupations and professions within the student's interests. His/her abilities would help determine the level of education and eventual concentration within a cluster.
- **Expansion of the concept of clustering** would serve the general education purposes of study of the broad functions of society as they interrelate within our technological society.
- **Career guidance** would be a continuing function of secondary education, assisting each student in a continual appraisal of abilities and interests matched with career options.
- **Flexibility and mobility** within secondary education would be a necessary ingredient. This concept matches the career guidance emphasis, permitting the student to make curricular adjustments based on interests and abilities.
- **Development of meaningful avocational, leisure, social, and personal pursuits** would help the student establish a set of goals which will contribute to self-fulfillment and a positive self-appraisal.
- Upon completion of secondary education (grade 12), each student would be ready to **enter useful and rewarding employment** or to **enter a program of higher education.**

An additional contribution of career education to the secondary schools is a strong effort to get the student out of the classroom and into the world for his/her education. While many aspects of education can best be taught in a classroom, it is also apparent that considerable effort has been expended in creating vicarious experiences to achieve goals that are more easily reached through real life experiences. The success of work experience programs has raised the question of how much career education can effectively be taught outside of the school and how much must remain for classroom instruction. It seems that the next ten-year period will find an increasing emphasis on the concept of "the school without walls," with the accompanying increase of educational activities conducted in the community and the world of work.

As career education developed in secondary schools, two concepts were introduced and tested: **career education in schools and career education with employers.**

School Programs

Career education in the secondary schools must build upon the program established in the elementary school. Since the elementary school program emphasizes career awareness and begins the process of career exploration, the secondary school must complete the process of career exploration and for many students, quickly move to career preparation. For these students (half or more), high school is terminal education and the only career preparation they will receive prior to entering the labor market.

Fig. 1-3. Career education programs prepare students for a variety of careers. This student is preparing for a position as "fingerprint classifier." (Belmont High School, Los Angeles)

One of the early concepts (Miller, 1972, 12) accepted by the planners of the secondary school program was that the program **outcomes** were —

> ... designed to equip the exiting student with an entry-level job skill and to prepare him for further academic or vocational education. The outcomes are:
> 1. Career Identity
> 2. Self Identity
> 3. Self Social Fulfillment
> 4. Career Decisions
> 5. Economic Understandings
> 6. Employment Skills
> 7. Career Placement
> 8. Educational Identity.

This list of outcomes was later expanded to include an emphasis on lifestyle goals and on serving the broad career preparation needs of learners.

The first two of the desired outcomes were left to the elementary school, as presented earlier. The others fall in the broad categories of exploration and preparation and are primarily the responsibility of the secondary school program.

Miller (1972, 31) further states that the curriculum objectives reflect, in student terms, the outcomes planned for career education. They are:

1. Assist youth to choose an individualized personal lifestyle and to establish and discover alternative paths for reaching goals commensurate with that lifestyle.
2. Prepare students to enter the world of work as contributing members of a productive society.
3. Assist young people to view education as a lifelong pursuit that is not restricted to schools, classrooms, or traditional institutions of learning.
4. Assist youth to develop problem-solving skills required to cope with an increasingly cybernated society.

The cluster concept, originally developed for some of the innovative programs in vocational education, was accepted as the basic framework for planning and developing the instructional program. Emphasis should be placed on the fact that **clustering is an educational concept.** Occupations and professions are grouped so that students can be provided information about the world of work and be given assistance in choosing a career which matches interests, aptitudes, and abilities. Clustering also structures the instructional program, identifying objectives and learning experiences common to all the occupations and professions represented within the cluster.

There is no single clustering arrangement which will meet the needs of all schools or districts. As a result, a number of systems are in use in secondary education. The clustering for career education consisted of an expansion and integration of vocational systems. The first structure was presented by the U.S. Office of Education and consisted of the fifteen clusters shown in Fig. 1-4. These fifteen clusters were restudied and reduced to twelve. The relationship of the two sets is shown in Fig. 1-4.

Career Education Clusters	Career Education Clusters
1. Natural resources	{ 1. Agri-business and natural resources 2. Marine science
2. Construction	3. Construction
3. Manufacturing	4. Manufacturing
4. Trade and finance	{ 5. Business and office 6. Marketing and distribution
5. Transportation and communication	{ 7. Communication and media 8. Transportation
6. Education	9. Public service
7. Health and welfare	10. Health
8. Government	
9. Personal services	11. Personal services
10. Product services	{ 12. Consumer and homemaking 13. Environment
11. Arts and humanities	14. Fine arts and humanities
12. Recreation and entertainment	15. Hospitality and recreation

Fig. 1-4. Comparison of CVTE Career Education Clusters with the Original U.S. Office of Education Clusters

Even twelve clusters was too large a number to use in elementary school. Also, the significance of the groupings could not be grasped by pupils in the lower grades. As a result, the elementary programs stressing career awareness and initial career exploration use the following formats:

- In grades K-3, students become aware of the world of work using the simplest possible division — two categories, goods and services.
- In grades 4-6, where students are able to understand more complex structure, the program is focused on five clusters — industry, commerce, social services, services, and the arts.
- In grades 7-9, students are ready to be introduced to the twelve-cluster system. Sampieri (1972, 19) suggests that each cluster exploration unit consist of approximately 45 hours of instruction.
- In grades 10-12, the students narrow their areas of interest and concentration so that career preparation becomes a major goal and students prepare for job entry or to continue with further academic or vocational education.

The cluster concept can be expanded to include more than **career development (awareness, orientation, exploration, and preparation)**. The career clusters indicate and reflect the economic structure and interrelationships of the many facets of society. A study of careers may well be based on the purposes of the cluster — the societal needs it fills and the structure of the system(s) to meet those needs. Many of the general education aims of industrial arts, home economics, business, and other programs of applied arts can be realized by expanding the concept of career clusters.

Employer Programs

A second major thrust in the development of secondary school programs of career education is the involvement of employers in planning and offering programs of career education. Employers are a logical group to involve in the planning and projection of career education programs since they provide the jobs for the graduates.

Employer involvement in education is an old concept, and the rationale and logic for it has been described well by Robert Peterson who is serving as a program director for an employer-based career education program. He states:

> [Employer involvement is] not only **not new,** but it represents an attempt to recapture some things about American education that were good but have somehow been lost. Lost not as a result of anything that the educational establishment has done, but lost as a result of some very profound social changes that have occurred in this country . . . Young people now spend less time at home, which someone recently said shuts down during the day, and less time in the work place, because the adult work has become too complex to let them explore. As they spend less time out in these places, they spend more time in classrooms. The result is that young people have been isolated from the world in which they are very shortly going to be asked to live, prosper, and lead productive and fulfilling lives. (Peterson, 1972, 25).

The involvement of employers is, therefore, an attempt to get the students back into the community for a portion of their education. In developing this concept into an instructional program, Hood and Banathy (1972, 20) define employers as "any individual or group who employ other people in profit-making, governmental, and other nonprofit enterprises."

The broad concept of an employer permits students to become involved in a variety of settings including places of work, community activities that involve social action, museums, recreational areas, and other real life community settings. As a result, the program is attempting to make the **community the classroom and involve the students with real life problems and activities.**

The following characteristics describe the program and the effort to involve employers:

- Most of the learning occurs in life experiences rather than educationally contrived settings.
- The program is comprehensive and provides for individual students' needs with respect to intellectual, social, and personal growth, as well as vocational and avocational preparation.
- Cognitive growth within the functional context of a real life activity is a basic premise of the program.
- Programs are individually tailored to each student's needs, aspirations, attitudes, aptitudes, abilities, and styles of learning.
- The program is not exclusive, serving all students in the 13-18 age

group. The program serves the college-bound student as well as those not college bound.
- Each student experience involves planned objectives. The experience is completed when the objectives have been met. Resource people are identified in each employer setting.
- After the objectives for a unit are established, the student is sent to work with a specific resource person in the employer's setting. The resource person is a person in the employer's setting who has a skill, a specific knowledge, or maybe just a well-developed interest that is needed by a student. Examples of resource people used include a lawyer, banker, printer, self-employed designer, child-care center director, artist, and airline representative.
- Each student has a planned program which builds his activities with resource people in employer settings into a complete and integrated program of instruction. Whenever necessary, employer instruction is supplemented by individual or small group instruction at the career center (the location of counselors and the base for the total program).

The resource person emerges as the key person in the development of this program. Since this person works on a one-to-one basis with the student, the opportunity to provide experiences to meet individual student needs is always present. Cast in a real life setting, motivation and learning can interrelate to provide maximum student growth and development.

Interrelationship — School and Employer Programs

Each program, school and employer, is presented as an individual effort. In establishing the development of **model programs,** the U.S. Office of Education set the structure which forced each program to develop independently. When the **models** are translated into operating models in school districts, the best efforts of each should be incorporated.

This integration is already taking place. Programs of career education being developed through the efforts of school districts and individual schools are taking the concepts developed by the **employer-based model** and incorporating them into **school-based programs.** The result is an increased use of employers (using the broad definition presented earlier) for a variety of educational needs, and the identification of specific individuals in the employer setting (resource people) to work with individual students. This integration should lead to a steady improvement of the cooperative education approach (discussed in Chapter 4) and career education programs in secondary schools.

The future may well see the development of employer-based programs by individual districts. These will, almost certainly, **integrate the best efforts of both programs, but build from an employer rather** than school base. If this occurs, the student has much to gain. At the present time, there is no alternative to the secondary school program. A student unable to profit from the school program either transfers to another school (probably little different than the first) or drops out of school. A real alternative might reach students now missed, as well as provide a program to meet special and unique educational needs.

Post-Secondary Education

Career education is a lifelong process. Beyond high school, it must expand into a multi-directional effort, including:
- Career preparation programs requiring **post-high-school instruction.**
- **In-service education** for people needing new information and abilities which will make them more effective in their occupation or profession.
- Career preparation **programs for adults** who need **new careers** or who are entering the labor market for the first time and do not possess job entry skills.

The first effort, **career preparation requiring post-high-school instruction**, is being met by the community colleges, area vocational skill centers, technical schools, and four-year and graduate colleges and universities. Career preparation at this level includes all the professions and all of the occupations which require special skills difficult to provide for high school students.

Many of the efforts taking place at secondary schools are also being considered for post-secondary schools. New systems of delivering higher education, expansion of cooperative education, individualized and self-paced instruction, and the "university without walls" are all changes which may improve career education programs at the post-high-school level.

The second effort, **in-service education,** is being expanded throughout the nation. This has always been a large program for high schools and community colleges. It is now growing in importance and significance at the four-year college and university level.

The knowledge explosion described at the beginning of this chapter has made in-service education a part of virtually everyone's career. Formal public school programs are the most visible but actually represent the smaller segment of in-service education. Other types of educational programs provide more in-service education than formal public schools. These include:
- **Business and Industry Instructional Programs for Employees.** Most major industries, and many small ones, maintain extensive programs of in-service education for their employees. This program, on a national scale, equals the public in-service education effort.
- **Proprietary Schools.** Private schools designed to provide both initial and in-service education are common throughout the country. These schools often provide programs of career preparation and in-service education not available from public schools.
- **Self-education by Technical and Professional Employees.** Reading and studying books, trade journals, and other publications and/or enrollments in correspondence courses represent another major form of in-service education.

The third effort, **programs for adults requiring new careers,** is the one receiving special attention as part of the total career education movement. The elimination of jobs due to automation and obsolescence; the increasing number of women seeking entry into occupations and professions for the first time; retired people seeking different, useful employment; and teenagers out of school but not settled in satisfying occupations — all show the need for career education programs for the adult community.

The early efforts of career education included two programs aimed at solving these unique career education problems of adults. The first recognized that many programs of adult career education already exist, including public and private adult education programs and correspondence courses. Also, instructional technology has made many new types of programs possible for adults. These include instructional television and various types of programed instruction.

However, people needing these programs were unable to utilize them. In many cases, they neither knew what was available nor their own interests and abilities. As a result, an early career education effort for these adults consisted of establishing a **career guidance center.** Such centers provide information regarding available careers and assist people in evaluating their own interests and abilities. Within these centers, the problems related to career choice and the difficulty in self-evaluation and the matching of interests and abilities to career options are given first consideration.

Once a person knows which occupations or professions he/she wants to explore, or the one seeming desirable to enter, the center helps the person identify the appropriate instructional program to meet his/her schedule, needs, and abilities.

Unfortunately, appropriate instructional programs are not always available. It is essential, therefore, that communities with good guidance programs work for the continuous development of instructional programs in areas where employment opportunities exist. These programs must meet the needs of the adult community, utilizing the developing methods of instruction whenever appropriate.

The **second early effort of career education** worked towards solution of the career needs of the adult population, but in a rural setting. Here, the problem of available career options is often acute since jobs are scarce. The efforts in these areas often must include developing industries or providing people with skills which fit into the economic development of the area. Often whole families or small communities can be brought into an educational program.

Inclusion of Industrial Arts

While the role of industrial arts in career education was quite obvious and supported by knowledgeable educators, development was handicapped during the first year by a lack of federal support. Congress recognized the need for funding industrial arts education and, through the Educational Amendments of 1972, amended the definition of vocational education to include industrial arts in Public Law 90-576, the Vocational Education Amendments of 1968. This change provided eligibility specifications for funding industrial arts programs. At the same time, Congress authorized funding the concept of career education as part of the funding for occupational education programs, as provided in the Educational Amendments of 1972.

Following inclusion of industrial arts in funding for career education, a special ad hoc committee[2] was appointed to establish appropriate guidelines. Within the guidelines, the committee identified five phases of industrial arts experiences for career education. These are:

- **Self and Career Awareness** — familiarize students with the many kinds of work people do and the interrelationship of such work in producing and using goods and services. Emphasis is placed upon attitudes and values and the relationship of manipulative activities to the total instructional program.
- **Career Orientation and Exploration** — gives students first-hand experience with the kinds and levels of work performed in a broad range of industry and occupations for which special skills are required; informs them of requisites for careers; acquaints them with the significance of changing and evolving technologies; instills in them an understanding and appreciation of the dignity of work; and assists them in making informed and meaningful career selections.
- **Career Exploration and Beginning Specialization** — provides transitional experiences to bridge the gap between the awareness/orientation focus and specialized in-depth offerings. Experiences provide students with opportunities to select and explore individual occupational clusters and thereby assess their own performance, aptitudes, and interests.
- **Career Specialization** — prepares individuals for enrollment in advanced, highly skilled, post-secondary technical education programs. It would provide experiences which should assist students in continuing to assess their interests, abilities, limitations, and potentialities in respect to industrial-technical occupations as well as to provide them with entry-level skills and knowledge from a selected occupation cluster or segment.
- **Adult and Continuing Education** — provides laboratory experiences for adults and out-of-school youth who may benefit from broad basic instruction related to industrial and technical occupations. (Report of the Ad Hoc Committee on **Criteria and Guidelines for Funding Industrial Arts,** 1972, 27).

The inclusion of industrial arts made all of the programs identified within VAE eligible for funding through the Vocational Education Act and appropriate amendments. Even though VAE programs are only **part of the total career education thrust,** they provide much of the occupational education, career guidance, and related instruction in grades K through 12 plus the community college.

---

[2]Committee membership: T. Gardner Boyd, Kansas City, MO; Karl Gettle, College Park, MD; James Good, Rochester, NY; Frederick Kagy, (co-chairman) Normal, IL; Rutherford Lockette, (co-chairman) Pittsburgh, PA; William Namel, St. Paul, MN; Howard Nelson, Minneapolis, MN; Herbert Siegel, Brooklyn, NY; Ralph Steeb, Tallahassee, FL; Leonard Sterry, Madison, WI; Robert Woodward, Sacramento, CA; George Lipman, Prince Georges Co., MD; Edward Kabakjian, Washington, D.C.; Lowell Burkett, Washington, D.C.

Instructional Emphasis

The concept of **applied** integrates the different disciplines of VAE and leads to the identification of a common **instructional** emphasis. The fact that most VAE programs are activity programs presents problems in both organization and instruction which are unique within the profession. The increased emphasis on problem solving, creativity, exploration and guidance, and technological development has produced many changes in curricular offerings. New methods of organizing and presenting instructional content have emerged. The Industrial Arts Curriculum Project (IACP)[3] is an example of a completely new program of instruction designed to meet the need for a change in instructional emphasis in the junior high school. The two programs developed — manufacturing and construction — attempt to update the junior high program so that instruction provides the student an initial understanding of the world of manufacturing and construction. Research and curriculum development projects similar to IACP are being encouraged by the U.S. Office of Education in other areas of education, such as the major divisions of business and distribution.

With the rapid increase of knowledge in both subject area content and instructional technology, it is necessary for teachers to become more competent in the professional aspects of teaching and in the technical skills and knowledges of their subject area.

A teacher not competent in his/her subject area or lacking the professional and technical competencies of the profession may easily permit a program to degenerate into a simple activity or busy work. Unfortunately, a few teachers have discovered that it is easy to demonstrate the basic operations in doing a project and then have all students in the class perform the same activity. Students in such classes master a few basic skills and little more.

Professional teachers have clearly demonstrated that successful programs require continual hard work. Such programs are only accomplished by capable and dedicated teachers working within the matrix of an established philosophy. The establishment of realistic course goals and behavioral objectives and the development of a delivery system to fulfill the behavioral objectives is difficult. Teachers often find desirable activities not possible due to lack of equipment. They observe that informational units or content lessons must be well integrated with activities, or many students lose interest and ignore this phase of their education. There are other factors — such as student capabilities, teaching load, and adequate supplies — that add to the difficulty of maintaining a good program. The path of least resistance is easy to find, but it offers little satisfaction to either student or teacher.

A number of **instructional emphases** are common to many areas of VAE and should be considered during the planning of an instructional program. Most good programs combine some characteristics of each of the following:

---

[3]This USOE funded project was administered through The Ohio State University Research Foundation and is described in Chapter 2 and Appendix A.

1. Exploration and guidance.
2. Occupational and professional development.
3. Problem solving.
4. Understanding technology and the world of work.
5. Creativity and design.
6. Generally useful knowledge and abilities.

Exploration and Guidance

The emphasis on career education brought with it a renewed emphasis on exploration and guidance. Traditionally, programs of industrial arts, business, and home economics provided some career information and group guidance. However, it was often relegated to the end of the term where it was given minimum emphasis, especially if the students were behind in other phases of instruction.

The responsibility for career awareness and exploration rests with all teachers. They, along with school counselors, must make certain that each student understands the need and importance for making intelligent career decisions. Students must be helped to identify and understand their own aptitudes, abilities, interests, and aspirations. They must also be provided with a large number of exploratory experiences designed to acquaint them with knowledge about available careers.

Fig. 1-5. Jacqueline Killam, industrial arts teacher, explains window frame construction to members of her class. The construction of this section of a wood frame structure permits the students to explore a large number of occupations and professions serving the construction industries. (Beverly Hills Unified School District, California)

Armed with knowledge of self and knowledge of careers, the student can begin the process of career selection which, in the beginning, should be the elimination of careers outside the interests and abilities of the student. This is a process which must be started in elementary school and continued throughout life. It not only identifies the occupation or profession the student enters, but helps him/her make decisions regarding avocational and leisure pursuits and the many activities which go into establishing a lifestyle which fulfills an individual's need for recognition and an appraisal of self-worth.

Occupational and Professional Development

Responsibility for occupational and professional development was once identified as the sole responsibility of the vocational educator and those in higher education. The introduction of career education has emphasized that this position is **invalid** in light of the current needs of students, and it quite possibly **has always been invalid.** At the elementary and secondary school levels the entire school staff has responsibility for career education, with major responsibilities for integration of instructional content resting with VAE teachers.

Programs for Specific Occupational Development

Once a student has the desire to enter a specific occupation or profession, instructional programs must be available which will provide the knowledge and abilities he/she needs. Specific instructional programs for occupational education are provided by many agencies. Many programs are provided by the high schools and community colleges in both day and evening programs. Additional programs are offered by private schools, sometimes in competition with public schools but more often in occupations not offered by the public schools. Many companies maintain their own schools for training and upgrading employees. Correspondence courses also provide occupational education in many specialized areas.

Even though numerous alternatives are available, the schools must maintain a strong program of occupational preparation. Since most high school students are unable to make a valid career choice early enough to complete an occupational preparation program in high school, most specific programs are left to the community college and adult programs. The high schools in turn provide instruction in occupational groups or clusters which permit the student maximum flexibility throughout high school.

Groupings and Clusters

Grouping of closely related occupations into clusters permits students to work toward development of knowledge and skills prior to making a commitment to a **specific** career. The clusters shown in Fig. 1-4 permit the student maximum flexibility within the cluster. For example, a student interested in a career in an occupation or profession within **Health and Welfare**, will gain information about individual and group health and welfare which is needed by nurses, medical doctors, nurses' aides, public health officers, dentists, orderlies, and the many additional occupations and professions within the **Health and Welfare** cluster. Notice that some occupations in this cluster can be entered directly from high school (nurse's aide) and some require many years of college (dentist).

Clusters are used for both exploratory and career development programs. In exploratory programs, students study to gain knowledge of the different occupations and professions represented within the cluster. During this study, they have an opportunity to analyze their own abilities and interests and determine whether they are interested in career development within the cluster.

Clusters also offer an opportunity to expand the student's knowledge of the functions of society, showing how the multitude of businesses and industries and public and private agencies interrelate to serve mankind. The future control of resources and preservation of a high standard of health and living will require all people to have a general understanding of these interrelationships for intelligent decision-making in environmental and ecological matters.

Occupations and Professions Requiring Collegiate Education

Many occupations and all professions require education beyond high school. The higher the level of education, the more specific instruction must become. As a result, the concept of clustering gradually gives way to specific occupational and professional preparation in collegiate education.

This is a gradual emphasis on specialization. For example, if a student wishes to become a computer programer, his/her initial education will equip this individual to be a machine operator. If the student's goal is computer systems analyst, he/she would first be equipped to be a machine operator, then a programer, and finally a systems analyst.

Problem-Solving Abilities

This emphasis is concerned with the methods of solving industrial or social problems. It is based on the assumption that society needs persons qualified to think constructively, quickly, and efficiently in solving everyday problems. Existing knowledge is continually being superseded by new discoveries and advancements. What is taught as practice today is often historical and obsolete tomorrow. The theory is that when students develop problem-solving ability they will then be able to adjust to a rapidly changing society and cope with its new and unpredictable problems.

There is currently much emphasis on problem solving in all areas of education. This emphasis provides a splendid opportunity for having individuals, or a group of students as a team, do research and plan for some meaningful project or problem, and then use the most appropriate materials and tools as they make an application of technological and scientific principles in completing the project or experiment. In this approach, predetermined essential content for all learners becomes secondary to the experiences that come to the individual who gets involved and engrossed in some exciting problem. The development of problem-solving abilities contributes to the growth and development of each student.

Understanding of Technology

An important emphasis in VAE is providing students with an understanding of the technology and its effects on people and the environment.

Quality of life has become an important concern of people all over the world. Air and water pollution, waste disposal, as well as sonic and thermal pollution, are all identified as by-products of our advanced technology. Many people are beginning to look at various types of limitations — industrial growth, population control, and restrictions on the use of energy — as ways of preventing further reduction in the quality of life in a Post-Industrial Age.

Education, and especially VAE subjects, must give special attention to the understanding of technology. The decades ahead will require numerous decisions which should be built on a firm understanding of how technology serves and assists man, how by-products harm him, and how alternative solutions to problems affect all interrelated aspects of technology. For example, a natural gas shortage might encourage people to switch to heating their homes with electricity — it is clean and quiet. However, most electricity is generated in coal burning power plants which use less than 50 percent of the heat energy produced. When gas is burned in the home, 90 percent or more is used to heat the home. The result of using only 50 percent of the heat generated from burning coal is:
- Nearly twice the fuel consumption.
- More than twice the air pollution since burning coal produces more air pollution than burning natural gas.

As a result, switching to electric heat at the present time doubles the air pollution and becomes an undesirable alternative to the problem. Solutions to complex problems of society will require a citizenry able to communicate intelligently about modern technology.

Creativity and Design

This emphasis deals primarily with fabrication areas where there is an opportunity for self-expression through design and original thinking. A major objective is to develop improved designs. Functional as well as aesthetic problems are undertaken. The problems that arise from this approach are numerous and require dedicated and capable teachers. It becomes easy for such a program to degenerate into a series of projects, all different, with none as well designed as the class model. Problems arising from class size and poor craftsmanship, as well as lack of student experience upon which to base new designs, plague this approach. Even so, teachers must realize the importance of this emphasis since design is prerequisite and essential to fabrication. Creativity and industrial design are also needed in the scientific and technical efforts in America.

Avocational and Leisure Activities

Industrial arts has always been a strong contributor to the development of avocational and leisure activities. Other VAE areas, such as home economics and agriculture, also provide for the development of avocational and leisure activities.

With the advent of the 30/35-hour work week, more people will have to derive personal satisfaction from pursuits away from their employment, such as creating works of art, beautifying their home and surroundings, and participating in sports. Many people find relaxation and gain self-satisfaction by creating things with their hands. Others accrue therapeutic values from meaningful physical and/or creative activities. In the years to come, this emphasis could become one of the most significant contributions of VAE programs to American education.

Integration of Instructional Programs

One of the strongest arguments favoring the development and expansion of career education is that **it is an integrating force which will unite education.** The need for integration of instruction has never been greater. Students need to know and experience how their educational programs will help them meet their present and future responsibilities and goals. The focusing of education around a broad concept of career education could fulfill this need.

VAE is, by its very nature, an integrated subject area. Students must use a wide background of mathematics, science, social science, and language arts in learning and using VAE instruction. VAE teachers should, therefore, exert leadership in the integration of all instruction into a meaningful program of education.

Programs to Meet Special Needs

Numerous VAE programs are designed to meet the special needs of people. Three of the most extensive and important are (1) industrial training programs, (2) special programs for the students with special needs, and (3) programs of continuing education.

Industrial Training Programs

Business and industry operate extensive educational programs designed to provide initial occupational information and continuing education for employees needing updated information. The need for well-educated employees is recognized by most companies since the ability to successfully compete in our free enterprise system is based on the ability to identify new and better ways of providing goods and services.

The fact that industry operates schools does not relieve the public school from providing instructional programs in VAE. In most cases, the programs of industrial schools are planned to meet the specific needs of company employees, and the skills are not easily transferred. Another important consideration is that no program of education should be controlled by a vested interest group. Education is the vehicle for job entry and the single most important way an individual can improve his/her position in life. Past history has shown that when career programs are placed in the hands of special interest groups, entrance is limited and the program controlled for the special interest group rather than the welfare of society.

Even though business and industry schools should not have exclusive control over VAE, they are a valued addition to the education process. Public schools often are able to cooperate with these schools for the benefit of all education. For example, General Motors Corporation, Ford Motor Company, other automobile manufacturers, and many manufacturers of test equipment make their schools and teachers available to public school automotive and power teachers. These teachers gain much valuable information which permits them to improve their instructional programs. The result is improved education for future employees of any and all companies.

Programs for Students with Special Needs

In recent years considerable attention has been given to the development of VAE programs for persons with special needs. One of the motivating forces has been the manpower programs designed to assist the socioeconomic handicapped. Programs have been developed to implement the provisions of the Manpower Development Training Act of 1962 and the Vocational Education Act of 1963. Federal funds are allocated for research and demonstration purposes, with 10 percent of the allocation assigned for experimental and demonstration programs designed to meet the needs of the handicapped.

The success of programs to train persons with special needs has been most rewarding. To illustrate, J. Earl Williams (1971, 61) reports:

> Job simplification and redesign are now making it possible to train retarded workers as data processors, electronic component assemblers, bank clerks, and offset press operators. One Midwest state developed an intensive job preparation and placement program which makes it possible to place long-time institution residents as nurses' aides, housekeepers, and food service workers. In fact, today nearly 5,000 mentally retarded persons work in 40 federal agencies and receive a higher percentage of outstanding performance rating than any other group of government workers.

VAE programs provide for the development of occupational skills and abilities, as well as craft and avocational activities. For some physically handicapped, especially those whose handicap has resulted from injury, physical activities in VAE may have a therapeutic value unrelated to the knowledge and skills gained.

Continuing Education

Continuing education is a term which is rapidly replacing the concept of in-service education. The broader concept of **continuing education recognizes that education is a lifelong process for all people.** In this sense, the broad concept of education must be used since education is not confined to **school instruction,** but rather includes self-education through reading, study, television, and activity. It includes formal and informal company meetings; a wide variety of ways people gain new knowledge.

In the past, formal continuing education was confined to the professions. Occupations changed at a very slow rate and all upgrading could be learned on the job. This condition no longer exists. The knowledge explosion has produced a rate of change that affects virtually all occupations and professions. In some cases, the occupation ceases to exist and employees need retraining for another occupation. In other cases, new knowledge requires participation in an educational program conducted by the employer. In many situations, the education is provided through adult education in one of the public schools.

Another important aspect of continuing education is the providing of opportunities for advancement. Often, more advanced jobs require knowledge the employee does not possess. Adult education programs are able to provide this instruction, thereby assisting people to improve their occupational positions.

The knowledge explosion has affected the professions, such as teaching, to an even greater extent. The teaching profession is continually looking for new ways to bring new information to teachers. The VAE teacher is especially affected by the knowledge explosion. The content being taught is continually undergoing change, as well as new knowledge being developed in instructional delivery systems and course planning and development. The problem can be acute when one considers that the teacher is the authority in the classroom and has no contact with the occupation or profession represented. For example, the electronics teacher is isolated from the electronics industry since he spends each day teaching. Continuing education is the principal means of keeping teachers current in both subject and professional knowledge.

Chapter Summary

Change and all the concomitants associated with this phenomena impinge upon the teacher from all sides. The need to implement new methods of **delivering** instruction to students, new structures for **the organization of content,** and new methods of evaluating **student progress** are combined into a system's effort to integrate instruction and make it relevant to the world in which the students live.

A new concept is emerging as vocational and occupational programs integrate with applied arts to form a unified program of vocational and applied arts education (VAE). At the present time, the integration exists in some programs of teacher education and is primarily a combination of administrative functions based on similar program goals. The combining of administrative functions into VAE has also taken place in some school districts and other levels of school administration. Even though the administrative functions are being combined, the unique contributions of each program of VAE are being maintained.

Career education, introduced by then Commissioner of Education Sidney Marland in 1971, has made significant contributions to the development of VAE programs. Career education has made elementary and secondary schools responsible for the development of career awareness in all students. Organized programs which help students understand their own interests, aptitudes, and abilities, become acquainted with a large variety of careers, and explore careers of specific interest have been developed as part of career education. The belief that every student leaving secondary education should have the ability to either enter the labor market as a productive employee or continue his/her education in collegiate instruction is one of the major contributions made by career education.

A broad concept of career education has been presented as an alternative to our existing structure of education. This concept **envisions career education as one's progress through life**, emphasizing the need to unite all programs of education around a central theme of helping people identify and develop career goals. For this concept, career education includes all the knowledge, attitudes, and skills needed to engage in meaningful vocational, avocational, leisure, social, and personal pursuits. Implementation of this concept requires strong leadership from those in control of the total school curriculum.

For Self-Assessment and Discussion

1. Which programs have been integrated to form a unified program of VAE?
2. Describe the ways in which a single program, such as industrial arts, retains its unique contribution within a unified VAE program.
3. Identify the three **periods or stages of change** which education has undergone since the fifties.
4. Explain the process of producing educational change.
5. What is the definition for career education that, if implemented, would unify all of education under a single concept?
6. What are the three major aspects of career awareness and exploration which must begin in the elementary school?
7. Identify characteristics of "self" which help one understand the abilities and interests which lead to an appropriate career choice.
8. Identify the outcomes planned for the school program of career education.
9. What is meant by "lifestyle goals"?
10. What is meant by "clustering occupations and professions for educational purposes"?
11. What is the definition of "employer" used in the employer program of career education?
12. What are the multiple directions for career education beyond high school education?

28   Planning and Organizing Instruction

13. Why is **problem solving** an important instructional emphasis in VAE programs?
14. Identify considerations to be included when the emphasis of the instructional program is on **understanding of technology**.
15. Why are avocational and leisure pursuits important areas to emphasize?

Assignments to Demonstrate Competency

1. Outline a career guidance program which would assist a student in making an appropriate career choice. Include both career awareness and career exploration as you develop the program with the following specific considerations:
   a. Objectives by grade level.
   b. Activities to develop awareness of self.
   c. Activities to develop awareness of occupations and professions.
   d. Activities which explore careers of interest to individual students.
   e. Considerations for career selection.
2. Compare the school and employer programs of career education. Describe the differences between the two programs. If integrated, which elements of each do you believe should be kept? Explain your answer.

References* and Resources

Books

Abstracts of Instructional Materials for Career Education. Columbus, Ohio: CVTE, The Ohio State University, 1972, Pp. xii + 102.

Campbell, Robert E., and Vetter, Louise. **Career Guidance: An Overview of Alternative Approaches.** Information Series Number 45. Columbus, Ohio: CVTE, The Ohio State University, 1971, Pp. 22.

Career Education — A Handbook for Implementation. Washington, D.C.: U.S. Government Printing Office (0-471-485), 1972, Pp. 102.

Gibson, Robert L. **Career Development in the Elementary School.** Columbus, Ohio: Charles E. Merrill Publishing Co., 1972, Pp. 81.

*Goldhammer, Keith, and Taylor, Robert E. **Career Education — Perspective and Promise.** Columbus, Ohio: Charles E. Merrill Publishing Co., 1972, Pp. viii + 296.

Herr, Edwin L. **Review and Synthesis of Foundations for Career Education.** Information Series Number 61. Columbus, Ohio: CVTE, The Ohio State University, 1972, Pp. 85. ERIC Reference No. ED 059 402.

Hoyt, Kenneth B.; Evans, Ruppert N.; Mackin, Edward F.; and Mangum, Garth L. **Career Education, What It Is and How to Do It.** Salt Lake City, Utah: Olympus Publishing Co., 1972, Pp. vii + 190.

Hoyt, Kenneth B.; Pinson, Nancy M.; Laramore, Derryl; and Mangum, Garth L. **Career Education and the Elementary School Teacher.** Salt Lake City, Utah: Olympus Publishing Co., 1973, Pp. 208.

Kenneke, Larry J.; Nystrom, Dennis C.; and Stadt, Ronald W. **Planning and Organizing Career Curricula: Articulated Education.** Indianapolis, Indiana: Howard W. Sams and Co. Inc., 1973, Pp. xv + 431.

Lauda, Donald P., and Rayn, Robert D. **Advancing Technology: Its Impact on Society.** Dubuque, Iowa: William C. Brown Publishing Co., 1971.

*Items with an asterisk have been cited in this chapter.

Long, Thomas E., Editor, **Essays on Career Education.** Pennsylvania State University: Department of Vocational Education, 1973, Pp. ii + 86.
McClure, Larry, and Buan, Carolyn, Editors, **Essays on Career Education.** Portland, Oregon: Northwest Regional Education Laboratory, 1973, Pp. xi + 265.
Stadt, Ronald W.; Bittle, Raymond E.; Kenneke, Larry L.; and Nystrom, Dennis C. **Managing Career Education Programs.** Englewood Cliffs, New Jersey: Prentice-Hall, Inc., 1973, Pp. xv + 224.
Stadt, Ronald W., and Bailey, Larry J. **Career Education: Approaches to Human Development.** Bloomington, Illinois: McKnight Publishing Co., 1973, Pp. xviii + 430.

Periodicals

American Association of Colleges for Teacher Education. "Career Education and Teacher Education." **Journal of Teacher Education.** Vol. 24, No. 2 (Summer, 1973), six articles, pp. 84-112.
American Vocational Association. "Career Development: K-14." **American Vocational Journal.** Vol. 44, No. 9 (December, 1969), entire issue.
_____. "Career Education — Is It a Fad or a Major Development?" **American Vocational Journal.** Vol. 47, No. 3 (March, 1972), entire issue.
Arnold, Walter M. "Career Education Model Gathers Momentum as Six School Districts are Selected for Test Programs." **Industrial Arts and Vocational Education,** Vol. 60, No. 9 (December, 1971), pp. 4-6.
Baker, G. E. "Attitudes of Vocational Teachers, Academic Teachers, and the General Public Towards Career Education." **Journal of Industrial Teacher Education,** Vol. 10, No. 1 (Fall, 1972), pp. 24-31.
Boone, James L. "Postsecondary Educators Discuss Role in Career Education." **American Vocational Journal,** Vol. 48, No. 2 (February, 1973), pp. 32-33.
Burkett, Lowell A. "AVA Formulates Positions on Career Education." **American Vocational Journal,** Vol. 47, No. 1 (January, 1973), pp. 9-14.
Campbell, Robert E. "A Procedural Model for Upgrading Career Guidance Programs." **American Vocational Journal.** Vol. 47, No. 1 (January, 1972), pp. 101-103.
"Career Education." **Industrial Education,** Vol. 62, No. 1 (January, 1973), series of articles, pp. 21-29.
"Career Education." **Journal of Industrial Teacher Education,** Vol. 10, No. 2 (Winter, 1973), series of articles, pp. 3-49.
"Career Education and You." **School Shop,** Vol. 32, No. 8 (April, 1973), entire issue.
"Career/Vocational Education." **D and R Report,** Periodical of the Council for Educational Development and Research, Inc., Vol. 2, No. 1 (December, 1972), pp. 1-19.
Church, O.; Labarre, J.; and Scrittorale, L. "Exploring the Business Teacher's Career Education Role." **American Vocational Journal,** Vol. 48, No. 2 (February, 1973), pp. 47-51.
Cravarella, Michael A. "We Do Need Elementary School Guidance, Mr. Ginzberg," **Phi Delta Kappan,** Vol. 54, No. 6 (February, 1973), pp. 384-385.
Deiulio, Anthony M., and Young, James M. "Career Education in the Elementary School." **Phi Delta Kappan,** Vol. 54, No. 6 (February, 1973), pp. 378-380.
Feirer, John L. "What You Can Do for Career Education." **Industrial Education,** Vol. 61, No. 7 (October, 1972), Pp. 27.
Ginzberg, Eli. "The Interface Between Education and Guidance." **Phi Delta Kappan,** Vol. 54, No. 6 (February, 1973), pp. 381-384.
Holland, John L., and Whitney, Douglas R. "Career Development." **Review of Educational Research.** Vol. 39, No. 2 (April, 1969), pp. 227-237.
Kazanas, H. C. (Editor). **Journal of Career Education.** Columbia, Missouri: College of Education, University of Missouri. Each volume consists of four issues. First published in 1973.

Laramore, Darryl. "Career Education Concepts Filter Down." **American Vocational Journal**, Vol. 47, No. 6 (September, 1972), pp. 45-47, 78.

McDowell, Glen. "A Concerned Look at Career Education." **American Vocational Journal**, Vol. 48, No. 2 (February, 1973), pp. 30-31.

Marland, Sidney P., Jr. "Marland on Career Education," **American Education**, (November, 1971).

Matheny, Kenneth B. "The Role of the Middle School in Career Development." **American Vocational Journal**, Vol. 44, No. 9 (December, 1969), pp. 18-21.

Muirhead, Peter P. "Career Education: The First Steps Show Promise." **Phi Delta Kappan**, Vol. 54, No. 6 (February, 1973), pp. 370-372.

Nash, Robert J., and Agen, Russel M. "Career Education: Earning a Living or a Life?" **Phi Delta Kappan**, Vol. 54, No. 6 (February, 1973), pp. 373-378.

Odom, James A. "The Open-Door High School to Junior College to Senior College." **College and University**, (Summer, 1970), pp. 513-524.

*Report of the Ad Hoc Committee on "Criteria and Guidelines for Funding Industrial Arts." School Shop, Vol. 31, No. 5 (January, 1972), pp. 26-27.

Resnick, Harold S., and Ricciuti, Renzo. "The Role of Industrial Arts in Career Education." School Shop, Vol. 31, No. 10 (June, 1972), pp. 17-18.

Steeb, Ralph V. "The Role of Industrial Arts in Career Education." **Man/Society/Technology**, Vol. 31, No. 8 (May-June, 1972), pp. 260-265.

Wells, Carl E. "Will Vocational Education Survive?" **Phi Delta Kappan**, Vol. 54, No. 6 (February, 1973), pp. 369-380.

*Williams, J. Earl. "Research Implications of Vocational Education for the Disadvantaged." In **Contemporary Concepts in Vocational Education**. Edited by Gordon F. Law. Washington, D.C.: The American Vocational Association, 1971, pp. 59-66.

Wolansky, William. "Career Development Skills for Industrial Teachers." **American Vocational Journal**, Vol. 48, No. 2 (February, 1973), pp. 72-74.

*Worthington, Robert M. "An (Over) View From the Top," School Shop, Vol. 32, No. 8 (April, 1973), pp. 58-61, 93.

Other Published Materials

*Banathy, B. H., "Employer Based Career Education (EBCE)" in **The Proceedings of the Eighth Invitational Conference on Systems Under Construction in Career Education and Development**. American Institute of Research, Palo Alto, California, 1971, pp. 26-36.

*Beck, James R., Editor, **Conference Proceedings, Community Dialog in Career Education**. Continuing Education, San Jose State University, California, 1973, Pp. 60.

Gillie, Angelo C., Editor, **The Fifth Annual Pennsylvania Conference on Post-Secondary Occupational Education**, Center for the Study of Higher Education, The Pennsylvania State University, 1974, Pp. xvi + 247.

*Hood, Paul D., and Banathy, Bela A. **An Employer-Based Career Education Model: A Description and Operational Plan**. Far West Laboratory for Educational Research and Development, San Francisco, California, 1972, Pp. iii + 97.

*Maley, Donald, et al. **Career Education Through Industrial Arts**. Division of Vocational Education, Maryland State Department of Education, 1972, Pp. 28.

*Miller, Aaron J. **The Comprehensive Career Education Model**. Columbus, Ohio: CVTE, The Ohio State University, 1972, Pp. 44.

*Peterson, Robert. "Employer-Based Career Education Model" in **Conference Proceedings, Community Dialog in Career Education**. Compiled and edited by James R. Beck. Continuing Education, San Jose State University, California, 1973, pp. 25-31.

*Sampieri, Robert A. "School-Based Career Education" in **Conference Proceedings, Community Dialog in Career Education**. Compiled and edited by James R. Beck. Continuing Education, San Jose State University, 1973, pp. 15-24.

Unpublished Materials

Butler, Cornelius F. "The Home-Community Based Model (Model Three) of the U.S. Office of Education's Career Education Research and Development Program — A Synopsis." Paper presented at the 1972 Annual Meeting of the American Educational Research Association, Chicago, Illinois, 1972, Pp. 49. ERIC Reference No. ED 062 539.

Kunzman, Leonard E. Career Education in Oregon. A Statement in Improvement of Vocational Instruction in Oregon Schools. Salem: Oregon State Board of Education, 1970, Pp. 11. ERIC Reference No. Ed 051 432.

Laws, Lee. Elementary Guide for Career Development: Grades 1-6. Austin, Texas: Education Service Center, 1970.

Miller, Aaron J. "Strategies for Implementing Career Education: A School Based Model." Paper presented at the 1972 Annual Meeting of the American Educational Research Association, Chicago, Illinois, 1972 Pp. 49. ERIC Reference No. ED 062 539.

Morgan, Robert L., et al., eds. Synopses of Selected Career Education Programs: A National Overview of Career Education. Raleigh: The Center for Occupational Education, North Carolina State University, 1972, Pp. 79. ERIC Reference No. ED 063 461.

Palo Alto Educational Systems, Inc. A First Step Toward Career Education. Vol. 1. Appendices — Vol. II. Palo Alto, California: Palo Alto Educational Systems, Inc., 1972, Pp. 251. ERIC Reference No. ED 060 224.

Swanson, Gordon I. "Facts and Fantasies of Career Education." Paper presented at the 1972 Annual Meeting of the American Educational Research Association, Chicago, Illinois, 1972, Pp. 49. ERIC Reference No. ED 062 539.

2 chapter

Identifying and Selecting Content

This chapter is concerned with what is taught in vocational, technical, and applied arts education. It identifies and explains various approaches and strategies either employed or advocated by curriculum builders for the selection of content to fulfill identified goals for a program, curriculum, subject, course, or module of instruction. The chapter presents strategies now employed in vocational and applied arts education (VAE) for the identification of content at the various educational grade levels (i.e., K through 6, middle or junior high, senior high, post high, and adult programs). It focuses on the substance of education — what students study about — to further the objectives of career education. Examples have been cited to illustrate recommended approaches now in use for the identification of content for needed programs, courses, or modules of instruction.

Occupational Surveys Provide General Direction and Scope

Educators in many states, or areas within a state, have conducted occupational surveys before planning and developing area vocational centers, technical institutes, or the vocational-technical offerings for a community college. Data from these studies are especially helpful in determining:
1. The needs and support of industry, business, and the government for an expanded occupational education program.
2. Occupations that might be organized as educational clusters.
3. Articulation needed between academic and vocational offerings to relate cognitive and manipulative skills.
4. Viable guidelines for the selection of content for occupational or manpower courses and programs.

It is essential that the educator directing these state or community occupational surveys be competent in research skills to direct the collection, tabulation, summarization, and presentation of needed data. The individual must be able also to present and interpret a modern philosophical approach and role for occupational and career education in a post-industrial society.

Identifying and Selecting Content

To accomplish the survey objectives, Silvius and Curry (1971, 228-230) suggest that it is often necessary to provide answers to these questions:

1. What are the occupations of the young people in the 17 to 21 age bracket who reside in the proposed service area? What will they be doing in five years? In ten years? This phase of the survey will provide data on how many young people in the community enter employment rather than continue their education on a full-time basis, and what percentages are: a) in schools or colleges, b) unemployed and seeking work (what kind), c) in the military service, d) married women temporarily out of the labor force raising a family, e) in penal institutions, or f) unemployed and not seeking work.
2. What skills and other competencies are expected by employers and need to be acquired by young people who hope to enter the labor market from high school? From a community college or area vocational school? From a baccalaureate degree program? With a graduate degree?
3. What skills were acquired in high school that now benefit these persons on the job?
4. What kind of work is being done by young people who have attended high schools in the community? What are their present occupational training needs and preferences to extend career opportunities?
5. What are the occupational growth trends for the community, state, and nation?
6. What are the projected growth patterns of the community in the next five years? Ten years?
7. What are the projected personnel needs of businesses, industries, government, and distributor and service firms in the proposed service area (qualified employees for progressive companies)?
8. What skills and competencies are being advocated by society and need to be acquired by young people in full-time attendance in school so that they may become happy and productive citizens as they move on a career ladder in the world of work?
9. What are the projected needs for workers in occupations under consideration (or occupational clusters), over five, ten, and fifteen years? These data can be determined from reports of the U. S. Department of Labor.
10. What are the existing programs and facilities and their articulation for occupational education in the public schools and colleges in the area? In private schools? In the Industries and businesses of the community?
11. Where should vocational facilities be located and structured to provide for the needs of the community?

Eliminate Dichotomy between "Vocational" and "Academic" Education

Educational leaders concerned with VAE have recognized the importance of having educational programs structured by all of the representatives of the basic phases of the total educational program. This calls for the involvement of interested individuals representing various areas of education, including those concerned with world of work programs.

Vocational education that is developed apart from general or basic education is too narrowly conceived to meet the total needs of the individual or society. Technical and manipulative skills essential for job-entry employment are only a part of the total concept being promulgated for career education. The career development concept is concerned with the total development of each person. Those advocating that the curriculum be built by a team representing essential interests in career education hope that educators will work to eliminate the dichotomy that has separated vocational and general education.

Donald G. Lux (1970, 312), one of the principal developers of the Industrial Arts Curriculum Project (IACP)[1], has stated:

> Every possible effort should be expended to break down the barriers between the practical arts and academics, and vocational education must be enjoined not to widen the breach through separate planning, programming, and budgeting.
> If these actions are taken, communications should improve. More importantly, youth will [then] be better served by the practical arts and vocational education.

In a special report to summarize the highlights of a National Conference for the Study of Curriculum Development in Vocational and Technical Education, Melvin L. Barlow, et al, (1969, 8) included these recommendations for curriculum development, dissemination, and coordination:

- Vocational-technical education curriculums should be an integral part of the total school program.
- Realistic preparation for the world of work must be accepted as a basic responsibility of public education.
- Cooperative planning should be implemented between general and vocational educators to:
    Examine the total needs of students;
    Provide for coordination of vocational-technical and general educational programs;

---

[1]IACP has been a joint effort of The Ohio State University and the University of Illinois with funds from U.S. Office of Education, beginning in 1965 and ending in 1971. The office for IACP was located at The Ohio State University, Columbus, Ohio 43210. The text materials and teacher guides for both **The World of Construction** and **The World of Manufacturing**, each covering one school year of instruction (originally planned for the junior high school level), are distributed by the McKnight Publishing Company, Bloomington, Illinois 61701.

Provide for team planning of curriculum teaching;
Provide for the establishment of behavioral objectives for the total educational program; and
Insure maximum involvement of administrators.
- Teachers must be involved in planning for curriculum development to the maximum extent possible.
- Curriculums must be concerned with the learning ability, social and economic needs, and maturity of the student as well as the specific training demands of the occupation.
- Objectives should be specific in terms of performance goals, and criteria should be prepared for evaluating behavioral characteristics.
- Curriculums should permit instruction utilizing a variety of teacher modes applicable to the individual learning needs of the student and should provide for a maximum of generalization and transfer.
- Evaluation must become a continuous part of the maintenance and improvement of the curriculum.
- Development of vocational-technical curriculum must begin with an analysis of the employment requirements and demands.

In support of the career education concept and to work toward the elimination of the dichotomy that has existed between general and vocational education, Rupert N. Evans (1970, 283) has said:

The goal should be development of an integrated program of general and vocational education extending from early childhood through retirement. Separate, parallel, antagonistic education systems are not the answer.

Content Selected in Relation to Goals, Behavioral Objectives, Methods, Evaluation, and Physical Facilities

Content for a course or program may be isolated, analyzed, and specified by curriculum planners but only as the builders consider:
1. The overall goals and the operational behavioral objectives for a program.
2. The methods and strategies that make it possible for a learner to attain the established goals.
3. Evaluation procedures to be employed so that each learner may demonstrate the competencies specified in the behavioral objectives.
4. Needed software and hardware to facilitate instruction for each unit or module of instruction.

The five major identifiable parts of any program (or curriculum) are:
1. Overall course goals.
2. Learner objectives and content.

3. Strategies and learning methods.
4. Evaluation.
5. Essential materials and equipment.

Each of the parts have entity and may be separated from the other four for analysis and development. While this is being done, there must be continuous consideration for the interrelationships and influences that may be inherent in even a minor change in one of the elements (like content) of the other four parts of the program. Through the systems approach, as explained in Chapter 3, it is possible to give careful consideration to any one of the major elements of the program, as an entity of the curriculum, while there is concurrent evaluation of chain reactions that may be set off by a change in one of the major parts. For example, a change in content may affect the other four parts of the program.

The remainder of this chapter is concerned with the identification and isolation of content for VAE. The procedure selected for identifying content will be effective only when the total process leads to the fulfillment of the selected overall goals of the program. It must provide also for the attainment of essential behavioral objectives specifically written to identify and measure what each student is to learn from the unit or module of instruction. The needs of individual learners are met as the performance tasks specified in the behavioral objectives are evaluated against criteria or standards specified for learner accomplishment.

Approaches for Identifying Content

This section describes the seven major approaches currently employed by curriculum builders in identifying content. After each approach is described, examples illustrating it are shown. The examples include selections from innovative occupational programs that have been promulgated and evaluated in recent years. The seven approaches are:

1. Identifying content using the praxiological domain of man's knowledge.
2. Identifying and selecting content to fulfill established overall goals for a curriculum area, program, or course.
3. Identifying and selecting work tasks that relate to human roles in the work force.
4. Identifying and organizing job clusters for a basic occupational education program.
5. Identifying and selecting content for a general vocational program.
6. Identifying and selecting content through an inventory of payroll tasks.
7. Identifying content through instructional analysis.

Identifying Content Using the Praxiological Domain of Man's Knowledge (A Comprehensive Knowledge of Practice or Efficient Action)

As a prelude to IACP, the original investigators (Donald G. Lux, Willis E. Ray, Jacob Stern, and Edward R. Towers) undertook an extensive review of systems for classifying knowledge and bringing order to accumulated bodies of knowledge. While these investigators were basically searching for a broad-based approach to the study of industry and technology, they uncovered a knowledge base that underlies all practical arts subject areas (Lux and Ray, 1970, 301). This knowledge base for all of vocational and applied arts education was first presented as a preliminary report to selected national leaders for reaction and comment and is now available through the ERIC system (Reference No. ED 013 955).

After reviewing the knowledge classification systems advocated by educational theorists beginning with Aristotle up through contemporary scholars of educational thought, Lux and Ray[2] concluded that all of man's knowledge can be effectively classified under the four domains of knowledge shown in Fig. 2-1.

In the four domains of man's knowledge —
- **Descriptive Knowledge,** the first domain, covers the established facts about phenomena and events, and their interrelationships in the sciences; including the physical, biological, and social sciences.
- **Prescriptive Knowledge,** the second domain, includes the fine arts and humanities and seeks to provide a system(s) of values — judgments as to whether phenomena or events are true and/or good and/or beautiful. Philosophy, literature, and the nonperforming dimensions of music and art are included in this domain.

[2]See also entries listed in this chapter by E. S. Maccia, E. S. Maccia and G. Maccia, and T. Kotaroinski.

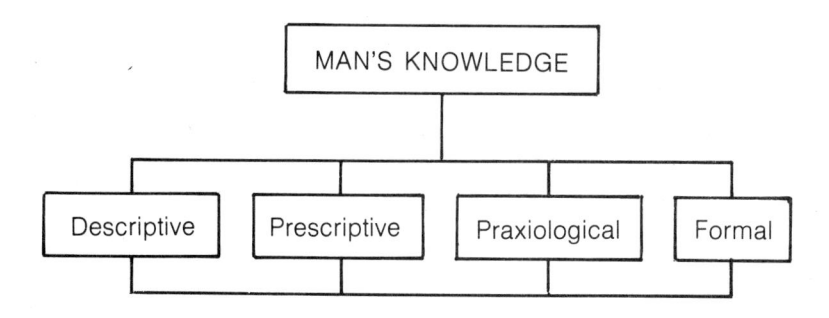

Fig. 2-1. Vocational and Practical Arts Education is classified under the Praxiological Domain of Man's Knowledge. (Lux and Ray, 1970, 302)

- **Formal Knowledge,** the fourth domain, includes the fundamental disciplines, like mathematics and logic, that provide for ordering all knowledge. This domain could therefore be considered the vehicle for coordinating or synthesizing knowledge classified in the other three domains.
- **Praxiological Knowledge,** the third domain, encompasses the knowledge of practice, "ways of doing which bring about, through efficient action, what is valued." This domain is represented by the professional schools in higher education. Examples would be the professional schools and departments in medicine, journalism, law, marketing, education, dentistry, dairy technology, and pharmacy. While these fields also draw from the other three domains ("descriptive," "prescriptive," and "formal") for their basic knowledge, they do demand a clinical and professional body of content cast in efficiency of practice or the praxiological domain (Lux and Ray, 1970, 302-303).

Classifying Knowledge in Higher Education and in Elementary and Secondary Education

Lux and Ray point out basic differences in classifying the structure of knowledge at the higher education and elementary and secondary school levels. In higher education the scholars search for the answers to basic and applied problems, develop order, and record accumulated knowledge according to the guidelines which govern their discipline. They in turn transmit the knowledge they have identified and organized to their students and to the profession through professional journals. Researchers in business and industry, and in the government, also contribute to the knowledge base for these disciplines.

In elementary and secondary schools, subject matter is generally classified in the sciences (descriptive knowledge), in the fine arts and humanities (prescriptive knowledge), and in mathematics (formal knowledge). Such disciplines as psychology, philosophy, and logic are not generally scheduled in elementary and secondary schools and are held in abeyance for higher education programs.

Progress in Classifying Knowledge within Praxiological Domain

Apprenticeship, which antedates formal education, is an example of "knowledge of practice" and is classified under the praxiological domain. The organized bodies of knowledge in applied arts and vocational subject matter areas come under this classification (i.e., agricultural education, home economics and family life, business and distributive education, health occupations, trade and industrial education, and industrial arts).

Lux and Ray point out that these subject areas have been added to the curriculum in recent years. This has been done to expand the total school offerings and make the program comprehensive. Because of this rather recent development, there has been very limited human and financial resources channeled into making a complete and thorough systematic study of man's "knowledge of practice" within each of these areas.

Industrial Arts Curriculum Project within Praxiological Domain

A notable example of "knowledge of practice" that is a part of VAE is the body of knowledge that supports IACP. In this instructional system, broad concepts and principles of contemporary industrial technology have been organized, tested, and refined with an emphasis on industrial-cultural orientation. This is usually a junior high school program established as two one-year courses. The first year studies **The World of Construction** and the second **The World of Manufacturing**. The program is readily classified within the praxiological domain since these two courses have been thoroughly developed, validated, and tested to offer learners exploratory experiences in how to become efficiently oriented within an industrialized society. In this context "Industry" is defined as that economic institution that changes the form of materials to satisfy man's material wants. "Industry" in this definition is further divided into the activities of **Construction**, those structures (goods) produced on a site, and **Manufacturing**, those goods created in a plant.[3]

These two one-year courses were initially tested over a three-year period. Carefully selected participating teachers were involved in writing, continuous evaluation, and subsequent revision of course content. They did this during the summer months following their experiences in actually teaching the courses during the school year. In addition, the content for both courses was validated by many experts from construction and manufacturing to assure its authenticity.

The planned instruction for **The World of Construction** and **The World of Manufacturing** was field tested annually for three years by 48 teachers and approximately 6,000 junior high students spread throughout the nation. The schools included both inner-city and suburban areas. In addition to the field evaluation centers, eleven demonstration centers in ten states were established to assist in the projection of the program and in the upgrading of teachers qualified to organize, manage, and present ICAP instruction.

Many industrial teacher education institutions are now scheduling workshops to orient and prepare teachers in the content, methods, and materials employed in IACP. Teachers initiating the IACP systems are expected to complete an approved IACP Teacher Education Workshop as a prerequisite to their undertaking either of these two courses.

The IACP system utilizes textbooks, laboratory manuals, teacher's guides, and achievement tests. The needed apparatus, equipment, and supplies, along with their costs, have been identified.

To make the results of major curriculum development projects (e.g. IACP) available to teachers and students throughout the nation, the United States Office of Education (USOE) encourages leading

---

[3] A descriptive bulletin on IACP is available without cost upon request from McKnight Publishing Company, Bloomington, Illinois 61701.

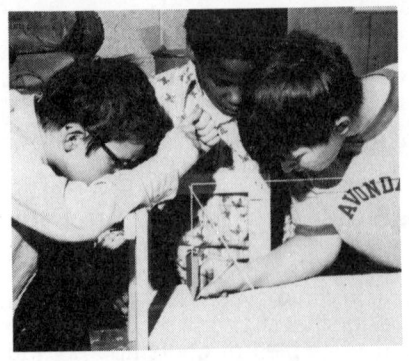

A. Using a sight board and plumb bob, students simulate the location of foundation corners.

B. Framing a house section.

C. Fitting a window frame into the rough opening.

Fig. 2-2. Students engage in a variety of construction activities within the IACP World of Construction program. (Courtesy Stanley G. Lyons, Jefferson Junior High School, Pontiac, Michigan)

publishers to disseminate materials developed with government grants. As a result, IACP instructional materials are available for school use.[4]

The content that has been identified through the research for the IACP, in the form of a listing of the titles for the units and learning experiences (for each of the IACP courses) is shown in **Appendix A**. This appendix also contains a description of the plan for organizing these modules of instruction into a developmental continuum for each of these two courses.

Identifying and Selecting Content to Fulfill Established Overall Goals for a Curriculum Area, Program, or Course

It has been common practice for educational leaders in the applied arts to establish and define major goals for courses in the general areas of agriculture, business, homemaking, and industrial arts education and then to identify a body of content essential and appropriate to the fulfillment of these major goals. In general, these goals for applied arts courses have been centered around exploration and guidance, creative expression, family living, development of basic and essential manipulative and foundational skills, an understanding of industry and/or technological development, an application of applied science and technology, problem solving, and avocational activities.

An example of identifying content and tasks to fulfill established goals is the work of the national committee that prepared **A Guide to Improving Instruction in Industrial Arts**. This committee (Minelli et al., 1968, 9-11) established five major goals for industrial arts education:

GOAL I — Develop an insight and understanding of industry and its place in our culture.

GOAL II — Discover and develop talents, aptitudes, interests, and potentialities of individuals for the technical pursuits and applied sciences.

GOAL III — Develop an understanding of industrial processes and the practical application of scientific principles.

GOAL IV — Develop basic skills in the proper use of common industrial tools, machines, and processes.

GOAL V — Develop problem-solving and creative abilities involving the materials, processes, and products of industry.

---

[4]The software for IACP, developed and refined at The Ohio State University by Donald G. Lux et. al., between 1965 and 1971, has now been copyrighted by USOE with five-year exclusive publishing rights assigned to McKnight Publishing Company. Royalties from the IACP books and manuals accrue to USOE and The Ohio State University Research Foundation for use in further curriculum development and teacher education as approved by the U.S. Commissioner of Education. Needed hardware for the two IACP courses also is available. Descriptive information may be obtained from the McKnight Publishing Company.

The committee then recommended the following body of content for industrial arts education as it focuses on the nature, functions, processes, and products of industry with special consideration for personal, social, and economic conditions that, in turn, provide for the fulfillment of these five major goals (Minelli et al., 1968, 25-26).

- Industry and Civilization
  — Historical view of man and industrial technology.
  — Evolution of modern industrial technology.
  — History of materials.
  — Technical heritage.
  — General education.
- The Industry
  — Relative importance.
  — Historical background.
  — Opportunities.
  — Allied industries.
- Organization
  — Enterprise.
  — Administration.
  — Management.
  — Labor.
  — Associations.
  — Production departments.
  — Plant organization.
- Research and Development
  — Original concept.
  — Market evaluation.
  — Product research and development.
  — Process research and development.
  — Materials research and development.
  — Market research.
- Planning for Production and Manufacturing Operations
  — Idea visualization.
  — Design and preparation of visual information.
  — Production drawings.
  — Material specifications.
  — Design of tools, jigs and fixtures, and special machinery.
  — Plant layout.
  — Plant organization.
  — Estimating and cost accounting.
  — Procurement and inventory.
  — Automation and numerical control.
  — Quality and production control procedures and scheduling.
  — Production flow.
- Production or Manufacturing
  — Custom.
  — Continuous or mass.
  — Materials.
  — Processes.
  — Energy and power.

- Distribution
  — Advertising (promotion).
  — Packaging and shipping (materials handling).
  — Marketing.
- Servicing Industrial Products
  — Diagnosing.
  — Correcting.
  — Testing.

In addition to the description of the five major goals and the eight major areas of content for industrial arts education, the national committee has:
- Specified the objectives, by operational levels, that serve as the stepping stones for the attainment of the five major goals (i.e., for industrial arts in elementary schools, in junior high schools, in senior high schools, in community colleges and technical institutes, in universities, and for graduate study beyond the baccalaureate degree).
- Provided information on essential facilities needed for the implementation of industrial arts education.
- Presented detailed content for each of the eight major areas of instruction in the form of industrial concepts followed with detailed content for each.

The Guide to Improving Instruction in Industrial Arts shows how a body of content, in the form of essential learning experiences for students, is delineated and organized to precisely result in student competencies to fulfill specified major goals for an educational program.

Identifying and Selecting Work Tasks that Relate to Human Roles in the Work Force

Moss and Smith (1970, 1-5) identified and reported on three basic steps in vocational curriculum development that deal primarily with the identification and selection of content. They summarize these and other steps of the process in the **Report of the Minnesota Seminar on Process and Techniques of Vocational Curriculum Development.** The steps that related to content selection are:
- Specify the Role
  There are several factors to be considered in addition to satisfying manpower requirements when specifying roles for which occupational training is to be provided. In defining these roles, consideration for citizenship and factors that contribute to self-fulfillment of the individual must be considered. It is also desirable to focus on "nonwork" as well as "work" roles in the broader perspective for vocational education. One of the difficulties in public vocational programs is to identify the work role of potential employees when the educational emphasis is on maximizing the potential of every student. Also involved is the social value structure and labor market barriers (i.e. discriminating practices, inefficient placement systems, union or management controls over entry points in certain career fields).

- **Identify the Tasks in the Specific Role**
  The boundaries for the total domain of the curriculum are established with the role to be performed by individuals receiving the training. After this is done, it is then possible to identify the specific work tasks[5] that comprise the role. Moss and Smith cite these examples of work tasks: perform blood count, establish work priorities, plan work flow, make local purchase of supplies, audit cash payments, maintain files of plans and programs, and receive and distribute outputs.

  The seminar participants identified three questions that need to be considered in task identification:
  1. What tasks within the role are educationally relevant?
  2. What task sampling frame should be used?
  3. What techniques of task identification are most efficient?

  In discussing these questions, it was mentioned that the technical tasks of the work roles (or task analysis) usually call for cognitive and psychomotor skill performance.[6] But what about affective behaviors that are involved in occupational adjustment and tasks that relate to human relationships? Are these affective behaviors to be included? Another perplexing question is: What kinds of tasks are inherent in one's role as a citizen?

  It was recognized by the seminar participants that it is indeed difficult to identify all of the relevant tasks in some roles, and that it might well be impractical to teach them even after they have been identified. To illustrate, Moss and Smith cite the issues that come with work roles becoming more complex as there is need for judgment rather than knowledge of procedures, as cognitive performance increases in relation to psychomotor performance and as task generalization becomes more important to performance. Also, as the number of relevant tasks increases, and with possible restrictions in training time and costs, it may not be possible to teach all of the identified tasks. It is suggested, therefore, that a task sampling frame be developed and used which would classify the total domain of relevant tasks and that would make the criteria for the selection of tasks to be taught explicit. Moss and Smith suggest that it is likely that such task-sampling frames should be multidimensional and consider such factors as:
  1. Work vs nonwork tasks.
  2. Entry job vs career development.
  3. Specific vs related job tasks.
  4. Predominately cognitive vs psychomotor vs affective tasks.
  5. Tasks organized according to a learning or performing hierarchical process as suggested by such psychologists as Gagne.[7]
- **Select the Tasks to Be Taught**
  Since it is not generally feasible to teach all of the relevant tasks that may be identified with a role, a criteria for selecting those to be taught

---

[5]They define "tasks" as groups of activities that generally occur together and which have a common purpose which is valuable in and of itself.
[6]The cognitive, affective, and psychomotor domains of man's knowledge are discussed on pp. 205-212.
[7]Explained in Psychological Principles in System Development, listed with references for this chapter.

is needed. The participants at the Minnesota Seminar suggested these considerations in task selection:
1. The practical limit on the number of tasks to be taught should be based on the available time to teach those selected to a reasonable level of functional utility. It was pointed out "that teaching about tasks is not conducive to adequate task performance nor to task generalization, and is therefore an inefficient instructional approach."
2. Tasks should be selected that permit the greatest generalizability (i.e., that develop the desired conceptual structure and optimize the response repertory).
3. Tasks which have the greatest frequency of use in the role (or time spent on them) might be selected.
4. Tasks which have emergency value or result in grave consequences if not included should be selected (e.g., those that result in safe work habits).
5. Tasks which have the lowest "perishability" role might be selected (i.e., those that are fundamental and basic to the role).
6. Tasks that are more economical to learn in formal training programs than on-the-job should be selected.
7. Tasks whose performance might reasonably be considered prerequisite to the training program should not be selected (Moss and Smith, 1970, 4-5).

Identifying and Organizing Job Clusters for a Basic Occupational Education Program

This topic, as one of the seven approaches for identifying VAE content, considers the national and basic concepts that underlie the structuring of occupational clusters. This is followed by the approach employed in the city of Pittsburgh and in the state of Oregon in making an application of the concept of clustering occupations.

Basic and Fundamental Instruction for a Group of Occupational Titles

Curriculum builders in occupational education have been experimenting with systems for identifying skills and knowledges (work tasks) that are common to a grouping of related titles as identified and described in the **Dictionary of Occupational Titles** (DOT).[8] These systems are facilitated by identifying, analyzing, and organizing the common work tasks in these occupational titles for the purpose of establishing a common instructional program. As mentioned in Chapter 1, it needs to be pointed out to those studying these various systems that job

---
[8]U.S. Department of Labor, **Dictionary of Occupational Titles** (Washington, D.C.: Government Printing Office) 1965, Third edition, Volumes I and II, 1965.

clustering is an educational scheme and not one that is found in business, industry, and commerce. Job clustering is, therefore, an educational system to provide for occupational adaptability, work adjustment, transferability of workers, transfer of skills, and changing work roles in a dynamic society. Educational economy is provided through job clustering in respect to the time needed by a student to explore several titles in an occupational cluster and then concentrate on one or more of them.

Douglas Sjorgren, in his **Review and Synthesis of Research on Occupational Adaptability** (1971, 1-30) analyzed 144 selected publications that relate to occupational exploration, career development, and the concept of occupational adaptability. Anyone interested in reviewing the rather large number of available papers or publications on job-clustering systems and techniques is referred to the listing in the "References and Resources" section by Sjorgren as the concluding part of his report (Sjorgren, 1971, 19-30).

Sjorgren's review (1971, 6-8) of available papers and reports on job clustering includes these observations or conclusions:

1. The most common method employed to identify job clusters is to conduct a job analysis and then form the clusters on the basis of an arbitrary criterion or on the basis of perceived similarity on the job analysis.
2. In general, the systems reported have been based on statewide programs. There have been enough of these, however, to suggest that one might well find a model that would be useful.
3. Most of the job analysis type studies were focused on the commonalities among jobs. While they gave consideration to implications for curricula, no study was reported in those reviewed by Sjogren, that included the building and testing of curricula based on the job clusters.
4. Several investigators have focused their efforts on the identification of the knowledge and competencies needed by workers for successful performance in an occupation.
5. Occupational adaptability is not just a function of being able to perform a variety of tasks. There are affective dimensions to adaptability that are also important.
6. Much of the job-clustering research has been predicated on the assumption that clusters can be identified that will serve as a basis for building a more viable curriculum than one based on teaching for a specific job.
7. When students consider various jobs that require certain skills, abilities, and interests, they acquire a broad information base for making educational and vocational decisions.
8. Job-clustering studies are not immediately applicable to curriculum building. Perhaps this is why there are several clustering studies but only a few that have been carried through the curriculum development state (such as the Oregon plan reported in this chapter).
9. In many cases the research and development effort to provide job clusters has not focused on objective criteria for deciding if a grouping of jobs is, or is not, a cluster.

10. It is hoped that job clustering methodology can be projected and applied to defining future job requirements. General adaptability would seem to be quite dependent on ability to adapt to a job in the future that is not yet defined.

Sjogren (1971, 12) summarizes the purpose for job clustering:

> Within the field of occupational education, the typical approach to resolving the problem of developing curricula for occupational adaptability has been that of job analysis — job clustering. The focus has been on the identification of common skills, behaviors, knowledges, etc., across jobs in order to design curricula that are generalizable, or, in effect facilitative of adaptability.

Curriculum Commonalities Identified in Pittsburgh

The Pittsburgh Public Schools, under the leadership of Jerry C. Olsen,[9] have developed a career education program based on (1) the development of a program continuum (K-12 and then adult programs), (2) research leading to curriculum commonalities, and (3) a systems approach for the implementation and management of the program.

[9] Jerry C. Olsen, Superintendent for System-wide Programs, Division of Occupational, Vocational, and Technical Education, Pittsburgh Public Schools.

COMMONALITIES

Educational Programs   Spin-Off Levels   Licensing and/or Employment Alternatives

Nurses Aid, 93 Tasks

Practical Nurse 148 Tasks

COMMON TASKS 61

Surgical Technician 136 Tasks

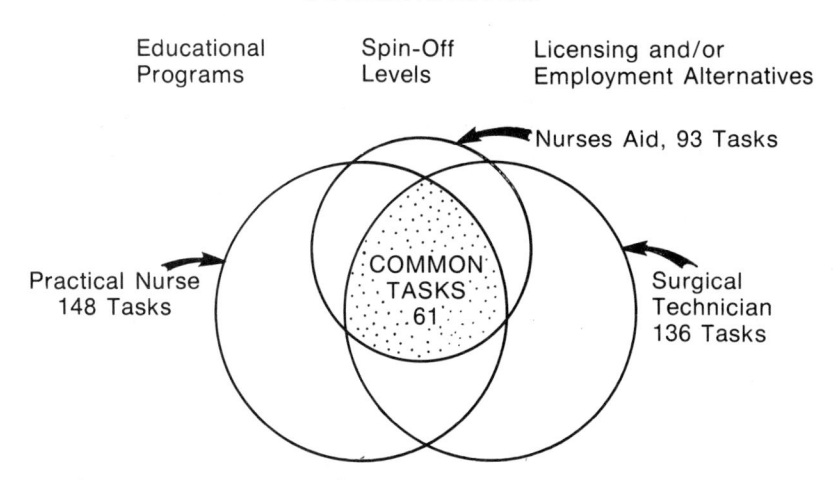

Fig. 2-3. Sixty-one tasks are common and basic to the fundamental instructional program in this job cluster of health occupations. (Pittsburg Public Schools)

Figure 2-3 illustrates the commonalities, consisting of sixty-one common tasks, in the job cluster covering the work of the practical nurse, nurse aide, and surgical technician. These commonalities serve as a base for the development of saleable skills and competencies in grades 10, 11, and 12 that are commensurate with a student's ability. The spin-off and placement opportunities within a job family cluster are tied closely to licensing and/or employment opportunities.

Figure 2-3 illustrates only one of the many clusters in Pittsburgh's program. To further exploratory experiences in grades 7 and 8, learners respond to hands-on activities relating to Business Communications, Information Processing, Merchandising, Clothing and Textiles, Foods and Nutrition, Home, Health and Community, Construction, Manufacturing, Power and Transportation, and Visual Communication. In grade 9 a student participates in any one of the mentioned ten cluster areas by organizing concepts that relate to his/her chosen occupational area. Then in grades 10, 11, and 12, the students participate in a specified skill-centered program designed to develop saleable competencies. The purpose of advanced experiences in the 13th and 14th grades is to enable students to study problem solving and strategy techniques and to apply these in a clinical skill development program as they study in depth in a particular field.

The task analyses for the jobs comprising a cluster are studied to determine the theoretical knowledge, technical skill, applied math skill, applied science skill, and communication skill necessary to function at various spin-off levels within the cluster. In commenting on this program for one of America's great cities, Jerry C. Olsen (1971, 310) has said:

> The purpose in studying commonalities is to develop educational programs that are open-ended and allow students to develop saleable skills and competencies that are commensurate with their abilities. Such a design allows for the identification of spin-off levels within a job family cluster. The identification of these levels is very closely tied to licensing and/or employment alternatives that are open to students who participate in the instruction in a specific cluster of occupations that show a wide range of commonalities.
>
> A wide range of clustered programs is necessary to provide the flexibility to serve the range of individuals seeking opportunities and to meet the needs of the total business/industry and service agencies existing in our community today.

The Oregon Way

Oregon has been one of the leaders in pioneering the career education movement. In describing "The Oregon Way," Dale Parnell, Superintendent of Public Instruction, has said that secondary schools should be preparatory institutions for all students. In addition to preparing students to go on to college, secondary schools should provide instruction that would prepare students to enter the world of work directly from high schools in positions that require less than a baccalaureate degree.

Parnell (1972, 57-58) has highlighted their plan in this way:

> A secondary school "preparatory" program should tie the curriculum to the goals of students in such a way that they are motivated while in school and also better equipped to choose from among many alternatives as they take the next step, whether it be on-the-job training, apprenticeship, community college, preparatory schools, a four-year college [or beyond].
>
> In Oregon, we are building an approach aimed at the development of skills and understanding which relate to a family of occupational fields. To put it another way, a cluster of occupations is a logical group of selected occupations which are related because they include similar teachable skill and knowledge requirements.
>
> Obviously, the implication is that most high school experiences will be centered upon the knowledge and skills common to the occupations which comprise a cluster or family. This structure not only has a motivational effect but will prepare students for entry into a broad family of occupations rather than a specific occupation.

While the primary goal is to organize appropriate career education for secondary schools, the Oregon plan is concerned also with a total coordinated approach for the vertical and horizontal articulation of career education, at all educational levels (i.e., kindergarten through productive life). To illustrate, specialized occupational training, over and above the generalized occupational instruction (that is based on occupational clusters) is largely the responsibility of post-high school institutions (i.e., community colleges, on-the-job training, apprenticeship programs, or private technical schools).

While the instruction for the thirteen-cluster high-school program is planned to provide entry-level employment opportunities, it provides also for the student who plans to go on and specialize in post-secondary occupational programs. Thus, through a greatly strengthened guidance and counseling program, students in Oregon will:
1. Be introduced to occupational life in grades K-6 with the focus on **Career Awareness.**
2. Have an opportunity for **Career Exploration** in grades 7-10.
3. Be acquiring general **Career Education Competencies** within a chosen occupational cluster in grades 11 and 12 for entry-level employment and/or advanced occupational training in a post-secondary setting.
4. Be provided with numerous possibilities for more **Specialized Occupational Education** courses and programs before or after entering the labor force.

Parnell (1972, 55-61) stresses that Oregon's articulated occupational program is being projected with the objective of not having any student "locked in" to any single career choice. The process is being kept flexible so that it is possible for a student to change from one occupational cluster to another with minimal frustration.

The Oregon System Translates Manpower and Employment Data into Essential Instruction

The process employed in this model to develop the career education clusters is shown in Figs. 2-4 and 2-5. These diagrams illustrate the steps that are followed in translating world-of-work data into instruction needed for the implementation of the program in the Oregon schools.

GENERAL MODEL OF CLUSTER DEVELOPMENT

```
WORLD OF WORK
      ↓
IDENTIFICATION OF CLUSTERS
      ↓
OCCUPATIONAL ANALYSIS TO IDENTIFY KEY AND RELATED
OCCUPATIONS WITHIN CLUSTERS
      ↓
TASK-COMPETENCY ANALYSIS OF KEY OCCUPATIONS
      ↓
INSTRUCTIONAL ANALYSIS
(CLUSTER GUIDE)
      ↓
IMPLEMENTATION
```

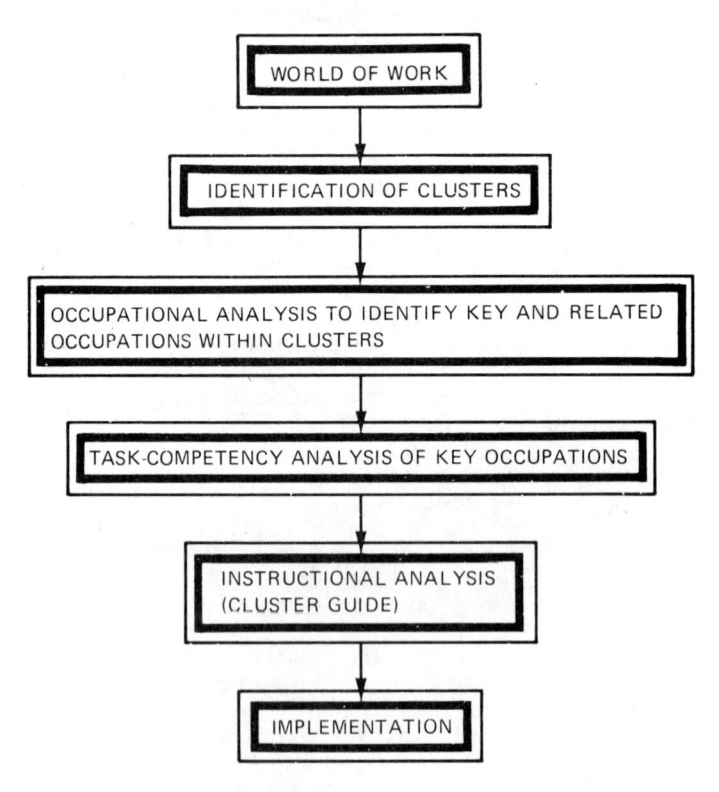

Fig. 2-4. Process employed in Oregon Career Education Cluster to translate manpower data into essential instruction (Multanen, 1973, 98)

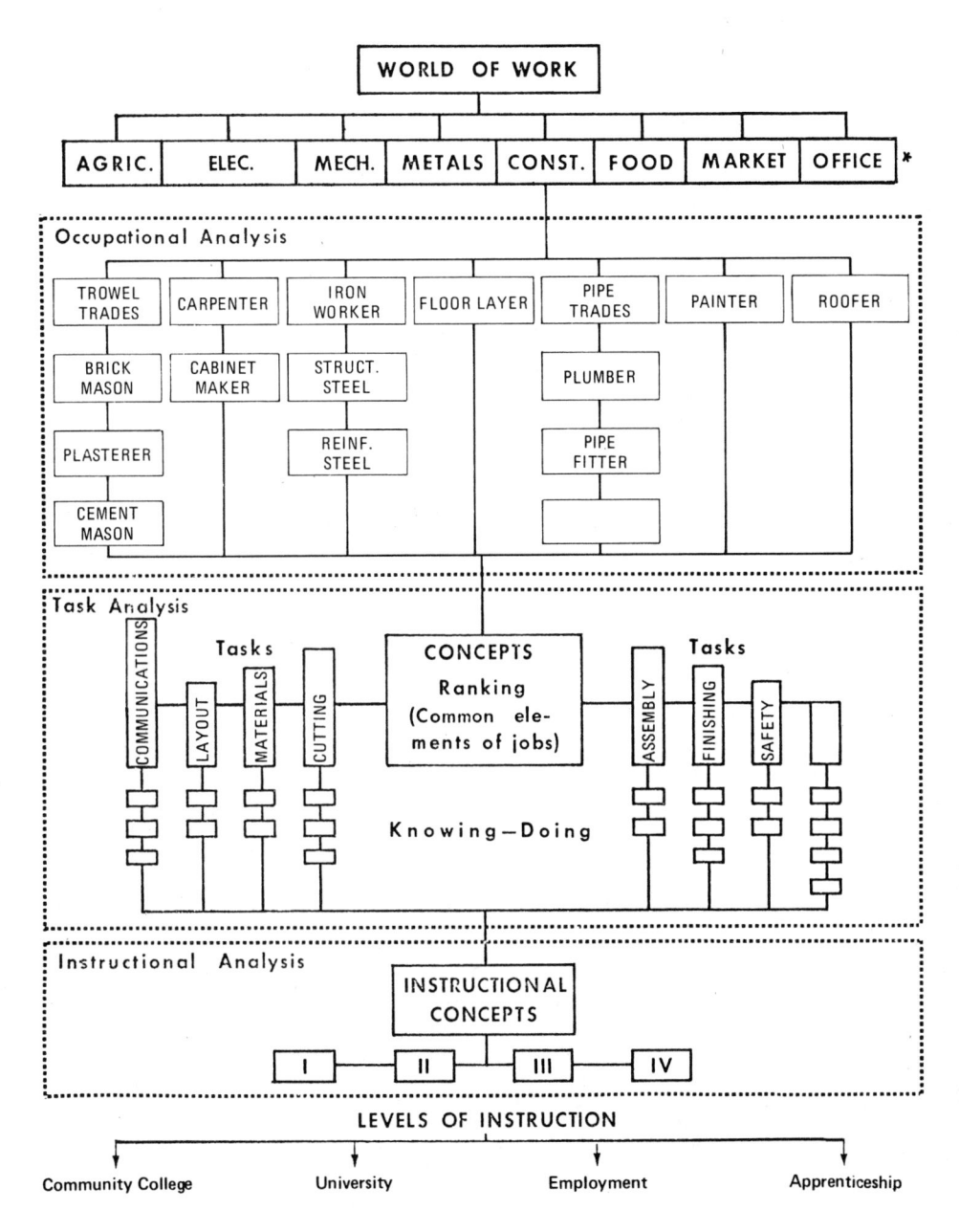

Fig. 2-5. Key occupations included in the Oregon building construction cluster. This diagram illustrates the process followed in the occupational analysis, the task analysis, and in establishing the instructional program.

*Only eight of the thirteen clusters are shown in this figure.

Planning and Organizing Instruction

In the identification of clusters, more than 20,000 possible careers, as listed in the DOT, are represented under the following thirteen career clusters:[10]

Accounting — Bookkeeping	Electricity — Electronics	Marketing
Agriculture	Food Services	Metals
Clerical	Forest Products	Service Occupations
Construction	Health	Secretarial
	Industrial Mechanics	

General Model of Oregon Plan

Multanen (1973, 96-97) explains that cluster development begins with the overall world of work and proceeds through the steps of cluster identification, occupational analysis to identify key occupations, task-competency analysis, instructional analysis, and, finally, implementation. These steps are explained in this manner:

1. **Identification of Clusters**
   The criteria for the identification and establishment of a cluster area in Oregon includes a grouping of occupations having similar competency requirements with 10,000 or more people employed in the occupational cluster group. In addition, it requires a projected expansion and/or replacement need of at least 2,000 in the next five years.
2. **Occupational Analysis**
   The purpose of the occupational analysis is to identify key and related occupations. The criteria for a key occupation specifies an employment of a minimum of 250 people, with a five-year expansion and replacement of 100 or more in the state. Related occupations are those with similar competencies in which 100 or more people are employed. [The top section of Fig. 2-5 shows the key occupations that have been identified for the Construction Cluster.]
3. **Task-Competency Analysis**
   Task analyses are completed on key occupations [as shown in Fig. 2-6]. These task inventories are compared to identify competencies common to all the key occupations involved and to the cluster in general. At this analysis stage the original inclusion of an occupation within a cluster can be validated on a detailed competency basis.
   Examples of a task-competency analysis:

---

[10]Guides for each cluster have been prepared by The Division of Community Colleges and Career Education through the involvement of the key officers of the Oregon Department of Education and a State Advisory Committee for each of the cluster areas. The documents are published by The Oregon Board of Education and are available through Leonard Kunzman, Director of Career Education, 942 Lancaster Drive NE, Salem, OR 97310.

TASK-COMPETENCY ANALYSIS

1. Inventory tasks for key occupations
2. Analyze tasks for similarity between occupations and rank tasks
3. Determine competencies common to the occupations and the cluster
4. Validate inclusion of occupation in cluster on a common competency basis

TASK INVENTORY

Job Title _____

Analyst _____

	Processes				
	Communication				
	Measurement				
	Problem-Solving				
	Decision-Making				
	Rule Using				
	Logical Manipulation				
	Synthesis				
	Estimating				
	Classifying				
	Coding				
	Discriminating or Identifying				
	Manipulative Sequencing				
	Detecting				
	Sensing				
Frequency	Great Amount				
	Average Amount				
	Small Amount				
Level of Difficulty	Difficult				
	Moderate				
	Easy				
Entry Level	On The Job				
	Entry				

INSTRUCTIONS:

List each manipulative and knowledge skill relating to the job noted above. To the right of each task is a series of columns asking specific questions about the entry level, level of difficulty, frequency, and type of skill involved as indicated on the sample sheet.

Block No.	Task No.	Task Description				

Fig. 2-6. There are four steps in the Task-Competency Analysis.

Task	Competency
a. Lubricate automobile.	Use lubrication equipment.
b. Lubricate typewriter.	
c. Lubricate washing machine.	
d. Lubricate food processor.	
e. Lubricate refrigeration system.[11]	

4. Instructional Analysis

    This step involves the identification of entry level tasks and those that should be learned in school rather than on the job. Expected behaviors are identified and objectives written based on the task competency analysis. Classroom activities are organized and curriculum materials developed to accomplish the instructional objectives [examples of manpower and needs data translated into essential curriculum content and materials is shown in Appendices B and I].

5. Implementation

    An important organizing principle in the Oregon plan is that occupations be grouped on the basis of common competencies. In this context a worker possesses a competency when he/she has the ability to efficiently perform the tasks under consideration. Implicit in this point of view is a consideration of all of the recognized aspects (cognitive, psychomotor, and affective) of the tasks performed.

Identifying and Selecting Content for a General Vocational Program

A review of the literature in applied arts and vocational education will reveal that considerable space has been devoted to proposals and programs to further prevocational education goals and objectives. These programs were promulgated after the passage of the Smith-Hughes Act (1917) and were somewhat popular until about 1960. In general, they were planned as junior high school programs and to serve as feeders for the specialized vocational courses offered selected students (those identified as able to profit from vocational programs) at the senior high school level. While a good number of these programs sprang up throughout America, there was opposition to them since they had such limited objectives. The professionals in the applied arts fields of homemaking, general business, and industrial arts education opposed having their courses promulgated exclusively as feeders for specialized training in senior high schools. They advocated much broader goals, identified with "general" rather than "specialized" education for their programs.

The need for these prevocational courses, as they were originally and narrowly conceived, was eliminated with the passage of the Vocational Education Act of 1963 and the Amendments of 1968. This recent legislation calls for a broader focus on clusters of occupations, such as the Pittsburgh and Oregon plans just described.

[11]Reprinted from p. 4 of **Occupational Career Clusters** "The Oregon Way", October, 1972, Oregon State Department of Education, Salem, Oregon 97310.

The Need for Identifying Programs: Objectives and Content for General Occupational Development

With the advent of the career education movement (Chapter 1) and National Assessment of Educational Progress[12] (Chapter 11), there has been a new interest and focus on general objectives and programs for career and occupational development. Three reports are briefly mentioned to illustrate present concerns for identifying a body of content that would support objectives, skills, and knowledges fundamental to occupational development. They are (1) **Research on General Vocational Capabilities** (Altman, 1966), (2) **Career and Occupational Development Objectives** (Nichols, 1970), and (3) **An Instructional Program for Employability Orientation** (Osborn, 1972).

The brief resumé of the report (prepared by Altman) on the **Research on General Vocational Capabilities** (skills and knowledges) conducted under a grant from the Ford Foundation, states:

> The objectives were to 1) develop and verify methods for determining general capabilities required for jobs, 2) describe the general vocational capabilities of high school students and relate them to intellectual aptitudes and educational experience, and 3) derive educational implications from an analysis of these general vocational capabilities. Task behaviors for each of 31 occupations having major employment opportunities in the future were translated into multiple choice test items. The items, rationally organized into a set of tests resulting in a total of 24 tests, were administered to about 10,000 students from grade 9 through junior college in the Woods County (Parkersburg), West Virginia and Quincy, Massachusetts Schools Systems. Analyses were performed for girls and boys separately and for the combined group scores of all tests for each occupation were analyzed in terms of relative male versus female mean performances.
>
> One of the major findings was that there is a definable and well-structured domain of vocational capabilities which has not previously been well defined and which is not being systematically taught by educational institutions. This domain promises to enhance the flexibility with which students can apply the results of their educational experiences. The appendix (in the report by Altman) includes samples of products from interim stages of the project and some of the detailed statistical results.[13]

---

[12]National Assessment of Educational Progress is a national census-like survey of the knowledge, skills, understandings, and attitudes of children and young adults. It is a project of The Education Commission of the States, 1860 Lincoln Street, Denver, Colorado 80203.

[13]This resumé was reprinted from the ERIC abstract.

The report covering **Career and Occupational Objectives** for the National Assessment of Educational Progress (NAEP) identifies Career and Occupational Development (COD) objectives that belong to a number of disciplines. The objectives identify knowledge and abilities which result from guidance and counseling, general education, and life experiences. These achievements "include self-evaluation, thoughtful career planning, realistic attitudes toward work, employment-seeking skills, effective work habits, and the development of skills generally useful in a variety of occupations."

This report from the committee classifies career and occupational development objectives under the following five major classifications:

I. PREPARE FOR MAKING CAREER DECISIONS
  A. **Know own characteristics relevant to career decisions.**
    1. Are aware of own current abilities and limitations.
    2. Are aware of own current interests and values.
    3. Seek knowledge of themselves.
  B. **Know the characteristics and requirements of different careers and occupations.**
    1. Know major duties and required abilities of different careers and occupational families.
    2. Know differences in work conditions among and within occupational families.
    3. Know entry requirements for occupations.
    4. Are aware of the impact of social and technological changes on occupations.
    5. Know important factors that affect job success and satisfaction.
    6. Seek information about occupations in general or about specific jobs.
  C. **Relate own personal characteristics to occupation requirements.**
    1. Associate own abilities and limitations with possible success in present or future occupational pursuits.
    2. Relate personal interests and values to job characteristics and occupations.
  D. **Plan for career development or change.**
    1. Consider relevant factors in planning toward an occupation or career.
    2. Are aware of alternative career choices or occupations and consider the consequences of career changes.
II. IMPROVE CAREER AND OCCUPATIONAL CAPABILITIES
III. POSSESS SKILLS THAT ARE GENERALLY USEFUL IN THE WORLD OF WORK
  A. Have generally useful numerical skills.
    1. Perform calculations and transactions involving money.

Identifying and Selecting Content **57**

   2. Understand numerical values in graphs, charts, tables.
   3. Use measurement equivalents, ratios, and proportions.
   4. Estimate numerical quantities.
   5. Compare numerical values.
   6. Calculate amounts needed to do practical jobs.
   7. Make graphic representations of numerical quantities.
   8. Interpret statistical data.
   B. **Have generally useful communication skills.**
      1. Communicate understandably (speak, write, demonstrate, and use nonverbal means).
      2. Understand communications.
      3. Interact verbally with others.
   C. **Have generally useful manual-perceptual skills.**
      1. Use common tools and equipment.
      2. Make and assemble, using appropriate materials.
      3. Adjust, repair, and maintain.
      4. Read displays and scales.
      5. Make visual representations.
   D. **Have generally useful information-processing and decision-making skills.**
      1. Learn efficiently and remember specifics, procedures, and principles which are basic to further learning or which are frequently needed in their work.
      2. Apply concepts, principles, and procedures in circumstances different from those in which learned.
      3. Analyze information and define problems.
      4. Collect and organize data.
      5. Develop and evaluate alternatives.
      6. Make decisions or choose alternatives in terms of relevant criteria.
      7. Devise plans, new ideas, and better ways of doing things.
      8. Implement and modify plans on the basis of feedback.
   E. **Have generally useful interpersonal skills.**
      1. Interact constructively with supervisors.
      2. Provide effective leadership.
      3. Work effectively with peers, co-workers, and others.
   F. **Have employment-seeking skills.**
IV. PRACTICE EFFECTIVE WORK HABITS
   A. **Assume responsibility for own behavior.**
   B. **Plan work.**
   C. **Use initiative and ingenuity to fulfill responsibilities.**
      1. Use initiative but seek assistance when needed.
      2. Are resourceful in accomplishing work.
   D. **Adapt to varied conditions.**
   E. **Maintain good health and grooming.**

V. HAVE POSITIVE ATTITUDES TOWARD WORK
   A. Recognize the bases of various attitudes toward work.
   B. Hold competence and excellence in high regard.
   C. Seek personal fulfillment through own achievements.
   D. Value work in terms of societal goals (Nichols, et al, IV-VI).

The broad goal of the research on **An Instructional Program for Employability Orientation** by Osborn et al (1972, 3) for the Human Resources Research Organization (Hum RRO) "was to increase awareness, understanding, and development of attitudes, other than job skills, that are necessary to obtain and hold a job and to advance, commensurate with ability within a career field." There were four subgoals with an implied order for implementation, as illustrated in Fig. 2-7. They state that the enrollee must —

Subgoal I

To enable an enrollee to meet home and family responsibilities so that he (she) is able to attend to the demands of employment

- Food
- Clothing
- (Residency)
- Health
- Child Care

- Family Relations
- Money Management
- (Transportation)
- Community Resources

Subgoal II

To enable an enrollee to develop an understanding of factors affecting career choice, and to acquire attributes prerequisite to the attainment of employment goals.

- Self-Concept
- Vocational Goals
- { Personal Hygiene
- { Grooming

Subgoal IV

To enable an enrollee to sustain employment and to advance, commensurate with ability, within a chosen field.

- Job Performance
- Employee Relations
- { Company Policies
- { Union Policies

Subgoal III

To enable an enrollee to seek and obtain full-time employment appropriate to capabilities and career expectations and interests.

- Job Searching
- Application
- Test Taking

- Interviewing
- Job Assessment

Note: ( ) indicates item omitted on basis of survey results;
{ indicates items combined on basis of survey results.

Fig. 2-7. Orientation Subgoals and Subject Areas of Employability Orientation (Reproduced from p. 4 of Handbook by Hum RRO for U. S. Department of Labor)

1. Be able to cope with home environment.
2. Be able to realistically assess his or her vocational goals.
3. Be able to obtain an appropriate job.
4. Be able to perform successfully within a vocation.

The instruction suggested in the manual containing the guidelines for the WIN Orientation Training Program[14] has been organized under these eighteen subject areas or modules of instruction[15] (Osborn, et al, 1972, 5).

A. Food	J. Grooming Hygiene
B. Clothing	K. Job Searching
C. Health	L. Job Application
D. Child Care	M. Test Taking
E. Family Relations	N. Job Interviewing
F. Money Management	O. Job Assessment
G. Community Resources	P. Job Performance
H. Self-Concept	Q. Employee Relations
I. Vocational Goals	R. Company and Union Policies

Fifty-one relevant behaviors (shown in first column of Table 2-1) were identified and translated into behavioral objectives. Each of the eighteen modules is organized so that it may be tailored to the specific needs of a trainee. Table 2-1 illustrates how this instruction in employability orientation has been organized according to the sub-goals of the program. The topics for the eighteen modules are analyzed and coordinated with the fifty-one identified behaviors. The reference numbers that have been assigned to the instructional units for each of the fifty-one behaviors are also shown in Table 2-1. Topics listed as "Essential" are considered to be the core program to be presented to all trainees.

Identifying and Selecting Content through an Inventory of Payroll Tasks

The content of much of occupational education is based on an analysis of tasks performed for a payroll designation. The instruction to prepare persons for such service is predicated on a selection of the tasks that are most basic and essential in the occupational area. This approach for identifying VAE content will be illustrated by two rather diverse applications. First is a sophisticated computerized system for identifying and codifying the essential work tasks of medical laboratory specialists. Second is a system to identify and validate the competencies needed to meet on-the-job standards in an entry-level position.

---

[14]The national WIN Orientation Training Program was conceived by the U.S. Department of Labor in recognition of the fact that finding, keeping, and advancing in a job requires knowledges and skills over and above and basic to those of a purely job-function nature.

[15]A module is used in the systems approach to curriculum development to describe a functional package of instruction organized to be undertaken by the learner on an individual basis. The behavioral objectives, instructional materials, prerequisite skills tests, the learning experiences, and the exit tests are included in a module of instruction.

Table 2-1
Fifty-One Desired Behaviors Indexed Against the 18 Modules and the 4 Subgoals for the Employability Orientation Program

Subgoal I To Enable an Enrollee to Meet Home and Family Responsibilities so That He (She) is Able to Attend to the Demands of Employment

	Trainee Need			Instructional Unit
	Essential	Desirable	Pretest	
A. Food			✓	
1. Menu Planning		F		A1, A2
2. Comparative Shopping for Food		F		A3
B. Clothing			✓	
3. Selecting Work Clothes		MF*		B1, B2
4. Comparative Shopping for Clothing	M	F		B3
5. Maintaining Clothing		MF*		B4, B5
C. Health			✓	
6. Preventing Unwanted Pregnancy	M	F*		C1, C2
7. Health Practices in the Home		MF		C3
8. Safety Hazards in the Home		MF		C4
D. Child Care			✓	
9. Arranging Child Care Services	M*	F*		D1
10. Evaluating Quality of Child Care	M*	F*		D1
E. Family Relations			✓	
11. Needs and Rights of Family Members		MF		E1
12. Scheduling Family Activities	MF			E1
13. Scheduling Household Chores	MF			E2
F. Money Management			✓	
14. Budgeting Expenses	MF			F1
15. Recording Expenses	MF			F1
16. Savings Accounts	M			F2
17. Sources of Credit	MF			F3, F4
18. Establishing a Credit Rating	MF			F5
G. Community Resources			✓	
19. Contacting Community Service Agencies	M*	F*		G1, G2, G3
20. Recreational and Cultural Facilities	MF			G1, G2, G3
21. Educational Facilities	MF*			G1, G2, G3
22. Legal Services		MF		G4

(continued on next page)

Identifying and Selecting Content   **61**

Table 2-1 (continued)

Subgoal II To Enable an Enrollee to Develop an Understanding of Factors Affecting Career Choice and to Acquire Attributes Prerequisite to the Attainment of Employment Goals

	Trainee Need			Instructional Unit
	Essential	Desirable	Pretest	
H. Self Concept				
23. Self-worth	M*F*			H1, H2, H3
24. Ability to Improve	M*F*			H4, H5, H6
25. Contributing to Others	MF			H7
26. Desire to Obtain Employment		M*F*		H8, H9
I. Vocational Goals				
27. Awareness of Job Opportunities	M*F*			I1
28. Personal Strengths and Weaknesses	MF			I1, I3, I4, I5, I6, I7, I8, I9
J. Grooming and Hygiene			✔	
29. Personal Cleanliness		M*F*		J1
30. Effects of Body Condition		M*F*		J1

Subgoal III To Enable an Enrollee to Seek and Obtain Full-Time Employment Appropriate to Capabilities and Career Expectations and Interests

	Trainee Need			Instructional Unit
	Essential	Desirable	Pretest	
K. Job Searching				
31. Potential Job Openings	M*F*			K1, K2
32. Initial Employer Contact	M*F*			K1, K2
L. Application			✔	
33. Employment Forms	M*F*			L1
34. Employer Criteria	MF			L1
M. Test Taking			✔	
35. Test Taking Procedures	MF			M1
36. Responding to Question Types	MF			M1
37. Standardized Answer Sheets	MF			M1
N. Interviewing			✔	
38. Supplying Interview Information	F	M		N1
39. Evaluating Job Offer	MF			N1
40. Interviewer Criteria	MF			N2
O. Job Assessment				
41. Transportation Requirements	MF*			O1
42. Long-Term Opportunities	MF			O2, O3

Table 2-1 (continued)

Subgoal IV To Enable an Enrollee to Sustain Employment and Advance Within a Chosen Field Commensurate With Ability

	Trainee Need Essential	Trainee Need Desirable	Trainee Need Pretest	Instructional Unit
P. Job Performance				
43. Established Work Standards	M*F*			P1
44. Attendance and Punctuality	M*F*			P1
Q. Employee Relations				
45. Fellow Employees		M*F*		Q1, Q2
46. Supervisors	M*	F*		Q1, Q2*
R. Company and Union Policies				
47. Employer Rights	M*F*			R1
48. Fringe Benefits	F*	M*		R2
49. Advancement Opportunities	M*F*			R3
50. Employee Rights	MF			R4
51. Union Regulations	MF			R4

Reference numbers (1 through 51), as identified under the 18 modules, are shown for instruction developed for each of the 51 behaviors. The * indicates that the instruction is to be checked for possible duplication as programs are tailored for each trainee. Table 2-1 was reproduced from pp. 13-15 of the Handbook by HumRRO for the U.S. Department of Labor.

Task Analysis Techniques Employed by the Air Force

For the past several years, the Occupational and Career Development Branch of the Personnel Research Division (AFHRL) at the Lackland Air Force Base in San Antonio, Texas, has been developing methods in job analysis, job evaluation, work organization, career planning, reassignment systems, performance evaluation, and job requirements. It has been especially concerned with military technical school curricula and methods for translating occupational information into a form useful for curriculum definition.

In reporting the Lackland research program, Christal observed that planning an educational program for a military technical training school is considerably less difficult than planning a vocational-technical program for the public sector. According to Christal (1970, 27-28) the reasons are that:
1. The majority of individuals entering the services have already graduated from high school.
2. Most of the military technical courses are of short duration.
3. When a person is in service and sent for technical training, the decision has already been made that he/she is being trained to perform work in a particular occupation.

4. The military services do not need to protect individuals against their skills becoming obsolete. If an occupational area shrinks in size or is eliminated, individuals are simply retrained for service in other areas.
5. The services usually have considerable advanced warning before jobs are established requiring new occupational skills.
6. Technical training for the services does not end when the trainee leaves the technical school since there may well be formalized on-the-job training and advanced training when it is warranted.

Christal indicates that:

> ... there are about 600,000 enlisted personnel (in the Air Force) performing thousands of different types of jobs at hundreds of locations throughout the world. Each of these jobs has been established by some local commander who can, within limits, assign work to men any way he sees fit to accomplish his mission. It is the function of the Air Force training establishment to provide individuals with the knowledges and skills they will need for performing the jobs they will encounter. This means that the local commander needs some way to communicate the nature of the jobs he has established to trainers. Until recently, his only means for communication was through the assignment of a five-digit specialty number to each job, classifying it into one of approximately 250 career ladders, at the apprentice, journeyman, first-line supervisor, or superintendent level. This system is grossly inadequate, because it does not provide information at a sufficient level of detail for curriculum designers.
>
> Because of the serious lack of information, the first goal we established for our occupational research program was to develop techniques by which the Air Force could collect more detailed and specific information about the jobs being assigned to personnel. We finally settled on a technique involving the administration of job inventories to workers in the field (Christal, 1970, 28-29).

Job Inventory Plan Employed by Air Force

The first section contains background questions relating to such items as previous education, time on the job, tools utilized, equipment worked on, interest in the job, and pay grade. If this approach were used in civilian life, there might be questions that would provide essential information about the occupational area, such as working hours and products manufactured.

The second section contains the master inventory listing of all significant tasks performed by workers in the vocational area being surveyed (i.e., all of the tasks being performed by apprentices, journeymen, first-line supervisors, and superintendents) in the single occupational area under study (e.g., automotive repair or firefighting). If the listing of tasks is properly constructed and complete, then every worker in the occupational area will be able to define his/her job by checking a selected subset of tasks in the inventory.

The inventory of tasks is then administered to all workers in the career ladders of the occupation under study. In the heavily populated occupational areas this would include several thousand workers. This is done as each worker completes the background questions, checks the tasks he/she performs, writes in any significant task accomplished that may not be on the list, and indicates how his/her work-time is distributed across the tasks in the job.

These data are then sent to a central agency to be analyzed by a computer. A number of computer programs have been developed for use in organizing and reporting the job inventory data in a form that is convenient and useful for those developing curriculum materials for the technical training programs. The typical record generated for each case contains identification information, answers to background questions, and the amount of time spent on each of the identified tasks that, in turn, accounts for 100 percent of the person's time. An information bank is, therefore, generated as these data for all individuals in an occupational area are fed into the computer.

Appendix C of this book includes two tables showing the analysis of duties (Table C-1) and of the tasks for 394 Journeymen Medical Laboratory Specialists (Table C-2). The introductory paragraphs for **Appendix C** mention considerations for the possible use of these data in developing a training program to prepare medical laboratory specialists.

Individualized-Task Instruction Packet (I-TIP)

The NOBELS research project (Lanham et al., 1972)[16] provides direction and content for curricula in office occupations. This project identifies and validates 373 task statements (in behavioral terms) to be employed in structuring a learning system for office occupations curricula. While the NOBELS outcomes are most helpful in planning curricula, leaders and teachers in business education observed that these office task statements need to be broken down for instructional purposes, with their subpoints analyzed and validated. This is the major mission, therefore, of the Individualized-Task Instruction Packet (I-TIP) research project carried on at Wayne State University under the leadership of Kathleen M. Herschelmann et al., since September, 1970.

Mrs. Herschelmann has developed over 700 task packets through the involvement of business education teachers, students at the University in preparation to become teachers, and cooperating personnel from the business offices of the community. Each packet provides the specificity that outlines what a student must do to acquire the competency that will meet on-the-job work standards in the performance of the task. A "task" in this project is defined as a collection of activities performed by one person and directed toward the achievement of a single objective or output. Each task description must be planned to cover enough of the content (skills and knowledges) to justify its place in the instructional program. The following task and steps sheet, Fig. 2-8, titled "Types Letter from Handwritten Copy" illustrates thirteen steps in the breakdown (the analysis) of this one task.

[16]The NOBELS study is described in Chapter 3.

Name _____ Estimated Time (15.9m) _____

Date _____ Actual Time _____

Additional Materials Needed Carbon paper, stapler _____

Task Setting The office employee types for the Detroit branch of a

New York insurance company. _____

TASK: Types Letter From Handwritten Copy.

STEPS:

1. Receives handwritten copy of letter from insurance agent.
2. Edits handwritten copy.
3. Types letter in triplicate using agent's stationery.
4. Proofreads letter.
5. Obtains agent's signature on letter.
6. Types mailing envelope.
7. Proofreads envelope.
8. Obtains loan application card from desk.
9. Inserts original copy of letter and two enclosures in mailing envelope.
10. Places mailing envelope in mail tray.
11. Places one copy of letter in desk file.
12. Staples handwritten letter to third copy of letter.
13. Places stapled letters in agent's file.

Fig. 2-8. Typical "task and steps sheet" from the I-TIP project.

Each of the packets is made up of the following:
1. A page of I-TIP instructions.
2. A task and steps page showing the subpoints in the performance of the task (such as sample shown as Fig. 2-8).
3. The source documents from which the worker performs the task (such as copy of a handwritten letter).
4. Materials needed by the worker to complete the task.

5. A model of the finished product that meets on-the-job standards acceptable to the office worker involved in the development and approval of the product for the packet.

One of the unique aspects of I-TIP is that working supplies in these packets are replicas of actual forms and letterheads used in the business world, so that the student can present his/her product under conditions which simulate those in the world of work.

Procedures employed in the development of an Individualized-Task Instruction Packet and the storage of these materials in the I-TIP Computer Bank are these:

1. First-year entry workers (16-18 years of age) are interviewed by business education teachers to determine what tasks these workers perform.
2. The I-TIPS are then made by the business education teachers, tested in their classes, and given back to the employees in the business world (who are cooperating in the development of an I-TIP). This is done to determine which students met employment standards and criteria for the particular task. When all aspects of a model are acceptable which may call for reworking and revising the steps and again checking them with the cooperating employee from the world of work, the packet for the task is then added to the I-TIP Materials and Computer Banks for completed and approved I-TIPS.
3. The I-TIPS are stored in a Materials Bank at Wayne State University so that they are readily available to teachers who have participated in the I-TIP program and who bring reflex masters to the University to make copies of the originals for use in the community schools.
4. Typical questions raised by teachers in the identification, selection, and use of I-TIPS on file were helpful in the development of the coding form for the I-TIP Computer Bank. The completed form is used to place information about an I-TIP in the Basic Indexing and Retrieval System (BIRS)[17] employed to facilitate the I-TIP Computer Bank. Answers to queries now directed to the computer through BIRS program aid business education teachers in locating needed I-TIPS for a desired instructional program.
5. To facilitate the use of the I-TIP materials outside of the Detroit Metropolitan Area, arrangements have been made to publish 100 I-TIPS in four units. Persons interested in a list of the tasks included in each of these four units are encouraged to contact Kathleen M. Herschelmann at Wayne State University. Additional I-TIPS will be published for national use when the demand dictates.

Business education teachers who have assisted with the development of the I-TIPS hasten to mention the significance of the I-TIP approach for bringing the world of work into their classrooms. They recognize that this is a sound system for preparing young people in the high schools for entry-level employment in the business occupations. To illustrate, Rosetta L. Royster, a business education teacher at the Hunter

[17]BIRS is a collection of computer programs written in FORTRAN for implementing the design and development of information systems for education and related social sciences. BIRS was used in establishing the retrieval system for the I-TIP Computer Bank.

School in Detroit, Michigan, reports on her experiences in developing I-TIPS for four beginning clerk-typists employed in the Detroit area at the Kirkwood General Hospital, Henry Ford Hospital, McCord Corporation, and Ex-Cell-O Corporation:

> For this project, I considered a beginning clerk-typist as a person who started on the job after the completion of high school and who had not worked over one year on that particular job. It is also important to note that the area chosen — whether it be clerical, computing, recording, or something else — is left entirely up to the individual interviewer.
>
> After locating the various businesses with workers that met my criteria and making the necessary arrangements for the interviews, I used the standard form for recording the data gathered. During each interview, I was able to observe the worker step-by-step as she performed her tasks. Thus, through this observation, I was able to record the steps necessary for preparing the I-TIPS; and at the end of each interview, the worker as well as the employer was very helpful in giving me the forms, letterheads, envelopes, and copies of handwritten rough draft to accompany the steps.
>
> Once the I-TIPS had been tested by the students, they were taken back to the workers for their evaluations in terms of what would be acceptable to their employers.[18]

Identifying Content through Instructional Analysis

Instructional analysis is the process by which educators study a trade subject such as welding or an applied arts activity such as plastics and identify the repetitive operations and the informational content to be taught to a learner, whose goal is to become proficient or develop understanding in the subject or activity. The manipulative phases of occupational education are organized as operations with each operation further broken down by listing procedures and other essential data for teaching purposes. Content, informational in character and not included in the breakdown of operations, can be organized in an instructional analysis as informational topics.

When a complete instructional analysis for a subject or activity has been made and each of the operations and informational topics outlined, the total content for a subject or activity has been identified. Such an analysis then serves as an encyclopedia, or as the resource material, for the selection of content to be taught. Content for a single course can be selected from the total instructional analysis of the subject or activity. For example, the high school teacher of machine shop would need a complete instructional analysis for the subject, with the operations and the independent informational topics broken down in outline form. From such

---

[18]Rosetta L. Royster report presented on the I-TIP system to members of a graduate seminar at Wayne State University, 1972 summer quarter.

an encyclopedia of content for machine shop, the teacher, possibly with the help of an advisory committee, could select the operations and informational topics to be placed in each of the machine shop courses in his/her school. It should be clear that some of the advanced or involved operations and independent informational topics appearing in the analysis for machine shop would undoubtedly not be selected for the basic course which would aim to teach the fundamentals of machine shop practice. The content selected by the teacher, or a committee, for a specific course of study would depend entirely upon the aims for that course.

Instructional Analysis as a Research Technique

Vocational leaders during the early years of the twentieth century realized the need to analyze the trades so that teaching units could be identified and selected. A course in trade analysis was basic in the professional preparation of tradesmen recruited to teach vocational subjects. C. R. Allen identified and reported these techniques for making an analysis of a trade in **The Instructor, the Man, and the Job** published in 1919.[19]

In 1923 Robert W. Selvidge clarified the process of instructional analysis in his book **How to Teach a Trade** which received wide acceptance.[20] Verne C. Fryklund, who had worked closely with the late Professor Selvidge while he was at the University of Missouri, did further refining and simplifying of the process of instructional analysis. He developed a more functional classification for informational topics when he authored **Trade and Job Analysis** in 1943. Fryklund has continued to revise his book and keep it up to date. It is now published under the title **Occupational Analysis: Techniques & Procedures**, as the fifth edition, and is widely used as a basic textbook for professional college courses where the objective is to teach teachers to identify content through instructional analysis for a subject or activity.

Manipulative Work Analyzed as Operations

One of the unique features of industrial education (and some of the other vocational curriculum areas) is that it has been basically an activity program. The learners are taught to use tools and machines and learn industrial processes as they plan, form, inspect, operate, shape, disassemble, repair, assemble, and test work. The **manipulative phase of the activity is analyzed as operations**, and it is the operations that are repeated by workers as they perform different jobs. The subject or activity determines the degree to which the content is manipulative. For example, a high percentage of an instructional analysis for machine shop is concerned with operations, with the informational topics more and more essential but fewer in number. On the other hand, an instructional

---

[19]Published by Lippincott Company of Philadelphia (373 pages).
[20]Published by The Manual Arts Press (now the Chas. A. Bennett Co., Inc.) of Peoria, Illinois (111 pages).

Identifying and Selecting Content 69

analysis of electronics will consist primarily of technical and vital informational topics, while the operations will be of secondary importance.

Before applying the research procedures for identifying the repetitive manipulative operations for a vocational subject[21] or a practical arts activity, one needs to understand:
1. That the title for an operation is a statement to describe a segment of what the student should be able to do in using his hands, tools, and machines, to do such things as shape, form, repair, assemble, and test work.
2. That an operation is one unit of the manipulative work in an instructional analysis which should not be considered synonymous with a unit of instruction for some course. The unit of instruction in industrial arts, for example, may consist of all of the instruction that is tied to some exciting and meaningful project or other activity. This means that it might be necessary for the teacher to demonstrate a number of tool and machine operations involved in completing a particular activity or project that was being used as the basis for a unit of instruction.
3. That the operations are the basic fundamentals of a vocational or technical subject or an activity in the practical arts. The operation is the transferable unit from one job or project to another.
4. That an operation is repeated as learners or persons, competent in the field, go about their work. For example, the operation, to turn between centers on an engine lathe, is repeated by the learner as he/she constructs projects in a machine shop course or by a skilled machinist as he/she works in industry.
5. That the learner develops skill only where there is meaningful repetition of an operation. For example, if the student's only experience with the operation, **turn between centers on an engine lathe,** was to have seen the teacher's demonstration of that operation, he/she surely would have little more than an appreciation of the steps involved in that operation. Only after the learner has performed the operation two or more times under the direct supervision of the teacher (or associates), to insure meaningful repetition, could there be any assurance that any degree of skill has developed in doing that particular operation.

The operation used in the example is performed by students in general metal courses to contribute to their basic education, as well as those taking vocational machine shop, where the objective is occupational competence. The difference lies in the desired degree of skill. In most communities, the practical arts teacher's objective will be to have the learner develop an appreciation or use level of skill with such operations. Where the goal is occupational competence, it calls for the development of a degree of skill sufficient so the student is ready to take his/her place on an initial job, performing the basic operations at an acceptable rate and quality. Where the objective is

---

[21] In the analysis of a trade, the work is first broken into the blocks of the trade. The operations are then listed for each block (i.e., The blocks of the trade in toolmaking are shown in Fig. D1 on page 414).

advanced occupational training, emphasis must be placed on bringing the skill of the student in performing the operation to an acceptable occupational level. This would take place only through meaningful repetition.

Students learn by doing when they clearly understand what they are working to achieve or correct. The key is **meaningful repetition**. The slogan, "learn by doing," may not, therefore, be psychologically sound. Many programs in vocational and practical arts education have been little more than custodial schools where students are kept busy doing work. Unless there is diligent and consistent concern for meaningful repetition to develop a degree of skill in the basic operations, whether it be on a use or occupational level, there can be little sound education. One might play ping pong for years and continue to make the same mistake while serving. To become a champion, one must always understand what he/she is doing incorrectly and work to correct such deficiencies as the individual strives to attain his/her goal.

6. That most tools and machines are used in more than one operation. This is why it is unsound to analyze the manipulative work completely around the use of each of the individual tools or machines. Several tools are used, for example, in the woodworking operation, **plane a surface true and smooth**, and to draw **a line tangent to an arc** in drafting. If the name of the tool or machine is included in the title for an operation, then there needs to be a description explaining how that particular machine or tool is used in doing the operation. It is recommended, therefore, that naming the tool be bypassed to the degree possible. Here are examples:

Drafting . . . . To transfer distances (with dividers).
Machine Shop . . . . To face and turn work (mounted in a lathe chuck).
 To cut keyways and other stop cuts (on a shaper).
Woodworking . . . . . To trim (with a chisel).

7. That where a particular tool is used for only one operation, the statement should describe what is done with the tool, such as:

Measure outside dimensions (with a micrometer)
rather than
Use a micrometer.

8. That operations are often listed with the prefix, "how to," thereby designating that manipulative work is to be taught. **How to mill flutes or grooves** illustrates this practice. Where there is consistency in this practice, the "how to" could be understood or placed at the top of the list, preceding the list of titles of operations. The titles for operations often appear in the literature, especially where their breakdowns are explained in the textbooks for occupational education, in the "ing" participle form. For example, the operation just described would then be written:

Identifying and Selecting Content 71

Milling flutes or grooves.
This makes good sense, in the "ing" form, when one is describing an ongoing activity, rather than something that has been identified to be taught.

9. That the verbs in the wording of operations are the keys that designate the type and character of the activity performed by the person doing an operation. For example:

Sharpen a drill.
Light and **adjust** a torch for cutting metal.
Make vertical and angular cuts.
Read a working drawing.
Bisect a straight line.
Grind and whet milling cutters.
Calculate cutting speed.

10. That it is desirable to keep the title for an operation to as few words as possible. The wording delimits the amount of instruction that would be included in the breakdown of an operation, the size of an instructional package for that particular operation. This reason has made it difficult to standardize analyses for vocational-technical and practical arts subjects and activities. The analyst needs to know about the experience and capacity of the learners, school and community conditions, and the overall aims for education so he/she may apply sound professional judgment in deciding how much instruction should be "packaged" as an operation or an informational topic.

To illustrate this point, one might be making an instructional analysis to be used later in planning an instructional program for a high school course in woodworking. Under such learning conditions, it seems reasonable that the operation, **get out stock**, might well encompass this amount of content in a breakdown: (1) measure with a rule, (2) select and lay out stock, (3) saw to a line with a rip saw, (4) saw to a line with a crosscut saw. In contrast, let us assume that the analyst was making an instructional analysis of woodworking to be used later as the basis for the content for a basic woodworking course for mentally retarded persons in special education. Surely, the packages of instruction for such learners should not become involved. It seems reasonable, then, that the analyst might decide, for such a learning situation, to break the amount of instruction described under "get out stock" in the example above, into these four operations:

Measure with a rule.
Select and lay out stock.
Saw to the line with a rip saw.
Saw to a line with a crosscut saw.

Here are some examples of typical errors made when titles for operations are listed:

a. Do inclined and vertical lettering. (Could not teach them concurrently.)

b. Use drawing instruments. (Used in many operations, such as: **Make a three-view drawing. Draw irregular curves.**)

c. Fill a ruling pen.
Ink with a ruling pen.
Ink regular and irregular curves. (These are points in the breakdown of the operation — **Ink with a ruling pen.**)

d. Prepare a surface for a layout. (A step in making a layout.)

e. Remove, rebuild, and install an engine. (Too much material to be covered in one operation.)

11. That in some of the service trades and applied arts activities, such as automotive mechanics and household mechanics, some of the operations are synonymous with jobs. To illustrate, it is now generally accepted that a job is the activity for which a person in industry is paid. Large industries have their jobs classified and analyzed. These job analyses cover such factors as responsibilities; educational background; job training — mental, visual, and physical effort; and responsibility for materials, tools, equipment, and safety. In practical or applied arts the term "job" is used interchangeably with **project** or **activity**. Students in these programs often refer to what they do as their "jobs." A very high percentage of the jobs done by students in vocational and applied arts subjects involve two or more operations. There are some exceptions, however, that can best be analyzed and treated as one operation. These include:

Repair a faucet.
Hang a door.
Adjust a carburetor.
Sharpen a knife.

Analyzing the Operations

After the titles have been identified and listed for each of the operations, it is necessary to analyze each title by preparing an outline for it. An example is shown in **Appendix D** on page 412. This analysis consists of listing the procedural steps and other significant data that would be useful. The steps and points placed on cards or sheets for each operation represent the content for that operation that may be used later by the teacher in selecting content for some particular course, in demonstrating the operation to an entire class or a small group within a class, or as the outline for an operation sheet, or as the outline for a film loop to teach the steps in the operation.

As the analyst starts thinking of what needs to be taught for one of the operations, he/she soon sees that there is essential information as well as steps to be followed in performing the operation. These need not be separated since they can be listed on a sheet or card in the order in which they might be presented during a demonstration or described on an operation sheet.

Several of the early practices in instructional analysis called for separating the "knowing" from the "doing" in the breakdown of an operation. The theory was that the shop teacher should only be concerned with teaching the "doing" while the "knowing phase" was withdrawn and later taught in the related courses. This dichotomy of separating the "doing" from the "knowing" is now considered psychologically unsound. It is therefore recommended that the breakdown for each of the operations include essential and significant informational content that could be integrated in a natural and logical manner with the operating steps. This practice should help to keep the independent informational topics to the very minimum. Selection of informational content for inclusion with operations should be carefully done to prevent the operations from becoming so loaded with informational content that a shop or laboratory course becomes too academic in approach. A unique characteristic of popular and effective occupational education courses is that they have been fast-moving and informative activity programs.

While these integrated operational outlines are being formulated, the analyst may want to consider one or more of the following additional factors as he/she identifies significant data:
1. What the learner should know to perform the operation intelligently.
2. Safety precautions.
3. New technical terms.
4. Care of tools and machines.
5. Quality requirements in respect to finish, limits, and time.

Independent Informational Topics

The case has been made for including essential information as an integral phase of the points listed in the breakdown of an operation. A good block of the essential informational content which is necessary to perform and understand an operation intelligently is, therefore, integrated with the manipulative work. As stated before, it is psychologically unsound to separate the "doing" from the "knowing" and encourage a dichotomy in education between "manipulative" and "informational" units. The ideal time to teach informational content is when the learner clearly sees that it is essential. It gives insight and meaning to what he/she is doing in a laboratory. This close integration is possible, however, with only a limited quantity of the informational content for any one course.

Since some of the informational content will be only remotely related to the breakdown of an operation, there is need to identify independent informational topics. The aims and character of the course will determine the appropriate number of these topics. For example, the number of independent informational units for the machine tool phase of a ninth grade general metalworking course would be limited by the time requirements for the other major activities. On the other hand, there probably would be many independent informational topics, in addition to the supporting information woven into the operations, to meet the aims of an engineering machine tool course directed toward an understanding of modern industrial processes. An instructional analysis of units for related subjects in vocational education, such as related mathematics or related English, will consist largely of informational topics. Many courses now designed to cover related instruction for those in registered apprenticeships in the building trades and manufacturing industries contain only a limited amount of manipulative work. The emphasis makes these courses primarily informational in character. In electricity, the independent informational topics may far outnumber the operations. Where industrial arts courses are designed to interpret American industry and contribute more and more to the guidance function, it will surely call for a greater emphasis on informational content.

With the technological developments of this century, the unique contribution of vocational and applied arts education must be tied closely to scientific principles that underlie operations and processes. For example, the ability to disassemble and assemble the component parts of an automobile is no longer as significant as it was in the early years of automotive mechanics. Today's learners in automotive mechanics must understand and appreciate scientific fundamentals. There are numerous applications of physics and chemistry in the functioning components of modern automobiles.

Fryklund has provided a simple and practical classification for independent informational topics. He calls for the classification of units as (1) technical, (2) general, or (3) guidance (1970, 70-77). This system classifies as "technical" those topics which cover the information that the worker must know to form judgments on the job. Topics are classified as "general" when the information would be desirable to know but is not essential to the performance of the operations. The "guidance" classification is for those topics that contribute to vocational, education, and personal guidance. Examples of these three types of informational topics are shown in **Appendix D** on pp. 417.

Curriculum Content That Does Not Discriminate Against Minority Groups

The larger school systems, especially those with a high percentage of minority students, are now giving every encouragement to the development of curriculum and text materials that will properly reflect the equal rights of Blacks, Latinos, and other minority groups in America. According to John J. Green (1968, 12) the Negro's drive for recognition is based on more than a century of precedent established by other ethnic and cultural groups, beginning with the Catholics 120 years ago.

The Detroit Public Schools have published evaluative criteria to screen proposed curriculum and text materials to ascertain that they deal adequately, and in a wholesome manner, with the issues that relate to discrimination. The factors considered encompass race, religion, and

Identifying and Selecting Content 75

socioeconomic background. Nine of the fifteen questions in their criteria have been selected to illustrate the criteria used to determine that curriculum materials are suitable for use in schools. These are the questions: Do the curriculum materials —

1. Suggest, by omission or commission, or by over-emphasis or under-emphasis, that any racial, religious, or ethnic segment of our population is more or less worthy, more or less important in the mainstream of American life?
2. Provide abundant, but fair and well-balanced, recognition of male and female children and adults of Negro and other minority groups by placing them in positions of leadership and centrality?
3. Delineate life in contemporary urban environments as well as in rural or suburban environments, so that today's city child can also find significant identification for himself, his problems, and his potential for life, liberty, and the pursuit of happiness?
4. Emphasize the multicultural character of our nation as having unique and special value which we must esteem and treasure?
5. Assist students to recognize clearly and to accept the basic similarities among all members of the human race, and the uniqueness and worth of every single individual, regardless of race, religion, or socioeconomic background?
6. Help students appreciate the many important contributions to our civilization made by members of the various human groups, emphasizing that every human group has its list of achievers, thinkers, writers, artists, scientists, builders, and statesmen?
7. Supply an accurate and sound balance in the matter of historical perspective, making it perfectly clear that all racial, religious and ethnic groups have mixed heritages, which can well serve as sources of both group pride and group humility?
8. Analyze intergroup tension and conflict fairly, frankly, objectively and with emphasis upon resolving our social problems in a spirit of fully implementing democratic values and goals in order to achieve the American dream for all Americans?
9. Seek to motivate students to examine their own attitudes and behaviors, and to comprehend their own duties and responsibilites as citizens in a pluralistic democracy — to demand freedom and justice and equal opportunity for every individual and every group?[22]

---

[22]"Evaluation Criteria: Minority Treatment", **Detroit Schools** (official publication of the school system), October 29, 1968, p. 30.

Use of Advisory Groups to Validate Programs and Content

For more than fifty years vocational educators have led the way in American education in the involvement of community leaders in the projection and development of their programs. In recent years (especially since the passage of the Vocational Education Amendments of 1968), it has become essential to establish and maintain advisory councils or committees for occupational education programs at the national, state, and local levels. The National Advisory Council, created by Congress in 1968, is composed of twenty-one persons appointed by the President from diverse backgrounds in labor, management, and education.[23] It is charged by law to advise the Commissioner of Education concerning the operation of vocational education programs, make recommendations concerning such programs, and make annual reports to the Secretary of Health, Education, and Welfare for transmittal to Congress. Each state has an Advisory Council for Vocational Education whose activities are coordinated with the National Council and gives direction to, and assists with the evaluation of, vocational education within the State.[24] There are also local advisory committees for the overall occupational program within an administrative unit of the state education system, as well as committees for each instruction program.

Samuel M. Burt (1971, 280) points out that advisory committees or consultants at the local program level are especially helpful in these ways:

1. Providing information concerning desirable aptitudes and educational and experience background needed by students in an occupational area to be qualified for entry-level employment.
2. Evaluating physical conditions, adequacy of equipment, and layouts of laboratories and shops.
3. Assisting in the development and evaluation of course content to assure its currency in meeting the changing skill and knowledge needs of industry and business.
4. Assisting in the development of evening school skill-improvement and technical courses for employed plant personnel.
5. Assisting in the development of apprenticeship and on-the-job training-related educational courses.
6. Compiling and publishing directories of community resources and personnel available to teachers, schools, and the school system for various volunteer services.

---

[23]The office of the executive director of The National Advisory Council on Vocational Education is Suite 852, 425 13th Street N.W., Washington, D.C.
[24]Persons interested in the work and program of their State Advisory Council for Vocational Education should contact their state director of vocational-technical education.

He[25] further states that:

> A great deal of industry-education cooperation takes place informally through personnel contacts between vocational educators and industry people. However, the most effective way to arrange for long-range extensive in-depth involvement of industry in education is for school people to work with and through formally organized advisory and cooperating committees (1971, 281).

Summary

The approaches now employed by curriculum builders to identify and select content for the different levels and ramifications of occupational education have become involved and sophisticated. The needs of man and society, in light of technological literacy, have made it mandatory to involve a great array of knowledgeable persons from the changing technologies, outside the profession of education, in the development and selection of content for vocational and applied arts education. To illustrate, Edward Kabakjian (1970, 8) has pointed out that the understanding and skillful applications of technology in solving today's technical and ecological problems call for "the expansion of our body of knowledge" over that represented by traditional secondary school subjects.

This body of knowledge becomes involved with content from the occupational areas used as the vehicle for motivation and for making education meaningful and relevant for learners with varied competencies and backgrounds. Content and methods need to be employed, therefore, that influence positive affective behavior, as well as cognitive goals and essential psychomotor skills. The content of prevailing career education programs needs, therefore, to embrace (1) an introduction to occupations; (2) exploration in clusters of occupations; (3) occupational guidance; (4) basic preparation in skills and other competencies needed for initial job placement; (5) placement and follow up; and (6) upgrading to cope with technological development, the emerging occupational opportunities, and retraining where skills and competencies have become obsolete.

---

[25]Mr. Burt, an authority on industry-education cooperation, is the author of **Industry and Vocational-Technical Education** (New York: McGraw-Hill Book Company, 1967), a publication to report a study of **Industry-Education: Advisory Committees** conducted by Samuel M. Burt for the W. E. Upjohn Institute for Employment Research with funding from the Fund for the Advancement of Education, Ford Foundation. Mr. Burt defines the term "industry" or "industry-people" generically, for purposes of convenience, to include representatives of business, labor, agriculture, manufacturing, homemaking, and the professions.

For Self-Assessment and Discussion

1. Identify the kinds of information that might be collected in an occupational survey that would influence course content of occupational education programs.
2. Describe the dichotomy that has existed between "academic" and "vocational education." What factors brought about this condition? Suggest three actions that will help eliminate this dichotomy.
3. What is meant by "Descriptive Knowledge"? By "Prescriptive Knowledge"? By "Formal Knowledge"?
4. What is meant by the "Praxiological Domain of Man's Knowledge"? Explain how the Industrial Arts Curriculum Project (IACP) serves as an example of "knowledge of practice".
5. What are the strengths of the IACP? What do you consider to be some limitations or weaknesses of the IACP?
6. Briefly describe approaches used to identify and select —
   a. Content to fulfill established goals for an educational program.
   b. Work tasks that relate to human roles in the work force.
   c. Job clusters for a basic occupational education program.
   d. Content for a general vocational program.
   e. Content through an inventory of payroll tasks.
   f. Content through instructional analysis.
7. What criteria may be used to insure that curriculum materials do not discriminate against minority groups?
8. Cite examples of the use of advisory committees to assist in the selection and validation of content for specific occupational education programs.
9. What are the unique features of the Individualized-Task Instructional Packet (I-TIP) system?
10. How is a "work task" defined in the I-TIP system?
11. Explain how Oregon manpower and needs data are translated into a job-clusters instructional program.
12. What is the basic difference in industry and business between a "job analysis" and a "task analysis"?
13. What distinctions are made between a job in industry or in the business world and "a job" in a VAE instructional program?
14. In analyzing content for VAE, what distinctions are made between "a process" and "an operation"? Between "an operation" and "an informational topic"?
15. What is the basic difference between job analysis in industry and the process of instructional analysis in VAE?
16. Why is it professionally unsound to standardize instructional analyses for vocational, technical, and practical arts education?
17. List the characteristics of an operation.
18. Explain the procedure for developing a reasonably complete list of the titles for the operations in a trade or technical subject or some applied arts activity.
19. Illustrate what is meant by "the blocks of a trade."
20. Give examples, in your area of specialization, of informational topics that could be classified as (a) "general," (b) "technical," and (c) "guidance" (Fryklund's classification).

An Assignment to Demonstrate Competency

Using the descriptions and examples of the seven approaches for identifying VAE content, prepare a statement of not over 250 words describing the approach that would be most appropriate for your area of specialization. The first paragraph should describe your present or proposed teaching assignment (i.e., VAE subject areas, mission of courses, and teaching level).

References* and Resources
Books

Bollinger, Elroy W., and Weaver, Gilbert G. **Trade Analysis and Course Organization.** New York: Pitman Publishing Co., 1945, Pp. 135.

*Burt, Samuel M. "Involving Industry and Business in Education," in **Contemporary Concepts in Vocational Education** (edited by Gordon F. Law, First Yearbook of AVA). Washington, D. C.: American Vocational Association, 1971, pp. 276-282.

Friese, John F., and Williams, William A. **Course Making in Industrial Education.** 3rd edition. Peoria, Illinois: Chas. A. Bennett Co., 1966.

*Fryklund, Verne C. **Occupational Analysis: Techniques and Procedures.** 5th edition. New York: The Bruce Publishing Co., 1970, Pp. vi — 213.

*Gagné, Robert M. (ed.). **Psychological Principles in System Development.** New York: Holt, Rinehart, and Winston, Inc., 1972.

Gagné, Robert M. **The Conditions of Learning.** New York: Holt, Rinehart, and Winston, Inc., 1965.

Giachino, J. W., and Gallington, Ralph O. **Course Construction in Industrial Arts, Vocational and Technical Education.** 3rd edition. Chicago: American Technical Society, 1967.

Henderson, John T. **Program Planning With Surveys in Occupational Education.** Washington, D. C.: American Association of Junior Colleges, 1970.

*Kotarbinski, T. "Praxiological Sentences and How They are Proved," in Section IV, **Logic, Methodology, and Philosophy of Science** (edited by E. Nagel, et al). Stanford, California: Stanford University Press, 1962.

*Lux, Donald J.; Ray, Willis E.; Hauenstein, A. Dean. **The World of Construction: Teacher's Guide.** 4th edition. Bloomington, Illinois: McKnight Publishing Co., 1970, Pp. viii + 309.

*_____. **The World of Manufacturing: Teacher's Guide.** 4th edition. Bloomington, Illinois: McKnight Publishing Co., 1971, Pp. vi + 367.

*Moss, Jerome, Jr., and Smith, Brandon B. "Some Steps in the Curriculum Development Process," in **Contemporary Concepts in Vocational Education** (edited by Gordon F. Law, First Yearbook of AVA). Washington D. C.: American Vocational Association, Inc. 1971, pp. 130-138.

*Osborn, William C., et al. **An Instructional Program for Employability Orientation.** Alexandria, Virginia: Human Resources Organization (HumRRO), 300 North Washington Street, February 1972, Pp. v + 303. Research performed for Manpower Administration, U.S. Department of Labor, Contract No. 51-49-70-06.

*Parnell, Dale. "The Career-Cluster Approach in Secondary Education," in Goldhammer, Keith, and Taylor, Robert, **Career Education: Perspective and Promise.** Columbus, Ohio: Charles E. Merrill Publishing Co., 1972, pp. 55-61. Article originally appeared in the December, 1969 issue of the **American Vocational Journal** titled "The Oregon Way."

*Silvius, G. Harold, and Curry, Estell H. **Managing Multiple Activities in Industrial Education.** Bloomington, Illinois: McKnight Publishing Co., 1971, Pp. xxiv + 648.

Singer, Edwin J., and Ramsden, John. **The Practical Approach to Skills Analyses.** New York: McGraw Hill Publishing Co., 1969, Pp. 170. ERIC Reference No. ED 040 319.

*Items with an asterisk have been cited in the chapter.

Periodicals

American Vocational Association. "Developing, Reviewing and Updating Curriculum to Meet On-the-Job Needs," in Bread and Fire series. **American Vocational Journal,** Vol. 47, No. 8 (November, 1972), pp. 89-98.

Ciancone, Elmer S. "New Techniques for Instructional Analysis." **Industrial Arts and Vocational Education,** Vol. 57, No. 4 (April 1968), pp. 35-39.

Cook, Fred S., and Lanham, Frank W. "Job Analysis Yields Individualized-Task Instruction Packets." **Business Education World** (September-October, 1971), p. 12.

*Evans, Rupert N. "How to Live With Change Without Being Corrupted by Money." **Theory Into Practice (TIP),** Columbus, Ohio: College of Education, The Ohio State University, Vol. 9, No. 5 (1970), pp. 280-283.

*Green, John J. "Finding the Missing Chapter in American Textbooks." **The Detroit News Magazine** (November 24, 1968), p. 12.

*Kabakjian, Edward. "The times, they are a-changin." Man/ Society/ Technology, Vol. 30, No. 1 (September-October, 1970), p. 7.

*Lux, Donald G. "A Call for Action." **Theory Into Practice** (TIP), Columbus, Ohio: College of Education, The Ohio State University, Vol. 9, No. 5 (1970), pp. 309-312.

*Lux, Donald G., and Ray, Willis E. "Toward a Knowledge Base for Practical Arts and Vocational Education," in **Theory Into Practice (TIP).** Columbus, Ohio: College of Education, The Ohio State University, Vol. 9, No. 5 (1970), pp. 301-308.

Staff of IACP. "The Industrial Arts Curriculum Project." **Journal of Industrial Arts Education,** Vol. 29, No. 2 (November-December, 1969), pp. 10-40.

Wolansky, William D. "Oregon Musters a Statewide Commitment to Clusters." **School Shop,** Vol. 29, No. 4 (May, 1970), pp. 33-35, 54.

Other Published Materials

*Altman, James W. Final Report: Research on General Vocational Capabilities — Skills and Knowledges. Robert M. Gagné, Principal Investigator. Pittsburgh, Pennsylvania: American Institute for Research in Behavioral Sciences, 1966, Pp. 159. ERIC Reference No. ED 013 870.

*Barlow, Melvin L., et al. A Guide for the Development of Curriculum in Vocational and Technical Education. Report of National Conference on Curriculum Development, held in Dallas, Texas, March 5-7, 1969 under direction of David Allen and James R.D. Eddy. Los Angeles: Division of Vocational Education, UCLA, 1969.

Buffer, James L., et al. A Junior High School Industrial Technology Curriculum Project: A Final Evaluation of the Industrial Arts Curriculum Project (IACP) from 1965-1971 (August 31, 1971), Pp. 395. ERIC reference No. ED 05 438.

*Christal, Raymond E. "Implications of Air Force Occupational Research for Curriculum Design" in Report of Seminar on Process and Techniques of Vocational Curriculum Development. Minneapolis, Minnesota: Research Coordinating Unit for Vocational Education, University of Minnesota, April, 1970, pp. 27-61.

*Lanham, Frank W., et al. Development of Task Performance Statements for a New Office and Business Education Learnings System (NOBELS), 2nd edition. Columbus, Ohio: CVTE, Centered Related Series No. 16, September, 1972, Pp. xii-361. (1st edition, April, 1970) ERIC Reference No. ED 041 134.

Larson, Milton E. Review and Synthesis of Research: Analysis for Curriculum Development in Vocational Education. Columbus, Ohio: CVTE, Research Series No. 46, October, 1969, Pp. 69. ERIC Reference No. ED 035 746.

Maley, Donald. The Preparation of Curriculum Materials and the Development of Teachers for an Experimental Application of the Cluster Concept of Vocational Education at the Secondary School Level. 1967, Pp. 306. ERIC Reference No. ED 016 841. Other ERIC numbers covering subsequent materials developed for this project are ED 014 554, June 1967, Pp. 17; ED 016 843, August, 1967, Pp. 157; ED 016 843, August, 1967, Pp. 178; ED 016 844, August, 1967, Pp. 125; and ED 022 965, August, 1968, Pp. 438.

Melching, William H., and Borcher, Sidney D. **Procedures for Constructing and Using Task Inventories.** A CVTE Publication, The Ohio State University (R + D No. 9), 1973, Pp. v + 56.

Michigan Department of Education. **Early Elementary-Level Social Studies Testbooks: A Report in Regard to Their Treatment of Minorities.** Lansing, Michigan: 1972, Pp. vi + 51.

*Minelli, Ernest L. (Chairman of Committee), et al. **A Guide to Improving Instruction in Industrial Arts,** 2nd edition. Washington, D.C.: American Vocational Association, 1968, Pp. 67.

Moss, Jerome, Jr., and Pucel, David J. et al. "An Empirical Procedure for Identifying the Structure of the Technical Concepts Possessed by Selected Workers" in **Process and Techniques of Vocational Curriculum Development.** Minneapolis, Minnesota: Research Coordinating Unit, University of Minnesota, 1970, pp. 71-90. ERIC Reference No. ED 042 917.

*Moss, Jerome, Jr., and Smith, Brandon B. "Summary and Discussion" in **Report of Seminar on Process and Techniques of Vocational Curriculum Development.** Minneapolis, Minnesota: Minnesota Research Coordinating Unit for Vocational Education, April, 1970, Pp. 1-8.

*Multanen, Monty E. "Occupational Career Clusters the Oregon Way," in **Proceedings, 6th Annual Vocational Technical Teacher Education Seminar** (Edited by Anna M. Gorman and Joseph F. Clark). Columbus, Ohio: A CVTE publication (LT No. 38), March 1973, pp. 95-102.

*Nichols, Daryl G., et al. **Career and Occupational Development Objectives.** National Assessment of Educational Progress, The Education Commission of the States, 300 Lincoln Tower, 1860 Lincoln Street, Denver, Colorado, July, 1970, Pp. vi + 47.

*Olsen, Jerry C. "Three Major Components of Pittsburgh's Occupational, Vocational, and Technical Program" in **Improving the Preparation of Professional Persons for Vocational Education in Eastern Metropolitan Area.** (Final report by Adolph Panitz). Philadelphia, Pennsylvania: Temple University, Division of Vocational Education, Feb. 1, 1971, pp. 309-313.

Schill, William J., and Arnold, Joseph J. **Curriculum Content for Six Technologies.** (Research Study funded in part by U.S. DHEW). Urbana, Illinois: Department of Vocational Technical Education, University of Illinois, 1965, Pp. vi + 118.

*Sjogren, Douglas. **Review and Synthesis of Research on Occupational Adaptability.** Columbus, Ohio: A CVTE Publication, (IS No. 42) 1971, Pp. iii + 30. ERIC Reference No. ED 057 182.

*Towers, Edward R.; Lux, Donald G.; Ray, Willis E.; and Stern, Jacob. **A Rational and Structure for Industrial Arts Subject Matter.** Columbus, Ohio: IACP, November, 1966, Pp. 382. ERIC Reference No. ED 013 955.

U.S. Department of Labor. **Handbook for Analyzing Jobs.** Washington, D.C.: Superintendent of Documents, Stock No. 2900-0131, 1972, Pp. v + 345.

Unpublished Material

*Fretwell, Dave. **Manpower Analysis for the Industrial Mechanics Cluster.** Report for Oregon Board of Education by Employment Division, State of Oregon, May, 1972, Pp. 27.

*Herschelmann, Kathleen M. **Adopting a Retrieval System for Individualized-Task Instruction Packets (I-TIPS) Using the Basic Information Retrieval System (BIRS).** In two documents. Part One, Pp. 31 and Appendices A-H; Part Two, Appendices I and J (abstracts of the I-TIP Computer Bank and the I-TIP Materials Bank), October, 1972. Division of Teacher Education, Vocational and Applied Arts Education, Wayne State University, Detroit, Michigan 48202.

*Maccia, E. S. **Curriculum Theory and Policy.** Occasional Paper 65-176, Educational Theory Center and Social Studies Curriculum Center. Columbus, Ohio: The Ohio State University, 1965, mimeographed.

*Maccia, E. S., and Maccia, G. **The Way of Educational Theorizing Through Models.** Occasional Paper 62-111, Educational Theory Center. Columbus, Ohio: The Ohio State University, 1962, mimeographed.

3 chapter

The Systems Approach

To organize educational programs which consider the growth and development of each learner, educators have turned to practices employed in industry, business, and the armed forces in systems design, analysis, management, and evaluation. Such practices permit educators to employ behavioral objectives and measure specific student performances against pre-established criteria (or outcomes).

According to Banathy (1968, 2) —

> the systems concept and systems approach emerged during and after World War II as a result of research and development in problem solving, efficiency analysis, and, most significantly, the development of complex man-machine systems.

These applications in the lives and work of people have become more and more essential with increased knowledge, the human needs and societal needs and technological advance. Banathy (1968, 1) points out that there are three fundamental systems:

1. Natural systems (like the solar system).
2. Systems designed by men and women (like the educational systems described and used as examples in this book).
3. Hybrid systems, a combination of natural and man-made systems (like the outer space system, with all of its involved components that made it possible for man to go to, and return from the moon).

In discussing applications of the systems approach, Banathy (1968, 2) states:

> It is the system as a whole — and not its parts separately — that must be planned, designed, developed, installed, and managed. What is really significant is not how the individual components function separately, but the way they interact and are integrated into the system for the purpose of achieving the goal of the system.

The Systems Approach Defined

As one of the leading authorities on the systems approach, Banathy (1968, 12) defines systems as

... assemblages of parts that are designed and built by man into organized wholes for the attainment of specific purposes. The purpose of a system is realized through processes in which interacting components of the system engage in order to produce a predetermined output. Purpose determines the process required, and the process will imply the kinds of components that will make up the system.

The definition for the systems approach by Fine (1969, 27) is also helpful.

A systems approach focuses on the achievement of a specific purpose or goal simultaneously seeking (a) to organize technology, manpower, and money within a specified time frame, and (b) to respond to changes in the environment of the goal, including needs and values that are important to its achievement. In short, the systems approach originates in needs and values, focuses on a goal, responds to its environment, and presumes to measure progress toward the goal.

Two or more systems may be planned as integral facets of a suprasystem. In this context, each major component is then designed as a subsystem to carry out its mission(s) as an essential part of a suprasystem. In this setting each of the subsystems is organized with its own purpose, resources, demands, and limitations. The "effectiveness (of the suprasystem) depends on how well these subsystems are integrated and how well they interfunction" within a suprasystem (Banathy 1968, 6). In commenting on the relationships between the suprasystem and its subsystems, Banathy (1968, 12) has said:

A system receives its purpose, its input, its resources, and its constraints from its suprasystem, a larger entity, designed for a specific purpose, which is comprised of two or more stystems. In order to maintain itself, a system has to produce an output which satisfies the suprasystem.

The Systems Approach in Education

The developments of the twentieth century have greatly increased the general body of knowledge, and specifically, the minutiae of facts. These as well as social and political influences have made it essential for educators to turn to the systems approach as they are continuously engaged in evaluating goals (expressed as measurable performance objectives), content, teaching strategies, and evaluation procedures to be employed in their courses or programs.

Through a careful analysis of educational problems and processes, the systems approach is emerging with a standardization of terminology. It is used as a process to attain:
1. The overall development of a curriculum (e.g., "A System Model" by Resnick);
2. A specific vocational and applied arts education (VAE) program (e.g., "Learner Controlled Education" by Jelden);

3. The identification of performance tasks for occupational education (e.g., the NOBELS study by Lanham).

These three examples of an application of the systems approach in education will be found later in this chapter.

The systems approach in education has attempted to take the good precepts of curriculum planning and integrate them into one discrete scheme. While most of the precepts employed in education with the systems approach have been identified in the literature, it is the system that gives structure and form to the steps that should be taken in curriculum or program development, evaluation, and improvement. The reader is referred to the schematic diagrams of the Resnick, Jelden, and Lanham models: Figs. 3-1, 3-2 and 3-3.

Systems approach and analysis facilitates increased educational effectiveness and efficiency by encouraging, even demanding, that the teacher or manager:

1. Identify needs and constraints for the system.
2. Clarify educational objectives.
3. Select pertinent and relevant content to fulfill objectives.
4. Determine the best methods and strategies for reaching objectives.
5. Use feedback to adjust the system where necessary.[1]

Behavioral Objectives Are the Heart of the Systems Approach

A behavioral objective[2] is a precise statement of the performance, behavior, or action to be attained by a learner. The objective must specify the behavior that can be observed, demonstrated, or measured in some suitable manner at the conclusion of a particular module of instruction. Such an objective describes:

1. The **conditions** that will prevail and control the learning climate (such as entry performance or skills, time limits and other restrictions, use of specialized machines that may be needed for testing or diagnosis in technical courses, and facilities for instruction).
2. The **performance task** that determines whether the learner has acquired the specified knowledge, attitudes, or motor skills to be specified in the **criteria** or **standards** for evaluation of the learner's accomplishments (e.g., quality, time, and/or specified readings on testing equipment).[3]

[1] Several points under "The Systems Approach in Education" were taken from a paper titled "Systems Approach to Curriculum Development: An Overview", by R. Terry Messenger, done under the direction of G. Harold Silvius at Wayne State University in 1971.

[2] The term "behavioral objective" is used synonymously with the terms "instructional objective" and "performance objective."

[3] For a more expanded explanation and classification of **Behavioral Objectives**, the reader is referred to the books by Mager (1962-1972), Mager and Beach (1967), Mager and Pipe (1970), Gronlund (1970), Armstrong et al. (1970), Kibler et al. (1970), and Byers et al. (1971). See "References and Resources" section in this chapter.

Plan for Assessing Initial Competence

A basic premise that underlies the systems approach is that there must be a sound plan for determining what the student knows and can do in respect to each identified end-performance objective (or outcome). This may be done in any of these ways:
1. A pretest.
2. A trial run by the student under observation (where safety factors permit).
3. Student assessment (a judgment made by the learner or his peer group).
4. A combination of these.

Learners Move at Their Own Rate

A unique feature of the instructional system is the provision for each learner to move at his/her own rate through a sequence of learning experiences, and then demonstrate behavior (with consideration for individual differences) that meets defined criteria. The system focuses responsibility on the initiative of the learner rather than the activities of the teacher. It is a practical approach to learning since it may simulate an occupational situation and employ a great variety of communication and learning principles, thereby facilitating the matching of individual students with effective learning styles.

Men and Machines Utilized

The learner directs his/her own activities and is given opportunity to demonstrate behavior that meets progressive steps leading to specified post-training proficiency. The system is predicated more on the responses of the learner than on what the teacher does in directing the educational process. This is done as the process utilizes both people and machines and attempts to maximize mediated instruction. This is where the learner is self-taught, on a highly individualized or small group basis, with available or teacher-developed instructional materials such as single-concept films, videotapes, motion picture films, and programed instruction. The intent here is that mediated instruction will create the time that is needed by professionals for their roles as managers of the system. It provides more time also for the teacher to work with individuals and small groups.

In the systems approach, there should be constant concern for matching the learning style of the individual student with the presentation modes[4] that motivate him/her. In the design and management of the system there is, therefore, provision for needed live demonstrations by the teacher, simulated life and work experiences, supervised performance for skill development, discussions of pertinent issues, computer-assisted instruction, on-the-job training, and the like. This implies that accountability for the learning process becomes the joint responsibility of the teacher and the learner.

[4] Term used in the systems approach that is synonymous with "teaching method."

A Curriculum Development Model

Figure 3-1 is a flow chart model for a systems approach developed by Harold S. Resnick, Director, Planning and Evaluation, Minuteman Regional Technical School District, Lexington, Massachusetts. He would be the first to stress, however, that this is not "the" model for all situations but merely an illustration that depicts one method of organizing a curriculum emphasizing a systems approach.

This suggests that before using an existing model, the user analyze it carefully, step by step. Upon careful analysis, it may be necessary to alter the model to meet varying requirements of curriculum development. The two top boxes of Resnick's model suggest general specifications for instruction. The next major step in his systems approach is to establish the overall and major behavioral objectives for each course of study. The development of such objectives is discussed in Chapter 8. Resnick suggests that the teacher's, or teaching team's, next step be a task-activity analysis to identify content and activity that would provide the vehicle for the needed educational experience. This instruction is essential for moving the student from the competence that he/she brought to the course, to that specified in the terminal performance objectives (or outcomes). It should be noted that Resnick provides for a subsystem (upper right corner of his model) where a subperformance objective, with its content identified, can be instituted for each major task within the hierarchy of the course.

At this point in Resnick's plan, a decision needs to be made for each behavioral objective and the task identified for its fulfillment (a diamond-shaped box in the model indicates where decisions need to be made in the design of a system). In this case, the question for decision is: **Could mediated instruction, where the student is self-taught, be used to reach the specific terminal objective?** If so, then the professionals developing the program need to determine whether the software and hardware to facilitate such instruction are commercially available, or whether they will need to be developed. If mediated instruction is not available for teaching a package of instruction, there are two other alternatives: The first one would be to rewrite the behavioral objective so that the instruction might be provided with available film loops, movies, videotapes, or programed instruction. The second solution is to have that behavioral objective attained through teacher-directed instruction.

There is a provision in Resnick's model to refine and improve the effectiveness of each package of instruction by (1) evaluating content and activities against the objective, (2) testing the students, and (3) revising where desirable. Finally, all of the packages are merged and put together as one course or a major curriculum. The final product, then, needs to be field tested with a trial run and then further refined as the teacher continues to use the system with subsequent students.

A SYSTEM FOR CURRICULUM DEVELOPMENT

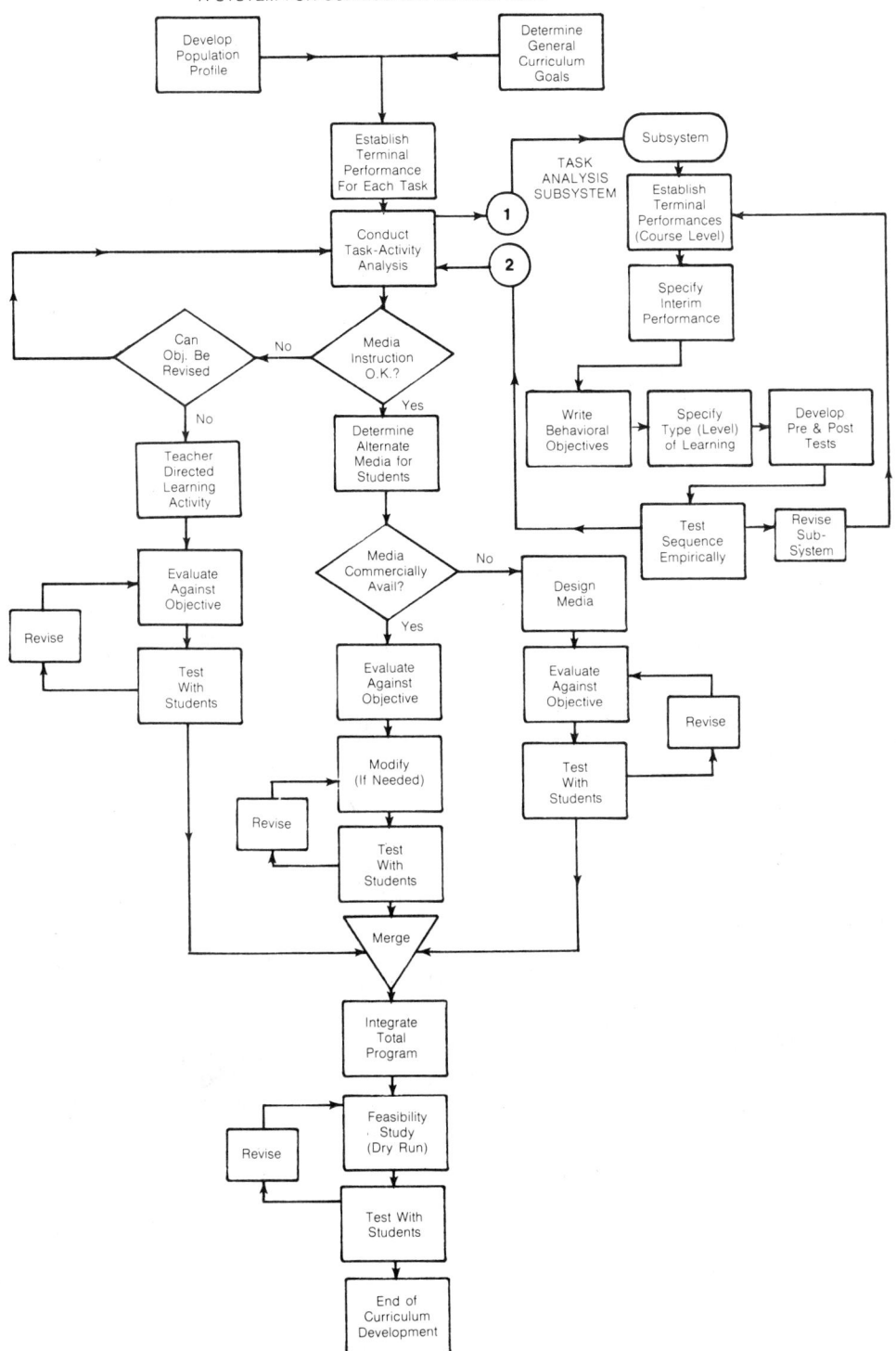

Fig. 3-1. The Resnick Model for a Systems Approach for Curriculum Development (Developed by Harold S. Resnick)

Learning Packets for an Electronics Course

David L. Jelden has applied the systems approach in the teaching of electronics at the University of Northern Colorado. The major units in the basic course have been developed as a series of Learner Controlled activity packets. Each packet is organized as a major unit of the course (e.g., #6 Resistance, #7 Voltage, #8 Current, #15 Meter Movements, and #16 Operation and Calibration of Oscilloscopes). Figure 3-2 is a basic flow chart illustrating the sequence followed as a student proceeds through the unit. Jelden explains this "Learner Controlled Education" (LCE) system as one that does not impose the teacher's method of learning on the student. He (Jelden, 1970) describes LCE as:

> ... individually oriented, self-instructional, and multimedia in approach. It is based on the premise that students can be taught to interpret the behavioral goals of a course, determine procedures that will permit attainment of the goals, and select and carry out the procedures which they consider desirable for attaining the goals. The learner controlled method is in contrast to the teacher-controlled method in which the teacher establishes the goals and determines the approach by which the outcomes can be reached. In both methods, the content, in the main, is determined by the teacher. The methods differ in terms of who determines the procedures for attaining the goals. Putting it bluntly, the teacher does not impose his [or her] methods of learning on the student.

Each of the packets in Jelden's system has behaviorally stated educational goals, recommended sources of information to achieve these goals, choices of sequences to be employed by students (alternative routes to reach the goal), self-evaluations integrated into the lesson, and a packet evaluation designed to have the students explain, in their own words, their understanding of the task leading to the attainment of the goals.[5] Each packet is organized with an independently color-coded syllabus on 8½" x 11" paper. Different colored paper is used for "objectives" and "student assessment," "self-tests," and "laboratory activities." A single color is used for "rationale," "recommended media," and "study guides." The pages are coded by packet numbers and designated so that the learner is readily directed to the needed material (e.g., "lab activity" in Packet 8, covering "Ammeter Measurement of Current" is on page 8-8).

The reader is directed to the wording of the symbols in Jelden's flow chart, shown as Fig. 3-2.

---

[5]Taken from p.1 of the Descriptive Materials prepared by David L. Jelden to accompany the series of packets covering his LCE program in Electronics.

LEARNING ACTIVITY PACKAGE

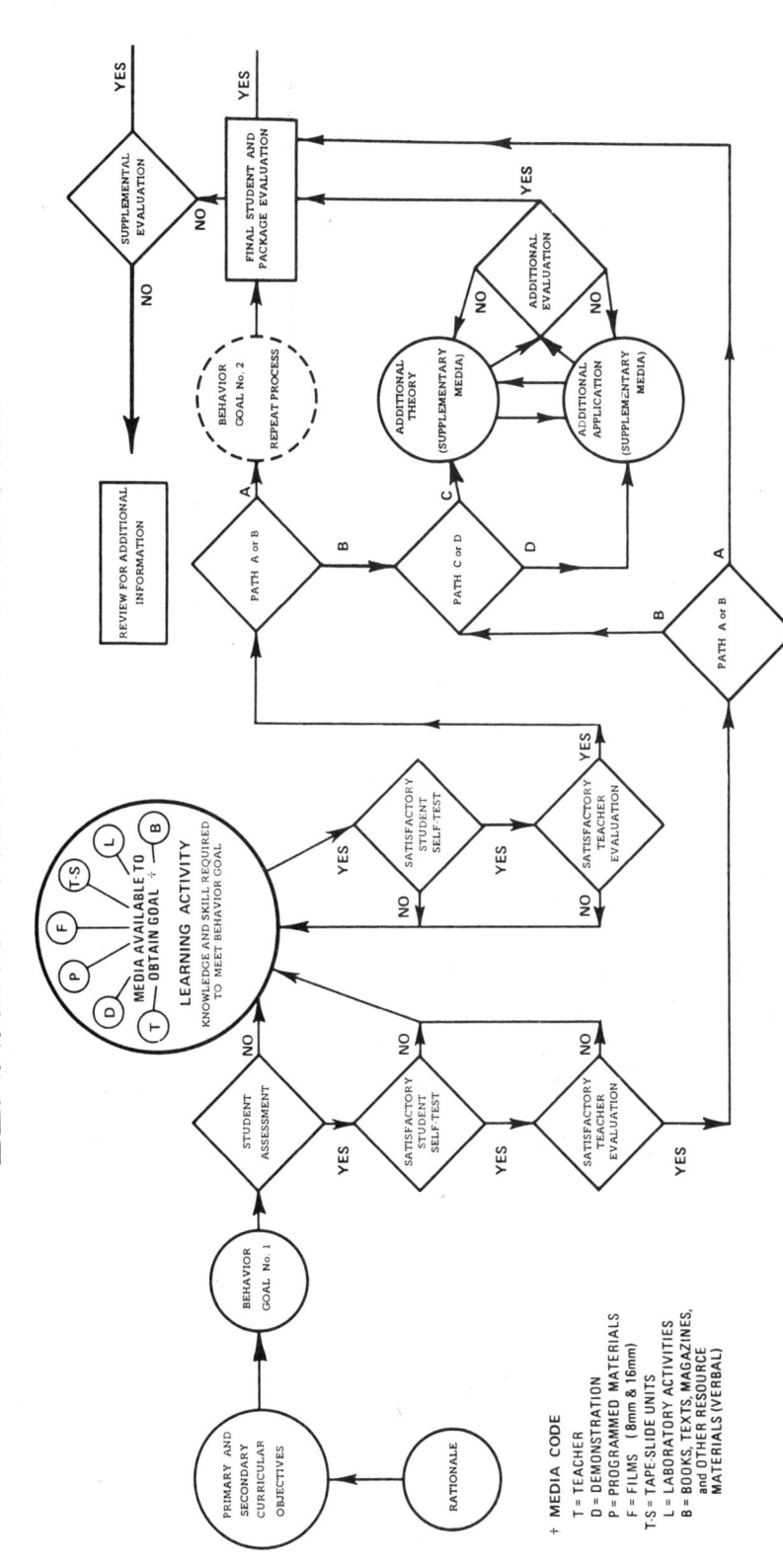

Fig. 3-2. Flowchart Showing the Instructional Steps Followed in the Jelden's "Learner Controlled Education" (From material distributed by David L. Jelden)

† MEDIA CODE
T = TEACHER
D = DEMONSTRATION
P = PROGRAMMED MATERIALS
F = FILMS (8mm & 16mm)
T-S = TAPE-SLIDE UNITS
L = LABORATORY ACTIVITIES
B = BOOKS, TEXTS, MAGAZINES, and OTHER RESOURCE MATERIALS (VERBAL)

Primary Objective

This is the statement of the overall purpose of a block of instruction describing what the student should be able to do when he/she has finished the module of instruction. It is the title of the unit and would be similar to the chapter heading in the usual technical book in industrial education. (e.g., the "primary objective" (mission) of Jelden's first activity packet is an **Introduction to Electricity**).

Rationale

This is a statement to motivate a student and stress the significance of the unit. For example, the rationale for **Current,** Jelden's Packet No. 8, is —

> Electrical current is the flow of electrons. To describe the nature of an electrical circuit, it is often necessary to measure and understand the effects of current in the circuit.
> Three sections are included in this packet. Section **One** presents an understanding of current — its practical unit, its measured units, and its exact nature. Section **Two** investigates lab measurement of the ampere. Section **Three** investigates "Kirchhoff's Current Law," which serves as a fundamental basis for circuit analysis and troubleshooting.

In dealing with the rationale for a unit in LCE, it is essential, according to Jelden, that the student recognize the importance of understanding this phase of the instruction, the relevance of the unit, and the benefits to be derived from the time spent studying the packet. Jelden suggests that it may be necessary for the teacher to verbally supplement the written statement of rationale to help unlock the student's internal drive so that he/she can obtain an essential learning experience.

Behavioral Objective #1

This is a functional statement explaining how the student is expected to behave after he/she has learned. This statement describes the conditions for the learning experience and to what degree the task is to be mastered.

For example, the first behavioral objective for **Topic One** in Packet No. 8, on **Current** is:

1. The learner will define "current" in writing, list its practical units of measurement, and explain the conditions necessary before electrical current will flow.

Student Assessment

The next step in Jelden's plan provides learners with three choices as they make a self-assessment of their competence. The following is an example of this self-assessment:

Directions: Check (✓) one of the following courses of action and pursue the plan indicated.

(_____) I understand **All** of the tasks indicated in the above objective and therefore wish to take the self-test found at the end of this section (p. 8-4).

(_____) I understand **Part** of the tasks identified in the above objective and will study those with which I am unfamiliar. When completed, I will take the self-test.

(_____) I understand **None** of the tasks identified in the objective and will proceed in order recommended in this packet, beginning on the next page. When completed, I will take the self-test (Packet 8, 2).

The Accelerated Track

This track is for the learner who checks the first choice in the "Student Assessment" form and thinks he understands **All** of the tasks indicated in the first behavioral objective. The self-test for this choice usually consists of objective questions, and in some instances, essay items. When essential, a performance or manipulative experience is specified with provision for the teacher's participation. It is only when both the learner and the teacher agree that the student has met the minimum requirements of the objective that the learner moves ahead on this accelerated path. The self-test for determining whether the student has the competence specified in Objective One, and should be encouraged to pursue the accelerated route, for Packet No. 8 on **Current**, is as follows:

EXAMPLE

TOPIC ONE
DEFINITION OF ELECTRICAL CURRENT[6]

Directions: This self-test is to be completed when you feel the objectives for this section have been fulfilled. Answers are to be placed on the test. Scoring will **Not** affect your term grade; it is an opportunity for you to identify tasks that you have mastered, or to determine your possible deficiencies. If the score is above 80 percent, continue to the next topic. A score below 80 percent indicates that additional study is required. See the instructor for assistance.

1. A "COULOMB" is ___?___
   a. a number of electrons.
   b. a rate of electron flow.
   c. a unit of electrical force.
   d. determined by multiplying electrons x time.

[6]From Packet 8, page 4.

2. The unit of electrical current is ___?___
   a. ohm.
   b. watt.
   c. coulomb.
   d. gauss.
   e. amp.
3. The unit of electrical current is most similar to ___?___
   a. pounds.
   b. pounds/in^2
   c. gallons/minute.
   d. cubic feet.
   e. heaven knows; I don't!
4. As voltage increases, current ___?___
   a. increases.
   b. does not change.
   c. decreases.
5. As resistance increases, current ___?___
   a. increases.
   b. does not change.
   c. decreases.

When the student pursuing the accelerated path finds that there are aspects of the self-test in which he/she is not proficient, the student returns to the learning activity to recommended materials listed in the study guide. If the self-test is satisfactory, then the teacher can suggest additional **in-depth** study of interest to the student, and beyond the minimum requirement specified in the behavioral objective. This is identified on Jelden's flow chart as Path "B", **Additional Theory** or **Additional Application**, and is undertaken only after a "satisfactory teacher evaluation."

Provisions for Learning Activity

Those who check **Number two** on the form for Student Assessment (understood part of the tasks) or **Number three** (understood none of the tasks) are referred to available media covering information and skills required to meet the behavior goal. The Learning Activity Packets include:
1. A list of recommended media available where data can be obtained which will allow the learner to gain information about the task.
2. A list of helpful study guide questions that, when answered by the student, will allow him/her to understand the objective or information related to it.
3. A laboratory experience, if feasible, that will give an opportunity to apply certain ideas or knowledge on a practical basis.

4. An information sheet that will summarize the basis of the task or its essential parts. (Jelden, Descriptive Materials, 4 & 5).

To illustrate, the learning activity sheet, for Topic One, Packet No. 8 on **Current** is as follows:

EXAMPLE

TOPIC ONE
DEFINITION AND FUNDAMENTALS OF
MEASUREMENT FOR ELECTRICAL CURRENT[7]

Recommended Media — Select any one of the following:

(_____) 1. **Electricity 1-5**, Van Valkenburg, pp. 1-60 to 1-73. (Excellent reference and best source to fulfill Objective #1.)
(_____) 2. **Electricity 1-7**, Mileaf, Vol. 1, pp. 57-58. (Recommended class test.)
(_____) 3. **Current Flow.** 16mm film, #108B, 12 min. (Good review. Found in Resource Center.)
(_____) 4. **Basic Electricity 1**, DC Fundamentals, Orla E. Loper, pp. 10-16, 1959. (Excellent reference.)
(_____) 5. **Measurement of I with VOM**, 35mm tape-slide presentation. (Best source for Part I of Lab. Activity found in Resource Center.)
(_____) 6. Additional media selected by student:

_____

_____

STUDY GUIDE QUESTIONS

Objective #1
(Listed on p. 9)
1. Define **Coulomb:** _____
   Electrical Current: _____
   Ampere: (give answer in terms of "coulomb")

_____

2. **Thought-Question:** Review the definition of electrical current. What effect does **Voltage** have on current flow?
3. What effect does **Resistance** have on current flow?
4. Identify the unit used in measuring the rate of flow of an electrical current: _____

[7]From Packet 8, page 3.

An example of "Lab Activity" on the **Ammeter** (reproduced on green paper) **Measurement for Objectives.**[8]

2. Given a lab VOM and milliamp meters, the learner will accurately measure electrical current.

and

3. The learner will use the VOM and lab milliamp meters in a safe manner.

In Packet 8, is found

Introduction: The purpose of this lab exercise is to furnish you with the opportunity to measure current through use of the VOM and the 1 ma panel meter.

Equipment Listing:	VOM VTVM Resistors:	1 MA Meter 2 — 1.5V cells 500 ohm, 5K ohm, 10K ohm NOTE: All resistors are brown in color and have the ohmic value clearly marked on each with color bands.
	1-3V Lamp Electrical Leads	

PART I — Use of the VOM for Measuring Current

Procedure:

(_____) Step #1. Plug in the VTVM. Allow it time to stabilize for future use on this exercise.

(_____) Step #2. Construct the circuit shown in Figure A. The Ammeter is a lab VOM. Caution: Set the VOM to the least sensitive current range (500 MA). Observe polarity of the meter.

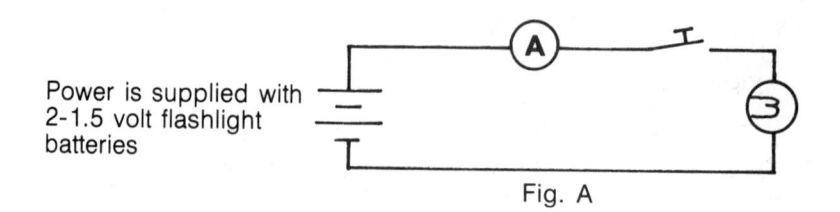

Power is supplied with 2-1.5 volt flashlight batteries

Fig. A

---

[8]Jelden's five behavioral objectives for the unit on **Current** are listed on p. 190 of Chapter 7.

(_____) Step #3. Close the switch. The lamp should glow.
(_____) Step #4. Measure and record the current flow in the circuit in the space provided.

_____ ma

Problem:
What controls the amount of current in the circuit?

PART 2 — Use of 1 MA Meter to Measure Current
Procedure:

(_____) Step #1. Connect the circuit shown below. **Note:** All resistors are large in size and located in the left drawer of each lab position. The ohmic values of each resistor are clearly marked on each.

Fig. B

(_____) Step #2. If the circuit has been properly constructed, the ammeter should indicate approximately .8 ma. (Tolerable error: ± .1 ma)

Record the ammeter indication: _____ ma

Problem: If you didn't get the proper value, give some reasons or explanation of what may be wrong.

Once the student has undertaken the learning activity, he/she can proceed to the self-test when there is confidence in achieving the tasks specified in the behavioral goal. If the student fails to meet the level of proficiency specified in the objective, he/she is re-cycled back into additional learning activities. This process is continued until the student and teacher have agreed that the demonstrated **performance** by the student is sufficient **to proceed** to the next objective.

There is provision, of course, in Jelden's system for additional in-depth study by the more able students who have the ability to pursue the accelerated track. This additional in-depth study is possible through path "B" if the need exists.

When all of the objectives (lessons) are completed, the learner and teacher schedule an exit test, a comprehensive evaluation session covering all of the instruction in the packets. This may take the form of an oral interview, an essay examination, a laboratory performance test, or a combination of these.

Jelden summarizes his system (Descriptive Materials, 4 & 5) of Learner Controlled Education (LCE) in this manner:

> The **Learning Activity Packet** is designed to provide the learner with a self-pacing, individualized, multi-media system of education. It frees the teacher from highly structured classroom lectures and provides the needed time to guide the learning process of the students.
>
> Most of the materials in the **Learning Activity Packet** provide for self-study. On occasion, a teacher demonstration or lecture may be the best way to present certain kinds of information to a small group of students within the class. What the **Learning Activity Packet** will do best is provide for the individual differences of the students and place the teacher in the professional role of being a diagnostician or prognosticator of the educational process rather than a regurgitator of factual information which a machine or some form of educational media might do better.

The Systems Approach Employed in the NOBELS Study

One of the most comprehensive examples of an application of the systems approach in occupational education has been the NOBELS study (Lanham et al., 1970, vii + 342), reported in April 1970, with a second and refined edition (Lanham et al., 1973, xii + 361) in August, 1972.

The long range goal of NOBELS was to cast office learnings into a system of instruction, involving design criteria, performance goals, a delivery system, and evaluation with a closed feedback loop. This systems approach is illustrated in Fig. 3-3. The first phase of the report provides the foundation for a complete system of instruction in the office occupations.

The outcomes of the research are in the form of 373 Task Performance Statements to be employed in the development of curricula for office and business education.

1. DESIGN CRITERIA

General Objectives for:

- Persons
- Processes
- Properties

of the system under consideration.

2. PERFORMANCE GOALS

Operational Objectives for:

Persons, expressed in terms of specific skills, and role expectations; Processes and Properties, expressed in terms of rules and regulations (the normative structure under consideration)

3. INPUTS (OUTPUTS)

Description of:

- Persons
- Processes
- Properties

included in the system under consideration to arrive at goals.

4. OUTPUTS (INPUTS)

Performance Measures of:

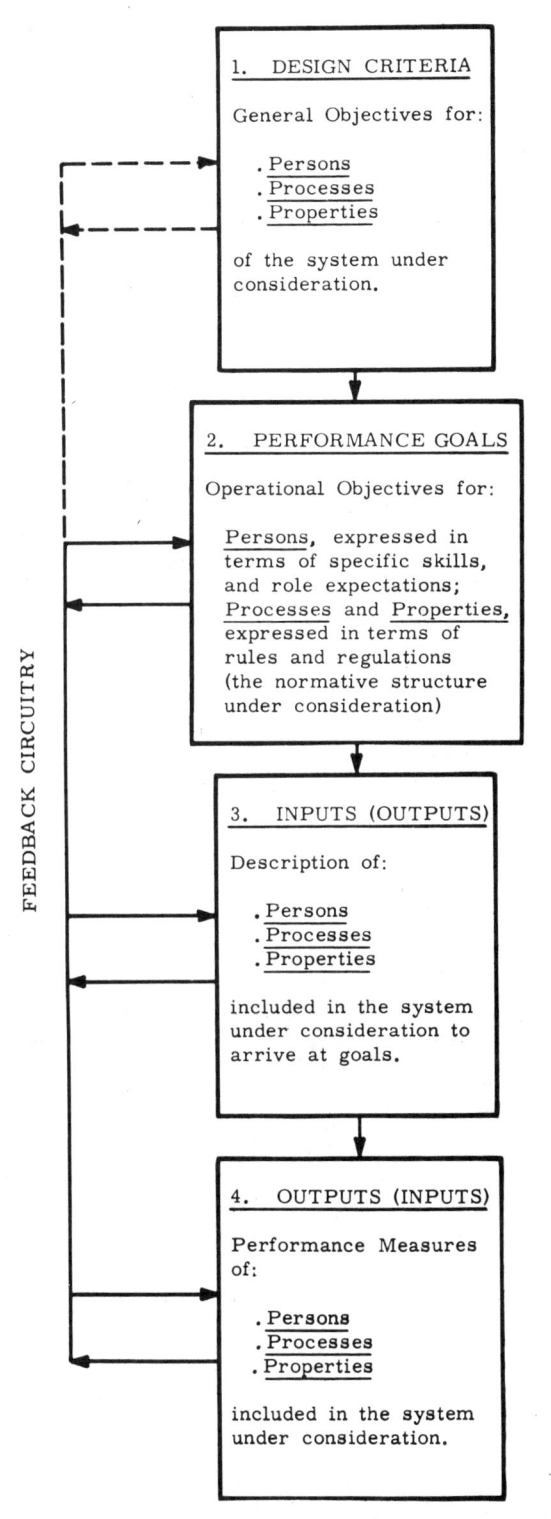

- Persons
- Processes
- Properties

included in the system under consideration.

FEEDBACK CIRCUITRY

Fig. 3-3. The Analog Systems Approach for NOBELS

Planning and Organizing Instruction

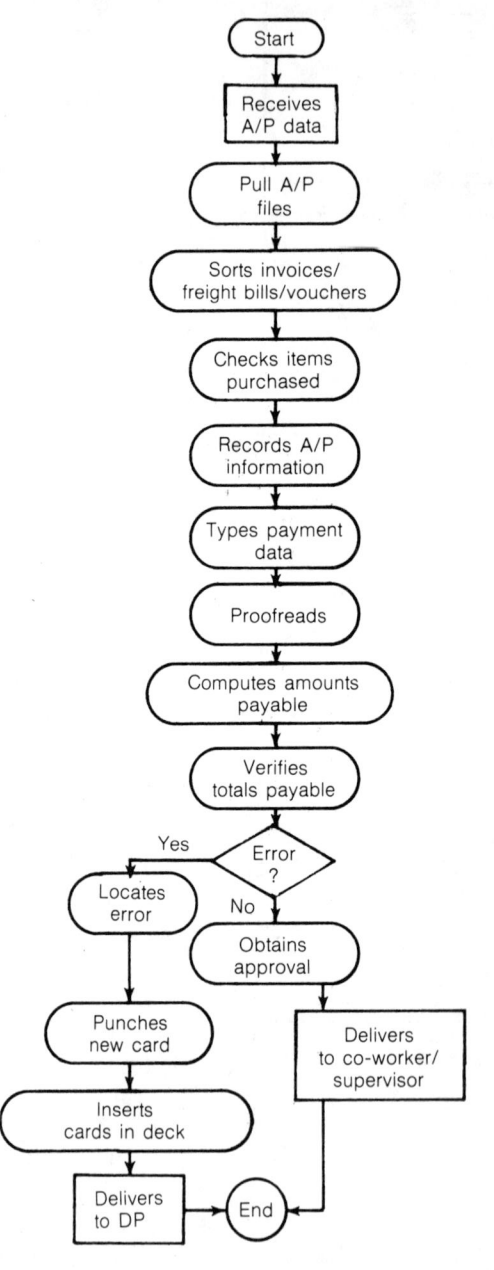

```
           Start
             │
             ▼
      Receives A/P data
             │
             ▼
       Pull A/P files
             │
             ▼
      Sorts invoices/
     freight bills/vouchers
             │
             ▼
       Checks items
        purchased
             │
             ▼
       Records A/P
        information
             │
             ▼
      Types payment
          data
             │
             ▼
       Proofreads
             │
             ▼
     Computes amounts
         payable
             │
             ▼
        Verifies
      totals payable
             │
             ▼
    Yes ◄── Error? ──► No
     │                  │
     ▼                  ▼
  Locates            Obtains
   error             approval
     │                  │
     ▼                  ▼
  Punches           Delivers
  new card        to co-worker/
     │             supervisor
     ▼                  │
  Inserts               │
 cards in deck          │
     │                  │
     ▼                  │
  Delivers              │
   to DP                │
     │                  │
     └────► End ◄───────┘
```

HARDWARE
Typewriter
Adding machine (10-key)
Calculator
Hand stamp

SOFTWARE
Catalog
Accounts payable documents
Code book

EDUCATIONAL CUES
Computational skills
Accuracy
Checking
Typing
Filing

SUPPLEMENTARY STEP: Photocopies transmittal sheet and bill.

REPORTED CRITERIA: "Must be exact and accurate; Aptitude with figures is essential; Must have the ability to reason well and be good in math; Knowledgeable in filing procedures; Correct typing of prices and shipping destination; Good handwriting; High accuracy in transferring figures; Work under pressure; Decimal placement very important; Some knowledge of bookkeeping; Check numbers carefully; Understand percentages and discounts; Add, subtract, multiply, and divide easily; Should take pride in work done; Ability to withstand monotonous, repetitive work."

Fig. 3-4. A sample flowchart for one of the performance tasks, "The worker computes accounts payable from source documents (01.02.01)" in NOBELS study. (This example was developed by Frank W. Lanham, director of NOBELS.)

Fig. 3-4. Continued

This accompanying sheet identifies the steps of performance (for task 01.02.01) arranged in three major divisions: (1) **acquisition**, i.e., the source or sources of/or materials on which the task is to be performed; (2) **process**, i.e., the sequence of actions taken by the worker to perform the task; and (3) **disposition**, i.e., what the worker does with product or output generated.

ACQUISITION

RECEIVES
    Computer listing of accounts payable / purchase orders / invoices / punched requisition cards / statements / purchase tickets / tickets on accounts payable from branch stores / computer time use report.

PROCESS

PULLS
    Logs in machine operating time / invoices / accounts payable ledger sheets.
SORTS
    Invoices / freight bills / vouchers (over $1,000, under $1,000).
CHECKS
    Items that correspond / prices / retail figures / costs / invoice amounts / errors.
RECORDS
    Information on make-up sheets / date received / vendor number / discounts / delivery carrier / date due / terms / information on transmittal sheet.
STAMPS
    Date, "OK" on invoices.
ATTACHES
    Purchase order, receiving slip, invoice / blank check to each bill / list to check request.
TYPES
    Authorization slip to pay / check request / schedule of payments / credit memo / purchase orders.
PROOFREADS

COMPUTES
    Discounts / extensions / net amount due.
VERIFIES
    Totals payable.
PUNCHES
    New card when error is found.
OBTAINS
    Initials, approval, signature on invoices.

DISPOSITION

DELIVERS
    Punched cards, vouchers to Data Processing / accounts payable data to co-worker, supervisor.

One of the missions of NOBELS was to develop guidelines for curriculum that would be congruent with the concepts of organic curriculum theory which was promulgated in connection with the ES '70 Project (Bushnell, 1969, 200) to achieve these objectives:
- A learner-centered curriculum, highly relevant to the adult roles which the student would be expected to play upon graduation.
- Individualized or "customized" education for each student.
- Utilization of appropriately tested and educationally oriented technology.
- Employment of suitable organizational and administrative patterns.
- Economic practicality within available resources.

The basic tasks performed by office workers, in the 16-24 year bracket, were identified in the NOBELS study from empirical data collected in interviews with 1,232 office employees and their supervisors from four areas of the United States. The educational specifications for each of the 373 performance statements, as illustrated in the sample shown as Fig. 3-4, were drawn from 4,564 basic tasks and 32,447 steps of task performance. This inventory of 373 task performance statements is cast in light of the classroom practitioner as a business education learner in public secondary schools and community colleges. The inventory of performance tasks, with their educational specifications, have been employed to give direction to instruction developed by media developers, curriculum committees, and teacher educators in business education. Additional outputs of NOBELS include (1) a Taxonomy of Office Activities (Ed 021 140); (2) two correlative studies on Interaction Critical Incidents and Hardware Used in Office Task Performance; (3) a Talent Inventory; and (4) the NOBELS Verbs and Synonyms.

The Second Edition of NOBELS

The revised and refined edition of NOBELS, published by The Ohio State Center for Vocational and Technical Education (CVTE), two years after the original document, reflects consideration of "public pressures for accountability in education, movements toward career education, and a strengthening of federal and state staffing in support of the thrust in career education."[9] Frank W. Lanham has pointed out that these contemporary thrusts in occupational education have necessitated "the revitalization of office occupation preparation with current and job-related task performance, the major output of the second edition of NOBELS."

The "performance goals" used in the terminology of the original report have been changed to "Task Performance Statements" or "Task Statements" since the director of the study now recognizes that performance goals must be developed from validated tasks performed in the office occupations.

---

[9]Quotation from Prologue to second edition.

In the reconsideration of the revision of NOBELS and in the reclassification of the task sheets, the 375 generalized "performance goals" (identified in the original report) were reduced to 373 generalized "task statements."

The three special listings of task statements, in the revised edition, will be especially helpful to classroom practitioners and curriculum developers in business occupations. These special listings of task statements are (1) The "51 High Frequency Performances" (for clustering curriculum content), (2) "Medical Task Statements," and (3) "Banking Task Statements."

These symbols were used in constructing the flow charts for a task performance in the report of the NOBELS study (as employed in Fig. 3-4).

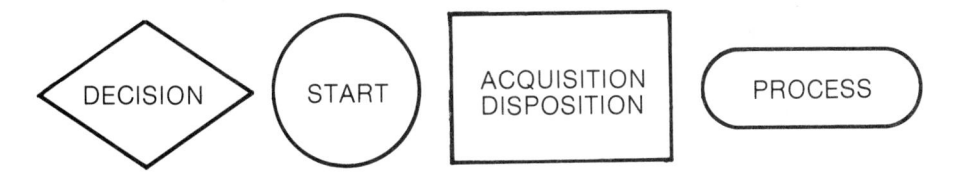

Concomitants of the Systems Approach

The systems approach makes it possible to plan and develop curriculum in an organized and logical manner. Specific values which come from an application of the systems approach in education include:
- The systems approach in education attempts to take all of the good precepts of curriculum development and integrate them into one interrelated scheme.
- The systems approach in education became essential with increased knowledge, the needs of individuals and society and the outcomes of technological advance.
- With the systems approach in education, it is possible to consider the components of curriculum planning: the goals, behavioral objectives, content, methods, and evaluation procedures — collectively and as an organized whole.
- With the systems approach in education, the elements of the curriculum can be organized and projected in an integrated manner while they are considered mutually discrete.
- Accountability is introduced in a competency-based educational system as the student demonstrates mastery of the behavioral objectives.

In sum, a well-planned and organized educational system makes it possible to focus on the goals of the student, to respond to the input of educational activities, to consider the environment generated by the school and society, to measure learned progress and achievement, and to modify and improve the system as it is being used.

For Self-Assessment and Discussion

1. What are the unique features of the systems approach to curriculum development?
2. How is the systems approach to curriculum development different from planning and organizing instruction using a more traditional method?
3. The following terms are found in the literature to provide a precise description of what a student will be able to do after completing a prescribed unit of instruction:
    - Performance Objective
    - Behavioral Objective
    - Instructional Objective
    - Learning Outcome
    - Learning Goal
    - Performance Goal

    a. Which of these terms would you use, and why, in developing VAE curriculum materials?
    b. What distinctions, if any, should be made in the definitions for these terms?
4. Describe the provision for an accelerated track in the Jelden model.
5. What is meant by criteria-referenced instruction? How does it differ from norm-referenced instruction?
6. Explain what is meant by the provision for standards and criteria of acceptable performance as an integral part of a behavioral objective.
7. What is meant by a model of instruction?
8. Explain how the systems approach to curriculum development provides for the evaluation of actual performances attained (outputs produced from inputs).
9. Explain how the Jelden model has a provision for the testing of needed essential prerequisite skills before a student moves ahead with the instruction for one of the packets (modules of instruction).
10. Why are behavioral objectives considered to be the heart of the systems approach?

Assignments to Demonstrate Competencies

A new set of terms has come with the systems approach to curriculum development. It is necessary, therefore, for the VAE student, teacher, or leader to demonstrate an understanding of these terms and phrases.

I. Using the content of Chapter 3 and the selected references and resources listed at the end of this chapter[10], write in your own words short and precise operational definitions for the following terms and phrases. Check these definitions with your peers and the instructor responsible for your personal development to make sure that they are acceptable.

---

[10] The books by Banathy, Butler, and Kaufman are especially recommended.

The Systems Approach   **103**

1. Behavioral Objective
2. Components
3. Constraints
4. Criterion-Referenced Evaluation
5. Educational Media
6. Exemption Test
7. Exit Test
8. Feedback
9. Flow Chart
10. Hardware
11. Input
12. Interface
13. Instructional System
14. Learning Experience
15. Learning Task
16. Learning Sequence
17. Mediated Instruction
18. Model
19. Mission
20. Needs Assessment
21. Output
22. Parameters
23. Prerequisite Skills
24. Software
25. Student Assessment
26. Subsystem
27. Suprasystem
28. Systems Approach
29. Systems Design
30. Systems Testing
31. Task Analysis
32. Task Hierarchy

II. Use the following schematic diagram of the instructional system employed in a typical VAE competency-based teacher education program.

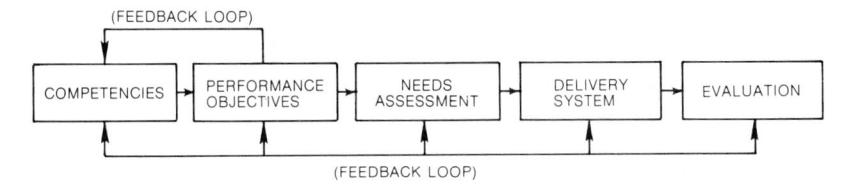

(FEEDBACK LOOP)

COMPETENCIES → PERFORMANCE OBJECTIVES → NEEDS ASSESSMENT → DELIVERY SYSTEM → EVALUATION

(FEEDBACK LOOP)

Define and describe, in your words, the following components designed to produce the competencies which a potential teacher must demonstrate before initial and/or continuing certification.[11]

1. Competencies
2. Performance objectives
3. Needs assessment
4. Delivery system
5. Evaluation
6. Feedback loop

Your efforts with Assignment II must meet the approval of the instructor directing your consideration of the systems approach and its application in VAE programs.

References* and Resources

Books

*Armstrong, Robert J., et al. The Development and Evaluation of Behavioral Objectives. Worthington, Ohio: Charles A. Jones Publishing Co., 1970, Pp. x + 99.

---

[11]Three Wayne State University publications which describe this VAE competency-based teacher education program are listed with the references for this chapter.

*Items with an asterisk have been cited in the chapter.

*Banathy, Bela H. **Instructional Systems.** Palo Alto, California: Fearon Publishers, 1968, Pp. v + 106.

*Butler, F. Coit. **Instructional Systems Development for Vocational and Technical Training.** Englewood Cliffs, New Jersey 07632: Educational Technology Publications, Inc., 1972, Pp. xviii + 360.

*Byers, Edward E., et al. **Writing Performance Goals: Strategy and Prototypes** (A Manual for Vocational and Technical Educators). New York: McGraw-Hill Book Co. In the Ohio State CVTE Related Series No. 15, 1971, Pp. 101.

Frantz, Nevin R., Jr. **Individualized Instructional Systems for Vocational and Technical Education: A Series of Instructional Modules.** Athens Georgia: Vocational Instructional Systems, 1974, Pp. vi + 136.

Gagné, R. M. **The Conditions of Learning.** 2nd ed. New York: Holt, Rinehart, and Winston, Inc., 1970, Pp. viii + 407.

*Gronlund, Norman E. **Stating Behavioral Objectives for Classroom Instruction.** New York: The MacMillan Co., 1970, Pp. vi + 58.

Hauenstein, Dean A. **Curriculum Planning for Behavioral Development.** Worthington, Ohio: Charles A. Jones, 1972, Pp. iv + 64.

Kaufman, Roger A., **Educational System Planning.** Englewood Cliffs, New Jersey: Prentice-Hall, Inc., 1972, Pp. x + 165.

*Kibler, Robert J., et al. **Objectives for Instruction and Evaluation,** 2nd ed. (under a new title). Boston: Allyn and Bacon, Inc., 1974, Pp. x + 203.

*Mager, Robert F. **Preparing Instructional Objectives.** Palo Alto, California: Fearon Publishers, 1962, Pp. x + 60.

*_____. **Goal Analysis.** Belmont, California: Fearon Publishers, 1972, Pp. vi + 136.

*Mager, Robert F., and Beach, Jr., Kenneth M. **Developing Vocational Instruction.** Palo Alto, California: Fearon Publishers, 1967, Pp. viii + 83.

*Mager, Robert F., and Pipe, Peter. **Analyzing Performance Problems or "You Really Oughta Wanna."** Belmont, California: Lear Siegler, Inc., Education Division, Fearon Publishers, 1970, Pp. vi + 111.

Popham, James W., and Baker, Eva L. **Systematic Instruction.** Englewood Cliffs, New Jersey: Prentice-Hall, Inc., 1970, Pp. ix + 166.

Stadt, Ronald W., et al. **Managing Career Education.** Englewood Cliffs, New Jersey: Prentice-Hall, Inc., 1973, Pp. xv + 224.

Periodicals

*Bushnell, David S. "An Educational System for the '70's." **Phi Delta Kappan,** Vol. 51, No. 4 (December, 1969), pp. 199-203.

Boston, Robert E., and Monzo, Roy, "Industrial Education for the Individual." **School Shop,** Vol. 31, No. 1 (September, 1971), pp. 35-37.

Childs, John W. "A Set of Procedures for the Planning of Instruction." **Educational Technology,** Vol. 8, No. 16 (August, 1968), pp. 7-14.

Hauenstein, A. Dean. "Developing Performance-Based Courses." **Man/Society/Technology,** Vol. 32, No. 4 (January, 1973), pp. 185-188.

Jelden, David L. "Learning Activity Packets for Indivualized Instruction." **Man/Society/Technology,** Vol. 31, No. 5 (February, 1972), pp. 138-140.

_____. "Individualized Instruction: A Meaningful Educational Experience." **Journal-Michigan Industrial Education Society, Inc.,** Vol. 29, No. 4 (June, 1970), pp. 3, 10, & 14.

Kraft, Richard H. P., and LaHa, Raymond F. "Systems Engineering Techniques Embarrassment or Opportunity for Today's Educators?" **Educational Technology,** Vol. 9, No. 9 (September, 1969), pp. 26-30.

Lawson, Tom E. "Designing Competency-Based Instruction." **Journal of Industrial Teacher Education.** Vol. 11, No. 4 (Summer, 1974), pp. 5-18.
Lee, A. M. "Instructional Systems — Which One?" **Audio-Visual Instruction,** Vol. 15 (January, 1970), pp. 30-31.
Moore, J. William. "Instructional Design: After Behavioral Objectives What?" **Educational Technology,** Vol. 9, No. 9 (September, 1969), pp. 45-48.
Morgan, Robert M. "ES '70 — A Systematic Approach to Educational Change." **Educational Technology,** Vol. 9, No. 9 (September, 1969), pp. 49-53.
Paulter, Albert J. "Computer-Based Curriculum Planning." **Man/Society/Technology,** Vol. 31, No. 5 (February, 1972), pp. 150-151.
Phi Delta Kappa. "Competency/Performance Based Teacher Education." **Phi Delta Kappan.** Vol. 55, No. 5 (January, 1974), pp. 289-337, series of articles.
Popham, W. James, et al. "Instructional Objectives." **Educational Research** Vol. 1, No. 9 (September, 1972), pp. 8-12.
Resnick, Harold S. "Implementing Instructional Technology: A Systems Approach." **Man/Society/Technology,** Vol. 31, No. 5 (February, 1972), pp. 155-161.
Silvern, Leonard C. "System Approach — What Is It?" **Educational Technology,** Vol. 8, No. 16 (August, 1968), pp. 5-6.
Schmitt, Marshall, "Eight Steps for Developing Performance Contracts." **Industrial Education,** Vol. 61, No. 4 (April, 1972), pp. 31-32, 34.
Tost, Donald T., and Ball, John R. "A Behavioral Approach to Instruction Design and Media Selection." **Audio Visual Communication Review,** Vol. 17, No. 1 (Spring, 1969), pp. 5-9.
Yee, Albert H.; Shores, Jay; and Skuldt, Karen. "Systematic Flow-charting of Educational Objectives and Processes." **Audio Visual Communication Review,** Vol. 18, No. 1 (Spring, 1970), pp. 72-83.
Williams, William H. "Major Steps in Developing Curriculum." **Industrial Arts & Vocational Education,** Vol. 60, No. 6 (September, 1971), pp. 79-82.

Other Published Materials

*Vocational and Applied Arts Education. **Competencies and Performance Objectives.** Competency-Based Teacher Education Series No. 1. Detroit, Michigan: Teacher Education Division, Wayne State University, November 1973, Pp. iv + 81.
*Vocational and Applied Arts Education. **Two VAE CBTE Project Models,** CBTE Series No. 2. Teacher Education Division, Wayne State University, November, 1973, Pp. iv + 26.
*Vocational and Applied Arts Education. **Designing a CBTE Instructional System: VAE Case History.** CBTE Series No. 3. Detroit, Michigan: Teacher Education Division, Wayne State University, May 1974, Pp. v + 36.
Fine, Sidney A. "A Systems Approach to Manpower Development in Human Services" in A Systems Approach to New Careers by Wretha W. Wiley and Sidney A. Fine, Kalamazoo, Michigan: The W. E. UpJohn Institute for Employment Research, 1969, pp. 27-37.
Gindele, John F., and Gindele, Joseph G. **An Instructional Package on How to Make an Instructional Package.** Minneapolis, Minnesota 27101: EDU-PAC of Minnesota, 1972, Pp. 32.
*Jelden, David L. Packets for a University course in Electronics (e.g., #6 RESISTANCE: #7, VOLTAGE; #8, CURRENT; #15, METER MOVEMENTS; and #16, OPERATION AND CALIBRATION OF OSCILLOSCOPES). Greeley, Colorado: Department of Industrial Arts, University of Northern Colorado, n.d.
*Lanham, Frank W.; Cook, Fred S.; Herschelmann, Kathleen M.; and Weber, Cathryn P. **Development of Performance Goals for New Office and Business Education Learning Systems.** Report to HEW, Office of Education, Bureau of Research, April, 1970, pp. viii + 343. Project No. 8-0414. ERIC Reference No. ED 041 139.

*Lanham, Frank W., et al. **Development of Task Performance Statements for a New Office and Business Education Learning Systems** (2nd edition under a minor change in title and sponsorship of The Ohio State CVTE), August, 1972, Pp. xii + 361. ERIC Reference No. ED 068 728.

Wiley, Wretha W., and Fine, Sidney A. **A Systems Approach to New Careers: Two Papers.** Kalamazoo, Michigan: The W. E. UpJohn Institute for Employment Research (300 South Westridge Ave., Kalamazoo 49007), 1969, Pp. vii + 37.

Unpublished Materials

Campbell, Robert E., et al. **The Systems Approach: An Emerging Behavioral Model for Vocational Guidance.** Columbus: The Ohio State CVTE publication RD 45. January, 1971, Pp. vii + 29. ERIC Reference No. ED 047 127.

Ullery, J. William, and Nicastro, Joseph S. **Development and Evaluation of an Experimental Curriculum for the New Quincy (Mass.) Vocational-Technical School.** Project ABLE, Final Report. American Institute for Research, Pittsburgh, Pa. and Quincy Public Schools, September, 1970, Pp. 163. ERIC Reference No. ED 048 492.

CHAPTER 4

Organization and Administrative Strategies

There has been considerable experimentation and evaluation of effective strategies for the organization and administration of vocational and applied arts education since 1960. A major shift in the role of the professional teacher has been from **being the key and sole organizer and presenter of basic instruction** to that of **being a facilitator or manager of a learning system.** In many places this is being done by an educational team headed by a master teacher. The team plans, organizes, and delivers an instructional program that is timely, meaningful, and motivating for each learner.

In addition to this team, the computer has served as a facilitator of organizational and administrative strategies in American education (Novosad, 1971). This tool has made possible the following:
1. Organizing and managing an educational program with a flexible modular schedule.
2. Undertaking a monumental research effort such as the NOBELS study, cited as an example in Chapter 3 of an application of the systems approach in education.
3. Employing the cognitive mapping strategy and in turn providing personalized educational programs, such as the program at the Oakland Community College (described later in this chapter).

The authors recognize the limitations of the organizational and administrative strategies chosen to illustrate considerations basic to a management system for VAE (vocational and applied arts education). While many other examples might have been selected to illustrate the selected strategies, those selected are believed to have far-reaching implications for the projection of curricula for occupational and applied arts education.

A Personalized Approach to Education

The unique feature of the educational program at the Oakland Community College (OCC), Michigan, with its four campuses and 15,000 students, is the provision for matching a student's learning style (the way he/she learns best) with effective instructional strategies. This experimental development program that matches a learner's cognitive learning style with suggested and effective modes of instruction is under the personal direction of Joseph E. Hill, OCC president, and Derek N. Nunney, vice-president for academic affairs. It is now being studied by many educators throughout the United States. Two Canadian colleges, Dawson College in Montreal and McGill University in Toronto, as well as a number of schools in Michigan, are experimenting with this approach. This plan is predicated on personalizing educational programs by utilizing cognitive style mapping. Students at all levels from preschool through college, including those in vocational-technical education, are involved in the refinement and further development of this personalized approach.

Diagnostic Testing and Cognitive Mapping

When a student seeks admission to OCC he/she finds that, in addition to the more traditional entrance examinations, there is a three-hour battery of tests that provides the needed information for his/her **Cognitive Style Map**, produced by data fed into a computer. Each tabular map is based on a consideration of eighty-four traits that describe how the student thinks and learns — his/her **own** cognitive style. In reporting on the OCC program, Hampton (1972) noted that "the measured traits can produce 2,304 combinations that show how he (the student) handles qualitative and theoretical symbols, how cultural influences affect the way he gives meaning to symbols, and how he derives meaning from the symbols he perceives." Nunney and Hill, in their circular describing **Personalized Educational Programs** (PEP),[1] state that the diagnostic testing and cognitive mapping phase of PEP determines:

1. How the student uses symbols to solve problems.
2. How the learner uses his/her senses and inference processes when faced with a situation which has no existing meaning for the student.
3. How the student searches for meaning in his/her environment.
4. Whether the learner prefers to listen or read.
5. If the student sees things as they affect him/her or as family or associates would see them.
6. If the learner has ability to categorize, contrast, or relate information.

An Educational Prescription for Each Student

The next step in PEP provides for a team of teachers, working in conference with the student, to develop a study plan designed to assure the student of performance success. This educational prescription is

---

[1]This circular and others describing PEP at the OCC are available upon request from the office of Dr. Derek N. Nunney, 2480 Opdyke Road, Bloomfield Hills, Michigan 48013.

geared to the strengths and weaknesses of the learner and is based on data gathered through diagnostic testing and in private conferences with the student. The learner, with this prescription, can personalize his/her approach to studying by employing modes for learning that are personally effective. He/she can "burst out" of the typical classroom setting into prescribed study in one or more of the OCC prescription centers, such as (1) the Individualized Program Learning Laboratory (IPLL), (2) Carrel Arcades (CA), or (3) Learning Resource Center (LRC). There are also these provisions for students:
1. To attend seminar "rap" sessions with teachers and/or other students.
2. To be tutored on a one-to-one basis by other students who are on the college payroll and who have already mastered the content and have been especially trained for the Youth-Tutor-Youth (YTY) phase of the program.
3. To work independently in the IPLL.

In practice the cognitive maps and prescriptions have produced up to nineteen ways of teaching the same course materials, with each one based on a particular learning style (Hampton, 1972, 10).

In the PEP circular, Nunney and Hill (n.d., 1) state:

> The decision to design and begin implementing a new educational program on an institutional scale grew out of frustration with the assumptions and attitudes that have pervaded the educational arena for the past 70 years. The overriding impact of these assumptions has led to a situation well described by Bloom (1968), when he said, "Only about a third of the nation's students really master the skills and concepts presented to them in school, but ninety-five percent are capable of doing so." Our position is that if we are to change this situation, we must stop using individual differences as a means of determining who succeeds or who fails in group competition, and instead, adapt to differences in cognitive styles and vary teaching techniques to insure the individual's success in his educational program.
>
> Furthermore, we believe that by using cognitive style mapping, we can determine which students can and do learn well from TV, for example. Also we can determine which students will probably have difficulty learning from TV, or textbooks, or audiotape, and so on. Our position, simply stated, is that different elements of educational technology can be used with varying effectiveness with students; none is superior for all students.
>
> An aim of the teacher is to diagnose the style of the student, determine his strengths, and begin to instruct him, utilizing media which will capitalize on his strengths. The student who is comfortable with a filmed presentation on metosis should have the film available to him and should not waste time in a lecture.
>
> The task, then, is one of matching the cognitive style of the student to the mode of presentation of information. To date at

Oakland Community College, we have mapped the cognitive styles of 33,000 students, and have developed distinctive prescription centers in which cognitive style and mode of presentation style can be matched.

Unitized Courses Make the Monitoring of Achievement Possible

By employing exit tests, it is possible in PEP to assess the competence of each student and determine if he/she is ready to move ahead with a program. Constant feedback keeps the student apprised of personal progress with his/her educational objectives and on target.

Student achievement is fed into the computer to facilitate the management of personalized instruction. These data provided by the staff, including those who direct the prescription centers, make it possible to test the validity of the student personalized prescription and to determine whether it needs to be modified. The overall goal is to guarantee the student a ninety percent success level of performance. That is, ninety percent of the students will earn a grade of C or better. Before PEP, only sixty-four percent gained this level of success.

Conclusions Based on Experiences with the PEP

Experiences at OCC with PEP clearly show that the way a student responds to instruction may be quite different from that of his/her peers. The student who responds well to structured step-by-step instruction may be comfortable and successful with programed materials, as he/she moves at a comfortable speed under the direction of a professional who has expertise in individualizing student development. The traditional formal classroom and lecture setting still works well for some learners. At the same time there are students who are motivated and become alive in the dynamics of group interaction as they participate in free and easy "rap" sessions with teachers and other students. Learners who relate to teachers on a one-to-one basis may work through conferences with teachers who are versed and enthusiastic about an open approach to education. Learners who respond well to help from selected and specially trained students may be assigned to advanced students serving as tutors.

Scheduled classes remain an essential element in the OCC instructional approach to personalized instruction. A major factor in the success of PEP at OCC is having qualified staff (teachers, paraprofessionals and tutors) specially trained for the mode of instruction for which they are responsible.

Students in the OCC program remain responsible for the content of their courses as they are encouraged to "burst" into any of the several available instructional modes appropriate to their needs, ability, and cognitive style.

Acceptance and Success of the PEP

To date, approximately thirty percent of the faculty is involved in PEP as a voluntary and experimental program. The PEP program was launched in 1968, shortly after Dr. Joseph Hill became president of OCC and Dr. Derek N. Nunney (a psychologist) was employed as vice-president for academic affairs and principal coordinator of PEP. The implementation of PEP has been facilitated as faculty have been recruited who are enthusiastic about the possibilities of personalizing educational programs, and as the present staff has had the opportunity to participate in special institutes focused on the specifics of individualized instruction. The present rate of growth of the program now suggests that more than fifty percent of the professional staff will be directly involved one way or another in PEP by 1976.

All incoming students at the OCC participate in the diagnostic testing and cognitive mapping phase of this program so that they may take advantage of possible modes of instruction through the various facilities for learning. The Carrel Arcades have been designed to provide instruction in social science, English, psychology, history, mathematics, and vocational-technical education (in electronics, automotives, and climate control systems). An eighteen-minute film on "Personalizing Educational Programs Utilizing Cognitive Style Mapping"[2] is used to present the total process to entering students in the freshmen General Orientation courses that are directed at helping each student understand self in relation to cognitive achievement. The film is also used to brief new faculty in conjunction with the ongoing in-service program.

In commenting on the success of the PEP at the OCC, Hill and Nunney have said:

> A striking example of the results which can be anticipated from such an approach has been demonstrated with a social science program in which 93 percent of the students received grades of "A", "B", or "C".

The Changing Role of the Professional Teacher and Supporting Staff in Mediated Instruction

Educators who have employed technology to optimize individualized instruction (Silvius and Curry, 1971, 480-522) are now concerned with personalizing the process. The issues that have come with this move relate to the role of those who are in direct contact with the learner in the implementation of such modes of instruction, i.e., teachers, paraprofessionals, teacher aides, student assistants, school staff for audiovisual services, experts from the community for some unit under study, and class officers performing leadership and service functions. The major

---

[2]This 16mm color film, approximately 20 minutes in length, is available for a rental fee ($20.00) or for purchase ($150.00) from Dr. Derek N. Nunney.

issues relate to the humanizing factors that encourage a strong bond between a student and the teacher.

Too many teachers have abrogated their responsibility for the instructional program in these ways:
1. Simply turning over the teaching of selected units (or modules) to a teaching machine.
2. Assigning a programed text.
3. Having the learner tutored by a person who has not been trained for the task.
4. Referring the student to computerized instruction that is cold and impersonal.
5. Referring the learner to a learning carrel to listen to or to view a presentation that is not really related to the immediate and central objective on which the learner is concentrating.

This topic reports promising and selected practices now being employed in the implementation of mediated instruction, and in keeping the teacher's role central and paramount. Also, consideration is given to humanizing the development of learning materials and the setting for the use of the equipment so that the learners are in an environment where they feel that they are viewing and/or listening, participating, and applying instruction, to the highest degree possible, that is tailored to their specific needs. It is essential that each student feel that mediated instruction is being directed or presented by the professional teacher, or some other person officially involved, with whom the learner relates and has personal contact and confidence. The goal is to maximize the use of humanized learning materials and relate them to the students and their objectives.

The Individualized Program at Michigan's Oakland Community College

Earlier in this chapter, there is an explanation of the unique personalized programs at the Oakland Community College (OCC). In examining the programs, one discovers that PEP is being projected against a theoretical base and structure known as **The Educational Sciences** (Hill, 1968). The following assumptions are essential to **The Educational Sciences:**
1. Man is a social creature with a capacity for deriving meaning out of his environment and personal experiences.
2. Not content with biological satisfactions alone, man uses symbols in his search for meaning.
3. These symbols acquire meaning through man's cultural experience. (Nunney & Hill, n.d., 1 & 2).

As mentioned in the earlier description of programs at OCC, participating staff have volunteered to take part or have been specially recruited. Also, there is an in-service training program for staff covering the underlying philosophy of PEP and the procedures followed in cognitive mapping and in the preparation of a personalized learning prescription for each student.

The use of staff who volunteer or are especially recruited and have had special training, may well be a cardinal principle to be observed in launching any innovative educational program. It is hard to see how staff members could reflect enthusiasm and interest in their contacts with students if they did not have their heart in the program and/or were poorly informed about it.

Individualized Program Learning Laboratory

The Individualized Program Learning Laboratory (IPLL) at the OCC is designed for the student who would rather work alone than in groups. In IPLL learners use programed texts as they progress through course materials that are structured in steps of increasing complexity. There is provision for students to check their answers before going on to the next step. If their answers do not match with those specified, the program leads each student through remedial instruction needed to again undertake the step. Also, the student may receive needed help to move ahead from available faculty in the IPLL. Many of the programed texts utilize programed filmstrips, slides with a synchronized tape recording, audio notebooks, three-dimensional models that may be studied and manipulated to make abstract concepts clear, and various kinds of other films to reinforce the understanding of the program under study.

When students first enter the IPLL, diagnostic tests aid the learners in choosing programs that would be appropriate for them and extend their competencies.

The programed texts cover a wide range of programs. Sample titles include Work Attack Skills, Vocabulary Development, Trigonometry, Slide Rule, Balancing Equations, Basic Electricity, Basic Electronics, Engines, Drafting, How to Measure Board Feet, How to Use a Micrometer, Nutrition, and Interior Decoration.

One of the unique features of the IPLL is that this phase of the OCC program is directed and coordinated by full-time faculty who are specially trained in the techniques of individualized instruction. Also, these full-time staff members are competent in the instructional areas embraced by the programed texts. Individual tutoring is instantly available in IPLL from 9:00 a.m. to 5:00 p.m. and some evenings each week.

Some of the IPLL programs can be loaned to students to be done at home. Where this is possible, the participating students check in with the IPLL on a weekly basis.

Carrel Arcades

The Carrel Arcades (CA) at OCC are large areas for informal individualized study, small group discussions, and tutorial sessions. These CA areas contain audiovisual resources that are needed for the implementation of the educational activities specified and planned by regular members of the faculty.

Some of the programs with cognitive goals at OCC, such as those planned by the English Department, are facilitated through the Carrel Arcades. This is done as students work in groups with their instructor for a course and then use other improvement devices for reinforcement. One of the unique features of the OCC arcades is that it is possible to have several different prescription centers operating concurrently in the same physical area with the use of wireless headsets.

Paraprofessionals have been specially trained to work in a supporting role in the arcades as they help students study and learn at their own speed. Students listen to audio tapes, review videotaped lectures, view films, or study other packets of instruction. To follow through and to provide reinforcement, students meet in the CA in small groups for informal "rap" sessions with their teachers, their peers, or resource persons (e.g., experts from business, industry, or the government).

Students who are "turned on" as they interact with lmeir peers, their teachers, and/or experts from their area of specialization find their informal group experiences in the congenial environment of the CA to be rewarding. Also, many of the students at the OCC have availed themselves of the opportunity to work with the CA staff in using the equipment for the improvement of their reading skills — speed and comprehension.

Learning Resource Center

At the OCC, the Learning Resource Center (LRC) includes the college library, but with more than the traditional services. This facility is a clearinghouse for a large variety of instructional packages. In addition to the usual books and periodicals, the LRC collection includes microfilms, special displays, and research materials in many forms.

Youth-Tutor-Youth

As mentioned, the CA at the OCC are used also for the Youth-Tutor-Youth (YTY) program that provides for having an experienced student tutor another learner on a one-to-one basis. This phase of the prescription program was established at OCC to make it possible for those students who may be intimidated by more formal teaching methods to receive informal guidance in a less threatening atmosphere.

The student tutors are:
1. Available on a regular basis.
2. Persons who have successfully completed the course and mastered the content under study.
3. Specially trained as tutors by the professional staff.
4. Paid by the college for their services.
5. Held accountable as they assist in reporting feedback to the professional staff on the student's progress with his/her personalized instructional program.

Since the youth tutors may have experienced pitfalls with course materials, they are often in a position to spot problems and suggest solutions that might escape an experienced faculty member.

Organizational Strategies and Curriculum for Implementation of Flexible Modular Scheduling

Flexible Modular Scheduling (FMS) is a system by which the school day is divided into time modules[3] (called "mods"), approximately twenty minutes in length, so that each student may be individually scheduled, with the assistance of a computer, for the kind and amount of instruction needed to fulfill his/her educational goals. In FMS, needed time for each kind of instruction becomes a variable. This is in contrast to the traditional plan where a student is scheduled for a course during the same period each day. With FMS, suitable combinations of the mod are used for the kind of instruction that would be most helpful to facilitate the learner's educational objectives. To illustrate, a student studying automotive mechanics may be scheduled for a number of different automotive programs each week. They might include (1) a two-mod period of large group instruction; (2) two three-mod periods each week for skill development in laboratory instruction; (3) one two-mod period especially planned for small group discussion; and (4) considerable blocks of time each week for individual development accomplished through independent study. Similar programs would be planned for each of the other subjects under study.

Generally the all-school program is organized around four types of basic instruction:
1. **Large Group Instruction.** Formal instruction is presented in a lecture-type facility to a minimum of forty students brought together for a predetermined length of time (such as two mods) for a presentation or activity directed by one or more teachers.
2. **Small Group Instruction.** A small group of students, generally held to not more than fifteen, meets with a teacher (or student leader), for a predetermined length of time, such as two mods, to discuss and think through some topic being studied in depth. In VAE programs, small group discussions may be introduced by a teacher's demonstration (or videotape) on some specialized hand or machine tool operation. Usually in small group discussions there is a high, positive psychological motivation for a learner to interact with others in his/her peer group, especially when the number can be kept to something like seven to eleven students.
3. **Laboratory Instruction.** A group of students (the number depending upon available work stations) meet for a predetermined period of time in a facility especially equipped to pursue an experiment, construct a project, or engage in skill development through the meaningful repetition of a hand or machine tool operation. The learning process is usually directed by a professional teacher with

---

[3]In the Resnick study (1970, 117-118) of 64 schools organized with FMS, the average length of a mod was 19.9 minutes (with a range of 13-30). The average number of mods per day was 20.5 (with a range of 13-28) for an average length school day of 6 hours and 37 minutes.

assistance from one or more paraprofessionals, student officers, experts from the community, or technicians employed to maintain the facility.
4. **Independent Study.** The student assumes responsibility as work begins with the staff in planning and undertaking activities that will fulfill his/her educational and personal goals. In FMS, from thirty to forty percent of the school week is allocated to the individual development of the usual learner, while the remainder of the school week is devoted to the other three types of instruction. Advanced and conscientious students may have as much as seventy to eighty percent of their time allocated for individual development. Such opportunity may be highly desirable for VAE students hoping to acquire the competencies needed to enter the labor force directly from high school.

Strategies and Curriculum for Large Group Instruction

Resnick (1970, 57) concluded that large group instruction was not being used by VAE teachers to the degree that it could be (and perhaps should be) in schools now organized with FMS. He conjectures that this is probably because of staff time required to organize and prepare for an outstanding presentation.

The nature of large group instruction, with a minimum of forty to fifty participants, precludes even a minimum interaction to presented materials. While this limitation is recognized, large group instruction remains an ideal mode of instruction for an illustrated lecture by a master teacher, a guest lecturer, or by an expert from the community on some technical subject under study. This mode of instruction seems ideal also for general testing, a pertinent and timely motion picture, televised instruction, carefully planned demonstrations covering basic instruction (to be followed by a scheduled laboratory experience for skill development).

Purposes advanced for large group instruction are:
1. To conserve teaching time.
2. To improve the quality of the presentation.
3. To make effective use of resource persons.
4. To capitalize on special talents of staff on the teaching team.
5. To make efficient use of a motion picture, television, or other audiovisual aids.
6. To use equipment and facilities efficiently.

It would seem that curriculum planners for VAE modules or courses need to screen their total outlines for an instructional program to determine those lessons that might be effectively delivered through large group instruction.

This mode of instruction in VAE seems efficient for the following types of instruction:
1. The introduction of new materials.
2. The demonstration of new equipment (that might be borrowed temporarily from industry or business).

3. Presentations to introduce major concepts.
4. A directed field trip to study aspects of the world of work. (The mods for such a session may need to be extended to approximately half of the school day).
5. General announcements and assignments.
6. General safety precautions (those that pertain to good personal habits and general laboratory activity).
7. Informational topics[4] (general, technical, and guidance).
8. An introductory presentation by a student panel with provision that the topic may be further explored as the audience is broken down and rescheduled for follow-through in small group sessions.

Since most illustrated lectures or visual presentations can be presented within thirty minutes, it works well to schedule such large group instruction for two twenty-minute mods. Such an allocation of time allows for the needed introduction and concluding remarks for the lesson. An important facet of large group instruction is to orient students on the techniques of taking notes and then to help them develop the skills to do so.

Resnick (1970, 60) found that persons planning schools for FMS advocate that there is provision for one large group facility adjacent to each subject area resource center. In this way the specific materials needed for large group presentations are readily available. Too often, the number of learners who can be assembled for large group instruction is restricted by the capacity of the available facility.

Since the key to the success of large group presentations is predicated on the ability and finesse of the teacher-presenter, it is important that this phase of the instructional program be done by a person who has developed such skills. Variety and suspense are two attention-attracting techniques employed in large group instruction. It must be expected, therefore, that some teachers have the talents and creativity to be effective with large group instruction, while others do not. It is important that the plan for computing faculty load provide for the inordinate amount of time needed to prepare teaching plans and materials for large group instruction. It may be desirable to divide the responsibility for the preparation and delivery of large group instruction among two or more persons on a teaching team to take advantage of their interests and areas of specialization.

Strategies and Curriculum for Small Group Instruction

There needs to be opportunity for learners to interact and participate with their peers, teachers, and experts on timely and pertinent issues and concepts. It is essential, therefore, that curriculum coordinators and teachers plan and schedule small group discussions needed to continue the study of a concept or issue considered timely by

[4]Fryklund's classification (1970, 70-77).

118 Planning and Organizing Instruction

the participants in respect to their educational objectives. To illustrate, the subject matter that supports the career education movement provides much opportunity for interaction and individual development through a further discussion of ideas introduced in large group presentations, or in special demonstrations scheduled to support experimentation or skill development in laboratory sessions.

Carefully planned and conducted discussions provide the setting for leadership development when the group is not too large (such as five to fifteen students). Such instruction provides the vehicle for testing:
1. The effectiveness of what is being presented in large groups.
2. The student's participation in laboratory experiences.
3. The work the student is doing to attain objectives through independent study in the open laboratory program, library, and other aspects of the program for individual development.

With proper planning, and by employing the systems approach to education, small group sessions serve a coordinating function for all experiences in an educational program.

Fig. 4-1. This small group discussion is a role-playing situation as two student groups represent labor and management in the negotiation of a labor contract. (Courtesy Stanley G. Lyons, Jefferson Junior High School, Pontiac, Michigan)

Educators have observed that students derive the capacity to modify, refine, and evaluate their positions as they probe into issues more deeply, and assume a more critical posture during small group discussions. It is essential, therefore, that curriculum planners plan assignments and interaction that will tie together all planned activity for an educational objective. Such interaction and reinforcement may be scheduled prior to manipulative activities or experimentation in a VAE laboratory, or possibly as a concluding experience if they are concerned with the overall evaluation of the unit of instruction.

In suggesting methodology that might be used with small group instruction, Allen (1964, 2) identifies (1) analytical discussions, (2) exploratory discussions, (3) reporting, (4) debating, (5) seminar groups, (6) role playing, and (7) testing of understanding. Participants in a summer workshop on modular scheduling at Salem, Virginia (**The Use of Modular Scheduling in Curriculum Improvement,** 1967, 2), suggested that there be provision in small group instruction for (1) an exchange of ideas, (2) individual reports, (3) a clarification of content as it is examined in depth, and (4) a discussion of tests.

Resnick (1970, 65) has recognized that the role of the teacher has changed with the mission that has been identified for small group instruction. He states:

> No longer in a dominant position in the small group, the teacher becomes a listener, participant, consultant, observer, discussion leader, or general healer. For teachers accustomed to doing a great deal of talking in classes, this adjustment is not easily made.

The following advantages for small group instruction were excerpted from those identified by Petrequin (1968, 46-47) from the outcomes of the program at Marshall High School in Portland, Oregon:
1. Students develop a sense of responsibility for their own learning as they make plans and evaluate outcomes.
2. Students learn to think independently of teachers.
3. Students become more confident in the validity of their own ideas and in themselves as individuals.
4. Students learn from each other as they raise questions. Issues that were once directed only to the teacher are now directed to other members of the group.
5. Teachers have become more acutely aware of individual and group problems as they have come to accept themselves as listeners.
6. Discipline problems found frequently in classes of a traditional size are nonexistent in small groups.
7. Students and teachers alike become more aware of the goals and objectives toward which they are working.

Instructional Program in Special Laboratories

Special school laboratories are now needed for nearly every curriculum area. Such facilities are no longer limited to VAE programs or to rooms where students do experiments with apparatus for physical science.

The new role for the school laboratory is described as a facility that includes the equipment and tools needed to enable learners to work independently and in small groups to (1) practice and acquire skills, (2) experiment, (3) do research, or (4) develop projects that make an application of concepts and principles covered in formal instruction. Laboratories provide the facilities for learners to acquire an essential competency (knowledge, skill, or judgment).

Dual Purpose for Laboratories

With FMS the laboratories are used as open labs or for scheduled educational experiences. The open labs are used by students, on a voluntary basis, for the unstructured part of their programs. The struc-

Fig. 4-2. This special laboratory is equipped to provide instruction in office practices for occupational and general education programs. (West Valley Occupational Center, Los Angeles)

tured phase of laboratory instruction facilitates skill development and other formal objectives that are promulgated as a part of the organized instructional program.

To the degree possible, most laboratories in the school are "open" to the students when they are not scheduled for the formal program. There are organizational problems in connection with the open labs that need to be considered by VAE teachers. Resnick (1970, 218) found that open labs posed problems in respect to safety instruction, cleanup, tool storage, and attendance records. To cope with these problems, some VAE teachers have experimented with a student-directed organization planned for those who find their way into one of the open labs during a specific block of time (Silvius and Curry, 1971, 516-518).

The Unscheduled Time

Some educators consider the unscheduled part of the school day to be a unique feature of FMS. During this part of the school week the typical student is allocated a significant percentage of his/her time to further and pursue personal goals for individual development. The rationale for this is that students can and should assume greater responsibility for their personal development. Most schools on FMS now provide a significant number of options to enable students to fulfill such personal objectives. These options include:
1. Working in available labs for the various curriculum areas on meaningful projects, experiments, research, or skill development.
2. Conferring with a teacher, counselor, or other available school specialist.
3. Studying in one of the various curriculum resource centers.
4. Studying in the library.
5. Conferring with an authority in the subject area.
6. Participating in an enrichment noncredit experience, such as a short mini course, or in a remedial program to improve reading skills.
7. Serving as an assistant to a teacher or as an assistant in a resource center.
8. Visiting sessions of selected large or small group instruction where the topic is of personal interest.

A distinction is made in the FMS approach between **individual study** and **independent study**. Bush and Allen (May, 1963, 82-83) point out that the term **individual study** is used to describe learning activities assigned and directed by teachers while **independent** study refers "to learning activities planned jointly by teachers and students and carried out by students with a minimum of faculty direction." In commenting on these distinctions, Resnick (1970, 71-72) wrote:

> Independent study is an attempt to find ways of making the student's individuality the most important part of the educational experience. It tries to deal as adequately as possible with real individual differences and to provide exciting learning experiences for every student, regardless of his ability or his interest.

The nature of what is done and advocated during the unscheduled part of a student's program varies with the philosophy and approach of those responsible for the overall educational program. In some schools, organized with FMS, the student is left to develop a major objective and then utilize any means he/she deems satisfactory to achieve that objective. At the other end of the continuum, such instruction is focused on individual development and is highly structured as key teachers assist the student in these ways:
1. In establishing each objective.
2. By suggesting activities to be pursued.
3. By providing for the supervision and assessment of his/her progress.
4. By specifying the performance level of the competence to be attained.

An example of a structured program for individual development would be the personalized prescription program at Michigan's Oakland Community College described in an earlier section of this chapter.

Differentiated Staffing in Occupational and Applied Arts Education

Differentiated staffing (DS) developed from the need to make maximum use of the talents, influence, and effectiveness of great teachers. This objective is accomplished as instruction for a specific educational program is planned, directed, and evaluated by a team of individuals who have precise and complementary roles needed to provide the essential staff functions for a motivating and effective educational program.

There are many possible models for the instructional teams. Allen and Wagschal (1969, 55-58) suggest four possible models for differentiated staffing in vocational-technical education.

- The first of these is a very simple plan where a teacher aide is employed to help the teacher with the noninstructional activities.
- The second model is somewhat more involved with the team made up of a teacher, an assistant team leader (with major responsibility for the technical content), two paraprofessionals, two interns, and two teacher aides.
- The third model provides for having the program coordinated by a curriculum council. The key persons in the third model are a curriculum associate and two senior teachers as shown in Fig. 4-3. Three staff teachers and three associate teachers work under the leadership of each senior teacher. In addition, model three calls for an auxiliary, noncredentialed support staff consisting of a clerk, a graphic artist, resource persons, and others as needed.
- The fourth model is shown in Fig. 4-4. In this plan there is need for specialists in curriculum, research, testing and diagnosis, guidance, logistics, and media. Instructors are specially trained for the various types of instruction employed with a flexible modular schedule (i.e., "large group," "small group," and "individual study"). Each major program is coordinated by a "master teacher."

Strategies **123**

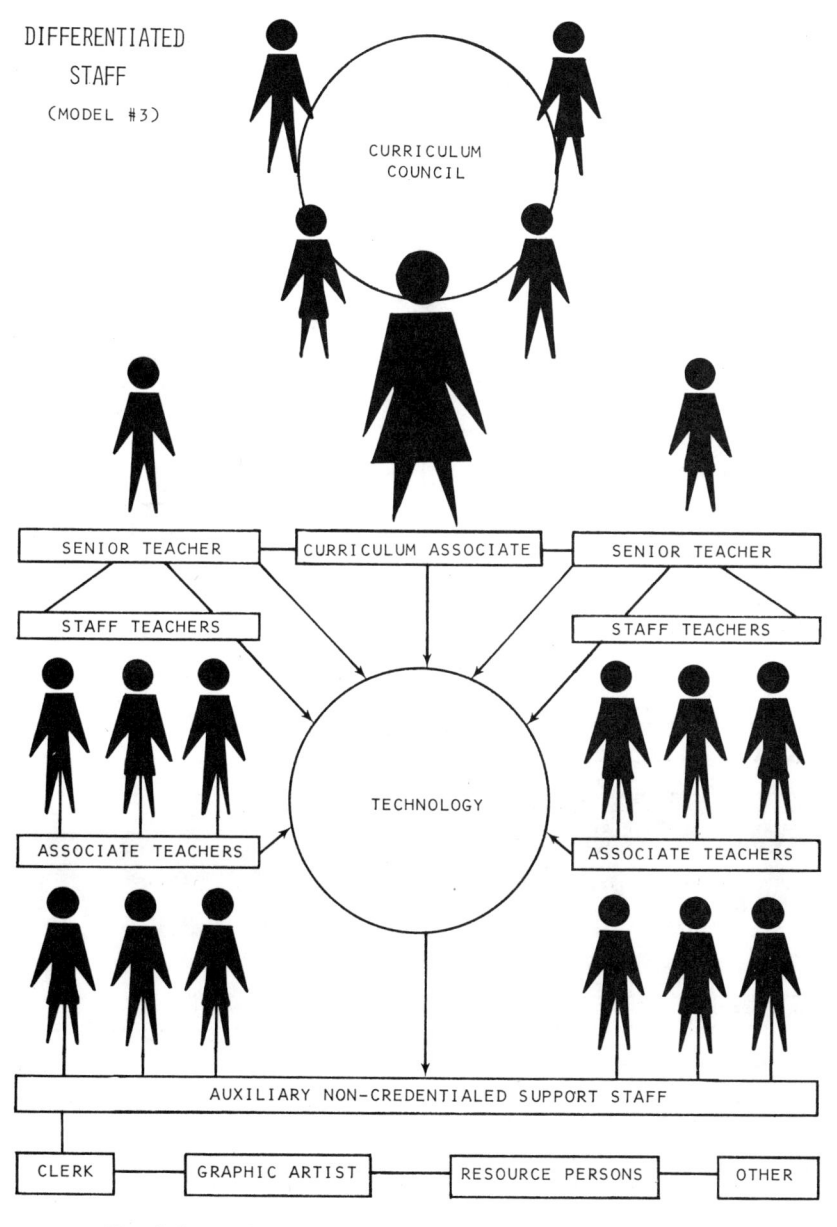

Fig. 4-3. A Suggested Model for Differentiated Staffing by Dwight Allen and Peter Wagschal (Reprinted from p. 57 of proceedings of Second Annual National Vocational-Technical Education Seminar sponsored by CVTE, The Ohio State University.)

124   Planning and Organizing Instruction

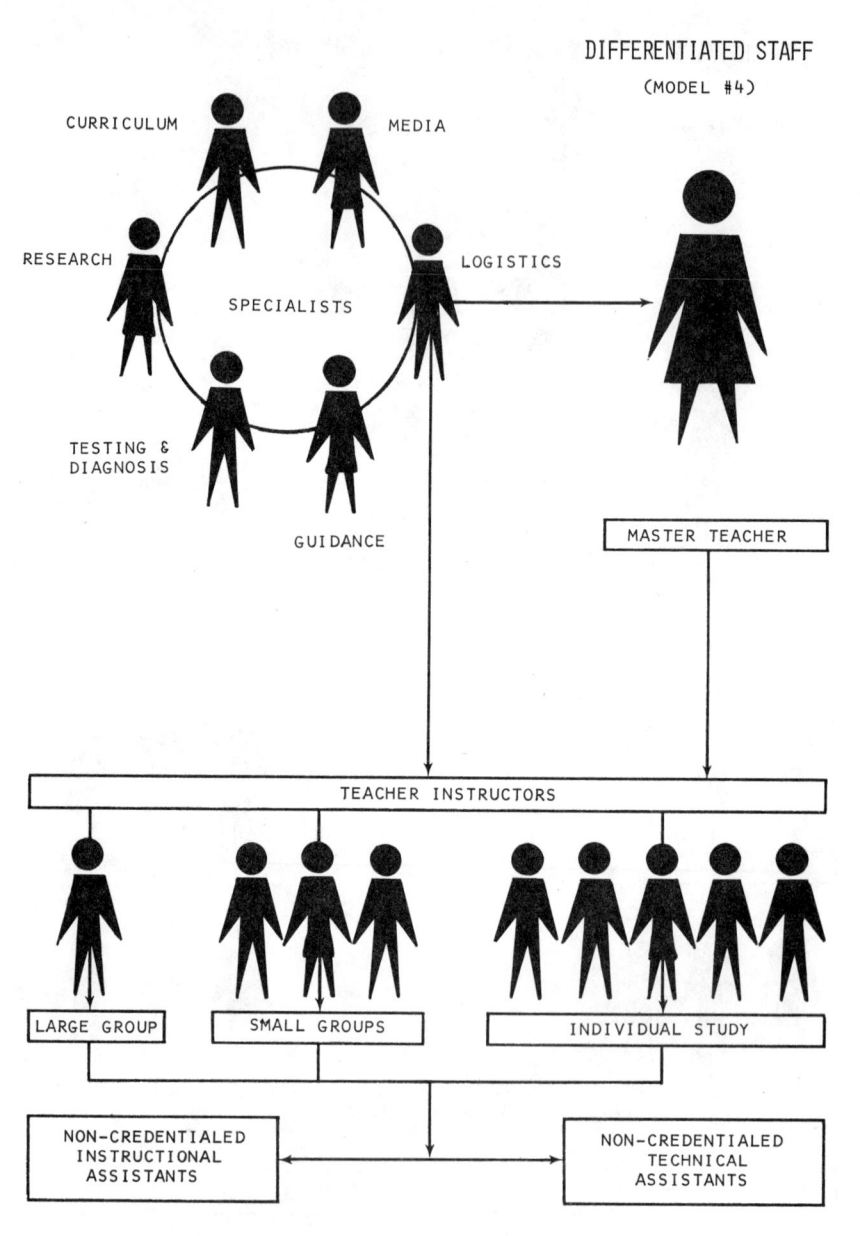

Fig. 4-4. Model for Differentiated Staffing Where School Is Organized with a Flexible Modular Schedule (This model was presented and designated as #4 by Allen and Wagschal for seminar proceedings mentioned in caption for Fig. 4-3.)

Takis, (1972, 14) defines DS as a staffing arrangement whereby education personnel are selected, educated, and deployed in ways that make optimum use of their interests, abilities, and commitments to education. Also, it affords teachers greater autonomy in directing their professional development. In many of the plans now in operation, status and financial rewards are based on complexity and level of responsibilities assumed by a person, as well as his/her professional preparation.

In DS a distinction is made between a "paraprofessional" and a "teacher aide." Paraprofessionals assume such duties as operating equipment, requisitioning supplies, repairing equipment, and constructing teaching aids. They are given either preservice or in-service training, often by the immediate professional staff, before they assume responsibility for designated tasks. Teacher aides assist with such non-teaching tasks as monitoring corridors and cafeterias, proctoring study halls, operating duplicating machines, and running errands. A teacher aide is not given special training for his/her duties. Both classifications, however, are for noncertificated personnel (Takis, 1972, 13-14).

The diversity of responsibilities and tasks that need to be performed in connection with the instructional program for occupational and applied arts education, including the learning experiences in the laboratories, provide untold opportunity to have significant roles identified for these individuals:

1. Special class officers, such as a student superintendent, a student safety engineer, or a student foreman in laboratory courses for curriculum areas, such as industrial education.
2. Student tutors, such as those selected advanced students who are trained by the professional staff and employed by the Oakland Community College for the Youth-Tutor-Youth program.
3. Teachers on school staff other than those from department of vocational and applied arts education, such as a physics, math, or chemistry teacher who would be well qualified to assist with selected units under study in a VAE course.
4. Experts from the community who would be employed when needed to assist with the technical aspects of some unit or problem.
5. Interns (one or more persons) who are in the final stages of their professional preparation.
6. Associates to the master or head teacher, such as advanced students who have already passed a course and are hand-selected and are invited to return to a course to be closely associated with a teacher (on a one-to-one basis). Such persons can work closely with the teacher on research and development projects and in assisting the teacher where appropriate in the implementation of his/her role as a professional (such as working under the close supervision of the teacher on an item analysis of an examination).
7. Student assistants who may be employed to assist with service activities that are needed for the implementation of a laboratory instructional program.

Community Resources Employed to Expand Occupational Education

Since the passage of the Vocational Education Act of 1963 and the 1968 Amendments there has been a renewed thrust to involve community leaders from industry (both management and labor), business, and the government in occupational education. This has come with the need to provide expanded opportunities in career education and to take advantage of the great array of available talent and facilities that now exists in many communities.

This topic addresses itself to five selected administrative and organizational strategies for optimizing such involvement which, in turn, expand the concept of "education without walls."

1. Expanding cooperative education programs at the secondary school level.
2. Procuring auxiliary facilities from companies to house expanding vocational programs.
3. Providing regional facilities for highly specialized programs, such as the Los Angeles Regional Occupational Centers and Programs.
4. Involving advisory craft committees in determining competencies for job-entry employment.
5. Negotiating contractual vocational programs with companies or individuals to expand the options in occupational education.

In addition to these five strategies there are many other ways in which VAE leaders and teachers are now working to optimize opportunities in career education. These would include these approaches:

- Securing equipment and instructional supplies for selected occupational programs from industry, business, and the government.[5]
- Working closely with persons in business who are interested in producing and merchandising the hardware and software needed to facilitate mediated instruction.
- Identifying and making available the facilities of industry, business, and government for organized field trips to further career education objectives.
- Identifying experts (technicians, engineers, businessmen, and other specialists) in the community who would be honored and willing to volunteer and share their expertise with students at work in schools on some unit of instruction.

Human and community resources for VAE programs appear to be limited only by the quality of educational leadership for school and community involvement.

---

[5]Much surplus equipment has been procured from the government for vocational education through the National Industrial Equipment Reserve (NIER). For information, contact: Office of Surplus Utilization, DHEW, 330 Independence Avenue, S.W., Washington, D.C. 20201.

Expanding Cooperative Work Education Programs

Evans (1971, 282) points out that Cooperative Work Education (CWE) was launched in the United States more than fifty years ago when the University of Cincinnati decided that it would be desirable for engineering students to spend part of their day in meaningful employment. The school program was thereby tailored to educational experiences that supported what these persons were doing on the job.

Because of the rather wide publicity covering the success of the experimental engineering CWE program at the University of Cincinnati, schools in the southern region of the United States were motivated, with their limited budgets for vocational education, to employ the CWE plan, especially at the secondary school level. Huffman (1971, 303) reports that this form of vocational education has been classified under these seven headings:
1. Business and office procedures.
2. Distributive services.
3. Home economics.
4. Trade and industrial skills.
5. Off-farm agriculture skills.
6. Interrelated programs.
7. Special purpose programs.

While CWE programs are acknowledged as being a most effective approach, they have not spread as rapidly in the United States as might have been anticipated. Three of the reasons are:
1. CWE can only be promoted and continued where there is optimum cooperation and working relationships between community employers and educators.
2. The school district must make an adequate investment in the employment of one or more coordinators with the needed professional preparation and work experience to launch and maintain the CWE program.
3. Too few educational leaders, from about 1950 through the early years of the 1960's, were ready to accept the CWE concept and work for the implementation of educational experiences outside schoolhouse walls.

Samuel M. Burt (1967, 13-14), one of the foremost authorities on industry-education cooperation, defines the term "industry," or "industry people" generically, for purposes of convenience, to include the representatives of business, labor, agriculture, manufacturing, homemaking, and the professions. Burt has concluded that the success of CWE depends most heavily on the adequate preparation and use of able coordinators. In summarizing qualifications for coordinators, Evans (1971, 284) mentions ability to plan in advance, initiative, outgoing personality, and organizational ability as essential for success as a coordinator.

The size of the school system and recent legislation for vocational education have been controlling factors in the character of the coordinator's responsibilities. To illustrate, larger school systems have often had multiple CWE programs with a coordinator for each family of occupations (e.g., a coordinator for distributive education, another for office occupations, a third for industrial occupations, etc.).

Several of the state plans for vocational education, especially in the smaller states, have made provision for a coordinator for Diversified Occupations (DO). A deterrent, however, in furthering the DO concept has been that traditional vocational leaders (including some state directors) have been slow to accept and implement the DO organizational plan. These traditional leaders have taken a strong position in favor of a coordinator for each major area of specialization, like distributive education. With the need for vocational education for all persons and a focus on the total occupational spectrum, it seems reasonable that CWE coordinators will be needed who are prepared to operate on a base broader than one major occupational grouping.

In general, CWE teacher-coordinators advise students, identify and arrange for suitable and pertinent training stations, develop or procure the related instruction, teach one or more courses for the school phase of the program, and direct and supervise the on-the-job experiences. A major goal of the teacher-coordinator is to assist the student and employer in establishing and maintaining a plan for criterion-referenced evaluation (see Chapter 11). Evans (1971, 284) stresses that the responsibilities of the teacher-coordinator include the building of community relationships for CWE and dealing with difficulties which may arise in maintaining equitable relationships among parents, students, employers, unions, and schools.

It is most essential that VAE leaders recognize the essential differences between CWE and Work-Study (WS). The goal for WS is simply employment for economic assistance so that the student may remain in school. While there are educational values that come from general employment in socially useful occupations, the major objective in WS is simply to provide a means of subsistence so that the learner may concentrate on his/her educational objectives. In CWE, the major objective of the on-the-job work experiences is **the learning which takes place.**

Procuring Auxiliary Facilities from Companies or Agencies to House Vocational Programs.

During six years between 1966 and 1972, the enrollment in technical-vocational education in Cleveland increased by 600 percent.[6] While the citizens in most of the great cities of the United States were voting down proposals for funding public education, the citizens of Cleveland supported a number of proposals that have made it possible to expand facilities and programs for occupational education.

---

[6]These data appear on p. 15, *Technical Vocational Education in the Cleveland Schools*, listed as a reference for this chapter.

Paul W. Briggs, Cleveland's superintendent of schools, recognizes that the solution of our great problems will continue to rest with scholars and scientists. He observes, however, that if there is to be a solution to these problems there will need to be a sufficient number of highly skilled and specially trained persons to carry through on what is being planned and projected by scholars and scientists. Paul Briggs believes, therefore, that the public schools have an important mission in providing educated workers for technological advance.

Paul Briggs speaks vigorously also about the role of occupational education in dealing with the burgeoning group of unemployed and underemployed adults, and their youth, who are experiencing misery and alienation in the midst of plenty.

There are more than 300 advisory committee members working with the Cleveland Public Schools. They review and make recommendations regarding courses of study, equipment and supplies, new training programs, and facilities for housing the expanding vocational programs. The AFL-CIO is sending able leaders to participate on these committees. Participating companies and organizations include The Cleveland Growth Association, Metropolitan Cleveland JOBS Council, General Electric, Addressograph-Multigraph, Higbee Company, General Motors, Ford Motor Company, Sherwin Williams Company, Central Data Systems, and many others.

Donald V. Healas, director of technical-vocational education in Cleveland, describes seven of the auxiliary facilities that have been established in Cleveland in recent years to extend occupational education:

1. The Lincoln Annex is a building formerly owned by the Ohio Bell Telephone Company, donated to the Cleveland Public Schools and located on the near west side of Cleveland. This facility serves the white Appalachian, Spanish-speaking and American Indian through the following programs: machine shop for Spanish-speaking; power sewing for the American Indian; English as a second language for the Spanish-speaking; a work-study program for the total community; and specialized high-impact programs in related technology based upon need.
2. The John Hay Annex is a building donated to the Cleveland Public Schools by The National Malleable Iron Corporation and serves the mid-east side, specifically the John Hay High School. The John Hay Annex serves the students from the high school through the following programs: machine shop, drafting, building maintenance, and office machine repair. The students are predominately black and this program is under the watchful eye of the General Electric Company's Special Equipment Manufacturing Division.
3. The East High Annex, formerly an A & P supermarket, is rented by the Cleveland Public Schools to provide increased vocational offerings for the East High School. This facility provides room for a machine shop program, an automotive mechanics program, and a building maintenance program.

4. The John F. Kennedy Annex was a utility garage and storage area for Shaker Heights municipal vehicles and was purchased by the Cleveland Public Schools to provide increased vocational programs for the students at the J. F. Kennedy High School. The facility houses programs in diesel engines, auto mechanics, carpentry, drafting, air-conditioning and heating, mechanical and industrial electricity, and occupational work experience.
5. The Woodland Job Center was donated to the Cleveland Public Schools by the General Electric Company and is providing a series of industrial-based vocational education programs. This facility is used for automotive mechanics, truck mechanics, auto body repair, building maintenance, machine shop, work-study, and related technical education. In addition, the General Electric Company has established their own mini manufacturing company to train new employees, as has the Chevrolet Division of General Motors. Other companies, such as Eaton, East Ohio Gas, Cleveland Electric Illuminating, Otis Elevator, and Ohio Bell utilize the Woodland Job Center to train additional employees at freqent intervals. This facility also contains supportive units from the Ohio Bureau of Employment Services; Work Incentive Program (WIN); the Ohio Division of Vocational Rehabilitation, State Department of Education; and the Counseling and Technical-Vocational Divisions of the Cleveland Public Schools.
6. The Woodbine (Fig. 4-5), a former Coast Guard buoy tender, was presented to the Cleveland Public Schools and is now serving as a Maritime School for diesel electric, navigational aids (electronics), deck operations, and water ecology. The Woodbine is valued at one million dollars and is utilized for their education program on the lakes during the shipping season.
7. The new Aviation High School in the heart of Cleveland at the Burke Lakefront Airport contains space and equipment to serve the aviation industry and interested students from Cleveland and the surrounding suburbs. A two-year program meets the requirements of an increasing aviation market. Accounting-computing, inventory control, parts room operation, wholesale and retail sales, and distribution are segments of this program. Utilizing a control tower, simulators, and computers, air traffic control programs prepare students for this sophisticated branch of aviation. There is a three-year program that prepares graduates to take the F.A.A. examination for their airframe and powerplant (A & P) license.[7]

---

[7]Excerpted from a letter from Donald V. Healas to G. Harold Silvius.

Fig. 4-5. The Woodbine was provided by the U.S. Coast Guard and is now being used as a training facility for the maritime trades. The ship is 180' long, 37' beam, and has a 10,000-mile cruising range. (Photograph provided by Donald V. Healas, Director of Technical-Vocational Education, Cleveland.)

The Los Angeles Regional Occupational Centers and Programs

The School Board for the Los Angeles City Unified School District, with valuable assistance from more than 500 large and small businesses and industries, has developed several Regional Occupational Centers (ROC) with timely and needed Regional Occupational Programs (ROP).

Support for the ROC/ROP program was expressed by the School Board with the following declaration on October 28, 1971:

> We believe that it should be the policy of our school district to provide career education for all youth and adults of the district to the end that . . .
> . . no student drops out of school who is not prepared to enter the world of work.
> . . no student graduates who does not have saleable skills for productive work or college education.
> . . no adult is denied an educational opportunity to become properly employable (**16 To 60**, 1972, 3).

132 Planning and Organizing Instruction

Shortly after this declaration, Superintendent William J. Johnston (1972, 3) told those attending a Town Hall meeting in Los Angeles that this action had been taken to deal with the occupational training gap. He pointed out that:

Of every 100 Los Angeles youth who start high school only 75 graduate, while a mere 20 go on to finish college. Nationally, he added, 750,000 dropouts a year, from high school and college, add to the unskilled labor glut. Of the 31.5 million who obtain entry-level jobs in the years 1967 - 1975, he estimates that three out of four — or 23 million will need vocational preparation.

The Los Angeles Regional Occupational Centers have been an overnight success. For example, a former supermarket was opened as the city's first paramedical occupational training center in 1970 in an underemployed, low income, welfare, and largely black community. Some persons questioned whether the community would be interested in courses like X-ray technology, inhalation therapy, medical and business terminology, hospital admitting clerk, licensed vocational nursing,

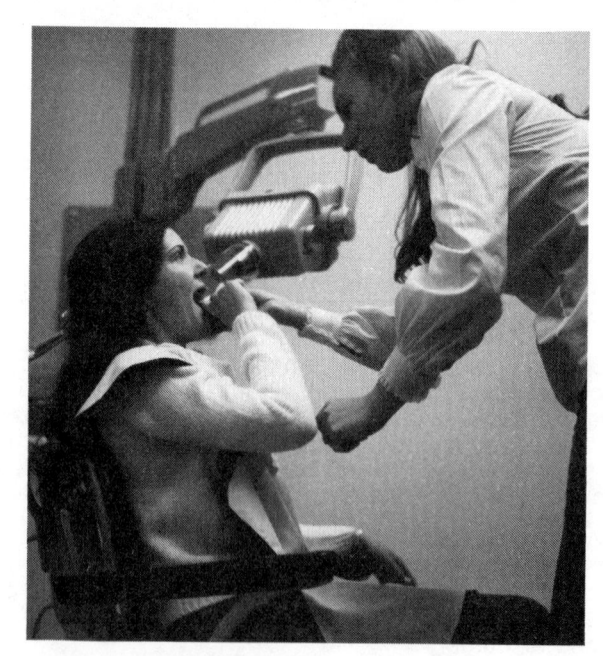

Fig. 4-6. Students enrolled in the dental assistant program, one of the "Para-Med" programs, learn how to take X rays of teeth and adjunct jawbone. (East Los Angeles Occupational Center)

operating room technician, medical diet aide, and other hospital-related subjects. It was gratifying that success was immediate. "Paramed's" first classes were quickly filled with more than 500 enrollees. One out of three walked long distances to class, while one drove 30 miles to participate. The student body was a mixture of serious teenagers and adults. The "Paramed" program attracted wide attention in its success in placing students after graduation. For example, the first ten inhalation therapy graduates in 1971 found immediate jobs, and five were quickly promoted to supervisory positions. Before "Paramed" all ten had been on relief.

Unique Features of the Los Angeles' ROC/ROP

1. The student selects his/her own course. No one forces the student to enter any particular field. Trained counselors help students find subjects that match interests and aptitudes.
2. There is no age grouping in ROC programs. Teenagers, young adults, middle-aged persons, and elderly students work side by side.

Fig. 4-7. Student operating a fork lift as part of his training to become a warehouseman. Instruction is provided in a real warehouse, a facility difficult to duplicate in a school. (Regional Occupational Program, Los Angeles)

A sixteen-year-old youth may be working with a sixty-year-old person.
3. Many ROP classrooms are located in high schools where special and unique laboratories are shared weekdays, late afternoons, and Saturdays by students from two or more high schools. Whenever strategic, they are located in well-equipped plants of private enterprise, whose competitive management spends large sums to facilitate production. This strategy provides classroom laboratories that could never be duplicated by a school district.
4. The ROP plan provides courses scheduled up to six hours on Saturday between 8:30 a.m. and 5:00 p.m. and/or two late afternoon sessions from 3:30 to 6:30 p.m., generally on Tuesday and Thursday. Students elect either the weekday or Saturday program to secure their six hours of "hands on" career training per week.
5. Placement is high since only courses that meet the needs of the job market are scheduled. Programs with doubtful job opportunities are dropped.
6. Students provide their own transportation. For some, it's a long bus ride, possibly with transfers.

Outcomes of the Los Angeles' ROC/ROP

1. In four and one half years, from the start in 1967 to early 1972, Los Angeles' ROC/ROP grew from zero to over 50,000 students educated each year in scores of training locations.
2. The ROC principal and his staff work closely with advisory committees of leaders and experts to develop programs, plan for future courses, and find the experts to do the teaching. These unpaid advisory committees are considered as much a part of the ROC system as the school board's staff. They provide world-of-work know-how, act as an early warning system on employment trends, keep ROC courses timely, and turn up job leads for graduates. These committees also help locate needed equipment, often obtaining it at little or no cost to the school district.
3. Employment rates for graduates run from 70 to 100 percent. The lower percentages are often caused by student transfer from one program to another, often after exposure to an initial selection.
4. Students are motivated in knowing that their ROC teachers are working experts in their own field and are listened to when they recommend their students for placement.
5. Those who have studied the Los Angeles ROC programs (**16 To 60,** 1972, 5) have concluded that:

> there is no substitute for an instructor who is a master of his own craft, who can create his own textbook as he goes along, and who can revise it overnight, if necessary, to keep up with [Technological Advance].

Advisory Craft Committees Help Set Competencies for Job-Entry Employment

Recent legislation for vocational education calls for the involvement of local advisory craft committees in formulating and validating curriculum specifications for occupational education programs. Such committees are composed of persons in the community who are currently working at a productive, service, or leadership level in the occupation under consideration and are in a position to volunteer their services. To illustrate, advisory craft committees function for each of the thirty-two occupational education programs offered by the four Area Vocational Education Centers in Oakland County, Michigan. An example of the curriculum information for the Oakland County programs is presented as **Appendix E** of this book. Such information is cooperatively developed by the Vocational Education Consultants for the Oakland Schools, the Craft Advisory Committee, the Area Center Vocational Directors, and Area Center teachers.

One of the unique aspects of formulating educational specifications for an occupational education program is the opportunity to involve members of the Craft Advisory Committee in formulating the behavioral objectives. These persons are very concerned about competencies, as expected outcomes, to be demonstrated by students. Because of the personal involvement and experience of these persons in the occupations, they take strong positions on the competencies needed for entry-level employment.

One of the concomitants of the program is that there will be little question about placement opportunities for those students who successfully complete the program and are able to demonstrate the competencies that accrue from the outcomes of instruction.

Contractual Vocational Programs

The directives in the Declaration of Purpose in the 1968 Amendments to the Vocational Education Act of 1963 state:

> ... that persons of all ages in all communities ... will have ready access to vocational training or retraining which is of high quality, which is realistic in light of actual or anticipated opportunities for gainful employment, and which is suited to their needs, interests, and ability to benefit from such training.

In the thrust to expand the options for occupational education and provide the services that are mandated by the 1968 Amendments, school districts have entered into contracts with individuals, private occupational schools, community colleges, area vocational centers, companies, or corporations to extend occupational preparation. Such companies as Westinghouse, Educational Development Corporation, and Thiokol Chemical Corporation have established divisions to facilitate contractual educational programs with school districts. Thiokol's initial venture in providing vocational education through a contractual arrangement was at the Clearfield Job Corps Urban Center in Utah. Thirteen hundred young men received vocational training in sixteen areas that included automotive repair, food service, social work, carpentry, and landscaping. Thiokol has also had a contract with the Bureau of Indian Affairs to provide vocational and social skills for single adults and families from virtually every tribe in the United States. This program is carried on at Thiokol's Roswell Training Center at Roswell, New Mexico. An Indian Police Academy is also operated at Roswell for the training of law officers. The Thiokol Chemical Corporation is interested in considering a contract and in preparing a proposal to provide occupational training in any area for which a school system might prepare educational specifications.[8]

School districts throughout the nation are contracting with private schools of cosmetology. Contracts provide that the instruction qualify the student, at the close of the program, to pass an examination administered by a State Board of Cosmetology as required for a license to practice. During the 1971-72 school year, seven such contracts in Michigan schools provided 750 hours of instruction in cosmetology. Eugene Simms reports[9] that the range in costs per student for the seven programs in Michigan was from a low of 26¢ to a high of 50¢ per hour. The average cost was 36.7¢ amounting to $275.25 per student for the 750 hours per year of instruction. These costs are in line (or less) than the cost for an area vocational center or a community college to plan, equip and operate a cosmetology program.

In addition to cosmetology, school districts are contracting for a variety of programs including such typical areas as automotive mechanics, clerical functions, data processing, and welding. In an article by Howard Smith, "New Approaches in Training" (November, 1972, 28-29), there is mention of how Manistique Area High School, with a student enrollment of 650 in a sparsely populated area of northern Michigan, is contracting for needed occupational education programs with business enterprises in the community, just like they would for a new roof on the school. The contracts provide for skill training in small engine repair, printing, sign painting, radio announcing, airport management, auto parts management, and meat cutting. Programs are being projected to include training in food preparation, dry cleaning, and baking. The contracts are negotiated for multiple blocks of ninety hours of instruction (needed to prepare the student so that he/she may secure a job after completion of the program). This is the time allocated for a unit of credit in a traditional high school program. The training station operators receive $2.50 an hour for each student hour of instruction. The students are not paid for the training since it is considered an integral part of the

---

[8]Thiokol's Education and Training offices for their Economic Development Operations are P. O. Box 1619, Ogden, UT 84401.
[9]Simms, Eugene J., Contractual Agreements, a research paper presented at the Michigan Career Education Conference held in Grand Rapids in August, 1972. At that time Mr. Simms was an occupational specialist, Vocational Education and Career Development Service, Department of Education, State of Michigan.

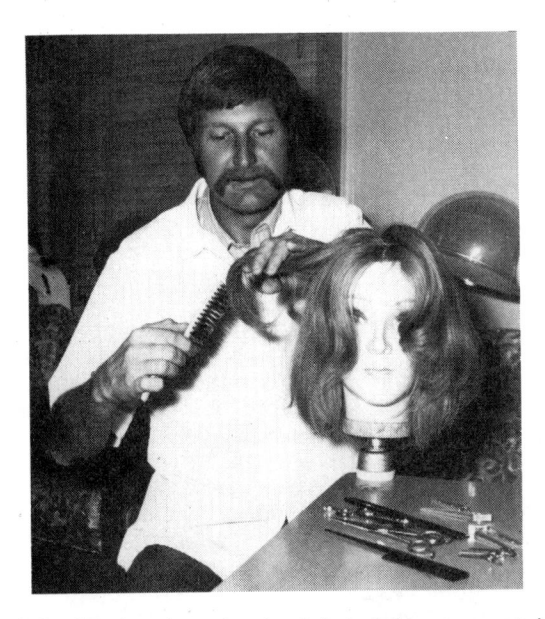

Fig. 4-8. Student learning to style hair in a cosmetology program. (West Valley Occupational Center, Los Angeles)

area high school program. The project director assumes responsibility for the coordination and supervision of the program.

To qualify as a training station, a businessperson in the Manistique community submits an outline for a proposed program. These proposals are scrutinized with great care, and then outlines for each program are cooperatively developed to assure that there is ample provision for classwork, laboratory experiences, and field experiences. The project director is provided with a weekly log of activities at each work station. From these reports the director is then in a position to be helpful as he/she undertakes to facilitate the ordering of needed textbooks, periodicals, supplies, equipment, and in providing needed related instruction. Students are counseled into electing related courses. The trainees at the radio station are scheduled for speech; those in meat cutting are encouraged to take courses in distributive education; and those in sign painting find courses in art helpful.

While costs of $720 to $773 (normally for ½ day for one semester) to prepare a student in the contractual program at Manistique, Michigan, may appear high, the school system is providing this instruction without a major investment in equipment and the cost that comes with full-time personnel for extending occupational education.

The schedule for the student in a contractual vocational program does not follow the traditional school day. It is, in fact, similar to a flexible modular schedule. To illustrate, the contract in cosmetology between the University School of Beauty Culture and the Bloomington, Illinois, school district provides released time from high school so students may attend classes at the school from 10:00 a.m. to 12 noon, Monday through Friday; 8:30 a.m. to 5:00 p.m. on nonschool days and on Saturday. Where there are few students involved, training station time is often arranged by the students and the persons responsible at the training station. Saturday schedules are popular and some of the instruction may be offered in the evening.

Contractual vocational programs are an example of Differentiated Staffing. The school-coordinator or the project director is responsible for planning and projecting the various contractual programs. This responsibility includes the planning and approval of courses of study, planning for the delivery system, and planning for evaluation and placement. The personnel at the various work stations provide expertise in the occupational areas and facilitate instruction. In addition, there is usually provision for technicians to facilitate the maintenance of the program.

School districts moving to initiate contractual arrangements to extend training opportunities should proceed with caution. They need to make a careful cost analysis of projected instruction and specify learning conditions that will virtually guarantee opportunity for employment upon the completion of the program. It seems desirable that State Departments of Education provide guidelines for negotiating agreements with business enterprises and private trade schools. They can provide sample contracts, comparative cost and specification data, and serve as the clearinghouse for the review of all proposals under consideration for approval and funding.

For Self-Assessment and Discussion

1. Describe the plan at Michigan's Oakland Community College (OCC) for cognitive mapping.
2. Cite examples of VAE organizational strategies.
3. Describe the plan for personalized learning at the OCC that makes it possible for a learner to employ modes for learning that are predicated on his/her cognitive mapping data.
4. What are the advantages of the "Personalized Education Program" at the OCC? What would be some of the disadvantages of this plan?
5. How would you define "mediated instruction"?
6. Describe techniques now being employed to humanize mediated instruction.
7. How would you define "Differentiated Staffing"?
8. What are the advantages of Differentiated Staffing (DS)?
9. What are the factors or the conditions that make it difficult to implement DS in the schools?
10. Define "Flexible Modular Scheduling" (FMS).

Strategies   139

11. Describe the typical plan in Flexible Modular Scheduling where instruction and the student's program are organized around modules of time.
12. What are the unique features of the following learning centers at the OCC:
    A. Individualized Program Learning Laboratory (IPLL).
    B. Carrel Arcades (CA).
13. What is the rationale for the Youth-Tutor-Youth (YTY) program at the OCC?
14. Cite instruction and lessons that might be scheduled by VAE teachers through these learning periods:
    A. Large group instruction.
    B. Small group instruction.
    C. Laboratory instruction.
    D. Independent study.
15. What problems come with a Flexible Modular Schedule in that portion of a student's time that is set aside for unscheduled activities?
16. What are the distinctions between "Cooperative Work Education" (CWE) and "Work-Study" (WS)?
17. What distinction, if any, would you make between "individual study" and "independent study"?
18. Identify three examples of VAE administrative strategies employed for extending opportunities in occupational education.

Assignments to Demonstrate Competencies

Using the content and selected References and Resources[10] for Chapter 4:
1. For your area of specialization, describe in precise statements the kinds of lessons, with estimated modules of time, that might be facilitated during these learning periods:
    a. Large group instruction.
    b. Small group instruction.
    c. Laboratory instruction.
    d. Independent study.
2. Prepare a proposal, not to exceed 250 words, for the use of a differentiated staff within your VAE area of specialization. Such a plan should consider the use and roles of two or more classifications of personnel.
3. Prepare a proposal, not to exceed 250 words, for the use of a Cooperative Work Education (CWE) plan for your area of specialization. Such a plan should consider the role of the teacher-coordinator, grade levels for CWE, plans for placement and supervision at training stations, involvement of community leaders in CWE, and advantages of the CWE program.

---

[10]References and Resources by English and Sharpes, Evans, Huffman, Petrequin, Silvius & Curry, Wolansky, Allen and Wagschal, Stocker, Resnick, and Takis are especially recommended.

These assignments are to be developed to the degree that they will meet with the approval of the person directing your development to become a VAE teacher or leader.

References* and Resources

Books

Brown, Robert Louis. **Cooperative Education.** Washington, D. C.: American Association of Junior Colleges, 1971.

*Burt, Samuel M. **Industry and Vocational-Technical Education.** A study of Industry Education-Advisory Committees. New York: McGraw-Hill Publishing Co., 1967, Pp. xx + 520.

Bush, R. N., and Allen, Dwight W. **A New Design for High School Education: Assuming a Flexible Schedule.** New York: McGraw-Hill Publishing Co., 1964.

English, Fenwick W., and Sharpes, Donald K. **Strategies for Differentiated Staffing.** Berkeley, California 94704: McCutchan Publishing Corporation, 1972.

*Evans, Rupert N. "Cooperative Programs: Advantages, Disadvantages, and Development" in **Contemporary Concepts in Vocational Education** (edited by Gordon F. Law, First Yearbook of AVA). Washington, D. C.: American Vocational Association, 1971, pp. 282-290.

*Fryklund, Verne C. **Occupational Analysis: Techniques and Procedures.** 5th edition. New York: The Bruce Publishing Co., 1970, Pp. vi + 213.

*Huffman, Harry. "Is Cooperative Vocational Education Unique?" in **Contemporary Concepts in Vocational Education** (edited by Gordon F. Law, First Yearbook of AVA). Washington, D. C.: American Vocational Association, 1971, pp. 300-306.

Kimbrell, Grady, and Vineyard, Ben S. **Strategies for Implementing Work Experiences Programs.** Bloomington, Illinois: McKnight Publishing Co., 1972, Pp. 400.

Tomlinson, Robert M. "Implications and Reflections: The Vocational Education Amendments of 1968," in **Contemporary Concepts in Vocational Education** (edited by Gordon F. Law, First Yearbook of AVA). Washington, D. C.: American Vocational Association, 1971, pp. 26-34.

*Petrequin, Gaynor. **Individualizing Learning Through Modular-Flexible Programing.** New York: McGraw-Hill Publishing Co., 1968, Pp. xv + 180.

*Silvius, G. Harold, and Curry, Estell H. **Managing Multiple Activities in Industrial Education.** Bloomington, Illinois: McKnight Publishing Co., 1971, Pp. xxiv + 648.

Periodicals

Anderson, Herbert A. "What is Instructional Technology?" **Man/Society/Technology,** Vol. 31, No. 5 (February, 1972). Pp. 137.

Arnold, Joseph P. "Applying Differentiated Staffing to Vocational-Technical Education." **Journal of Industrial Teacher Education,** Vol. 7, No. 1 (Fall, 1969), pp. 13-20.

*Bush, R. N., and Allen, D. W. "Flexible Scheduling." Bulletin of **National Association of Secondary School Principals.** Vol. 47 (May, 1963), pp. 73-98.

Buzzell, Charles H. and Hollander, Sophie S. "The Place of the Post-Secondary Institutions in Vocational Education." **Journal of Industrial Teacher Education.** Vol. 11, No. 2 (Winter, 1974), pp. 7-12.

*Items with an asterisk have been cited in the chapter.

Cochran, Leslie H. "Charting the Changing Directions of Industrial Education, Part I." **School Shop**, Vol. 29, No. 1 (September, 1969), pp. 47-50.

_____. "Charting the Changing Directions of Industrial Education, Part II." **School Shop**, Vol. 29, No. 2 (October, 1969), pp. 53-56.

Gillie, Angelo C., Jr. "The Area Vocational Schools and Community Colleges: Cooperation on Confrontation?" **Journal of Industrial Teacher Education**, Vol. 11, No. 2 (Winter, 1974), pp. 13-21.

*Hampton, William. "Students Find Their Way to Learning With Cognitive Style Mapping." **College & University Business**, McGraw-Hill Publishing Co., (February, 1972), pp. 10 + 14.

Resnick, Harold S. "Communications Systems." **Man/Society/Technology**, Vol. 31, No. 4 (January, 1972), pp. 104-105.

*Smith, Howard, "New Approaches in Training." **Industrial Education** (Formerly **Industrial Arts and Vocational Education**), Vol. 61, No. 8 (November, 1972), pp. 26-29.

Vassallo, Wanda. "Learning by Tutoring." **American Education**, Vol. 9, No. 3 (April, 1973), pp. 25-28.

Wolansky, William D. "Teacher Aides — A First Step to Differentiated Staffing." **School Shop**, Vol. 32, No. 4 (December, 1972), pp. 30-31.

Other Published Material

*Allen, Blaine W. Individualized Learning Through Computerized Modular Scheduling. Second report of scheduling project at Virgin Valley High School, Mesquite Nevada. (1964), ERIC Reference No. 021-669.

*Allen, Dwight W., and Wagschal, Peter. "Differentiated Staffing for Vocational-Technical Education" in proceedings of **Second Annual National Vocational-Technical Teacher Education Seminar** by James W. Hensel and Garry R. Bice, Columbus, Ohio: CVTE (January, 1969), Pp. vii + 190, ERIC Reference No. ED 027-424.

*Bloom, Benjamin S. "Learning for Mastery." VCLA **Evaluation Comment** (May, 1968).

*Hill, Joseph E. The Educational Sciences. Bloomfield Hills, Michigan 48013: Oakland Community College Press, 1968, Pp. 21.

*Nunney, Derek N., and Hill, Joseph E. **Personalized Educational Programs.** A circular published by the Oakland Community College. Bloomfield Hills, Michigan 48013 (n.d.), Pp. 6.

*16 To 60, a ROC/ROP Publication of the Division of Career and Continuing Education, Los Angeles Unified School District, P.O. Box 3307, Los Angeles, CA 90051, 1972, Pp. 31.

Stocker, Joseph. "Eighteenth Special Report on Differentiated Staffing in Schools." **Education USA**. Washington, D. C. 20036: National School Public Relations Association, 1970, Pp. 48.

*Technical Vocational Education in the Cleveland Schools. Cleveland, Ohio, 1380 East Sixth Street 44114: Cleveland Public Schools, 1971-72, Pp. 20.

Wallace, Harold R. Review and Synthesis of Research on Cooperative Vocational Education. Publication of The Ohio State CVTE, June, 1970, Pp. 124. ERIC Reference No. ED 040 247.

Unpublished Material

*Novosad, John P. Implications of Computer Technology for Industrial Education. Ed D. doctoral dissertation, Wayne State University, 1971, pp. x + 298. Microfilm No. 71-29778.

*Resnick, Harold S. Implementation of Flexible Modular Scheduling for Industrial Education. Ed D. doctoral dissertation, Wayne State University, 1970, pp. viii + 304. Microfilm No. 71-17306.

*Takis, John P. A Survey of Differentiated Staffing in Industrial Education. Ed D. doctoral dissertation, Wayne State University, 1972, pp. xiii + 409. Microfilm No. 72-28495.

*The Use of Modular Scheduling in Curriculum Improvement. A report of the Summer Workshop, an activity of the Title III Project, Salem, Virginia (June, 1967). ERIC Reference No. ED 022 241.

chapter 5

First Considerations in Course or Program Planning

Behind every well-presented discussion or demonstration, every well-run student organization, and every neat and orderly laboratory or shop will be found a teacher or a teaching team that has carefully planned the instructional program. This planning may include the course or program goals, behavioral objectives and needed subject matter, plans for lessons and demonstrations, plans for a student-directed organization, necessary references, and other written materials believed necessary for the instructional program.

These materials may all be placed between two covers and titled "A Course of Study," or they may be organized in a less formal manner and located in the teacher's home, office, or laboratory. For example, plans for demonstrations and other lessons may be kept on cards and housed in a card file in the office; examinations may be kept at home; equipment and supply lists and identified references may be kept in the office file cabinet; and duplicated materials for distribution to the class may be kept in a file close to a planning center. Whether the teacher or teaching team keeps the planned materials in an organized volume or whether they are kept in various places determined by need and convenience, capable VAE teachers must continually plan, revise, and prepare written materials for the instructional program.

In developing and organizing instructional material, the teacher or teaching team must first determine and analyze beliefs held for education, and in the light of these beliefs, prepare the overall goals[1] for the instructional program. These goals will then serve as the foundation for the development of behavioral objectives and course content, instructional methods, evaluation procedures, and laboratory facilities.

Consideration must be given also to the relationships that exist between the identified elements of instructional planning. The integration of the basic parts of an instructional program must be given careful consideration in order to prepare a course or program that will, in turn, be an integral phase of the school curriculum.

---

[1] "Aims" or "major objectives" are other terms used to delineate the parameters of an educational program, curriculum, subject, or course and are hence considered as synonymous with educational goals.

144 Planning and Organizing Instruction

This chapter gives an overview of the entire process of organizing instructional materials for a specific teaching situation in applied arts, technical, or vocational education. In other words, it shows what the teacher or teaching team must consider to plan adequately for one program.

What Is a Course of Study?

In this book a course of study is defined as the written materials designed to describe accurately the instructional plan for a course that has been planned for a specific teaching situation. The organization and handling of instructional materials must be arranged to complement and assist the teacher[2] in managing the activities of the class. If a teacher keeps the course of study disassembled, with some of it on cards or sheets placed in the office or laboratory for efficient use in teaching, the person or individuals managing the program should also consider keeping a second copy organized and placed between two covers. This organization provides, in one volume, an accurate description of the entire program, a single source for making revisions or noting contemplated changes, and a document that can be shown to professional educators or community representatives to describe and publicize the program of instruction. In this book, the course of study will be considered a single volume. As the various materials are described, their use and integration into a program of instruction will be discussed.

The concept of a single document **designed to describe accurately the plan for a course calls for having this document tailored by the professional teacher to a specific teaching situation.** Before such information can be put on paper, the conditions that control the course of study must be known. This calls for such specific data as the following:

1. Philosophy of administration.
2. Aims of the school.
3. Pertinent data concerning students.[3]
4. Time allocated per day and week to the course.
5. Community resources.
6. Amount and condition of equipment.
7. Education and background of the teacher.
8. Outcomes to be demonstrated by learners at conclusion of instruction (such as shown on pp. 422-425 of Appendix E).

These are only examples of what must be known before a teacher can prepare a course of study for a teaching assignment. Courses of study

---

[2]The "teacher" in this context may be working completely alone or as a member of a teaching team.

[3]These pertinent data include (1) individual interests as they can be associated with the course to be offered; (2) physical conditions (such as left-handedness, poor vision, and impaired hearing); (3) socioeconomic background; (4) competencies acquired in previous VAE programs; (5) measures of general intelligence; and finally; (6) special aptitudes. See **Teaching Successfully**, by Silvius and Curry, pp. 14-31, for the specifics of these data.

cannot, therefore, be written intelligently for a hypothetical teaching assignment.

Now let's examine what might be placed between two covers and labeled a course of study in VAE. First of all, the teacher would surely be concerned with a statement of the overall goals for the specific course and how these goals contribute to the total educational program. Attention should be given to behavioral objectives and the units (content) selected to contribute to their fulfillment. Supervisors and administrators would be interested in knowing about the methods, techniques, and teaching aids to be used when each unit (or module) of instruction is taught. To make the course of study complete, information should be furnished to explain how the student would demonstrate at the conclusion of a unit, the competencies specified in the behavioral objectives. Many courses of study also describe devices for helping the teacher evaluate his/her role. In VAE subjects it is most essential that adequate instructional supplies, tools, and equipment be provided for a course; as a result, many teachers include information of this type in a course of study.

As mentioned, the degree to which these items may be found in a course of study will depend on the teacher preparing the material. It should be mentioned, also, that it takes years to complete all ramifications of a course of study, so it may be necessary to start a new course with a rather sketchy outline that will be filled in and developed as it is used. Even when a course of study is reasonably complete, changes come to mind that seem essential. The functional course of study, then, is an ever-changing and evolving document.

Often one is asked, "Should the course of study describe only what is now feasible, or should it describe what the teacher thinks the program should be?" This is a critical issue in VAE where such factors as room size or lack of instructional supplies or equipment may govern what can be offered. Since teachers must be practical, it is recommended that they describe instructional programs that are feasible at the time of writing, but include specific sections describing what needs to be done or purchased to facilitate what is believed to be an optimum program. When a course of study containing such recommendations is transmitted to the administration, the teacher or teaching team has then officially placed responsibility with administration to evaluate what is being suggested.

In summary, a course of study is a document written by the teacher for a specific course to explain philosophy, aims, behavioral objectives and content, methods, and plans for evaluation. It may also include specifications for instructional supplies and equipment. It may be considered a quasi-legal document if it is officially presented to the administration, as it might describe matters important to shop or laboratory safety and teacher liability. Its content must be selected to satisfy service area needs, and it must be designed to be read by substitute teachers, supervisors, administrators, advisory and accreditation committees, and other teachers. The course of study is often used as an instrument for public relations as it is displayed at an open house or other activity for parents. It is not a text, nor is it intended to be read by students. The text, reference materials, study guides, and other materials needed by students should only be described and illustrated in the course of study.

An Educational Philosophy Gives Direction to Education

A teacher's philosophy of education may be described as the beliefs that govern the character of the approach to education; the concepts that give direction to the program of education; and the foundation upon which the teacher builds and develops the overall goals for education, formulates behavioral objectives, selects the content for the courses, and considers approaches against which the progress of students and the teacher's performance may be evaluated.

A personal philosophy of education is not static since it is based upon the sum of many educational and personal experiences. These experiences may be as simple as normal classroom routine or as stimulating as discussions of professional problems with fellow teachers and administrators, or they may be the study of educational literature. On the other hand, the experiences controlling a changing philosophy may be only remotely connected with education, such as the changing pattern of world politics or the economic conditions of the United States. The result of all the teacher's experiences should be a continually growing philosophy, which in turn results in a constant development of the teacher's individual program of instruction. Even though one's philosophy is in a continual state of development, basic beliefs tend to change slowly, thus providing the desirable stability and continuity in the behavioral objectives and methods of instruction.

Since a philosophy of education is developed from past experience, many teachers first state their philosophies for education in terms of their vested interests or present position. One who teaches in public schools, for example, will be anxious to report the basic tenets for American public education. A professor in an institution of higher learning is likely to be thinking most about a foundation for collegiate education, while the teacher in a private school would undoubtedly have thoughts directed more toward the basic purposes of education in such an institution. When developing a philosophy, a teacher must be on guard to keep from overemphasizing any personal or vested interest. The instructional program developed from an individual teacher's philosophy and utilized within the classroom must fit into the entire program of education.

In developing a philosophy, teachers must first state their beliefs so colleagues, administrators, and others may be invited to examine what they have perceived for the total educational effort. Teachers could not hope to be influential in helping other teachers establish overall aims for education, nor would the specific aims for their courses be appropriate if their beliefs for education were in basic conflict with those of their colleagues.

An analytical examination of statements of educational philosophy prepared by VAE teachers revealed the following concepts interwoven in what they believed should underly the total program of American education. Education should:
1. Be continuous from birth and available to everyone.
2. Educate the whole individual for a balanced, well-rounded, and complete life.
3. Provide for an equality of individual opportunity in accord with the limitations of in-born capacities, so no individual is deprived of educational advantages because of race, religion, age, or physical, social, or economic conditions.
4. Foster democracy through tolerance, good will, respect for others, and cooperative endeavors.
5. Encourage questioning, experimentation, creativity, and evaluation.
6. Strive to provide pleasant associations with success, rather than frustrating experiences of failures.
7. Fit the individual to live successfully in a democratic society.
8. Provide not only for cultural reproduction, but the improvement of culture.
9. Provide for social and economic mobility.
10. Provide experiences through which the individual may become adapted to the environment.
11. Provide for career development and broad and adequate occupational training limited only by interest and ability.

The following are examples of statements of philosophy of general public education prepared by VAE teachers.

EXAMPLE

By R. Terry Messenger
I believe in education for each rather than education for all. To reach this goal, each student should be helped to assess his/her individual abilities, interests, and potential. Through direction and guidance, education should help develop these attributes for each student:
- Ability to think independently, reflectively, creatively, and responsibly.
- The ability to interpret and control experiences.
- New attitudes toward, and new interest in, life and the world of work.
- Increased capacities to appreciate and enjoy many areas of culture.

The educational program must maintain a balance between **freedom** for individual creative expression and discipline to meet social standards. The goals of education are not and cannot be fixed, but must be continuously altered, interpreted, and modified in response to changes in society and the environment.

By Barbara R. Koscierzynski
Education should help a student clarify and amplify values, aspirations, and goals. Education should then provide the learner with an atmosphere which would help focus on, develop, and perfect the competencies the learner wishes to attain. It should prepare the individual for the world of work in such a way as to highlight skills and strengths. Education should aid in promoting personal, social, and cultural growth and development. These experiences should produce a well-rounded individual who is able to attain a level of personal fulfillment, who can readily adapt to the environment, who can function in and gain self-support through productive work, and who can contribute to society. Education should be freely and easily accessible to everyone — with no reservations. Education should begin with birth and should end with death.

By Theodore L. Sipes
Education must meet the ever-changing needs of the individual in a constantly shifting environment. Touching every aspect of the student's existence, it should develop a product that is self-sufficient, self-confident, self-disciplined and acutely aware of the needs of self, as well as the desires and necessities of others. Education must be free of human bias to allow for maximum creativity, investigation, and evaluation. With prejudices removed, success will come more frequently, interests and abilities will develop uninhibited, and adjustment to the social and economic worlds will be with a smoother transition. Education must be reality not pious platitudes.

No one of these statements includes all of the previously listed concepts. At the same time, a statement may include many concepts not listed. Regardless of length, the important consideration is that the statement truly represents the philosophy of the author at the time of writing. Furthermore, it should be in general terms and encompass all education since the VAE teacher, as all others, must first look at the entire educational effort for students and then fit the planned segment of instruction into the entire program.

It is recommended, therefore, that every teacher prepare a statement of philosophy and solicit the reactions of fellow teachers and administrators before undertaking the development of teaching plans and instructional materials. After due consideration, the teacher should know whether his/her philosophy and aspirations for an educational program are acceptable in a democratic and dynamic society.

The **Dictionary of Education** (1973, 420) defines educational philosophy as:

> A careful, critical, and systematic intellectual endeavor to see education as a whole and as an integral part of man's culture, the more precise meaning of the term varying with the

systematic point of view of the stipulator; any philosophy dealing with or applied to the process of public or private education and used as a basis for the general determination, interpretation, and evaluation of educational problems having to do with objectives, practices, outcomes, child and social needs, materials of study, and other aspects of the field.

Frederick C. Neff[4] (January, 1963, 59) has pointed out that education is inescapably a value-centered enterprise. He states:

> Like democracy, education can tolerate diversity only up to the point where such tolerance becomes a danger to the very structure that makes diversity possible. If such a framework is to be viable and at the same time consonant with democratic principles, it must possess at least three characteristics: (1) it must be flexible enough to include a rich variety of views, (2) it must be sufficiently unyielding to reject those outlooks that would threaten the framework itself, and (3) it must emerge from operational procedures of consensus rather than from sacrosanct doctrines of metaphysics.

It is easy to see from the definition of educational philosophy and the characteristics for a frame of reference suggested by Neff that a statement of philosophy could serve as a guidepost for the development of the entire instructional program and, basically, serve as the first step in the development of a functional program of instruction. The second step involves the development or acceptance of general aims of education which must stem from, or be in harmony with, the teachers' philosophical statements. The general aims for education must, in a direct manner, show the contributions that the entire educational program will make in the development of the learner. Many sets of educational aims have already been developed and published; they will be discussed in Chapter 8.

Course Goals Are Formulated for the Unique Contributions of Each Course

After a teacher or teaching team has considered the complete educational program of students in the light of his/her own philosophy of education and aims for education, the teacher is then ready to fit the instructional program into the overall program of instruction. To accomplish this, the teacher must determine exactly what contributions each course will make to the growth and development of students. When the goals are determined, written, and checked to see whether they are in full agreement with the teacher's educational philosophy and the general aims for education, they become the "goals of a course." They simply describe the aspirations held by the teacher for each course and

---

[4]Frederick C. Neff is Professor of History and Philosophy of Education at Wayne State University.

delineate the parameters for instruction. They should not be unrealistic ideals or goals, but should be within the limitations of the student's abilities, laboratory facilities, and the teacher's teaching ability. **The course goals should accurately describe to the administration, students, and community the contributions the course will make to the growth and development of each individual class member.**

The following course goals illustrate what is being suggested. These goals were written for an industrial arts course designed to provide exploration and contribute to career education.

Goals for Junior High School Power Mechanics[5]

- To develop an understanding of the total process of "energy conversion." Specific emphasis is placed on how man has learned to control energy and convert it into power.
- To develop knowledge and understanding of the principles and concepts of energy sources plus methods of transmission: (1) mechanical, (2) fluid, and (3) electrical.
- To develop an understanding of the variety of career opportunities available in the area of power development, transmission, and utilization.
- To gain sufficient first-hand experiences with power components by constructing a variety of power circuits and systems, using basic components for developing, transmitting, and controlling power.
- To gain knowledges and experiences in the broad subject area of power which will provide meaning and understanding for future study in other technical education areas.
- To gain a sufficient and accurate understanding of power so that intelligent judgments can be made relative to the most desirable role of power in modern ecological, social, and economic trends.

As each course goal is written, the teacher(s) needs to be continually thinking of the kind of activity students need to experience to grow and develop in terms of the established goal. Unfortunately, there is too little relationship in many courses of study between the goals for the course, the behavioral objectives and units of instruction, and the methods selected to teach the proposed course content. Course goals should be kept general, practical, and functional. The total for any one course should be limited to five or six statements. When course goals are broken into numerous fine divisions, they become difficult to remember and manage. The course goals, then, describe the expected accomplishments for the program of instruction and delineate what is to be covered.

---

[5]Formulated by Angus J. MacDonald, Professor, San Jose State University.

Behavioral Objectives Determined After Course Goals

After the overall program goals are established to delineate the parameters for a program (or course), the instructional planners are ready to specify student behavioral objectives that are closely identified with the instructional units. There may be one or more student behavioral objectives for each unit of instruction, or in some cases, one or more behavioral objectives for each lesson within a major unit of instruction.

Each behavioral objective may be broadly classified as specifying cognitive, affective, or psychomotor behavior. In addition, each behavioral objective may be further classified according to one of the six levels of cognitive behavior, one of five levels of affective behavior, or under one of seven classifications in the psychomotor domain. These are described and discussed in Chapter 8.

Course Goals Give Direction for Behavioral Objectives and Content, Methods, and Evaluative Procedures

After the goals for the course are established and checked against the goals of education and the educational philosophy of the author the entire course or program should contribute to the fulfillment of the course goals. Behavioral objectives, course content, methods of instruction, and evaluation procedures must all share in the fulfillment of established goals.

Course content for VAE programs must be selected with extreme care since it constitutes the "heart" of the student's program. When the content consists of a series of stereotyped or uninteresting projects, student interest drops; this in turn retards learning. The content for vocational or technical subjects should be selected from an analysis of the occupation and be taught in an instructional order determined with the assistance of this process. Content for the applied arts programs must be selected more subtly. The practice of selecting a series of **standard projects** deemed by the teacher to be useful and "full of essential learning experiences" is now being discouraged by many educational leaders. Much attention is now focused in applied arts courses on the values that accrue from placing emphasis on exploration, creativity, and problem solving as students undertake projects or modules of instruction. The activities selected for applied arts, the resulting content, and the methods used must be determined by studying the established goals for a course in light of their contributions to career education and general capabilities.

Methods are normally considered as tools to convey content. This, however, is only one of the functions of teaching methods. They can also be used to fulfill goals and, in many cases, provide some of the finest opportunities for fulfilling certain behavioral objectives. For example, a goal dealing with the development of leadership and responsibility can be accomplished effectively through the use of a student-directed organization. The student-directed organization has many functions, such as checking progress of students, assisting learners with their laboratory activities, maintaining order, and encouraging safety in a shop or laboratory. While these functions of the student-directed organization contribute to smooth and efficient operation, the services are of only minor importance when compared with the learning experiences obtained by the members of the student organization. Such learning experiences, when properly planned and directed, simulate human relations — conditions that will later be found by the learner when taking his/her place in the world of work. Students who help others with their projects, supervise the operation of the program, and look out for the safety of class members are learning to accept responsibility and serve in leadership positions within their peer group. Other methods of instruction may be equally useful in fulfilling established goals.

The same is true of evaluative procedures. Testing and evaluating in many schools are functions of the teacher and are designed only to test mastery of course content. It is possible, however, to involve students in their own evaluation, thereby helping them learn how to appraise their accomplishments realistically. In addition, the student organization can become involved in evaluation. A student profits from participation in criterion-referenced evaluation when properly conducted.

Written tests administered and graded by the teacher also contribute to the growth of the student when the results are analyzed and studied by members of the class. Each student, then, has an opportunity to determine individual strengths and weaknesses. In addition, weak areas can be strengthened by the teacher through review and follow-up. Tests and other evaluation procedures may also serve as an indication of how successful the instructional program has been. The teacher may receive clues as to what areas of instruction need strengthening and further study.

These are ways in which methods and evaluative procedures, along with content, and the behavioral objectives for the units become involved in the fulfillment of established course goals. Every care should be exercised when designating behavioral objectives and selecting course content, methods of instruction, and evaluative procedures to make certain that they represent the best approach for the fulfillment of the specific goals for the course.

The example shown in Appendix H illustrates how titles for course units in a technical course were carefully planned to contribute to the fulfillment of specific course goals.

Course Goals, Behavioral Objectives and Content, and Methods Determine Needed Physical Facilities

Many VAE laboratories are built and equipped with little or no thought given to the goals, behavioral objectives, content, and methods of the programs to be conducted in them. Many teachers order equipment by simply requesting what "they haven't got" rather than looking at their instructional program and determining the facilities needed to support and implement the instructional program. Too often shops and laboratories have been equipped with tools and materials, and then the courses of study are written. Such methods of planning for physical facilities result in a waste of public funds and the development of inadequate plant facilities.

Every teacher needs a written list of supplies, tools, and equipment necessary to implement the instructional program. The list will then serve as a guide to the teacher when preparing periodic purchase requests, taking inventories, and planning for expansion of educational facilities.

Professional teachers are interested in recommending only the purchase of equipment, instructional supplies, and room facilities needed for the activities to implement the units of instruction. This is accomplished by considering the methods, techniques, and teaching aids

Fig. 5-1. The laboratory facilities for this commercial baking program are highly specialized. They were planned to provide the physical setting needed to implement the instructional program as determined by the course goals, behavioral objectives, content and methods. (West Valley Occupational Center, Los Angeles)

needed for each module of instruction or unit and determining the equipment, tools, and supplies necessary to provide the learning activities. The quantity of each item is determined by the optimum class size and the number of students to be engaged in the activity or operation at one time. The specific goals for a course also give direction to purchasing specifications and the arrangement of equipment. For example, a program having as a goal "to provide instruction in home workshop activities" would need to be carried on in a shop equipped with power tools similar to those recommended for home workshops rather than heavy duty industrial production machines of the type designed to train students for a vocational pursuit.

Where it might be too costly to equip school shops with industrial equipment for vocational-technical education, it may be possible to plan these programs around the cooperative work-study plan or to schedule them in leased or loaned facilities as is done in the ROP in Los Angeles (see pp. 131-135). The coop programs provide for having the students secure their manipulative skills on the job and their related instruction in school. Many good vocational programs as described in Chapter 4, are being planned around the concept, "the community is the classroom."

When needed physical facilities to implement a course of study are determined, it is easy to overlook such items as location of text and reference library, storage of supplies and materials, location of student planning areas, and provisions for safety zones. Numerous lists of items to be considered in planning physical facilities for a shop or laboratory have been developed and are easily obtained. A list of fifty-seven items to consider in planned physical facilities for a VAE laboratory may be found in Silvius and Curry (1971, 182-184).

Systems Approach Provides the Coordinating Agency

A performance-based VAE course or program is most effectively developed through a systems approach as described and illustrated in Chapter 3. Various entities for course or program development need to be considered, through the systems approach, and the functional relationships delineated. These include:
1. The educational statements of teachers covering their philosophies of education.
2. The overall aims for all of education.
3. The specific course or program goals that delineate the parameters of some part of the educational effort.
4. The formulated behavioral objectives with their modules or units of instruction (content to fulfill these objectives).
5. The methods and instructional aids to facilitate modules or units of instruction.
6. The evaluation procedures to determine student progress, growth, development, and competency in terms of the course or program outcomes specified in the behavioral objectives.

7. The essential physical facilities and materials needed for the implementation of course or program.

The systems approach is a tool for conceptualizing the relationships of these entities within the system. The system is characterized by a consideration of the constraints, inputs, processes, and outputs and their resulting influence on the totality of the effort.

For Self-Assessment and Discussion

1. What is an educational philosophy? On what should it be based?
2. Define a "course of study."
3. Should a course of study be written for a particular situation, or should it be general enough to be used in several different teaching situations?
4. Should the course of study describe a course as it now exists or as the teacher would like it to be?
5. Who should be familiar with the goals for a course?
6. How can a teacher determine what content should be included in a course?
7. In what other form besides book or notebook may a course of study be presented?
8. To what degree do the goals for the course or program guide the preparation of the course of study?
9. What distinctions would you make between the "goals for the course" and "behavioral objectives"?
10. In what way are behavioral objectives identified with the units or modules of instruction?
11. Explain how the systems approach becomes the vehicle for conceptualizing the relationships that must be considered in respect to the entities or elements of course or program development identified in this chapter.

An Assignment to Demonstrate Competency

After studying the chapter and selected resources, prepare a statement of not more than 150 words setting forth your personal philosophy of education. It is suggested that before writing you do the following:
- List the basic points, principles, or concepts to be included.
- Check this list against underlying concepts on p. 147.
- Take sufficient time to group thoughts and ideas.
- Give careful attention to the selection and use of words; keep to the point and avoid complex sentence structure.

Secure the reaction of at least two of your peers to what you have written. If necessary continue to work on your statement until it is acceptable to other educators and reflects a sound approach for education in a democratic society.

References* and Resources

Books

Baird, Ronald J. Contemporary Industrial Teaching. South Holland, Illinois: The Goodheart-Willcox Co., Inc. 1972, Pp. 200.

Barlow, Melvin L. "Changing Goals" in Vocational Education: Today and Tomorrow. Edited by Gerald G. Somers and Kenneth J. Little. Madison, Wisconsin: Center for Studies in Vocational Technical Education, The University of Wisconsin, 1971, pp. 9-32.

Evans, Rupert N. Foundations of Vocational Education. Columbus, Ohio: Charles E. Merrill Publishing Co., 1971, Pp. xi + 292.

Friese, John F., and Williams, William A. Course Making in Industrial Education. Peoria, Illinois: Chas. A. Bennett Co., 1966, Pp. 301.

Giachino, J.W., and Gallington, Ralph O. Course Construction in Industrial Arts, Vocational and Technical Education. Chicago: American Technical Society, 1967, Pp. 314.

Good, Carter V., (ed). Dictionary of Education, 3rd edition. New York: McGraw-Hill Publishing Co., 1973 Pp. xix + 681.

Green, Thomas F. Work, Leisure and the American Schools. New York: Random House, 1968.

Hammonds, Carsie, and Lamar, Carl F. Teaching Vocations. Danville, Illinois: The Interstate Printers & Publishers, Inc., 1968, Pp. viii + 256.

Householder, Daniel. Review and Evaluation of Curriculum Development in Industrial Arts Education. Bloomington, Illinois: McKnight Publishing Co., 1972, Pp. iv + 59.

Mager, Robert F., and Beach, Kenneth M., Jr. Developing Vocational Instruction. Palo Alto, California: Fearon Publishers, 1967, Pp. viii + 83.

McMahon, Gordon G. Curriculum Development in Trade and Industrial Education. Columbus, Ohio: Charles E. Merrill Publishing Co., 1972, Pp. vii + 134.

Harland, Sidney P. "Career Education Now" in Contemporary Concepts in Vocational Education. Edited by Gordon F. Law. Washington, D.C.: American Vocational Association, Inc., 1971, pp. 41-49.

*Silvius, G. Harold, and Curry, Estell H. Managing Multiple Activities in Industrial Education. Bloomington, Illinois: McKnight Publishing Co., 1971; Topic I, pp. 2-9; Topic 2, pp. 11-21; Topic 3, pp. 23-44; Topic 4, pp. 47-58; and Topic 16, pp. 181-205.

*Silvius, G. Harold, and Curry, Estell H. Teaching Successfully in Industrial Education. Bloomington, Illinois: McKnight Publishing Co., 1967; Topic 2, pp. 14-30; Topic 3, pp. 34-47; and Topic 4, pp. 53-67.

Swanson, Chester J. "Criteria for Effective Vocational Education" in Contemporary Concepts in Vocational Education. Edited by Gordon F. Law. Washington D.C.: American Vocational Association, Inc., 1971, pp. 21-26.

Toffler, Alvin. Future Shock. New York: Random House, 1970.

Willers, Jack C. "The Quality of Life in the Seventies and Implications for Vocational Teacher Education" in Changing the Role of Vocational Teacher Education. Edited by Rupert N. Evans and David R. Terry. Bloomington, Illinois: McKnight Publishing Co., 1971, pp. 8-27.

---

*Items with an asterisk have been cited in the chapter.

Periodicals

Deex, Oliver J. "Philosophy and Evaluation." **North Central Association Quarterly,** Vol. 40, No. 4 (Spring, 1966), pp. 332-335.

*Neff, Frederick C. "Education-Yes, Metaphysics-No," **Educational Theory,** Vol. 13, No. 1 (January, 1963), pp. 59-64.

Patterson, S. D. "Utilizing Industry to Identify Objectives for Vocational Teacher Education Programs." **Journal of Industrial Teacher Education,** Vol. 11, No. 3 (Spring, 1974), pp. 65-71.

Willers, Jack C. "Reconstruction in Educational Philosophy," **American Vocational Journal,** Vol. 43, No. 3 (March, 1968), p. 62.

Other Published Materials

A Position Statement on Educational Accountability. Lansing, Michigan: State of Michigan, Department of Education, 1972.

A Common Goal of Michigan Education. Lansing, Michigan: State of Michigan, Department of Education, September, 1971.

6 chapter

Instructional Materials Needed by the Professional Teacher

This chapter is designed to give an overview of the task of professional teachers as they undertake to organize or produce functional instructional materials and teaching plans for each of their classes. Great teachers never teach "off the cuff." They spend many hours in research, study, and reflective thinking before placing their thoughts on paper. The results of these efforts are instructional programs that serve the needs of students through carefully determined course goals. The plans prepared by these teachers appear in many varied patterns, but there are identifiable elements that are common to all organizational patterns. Teaching plans appear under such titles as "Teacher's Guide," "Course of Study," "Syllabus," and "Curriculum Guide." The objective then of this chapter is to identify and describe the common elements in these supporting documents.

The instructional materials written by professional teachers or school administrators may be divided into four major classifications: materials for preplanning; materials for content, methods, and evaluation; student study materials; and specifications for physical facilities. These materials may be placed between two covers and labeled a "Course of Study" or kept in various locations governed by convenience. Every teacher and prospective teacher need not prepare each of these plans, but curriculum coordinators and the professional teacher(s) must be aware of these materials and utilize the ones needed for instructional purposes. Some of the items in these four classifications are prepared by administrators and supervisors or committees of occupational education teachers; some are applicable only to certain types of programs; and some must be developed by the teacher or teaching team for each course and reviewed and revised at periodic intervals. Regardless of use, it is important for the teacher to consider each of these components of VAE curriculum materials and provide for their development as plans are written for each course or program.

Materials for Preplanning

A review of course materials shows that ten items fit into the preplanning classification. These are the materials that need to be con-

sidered before curriculum coordinators and teachers select and plan the instructional units and other aspects of instruction for each specific course or program.
1. The ARM documents for pertinent research.
2. Standard terminology for instruction.
3. Available instructional materials from federal agencies.
4. DOT Codes with matching educational description.
5. Occupational surveys.
6. Provisions of negotiated contracts.
7. Occupational analyses.
8. The AIM documents for locating state and local manuals and guides for instruction.
9. Specifications for admission and curriculum.
10. Educational justification for each course.

Research in Subject Area

The best single source for locating reported and on-going research projects in VAE is through **Abstracts of Research Materials in Vocational and Technical Education** (ARM), now available in most libraries. These volumes of ARM have been published since 1967 by The Center for Vocational and Technical Education (CVTE) at The Ohio State University. Each volume is organized in three sections: (a) resumés of abstracts of completed VAE research, (b) comprehensive indexes for locating studies under general headings categorized with identified subjects, and (c) research projects in progress. The general headings in ARM cover areas such as business education, construction industry, industrial arts, federal legislation, guidance programs, hospitality education, homemaking education, paramedical occupations, program design and development, retailing, space utilization, vocational goals of urban youth, technical education, vocational agriculture, vocational rehabilitation, youth opportunities, and many other areas of interest to VAE teachers and leaders.

With the various ARM indexes, one can quickly locate the abstracts for such research as the Industrial Arts Curriculum Project (IACP) and the NOBELS study that are described in Chapter 3. The VT reference number[1] and the Educational Resources Information Center (ERIC) reference number are listed for each research project. Persons needing more information than that provided in the ARM abstract may study the complete report now available on microfiche (MC) or paper copy (HC) in most libraries. The microfiche and paper copies may be purchased for a nominal cost from the ERIC Document Reproduction Service (EDRS), Computer Microfilm Corporation (CMIC), P.O. Box 190, Arlington, Virginia 22210.

Another excellent source for quickly locating pertinent research in a subject area is to turn to a listing of the **Publications of the Center for**

[1]Reference number assigned by CVTE to every project reported in ARM or in their publication titled *Abstracts of Instructional Materials in Vocational and Technical Education* (AIM).

Vocational and Technical Education (CVTE). A pamphlet listing all of their publications is available upon request.[2] The CVTE publications listed in this document are classified under Research and Development, Leadership Training, Bibliography, Information, and Center Related. The Information Series contains many entries devoted to a review and synthesis of research in VAE subject areas. It should be noted that several of their publications covering a review and synthesis of VAE research have been selected and listed under a special heading with the "References and Resources" for this chapter.

Standard Terminology for Instruction

An early step in preplanning for a course or program is to investigate and identify recommended terminology for a contemplated VAE course or program. This information can be found in **Handbook VI on Standard Terminology for Curriculum and Instruction in Local and State School Systems** developed by the National Center for Educational Statistics (listed with the references for this chapter). This document was compiled with assistance of over seventy-five national cooperating associations, including most of those representing VAE subject areas. This handbook identifies and defines twenty specific subject-matter areas, utilizing an instructional code number to group and identify definitions. The first two digits of the ten digit system identify the subject area. Curriculum coordinators and VAE teachers should be especially interested in the designated codes for the following curriculum areas:

01 — Agriculture
03 — Business
04 — Distributive Education
07 — Health Occupations Education
09 — Home Economics
10 — Industrial Arts
14 — Office Occupations
16 — Technical Education
17 — Trade and Industrial Occupations
21 — Safety and Driver Education

While this standard classification system provides for the possibility of a ten-digit code, the definitions developed to date generally do not extend beyond six-digits. The explanation of this code is as follows:

First two digits designate the **subject-matter area** (e.g., 10— Industrial Arts).

Second two digits are for a **principal segment of subject matter** (e.g., 10.12 — Industrial Materials and Processes).

Third two digits are for a **division of the principal segment** (e.g., 10.1206 — Numerical Control).

---

[2]The address is CVTE, The Ohio State University, 1960 Kenny Road, Columbus, OH 43210.

Fourth two digits have been set aside for **first level detail of a division of the principal segment** (there was no need for this degree of specificity in industrial arts education; the classification for this subject-matter area is presently contained within six digits of the possible ten-digit classification).

Major uses of the coding system are to facilitate educational planning and accountability. With the recent expansion of VAE education to fulfill the mandates of legislation and the occupational cluster concept being promulgated to develop career education programs, a classification system became essential. Each of the states now has VAE instructional programs identified with several hundred occupational titles. This system integrates the national educational codes with DOT titles, thereby facilitating the combination of DOT titles and instructional programs.

Handbook VI provides an excellent source for occupational definitions used in curriculum and instruction within a subject area. The definitions for the subject area, segments of a subject area, and divisions of a segment of instruction are especially helpful in formulating the goals and delineating the parameters for a course or program. A concluding section of **Handbook VI** contains an excellent glossary of curriculum terminology.

Instructional Materials Available from Federal Agencies

The 1968 Amendments to the Vocational Education Act of 1963 authorized monies for surveying publications that would be especially useful in VAE education. A contract was let to the Northwest Regional Educational Laboratory to conduct a survey in 1970-71 and report instructional materials available from Federal Agencies in the areas of Agriculture, Distributive Education, Health Occupations Education, Home Economics, Office Occupations, Technical Education, and Trade and Industrial Occupations. The findings are now available in separate documents for each of these major vocational areas.

Entries in these volumes are organized and listed according to the national educational coding system of the Office of Education explained in the preceding topic, "Standard Terminology for Instruction." The annotation for each entry covers such data as author or corporate author, date, number of pages, form of instructional material (i.e., textbook, reference book, guide book, catalog, or pamphlet), appropriate educational level for use of material, cost (if any), reference order number, resumé of content, potential use with occupational codes specified, and the agency where it can be procured. The addresses are given for the thirty agencies that cooperated in the development of these seven volumes.

The closing section of each volume is devoted to Related Career Education Materials. These documents are classified under Basic Education, Related Education, Guidance and Counseling, Teacher

Education, Disadvantaged/Handicapped-Internal, and Disadvantaged/Handicapped-External.

Educational Descriptions Matched with DOT Codes

Another early step in the preplanning for a program in occupational education is to locate the DOT[3] title and code that matches the classified and coded instruction program listed in **Standard Terminology for Curriculum and Instruction in Local and State School Systems**. To do this, curriculum coordinators and teachers must turn to the publication titled **Vocational Education and Occupations** (listed as a chapter reference). Published in 1969, this book was compiled jointly by HEW and the Department of Labor in cooperation with the National Center for Educational Statistics. This publication was developed in response to mandates of the sixty-eight Amendments to the Vocational Education Act of 1963 that called for —

- The preparation of a qualified, well-trained labor force necessary for economic growth.
- The development of the individual's capabilities so that he/she may benefit from, participate in, and adjust to changes in the world of work.

Vocational Education and Occupations serves as a ready reference for matching instructional programs (consisting of national descriptions and codes) with titles and codes in the DOT.

Coding System for DOT

The DOT defines nearly 22,000 occupations. Jobs are assigned a six-digit code number to reflect the kind and level of work performed (e.g., 827.281 for a HOUSEHOLD APPLIANCE REPAIRMAN). Jobs are grouped according to a consideration of work field, purpose, material, product, service, subject matter, generic term, and/or industry. These data are reflected in the first three digits of the code number.[4] This arrangement groups jobs into these nine broad categories:

0)
1) Professional, technical, and managerial occupations.
2 Clerical and sales occupations.
3 Service occupations.
4 Farming, fishery, forestry, and related occupations.
5 Processing occupations.
6 Machines trades occupations.
7 Benchwork occupations.
8 Structural work occupations.
9 Miscellaneous occupations.

[3]Dictionary of Occupational Titles.
[4]For a more detailed explanation of this classification system see the "Introduction" to Volume I of the DOT.

The fourth, fifth, and sixth digits of the code refer to how the worker functions in respect to **data, people,** and **things.** Following are the job relationships to these three headings, arranged in hierarchies:

Data	People	Things
0 Synthesizing	0 Mentoring	0 Setting up
1 Coordinating	1 Negotiating	1 Precision Working
2 Analyzing	2 Instructing	2 Operating-Controlling
3 Compiling	3 Supervising	3 Driving-Operating
4 Computing	4 Diverting	4 Manipulating
5 Copying	5 Persuading	5 Tending
6 Comparing	6 Speaking-Signaling	6 Feeding-Offbearing
7 No significant	7 Serving	7 Handling
8 relationship.	8 No significant relationship.	8 No significant relationship.

To illustrate, the fourth, fifth, and sixth digits (281) for the HOUSEHOLD-APPLIANCE REPAIRMAN (example used in this topic) describe the work as follows:

Fourth digit: The worker function is **Analyzing** (2 in the **Data** hierarchy).
Fifth digit: The worker has **No Significant Relationship** (8 in the **People** hierarchy).
Sixth digit: The worker has a **Precision Working** relationship (1 in the **Things** hierarchy).

In 1967, the U.S. Department of Labor developed an additional three-digit suffix code system that was added to the six digit DOT codes.[5] This was done to facilitate the statistical and tabulating procedures for reporting manpower programs. The codes in **Vocational Education and Occupations** are presented with the suffix codes, producing nine-digit numbers. The suffix code (digits seven, eight, and nine) for the HOUSEHOLD APPLIANCE REPAIRMAN is 022 which then make the nine-digit DOT code number for this job 872.281-022.

Matching Instructional and Manpower Codes

The use of **Vocational Education and Occupations** provides two options for matching the instructional and manpower titles and codes. One can either:
- Look in **Part I** of the guide and match the instructional program with the occupational code and title as illustrated in TABLE 6-1.
- Use **Part II** of the guide and match the occupational titles with the instructional program.

---

[5]For more information see Suffix Codes for Jobs Defined in Dictionary of Occupational Titles, Third Edition, 1967.

Table 6-1
Examples of U. S. Instructional Programs
Matched with DOT Titles[a]

U.S. OFFICE OF EDUCATION CLASSIFICATION		DICTIONARY OF OCCUPATIONAL TITLES			
				Worker Trait Groups (Vol. II)	
Code	Instructional program	Code	Occupational Title (Vol. I)	Page	Title
17.0199	AIR CONDITIONING, OTHER Include here other specialized subject matter and learning experiences emphasized in air conditioning, refrigeration and heating which are not listed or classifiable above. (Specify.)				
17.02	APPLIANCE REPAIR Classroom and shop experiences concerned with the theory of electrical circuitry, simple gearing, linkages, and lubrication in the operation, maintenance, and repair of components including relays, time switches, pumps, and agitators used in appliances such as washers, dryers, vacuum cleaners, toasters, water heaters, and stoves. Related training is provided in the use of familiar tools, test equipment, and service manuals, and in making cash estimates for repairs.	827.281-022	HOUSEHOLD-APPLIANCE REPAIRMAN (any ind.)	312	Crafts & Rel. Wk.
		827.381-018	HOUSEHOLD-APPLIANCE-INSTALLATION MAN (any ind.)	312	Crafts & Rel. Wk.
17.0201	ELECTRICAL APPLIANCES Learning experiences specifically concerned with the repair, installation, and servicing of electrical appliances.	723.381-018	VACUUM-CLEANER REPAIRMAN (any ind.)	312	Crafts & Rel. Wk.
		723.884-010	APPLIANCE REPAIRMAN (elec. equip.)	322	Manipulating
		827.281-010	COFFEE-MAKER SERVICEMAN (any ind.)	312	Crafts & Rel. Wk.
		827.281-014	ELECTRICAL-APPLIANCE SERVICEMAN (any ind.)	312	Crafts & Rel. Wk.
		827.884-030	ELECTRICAL-APPLIANCE SET-UP MAN (any ind.)	322	Manipulating
		827.887-010	ELECTRICAL-APPLIANCE-SERVICEMAN HELPER (any ind.)	360	Handling

[a]Data used in this table were excerpted from information on pp. 105 of **Vocational Education and Occupations**.

Occupational Surveys

As a base for a viable occupational education program, many communities have conducted occupational surveys to provide general direction and scope for VAE programs. The type of data collected in such surveys is explained in Chapter 2. Teachers or teaching teams planning VAE courses or programs should give careful attention to the findings of any such available survey.

Provisions of Negotiated Contracts

Where there are negotiated contracts, covering agreements between administrators and the teaching staff, it is important to review these documents before planning courses to identify obligations pertaining to curriculum development and the quality of instruction. The more recent agreements cover such provisions as these:

- Each teacher shall develop and submit to the department head, for the approval of the departmental curriculum committee, course content and appropriate instructional materials for each course he/she is assigned to teach.
- Each teacher shall maintain records required by law, and cooperate in the planning of departmental (and where appropriate) interdepartmental programs and courses.
- Teachers who teach the same course shall have the responsibility to provide the department head — for the approval of the departmental curriculum committee — a collective statement of the course goals, course content, and prerequisite skill levels for sequenced courses.
- Those teachers who teach a common course shall submit to their department head a single common list of textbooks from those approved for use in the course.
- A teacher shall, within a specified period of time after the beginning of a new school term (e.g., two weeks), submit to the supervisor a course outline which demonstrates agreement with the statement of course goals, prerequisite skills, and the use of the selected textbook.
- When instructional innovations are planned, the teacher shall inform his/her administrator and other teachers who teach the same course of the plans to carry out the innovations. This should be done in a professional manner and within the limits of the prevailing budget.[7]

Occupational Analyses of Trade Subjects

As one of the seven methods for identifying content for VAE programs (as explained in Chapter 2), **occupational analysis** is used by teachers of trade subjects to identify and break down the operational and informational topics for the blocks of their trades. Such analyses then

---

[7]Such factors as these are included under "Teacher Responsibilities" in the **Agreement Between Board of Trustees of the Community College District of the County of Macomb and the Macomb Community College Faculty** in Michigan.

SCHOOL CITY OF SOUTH BEND
INDUSTRIAL EDUCATION DEPARTMENT

Student Analysis   Metals

Name _____ Date _____

Machine Shop: 1   2   3   4   5   6
(Circle one)

MILLING MACHINE
Operations

Feel I can do well
I need more practice
Feel I need more help
Have had no practice

1. Lubricate
2. Set up cutters on arbor
3. Adjust R.P.M. of cutter
4. Adjust cutter
5. Adjust knee position
6. Adjust table position
7. Set up work on table
8. Set up work on vise
9. Do plain milling
10. Do angular milling
11. Do side milling
12. Do end milling
13. Do face milling
14. Do spiral or helical milling
15. Do straddle milling
16. Use mill for drilling
17. Use mill for boring
18. Use mill for reaming
19. Use fly cutter
20. Locate centers
21. Use graduations on vertical & longitudinal feeds to locate holes

Feel I can do well
I need more practice
Feel I need more help
Have had no practice

22. Spot face
23. Machine key seat
24. Use slitting saw
25. Set up indexing head
26. Do plain indexing
27. Do direct indexing
28. Do differential indexing
29. Machine gear teeth
30. Machine a rack
31. Mill irregular contour
32. Use vertical head
33. Line up work with indicator
34. Line up vise with indicator
35. Do climb & conventional milling
36. Mill dovetail
37. Mill "T" slot
38. Mill a radius
39. Clean mill
40. Set feed trips
41. Mill flutes

Related Knowledge

Well informed
Doubtful
No knowledge whatever

1. Names of several milling machines
2. Types of mills
3. Types of cutters
4. Slotting attachment
5. Universal milling attachment
6. Tilting table
7. Rotary attachment

Well informed
Doubtful
No knowledge whatever

8. High speed milling attachment
9. Rack milling attachment
10. Use of line finder
11. Use of jig borer
12. Use of sine table
13. Gang milling operation
14. Gear hobbing

Fig. 6-1. The student makes an evaluation of his/her competencies with this instrument. (Courtesy Floyd M. Dickey, South Bend Public Schools, South Bend, Indiana)

serve as encyclopedias of content from which the teacher or teaching team selects units or modules of instruction that would be appropriate to fulfill the goals of each course. Parts of an instructional analysis of this type may be used also to develop a competency-based evaluation instrument to be used by students. Such an application is shown in Fig. 6-1.

Manuals or Guides for Teachers

State education departments and large school systems often publish manuals to assist VAE teachers as they undertake to plan and organize tailored courses of study for their specific teaching situations. These volumes normally contain the following:
- Overall aims for the department or division.
- Suggested subject goals and behavioral objectives identified with units or modules of instruction.
- School system policies, practices, and procedures.
- Examples of plans for successful experiments, lessons, or projects.
- Safety regulations.
- Lists of available supplies and equipment.
- Standards and criteria for evaluation.

Standardization of instruction in different schools in a city or state is not the objective. The information is furnished only to assist the professional teacher or teaching team in planning and organizing a course tailored to the needs of the student, school, and community. These teacher's manuals or guides are usually prepared by a committee of teachers working under the leadership of a local or state supervisor, curriculum coordinator, or consultant.

It is now possible for VAE teachers, leaders, and curriculum coordinators to quickly identify and review numerous instructional materials in their subject areas. These materials are in the form of curriculum guides, courses of study, student study guides, modules of instruction, manuals for teachers, guides for a subject area, and curriculum projects that have been reported in a VAE area of specialization and placed in the national data bank. This information is contained in **Abstracts of Instructional Materials in Vocational and Technical Education (AIM)**, published since 1967 by CVTE. These documents are organized into two parts:
- Abstracts that identify information by content, the VT and ERIC reference numbers for ordering microfiche (MF) or paper copies (HC) from ERIC Document Reproduction Service (EDRS), source and availability of each item, cost (if any), date, number of pages, and form of material (such as curriculum guide or module of instruction).
- Indexes for locating AIM page numbers which show abstracts with VT numbers; abstracts by subjects, person(s) and/or institution or agency sponsoring the material; and tables carrying the conversion of VT to ERIC numbers.

168 Planning and Organizing Instruction

As an additional service CVTE has released a compilation of abstracts from AIM documents from 1967 through 1971. These volumes are identified as the CVTE Bibliographical Series. They are listed with the references for this chapter.

It should be mentioned that several universities, state education departments, and consortia of agencies now have computer center services available to the educational community. Many of these centers have the ERIC information in their data banks and stand ready to do a computer search of the ERIC file documents on any timely VAE subject or problem.

The Division of Occupational Education, Massachusetts Department of Education has established a Career Education Document Information System for educators in their Commonwealth. To take advantage of this service, persons needing help simply write or call the office in Andover, directed by Henry A. Haroian. The service provides 4" X 6" microfiche cards containing up to seventy pages of document(s) regarding the study or project being investigated. The information comes from abstracts found in one of the ERIC indexes: ARM, AIM, or RIE (Research in Education). The service also provides for a general request for

Fig. 6-2. Resource information to help students with the design and development of complex projects, such as this canoe, can be found through the use of AIM and ARM documents. (Garfield High School, Los Angeles)

materials in a subject area (i.e., food service, nuclear medicine, and other career education programs). In response to such a request, the office sends a number of printouts of abstracts for review. The microfiche is ordered when the requester decides which of the summaries are relevant to his or her needs.

Specifications for Admission and Curriculum

With assistance from an advisory Craft Committee, teachers, administrators, and curriculum consultants (at the local and/or state levels) often work to establish the specifications and admission requirements for a VAE program, as described in Chapter 4.

Appendix E is an illustration of such data. In this case, the admission and curriculum data for **Radio Television Service** include:

- A description of the program with the educational code and the related DOT code numbers.
- A plan for organizing the program as one or more courses, with time allocations suggested for school day and week as well as the number of students who are to be accommodated.
- School prerequisites — general mathematics, industrial arts (one year or more), drafting, and basic electricity.
- Recommended electives — applied physics, algebra, and trigonometry.
- Academic skills required — ability to read and interpret written instructions carefully.
- Physical abilities required — good vision and color perception, correction permitted; good eye-hand coordination and finger dexterity.
- Social skills required — ability to work with a minimum of assistance and/or supervision.
- Unique skills and abilities required — strong interest in mechanical and electronic mechanisms, ability to learn and follow methodical procedures related to trouble-shooting malfunctions.
- Acceptable tests scores on factors considered in the General Aptitude Test Battery (GATB) and Differential Aptitude Test (DAT).
- Major instructional areas to be covered in the program — AM and FM radio, audio recorders and phonographs, television receivers, high-fidelity sound equipment, master antenna and sound systems, and electrical/electronic appliances.
- Expected student outcomes — behavioral objectives for a program in Radio Television Service.

Educational Justification for Each Course

These statements report functional course goals, their place in the curriculum, and their contribution to a total educational program. The next step then is to identify the behavioral objectives with the titles of the units or modules of instruction that contribute to the fulfillment of the course or program goals.

Materials for Content, Methods, and Evaluation

As teachers or teaching teams select the content and the units for each of their courses and then plan for the effective teaching and evaluation of this instruction, considerable information must be put in writing. Appropriate formats and good arrangements for storage and retrieval must be provided.

Units for the Course

Advisory committees, administrators, curriculum coordinators, supervisors, parents, and other teachers should be invited to review the behavioral objectives and the units or modules of instruction that have been identified for each course or program. Often this is presented as a plan for the term's work, that consists of the titles of units with their behavioral objectives and their topics or activities that are to be studied or programed during an entire course or program, usually arranged in instructional order.

Unit Teaching Plans

These are the detailed, written plans prepared and used by the teacher for each topic or unit listed in the plan for a term. Any one of them may require from only a few minutes to two or more weeks of instruction. Since, in many cases, the instruction that centers around the solving of a problem, an experiment, or a project becomes the module of instruction in VAE, the teacher's written notes for a module teaching plan might include:
1. Suggestions for introducing the activity.
2. Behavioral objectives for each unit.
3. Titles and breakdown of operations and/or informational topics involved in the module.
4. Useful teaching aids.
5. List of needed tools, instruments, equipment, and supplies.
6. Needed drawings and sketches.
7. Suggested procedure, with checking levels indicated.
8. A test on the module.

Student Organization

Many VAE teachers, especially those in the applied arts, have their classes organized in a manner similar to an industrial or business personnel organization. Descriptions of these organizational plans need to be placed on paper. Charts are often made to show the working relationships and levels of responsibility for student officers. There is a need, too, for spelling out the responsibilities of the needed officers such as student superintendent, foremen, record clerk, and safety engineer, as are often used in industrial education. A more detailed explanation of procedures for establishing and maintaining a student-directed organization will be found in **Managing Multiple Activities** by Silvius and Curry (1971, 61-80).

Safety Materials

Since safety is an integral phase of VAE instruction special written materials and instruments are needed to facilitate instruction and evaluation. These items include general safety precautions, study guides covering safety precautions for each machine or major piece of equipment, test on general safety precautions, safety tests for each major machine or piece of equipment, safety records, permission forms to use power machines, and safety posters.

Teaching Aids or Devices

Teaching aids or devices are specially planned to help students understand and learn. Illustrative of these are charts, posters, videotapes, televised instruction, student assignment board, and production jigs. They are material aids, employed as an adjunct to training or teaching, and may be classified in the following manner:
 1. Devices for the improvement of instruction.
 2. Administrative devices.
 3. Production aids.

Motion Pictures, Filmstrips, and Projecturals

For nearly every course there are many projecturals (filmstrips, overhead transparencies, film loops, and motion pictures) that need to be identified and previewed to determine whether they can be used effectively when student learning experiences for a unit of instruction are taught or directed. Through such indexes as those listed by Silvius and Curry (1971, 409-413) the teacher may quickly locate available films and secure them for preview to determine which of these may be brought into focus with the instructional units or modules for his/her course or program.

Bulletin Board Materials

Bulletin board materials are needed for these purposes:
 1. Create an attractive atmosphere in VAE laboratories or shops.
 2. Arouse creative desires in students.
 3. Display examples of students' work.
 4. Illustrate safety precautions under study.

5. Call attention to information that would be in support of some current module of instruction.
6. Point out related instruction through pictures, diagrams, and graphs.
7. Display guidance information, notices of school and community affairs, and selected publications.

Tests to Measure Student Competency

Objective and subjective tests for either norm- or criterion-referenced evaluation are needed to enhance learning, check on student competency, and determine the effectiveness of instruction. In VAE courses, such instruments may be used at the conclusion of a unit to evaluate achievement during the term, to ascertain whether the student has mastered the safety precautions, to check progress during a long unit, and to determine the adequacy of out-of-school preparation.

Evaluation Instruments to Improve Teaching

Professional teachers look forward to the reteaching of any unit, course, or program. It is important, therefore, that they develop and use instruments which achieve the following:
1. Show changes that need to be made in the physical plant (see the **National Standard School Shop Safety Inspection Check List** of the National Safety Council).
2. Identify instructional problems that can be "engineered out."
3. Provide opportunity for students to make suggestions for consideration when a unit, course, or program is retaught.

No VAE teacher can be successful unless desirable changes are continually evolving.

Plans for Substitute Teacher

The teacher who maintains a well-organized instructional program and a functioning student organization needs carefully prepared plans for a substitute. When teachers are incapacitated, in attendance at conferences, or away on personal business, substitutes are needed. Substitutes need to know how the class is organized, the ongoing activity, and what the teacher plans to do.

Records and Forms

Many forms and records are needed to admit and excuse students, operate the student-directed organization, prepare cumulative records, account for the purchase of materials, secure personal information, report accidents, facilitate student participation in evaluation, provide charts for recording individual progress, and give credit for homework.

Student Study Materials

Teachers devise or secure instructional materials to direct student activity. These items are used by the students as they participate in a course or program. They are the **instructional materials for the student** as contrasted with the items already listed which are instructional materials employed by educators to direct the learning experiences of students.

Text and Reference Materials

Suitable published materials are as essential for VAE courses and programs as are tools, equipment, and instructional supplies. The VAE teacher needs lists of the following:
1. Text and reference books.
2. Programed instruction.
3. Handbooks (such as the **Machinist's Handbook**).
4. Manufacturers' operation manuals.
5. Trade catalogs.
6. Plans for directing the work of students undertaking projects, experiments, or other learning experiences.
7. Trade journals and professional magazines for VAE subjects (guides for locating these periodicals are listed with chapter references).
8. Pamphlets describing occupations of interest to students.

Charts carrying page numbers with the titles for units of instruction cross-checked against the titles of these publications help students locate needed information. The publishers of VAE materials have produced many excellent and well-written texts. There are still a few areas of vocational and technical education, as well as training for a specific payroll job, where available published material is so sparse that teachers and school systems are forced to write and duplicate the text and reference material for the program. Such instructional material may be in the form of operation and information sheets. This means that specific directions are written for each operation and informational topic identified in the instructional analysis and included in the course(s).

Planning Sheets or Books

Planning sheets may be used by students in applied arts programs. When used, they assist the student in outlining the procedures, listing the specifications for needed supplies, determining checking levels, listing tools and other equipment, and making sketches or drawings. Such sheets are often bound in sufficient quantity to accommodate one student for an entire course.

Student Study Guides

In VAE subjects, many teachers develop study guides to direct the activities of students as they work from text and reference books. These study guides may involve only reading assignments followed by questions, or they may help the superior student study materials of an advanced nature.

Physical Facilities

Intelligent planning calls for identifying the physical facilities that are essential for an optimum instructional program. Only what is needed should be requested and purchased. Professional VAE personnel must specify, too, the required type and quality of equipment, machines, tools, and instructional supplies. Additional physical facilities often need to be added to on-going programs as they are changed and projected. The goal should be to have in writing everything which is essential and needed for maintaining and projecting every course or program. The following are brief descriptions of four headings for such instructional materials.

Supply and Equipment Lists

Instructional materials, including the supplies that are used by students in pursuit of their instructional activities, such as in the construction of projects or in completing assignments, are usually listed for each course. Such lists may carry prevailing costs for a unit of each item and recommendations regarding the amount needed. Equipment lists may be organized with such subheadings as room furniture, hand tools, power machines, and equipment.

Specifications for Ordering Supplies and Equipment

In VAE programs where considerable budget is channeled into the purchase of instructional supplies and equipment, it is imperative that the professional teacher (individually or through committee action) participate in the development of specifications for the purchasing of instructional materials, tools, furniture, machines, and accessories.

Device for an Inventory

A system needs to be devised to keep an accurate accounting of equipment, tools, and supplies currently on hand. A description of the forms and their use should be on file and, where possible, this activity should be programed for the computer.

Floor Plans with Equipment Layouts

Placing equipment on the floor plan to create an optimum learning climate calls for a consideration of many factors. Planning the arrangement of equipment is most effectively done with three-dimensional models. Templates are helpful in two-dimensional planning. After such visual planning has been done, the layout may be photographed and descriptive information prepared to accompany the pictures. Such materials are particularly helpful in presenting the case for needed and requested facilities to advisory or accreditation committees or administration.

Needed Instructional Materials Determined by the Teacher

The different types of materials needed for a specific VAE teaching assignment need to be developed by the professional teacher or teaching team. It is important that those items that apply be secured or developed. The format for presenting them to administration, curriculum committees, and others is of secondary importance.

Instructional Packages for Individual Development

Curriculum coordinators and teachers are now developing instructional kits for modules of instruction to facilitate the systems approach for individualized instruction. The packages of instruction for an electronics course by David Jelden, as explained and illustrated in Chapter 3, are a good example of this plan for instruction. Other examples are shown in Appendix M. Each module of instruction is made up of the following:

- An introduction covering the purpose of the instructional package (or kit).
- The estimated time for the usual student to complete the specified activity.
- Behavioral objectives for the module.
- Listing arrangements to be made in advance (e.g., viewing of a slide-tape presentation or reading specified references).
- A plan for self-assessment to determine what the student already knows and can do.
- Specified learning experiences to fulfill the behavioral objectives.
- Provision for enrichment experiences for those students who are in a position to do more than the required work.
- The plan for proficiency assessment (an exit test for the student to demonstrate the desired competencies as the module is completed).

For Self-Assessment and Discussion

1. What are essential factors to be considered in formulating specifications for admission and curriculum for a VAE instructional program?
2. What are the major headings of instructional packages being developed as modules of instruction for the individual development of students?
3. Identify several specific instructional materials for your area of specialization that could be procured with the use of the document titled **Vocational Education Materials Available from Federal Agencies.**
4. Cite some examples as to how the findings from a community occupational survey might influence course goals and content for a VAE instructional program.
5. Explain the function of CVTE publications titled:
   a. ARM.
   b. AIM.
   c. **Compilations of Abstracts of Industrial Materials in Vocational and Technical Education 1967 - 1971** (available for each of seven major VAE curriculum areas).
6. Describe the six-digit code used in the DOT.
7. Describe these acronyms:
   a. CVTE
   b. ERIC
8. Describe the specific kinds of data that may be procured from **Handbook VI, Standard Terminology for Curriculum and Instruction in Local and State School Systems.**
9. Describe the eight digit U.S. educational codes as applied in your area of specialization.
10. From a psychological point of view, would it be better to organize and present safety material as "safety rules" or "safety precautions"? Why?
11. What are the pros and cons of basing a vocational education program on a community work survey when such a low percentage of people remain in the community where they receive their basic education?
12. What distinction, if any, do you make between the following:
    a. Instructional supplies and instructional materials.
    b. Tools and equipment.
    c. Equipment and machines.
    d. Power tools and machines.
    e. Textbooks and reference books.
13. Describe some of the conditions that relate to the teacher's responsibilities for curriculum development now being written into negotiated contracts between teachers and their governing boards.

Assignment to Demonstrate Competencies

1. With the use of the ARM documents from the library, identify reported research that relates to your present or projected subject area.

2. With the use of the special volume for your curriculum area, consisting of a compilation from **Abstracts of Instructional Materials in Vocational and Technical Education** and the more recent issues of AIM (both listed with the references for this chapter), identify and report abstracts for courses of study, curriculum guides, student study guides, and modules of instruction that are pertinent to your specific VAE teaching situation.

References* and Resources
Books

*Silvius, G. Harold, and Curry, Estell H. Managing Multiple Activities in Industrial Education. 2nd edition. Bloomington, Illinois: McKnight Publishing Co., 1971, Topics 5, 6, 10, 11, 14, 16, 22, 31, and 32.

*Silvius, G. Harold, and Curry, Estell H. Teaching Successfully in Industrial Education. 2nd edition. Bloomington, Illinois: McKnight Publishing Co., 1967, Topics 4, 5, 6, 7, 8, 10, 21, 22, 23, 27, 28, and 29.

Special Compilations of AIM

Agricultural Education Instructional Materials from AIM 1967-1971. Bibliography Series No. 8, CVTE, 1972, Supt. of Docs., Pp. ix + 437.

Business and Office Education Instructional Materials from AIM 1967-1971. Bibliography Series No. 9, CVTE, 1972, Supt. of Docs., Pp. ix + 117.

Distributive Education Instructional Materials from AIM 1967-1971. Bibliography Series No. 10, CVTE, 1972, Supt. of Docs., Pp. ix + 140.

Health Occupations Education Instructional Materials from AIM 1967-1971. Bibliography Series No. 11, CVTE, 1972, Supt. of Docs., Pp. ix + 89.

Home Economics Education Instructional Materials from AIM 1967-1971. Bibliography Series No. 12, CVTE, 1972, Supt. of Docs., Pp. ix + 161.

Industrial Arts Education Instructional Materials from AIM 1967-1971. Bibliography Series No. 13, CVTE, 1972, Supt. of Docs., Pp. ix + 97.

Trade and Industrial Education Instructional Materials from AIM 1967-1971. Bibliography Series No. 14, CVTE, 1972, Supt. of Docs., Pp. ix + 536.

Selected CVTE Publications Covering Review and Synthesis of Research**

Ashman, Richard D., and Larson, Rodger A. Review and Synthesis of Research on Distributive Education, 2nd edition. ERIC Reference No. ED 038 498, April 1970, Pp. 89.

Bailey, Lena C. Review and Synthesis of Research on Consumer and Homemaking Education. ERIC Reference No. ED 048 482, April 1971, Pp. 78.

Carpenter, Earl T., and Rogers, John H. Review and Synthesis of Research in Agricultural Education, 2nd edition. ERIC Reference No. ED 040 275, June 1970, Pp. 90.

*Items with an asterisk have been cited in the chapter.
**These publications are revised often. Check with the library for latest editions.

Holloway, Lewis D., and Kerr, Elizabeth E. **Review and Synthesis of Research in Health Occupations Education.** ERIC Reference No. ED 029 982, May 1969, Pp. 97.

Householder, Daniel L., and Suess, Alan R. **Review and Synthesis of Research in Industrial Arts Education.** 2nd edition. ERIC Reference No. ED 034 898, October 1969, Pp. 69.

Lewis, Wiley B. **Review and Analysis of Curricula for Occupations in Construction.** ERIC Reference No. ED 044 496, October 1970, Pp. 34.

───── . **Review and Analysis of Curricula for Occupations in Health.** ERIC Reference No. ED 044 507, November 1970, Pp. 38.

───── . **Review and Analysis of Curricula for Occupations in Transportation.** ERIC Reference No. 045 814, December 1970, Pp. 38.

───── . **Review and Analysis of Curricula for Occupations in Food Processing and Distribution.** ERIC Reference No. ED 045 820, December 1970, Pp. 39.

───── . **Review and Analysis of Curricula for Occupations in Public Services.** ERIC Reference No. ED 045 813, November 1970, Pp. 39.

───── . **Review and Analysis of Curricula for Occupations in Environmental Control.** ERIC Reference No. ED 045 817, December 1970, Pp. 36.

Nelson, Helen Y. **Review and Synthesis of Research in Home Economics Education.** ERIC Reference No. ED 038 519, April 1970, Pp. 67.

Paulter, Albert J., and Schaefer, Carl J. **Review and Synthesis of Research in Trade and Industrial Education.** 2nd edition. ERIC Reference No. ED 036 638, September 1969, Pp. 56.

Phillips, Donald S., and Briggs, Lloyd D. **Review and Synthesis of Research in Technical Education.** 2nd edition. ERIC Reference No. ED 036 639, October 1969, Pp. 50.

Price, Ray G., and Hopkins, Charles R. **Review and Synthesis of Research in Business and Office Education.** 2nd edition. ERIC Reference No. ED 038 520, April 1970, Pp. 120.

Snyder, Thomas R., and Butler, Roy L. **Review and Analysis of Curricula for Occupations in Metalworking.** ERIC Reference No. ED 044 495, October 1970, Pp. 31.

Other Published Material

*CVTE. **Abstracts of Instructional Materials in Vocational and Technical Education (AIM).** Published quarterly since Fall 1967 by the CVTE. Available from EDRS on FM or HC. Recent individual issues available from the CVTE.

*CVTE. **Abstracts of Research Materials in Vocational and Technical Education (ARM).** Published quarterly since Fall 1967 by the CVTE. Available from EDRS on MF or HC. Recent individual issues available from the CVTE.

*National Center for Educational Statistics. **Standard Terminology for Curriculum and Instruction in Local and State School Systems.** State Educational and Records Series: Handbook VI. Compiled and edited by Putnam, John F. et al. Reference No. OE-23052, Supt. of Docs. Catalog No. HE 5.223:23052, U.S. DHEW, 1970, Pp. x + 317.

*Northwest Regional Educational Laboratory. **Vocational Instructional Materials Available from Federal Agencies.** Separate volumes for Agriculture, Distributive Education, Health Occupations Education, Home Economics, Office Occupations, Technical Education, and Trade and Industrial Education. Douglas C. Towne, Project Director. Washington, D.C.: Supt. of Docs., Stock No. 1780-0842, August 1971.

Northwest Regional Educational Laboratory. **Vocational Instructional Materials for Students with Special Needs.** Douglas C. Towne, Project Director. Portland, Oregon 97204: NREL, 700 Lindsay Building, 710 S.W. Second Avenue, August 1972, Pp. xii + 225.

*Publications of the Center for Vocational and Technical Education. A listing of all Center and Clearinghouse documents in two sections: One a "List of Publications by Series" — Research and Development (RD), Leadership Training (LT), Bibliography (BB), Information (IN), and Center Related (CR); and Two "An Index" organized by descriptions for identifying and locating these publications. Columbus, Ohio: CVTE, The Ohio State University. Updated at regular intervals.

*The Standard Periodical Directory. Published annually with a semiannual supplement. A listing of 20,000 periodicals published in United States and Canada. New York: Oxbridge Publishing Co., Inc. Library of Congress No. 64-7598.

*Ulrich's International Periodicals Directory. Edited by Eileen C. Graves. Revised every three years. A listing of 16,000 current periodicals (foreign and domestic). New York: R. R. Bowker Co. Library of Congress No. Z6941. U5.

*U.S. Departments of HEW and Labor. **Vocational Education and Occupations.** Reference No. OE-80061. Washington, D.C.: Supt. of Docs. (Catalog No. FS 5.280:80061), July 1969, Pp. xv + 292.

*U.S. Department of Labor. **Dictionary of Occupational Titles.** Third Edition. Volume 1, "Definition of Titles," 1965; Volume 11, "Occupational Classification and Industry Index," 1965; A supplement, "Selected Characteristics of Occupational (Physical Demands, Working Conditions, Training Time)," 1966; "Suffix Codes for Jobs Defined in the Dictionary of Occupational Titles," Third Edition, 1967; and Supplement 2, "Selected Characteristics of Occupations by Worker Traits and Physical Strength," 1968. Washington, D.C.: Supt. of Docs.

Unpublished Material

Joos, Loyal W. Computer Analysis of Reading Difficulty. A paper presented at the 11th Annual Convention of the Association for Educational Data Systems, at New Orleans, Louisiana, 1973. Available from Dr. Joos, Director of Systematic Studies, Oakland Schools, Pontiac, Michigan 48054. Pp. 6.

Novosad, John P. Implications of Computer Technology for Industrial Education. Ed. D. doctoral dissertation, Wayne State University, 1971. Microfilm No. 71-29778. Pertinent to this chapter are pp. 88-107.

7 chapter

Organizing Course Materials for a Specific Teaching Situation

Careful planning for the instructional activities helps ensure the development of teaching materials which will lead to instruction that will fulfill the goals for the program. This chapter is designed to outline preliminary considerations that are necessary before actually undertaking the development of instructional materials, including:
1. Preplanning materials to be reviewed.
2. The need to consider the community, the school conditions, and the students being served.
3. The use of behavioral objectives specifying performance that provides opportunity to start using life-long learning skills.
4. Terminology used in curriculum development.
5. The different types of organizational patterns which may be followed for courses or programs.

Review Preplanning Materials

Ten possible sources for preplanning materials were described in Chapter 6. A curriculum developer planning an instructional program would not have the time to examine all of the curriculum materials that would be identified from these sources. However, the more pertinent resource materials should be procured and examined.

Curriculum guides for teachers provide an excellent source for ideas and are invaluable when instructional materials for a program are organized. These prepared materials should, however, be adopted only after they are adjusted to the specific teaching situation.

When an instructional program is planned and organized, the teacher or teaching team may use the preplanning resource or reference materials that have been prepared and made available by administrators, supervisors, researchers, teacher groups, or individual teachers. In addition, consideration must be given to these items:
1. The ability of the students.
2. The use they will make of the course content.
3. The future educational plans of the students.
4. The specific interests of the learners.
5. The experiences and competencies they will bring to the program.

6. The community in which the school is located.
7. The industrial or business facilities available in the community.
8. The contribution that the planned course or program will make to the total school curriculum.

These considerations often require that the instructional program be tailored to meet the specific needs of students.

Some of the best references available are the state guides for VAE prepared by committees representing the profession. These guides are carefully planned and represent the current thinking of the state leaders. They are prepared in general (rather than specific) terms and are designed to stimulate the critical analysis of an instructional program being prepared. These guides often contain instructional outlines of representative programs and provide a brief and concise list of behavioral objectives identified with suggested units of instruction, teaching methods, and resource materials. In addition, some state departments of education recommend laboratory floor plans and equipment and supply lists. These guides are prepared with the hope that liberal use will be made of them while instructional materials are developed. They are designed neither to regiment or dictate the program nor to limit the freedom of the individual teacher (or school district) undertaking essential or experimental programs of instruction. Actually, they are minimum **guides** (rather than suggested courses of study) designed to assist and suggest rather than specify exactly what must be taught.

A second excellent source is reference material specially prepared by local committees representing teachers and/or supervisors. These committees are often charged with the responsibility of preparing instructional guides which supplement the work of state committees. Curriculum guides that come from the efforts of local groups generally represent the thinking of teachers responsible for specific teaching subjects. It is only natural, then, that they consider the needs of the community and available resources. Like the state guides, the local ones are not designed to serve a specific teaching situation. They are only to help the teacher or teaching team plan an instructional program for his/her school.

Adapt Instruction to Community, School, and Students

The starting point in tailoring instruction and instructional materials to teaching conditions is to appraise accurately the conditions where the program is expected to function. To do this the teacher must develop an understanding of the community, the school, and the students.

In respect to the community, the professional teacher should know:

1. Service area served by the school.
2. Parents' occupations.
3. Community organizations concerned with educational endeavors.
4. Avocational interests of students and parents.
5. Economic status of parents.

6. Employment opportunity for youth leaving school.
7. Available educational institutions for further study.
8. Prevailing attitude of parents, teachers, and students toward VAE programs.

In respect to the school, the professional teacher should understand:

1. Educational philosophy of the administration.
2. Overall aims for the school.
3. School population.
4. Overall policies and practices of the school system, with special concern for the following:
   a. Curricular patterns.
   b. Available staff and facilities.
   c. Extent and character of guidance programs.
   d. Students with special needs (i.e., disadvantaged, handicapped, and very able).
   e. Aims for department.
   f. Time allocation for courses.
   g. Faculty load.
   h. Size of classes.
   i. Available funds for supplies, equipment, and maintenance.

In respect to the students, the professional teacher should know:

1. Results of tests and other guidance data showing general intelligence, aptitudes, and special abilities.
2. Previous experiences and competencies acquired in VAE programs or from work experience. (Teachers develop instruments such as the one illustrated as Fig. 7-1 to determine what their students already know and can do.)
3. Prevailing interests.
4. Educational goals.
5. Status of prevailing program in minds of students.
6. Social influences and environment out of school.

The information suggested in the above statements is important to the teacher developing an instructional program to fit the needs of the community, school, and students. The aims of the program must be developed with a knowledge of the above conditions. Failure to do this will result in a set of aims and a program of instruction which will be unsuitable for the students being served.

Before developing the instructional program, the teacher should investigate each of the above items. If a formal course of study is being prepared, this information should be included in the introductory chapter in an attractive and readable manner. Otherwise, accurate notes should be kept on prevailing conditions and stored in the teacher's file for quick reference.

The following was developed by William F. Gayde as an overview for courses of study in all VAE curricular areas at the Fitzgerald Public Schools in Warren, Michigan. It is hoped that this analysis will serve as an example of what is being suggested.

Organizing Course Materials   **183**

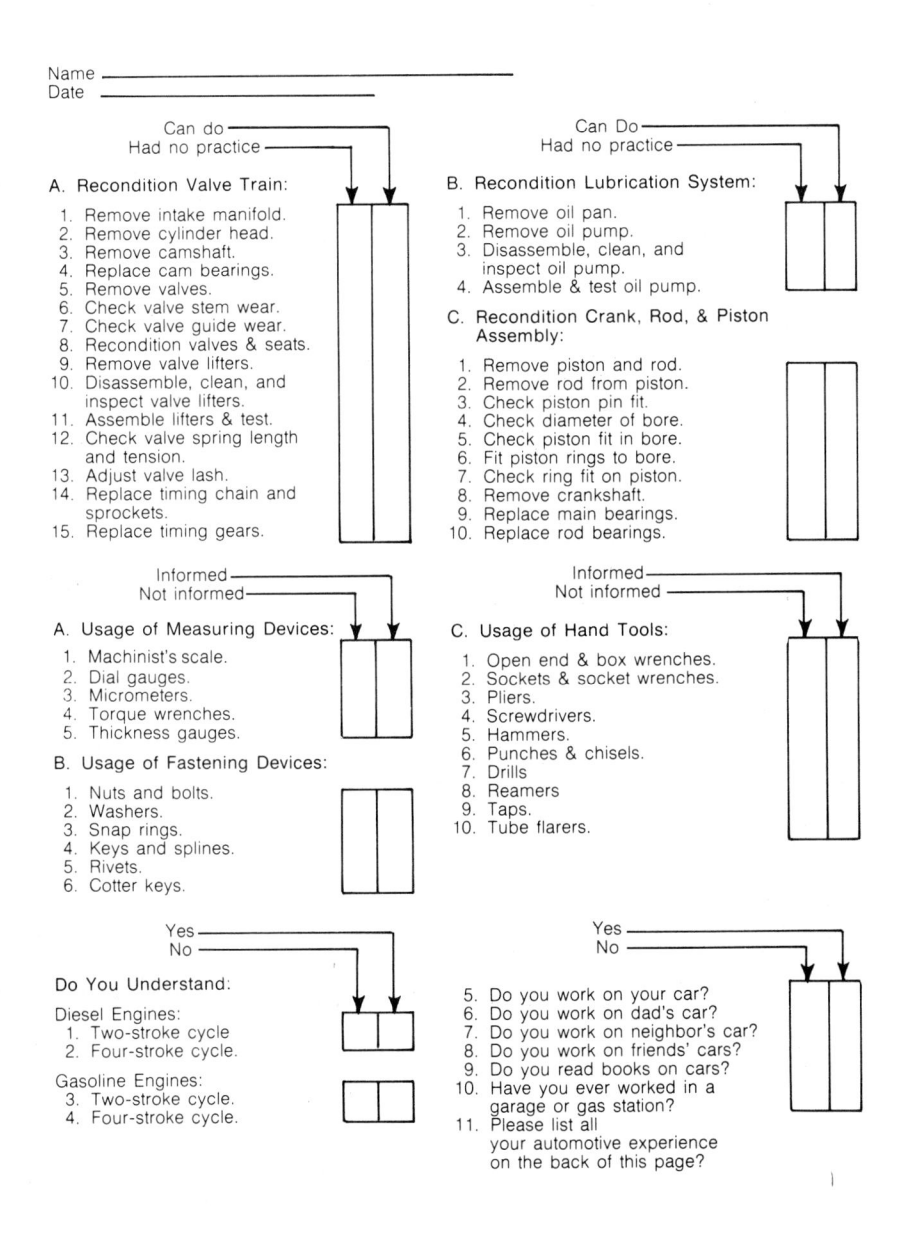

Name _____
Date _____

          Can do ─┐   Can Do ─┐
Had no practice ─┐   Had no practice ─┐

A. Recondition Valve Train:

1. Remove intake manifold.
2. Remove cylinder head.
3. Remove camshaft.
4. Replace cam bearings.
5. Remove valves.
6. Check valve stem wear.
7. Check valve guide wear.
8. Recondition valves & seats.
9. Remove valve lifters.
10. Disassemble, clean, and inspect valve lifters.
11. Assemble lifters & test.
12. Check valve spring length and tension.
13. Adjust valve lash.
14. Replace timing chain and sprockets.
15. Replace timing gears.

B. Recondition Lubrication System:

1. Remove oil pan.
2. Remove oil pump.
3. Disassemble, clean, and inspect oil pump.
4. Assemble & test oil pump.

C. Recondition Crank, Rod, & Piston Assembly:

1. Remove piston and rod.
2. Remove rod from piston.
3. Check piston pin fit.
4. Check diameter of bore.
5. Check piston fit in bore.
6. Fit piston rings to bore.
7. Check ring fit on piston.
8. Remove crankshaft.
9. Replace main bearings.
10. Replace rod bearings.

        Informed ─┐   Informed ─┐
Not informed ─┐   Not informed ─┐

A. Usage of Measuring Devices:

1. Machinist's scale.
2. Dial gauges.
3. Micrometers.
4. Torque wrenches.
5. Thickness gauges.

B. Usage of Fastening Devices:

1. Nuts and bolts.
2. Washers.
3. Snap rings.
4. Keys and splines.
5. Rivets.
6. Cotter keys.

C. Usage of Hand Tools:

1. Open end & box wrenches.
2. Sockets & socket wrenches.
3. Pliers.
4. Screwdrivers.
5. Hammers.
6. Punches & chisels.
7. Drills
8. Reamers
9. Taps.
10. Tube flarers.

           Yes ─┐   Yes ─┐
            No ─┐   No ─┐

Do You Understand:

Diesel Engines:
1. Two-stroke cycle
2. Four-stroke cycle.

Gasoline Engines:
3. Two-stroke cycle.
4. Four-stroke cycle.

5. Do you work on your car?
6. Do you work on dad's car?
7. Do you work on neighbor's car?
8. Do you work on friends' cars?
9. Do you read books on cars?
10. Have you ever worked in a garage or gas station?
11. Please list all your automotive experience on the back of this page?

Fig. 7-1. Student Analysis for Auto Mechanics Engines (Developed by Charles K. Paterson)

EXAMPLE

CONDITIONS CONSIDERED BEFORE WRITING A COURSE OF STUDY FOR A COMPREHENSIVE HIGH SCHOOL IN AN INDUSTRIALIZED COMMUNITY

Type of Community

The Fitzgerald Public Schools serve a small, highly industrialized community with comfortable, well-groomed homes. There is also a high concentration of mobile home courts.

Since there is no "downtown" in the city and since the school district existed long before the city was chartered, the school has become a community center. School facilities are available to various church and civic organizations, and an extensive adult education program is offered.

Employment opportunities for graduates are good, especially for those with industrial or business skills. Follow-up studies indicate that unemployment among the graduates is well below the regional, state, or national figures and that 75-80 percent of the graduates are in a post-high-school job or a related program for which they were prepared.

The vocational programs are continually expanded and revised and are well accepted by the students as evidenced by the fact that 60-65 percent are enrolled in a business, industrial, business/college prep, or industrial/college prep program.

Students wishing to further their education may enroll in any of four nearby universities, the Macomb County Community College, or any of a number of technical schools.

Type of School

"Fitzgerald Public Schools must provide to each individual the opportunity to select and prepare for a career of his/her choice consistent to the optimum degree with his/her capabilities, aptitudes, and desires and the need of society." This statement is included in the document "Goals of Fitzgerald Public Schools" which was adopted by the Board of Education in 1972 and forms the base for building the various vocational offerings.

Students have available to them programs in Industrial and Architectural Drafting, Machine Metalworking, Machine Woodworking, Printing, Electronics, Auto Service, Building Trades, Cosmetology, Homemaking, Secretarial, Bookkeeping, and General Clerical.

The staff consists of 11 members in the Business Department, 4 members in the Home Economics Department and 12 members in the Industrial Education Department. Each department has a chairman who deals directly with the director of vocational education.

Extensive facilities are provided for each of the curricular areas listed above except the Cosmetology program which is provided by a private beauty school under contract with the district.

Fig. 7-2. High school students acquire salable skills as they help construct a school patio. **At top,** First Pour—Members of building trades class swarm over forms as first concrete is poured to form foundation for the barbecue and pool. **Below,** Building trades students work after hours and learn to trowel with little difficulty. (Courtesy Fitzgerald Public Schools, Warren, Michigan)

Sufficient funds are provided for maintaining tools, supplies, and equipment needed to properly operate the programs.

Enrollments are limited, on the average, to 24 students per section.

The guidance program includes elementary teacher and counselor career development activities in classroom and large group situations, junior high teacher and counselor career exploration activities, and senior high career exploration. Career preparation activities for students include world of work meetings with business and industry personnel, meetings with graduates, individual and group guidance meetings with a counselor, and occupational information provided by the vocational staff.

Physically and mentally handicapped students are integrated into the regular vocational programs with supervision and consultation provided by the special education staff.

Interest of Student

Students enroll in vocational programs to develop entry-level skills or to prepare for post-high-school training. Since all programs in the vocational department are elective, the curriculum must meet student interests and needs. As a result of job market demands and student surveys there are presently 15 course offerings in Home Economics, 23 in Business Education, and 25 in Industrial Education (including Trade and Industrial Education, and Office and Distributive Co-op).

Relationship of Course to Subject and Subject to Curriculum

Before a teacher can start the preparation of materials for a course of study, the organizational breakdown of the instructional program must be understood. The words "course" and "subject" are used synonymously by many persons not familiar with the specific application of each of these words. When instructional materials are developed, the distinction and interrelationship of these words becomes important. **The subject is a division or field of organized knowledge which may be covered in one or more semesters or terms.** Food management, data processing, drafting, or diesel mechanics are examples of subject area. **A course is the subject matter which may be covered by learners in one term or semester.** For example, the subject of food management may be divided into course I, course II, and course III. A course of study would be written for each of the three **course divisions** of food management.

There is also the curriculum division in the organizational pattern for instruction. In this case **curriculum is defined by VAE teachers, as that group of subjects selected and arranged in a predetermined order to assist a student in the fulfillment of educational goals.** For example, there are graphic arts curriculums in area vocational schools that include, in a predetermined order, such subjects as typography, photo-offset, printing history, typesetting, and automatic presswork. Technical curriculums in high schools may call for such subjects as physics, algebra, geometry, chemistry, drafting, electronics, and English.

In summation, a teacher must know the curricular breakdown for the educational program of the school. This includes the knowledge of what already has been done to group and describe subjects as a curriculum, and the plans for dividing subjects or fields of study into courses.

Student Involvement with Life Learning Skills

It is imperative that students be placed in a setting where they start using and acquiring the skills of learning that they will need all of their lives. Learners must assume more and more responsibility for extending their educational experiences. Through this type of approach, persons now in school will acquire the learning skills needed for keeping abreast of the expanding knowledge that comes with technological advance. This is the reason some teachers word behavioral objectives in the second person, thereby making them more personal and the direct responsibility of the individual student. This is done by using the pronoun "you" (second person) rather than "learner" (third person).

Placing students in a setting where they are expected to share more and more responsibility for their own destiny is one of the major reasons why educators are employing flexible modular scheduling (FMS), as explained in Chapter 4. In many schools utilizing FMS, a learner is expected to intelligently plan for, and use, as much as forty percent of the time for activities that contribute to individual development. This is done through the fulfillment of educational goals established by the student or teacher and accepted by the learner.

Another technique for making instruction student oriented is to cast the verbs for the behavioral objectives in the present tense. For example, third person vs. second person and the use of present tense vs. future tense are shown in brackets in the following behavioral objective for a course in radio repair:

EXAMPLE

The student [you] demonstrates [will demonstrate] his or her [your] understanding of how sound waves are transferred from the source, via radio waves, to the receiver. Evidence of understanding is based [will be based] upon a paper to be presented which graphically explains and illustrates the process. The paper is [shall be] limited to a maximum of ten pages, including diagrams appropriately labeled.

The wording with the action verbs in the future tense is preferred by many VAE teachers since it implies behavior to be measured and demonstrated by the learner. Several of the examples of behavioral objectives included in this book have been written with their action verbs cast in the future tense.

Why Behavioral Objectives?

Many educators, including those in VAE, have been refining their courses by developing behavioral objectives[1] for units or modules of instruction. After the overall course goals have been established, the professionals responsible for organizing course materials are ready to specify the performance outcomes and organize behavioral objectives for each course or program. Behavioral objectives thereby become the stepping stones for the fulfillment of the overall goals for the course as illustrated in Fig. 7-3. This end-oriented approach is the basis for the specificity needed in curriculum development that, in turn, aids in obtaining desired or expected outcomes in learner performance. It also reduces instruction to essentials and is an approach for eliminating extraneous teaching content.

Behavioral objectives should have these aims:

1. Provide the learner with specification of the learning tasks so the student knows what is expected and can determine when the intended behavior has been achieved.
2. Give educators a sound basis for identifying prerequisites, planning content, selecting methods and strategies, formulating specifications for instructional supplies and equipment, and evaluating and accounting for the effectiveness and efficiency of instruction.
3. Help the teacher specifically determine the degree to which he or she has, or has not, attained success in teaching specific elements of content.
4. Provide a system for classifying and evaluating desired behavior within the three domains of learning (cognitive, affective, and psychomotor — discussed on pp. 205-212).

Robert E. Campbell **et al** (1971, 8-9) identify these values for behavioral objectives:

[1]Some educators use "Performance Objectives" or "Instructional Objectives" in place of "Behavioral Objectives"; in this book these terms are considered to be synonymous.

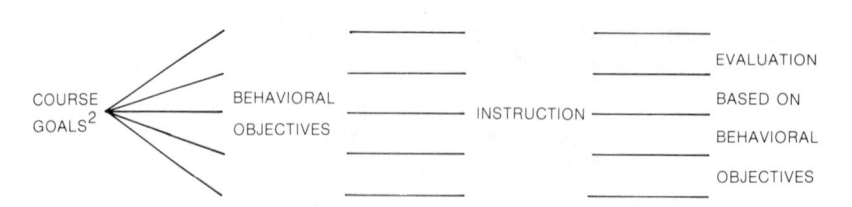

Fig. 7-3. Course goals delineate instruction and set the stage for behavioral objectives that determine learning tasks which are in turn later used to evaluate student growth and development.

[2]In place of "Course Goals," some educators use the terms "Aims for a Course" or "Major Course Objectives" as they refer to those more global statements and delineate the parameter of instruction for a course or program.

Program Efficiency: Very few school programs have unlimited time and resources to tackle every conceivable learning opportunity for the student. Programs must set some limits for what they can realistically hope to achieve within the resources of their school and community. Guidelines are needed for formulating realistic objectives for a program. The problem is one of conceptualizing program priorities [and establishing goals] which are realistically achievable by the school.

Clarity of Communication: A major advantage of defining behavioral objectives is clarity of communication. Statements of objectives, when properly written, leave no doubt as to what is to be expected. General goals and mission statements are often so general that the collective publics have been erroneously led to believe that [the school] could deliver much more than could reasonably be expected. Explicit communication is beneficial to all.

Assessment of Student Performance: It is essential, both for the student and the school, to have some barometer of the student's progress for a given subject matter area. For classroom subjects such as mathematics, graded exercises are given to assess the student's readiness for progressing to the next unit in a sequence of courses to achieve some math performance criterion. The same reasoning should apply to vocational development through vocational guidance. A well conceptualized set of behavioral objectives will provide a progressive series of performance targets for students.

Identifying Behavioral Objectives with Specific Instruction

Each lesson within a unit of instruction may be organized to satisfy one or more behavioral objectives. Some teachers organize instruction around a hierarchy of goals and objectives characterized by something like five or six unique course goals (or major objectives) with each goal in turn broken down with supporting behavioral objectives.[3] Each phase of instruction is then sharply identified with a specific objective that is planned to contribute to the overall fulfillment of one or more of the course goals (or major objectives) for the course or program.

The behavioral objectives identified as an early step in the development of each packet (unit of instruction) for Jelden's Learner Controlled Education Program (Chapter 3) will serve as example. For the unit on CURRENT, Packet 8, he identified five behavioral objectives and placed them in this order:

---

[3]Teachers also refer to such objectives as "minor" or "interim" behavioral objectives, connoting that they are in a subordinate position in the hierarchy for classifying objectives.

Fig. 7-4. This student is demonstrating his ability to meet the behavioral objective "The learner will be able to lay a simple brick wall, with ends and sides vertical, as measured with a mason's level." (Central City Occupational Center, Los Angeles)

1. The learner will be able to define "current," list its practical units of measurement, and explain the conditions necessary before electrical current will flow.
2. Given a lab VOM and milliamp meters, the learner will be able to accurately measure electrical current flow.
3. The learner will be able to use the VOM and lab milliamp meters in a safe manner.
4. The learner will be able to state Kirchhoff's Current Law in writing and illustrate its application through the diagramming of an example.
5. Given a combination of electrical components which constitute a circuit, the learner will be able to apply Kirchhoff's Current Law in analyzing current flow throughout the entire circuit.

As the behavioral objectives are being identified and formulated, curriculum builders work from a task analysis of the subject area and ascertain what instruction is essential for a unit or module of instruction.

For example, the unit on CURRENT (Packet 8) for the basic college course in electronics was organized by Jelden as three topics.

Topic One, "Definition of Electrical Current" was planned to fulfill the first of the five behavioral objectives for Packet 8.

The second and third of Jelden's five behavioral objectives, for the unit on CURRENT in Packet 8, are fulfilled through instruction organized as **Topic Two**, "Measurement of Current with VOM and Lab Milliamp Meters."

Topic Three, "Kirchhoff's Current Law" was organized for the fulfillment of Jelden's behavioral objectives 4 and 5.

Instruction for each of these topics (or lessons) includes the self-assessment form to identify a track to be pursued, a self-test to determine competency against objective(s), recommended media, study guide questions, and lab exercises for application.

Three Organizational Patterns

It is possible to organize instructional materials into various patterns, depending upon the length, schedule, level of instruction, and goals of the course or program; the subject area from which the course or program was derived; and the personal preference of the teacher. The decision as to the desired organizational pattern should be made during the early phases of course or program planning and before the content is organized for instruction. While it is possible to utilize a variety of formats, most arrangements of materials can be identified readily within three organizational patterns. These patterns vary primarily in the arrangement of content for the program. All have an introduction containing background information, goals, and behavioral objectives for the course or program; and they all permit the inclusion of a final unit on equipment, physical plant, and instructional supplies. The differences between the three systems lie in the organization of course content, methods of instruction, and evaluation procedures. The three basic patterns are these:

1. **Formal/Descriptive** — division of aims, content, methods of instruction, evaluative procedures, and needed physical facilities presented as individual chapters or subsections.
2. **Modules of Instruction** — integration of the content, methods of instruction, and evaluative procedures into plans for solving selected problems which in turn become the major modules of instruction.
3. **Class Session Units** — integration of content, methods of instruction, and evaluative procedures into units for each of the sessions of the course.

Formal/Descriptive Organization of Instructional Materials

The formal/descriptive method of organizing instructional materials is the oldest of the three approaches and is still advocated by many colleges offering work in organizing courses of study for VAE. This type of organization works well in vocational education where content is obtained from an instructional analysis of the trade with projects and operational lessons designed to provide desired experiences in course content. Programs in general merchandising, transportation, and electricity are readily organized by this format. In fact, any instructional program can be organized by this approach. The following outline shows the basic pattern:

I. Preliminaries.
   A. Title page — course or program, school, author, and date.
   B. Preface — explanation of how and why the course or program of study was written, and acknowledgments. (See suggested format in Appendix F).
II. Introduction.
   A. Background information related to community, school, and student.
   B. Physical characteristics of course or program — number of meetings per week, number of weeks per term, place in the curriculum, general nature of physical plant, advantages, or limitations.
   C. List of appropriate general aims of education (those used by the school system).
   D. List of aims of the department in which the course is taught, and their relationship to the aims of the school system.
   E. List of specific goals for the course and their relationship to the aims of the department.
III. Behavioral Objectives and Content.
   A. List of behavioral objectives identified with **titles of units for the course arranged in a teaching/instructional order.** Each of these units, in turn, is presented in outline form showing what will be taught in the unit. The list may include such topics as these:
      1. Presentation of course goals and behavioral objectives.
      2. General safety precautions.
      3. Operational lessons in outline form.
      4. Informational lessons — classified as general, technical, and guidance — in outline form.
      5. Administrative units, such as:
         a. Responsibilities of student officers.
         b. Use and checking of utensils, instruments, or tools.
         c. Marking or grading system.
   B. Chart or other device showing behavioral objectives and titles of units checked against the goals for the course.
IV. Methods, Aids, and Techniques.
   A. Charts showing titles for units checked against teaching methods and devices. See example on pp. 303-304.
   B. Description of each method used.
   C. Description of teaching aids for selected units (e.g., the one shown as Fig. 7-5).
   D. Description of effective teaching techniques used with a method or teaching aid.

A. Assembled Teaching Aid—Ready for Use

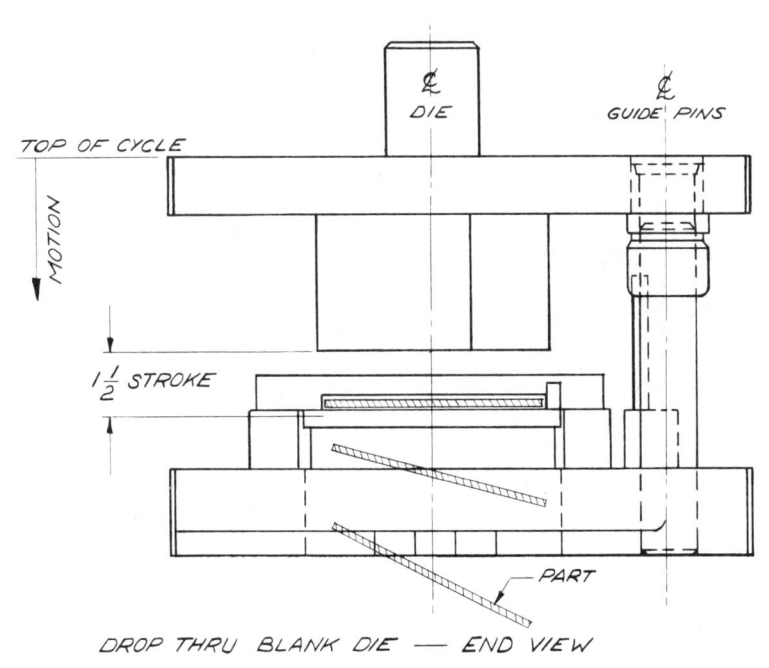

B. Side View, Showing the Die Open

Fig. 7-5. Teaching Aid to Show the Principle of the Drop-Thru Blank Die (Developed by Ronald J. Monfette)

E. Sample records and explanations of their use.
   F. Chart showing titles for units checked against pages in textbook or references for course.
   G. Directions for substitute teachers.
V. Evaluation.
   A. A routing order containing system for checking off lessons taught.
   B. Exit tests for each unit or module of instruction.
   C. Safety tests.
   D. Course examination.
   E. Method of arriving at periodic and final grades.
   F. Samples of assignments given students.
   G. Plan for evaluating the course — student demonstration of competencies specified in behavioral objectives.
VI. Physical Plant.
   A. List of tools, paraphernalia, and equipment.
   B. List of instructional supplies and plans for issuing these items to students.
   C. Floor and equipment plan.
   D. Plan for a perpetual inventory.
   E. Plan to maintain the physical plant.
   F. Specifications for equipment and power tools.

An individual course of study may contain all or any part of the above information. In fact, many courses of study with the formal/descriptive organization contain additional information about the course, such as descriptions of the teacher's plan for the student-directed organization and examples of instruction sheets.

Plan for Modules of Instruction

This organization integrates the behavioral objectives, course content, methods and teaching aids, and evaluation into one section. This approach is recommended where major units of instruction are oriented to solve major problems[4] with independent informational topics serving as supplementary instruction. A plan for solving a selected problem organized as a module of instruction permits the organization of teaching materials into a simple and functional plan. In the course of study using this format, the preface, introduction, and physical plant sections are identical to those shown for the formal/descriptive organization pattern. The following outline shows the organization pattern for the behavioral objectives, content, methods, and evaluation sections when the module approach as a method or organization is used:

I. Preliminaries (same as formal/descriptive).
II. Introduction (same as formal/descriptive).
III. Behavioral Objectives, Content, Methods and Teaching Aids, and Evaluation.

[4]In this context, the solving of a major problem is interpreted to include the carrying out of an essential experiment or the planning and constructing of a meaningful project.

A. Behavioral objectives and titles of units for the course or program arranged in a teaching instructional order. Each of these units, in turn, is presented in outline form. The list should include:
  1. Presentation of course goals and behavioral objectives.
  2. General safety precautions and safety tests.
  3. Administrative units, such as:
     a. Responsibilities of student officers.
     b. Use and checking of utensils or tools.
     c. Marking or grading system.
  4. Plans for each module, including:
     a. Behavioral objectives for the module.
     b. A list of the hand or machine-tool operations (if module of instruction is built around the construction of a project).
     c. A list of technical informational topics.
     d. A plan for introducing the module of instruction.
     e. A suggested procedure (the steps that a student might follow in solving the problem, doing an experiment, doing an exercise, or in developing a project).
     f. Materials needed by students to solve the problem, do an experiment, complete an exercise, or construct a project.
     g. Tools, paraphernalia, and equipment needed by the students to do the work.
     h. Materials, utensils, tools, instruments, and/or equipment, and teaching aids needed by the teacher for each lesson identified with the problem, experiment, exercise, or project.
     i. Needed drawings or sketches for the problem or project.
     j. A layout of diagrams or sketches to be placed on the chalkboard or presented by overhead transparencies before or during a lesson.
     k. Safety precautions to be emphasized.
     l. Suggested references for students.
     m. Discussion questions for students.
     n. An exit test to be given at the conclusion of the lesson or series of lessons for a module of instruction.
     o. A plan for breaking the module of instruction into a series of daily lessons (showing how much might be taught each day) with points to be stressed during each lesson.
  5. Informational lessons not included in the teaching plans for the modules of instruction classified as general, technical, or guidance. These lessons should be in outline form and include behavioral objectives, methods of instruction, teaching aids, and criteria for evaluative purposes.
B. Course examination.
C. Chart or other device showing behavioral objectives with titles of units checked against the course goals.

IV. Administration.
  A. Plan for a student-directed organization.
  B. Sample records and explanation of their use.
  C. Directions for substitute teacher.

D. Routing order containing system for checking off lessons taught.
E. Methods of arriving at periodic and final grades.
F. Plan for evaluating the course — to determine whether all course or program behavioral objectives have been fulfilled.
V. Physical Plant (same as formal/descriptive).

This approach permits the teacher to integrate the behavioral objectives, content, methods, and evaluation associated with the solving of a problem, doing an experiment, or planning and constructing a project as a major module of instruction. Each teaching plan for the module of instruction should contain all the information, instructions, and examinations necessary to teach and evaluate the module as a major unit of instruction. The administrative information pertaining to physical plant facilities may be organized as an independent chapter or section of the course or program as in the formal/descriptive format.

Units Organized by Class Sessions

Some instructional programs can be best organized by having the instruction planned by class sessions. Here are some of the specialized situations that lend themselves to this organizational pattern:

1. College or high school classes meeting once or twice per week. When only a limited number of class meetings is available, the session plan is probably the most suitable.
2. Courses in marketing analysis, human relations, nuclear energy occupations, industrial materials and processes, or power mechanics which contain large blocks of instructional materials from which the course content is selected. When these areas are compressed into units for a term or semester program, they must be taught as a survey course. In a survey program, it is extremely important to sample the whole field since the primary objective is to provide the student with the interrelation of the many phases of an advanced industrial society. The most efficient distribution of time is assured when the program is divided into session units.

Even though this system of organization has decided advantages for certain situations, **it also contains many pitfalls** which need to be considered.

1. This method of organization is very difficult for beginning teachers to apply if they have never taught the course or program.
2. It calls for careful planning to determine how much can be covered adequately in a given period.
3. If too little content is included for a session, the more able student loses interest.
4. If too much content is included (the general tendency) the less able and even the better students will not understand the lesson for that session.
5. The method lends itself best to homogeneous rather than heterogeneous groups.

6. The problem of reaching all members of the class with a single lesson creates a most difficult learning climate since many VAE classes are composed of students with a wide range of abilities.

Probably the strongest argument in favor of this method of organization is the need for careful planning that is imposed upon the teacher or teaching team in organizing the material into units for the sessions. Most subjects contain more content than can be covered adequately in the allotted time. As a result, when either of the first two organizational patterns just described is used, the beginning of the course may be thoroughly taught while the last part is either hurriedly covered or skipped altogether. In many cases, the latter part of the course is the most important since it tends to bring together the many units of the program into an integrated whole. A course in power mechanics, for example, might begin with a survey of the many different ways of developing and using power and end with the integration of this information, showing the function of power in our post-industrial society. In either of the first two approaches, if the teacher is not careful, too long a time may be spent on one phase, such as internal combustion engines, and then the remainder of the course taught in a hurried manner. In this example, many would consider the last unit the most important. The plan for individual sessions (the third approach) forces the teacher or teaching team to allocate time and give careful attention to each unit of instruction.

The unit session plan of organizing instructional materials has many strengths and many weaknesses. When it is used by a master teacher, however, it provides for an instructional program that is educational, interesting, stimulating, and fast moving — especially with mature or adult students. When an outline for this organizational pattern is developed, the preface, introduction, administration, and physical plant sections are the same as was described for the other two basic formats. Content, methods, and evaluation are considered collectively as an integrated plan for each of the sessions. The following outline describes the format:

I. Preliminaries (same as formal/descriptive).
II. Introduction (same as formal/descriptive).
III. Titles for each of the sessions become the headings for the units. Each of these units, in turn, is then presented in outline form. Factors to consider in preparing outlines for one or more of these sessions include:
   1. Presentation of course goals and behavioral objectives for course or program.
   2. General safety precautions.
   3. Safety tests.
   4. Administrative units, such as:
      a. Responsibilities of student officers.
      b. Use and checking of paraphernalia, utensils, instruments, and tools.
      c. Marking or grading system.
   5. Operational lessons in outline form.

6. Informational lessons — classified as general, technical, and guidance — in outline form.
7. Exit tests for units and course examination.
8. Description of the methods of instruction, teaching aids, and teaching techniques as each session unit is outlined. It may be helpful also to develop charts showing how the titles for the sessions, behavioral objectives, and the specific course goals are interrelated.

IV. Administration (same as modules of instruction).
V. Physical Plant (same as formal/descriptive).

Interrelationship of Organizational Patterns

A quick perusal of the three outlines used to exemplify the three variations of organizational formats will show that they contain many common characteristics. As previously emphasized, the basic or primary difference lies in the methods used to organize and present the content to a class. The subsequent chapters will delve more deeply into the many phases of course organization presented in this section.

For Self-Assessment and Discussion

1. What distinguishes a curriculum guide for teachers from a course of study for some specific VAE teaching situation?
2. To what sources should an individual turn to locate examples of specific courses of study in his/her area of specialization that have been developed by other professionals?
3. Describe community conditions to be considered by a VAE teacher before undertaking the development of a specific course or program of study. How should a new teacher undertake to become familiar with such factors?
4. What does a VAE teacher need to know about a school and the students before planning a course or a program for a specific teaching situation?
5. Describe the basic differences between the three formats or organizational plans that have been identified to assist teachers in developing tailored VAE courses of study.
6. What is the difference between a "subject" and a "course"?
7. What instructional techniques could be employed in organizing instruction that would make it possible for learners to be introduced to learning skills that they will need all of their lives?
8. Some educators advocate that the terms "Performance Objectives" or "Instructional Objectives" be used in place of "Behavioral Objectives." Give the advantages of each term over the other two.
9. Identify, in your words, at least two advantages for identifying behavioral objectives with units of instruction.
10. Would you advocate A or B for your area of specialization?

A. That behavioral objectives be completely identified and then, as the next step, that needed and related units of instruction be developed.
B. That behavioral objectives and the units of instruction be developed concurrently?

Assignments to Demonstrate Competencies

1. Prepare the description of a community, school, and student body for a course of study that you plan to write. The situation selected should be one with which you are thoroughly familiar. If you are a teacher, your current teaching assignment or the community in which you hope to teach are familiar situations. Consider items listed in the topic "Adapt Instruction to Community, School, and Students." Use either essay or outline form.
2. Develop short operational definitions, preferably in your own words, for the terms listed below. Where a definition is paraphrased or quoted, the source should be properly cited. **Handbook VI on Standard Terminology**, listed with the references in the previous chapter (Chapter 6), and "Selected Definitions" in **Managing Multiple Activities** by Silvius and Curry (1971, 587-601) will be helpful resources.
Group I — Generic Terms
   - Career Education
   - Occupational Education
   - Vocational Education
   - Applied Arts
   - Practical Arts

   Group II — Curriculum Areas
   - Agriculture
   - Distributive Education
   - Health Occupations Education
   - Home Economics
   - Industrial Arts
   - Office Occupations
   - Technical Education
   - Trade and Industrial Occupations

   Group III — Key Terms in Organizing Instruction
   - Course of Study
   - Aims of Education
   - Course Goals
   - Behavioral Objectives
   - Methods of Instruction
   - Teaching Techniques
   - Teaching Aids
   - Procedures for Evaluation

   Group IV — Terms for Curricula
   - Curriculum
   - Program
   - Subject
   - Course
   - Unit or Module of Instruction

References* and Resources

Books

Gronlund, Norman E. Stating Behavioral Objectives for Classroom Instruction. New York: The Macmillan Co., 1970, Pp. vi + 58.

Hough, John B., and Duncan, James K. Teaching: Description and Analysis. Reading, Massachusetts: Addison-Wesley Publishing Co., 1970, Pp. xv + 445.

Kapfer, Miriam B. Behavioral Objectives in Curriculum Development, Selected Readings and Bibliography. Englewood Cliffs, New Jersey: Educational Technology Publications, Inc., 1971, Pp. viii + 400.

Kibler, Robert J. et al. Objectives for Instruction and Evaluation, 2nd ed. (under a new title). Boston: Allyn and Bacon, Inc., 1974, Pp. x + 203.

*Silvius, G. Harold, and Curry, Estell H. Managing Multiple Activities in Industrial Education. Bloomington, Illinois: McKnight Publishing Co., 1971, Pp. 512-519; 587-602.

Periodicals

Bortz, Richard. "Studying the Behavior of Materials," Industrial Arts and Vocational Education, Vol. 59, No. 7 (October, 1970), Pp. 25-26.

Ebel, Robert L. "Behavioral Objectives: A Close Look," Phi Delta Kappan, Vol. LII, No. 3 (November 1970), Pp. 171-173.

Other Published Material

Byers, Edward E., and Huffman, Harry H. Writing Performance Goals: Strategy and Prototypes. A Manual for Vocational and Technical Educators. Publication of the CVTE: CR No. 15. ERIC Reference No. ED 061 413, 1971, Pp. 107.

*Campbell, Robert E. et al. The Systems Approach: An Emerging Behavioral Model for Vocational Guidance. A Summary Report. Publication of the CVTE: RD No. 45, ERIC Reference No. ED 047 127, January 1971, Pp. 33.

*Items with an asterisk have been cited in the chapter.

CHAPTER 8

Educational Justification of a Course or Program

Every instructional program must be organized so that it may be guided and measured. Before any particular course or program is offered to students, instructional planners should feel certain that it will meet the specific needs of students and the needs of society. If this is not the case, the course must be replanned so students will receive instruction to fulfill their needs more thoroughly. It is necessary to justify a course or program in terms of the **fulfillment of specific needs of students and the needs of society.**

To determine whether a course or program fulfills the needs of those who are to be scheduled for the instruction and thereby justify its existence, a set of goals must be established to describe the parameters and the major thrust of instruction. Such a listing of goals serves three purposes.
- First, counselors and students can determine whether it fulfills a need and contributes to a student's overall program.
- Second, the goals serve as a guide for the teacher while he/she develops the instructional program.
- Third, they serve as the basis for evaluation of student growth and development.

The course must always be designed to fulfill the goals established for it. In this way, the counselor, student, teacher and others concerned are assured of effective instruction.

Teachers of vocational and applied arts education (VAE) serve in two capacities: first as educators and second as specialists in their subject area. This implies that the first responsibility of VAE teachers is the education of the whole student rather than education for a specialized area only. The complete program of education is organized around the integration of its many specialized programs of instruction. Each teacher should assume responsibility for continually analyzing the entire program of instruction and evaluating how his/her special area might be adjusted to better fit the need of the students.

General and Specialized Education

The curriculum in American education is generally directed at two specific functions. The first is **general education.** This is defined as **that** education which is common for all students or as that instruction pursued by an individual for purposes other than occupational preparation. This general education function has significance for those responsible for developing VAE programs that contribute to the total program of education.

The second function is **specialized education, which is the special training needed by an individual student or by a selected group of learners, capable of profiting by such instruction.** Vocational courses would be classified as specialized education.

There are differences in the thinking of educational leaders regarding the organization of the total curriculum to provide for both general and specialized education. Some believe that education should be general up to a predetermined point and be specialized thereafter. Others think that the general and the specialized education of a learner should run concurrently with the emphasis on general education lessened as specialization becomes more paramount. Still others believe that a program of general education should include some provision for meaningful work experience, as advocated for the career education thrust. Finally, another group would have career education including vocational education and a provision for work experience as a substantial part of the school's program for all youth. Of these, the one most commonly accepted in educational circles is the vertical arrangement in which general education is given less and less emphasis as the student progresses through school. As general education is decreased, specialized education to prepare the learner for an occupation or profession gains in time and importance. This approach provides for a transition from a complete program of general education to a complete program of specialized education as the learner travels from elementary school through college. Formerly this transition was considered as taking place gradually and was represented by a straight line. However, with the consideration now being given to career education, there is an accelerated transition taking place so that high school students may acquire basic salable skills for a job-entry position. These career education programs are dual directed since they provide for the student who chooses to continue study in a community or senior college to further his/her occupational objectives. All of this is rapidly breaking down the long standing dichotomy between education considered "academic" and "vocational" in character (as discussed in Chapter 2). **The career education thrust provides for an integrated focus on "general" and "specialized" education.** In fact, there is an overlap in these functions for education as programs are directed to prepare people for the five life careers identified by Goldhammer and Taylor listed on pp. 214-215 of this chapter (1972, 129).

The process of curriculum building is one that should involve the whole school. While this concept is essential, it is equally important for each teacher to recognize and accept responsibility for planning the instructional program for each of his/her courses. In addition to planning their own program, it is important that teachers participate in the planning for all school curricula. To adequately do this, they would need to take part in the study and discussion of the overall aims for education as they would relate to the problems that teachers recognize and consider significant. Also, teachers would need to present their own views on the proposals for the all-school program and take an active part in the discussion of these issues. It is only through this type of cooperative effort between all of the professional staff within the school program that curricula will be developed to equip a student to meet and cope with the problems of society.

The Function of General Education

The first phase of the definition for general education presented in the previous section, namely "that education which should be common to all students" provides the basic or fundamental framework for elementary public education. In addition, the previous section explains the relationship between general and specialized education and describes how general education provides the full program of instruction in the early grades and gradually gives way to specialized education, which becomes more and more prominent, eventually encompassing all, or nearly all, of the curriculum activities.

One needs to take a more critical look at the term "general education" since it has almost become an educational cliché. Actually, the term is much easier to define than to put into practical application. If each area of instruction were to be critically evaluated in terms of whether it should be common to all students, the list of units that would meet this criterion might be very short. It is for this reason that general education now needs to be defined as:
1. Education that every student needs to know.
2. Education that contributes to the growth and development of an individual student.

A realistic inspection of these two phases of this definition will place such fundamental areas as English, mathematics, social science, and physical science in the need to know category. Many educators refer to these courses as the basic or required courses rather than what the learner needs to know. Regardless of terminology, these areas of instruction are required for existence in modern society. A student must master the fundamentals of these basic subjects either at school or in society. The student who misses will have difficulty in becoming a self-sufficient and contributing citizen.

The second phase of this proposed definition for general education, which is concerned with those experiences described as "contributing to the growth and development of an individual student," is somewhat nebulous since it depends on the evaluation of individual educators or educational philosophers. The applied arts which include industrial arts, homemaking, general business, and general agriculture; physical education; art; music; health; dramatics; and driver education are subject areas that are generally maintained to contribute to the growth and development of individual students. These subjects, when properly organized and taught, become vehicles essential for general education and the optimum growth and development of an individual. John L. Childs (1959, 22) has pointed out that the school should provide the conditions under which the young can learn from fruitful experiences and thereby progressively develop their competence to think, to evaluate, and to decide for themselves. Convinced that children can learn to think only as they are given opportunity to engage in the full act of reflective thought, Dewey strove to supplant a curriculum with primary emphasis on "listening," "memorizing," and "reciting," by an "activity," "functional," and "experience" curriculum in which the young learn significant attitudes and subject matters through their own purposeful interactions with things and people in actual life situations.

In his article, "Enduring Elements in the Educational Thought of John Dewey," Dr. Childs (1959, 23) observes that

> ... the acquisition of habits, skills, appreciations, and meanings — is a function of this process of doing, undergoing, inferring, and testing [as now suggested by behavioral objectives classified in the cognitive, affective, and psychomotor domains]. This process of interaction becomes educationally significant when it is so conducted that it "adds to the meaning of experience" of those involved in it, and "increases their ability to direct the course of subsequent experience." Life is good when it is characterized by the kind of functioning which produces this quality of growth.
> According to this functional point-of-view, mind is not an inborn psychological substance endowed with ready-made powers of reasoning. Nor is mind a system of mental faculties that can be developed by appropriate exercise on such academic disciplines as language, logic, and mathematics.

Occasionally, teachers consider their subject as being needed by everyone. When sufficient agreement is reached, an area may be moved into the need category. This is sometimes accomplished by state legislation. For example, many states have legislated required courses in driver education and physical education.

A second consideration in any discussion of general education involves the "level of instruction." It has already been emphasized that during the early stages of one's elementary education, all available time is devoted to general education. This permits the school to include many of the areas of general education which contribute to the overall growth and development of the child, thereby providing a complete and well-rounded education. As a result, one often finds experiences in industrial arts, music, art, and health a required part of elementary education. As the student advances in school his/her program of instruction usually provides for specialized instruction in a limited number of areas. In high school, able students may elect a college-preparatory program designed to prepare them for admission to a college or university, and/or pursue sequences directed at providing salable skills employment after high school.

At best, general education is a complex concept. Defining it is easy, but interpreting and carrying it out as an integral part of education is difficult. In a democratic society, the operating definition of general education and the resulting program will vary in different school districts. This is good, for it provides an opportunity to compare different programs and study the results.

Educators in VAE hasten to point out that **applied arts** is an integral part of general education. In **applied arts** the case is made for having all persons know societal functions and develop an appreciation for these:
1. Industry as it is represented in construction and manufacturing.
2. Food and fiber production.
3. Marketing, distribution, and office practices.
4. Hospitality, health, and the consumer.
5. Communication, transportation, and power.
6. Safety and environmental protection.

The Cognitive, Affective, and Psychomotor Domains

Desired behavioral objectives may be classified as cognitive, affective, or psychomotor learning. These classifications are helpful as professionals undertake to plan relevant instruction by matching the learning patterns of an individual with teaching strategies. The publications by Bloom, Krathwohl, and Simpson, listed with "References and Resources" for this chapter, deal with the taxonomies of educational objectives in each of these three domains.

The Behavioral Domains

Cognitive — refers to the mental and intellectual development that encompassses knowledge, comprehension, application, analysis, synthesis, and evaluation (Bloom, 1956, vii + 207). The behavioral objectives classified as "cognitive" deal with recall or recognition of knowledge and the development of intellectual abilities and skills. This is the domain in which most curriculum work to date has taken place with objectives phrased as student behavior. At present, these objectives are generally limited to "recall and recognition," with little application at the "higher order" of the cognitive domain (intellectual abilities and skills). Examples in VAE teacher education would be (1) the acquisition of "knowledge" (first level) of the Fryklund Classification of Informational Topics (1970, 70-85), namely technical information (essential to form judgments on the job), general information (nice to know), and guidance information (personal, educational, and occupational); and (2) the application (third level) by identifying and describing informational topics, in a teacher's area of specialization, in each of the three Fryklund categories.

Affective — includes behavior that centers around the attitudes, emotions, and values of the person, as reflected in the interests, appreciations, and adjustment of the learner (Krathwohl, 1964, ix +

196). Behavioral objectives classified as "affective" would describe desired changes in interests, attitudes, and values, and the development of appreciations and adequate adjustment (Krathwohl, 24-44). Examples in VAE are the student's attitudes toward (1) safety precautions, (2) absenteeism, and (3) care of tools and equipment in the laboratory; and his/her appreciation and respect for good design, craftsmanship, and technology's effect on the quality of life.

Psychomotor — refers to the teaching of motor abilities and the degree of skill involved in carrying out a physical activity. The factors involve neuromuscular coordination and the development of skillfulness in the learner.[1] An example is the degree of skill development (such as "understanding," "use," or "occupational" level)[2] that comes from the meaningful repetition of a basic hand or machine tool operation at the work station. According to Simpson (1970, 121-126) skill denotes that some learning has taken place. Thus, the psychomotor objectives should be stated in terms of abilities and skills to be acquired by the learner. Gronlund (1970, 24) points out that the key words in behavioral objectives classified in the psychomotor domain include such typical behavioral terms as these: assembles, builds, composes, dismantles, fixes, manipulates, sharpens, sketches, and uses.

In brief, each behavioral objective can be broadly classified as contributing to the intellectual outcomes (cognitive), attitudinal approach (affective), or manipulative skills (psychomotor) development of the learner. This classification of learning needs to be considered in these instances:

- Instruction is planned for the fulfillment of the goals for the course or program or the roles specified for instruction.
- The content for instruction is organized.
- Methods and teaching aids are selected.
- The organization is planned.
- Appropriate evaluation approaches and instruments are developed and used.
- Plans are made for appropriate physical facilities.

---

[1] These variables for the psychomotor domain are reported in a paper by David L. Jelden of the University of Northern Colorado, entitled "A Practical Approach to Individualized Instruction," p. 4.
[2] At the point that a learner has initially performed an operation, he would have little more than an "understanding" of the motor activity; after performing this same operation a few times, under meaningful instructional supervision, it is possible to bring the proficiency to a practical "use" level that would compare with that demonstrated by the home craftsperson; and through continued instruction and practice it is possible to bring the degree of skill in doing an operation to an "occupational" level where the rate and proficiency of performance is commensurate with industrial standards, with many of the steps performed automatically.

Classification of Objectives: Cognitive Domain

A study of any listing of behavioral objectives will quickly reveal that the cognitive outcomes are easy to formulate and use in program development, and the outcomes are often easier to measure than in the other domains. Teachers can readily see this development as they examine typical behavior classified in the major categories of the cognitive domain.[3]

1. **Knowledge** — involves remembering previously learned material such as recalling a structure, pattern, or setting. For measurement purposes it means little more than bringing to mind essential information from one's total bank of knowledge. It represents the lowest level of cognitive learning. Examples are recalling technical, general, or guidance information in a technical education course.
2. **Comprehension** — understands what is being communicated, can make use of the idea or material without necessarily relating it to other applications, or seeing its fullest implications. Examples are translating fractions to decimals, and estimating costs.
3. **Application** — is a higher level of understanding than comprehension. It is concerned with ability to apply principles, laws, safety precautions, methods, theories, and procedures.
4. **Analysis** — is the ability to identify the elements so an organizational structure is understood. Examples of such behavior are (1) ability to recognize unstated assumptions, (2) ability to identify kinds of materials used in the construction of a project, (3) ability to recognize the kind of three-dimensional method used in a pictorial rendering, and (4) ability to diagnose the trouble in a malfunctioning engine. It would include ability to predict trends and effects. Analysis is a higher level of learning than comprehension and application.
5. **Synthesis** — is the ability to put the parts or elements together, or make an application or proposal, in a way that a plan, project, or rendering is developed or created. It includes the communication process of the writer or speaker as he/she conveys to others ideas, feelings, and/or experiences. It includes skill in writing (organization of ideas and statements), ability to tell a personal experience effectively, plan a procedure for an experiment or project, and propose an approach for testing a hypothesis.
6. **Evaluation** — is making value judgments (both quantitative and qualitative) against internal or external criteria. It would include criterion-referenced measurement (where an individual's performance is evaluated against some established criterion rather than against other individuals) or norm-referenced measurement (where an individual's performance is evaluated against a normative group). Evaluation is the highest level of learning in the cognitive hierarchy

---

[3]A more complete description and breakdown of these major categories is given in Bloom's book (1956, 201-207).

and employs elements from the other major factors in this classification of the cognitive domain.[4]

Classification of Objectives: Affective Domain

The affective domain poses quite a different problem. An examination of the major variables in the affective classification reveals that it is more difficult to plan behavioral objectives to be objectively measured and which would contribute, with assurance, to the growth and development of the learner. It is encouraging, however, that attention is now being focused on procedures and techniques for the evaluation of affective objectives. An approach, illustrated with a number of examples that could be applied in VAE for evaluating affective objectives, is reported by Mager, in his book on **Goal Analysis** (1972, vi + 136). The reference by Banks (1973, 36-37) reports excellent procedures for evaluating objectives in this domain. The following categories are in the affective domain:

1. Receiving — is the learner's willingness to respond to stimuli and receive selected phenomena such as course goals, content, and activities or some subject area in general. Previous experience causes the student to bring to each situation a point of view or set which may facilitate or hinder attainment of the objective. The goal is to secure, direct, and hold the learner's participation. Examples of objectives in this classification are (1) listens attentively to all basic instruction and (2) gives careful attention to responsibilities as a student officer. This is the lowest level of learning in the affective domain.
2. Responding — is the level above that of merely attending to phenomenon. The student becomes involved and is committed to the activity at hand. While this category is at the lowest level of commitment, the learner expresses a value by receiving and displaying a wholesome attitude toward the subject phenomenon or activity. Examples are (1) serves willingly in a leadership role in the student-directed organization (2) obeys the safety precautions, and (3) follows through on assignments in the home workshop.
3. Valuing — is behavior categorized at a level that is sufficiently consistent and stable to be characterized as a belief or an attitude. The learner recognized the thing, phenomenon, or behavior as having worth in value or assessment judgments through attitudes and expressions or appreciations. Belief at this level involves a high degree of certainty. Examples are (1) appreciates good craftsmanship and (2) demonstrates ability to value good design while shaping and forming materials with tools and machines.

---

[4]Helpful illustrative examples of instructional objectives and specific learning outcomes for each of the levels or classifications of behavior under the three domains may be found in Gronlund's book (1970, 20-24).

4. **Organizing** — is the bringing together of different values, evaluating them and assimilating them in a system that is subject to change as new values are considered. Conceptualization is the first subdivision in the organization process, which permits the individual to see how a value relates to those already held. The organization of a total value system is second. An example of a value system is to formulate and accept a life plan for career development.
5. **Characterizing by a Value or Value Complex** — is the highest level of learning in the affective domain. It consists of the individual's value hierarchy, organized as an internally consistent system that controls behavior so that a person acts consistently and does not display emotion when threatened or challenged. Affective behavior at this level becomes a "lifestyle" as it becomes predictable and is consistent. Often, an unconscious set guides action without conscious forethought. Thus, an example is behavior relating to attitudes, values, beliefs, and ideas that is consistent with the individual's internal value system.[5]

Persons serving on advisory councils as well as other leaders are raising many questions that relate to the affective domain for a broad-based occupational education program. To illustrate, in the Report of the Minnesota Seminar on Vocational Curriculum Development, Moss and Smith (1970, 3 & 4) point out that

> . . . the technical tasks of the work role involving cognitive and psychomotor skill performance are typically considered relevant by all vocational educators. But what about the affective behaviors that are involved in occupational adjustment and human relations tasks on the job? Are these to be identified as work tasks to be taught (and built into the behavioral objectives)? The same issue can be extended; what kinds of tasks inherent in the citizenship and culture-carrying roles are to be included among the tasks to be taught in vocational curriculums?

At this Minnesota Seminar

> It was proposed that these behaviors are simply another type of "task," and may, therefore, be treated (after identification) in the same way as other tasks. The immediate difficulty seems to be that we currently lack adequate methods, instruments, and/or observation skills to reliably identify affective tasks and to specify the level of performance required for each.

Behavior which results in changes of interest, attitudes, and values and the development of appreciations and adequate adjustments is concerned with the humane outcomes of education and is not readily qualifiable in the education setting. Perhaps this has been a deterrent to

---

[5] A more complete description and breakdown of these major categories is given in Krathwohl's book (1964, 116-185). There are helpful illustrative examples of general instructional objectives and specific learning outcomes for each of the categories in the affective domain in Gronlund's book (1970, 22-23).

the systems approach since the growth factor cannot be as objectively measured as in the cognitive and psychomotor classifications. However, learning in the affective domain can now be evaluated in a satisfactory manner by employing the procedures that have been developed by Robert F. Mager, described in his book titled **Goal Analysis** (1972, vi + 136), and in the article by Banks (1973, 36-37).

Classification of Objectives: Psychomotor Domain

The relevance of many occupational and industrial education courses is predicated on the learning styles that are inherent with an activity-based progam. There is significant opportunity for degrees of skill development in the psychomotor domain, as learners use tools and machines in a **learn by doing** setting. Among the variables in psychomotor behavior are:

- **Frequency** — the planned repetition of a hand or machine tool operation for a desired degree of skill development.
- **Energy** — the steadiness, strength, and speed that influences precision in doing the task.
- **Duration** — the length of time at the work station for skill development.

Such variables as the rate at which an individual performs a skill, amount of strength or power needed to do a manipulative task, and the length of time that the learner continues to perform a tool or machine operation are paramount in such development. Fine motor acts are performed by small muscles, especially the fingers, hand, and forearm, and frequently involve eye-hand coordination. Gross motor skills involve the large muscle group of the body, especially shoulders, trunk, and legs.

Schema for the classification of educational objectives in the psychomotor domain (Simpson, n.d., 1-5) are:

1. **Perception** — is the process of becoming aware of objects, qualities, or relations by way of sense organs. Perception is essential before there can be purposeful motor activity. An example is to develop a feel for the differences in fabrics.
2. **Set** (readiness for action or experience) — is the mental set (such as knowledge of steps to perform an operation), physical set (positioning of hands and body for a manipulative task), or emotional set (desire to perform a hand or machine tool operation). An example is to demonstrate readiness to undertake a project by developing a plan of work, observing a demonstration of the hand and machine tool operations, and passing the safety test covering precautions to be observed at the work station.
3. **Guided Response** (directed by a person who has acquired the level of skill to be attained by the learner) — is the skillfulness attained through imitation and continual correction of errors. An example is to develop a use level of skill for a designated hand or machine tool operation through carefully directed and meaningful repetition at a work station such as cutting to a line with a crosscut handsaw.

4. **Mechanism** — is where the learned response has become habitual. At this level the learner has achieved confidence and the desired degree of proficiency. The act is then a part of his/her repertoire of possible responses to stimuli. Examples are hand-hemming a garment or mixing the ingredients of pancakes.
5. **Complex Overt Response** — is where a complex act, so classified because of the required movement pattern, is carried out smoothly and efficiently with a minimum expenditure of time and energy. The learner is no longer uncertain about any of the steps and the performance of the motor skill has become automatic. The motor activity includes all specific and generalized movements involved in motor coordination as it is done with ease and muscle control. Examples are a highly skilled person (1) operating a milling machine to face a surface, (2) laying a pattern on fabric and cutting out a garment, or (3) performing the basic steps of national folk dances.

Fig. 8-1. An adult student cuts material to match a pattern while studying in a power sewing program. (Central City Occupational Center, Los Angeles)

6. **Adaptation** — is altering motor activities to meet the demands of new problematic situations requiring a physical response. Examples are (1) new welding skills required to use newly developed welding equipment and materials or (2) developing a new dance routine by adapting mastered dance skills and abilities.
7. **Organization** — is creating new motor acts or ways of manipulating materials out of understandings, abilities, and skills developed in the psychomotor area. Examples are (1) creating and refining simulation equipment so that learners would have the facilities to demonstrate an essential VAE psychomotor response, or (2) designing and developing an involved project (i.e. "The Lawnminder" shown in Fig. 8-2).

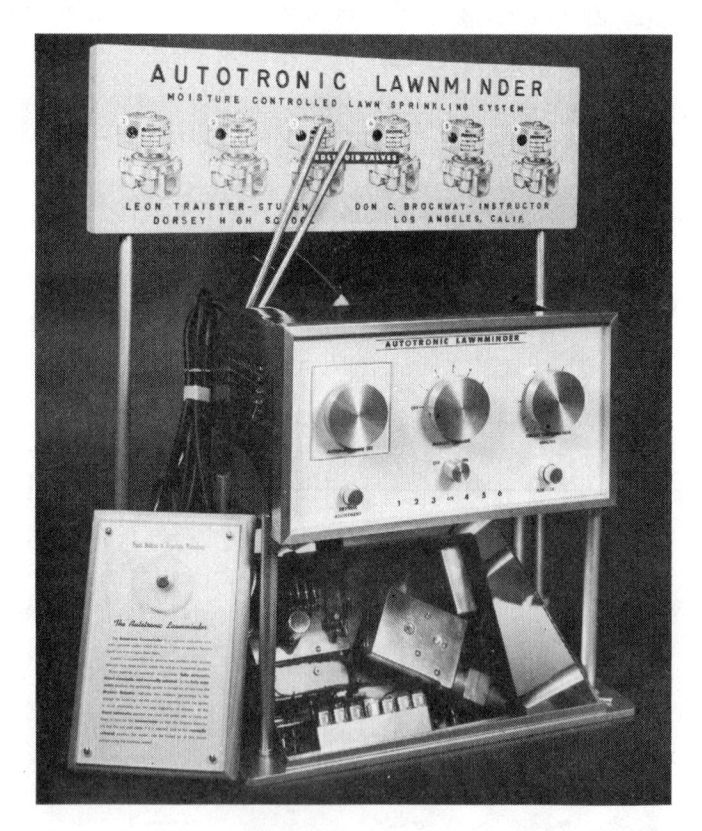

Fig. 8-2. When Leon Traister designed and built this lawnminder at Dorsey High School in Los Angeles, under the direction of Donald C. Brockway, he was dealing with the current problems of society.

A Possible Fourth Domain

In discussing the relationships among the cognitive, affective, and psychomotor domains, M. Ray Loree (1965, 75) suggested that the psychomotor domain might be better thought of as a part of a larger domain that he would call an

> 'action-pattern domain' for objectives in which some motor response constitutes the essence of the objectives. Psychomotor skills would constitute one category within this domain. [He suggests that] Competencies such as speech making, organizing a committee, and the like belong in the action-pattern domain.

Elizabeth J. Simpson (June, 1970, 122), in her report on **The Classification of Educational Objectives, Psychomotor Domain,** found Loree's proposal appealing and pursued it to some depth in her investigation and research. She concluded, however, that

> 'the action-pattern domain' was an all-encompassing one that might very well be a fourth domain extending beyond and including the three already identified in the original work on the classification systems. Even though the psychomotor domain involves behaviors of all three domains to a considerable extent, the primary concern is with abilities and skills which have motor activity as a focus; this is what the investigator regarded as the psychomotor domain.

Identify Overall Aims for Education

Persons responsible for course or program development need to be thoroughly familiar with prepared and available statements that give direction to the total educational effort. Many communities and states have had task forces determine the overall goals[6] for public education. Such projects are often directed by an advisory board and provide for the involvement of interested and influential citizens. To illustrate, early in 1970 the Michigan State Board of Education appointed an advisory task force of Michigan educators, students, and lay citizens to look into the purposes of public education. The charge to this task force was that of "identifying and delineating what was felt to be the common goals of an educational system capable of meeting the growing and changing needs of a contemporary society."

This task force made its report to the Michigan State Board of Education in June of 1970. The State Board received the report, made revisions and additions, and then arranged to have the proposed common goals published in tentative form and presented to the people of Michigan for further review and comment. Twenty-five public meetings

---

[6]"Goals" and "aims" are considered synonymous terms when used to delineate the overall purposes of education.

were held to elicit the opinions and concerns of local educators and interested citizens throughout the State. As a result of this effort, **The Common Goals of Michigan Education** were then accepted and published by the Michigan State Board of Education in September of 1971. These goals have been reprinted as **Appendix G** in order to provide an example of cooperative efforts at the state and local levels.

Surely no Michigan teacher or curriculum coordinator could afford to make specific recommendations regarding goals for any course or program, area of education, or a department until he/she was familiar with **The Common Goals of Michigan Education.** Many communities throughout the United States have had similar involvement of citizens in focusing attention on public education.

Many of the major school systems, professional organizations, councils, or commissions — on their own or in collaboration with state departments of public instruction or the United States Office of Education — have made pronouncements of general aims for public education. These lists cover such guiding principles as these:
1. Education serves all people in a democracy and should develop high democratic ideals.
2. Education continues throughout life.
3. Education aims at self-direction.
4. Education provides for intelligent adjustment to social change.
5. Education functions through many agencies.
6. Education changes behavior.
7. Education deals with all aspects of life.

The major functions of living which comprise the framework for the learning experiences include the following:
1. Practicing American citizenship.
2. Using the tools of communication effectively.
3. Acquiring vocational competence.
4. Building human relationships.
5. Improving family living.
6. Developing economic competence.
7. Protecting life and health.
8. Satisfying spiritual and aesthetic needs.
9. Enjoying wholesome leisure.[7]

There have been lists of general aims for education that have been advocated by the authors of professional books in education. To illustrate, in his treatise on "A Careers Curriculum," in the book by Goldhammer and Taylor (1972, 129), Goldhammer recommends that one prepare for all five of these careers:
1. A producer of goods or a renderer of services.
2. A member of a family group.
3. A participant in the social and political life of society.
4. A participant in avocational pursuits.

---

[7]These listings of **guiding principles** and **major functions**, to be helpful to those formulating the general aims for education, are based on similar listings developed by the Chicago Public schools.

5. A participant in the regulatory functions involved in aesthetic, moral, and religious concerns.

It should be obvious that it is not the responsibility of any one teacher to furnish the overall aims for a total educational program. Surely this must be a cooperative effort. Wherever the faculty for a school or a citizens' advisory group has been commissioned to evaluate the educational program and to formulate overall aims, teachers should be encouraged to participate and become involved. Where there is no such project, the teacher then needs to study the published lists of overall aims to see if he/she can locate statements that might be acceptable to the faculty of the school and to which the teacher can personally subscribe.

Before preparing the goals for any one course or program, it is necessary to locate overall aims for the total program. In some cases these would not be aims for primary and secondary public education, but aims designed to serve a special area or curriculum. For example, an industrial education teacher preparing a course of study for an engineering shop program in Manufacturing Processes would need to identify the overall aims for engineering education. A teacher organizing a course to prepare practical nurses would be looking for the overall aims for Health Occupations. Likewise, a person bringing together material for a course to prepare industrial education teachers would need to locate overall aims for industrial teacher education. Acceptable aims for primary and secondary education in public schools would hardly suffice as the springboard for these three examples.

Compare Well-Known and Published Aims for Education

During the past decades professional organizations and commissions, in cooperation with the state departments for public education and the U.S. Office of Education have, from time to time, published lists and descriptive literature regarding the aims for public education.

These lists have been appearing through the years. As early as 1918, the National Education Association, with the cooperation of what was then the United States Bureau of Education, published bulletin No. 35, **Cardinal Principles of Secondary Education.** These seven principles are well known to all who devote their lives to education. Bulletin No. 35 has been reprinted three times, most recently in 1962. In a survey conducted in 1967 the National Education Association found that the Cardinal Principles were still popular with teachers (see article in references for this chapter).

The Purposes of Education in American Democracy, which came from the efforts of the Educational Policies Commission in 1938, has had a profound influence on American education. In 1946 the NEA released **Policies for Education in American Democracy.** Under the authorship of L. A. Kirkendall, I. R. Kuengli, and F. Reeves, the American Federation of Teachers published **Goals for American**

Education in 1948. Then there was **Education for All American Youth** in 1944, which has been one of the most significant releases to have come from the Educational Policies Commission of the NEA, especially as it has given direction to the full development of comprehensive high schools in the United States. Robert J. Havighurst's Developmental Tasks, first published in 1948, have had a monumental influence on American education. A brief but important statement on the goals of American Secondary Education may be found in **The High School in a Changing World**, a 1958 publication of the American Association of School Administrators.

These lists of goals, aims, principles, policies, or objectives show that the representatives of professional organizations or commissions and state and national education departments have continued to scrutinize public education. With the tremendous concern for the effectiveness of the educational program in the United States today, it hardly seems that the original interpretation and emphasis placed on the items in any of these lists of aims developed during the first half of the twentieth century would serve to give adequate direction to an educational program to prepare American youth for their adult responsibilities during the last quarter of the twentieth century.

As one examines and compares these lists of aims it is soon discovered that they are basically the same but that it is a shift in emphasis that distinguishes one from the other. An interpretation of the **Cardinal Principles of Secondary Education** would be different today than when they were brought out in 1918. Let's examine these principles to see what interpretation might be given to them in light of what is currently being emphasized in education.

Cardinal Principles

Cardinal Principles of Secondary Education from the NEA Commission on the Reorganization of Secondary Education are:
1. Health (Personal and Public)
2. Command of Fundamental Processes
3. Worthy Home Membership
4. Vocation
5. Civic Education
6. Worthy Use of Leisure
7. Ethical Character

As one looks at principle one, **Health — a sound mind in a strong and healthy body**, it is quickly observed that the gains for Americans have been great as the life span has increased and many of the communicable diseases have been practically eliminated. A high percentage of Americans now enjoy vacations and participate in such recreation as bowling, golf, skiing, boating, hiking, and snowmobiling. Those in VAE are increasingly aware of the importance of safety education as it may affect people who must work, live, and adjust to our rapid technological developments. Our society is much more dynamic than it was in 1918.

With increased emphasis on career education for more and more Americans, there has been a renewed public awareness of the importance of a **Command of Fundamental Processes — ability to read, write, think, study, and act.** This has behooved those in the applied arts to evaluate their contribution to general education; that is, what they believe everyone should know about such fields as the industrial arts, homemaking, and general business.

With so many women in the labor force, there are truly many new and projected issued underlying Cardinal Principle Three, **Worthy Home Membership — a happy, unselfish, and democratic life.** Those in applied arts (especially family life and industrial arts education) have seen the desire on the part of Americans for basic instruction in the use of hand tools and power machines, and in the wise selection of materials for the development and upkeep of the home. There has been concern, also, about helping young men and women develop competencies that would assist them in the initial construction, refinishing, repairing, and rebuilding of their homes. Surely, these experiences should be concomitants of the applied arts as they contribute to the general education of people.

There are constantly evolving implications for Principle Four, **Vocational Knowledges and Skills Needed to Earn a Living.** In 1918 only a privileged few had opportunity for a high school education. Extensive vocational programs were, therefore, needed even at the junior high school level. The introduction of career education emphasizes the importance for today's youth to have a salable skill before leaving school to enter the labor market. Vocational and technical education in the public schools has been moved up by grade levels, as the years that students remain in schools have increased. As stated in Chapter 1 and 4, plans to utilize the facilities of local industries and business have become very effective in many school districts. The role of educational programs maintained by industry and business is being clarified. Through organized and indentured apprenticeships, highly skilled persons are being provided for the building trades and industries. Educational programs to prepare technicians to assist engineers, dentists, teachers, doctors, and other professionals are being carried on by public schools, especially as a function of comunity colleges. Automation in America's industries has focused attention on the accelerated need to upgrade or retrain skilled and technical workers on the job. These points illustrate that the appropriate features of a program for vocational effectiveness in 1918 would be practically antiquated at this time. The approach to vocational education is ever changing as it becomes more and more essential in American education.

Civic Education, the fifth of the Cardinal Principles, **calls for informed citizenship dedicated to the common good.** This is recognized in a free society as basic for democratic government. Our democracy will never be any better than the degree of involvement of its citizens. In the years since this Cardinal Principle was enunciated, teachers have become aware that this aim encompasses more than teaching youth about the organization and operation of their government on the local, state, and national levels. Most teachers now think that a primary aim of their courses should be to help each of their students become a well-integrated, cooperative, and participating citizen. Because of the structure and organization of VAE, teachers in these areas of education should quickly see the potential of their contribution to this Cardinal Principle.

With the continual decrease in time spent at work, renewed interest has been shown in the principle, **Worthy Use of Leisure — use of free time for worthy activities and pleasures.** How different this is today than it was in 1918 before radio, television, jet propulsion, and the nuclear era. Those in industrial and family life education see that they need to provide educational experiences to help persons derive personal satisfaction from the development of their homes and in repairing and building articles for their homes, families, and friends. Then too, more and more men and women need experiences in such activities as gardening; cooking; sewing; and craft activities related to metalworking, woodworking, plastics, electricity, and working with electrical mechanisms. It should be the role of applied arts to provide these competencies. As more and more persons are subjected to the emotional pressures of American productivity, the therapeutic values that come to those who work with tools, machines, and materials during their increased hours away from work needs to be emphasized in public education.

Ethical Character — the development of a spirit of service and character that is trusted and admired, the last of the seven Cardinal Principles, will always be of major concern to those who have the privilege of working with youth. Leaders in VAE education have focused attention on the significant contribution that teachers in this field should make to this aim. VAE teachers have, therefore, been concerned about providing opportunities for students to assume responsibility in organizing and maintaining instructional activities, and about helping students develop interpersonal relationships in work situations. Employment managers in industry and business stress that they are looking for persons who are cooperative, articulate, reliable, well-integrated, and willing to assume responsibility. Through the student-directed organization, VAE teachers have an optimum opportunity to help students develop these qualities.

Purposes of Education

The Purposes of Education in American Democracy, developed in 1938, were:

1. The objective of **Self-Realization**.
   a. The inquiring mind
   b. Speech
   c. Reading
   d. Writing
   e. Numbers
   f. Sight and hearing
   g. Health knowledge
   h. Health habits
   i. Public health
   j. Recreation
   k. Intellectual interests
   l. Esthetic interests
   m. Character

2. The objective of **Civic Responsibility**.
   a. Social justice
   b. Social activity
   c. Social understandings
   d. Critical judgment
   e. Tolerance
   f. Conservation
   g. Social applications of science
   h. World citizenship
   i. Law observance
   j. Economic literacy
   k. Political citizenship
   l. Devotion to democracy
3. The objective of **Human Relationship**.
   a. Respect for humanity
   b. Friendships
   c. Cooperation
   d. Courtesy
   e. Appreciation of the home
   f. Conservation of the home
   g. Homemaking
   h. Democracy in the home
4. The objective of **Economic Efficiency**.
   a. Work
   b. Occupational information
   c. Occupational choice
   d. Occupational adjustment
   e. Occupational efficiency
   f. Personal economics
   g. Efficiency in buying
   h. Consumer judgment
   i. Consumer protection

Surely these purposes helped to identify factors to be stressed in the optimum development of each student. With this breakdown, teachers were able to identify more readily those activities in their respective curriculum areas that would contribute to the fulfillment of the four major purposes: (1) Self-Realization, (2) Civic Responsibility, (3) Human Relationship, and (4) Economic Efficiency.

Imperative Needs of Youth

In 1944 the Educational Policies Commission of the NEA issued a statement on educational needs. These needs served as guide posts for the Commission's widely quoted 1944 report on **Education for All American Youth: a Further Look**. These ten **Imperative Needs of Youth** are:

1. All youth need to develop salable skills and those understandings and attitudes that make the worker an intelligent and productive participant in economic life. To this end, most youth need supervised work experience as well as education in the skills and knowledge of their occupations.
2. All youth need to develop and maintain good health and physical fitness.
3. All youth need to understand the rights and duties of the citizen of a democratic society, and to be diligent and competent in the performance of their obligations as members of the community and citizens of the state and nation.
4. All youth need to understand the significance of the family for the individual and society and the conditions conducive to successful family life.

5. All youth need to know how to purchase and use goods and services intelligently, understanding both the values received by the consumer and the economic consequences of their acts.
6. All youth need to understand the methods of science, the influence of science on human life, and the main scientific facts concerning the nature of the world and of man.
7. All youth need opportunities to develop their capacities to appreciate beauty in literature, art, music, and nature.
8. All youth need to be able to use their leisure time well and to budget it wisely, balancing activities that yield satisfactions to the individual with those that are socially useful.
9. All youth need to develop respect for other persons, to grow in their insight into ethical values and principles, and to be able to live and work cooperatively with others.
10. All youth need to grow in their ability to think rationally, to express their thoughts clearly, and to read and listen with understanding.

Havighurst's Developmental Tasks

The general aims for public education have been greatly influenced by Robert J. Havighurst's Developmental Tasks. These tasks were first identified and published in 1948 when Havighurst was serving on the Committee on Human Development, The University of Chicago. Since then Havighurst has authored many publications that focus on the implications of these tasks in American education. To illustrate, his treatise on "Youth in Exploration and Men Emergent" (1964, 216) will be of special interest to VAE teachers as it deals with life stages of vocational development. Kimbrell and Vineyard (1972, 67-68) deal with the six stages of vocational development that are predicated on Havighurst's thesis that "work is such an integral part of man's life that we can identify the stages through which an individual passes along the road to work."

Havighurst's Developmental Tasks are classified under these six major headings:

1. **Infancy and Early Childhood**
   This classification includes nine tasks. Typical are:
   1) "Learning to walk."
   6) "Achieving physiological stability."
2. **Middle Childhood**
   There are nine tasks in this category. Of significance to VAE are:
   6) "Developing concepts necessary for everyday living."
   8) "Achieving personal independence."
3. **Adolescence**
   There are ten tasks in this classification with four of them having major implications for VAE programs:
   3) "Accepting one's physique and using the body effectively."
   5) "Achieving assurance of economic independence."
   6) "Selecting and preparing for an occupation."

7) "Preparing for marriage and family life."
4. Early Adulthood
Five of the eight tasks in this category have implications for VAE courses and programs (especially family life education):
2) "Learning to live with a marriage partner."
3) "Starting a family."
4) "Rearing children."
5) "Managing a home."
6) "Getting started in an occupation."
5. Middle Age
Three of the seven developmental tasks in this classification have been selected for their implications in VAE programs:
2) "Establishing and maintaining an economic standard of living."
3) "Assisting teen-age children to become responsible and happy adults."
4) "Developing adult leisure-time activities."
6. Later Maturity
The first of five tasks under this classification has implications for VAE. It is:
1) "Adjusting to decreasing physical strength and health."

These seventeen developmental tasks, selected from Havighurst's forty-eight tasks, under the six major headings, should prove helpful to VAE curriculum builders.

Goals of Secondary Education

In 1958, The American Association of Secondary Schools stressed these two goals for American secondary education in their publication, **The High School in a Changing World:**
1. Self Realization:
   The maximum development of all the mental, moral, emotional, and physical powers of the individual, to the end that a rich life may be enjoyed through the realization of worthy and desirable goals.
2. Social Effectiveness:
   The maximum development of the ability and desire in each individual to make the greatest possible contribution to all humanity through responsible participation in, and benefit from, the great privileges of American citizenship.

Basic Aims Are Stable

These examples show that the basic tenets for the aims for American education remain somewhat stable. It is the emphasis that is shifting with our times. This condition is illustrated by the following story.

A father had gone to visit his alma mater, where his son was a college student. Upon his arrival on the campus, he discovered that his son was about to leave to attend a course in political science that was being taught by the same professor that had taught him when he was an undergraduate at that institution, thirty years before. The father decided to visit class with his son. As they arrived in class, the professor was passing out a mimeographed examination for the session. The father, therefore, had an opportunity to examine the questions before he left his son to complete the test. When the father met his son after the exam, he said, "Son, I think that Professor Jones had exactly the same questions on that sheet as he had thirty years ago when I was a student." To which the son replied, "Dad, that is correct — but he expects different answers today."

These examples of aims for education which have received wide acceptance through the years should serve to illustrate that such basic statements as "Command of Fundamental Processes" and "Economic Efficiency" are still essential aims for an overall program of public education. It is the tempo of change in the lives of individuals and the attitude of Americans toward this rate of change that influences what needs to be stressed in public schools of the United States to fulfill these essential goals for public education.

Committees Develop Aims for a Program within a School System

In many school systems, teachers are grouped together for administrative and supervisory purposes, to work cooperatively to identify and formulate aims for their subject area according to some departmental or divisional organizational plan, or for some specialized function in a total school program. This has often been a goal of the preschool workshops. Usually directors for an instructional division and coordinators give leadership to the effort. This might well result in a statement of the **Aims for Vocational Education and Applied Arts** (in a particular city or school system).

In other situations teachers have been grouped by subject areas. For example, those who teach the business subjects work together to formulate overall **Aims for Business Education.** Those who teach in such areas as industrial education, home economics, distributive education, health occupations, and agricultural education are grouped together to formulate statements that guide their contributions to education.

Where there are several teachers for the same curriculum area in a school, such as industrial arts, these teachers may work together under the leadership of a departmental chairman or division head to identify the aims for their portion of the total curriculum.

In charging committees with such responsibility it is important for the leaders (whether they be directors, supervisors, or coordinators) to point out that when two or more teachers undertake the formulation of written aims, there perhaps will need to be some compromise to reconcile individual points of view.

Often there are several teachers in a particular department who would welcome an opportunity to work on the establishment of aims for a program. In sparsely populated regions where there may be only one or two VAE teachers in a school system, these teachers from the geographical region have met and produced significant curriculum materials. High level and creative work emerges when professional teachers understand what is needed and are given optimum opportunity to participate.

Administrative leaders need to provide editorial and clerical service to facilitate committee effort. They need, also, to follow through and facilitate the publication and dissemination of these curriculum materials. All too often committee effort has been relegated to the files of the coordinator, department head, or supervisor. All teachers who contribute should be recognized for their efforts; often it is appropriate to carry the names and schools of those who have assisted. When needed, resource persons should be provided to assist a committee.

Departmental aims need to be written in somewhat general terms, thereby reflecting the philosophy of the whole program rather than a specific area. This is in contrast to the goals for a course which guide the development of the instructional program and describe the parameters for a specific course. Generalized statements of aims for three selected programs or institutions are presented as examples of what might be formulated as aims for a program by two or more qualified teachers.

EXAMPLE

AIMS FOR A HIGH SCHOOL COOPERATIVE WORK-STUDY PROGRAM[8]

1. To provide a cooperative coeducational program that will afford all qualified students an opportunity to gain an understanding of the technical knowledge and skill related to initial entrance into an occupational area such as the skilled or needle trades; hospital and commercial foods services; or office and distributive occupations.
2. To provide all eligible students with a high school education of such quality that upon graduation they may receive a standard high school diploma which may serve as the basis for recommendation for entrance to institutions of higher learning.
3. To provide industry and business with workers trained to enter the initial phases of technical, skilled trades, or general industrial and business levels of employments.
4. To develop in students the ideals of democracy, responsibilities for intelligent citizenship and civic participation, through an academic program and extracurricular activities that afford students an opportunity to practice desired civic behavior, develop personal initiative and ability, as well as character growth, talent, and good habits of personal hygiene.

[8]Compiled by Parke Huffman et al., Detroit Public Schools.

EXAMPLE

AIMS FOR PRACTICAL NURSING[9]

The practical nursing education program is planned to prepare a person to be a member of the health care team and share in the care of the sick, in rehabilitation, and in the prevention of illness. The program is planned to operate within the framework of state laws regulating the practice of nursing.

The general aims of the curriculum are to provide the student with these opportunities:

1. To understand the principles of healthful living.
2. To understand the structure, function, development and behavior of the human from birth to old age.
3. To understand the principles of normal and therapeutic nutrition.
4. To develop nursing skills and apply knowledge in the care of patients in the areas of medical, surgical, obstetric, and pediatric nursing.
5. To develop effective interpersonal and working relationships.
6. To appreciate the necessity for personal and professional growth and development.

EXAMPLE

AIMS FOR CAREER EDUCATION[10]

These aims for career education are organized by operational levels. They are predicated on the premise that vocational education is an integral part of career education. The School District of the City of Berkley, Michigan, describes career education as follows:

> The central purpose of career education is to relate learning to life roles and assist all individuals to develop values and skills which will improve their potential for more effective living as children, youth, and adults in their family and citizen roles.

These aims were developed and screened by numerous groups prior to approval by the Board of Education. Preparation, review, and approval involved the following groups:

- VAE teachers from Berkley's elementary and secondary schools.
- Elementary and secondary school principals.
- Parents Advisory Committee.

---

[9] These aims were developed by the staff of the Practical Nursing Center, Detroit Public Schools, under the leadership of Margaret Crager, R.N., Department Head.

[10] Developed under the leadership of Mrs. Alexandria Takis, Director of Career Education, Berkley, Michigan.

Educational Justification   **225**

Fig. 8-3. Five of the twelve members of the Berkley Curriculum Advisory Committee review aims for career education. Seated left to right: Theresa Novitsky (student), Ronald Murdock (student), Irving Ritter (parent), Dr. Mary Jane Bell (Principal, Tyndall Elementary School), and Mrs. Harriett Sawyer (parent). (Courtesy Mrs. Alexandria Takis, Berkley, Michigan)

- Curriculum Advisory Committee.
- Office of the Superintendent of Schools.
- Board of Education.

The following aims were the results of this thorough review and involvement of educators, parents, students, and interested representatives of the community.

1. **Career Orientation** — Self-Awareness and Career Awareness (K-6) should provide instructional activities that help students to:
   - Identify the feelings, attitudes, physical strengths and weaknesses, and differences in social abilities and environment that make each person truly an individual.
   - Develop feelings of self-pride and self-worth.
   - Become aware of the necessity and dignity of work.
   - Learn about the many different ways that people earn a living, become useful citizens, and spend their leisure time.
   - Become aware of themselves and their own feelings about the different activities of the world of work.
2. **Career Exploration** (Grades 7-10) should provide instructional activities that help students to:

- Continue their self-awareness and career-awareness experiences.
- Continue to develop feelings of self-pride and self-worth.
- Learn about the different job clusters (as identified by the United States Office of Education) and have exploratory experiences in each.
- Develop skills for career decision-making and planning.

3. **Career Decision-Making and Planning** (Grades 9 and 10) should provide instructional activities that help students to:
   - Make wise, meaningful, and flexible tentative career decisions and educational plans directed toward one of the job clusters.
   - Develop a foundation for further education in the tentatively chosen career field.

4. **Career Preparation** (Grades 10 through 12 and Continuing Education) should provide instructional activities that will give each student the opportunity to:
   - Develop and maintain self-worth, good citizenship, teamwork, and desirable work attitudes.
   - Select a specific occupational or preparatory program consistent with a tentative career decision and educational plan.
   - Gain saleable entry-level skills in a chosen specific occupational area.
   - Participate in actual work experiences in the real world of work.
   - Become a knowledgeable consumer of the available products and services of this country.

In addition to the District Aims, the District adopted a set of "principles" which will assist in the implementation of programs needed to fulfill the accepted aims.

- Determine the occupational needs of adolescents and adults within the school and community.
- Determine the manpower needs and resulting instructional needs of industry, business, government, and service organizations within the local community and beyond.
- Respond to identified needs by providing or recommending occupational preparatory programs for all segments of the school-community population.
- Ascertain that instructional activities developed for specific occupations within the program are realistic, salable, meaningful, and up-to-date.
- Base curriculum content on general goal statements and performance objectives that are written in clear, concise, and understandable language, and define the expected outcome from each career preparation course.
- Continually appraise written general goal statements and performance objectives to insure that objectives are being met and are consistent with current occupational activities.
- Help guide and place graduates from completed programs into entry-level jobs or into institutions of higher learning.
- Use both general advisory committees and occupational advisory committees for specific instructional programs in planning and evaluating career education programs at all levels.

The aims for the Henry Ford Community College included in Appendix H serve as an excellent example of group effort in developing aims for a school.

Develop Specific Goals for a VAE Course

The responsibility for developing the specific course[11] goals must be accepted by each individual teacher. This obligation justly lies with teachers since the entire course or individual program will be built around these overall goals. Teachers must, therefore, be thoroughly familiar with the aspirations held for the course. In addition no one is better qualifed to develop the specific goals since teachers are the recognized authority for the subject. They should have a thorough understanding of the needs of their students and the ways in which instruction will contribute to the fulfillment of these needs.

In developing course aims, the teacher needs to utilize the wealth of resource materials available.

Consider Philosophy of Education

A teacher must consider his/her own philosophy of education and that philosophy which would be acceptable to colleagues before starting the preparation of goals for a course. Then the teacher must justify the course as it contributes to extending the educational program of the students. The teacher should feel sure that what he/she is advocating will be acceptable in the community. In doing this, the teacher will develop many insights that should be considered when formulating the goals for a course.

Consider General Aims for Education — Departmental Aims

The aspirations held for the entire program of education or the total offerings for VAE should certainly be reviewed. Ways in which the course under preparation can help fulfill the general aims for education will become apparent as these general aims are analyzed.

If a vocational course of study is being prepared, the local aims for vocational education, whether they be for the state, district, or school, will indicate what has been envisioned for vocational education as a part of career education. Each specific vocational course should be developed within the framework established for the entire program. Where an applied arts course of study is being prepared, the local aims for the program should be reviewed so that the course being designed will contribute to the designated area.

It is not essential to have any one course contribute to the fulfillment of all the general or departmental aims — in fact, this would probably be impossible for a single course. The course should, however, contribute

---

[11]In this sense the term "course" is interpreted generically as one instructional program.

to the fulfillment of educational aims in some unique manner. For VAE courses, this uniqueness might be found in any of these:

1. **Teaching a body of knowledge covered only by a specific course** — the course content. For example, the processes of forming metals into various shapes are unique to metalworking.
2. **Methods that are effective in VAE** — different methods may be needed to convey instruction to individuals with varying education and social backgrounds and capacities for learning. For example, one person may understand how an electric motor operates from a lecture or chalk talk while another may develop this understanding by building a small motor.
3. **Development of interpersonal relationships** — providing an opportunity for students to assume responsibility for organizing and maintaining the laboratory activities can contribute to the development of these abilities.
4. **Integration of education** — for example, in applied arts such segments of education as science, mathematics, communications, and vocational skills may be integrated into a carefully planned instructional program.

Other examples are possible. Without uniqueness a course is difficult if not impossible to justify. The specific goals for the course should, therefore, show its unique contribution.

Review Goals Developed for Similar Courses

Reviewing the goals for similar courses developed by other teachers is an excellent method of obtaining ideas for developing a clearer understanding of purposes for a specific course. These goals may be reviewed in a college library where courses of study are on file, by contacting teachers in other schools teaching similar programs, by contacting teachers through local or state professional organizations, or by contacting a state consultant for VAE. The best single source for locating VAE instructional programs is through the abstracts published in the AIM documents (described in Chapter 5), CVTE, The Ohio State University.

Determine Needs of Students to Be Enrolled in a Course

The specific needs of the students to be enrolled in the course should be identified. The strengths and weaknesses of the students need to be studied to ascertain how the course might contribute to their growth and development. Generally, the goals for a specific course take on unique characteristics and individuality as they become concerned with the needs of students. Such factors as the previous experiences of the

Educational Justification 229

students have a real bearing on goals to be established. These data may be secured from such sources as school records, personal interviews, and data sheets. The needs of students become especially important in occupational education courses being designed to upgrade technical and skilled workers in a community.

Specific Goals Need to Be Simply Stated

When specific goals for a course are developed, it is important to remember that these statements should simply and accurately describe the course. They should not be general or vague but should be tailored to give direction to the behavioral objectives and the instructional program. When goals for a course of study are carefully developed, they completely delineate the parameters for instruction. This permits students, counselors, and parents to appraise the course accurately and thereby place it in proper perspective in the student's program. Course goals also serve as cornerstones for the development of the entire course. Figure 8-4 shows how specific course goals guide and direct the organization of a course.

It can readily be seen from Fig. 8-4 that the goals and behavioral objectives represent the focal point for the instructional program. Their importance in guiding the development of course content, methods of instruction, and evaluation procedures cannot be overemphasized.

As a teacher, or curriculum team, prepares a few specific goals for a course, the purpose should be to write statements which accurately describe the parameters of the course or program in terms of what the student is expected to achieve. The remainder of this topic will be given to a series of examples that show characteristics of a specific course goal and selected examples from VAE courses or programs of study or curriculum guides that illustrate what is being suggested.

Examples of Course Goals

Selected examples of course goals, under five headings, will illustrate the structure of these goals.

Course Goal — Exploration or a Desired Degree of Skill

Such factors as exploration and standards for skill may be incorporated. Examples:
- **General industrial arts in a junior high school** — To provide exploratory experiences in industrial materials and processes.
- **Junior high graphic arts** — To develop a "use level"[12] of skill with selected tools and processes employed in the graphic arts industry.
- **Senior high distributive education program** — To develop employment level competencies in general merchandising with special consideration given to advertising services, finance, and credit.

[12]Defined on p. 206.

Planning and Organizing Instruction

Philosophy of Education

General Aims
of Education

Departmental or Local
Aims of Education

SPECIFIC COURSE GOALS

BEHAVIORAL OBJECTIVES

Course Content

Methods of
Instruction

Evaluation
Process

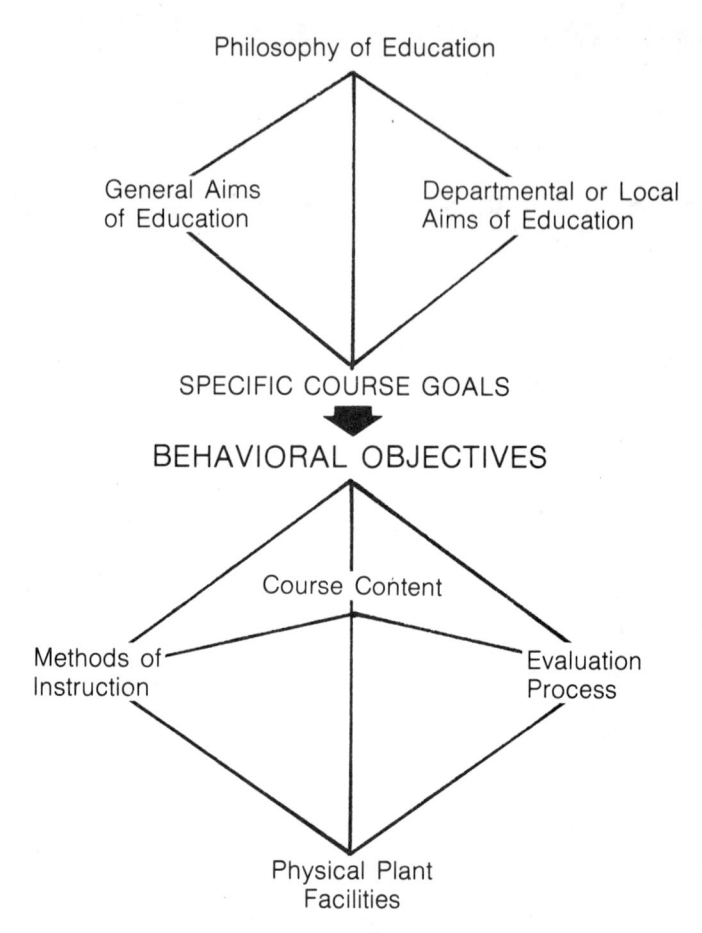

Physical Plant
Facilities

Fig. 8-4. This chart of the organizational development of a course of study shows how the various sections are interrelated. Materials are developed as teachers consider the steps from the top to the bottom of the chart. Connecting lines indicate dependency and integration.

The upper section describes the total course. The lower section, starting with behavioral objectives, represents the instructional units designed to fulfill course goals. Each instructional unit has behavioral objectives and may consist of any or all of the elements shown in the lower half of the figure.

- **Senior high homemaking** — To develop an understanding of the individual's role in the home and family living.
- **Welding at an area vocational school** — To teach the student a series of welding operations at a job-entry level to qualify for employment as a welder or in some other related field.
- **Nursing arts at a community college** — To develop the degree of skill in basic nursing procedures that will enable the student to practice as an aide or helper to professional and practical nurses in the hospital or in the home.
- **Culinary arts at a community college** — To acquire an occupational level of skill in the preparation of entrées: soups, salads, and sandwiches — as served in a commercial food establishment.

Course Goal — Related Informational Content

Such goals would encompass the considerations to be given to technical and general informational content.[13] Examples:

- **General drafting in a junior high school** — To develop an understanding of the drafting industry through interesting problems, experiences, and technical and general drafting information fundamental to industrial and architectural drafting.
- **High school occupational cluster program in building construction** — To develop an understanding of building functions, location, and design as they apply to industry, business, and residential activities.
- **Nursing arts at a community college** — To identify contacts regarding programs in nursing education, and to explore the opportunities for graduates in both the practical and professional fields of nursing.
- **Culinary arts at a community college** — To develop a functional employment level knowledge of cost control of quantity food preparation, portion control, menu formulation and terminology, and dining room operation.

Course Goal — Development of Desired Attitudes

These statements should be directed to such issues as attitude toward care of equipment, safety precautions, efficiency, honesty, integrity, and cooperation. Examples:

- **General industrial arts in a junior high school** — To develop desirable personal traits and attitudes, including good work habits and good social relationships.
- **Senior high school driver education** — To develop safety consciousness in using and caring for the automobile.
- **Senior high home economics program in child development** — To develop a wholesome and constructive attitude toward working with co-workers and supervisors through participation in a student-directed organization.
- **Senior high automotive mechanics** — To understand the value of knowing "why" as he/she is learning "how."

[13]The Fryklund classification for informational topics (1970, 70-77).

Fig. 8-5. An adult student learns automobile body repair. (East Los Angeles Occupational Center, Los Angeles)

- Senior high school distributive education program — To develop effective work habits, a feeling of responsibility, and ability to plan and execute work independently and in cooperation with others.
- Senior high school business education program in introduction to office machines — To teach the student to appreciate the use of time and budget it wisely so assignments can be accomplished in a businesslike manner during the class period.

Course Goal — Educational, Personal, and Career Guidance

Here the goals should be stated to provide opportunity for the students to discover their interests and aptitudes, as well as investigate further educational facilities. Examples:

- General industrial arts in a junior high school — To provide information about careers, needed capabilities, and the potential rewards of industry.
- Senior high automotive mechanics — To acquaint the student with the industry, working conditions, and occupational opportunities.
- Automotive body repair at an area vocational school — To provide

information about the advantages and disadvantages of positions in the automotive body repair industry.
- **General drafting in a junior high school** — To help discover aptitudes and abilities the student possesses in graphic communications which will assist in making a wise career choice.
- **Business education in a senior high school** — To provide information and experiences that will create an understanding of occupations related to the business world.
- **Distributive education course in marketing analysis at a community college** — To acquaint those enrolled with the scope of opportunities in the marketing field.

Course Goal — Desirable Appreciations

Under this heading should be goals directed towards developing appreciation for industrial design, craftsmanship, and working relationships. Teaching the student to be a critical and intelligent consumer is often listed as an important goal in applied arts. Examples:
- **Senior high school automotive mechanics** — To develop student ability in evaluating personal needs and desires, and selecting the automobile which best fulfills his/her established criteria.
- **Industrial drafting in a senior high school** — To develop an appreciation of drafting in industry as a form of modern graphic expression.
- **Instruction in apprenticeship for die constructing** — To require the apprentice to coordinate the machine and bench operations in the construction of a die so that the individual maintains a uniform method of construction to avoid wasting time in the construction of a die.

Other Goals

Other goals which may be used are (1) to provide for creativity and problem-solving experiences, and (2) to prepare for off-the-job activities.

Phraseology of Goal Statements

Note that the statements of goals are started with such phrases as "to provide," "to develop," "to acquaint," "to determine," "to foster," and "to show." By forcing the course goals into this pattern, the teacher is better able to present material in terms of expected accomplishment. Essentially, the teacher is saying, "This course or program is designed and developed to do these things for the student," and that he/she will provide the learning experiences so that the students may reflect this degree of attainment. The statement following the word "to" describes one important segment of the planned course or program. The goals, of course, set the stage for the next step which is to formulate the behavioral objectives in terms of expected behavioral development.

234 Planning and Organizing Instruction

In formulating a few goals for any course or program, teachers must be creative and practical in their approach. They need to have a sound philosophy of education as it contributes to a "good life," "good school," "good community," and a "well-integrated student." The teacher or teaching team needs to be fully acquainted with all the conditions that should be considered to tailor the course or program to the students' needs. The goals should be practical so teachers can clearly see the type of activity that would bring about student growth and development in terms of these statements. They should be phrased in the teachers' words, for it is then that they will fully understand them and champion the program that would provide for having these statements serve as "goal posts." All too frequently teachers have copied statements of aims from other courses of study. This often results in overall goals that are out of focus with the behavioral objectives, content, methods, and evaluation procedures for the course. Writing the goals, then, for any course or program is a creative job for professional teachers.

Goals for Selected Courses or Programs

A number of examples of goals are provided to illustrate the manner in which goals describe the instructional program. The first set of goals is shown on p. 150, Chapter V, where a high school power mechanics program is described.

The curriculum goals for the Oregon career cluster in Clerical Occupations are designed for a diverse group of students. These goals prepare students, according to their interests and abilities, (1) to become productively employed in clerical positions upon graduation from high school, or (2) to continue their training, if desired, in a post-high-school instruction. This cluster program is planned to develop these competencies:

1. To make and keep an accurate log of customer appointments.
2. To type and prepare correspondence according to current standards and practices.
3. To type forms and reports accurately and efficiently.
4. To handle mail properly, whether incoming our outgoing.
5. To file and retrieve correspondence and other business papers and documents.
6. To handle and keep accurate records of money transactions.
7. To observe proper telephone etiquette.[14]

The curriculum goals for the **forest products** cluster program for the State of Oregon provide for having students prepared (1) to become productively employed in an entry-level occupation in the forest products industry upon graduation from high school, or (2) to enter

[14]Reprinted from p. 17 of the **Oregon Occupational Cluster Guide for the Clerical Occupations**, courtesy Oregon Board of Education.

specialized post-high-school training programs. Students who complete a forest products cluster program should have:

1. Attitudes and knowledge necessary to accept responsibility as working members of the forest products industry.
2. Knowledge of the application, use, and maintenance of hand and portable power tools and machines common to the forest products industry.
3. Habits and attitudes that reflect an intelligent concern for safety in working with tools, machines, and equipment.
4. Knowledge of forest products, equipment, and raw materials — their uses and characteristics, and the basic processing flow.
5. A basic understanding of the various forest products industries and occupations, and their interrelationships.
6. Ability to understand and use the language symbols, mathematics, and science of the forest products industries.[15]

The following five goals are for a **drafting course** specifically designed for students in apprenticeship programs. This course is for students from a broad mix of trade curriculums at the Schoolcraft College:

1. To develop the ability to understand and interpret industrial drawings and to communicate through the drafting media.
2. To teach the fundamental drafting techniques and investigate their application in problem solving.
3. To develop neat work habits, systematic procedures, and proper use of drafting tools.
4. To test the depth of interest in drafting.
5. To be able to apply drafting in the trade areas, and to analyze the interrelationships of this media in the various trades.[16]

Relationship between General Aims for Education, Departmental Aims, and Goals for a Course

It has now been established how aims for the total educational effort are agreed upon, how departmental or subject aims may be cooperatively developed, and how professional teachers need to formulate operational goals for each of the programs or courses. Teachers, then, at this point need to think through the relationship that should exist between these three levels and be concerned with educational justification for instruction.

---

[15]Reprinted from p. 48 of the Oregon Occupational Cluster Guide for the **Forest Products** industry, courtesy Oregon Board of Education.

[16]These goals were developed by Kenneth M. Schultz when serving as coordinator of the apprenticeship program, Schoolcraft College, Livonia, Michigan.

Before teachers in any one of the major divisions of a school system, such as those in social studies or those concerned with the applied arts and vocational subjects, could defend the goals formulated to give direction to their phase of the program, they need to ascertain how their offerings and effort are contributing to the desired overall educational effort. This would suggest that representatives from major divisions of a school or school system — (1) fine arts, (2) exact science, (3) social science, (4) English and communication, (5) health education, (6) applied arts and vocational education — evaluate the contributions of, and establish responsibilities for, each of the divisions contributing to the overall educational program. If the aims for a major department or division of a school, school system, or college are out of focus with the total educational efforts — as envisioned and subscribed to by the administration, others in the profession, and the community — the program of that division or department could hardly expect to prosper.

It is obvious that it is equally important for each of the courses or programs within the division or department to contribute to the aims for the department and the expected outcomes from these courses. Often there are gaps between the published aims for a department and the outcomes from the courses that are maintained. Such gaps could well come from insufficient funds or staff to organize and maintain needed courses. Where desired aims cannot be fulfilled for such reasons, it is important that such conditions be made a matter of record and transmitted to administration.

There needs to be cooperative effort between all teachers to ascertain how envisioned aims for an organizational division may contribute to the total growth and development of learners. The teacher of industrial drafting, for example, should look upon his/her courses as they contribute to the total education of the youth who participate in the classes. The teacher needs to work quickly to remove the hypothetical walls that have sprung up around departments in America's schools. There is no place for "air-tight" instructional departments in public schools. This does not mean that behavioral objectives and subject matter are secondary, nor are they an end in themselves. They are the keys that enable teachers to work closely with the entire faculty in a school in providing an educational effort directed at the maximum growth and development of each of the learners in that institution.

Techniques for Showing How Course Goals Contribute to Fulfillment of Department Aims and Overall Aims for Education

Figure 8-6 shows the relationship between the various levels of aims for education and a philosophy of education. Since the **general aims for education** must support a statement of **philosophy of education**, an educator will be able to accept a list of general aims only after determining that they are in harmony with a statement of his/her **philosophy of education** and that held by leaders in the field.

Educational Justification 237

```
                    ┌──────────────────────┐
                    │ A PHILOSOPHY OF EDUCATION │
                    │         for a          │
                    │   DEMOCRATIC SOCIETY   │
                    └──────────────────────┘
                              ↑
                              ↓                    ┌──────────────────────────┐
                    ┌──────────────────────┐       │ Aims are needed for each of │
                    │ GENERAL AIMS FOR AN  │───────│ these organizational divi-  │
                    │ EDUCATIONAL PROGRAM¹⁷│       │ sions of a school that con- │
                    └──────────────────────┘       │ tribute to accepted general │
                                                   │ over-all aims.              │
                                                   └──────────────────────────┘
```

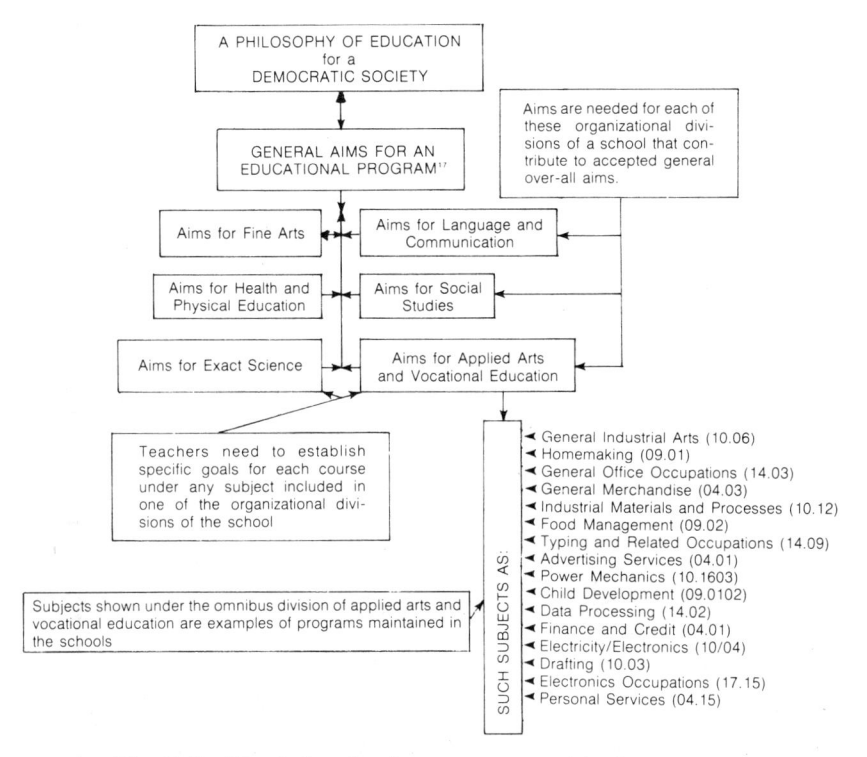

Fig. 8-6. Chart showing how any one subject may contribute to a total educational effort.

Aims for Fine Arts ↔ Aims for Language and Communication
Aims for Health and Physical Education ↔ Aims for Social Studies
Aims for Exact Science ↔ Aims for Applied Arts and Vocational Education

Teachers need to establish specific goals for each course under any subject included in one of the organizational divisions of the school

Subjects shown under the omnibus division of applied arts and vocational education are examples of programs maintained in the schools

SUCH SUBJECTS AS:
◀ General Industrial Arts (10.06)
◀ Homemaking (09.01)
◀ General Office Occupations (14.03)
◀ General Merchandise (04.03)
◀ Industrial Materials and Processes (10.12)
◀ Food Management (09.02)
◀ Typing and Related Occupations (14.09)
◀ Advertising Services (04.01)
◀ Power Mechanics (10.1603)
◀ Child Development (09.0102)
◀ Data Processing (14.02)
◀ Finance and Credit (04.01)
◀ Electricity/Electronics (10/04)
◀ Drafting (10.03)
◀ Electronics Occupations (17.15)
◀ Personal Services (04.15)

¹⁷Reference is made here to acceptance of one of the well-known and published lists of general aims or a list that is being proclaimed by some responsible professional group.

Most curricula are now administered by having subjects with similar activities grouped for organizational purposes, as illustrated by the VAE grouping in Fig. 8-6. Usually one teacher in each of these divisions or departments is designated by the administration, or elected by the personnel in the division, to serve as chairman or department head. This is done to facilitate communication and cooperation among staff within each organizational division. Where schools are organized in this manner, an early project for such a faculty group might well be the formulation of overall aims for the organizational division. These departmental aims should show the contribution that each division will make to the established overall aims for the total educational effort. This will automatically call for the interrelationships that should be established between the departments. In general, professional teachers are interested in showing how each department contributes to the whole

238 Planning and Organizing Instruction

educational program rather than considering the functions of any one program as an end within itself. It is important for all teachers to see that it is only when the essential courses are provided and taught in each and every division that the overall aims for the program are fulfilled. The aims that would be acceptable for a program of secondary education in most communities could never be attained without suitable offerings in exact science or any one of the other major instructional areas. Unfortunately with the present pattern of school districts, the high school population is still so small in many communities that many secondary schools have been unable to provide needed work in physics, mathematics, applied

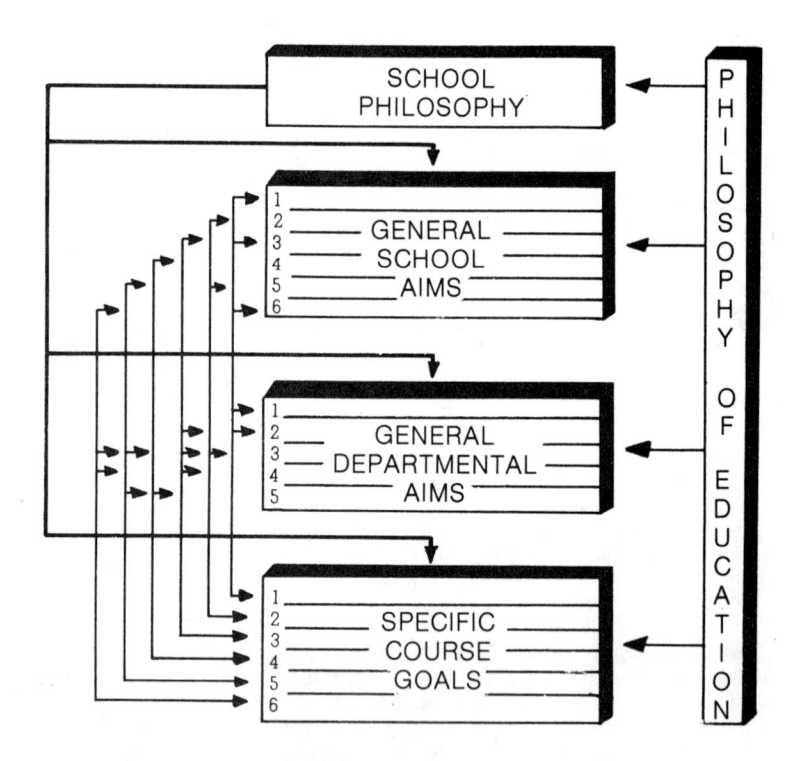

Fig. 8-7. This is an effective technique for showing the relationships between the aims for a school, department, and a course, and their relationship to a philosophy of education and the philosophy of the school. (Courtesy, H. C. Kazanas, Professor, Department of Practical Arts and Vocational-Technical Education, University of Missouri, Columbia, Missouri)

GOALS FOR AMERICAN EDUCATION

1. The schools must close the gap between scientific advance and social retardation.
2. The schools must prepare individuals to create and live in a cooperative independent society.
3. The schools must extend the interest and concern of people in international cooperation and maintenance of a just and durable peace.
4. The schools must help in securing acceptance of the ideals of democracy in social, economic, and political arrangements.
5. The schools must develop values that will serve to guide the individual toward high standards of moral conduct and ethical living.
6. The schools must provide for the development of creative abilities and afford avenues for expression in constructive activities.
7. The school must insure the mastery of the common integrating knowledge and skills necessary to effective living.

INDUSTRIAL EDUCATION IN THE COMPREHENSIVE HIGH SCHOOLS

Industrial Education in the comprehensive high schools of the United States, grades 10-12, should be maintained in shops, laboratories, or drafting rooms especially designed and equipped:

1. to provide a comprehensive curriculum to meet the specific needs of students with varying abilities, aptitudes, desires, and interests. This calls for an instructional program:

    a. for the student (or team of students) with a burning interest in one or more of the industrial arts activities to do intensive research and planning, to use modern tools and machines, and to use the most appropriate materials in the construction of a project. The emphasis should be on problem solving and the application of scientific principles through creative manipulative experiences.

    b. to provide fundamental and essential occupational preparation for selected students entering community occupations from high school.

    c. with basic courses in industrial mechanics with content cast in industrial chemistry, electricity and electronics, hydraulics, machine shop, industrial drafting and descriptive geometry, basic power system, instrumentation and automation, and applied physics and mathematics for college-bound students planning to become technicians, engineers, or industrial education teachers.

    d. that includes a home planning course to help young men and women develop skills and insights needed to intelligently plan for their homes.

    e. to provide information about industrial and related occupations, and an understanding of American industry for the educational and career guidance of youth.

2. to provide opportunity for students to assume responsibility in organizing and maintaining industrial arts activities to develop safe work habits, and desired interpersonal relationships in work situations.

3. to provide an interesting and effective learning climate for youth that may be adapted to their individual differences and needs.

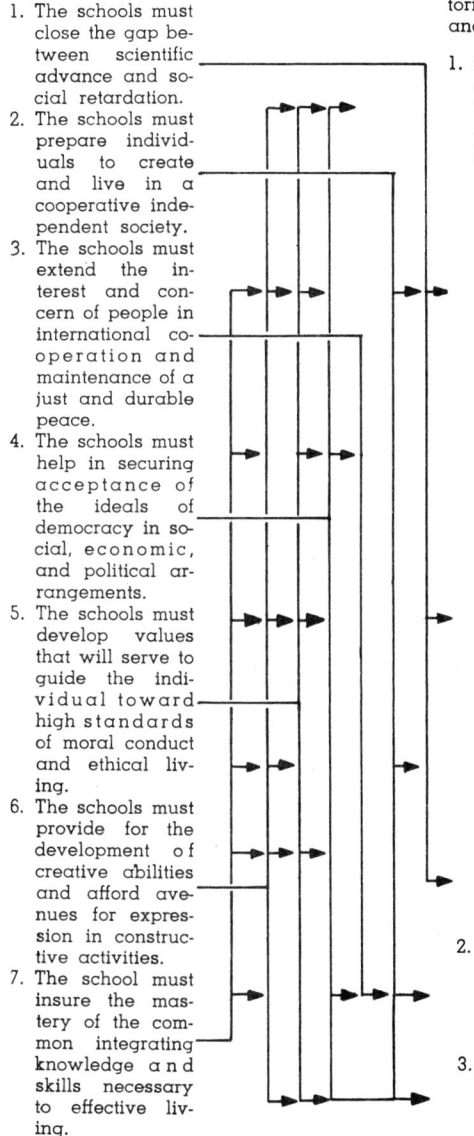

Fig. 8-8. This chart graphically conveys the interrelationships between general aims and aims for industrial education in comprehensive high schools. (**The Goals for American Education** were used, courtesy American Federation of Teachers.)

240 Planning and Organizing Instruction

Aims for Engineering Drawing Section of the Product Engineering Department at General Motors Institute

1. To provide the engineering student with sufficient engineering drawing knowledge so he may be prepared for study in advanced engineering design courses.

2. To provide the student with classroom and laboratory experience, combining theoretical with practical applications of engineering drawing techniques, needed for successful completion of plant drawing room assignments.

3. To develop student ability to accomplish progressively difficult assignments in engineering graphics, accept increasing responsibility, and exercise greater initiative.

4. To provide technical training and practice in the use of engineering graphics, needed by professional engineers, for a concept of and experimental approach beyond that of engineering formulas.

Specific Goals for Engineering Drawing I
(Stated in terms of student's ability)

1. To understand and properly use standard drafting equipment and instruments.

2. To produce, read, and analyze commercially acceptable detail product drawings complete with dimensions, notes, and specifications.

3. To understand and use the knowledge and techniques of engineering graphics including freehand drawings, pictorial drawings (oblique and isometric), and graphical presentation of data.

4. To work intuitively, to follow directions, and to respect supervisory authority.

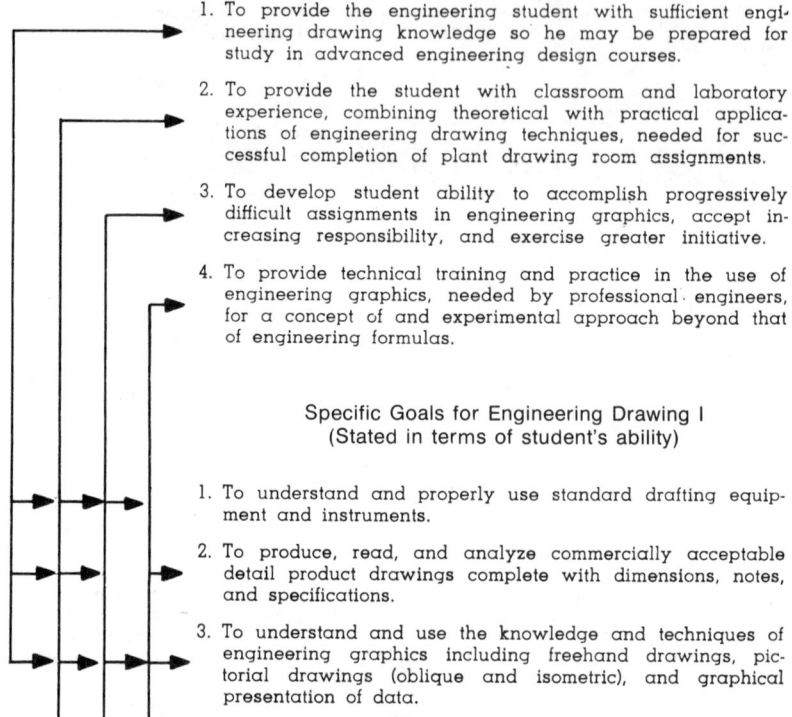

Fig. 8-9. This chart shows how goals for a specific course contribute to fulfillment of aims for a department. (Courtesy William C. Schneider, Teacher, Product Engineering Department, General Motors Institute, Flint, Michigan)

arts, vocational education, and chemistry. Citizens in such communities need to understand fully that their youth are being deprived of educational opportunity to develop in terms of the desired aims for the total educational effort. This should suggest that VAE teachers be well versed in the essential subjects for organizational divisions as now identified in **Handbook VI** (Putnam et al., 1970 x + 317) and entitled **Standard Terminology for Curriculum and Instruction in Local and State School Systems.**

Educational Justification

Functional techniques are needed for presenting the relationships between the general aims for education, the aims for a specialized program within a school system, and the specific goals for one course. The examples in Figs. 8-7, 8-8 and 8-9 were chosen as different approaches that have been used by teachers to show how their specific courses contribute to the fulfillment of accepted aims for an overall educational program. Appendix H of this book illustrates a contemporary approach for illustrating such relationships.

Stating Behavioral Objectives

A behavioral objective should describe the specific behavior to be demonstrated by the learner when the desired outcome has been achieved. This contrasts with the overall goals for the course which are stated in more general terms since they delineate the parameters for instruction. Behavioral objectives state how the learner should demonstrate or show evidence of what he knows or is able to do. Often the introductory phase of a behavioral objective specifies conditions or defines what is given to the learner. For example (conditions underlined):

2. Given several resistors to be connected in parallel, a power supply, voltmeter, VOM, and an ohmmeter, the learner will, with the aid of the meters:
   (a) find the resistance of each resistor and the total resistance of the circuit.
   (b) find the voltage at any point in the circuit.
   (c) find the current through each resistor and the total current.[18]

3. Given a test of aptitudes from the General Aptitude Test Battery (GATB), the student will be able to identify his (her) three highest aptitudes measured by the test.[19]

Robert J. Janeczko (1970, 48) has observed that the format and usefulness for measurable behavioral objectives varies from teacher to teacher depending upon the skill and ingenuity of the individual. In examples taken from a course in power mechanics, the statements consider (1) tasks, (2) conditions, and (3) performance criteria. For example:

---

[18] Behavioral Objective No. 2 from packet No. 11, on PARALLEL CIRCUITS, Electronics course at the University of Northern Colorado, Greeley, Colorado (explained in Chapter 3).

[19] The third behavioral objective from the materials organized as the INTRODUCTION, Packet O, to Jelden's Learner Controlled Education program. Dr. David L. Jelden schedules students in his Electronics program for the GATB and the **Edwards Personal Preference Schedule** (EPPS) to determine aptitude and personal adjustment measures for participation in self-pacing instruction for individual development.

TASK 2: Given a list of five technical magazine articles, the student will select two and prepare a written analysis.
Conditions: Time: one week, outside of class, typewritten, double spaced, not more than two pages each in length.
Criterion: Identify the author's major purpose, at least two subordinate themes and explain their relationship to the central purpose and the author's conclusions.

TASK 3: Given a four-cycle internal combustion engine with a pulse-jet carburetor, properly adjust the carburetor with a hydraulic dynamometer.
Conditions: Time: twenty minutes, temperature 75°, Atm press. 14.7 psi, 36% RH ± 5%.
Criterion: Idle speed: 1000 ± 50 rpm.
Vacuum: 18" @ idle ± 1" of Hg.
Load: 7.5 psi @ 3500 rpm ± .5 psi.
Fuel consumption: 9#/hr. @ 3500 rpm ± .5#/hr.

EXAMPLE

AN EXAMPLE OF A PERFORMANCE
GOAL FOR AVIATION MECHANICS AT
THE AERO MECHANICS VOCATIONAL SCHOOL
IN DETROIT[20]

Student Performance Goal (Level 2)
for Operation of a Basic Hydraulic System

Given:
Reference manuals, drawings, diagrams, mock-ups, or components installed in an aircraft hydraulic system.

Performance:
The student will diagram a basic hydraulic system, and explain the relationship, purpose, and function of each component in the system.

Standard:
Correct nomenclature and terminology will be used in all explanations and descriptions.

---

[20]Contributed by Welton L. Lawrence, teacher, Detroit Public Schools. Example selected from A National Study of the Aviation Mechanics Occupation, A Report by David Allen, Principal Investigator (1970, ERIC Reference No. 044 531).

A Definition of a Level 2 Performance Goal

Levels of instruction basically refer to the proficiency at which each performance goal in the curriculum must be taught. In the study conducted by Allen et al it was found that a three-level structure was needed. Briefly defined:

Level 1
> Know — basic facts and principles. Be able to find information and follow directions and written instructions. No skill demonstration is required.

Level 2 (applies to the example cited)
> Know and understand — principles, theories and concepts. Be able to find and interpret information and perform basic operations. A high level of skill is not required.

Level 3
> The third level focuses on the student's ability to abstract and synthesize material so that he/she can recognize common factors within a complex problem and draw upon many sources and types of information to formulate its solution. An entry level of occupational skill is required.

Each of the major instructional units is subdivided into a number of segments of instructions. These segments are complete entities in themselves and each has its own level of attainment.

Experienced teachers recognize that no two learners will perform the same task at the same rate or with equal proficiency. This is most apparent where tools are used to shape and form materials for psychomotor skill development. Rate and proficiency are, therefore, very significant variables that must be considered carefully when behavioral objectives are written. In considering these issues, David S. Bushnell (1970, 14) suggests that there be

> ... appropriately classified performance objectives [or behavioral objectives] that would describe with precision the minimal levels of performance that each trainee should be able to achieve. This does not ignore the fact that such trainees could go well beyond the minimally sufficient level. However, it [a catalog of appropriately classified performance objectives] would describe the adaptive, functional, and specific content skills needed to qualify for a given occupation.

Teachers about to write behavioral objectives for a module of instruction, course, or program will want to study the examples included in Appendix P and throughout this topic. These objectives may:

1. Mention "the **student**," "**learner**," or "**you**" (when the pronoun of the second person is used) in the introductory part of the statement. This

is done to make it clear that the student is expected to assume responsibility for the specified behavior to be acquired. This is in contrast to something to be performed (or taught) only by the teacher. It will be noted that some teachers simply bypass the words "student," "learner," or "you" in their objectives. They simply expect this to be understood.
2. Describe the **behavior** in relation to the task to be mastered by the learner. This is introduced with a verb that describes observable action and the results to be evaluated and possibly demonstrated.
3. Define the **conditions** covering restrictions and limitations (such as time limits) to be placed on the learner and the kind and specifications for instructional materials and equipment to facilitate the activity.
4. Define the **standards** to be met, or criteria, for acceptable performance (i.e., the degree of skill to be met in the performance of a task such as a hand or machine tool operation) unless perfection is attainable.

Edward E. Byers and Harry H. Huffman et al (1971, vii + 107) developed a manual for vocational and technical educators that is entitled: **Writing Performance Goals: Strategy and Prototypes.** This document was sponsored jointly by the McGraw-Hill Book Company and The Center for Vocational and Technical Education (CVTE) at The Ohio State University. This manual has prototypes of performance goals (behavioral objectives) for the VAE curriculum areas of agriculture education, business and distributive education, health education, home economics, education, technical education, and trade and industrial education.

Summary

Prior to identifying course content, a strong justification for the course or program must be established. A well-planned justification includes a set of course or program goals which carefully describe the expected attainment for each student. These course goals can then be used to identify the specific behavioral objectives and instructional content for each unit or module of instruction. The specific nature of behavioral objectives helps identify content, methods, and evaluation for each unit or module.

Course or program goals provide general justification for a course or program. Behavioral objectives are more specific and are prepared for each unit or module of instruction. Less specific and more universal in presentation are the subject area, school, and general aims of education. These aims describe total subject areas, such as industrial arts, or the overall aims of education, such as the Cardinal Principles. It is important that course goals relate to these broader aims since the justification of a course or program, and even a unit or module of instruction, is based on its fulfilling part of one or more of the general aims of education.

The justification for a course or program is, therefore, the degree it can be shown that an accurate and descriptive set of course goals contributes to an appropriate set of overall aims of education.

For Self-Assessment and Discussion

1. Define general education.
2. Explain how applied arts contributes to general education:
   a. In elementary education.
   b. In junior high schools.
   c. At the senior high school level.
   d. In adult education programs.
3. What is the basic difference between general and specialized education?
4. Does vocational education ever contribute to general education?
5. Is there a place for applied arts as specialized education?
6. Explain shifts in emphasis in vocational and technical education during the last fifteen years.
7. Identify lists of the well-known, overall aims for public education.
8. Are the "Seven Cardinal Principles of Secondary Education" outdated?
9. Is industry looking more and more to public schools to train workers?
10. With increased life expectancy, what should be the responsibility of applied arts education for senior citizens?
11. What should be the basic differences between the way an aim or goal is stated for a department and for a specific course or program within the department? To illustrate these differences, cite examples of such statements in your area of concentration.
12. Define the type of behavior that is identified with these domains:
    a. The cognitive domain.
    b. The affective domain.
    c. The psychomotor domain.
13. Why is it more difficult to assess learning outcomes in the affective domain?
14. Often it is difficult for a teacher to sharply classify a stated objective in one of the three major domains of learning. Why has this been so?
15. What is the basic difference between "criterion-referenced" and "norm-referenced" evaluation of learning outcomes?
16. The importance of having the goals for a VAE course make a unique contribution was discussed in this chapter. Describe these unique factors for courses that you are qualified to teach.
17. Where could a VAE teacher turn to find source materials that would be helpful when formulating the goals for a course of study?
18. What would be the disadvantage of bypassing the relationships that exist between course and departmental aims and simply showing the direct contribution that the aims for a course make to the goals for the total educational program?
19. Why do many educators now believe that it is imperative to organize instruction to fulfill specific behavioral objectives? Why do other educators take such a strong position against the use of behavioral objectives?

246 Planning and Organizing Instruction

20. Distinguish between "major" and "minor" (or interim) instructional objectives.
21. What are the essential factors to be included in the format of behavioral objectives for your area of specialization?

Assignments to Demonstrate Competencies

1. Examine all lists of overall aims for public education available from your local school, state department of education, or from professional councils or associations within your state. Where such lists are not available from local or state sources, examine those advocated by national associations, councils, or groups and the ones included in professional books.

    Select one of the lists that is in keeping with your philosophical approach to education, and to which you could personally subscribe as a professional teacher. Prepare copies for your course of study. Carry a complete footnote, in accurate bibliographical form, to give credit to those responsible for the development of the original materials.

2. With the assistance of other qualified teachers, a supervisor, and administration, formulate either:
    a. Departmental aims,
        or
    b. Aims for some specialized educational program within a school system such as the aims for some citywide vocational or technical school.

    For either the "a" or "b" assignment, a brief introductory statement is needed to describe adequately the conditions for these aims. In a very few sentences, or in outline form, provide the information about the school, community, and learner that the reader would need before he/she could intelligently appraise these aims. A footnote should be carried at the end of the statement of aims, giving credit to all persons who assisted or contributed.

3. Formulate specific goals for a VAE course you are qualified to teach. Preface this list with the following:
    1. Name of course.
    2. Prerequisites.
    3. Place of course in curriculum.
    4. Grade level of learners.
    5. Ability and experience of learners.
    6. Time allocation for instruction.

4. With a graphic illustration or a descriptive statement, present the relationships that exist between overall aims for education, departmental aims (or those for a specialized program within a school system), and the specific goals for your course of study. Techniques for showing such relationships will be found beginning on p. 237 and in **Appendix H**.

Educational Justification   **247**

5. Prepare behavioral objectives for a course (or several selected units or modules for the course) that you are qualified or preparing to teach. Your course or series of units or modules must contain objectives for each of the three domains, including:
   a. The cognitive domain (at the third level "Application").
   b. The affective domain (at the fourth level "Organization").
   c. The psychomotor domain (in the third category "Guided Response").

References* and Resources

Books

Beauchamp, George A., and Beauchamp, Kathryn E. **Comparative Analysis of Curriculum Systems.** 2nd Ed., Wilmette, Illinois: Kagg Press, 1972, Pp. viii + 166.

*Bloom, Benjamin S. (ed). **Taxonomy of Education Objectives Handbook I: Cognitive Domain.** New York: David McKay Co. Inc., 1956, Pp. vii + 207.

*Fryklund, Verne C. **Occupational Analysis: Techniques and Procedures.** 5th Edition. New York: The Bruce Publishing Co., 1970, Pp. vi + 213.

*Goldhammer, Keith, and Taylor, Robert E. **Career Education: Perspective and Promise.** Columbus, Ohio: Merrill Publishing Co., 1972, Pp. viii + 296.

*Gronlund, Norman E. **Stating Behavioral Objectives for Classroom Instruction.** New York: The Macmillan Co., 1970, Pp. vi + 58.

Hauenstein, A. Dean. **Curriculum Planning for Behavioral Development.** Worthington, Ohio: Charles A. Jones Publishing Co., 1972. Pages 18-22 cover functional relationships between the cognitive, affective, and psychomotor domains.

*Havighurst, Robert J. **Developmental Tasks and Education.** 2nd ed. New York: Longmans, Green and Co., 1952, Pp. vii + 100.

*_____. "Youth in Exploration and Man Emergent," in **Man in a World of Work,** ed. Henry Borrow. Boston: Houghton Mifflin Co. 1964.

Kibler, Robert J. et al. **Objectives for Instruction and Evaluation,** 2nd ed. (under a new title). Boston: Allyn and Bacon, Inc., 1974, Pp. x + 203.

*Kimbrell, Grady, and Vineyard, Ben S. **Strategies for Implementing Work Experience Programs.** Bloomington, Illinois: McKnight Publishing Co., 1972, Pp. xiv + 290.

Krathwohl, David R. et al. **Taxonomy of Educational Objectives, Handbook II: Affective Domain.** New York: David McKay Co. Inc., 1964, Pp. ix + 196.

*Mager, Robert F. **Goal Analysis.** Belmont, California: Fearon Publishers, 1972, Pp. vi + 136.

_____. **Preparing Instruction Objectives.** Palo Alto, California: Fearon Publishers, 1962, Pp. x + 60.

Mager, Robert F., and Beach Jr., Kenneth M. **Developing Vocational Instruction.** Palo Alto, California: Fearon Publishers, 1967, Pp. x + 84.

McAshan, H.H. **Writing Behavioral Objectives: A New Approach.** New York: Harper & Row, Publishers, 1970, Pp. xi + 116.

Popham, W. James, and Baker Eva L. **Establishing Instructional Goals,** New Jersey: Prentice-Hall, Inc., 1970, Pp. xvii + 130.

_____., and _____. **Planning an Instructional Sequence,** New Jersey: Prentice-Hall, Inc., 1970, Pp. vi + 138.

_____., and _____. **Systematic Instruction,** New Jersey: Prentice-Hall, Inc., 1970, Pp. ix + 166.

*Items with an asterisk have been cited in the chapter.

Periodicals

*Banks, Jane M. "Measuring the Immeasurables: Performance Goals for the Affective Domain." American Vocational Journal, Vol. 48, No. 4 (April, 1973), pp. 36-37.
Bortz, Richard. "Studying the Behavior of Materials," Industrial Arts & Vocational Education, Vol. 59, No. 7 (October, 1970), pp. 25-26.
*Childs, John L. "Enduring Elements in the Educational Thoughts of John Dewey," The University of Michigan School of Education Bulletin, Vol. 31, No. 2 (November, 1959), pp. 19-23.
Deiulio, Anthony M., and Young, James M. "Career Education in the Elementary School." Phi Delta Kappan, Vol. 54, No. 6 (February, 1973), pp. 378-380.
Ebel, Robert L. "Behavioral Objectives: A Close Look," Phi Delta Kappan, Vol. 52, No. 3 (November, 1970), pp. 171-173.
*Janeczko, Robert J. "Behavioral Objectives or Objections," Journal of Industrial Teacher Education, Vol. 7, No. 5 (Summer, 1970), pp. 47-50.
Millman, Jason. "Reporting Student Progress: A Case for a Criterion-Referenced Marking System," Phi Delta Kappan, Vol. 52, No. 4 (December, 1970), pp. 226-227.
Muirhead, Peter P. "Career Education: The First Steps Show Promise." Phi Delta Kappan, Vol. 54, No. 6 (February, 1973), pp. 370-372.
Nash, Robert J., and Agne, Russel M. "Career Education: Earning a Living or Living a Life?" Phi Delta Kappan, Vol. 54, No. 6 (February, 1973), pp. 373-378.
*NEA Research Division. "A New Look at the Seven Cardinal Principles of Education," NEA Journal, Vol. 56, No. 1 (January, 1967), pp. 53-54.
Popham, James W. "The Instructional Objectives Exchange: New Support for Criterion-Referenced Instruction." Phi Delta Kappan, Vol. 52, No. 3 (November, 1970), pp. 174-175.
Smith, Harry T. "Bridging the Grading Gap," School Shop, Vol. XXX, No. 5 (January, 1971), pp. 50-51.
Van Til, William (guest Editor) et al. "Curriculum for the 70's." A special issue of Phi Delta Kappan with Brameld, Foshay, Tanner, Metcalf-Hunt, Hamilton, Wright, Wilhelms, Havighurst, Robinson, Krutch, Engler, Doll, Crosby, and Shane contributing. Vol. 51, No. 7 (March, 1970), Pp. 345-411.

Other Published Materials

*Allen, David et al. A Report of A National Study of the Aviation Mechanics Occupation, Phase III. Project No. 5-0189, Vocational and Technical Education Contract OE-6-85-043, Bureau of Research, US OE, DHEW. Los Angeles, California: Division of Vocational Education, University of California, Los Angeles, 1970. ERIC Reference No. 044 531.
*Bushnell, David S. "A Systems Approach to Curriculum Improvement," a treatise in A Report of a Seminar on Process and Techniques of Vocational Curriculum Development, Edited by Brandon B. Smith and Jerome Moss, Jr. Minneapolis, Minnesota 55455: Research Coordinating Unit for Vocational Education, University of Minnesota, (April, 1970), pp. 11-19.
*Byers, Edward E., and Huffman, Harry H. et al. Writing Performance Goals: Strategy and Prototypes. A Manual for Vocational and Technical Educators. New York: McGraw-Hill Book Co. In The Ohio State CVTE related Series No. 15, 1971, Pp. vii + 101.
*Educational Policies Commission, The Purpose of Education in American Democracy. Washington, D.C.: National Education Association, 1938, Pp. 219.
*Educational Policies Commission, Education for All American Youth. Washington, D.C.: National Education Association. 1944, Pp. 421.
*Educational Policies Commission, Education for All American Youth: A Further Look, Revised Edition, Washington, D.C.: National Education Association, 1952, Pp. xi + 403.

Educational Policies Commission, **Policies for Education in American Democracy.** Washington, D.C.: National Education Association, 1946, Pp. 253.
*Loree, M. Ray. "Relationships Among Three Domains of Educational Objectives," in **Contemporary Issues in Home Economics.** A Conference Report. Washington, D.C.: National Education Association, 1965.
*Moss, Jr., Jerome, and Smith, Brandon B. "Summary of the Discussion." **Processes and Techniques of Vocational Curriculum Development.** Report of a Seminar. Minneapolis, Minnesota: The University of Minnesota, Minnesota Research Coordinating Unit for Vocational Education, April, 1970, pp. 1-8.
*National Association of Secondary School Principals. **The Imperative Needs of Youth of Secondary School Age.** Vol. 31, No. 145, Washington, D.C.: National Education Association, March, 1947.
*National Center for Educational Statistics. **Standard Terminology for Curriculum and Instruction in Local and State School Systems.** State Educational and Records Series: Handbook VI. Compiled and edited by Putnam, John F. et al. Reference No. OE-23052, Supt. of Docs. Catalog No. HE 5.223: 23052, U.S. DHEW, 1970, Pp. x + 317.
*National Education Association, Commission on Reorganization of Secondary Education, **Cardinal Principles of Secondary Education.** Bulletin 35. Washington, D.C.: U.S. Government Printing Office, 1918, Pp. 32.
*Porter, John W. (Superintendent of Public Instruction). **The Common Goals of Michigan Education.** Lansing, Michigan: State Board of Education, September, 1971, Pp. iii + 11.
*Simpson, Elizabeth J. **The Classification of Educational Objectives, Psychomotor Domain.** Reprinted from **Illinois Teacher of Home Economics.** Vol. 10, No. 4 (Winter, 1966-67) as an abstract of research carried on under Vocational and Technical Grant Contract No. OE 5-85-104 (July 1, 1965-May 31, 1966). Urbana, Illinois 61801: Department of Vocational and Technical Education, University of Illinois, June 1970, pp. 111-144.
U.S. Office of Education. **Career Education.** Washington, D.C. 20202: Inquiries Section, USOE, Reference No. OE 73-00501, 1973, Pp. 12. Discusses need for Career Education and describes USOE's school based model (single copies without charge).
U.S. Office of Education. **Comments on Career Education.** Washington, D.C. 20202: Inquiries Section, USOE, Reference No. OE 73-00503, 1973. Carries quotations from Plato to Whitney Young on a single-page foldout showing that philosophers through the ages have advocated education that trains people both to think and earn a living (single copies without charge).

Unpublished Materials

*Simpson, Elizabeth J. **Schema for Classification of Educational Objectives.** Xeroxed release provided by Author, Dean of the School of Family Resources and Consumer Sciences, University of Wisconsin, Madison (n.d.), Pp. 5.

9 CHAPTER

The Instructional Units

The content of the program represents the focal point for all planning, since an entire course revolves around what is presented in the instructional units.

Uniqueness, therefore, must be considered when course or program content is selected. Without this uniqueness, it is difficult to justify the existence of a course in a total instructional program. Education must be even more effective with the ever-increasing amount of content to be transmitted to youth and adults and the ever-increasing complexity of our post-industrial society. Fortunately, the numerous offerings in VAE provide unique contributions to the education of the learners they are designed to serve. The courses classified as applied arts accomplish this through the information and instruction needed to develop an understanding of the tools, skills, and methods that integrate science, the arts, English and communication, and social studies with industrial and business procedures and development for family life. The courses for occupational preparation are unique as they are organized to teach essential saleable skills and technical information used in occupational families. It is, therefore, the uniqueness of the content for any course or program that becomes the basis for its acceptance or rejection as an essential and justified part of a total school program.

Many of the established goals for a course are fulfilled by course content. The selection of the instructional units, the order in which they are taught, and the time devoted to each are all important factors in determining whether the specific course goals are to be properly fulfilled.

This chapter addresses itself to the following:
1. An operational definition for a unit (or module) of instruction.
2. A description of administrative units.
3. The selection and placement of units in an instructional order as a plan for the term's work.
4. The character and organization of instructional units within each of the three possible formats for a course of study as suggested in Chapter 7, namely:
    a. Formal/Descriptive
    b. Modules of Instruction
    c. Class Session Units

5. The arrangement (teaching sequence) of units for VAE programs.
6. Techniques for scheduling instructional units.
7. Factors to be considered in development of units of instruction.
8. Examples of VAE units of instruction.

The Unit of Instruction

A unit of instruction is a principal subdivision of a course of study, subject, or program. Essentially, **it is the smallest amount of instruction that has purpose, interest, unity, and meaning within itself.** In VAE, a unit of instruction involves educational activities centered around a problem (example — **money handling** in the clerical occupations), a sub-area of instruction (example — **patient relationships** in the health occupations), or the instruction that would be associated with a project (example — **thermo-electronic converter** in electronics). It represents a logical division point, a place where students in an instructional program may start and conclude their work for one of the blocks of the total instruction or activity for a course.

Figure 9-1 illustrates how the specific goals for the course provide parameters for needed units of instruction. Appendix H, p. 432, shows

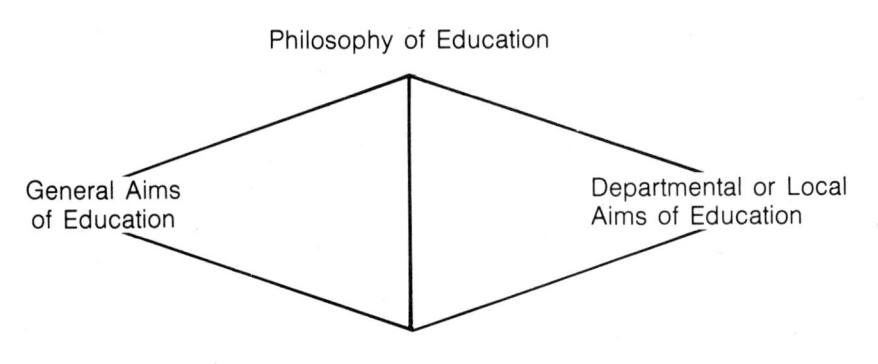

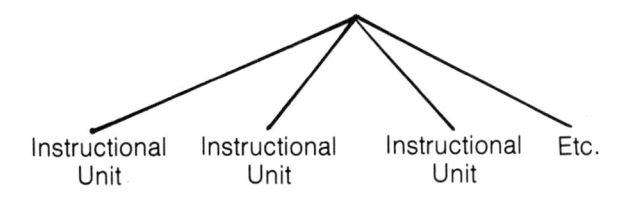

Fig. 9-1. Units of instruction that will fulfill the specific goals for the program need to be designed and developed.

252 Planning and Organizing Instruction

an example of units for a metallurgy course that have been developed from the four specific course goals for the program.

With the acceptance of the systems approach in Education, **the module of instruction** has become synonymous with **unit of instruction**. In this approach to course construction, the module becomes the major unit for a course or program. Each module is specifically designed to provide the educational experiences that will fulfill one or more behavioral objectives, as illustrated in Fig. 9-2. It will be noted from the examples of modules included in this chapter that the behavioral objectives suggest the nature and parameters for the content of such units.

VAE curriculum planners work from the specific course goals in identifying the behavioral objectives and the modules of instruction. Each unit is then carefully planned to provide the educational experiences prescribed by the behavioral objectives for the module. This is essentially what is done in the implementation of the second organizational planning format for instructional program titled "Modules of Instruction" (described in Chapter 7).

Identifying Administrative Units

In addition to subject content, there are other units of instruction that need to be identified and taught. They are concerned with the mechanics of organizing and offering the instruction. It is

BEHAVIORAL OBJECTIVE(S)

Course Content

Methods of Instruction

Evaluation: Product and Process

Facilities for Implementation

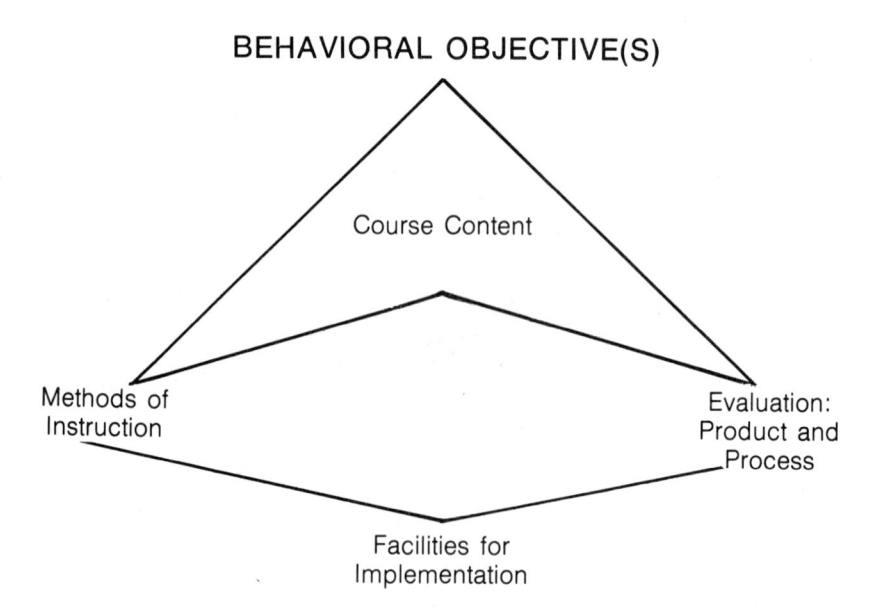

Fig. 9-2. Major factors interrelating in the development of a Module of Instruction.

recommended that they be thought of as the **administrative units of instruction.**

Administrative units become extremely important where selected essential goals for a course are fulfilled through student involvement in the supervision and direction of class activities. Where there is need for a student-directed organization, the plan for it must be carefully analyzed so that the system can be quickly and effectively taught to the learners. A teacher could hardly expect a student safety engineer or a student manager in a homemaking laboratory to be successful if the specific responsibilities were not known and if the members of the class had not been appraised of their cooperative relationships with such officers.

An example of another administrative unit would be the identification and careful analysis of a system for tool or instrument checking and accounting. Many applied arts teachers have developed devices and plans to facilitate the individual progression of students in multiple activity programs. Surely, these evaluation systems need to be clearly understood by students. An example would be the use that might be made of an individual progress chart to facilitate criterion-referenced evaluation (see Chapter 11). Often there is need for student involvement in the collection and utilization of salvage materials. Many VAE laboratories have plans for managing funds from the sale of instructional material. It may be opportune for the teacher to develop special lessons around the care of tools and materials. There are many educational values in having advanced students work as assistants to the teacher, as they assist with the utilization of audiovisual equipment. These examples illustrate typical activities that are essential as students are involved in the routine, supervisory, and administrative work for a course. It is recommended that they be carefully identified and analyzed as the **administrative units.**

Teachers should be cautioned not to be so organized that the "tail wags the dog." It is obvious that it is possible for a VAE teacher to have so many systems and to be so highly organized that too much of the allocated time for a course would be used in teaching the system, while there would be too little time for the subject content. On the other hand, successful teachers know that they need to give as careful consideration to a few well-chosen administrative units as they do to those units concerned with the subject content. Teachers of VAE subjects have often failed, even though well versed in their subjects, when they neglected to give careful attention to matters pertaining to the organization and teaching of their courses. They failed to recognize that administrative units need to be identified, analyzed, and then later taught as integral parts of a course of study.

It is only when students fully understand their role in class activities that a maximum learning climate may be created for studying the subject content. It is through student involvement, too, that the stage is set for the fulfillment of such important goals as these:
1. To provide opportunity for students to assume responsibility in organizing and maintaining class activities.
2. To develop safe work habits and desirable interpersonal relationships in work situations.

Selecting and Placing Unit Titles in an Instructional Order

To select unit titles, the VAE teacher must first study the appropriate content sources for his area of specialization as explained in Chapter 2. If these resource materials are not available, they should be prepared as outlined in Chapter 6. Such preparation calls for the review of many reported research projects, curriculum guides, journals, and other literature. This will bring the teacher (or teaching team) into focus with what others in the field are recommending. It is suggested that a faculty committee made up of those responsible for the VAE program could be of real assistance in reviewing the resource material, such as an instructional analysis, and helping with the development of the plans for the units. In addition, the teacher must determine the organizational format that he plans to use (formal/descriptive, module, or session, as explained in Chapter 7).

When these steps are completed, the curriculum builders are ready to select instructional units which will fulfill the goals established for the course. The units are first selected and listed without consideration for teaching order. After they are selected, the teaching order is then determined. Time requirements for each unit must be estimated as carefully as possible. The number of units must be realistic, for in many courses or programs it is just as important to have the students complete the last units as the first. To make allowances for the more capable students who progress more rapidly, optional units should be prepared which could be interjected during the course or after the basic units are finished.

Since the goals for vocational and technical education programs may be quite different from those in applied arts, the procedures for selecting and placing unit titles in an instructional order will be considered separately. Illustrations are included for both vocational and applied arts courses.

Units for Vocational Courses

Vocational courses need to be based on a carefully constructed occupational analysis. This is necessary to insure proper coverage of essential knowledge, saleable skills, and other competencies.

The organization of the instructional material selected from an instructional analysis may be either formal/descriptive, module, or session. In general, these factors need to be considered when the organizational format is selected.

1. If a vocational course calls for the teaching of manipulative tasks, as identified from an occupational or task analysis in such areas as office occupations, the trade areas of home economics, distributive occupations, or in the building and manufacturing trades, the **formal/descriptive** or **modular** formats could be used. In most cases in the past the formal/descriptive organizational pattern has been used for courses in vocational education.

2. In order to meet the mandates of career education, it seems likely that there will be a greater need for VAE educators to employ the **modular** approach in course construction. This is a logical approach for introducing elementary school children to the world of occupations and in providing for junior high school youth to have exploratory experiences in selected occupational areas.
3. If the vocational course being planned has a limited number of sessions — such as a mini-course in child care, related instruction for apprenticeship, or evening classes to upgrade skilled workers — **the session plan** can be used to advantage.

After the organizational plan is determined for a vocational course, the curriculum builder(s), with the help of an advisory committee, selects the titles for the units of instruction. In the **formal/descriptive** plan of organization, a dual list of units, operational and informational, should be selected from the instructional analysis. When the units for a course using the **formal/descriptive** format of organization is selected, the following must be considered:

1. **Operational Units.**
   a. An occupational or task analysis for the area should be obtained or a partial analysis made, using the procedure outlined in Chapter 2 for the vocational program under preparation. (e.g., The operations for the turning block of the toolmaker's trade are shown in **Appendix D**.)
   b. The number of clock hours of instruction for each course, the number of courses in the sequence, and the number of independent informational units will determine how many operations (manipulative tasks) from the instructional analysis may be selected. This selection will also determine the extent of repetition of operations permitted to develop skill, speed, and understanding. It may be necessary to omit some operations in the interest of essential repetition to develop an occupational level of skill in the basic performance tasks. Operations omitted might be left to on-the-job training. If so, they should be listed for the record.
   c. The methods for teaching the operational units must be determined. A number of operations may be grouped with a project serving as the vehicle for teaching them. It may be that repetitious drills will be needed to provide for an occupational level of skill. It is important, too, that the selected plan combine the desired learning experience with adequate provisions for motivation and student interest and due consideration for the maturity and experiences of the learners.
2. **Independent Informational Units.**
   a. These units are included in the lecture phase of the course and are taught independently of the operational activities. The word **independent** or **lecture** is used to differentiate between instruction essential to the operation and informational topics that are important yet not an integral part of what might be identified with a specific on-the-job manipulative task.

b. The number of hours of instruction for the entire program, the number of courses in the sequence that may be a part of a curriculum, and the number and organization of operational units will determine how many of these informational units from the occupational analysis may be selected.
c. It is important that administrative units necessary for the efficient operation of the program be listed and placed in the instructional order since they are essential for most courses.

Once the titles for the operational units are selected for the **formal/descriptive** format, the units may then be placed in an instructional order. This could be a dual listing with the titles for the operational units in one list and the titles for the independent informational units in the other. The independent informational topics may be an integration of the technical, general, and guidance informational units (Fryklund, 1970, 70-77) and the administrative units or there may be two separate lists — informational and administrative. In some situations, the total listing of units is integrated into a single listing containing all operational, informational, and administrative units in an instructional order.

The instructional order of operational units may be obtained from the occupational analysis or decided while organizing the course. It is extremely important that these units be so arranged that the early ones, particularly in basic or beginning courses, involve only a limited number of common operations or tasks from the occupation. Fryklund (1970, 98-104) recommends techniques for arranging operations to be taught according to their frequency of use. This arrangement permits shop activity to start after a few operations have been taught. In addition, instruction will be continuous over the entire course since each succeeding unit covers one or more additional tasks or operations.

Informational units should be arranged with the same consideration for basic and essential instruction. For example, in an electrical course, the principles of the electric motor, magnetism, inductance, and resistance may be taught. Since the principle of resistance is common to everything listed, it would be logical to have it covered first, followed by magnetism and inductance. Since the operation of the electric motor involves all of the principles, it could be last. Besides this consideration for a teaching order, a dependency of certain operational units on technical information units must be considered. In such areas as the distributive and health occupations, the informational units provide the technical background essential to an understanding of the operational units. This point must be given serious consideration as the complete instructional program is scheduled.

Units for Applied Arts Courses

Applied arts courses usually have broad objectives: to provide orientation, guidance, vocational background through exploration, etc. As a result, applied arts courses must reflect this increased breadth through the selection of units of instruction and the methods by which they are taught.

The organization of instructional materials for applied arts may be either **formal/descriptive, module,** or **session.** However, few applied arts courses are either short enough or have content which permits organization into sessions. In general, applied arts courses are organized using either the **modular** or **formal** formats (as described in Chapter 7). The **modular** format makes provision for demonstrations and experience at the work station in which hand and machine operations, group or individual activities, project construction, reference study, discussions on pertinent topics, and other related activities are utilized. Applied arts instructional programs which have operational and informational units not closely related, or areas having a large number of informational units may be organized formally. It is possible, therefore, to organize applied arts courses using either of these approaches. Traditionally, applied arts courses were organized in the formal/descriptive manner. In recent years, more and more applied arts teachers have turned to the **modular** format for arranging instruction with the units tied closely to problem solving, performing an experiment, making an application of scientific principles, and/or the planning and constructing of an individual or group project.

In selecting content for an applied arts activity, an instructional analysis of that activity, such as those shown in **Appendices A** and **D,** will prove helpful in arranging the instructional order and making certain that desired content is not overlooked. To insure content selection for applied arts which meets the needs of the students, the following should be considered:

1. Select content to fulfill established course goals. When selecting modules of instruction, study the course goals and only select units which contribute to their fulfillment.
2. Select methods in keeping with established course goals. Methods of instruction enrich the program and help fulfill goals concerned with problem solving, leadership ability, and desired attitudes (discussed in Chapter 10). Instructional units need to be selected with consideration for desired methods and class activities. For example, a small object might be selected as a production project to involve all class members. Or a research-type project involving the study of the structure of metals might be developed by one or more students who would later report their findings to the entire class.
3. Select content that is representative of the VAE area of concentration, such as the concept of interchangeability in industrial arts.
4. Content should be selected which challenges students and forces them to utilize their abilities. At the same time, content must be within the capacities of the students. Teaching beyond the capacities of students should be avoided as well as teaching below their ability.
5. The number of hours of instruction for entire course, abilities of students, and size of the class should determine the type and number of modules to be developed from all of the possibilities.

In selecting applied arts content, then, the curriculum builders should refer to available instructional analyses, textbooks, reference books, courses of study, curriculum guides, manuals, reported research, and other literature representative of the course being planned (as explained in Chapter 6). From all possible content, they must then choose that which will fulfill the established course goals, provide challenging and motivational experiences, and be within the abilities and physical limitations of the class members.

If the **modular** format is used, this instructional order will consist of just one list of units. Independent informational and administrative units will be integrated and listed in the order they will be presented to the class.

In arranging the order of instructional units, curriculum builders should keep the same considerations listed for vocational courses in mind. With a larger variety and breadth of units, there will need to be much concern for continuity. Likewise, consideration needs to be given to the methods of teaching the various units. For example, where a unit calls for student presentations, including demonstrations or group activities, classroom planning must start a considerable time before the selected students report their findings to the class. E.g., if a unit on "How Lumber is Cut from Trees" were planned as an activity for a group, the participants would need to start preparation a few weeks before their presentation since they would have to decide on how to present the unit, conduct the research, build demonstration equipment (if this were part of the plan) and/or prepare drawings and sketches before stepping in front of the class.

Examples of Titles for Units Arranged for VAE Programs

Automotive Body Repair

This example carries the titles for instructional units to be developed using the **formal/descriptive** format for a vocational course of study[1] in Automotive Body Repair at an area vocational school. The program provides fifteen hours of instruction per week with minimum time spent on lecture.

The descriptions following the unit titles are brief digests of the content as taken from the unit outline of the course of study. They are placed after the unit title to show the classification of the content and the reason for the order of the units. This information would not be in an actual course of study. It is included to clarify the classification of the units.

This program is primarily based on operational activities. Work is performed on either car panels or actual cars. A few administrative and informational guidance and general informational units are integrated with the operational units. Instruction is presented for nearly all units by teacher demonstration with all necessary information covered while the operations are being demonstrated. This results in only one list of instructional units.

[1]Developed by Richard Christian when an employee of the Detroit Public Schools.

EXAMPLE

1. Introduction-Course Goals, Program Description (administrative).
2. Safety Precautions (informational, general).
3. Shop Organization (administrative).
4. Principles of Body Construction (informational, general).
5. Educational and Occupational Guidance (informational, guidance).
6. Testing Procedures and Grading (administrative).
7. Metal Bumping (operational).
8. Measuring and Layout of Body Sheet Metal (operational).
9. Metal Forming (operational).
10. Metal Finishing (operational).
11. Shrinking Excessive Metal (operational).
12. Heat Treating (operational).
13. Grinding Metal (operational).
14. Leading (operational).
15. Automotive Acetylene Welding (operational).
16. Automotive Acetylene Cutting (operational).
17. Automotive Arc Welding (operational).
18. Automotive Spot Welding (operational).
19. Using Fiber Glass and Plastics (operational).
20. Sanding (operational).
21. Automotive Painting (operational).
22. Reconditioning Interiors (operational).
23. Reconditioning Exteriors (operational).
24. Replacing Window Glass (operational).

Telephone Communications Technology

This example outlines seven major subjects with time allocations for an eleven-month instructional program in Telephone Communications at the Wadena Area Vocational-Technical Institute.[2] The courses of study to implement this program to prepare a central office telephone technician could be developed with either the **formal/descriptive** or **modular** format.

The behavioral objectives for this program call for the student to demonstrate competencies in a broad area of theory and practice in Telephone Central Office Equipment (COE) so that he/she will be qualified to enter the job market as a COE Maintenance Person, COE Installer, PBX Maintenance Person or Installer, or a Key System Installer or Maintenance Person.

[2]This outline was provided by the management team of this institution at Wadena, Minnesota — consisting of Donald C. Hamerlinck (Director), Lowell M. Rasmussen (Assistant Director), and James B. Baymler (Coordinator).

260 Planning and Organizing Instruction

Fig. 9-3. Students in a telephone communication program learn through practical application of instruction. (Courtesy Wadena Area Vocational-Technical Institute)

EXAMPLE

This eleven-month program covers the following subjects:

1. Introduction to Circuit Analysis	220 Hours
2. Transistor Fundamentals	190 Hours
3. Advanced A-C and Vacuum Tubes	140 Hours
4. Advanced Semiconductors	140 Hours
5. Central Office Equipment	340 Hours
6. Carrier Equipment	130 Hours
7. Associated Telephone Equipment	160 Hours
TOTAL	1320 Hours

1. Introduction to Circuit Analysis   7 weeks — 220 Hours
    A. Atomic Structure
    B. Introduction to Direct Current
    C. D-C Circuits
    D. D-C Instrumentation
    E. Magnetism

   F. Introduction to Alternating Current
   G. Calculators and Mathematical Calculations
   H. Introduction to Algebra
   I. First Aid and Safety
   J. Shop Practices and Print Reading

This segment of the program provides the necessary introduction to basic electricity and consists each day of two hours of lecture, two hours of lab, one hour of math, and one hour of shop practices or print reading.

2. Transistor Fundamentals   6 weeks — 190 Hours
   A. Semiconductor Physics
   B. The P-N Junction
   C. Large and Small Signal Diodes
   D. Basic Power Supplies
   E. The Common-Base Circuit
   F. The Common-Emitter Circuit
   G. The Common-Collector Circuit
   H. Large Signal Operation
   I. Bias Arrangement
   J. A-C Operation
   K. Advanced Algebra and Trigonometry
   L. Print Reading and Shop Practices

This introduction to semiconductor technology emphasizes the state of the art. Students work with solid state amplifiers to secure a sound foundation in telephone circuitry. Daily instruction consists of two hours of lecture, two hours of lab, one hour of math, and one hour of print reading or shop practice.

3. Advanced A-C and Vacuum Tubes   5 weeks — 140 Hours
   A. RL Circuits
   B. RC Circuits
   C. RLC Circuits
   D. Resonant Circuits
   E. A-C Filters
   F. Vacuum Tube Power Supplies and Amplifiers

This segment of the program provides the student with a working knowledge of complex A-C circuits, filters, and basic vacuum tube operation. Daily instruction consists of three hours of lecture and three hours of lab work.

4. Advanced Semiconductors   5 weeks — 140 Hours
   A. Cascading Transistor Amplifiers
   B. Unijunction Transistor
   C. Silicon Control Rectifiers
   D. Field Effect Transistors
   E. Tetrode Transistors
   F. Triacs and Diacs
   G. Tunnel Diodes

This segment of the program provides the student with a working knowledge of all semiconductor devices that later will be applied to telephone circuitry. Daily instruction consists of three hours of lecture and three hours of lab work.

5. Central Office Fundamentals   12 weeks — 340 Hours
   A. Basic Telephone Operation
   B. Basic Central Office Operation
   C. Relay Adjusting, Mechanical and Electrical
   D. Adjusting of Switches, X-Y, Strowger and Crossbar
   E. Installation of Central Office Equipment
   F. Troubleshooting Central Office Equipment
   G. Maintenance Procedures

This segment of the program provides the student with a working knowledge of central office equipment and maintenance and troubleshooting of this equipment. Daily instruction consists of three hours of lecture and three hours of shop work.

6. Carrier Equipment   4 weeks — 130 Hours
   A. Principles of Transmission and Reception
   B. Modulation and Demodulation
   C. Multiplexing
   D. Introduction to Microwave
   E. Transmission Lines
   F. Related Test Equipment
   G. FCC License Preparation

This segment provides the student with an introduction to carrier equipment, use of transmission test equipment, and FCC license preparation. Daily instruction consists of three hours of lecture and three hours of shop work.

7. Associated Telephone Equipment   5 weeks — 160 Hours
   A. Key Systems, Installation and Maintenance
   B. Operator Turrets
   C. Switchboards

This last phase of the program provides the students with a working knowledge of key systems and an introduction to operator turrets and switchboards. Daily instruction consist of three hours of lecture and three hours of shop work.

    A unique facet of this program is that students have the option, after completing the first three segments of this program, of switching to an alternate remaining sequence to prepare to be a Combination-man Technician. Graduates of the Combination-man sequence find employment with operating companies working both inside and outside the telephone plant and with telephone construction companies. Job placements are in installation-repair work, cable splicing, and entry-level maintenance of central office equipment. Those remaining with the sequence for the Central Office Equipment Technician, outlined in this example, find employment primarily with firms which manufacture, install, and maintain telephone central office systems and with operating telephone companies.

AN INSTRUCTIONAL ANALYSIS FOR ORGANIZING LEARNING EXPERIENCES

CLASSIFICATION FOR UNITS

	Instructional Code	Typewriting	Office Procedures	Record Keeping	Office Machines	Communications
Receiving money	1.0		X	X		
Typing forms	1.1	X	X			
Routing items	1.2		X			
Sorting and filing records	1.3		X			
Compiling records and reports	1.4		X			
Preparing forms and reports	1.5	X	X	X		X
Answering the telephone	1.6		X			X
Posting data	1.7			X		
Making account computations	1.8			X	X	
Conveying messages	1.9	X				X
Ascertaining names and requests of customers	2.0		X			
Preparing outgoing mail	2.1		X			X
Opening mail	2.2		X			X
Ordering materials and supplies	2.3	X		X		
Verifying information	2.4		X	X		X
Counting, measuring, and weighing merchandise	2.5		X			
Maintaining custody of customers valuables	2.7		X			X
Interviewing customers	2.8		X			X
Preparing inventory of stock	2.9	X	X	X	X	
Compiling census of patients	3.0	X	X	X		X
Addressing envelopes and parcels	3.1	X			X	X
Running errands	3.2		X			
Stuffing envelopes	3.3	X	X			X
Proofreading	3.4	X	X			X
Keeping logs and appointment records	3.5		X	X		
Receiving supplies and materials	3.6		X	X		X
Making appointments	3.7		X	X		X
Answering correspondence	3.8	X	X			X
Resolving discrepancies in records	4.0			X	X	X
Issuing supplies	4.1	X	X	X		X
Administering petty cash fund	4.4			X		
Writing checks	4.5	X	X	X	X	X
Adjusting complaints	4.6		X	X		X
Recording of orders	4.7	X		X		X
Acting as overseer	4.8		X			
Stamping and numbering forms	5.0		X		X	
Depositing money in bank	5.4		X	X		X
Obtaining statement of responsibility	5.6	X	X			X
Arranging for payment of accounts payable	5.7			X		X
Collecting accounts receivable	5.8	X		X		X
Assigning room for patient	6.5	X	X			
Arranging escort for patient	6.6		X			
Explaining clinic or hospital regulations	6.7					X
Assisting in patient care and services	6.8		X			X
Copying information on patient's records	6.9	X	X	X	X	X
Preparing time cards and reports	7.0			X	X	
Preparing payroll reports	7.1	X	X	X	X	X
Forwarding insurance information	7.3	X				X
Reconciling general ledger	11.1			X		
Tracing delinquent accounts	11.2	X				X
Recording from source documents	12.0	X	X	X		
Operating key punch machine	13.0				X	

Fig. 9-4. Basic instruction to be covered in the Oregon clerical occupations. (Courtesy of Oregon Board of Education)

Oregon Cluster for Career Occupations

Figure 9-4, page 263, identifies on-the-job tasks from the Oregon clerical occupations to be taught as entry-level skills. The major mission is to prepare students for a cluster of related clerical jobs. The program is especially planned for students who foresee employment in the clerical occupations after completing high school.

Each job task has been assigned an instructional code number and classified under a heading for a major unit of instruction.

The Oregon **Guides** for each of the thirteen career clusters, identified in Chapter 2, carry outlines for each major unit or module of instruction. Units on Business and Office Machines that match the appropriate instructional codes as shown in Fig. 9-4 are carried in Appendix I. It will be noted that this module of instruction includes:
1. The mission of the unit.
2. Behavioral objectives.
3. Required knowledge and skills.
4. What the student can do at the conclusion of instruction.
5. Suggested learning experiences.

Task Analysis for Distributive Occupations

As explained in Chapter 2, many vocational courses are now predicated on an analysis of the tasks performed by successful workers on the job. Figure 9-5 shows a task analysis for distributive education. Note that these tasks are classified under (1) communication, (2) manipulation, and (3) individuation. This classification would be very helpful to curriculum builders in planning courses of study with either the **formal/descriptive** or **modular** format and in planning instruction that could best be covered through large group instruction, small group instruction, or individual development (see Chapter 4).

Units for Die Theory One

This example shows titles for eleven units to be developed and scheduled as a course of study according to the format for **class session units**. Apprentice tool and diemakers attend this related instruction program for a single two-hour session each week for eleven weeks.

EXAMPLE

1. Orientation, Introduction, and Assignment.
2. Die Shoes — Upper and Lower. Guide Pins and Bushings.
3. Inside Steels and Outside Steels. Composite Steel Sections.
4. The Punch and the Die.
5. Other Parts to a Blanking Die.

Communication

Co-workers;
: Discusses work procedures.
: Verifies prices.
: Requests assistance.

Supervisors:
: Obtains instructions of work functions.
: Obtains approval for certain duties.

Clientele:
: Greets customers.
: Assists customers.
: Thanks customers.
: Answers telephone.
: Answers customers' inquiries.

Manipulation

Operates cash register efficiently.
Checks cash in and out of register.
Changes cash register tapes.
Accepts money and makes change.
Bags and wraps merchandise.
Keeps area neat, clean and sanitary.
Verifies sales prices.
Records financial transactions.
Restocks merchandise.
Calculates tax.
Straightens merchandise.
Arranges interior displays.
Verifies merchandise listed on invoice.
Measures and prices customer selection.

Individuation

Utilizes initiative.
Has knowledge of merchandise.
Presents optimistic attitude.
Indicates "Customer" personality (empathy).
Keeps personal appearance neat and clean.
Has physical stamina and posture sufficient for job.

Fig. 9-5. Task Analysis in Distributive Education (Cook, et al. 1968, 10)

6. Solid Stripper — Drop Thru Die.
7. Spring Stripper — Drop Thru Die.
8. Return Type Die — Inverted.
9. Die Cast Dies.
10. Hammer Dies.
11. Course Examination.[3]

Other Examples for VAE Curriculum Builders

1. The units developed by the Industrial Arts Curriculum Project (IACP) in the **World of Construction** and **the World of Manufacturing** are listed in **Appendix A**.
2. A body of content is outlined in Chapter 2 for industrial arts education as presented in the report titled **A Guide to Improving Instruction in Industrial Arts** (1968).
3. The instructional analysis of the on-the-job tasks for the Oregon METALS occupational cluster is shown in **Appendix B**.
4. Objectives and content for general occupational development are listed in Chapter 2.
5. A task analysis of medical laboratory specialists is reported in **Appendix C**.
6. The task performance statements of the NOBELS study will be helpful in planning office and business education programs. This study is described in **Chapter 3**.

Scheduling of Instructional Units

While instructional units are selected, consideration must be given to the time required to complete the planned program. This may be accomplished by estimating the length of time each unit will take and listing this time following the unit. Since the units are listed in the order they will be taught, the total course can be studied to determine whether all planned units are feasible within the allotted time or whether additional units may be added to the course.

Since students within a class differ in their learning rates, it will be necessary to adjust the time allocations as the term progresses. Experienced teachers provide sufficient time for the various units, but in addition, hold supplementary instructional units in abeyance to provide challenging experiences for the more capable, faster-moving students. The slower students will be able to finish the basic course in the time provided while the more capable ones complete the basic requirements plus a number of advanced instructional units.

---

[3]Outline provided by Roger R. Carver.

Estimating Teaching Time for Each Unit

The following examples illustrate the planned time allotment per instructional unit. Two examples are shown. The first is an exploratory course in power mechanics. The second is a career guidance and exploration course.

Power Mechanics

This course is designed to provide integrated instruction of the scientific principles and industrial applications related to the development, transmission, and utilization of power.

This class meets 50 minutes per day, five days per week for a school semester of 18 weeks. **Modules of instruction** are developed for each of the ten units. The estimated time allocation for each unit is specified.

EXAMPLE

UNITS	Weeks	Hours
1. Orientation — course aims, course outline, overview of instruction, class and student organization, laboratory tour, use of laboratory facilities, and safety.	1	5
2. Harnessing energy — mechanical energy, nuclear energy, heat energy, light energy, chemical energy, electrical energy, friction and energy conversion, kinetic and potential energy, force, work, torque, power, pressure and measurement of power.	1	5
3. Power sources — solar, nuclear, wind, hydroelectric, heat engines, use of each source of power, efficiency, and principles of operation of power sources.	3	15
4. Mechanical power transmission — control, basic machines, mechanical advantage, control devices (gears, pulleys, clutches, etc.), and transmission devices.	3	15
5. Fluid power transmission — measurement of pressure, compressibility, gas laws, fluid power systems, input devices (pumps, reservoirs, filters, etc.), control valves, cylinders, and motors.	3	15
6. Electrical power transmission — magnetism, circuits, AC and DC current, electrical measurements, cells, generators, on-off control devices, solid state devices, circuit protection, transformers, solenoids and motors.	3	15
7. Power utilization — light, heat, motion, communication, conversion to heat and dissipated.	1	5
8. Conservation and environment — limit of fossils and nuclear fuels, potential for hydroelectric and other natural sources, air and thermal pollution, and nuclear waste disposal.	1	5
9. Power systems of the future — nuclear and solar power, laser transmission, fluidics, space exploration, automation and computers.	1	5
10. Career Opportunities — in generation of electricity, nuclear power, transportation, other power sources, power transmission and control, selecting and preparing for a career.	1	5
Total	18	90

Career Guidance and Exploration[4]

This course is planned to assist sixth grade students in exploring a number of different career areas. Emphasis is placed on having each student gain a better understanding of his/her interests and abilities, and relating this understanding to a variety of career options.

This class meets 80 minutes per day, one day per week for one semester. Modules of instruction are developed for each of the units.

EXAMPLE

UNITS	Time Allotment Weeks (one double period/week)
1. Orientation — course aims, course outline, class organization, use of laboratory, begin exploration of service careers (unit 5).	1
2. Self awareness — "Who Am I" questionnaire, interests, abilities, physical characteristics (height, vision, etc.), and relationship of understanding self with selecting careers, continue exploration of service careers.	1
3. Career awareness — abilities required for different careers, grouping of careers, preparation time, vertical and horizontal mobility, continue exploration of service careers.	1
4. Problem solving — four steps of decision-making, application to home, career and life situations, continue exploration of service careers.	1
5. Explore service careers — homemaking (nutrition, table manners, meal planning, timing, preparation, serving, etc.), home repair (lamps, switches, simple appliances, refinishing, etc.), service career opportunities, entry requirements, match of career requirements and individual interest and abilities.	4
6. Manufacturing and construction careers — individual craftsmanship (plan, design, construct, evaluate) cost and time analysis, mass production activity, establishment of a company (name, product, board of directors, job titles and applications, training program), product marketing, worker salaries, investor dividends, profit and loss analysis, career opportunities in manufacturing and construction, match of career requirements and individual interests and abilities.	8
7. Career selection and preparation — Kuder Interest Inventory, alternate careers, changing careers, continuing education, complete work on construction and manufacturing careers.	1
8. Course and student evaluation — suggestions for course improvement.	1
	TOTAL 18

---

[4]Prepared by Dr. Jacqueline Killam, Beverly Hills Unified School District, California.

Week	Monday	Tuesday	Wednesday	Thursday	Friday
1.	Registration	Orientation	Shop Tour Course Outline	General Safety Precautions	Safety Test Principles of Design
2.	Student-directed Organization—Principles of Design	Instruction—Module Teaching Plan—Free-Form Dish	Continue Instruction—Free-Form Dish—Shop Work	Planning for Lumber Yard Field Trip—Shop Work	Continue Instruction—Free-Form Dish—Shop Work
3.	Finish Instruction—Free Form Dish—Shop Work	Informational—Measuring Shop Work	Informational—Measuring Shop Work	Discussion and Final Arrangements for Field Trip—Shop Work	Field Trip Lumber Yard

Fig. 9-6. Typical Daily Schedule for First Three Weeks of a Beginning Course in Woodworking Technology

Scheduling Procedures

From the planned time allotment for the units of instruction, the teacher is able to plan his/her schedule of activities. This planning may involve establishing a daily lesson schedule as illustrated in Fig. 9-6. A review of this schedule will show how this course meets the problem of getting a new class started at the beginning of a term. During the first week or two, it is essential that the teacher provide for class orientation, student-directed and class organization, general safety precautions, and class and laboratory activities. In addition, initial instruction must be provided so the students may get started with the activity part of the instructional program.

It is also possible to outline the entire instructional program on a daily lesson schedule with all course content listed under the day of the week on which it should be taught. This method forces the teacher to consider what instruction he/she will cover each day. It is an adaption of the session plan for organization and is probably the most difficult to organize since it requires very accurate scheduling and estimating of student accomplishments. The Industrial Arts Curriculum Project (IACP) described in Chapter 2 and illustrated in **Appendix A** is precisely scheduled based on extensive field testing over a three-year period. One can see how this is done from the following selected units from the table of contents for the **Teacher's Guide for Manufacturing**. With this information, a teacher can quickly find the assignments, laboratory activities, and references for each topic and be apprised of the daily plan for instruction.

EXAMPLE

Day of the Course	Lab Assignment	Text Assignment		Page in Teacher's Guide
61	28	(5)	*Manufacturing Management Technology	109
62	29	6	Inputs to Manufacturing	116
63	30	7	Organization, Ownership, and Profit	119
64	31	8	Identifying Consumer Demands	120
65	32	(10)	*Designing Manufactured Goods	122
66	33	(17)	*Making Working Drawings	124
67	34	(18)	*Building the Production Prototype	125
68	35	(20)	*Planning Production	126
69	36	(25)	*Tooling Up for Production	128
70	37	27	Operating Quality Control Systems	129
71	38	23	Measuring Work.....................	132
72	39	24	Estimating Costs	134
73	40	35	Hiring and Training	136
74			Review 4 (Optional)	138
75			Test No. 4	138
76	41	34	Manufacturing Personnel Technology ..	139
77	42A-C		Manufacturing Production Technology .	141

On the other hand, many teachers work directly from their unit teaching plans, teaching according to the progress being made by the class. In this situation, demonstrations and necessary instruction are provided just prior to use, the most desirable time. The teacher is able to determine whether the members of the class are progressing at the proper rate of speed by comparing their progress with the time allotment for each unit. In this way he/she can guard against falling behind and omitting the last part of the course; or, if progressing at a faster rate, the teacher can plan the inclusion of units which will enrich the instructional program.

Planning for Major Concurrent Activities

Careful consideration needs to be given to the scheduling of units for VAE programs organized with two or more major activities running concurrently such as the career cluster programs at the senior high school level. An example of a multiple activity program would be a course in industrial materials and processes for seventh grade youth with exploratory experiences in woodworking technology, metalworking technology, and plastic technology. The teacher must plan to have these three distinct activities carried on simultaneously after the class has been

*Review of previous reading (as indicated by text assignment numbers in parentheses).

completely organized at the beginning of the term. One plan that the teacher could follow in providing the basic instruction for these three different areas follows:
1. Organization — enrollment aims for course, assignment of lockers, personal data needed, general safety precautions (administrative).
2. Present essential instruction (enough to get the three departments started) from the modular teaching plans for the first work to be undertaken by students starting in the woodworking, the metalworking, and the plastics departments (operational and informational).
3. Organize the class at work stations (administrative).
4. Explain plan for student-directed organization (informational).
5. Explain plan for evaluation (administrative).
6. Complete the instruction for each of the first modular teaching plans (including the unit tests) in woodworking, metalworking, and plastics. This series of lessons includes classroom planning plus demonstrations in different shop areas. Present a lesson each day before students report to their work stations to continue with individual or group assignments (informational and operational).
7. Present instruction for the modular teaching plans for the second units in woodworking, metalworking, and plastics, a lesson each day. Administer unit tests as students are prepared for them (informational and operational).
8. Present the instruction for the third and final basic projects in woodworking, metalworking, and plastics. Administer the unit tests that are a part of the three project teaching plans (informational and operational).
9. Administer the course examination (informational and administrative).

Developing the Units of Instruction

Once the units have been selected and arranged in an instructional order, they must be developed and expanded so that instruction can be provided. This development is the final step in organizing course content.

In planning units, emphasis must be placed on **thoroughness.** It is better to be too detailed in outlining instruction for student development or presentation than to be so sketchy that important points are missed. Many teachers feel that they have the ability to step in front of a class and present a lesson without aid of notes or preparation. In most cases, these lessons, with the possible exception of a demonstration on tool or machine usage, give a superficial treatment of the subject, and many times miss important concepts. A good teacher is well prepared with thorough and complete directions for student development and either teaches from prepared notes or, even better, speaks to the class, referring to notes from time to time to make certain that points are not being skipped and that a logical sequence is being followed. The teacher who follows this latter pattern is in a position to concentrate on student-teacher communication. This must, however, be coupled with well-prepared lessons (in the form of written directions for students and functional teaching notes) to be certain that the unit is thorough, accurate, and the information current.

The outline for the unit should contain all the information needed for the student's programed materials and for class presentations. Typical plans include:

1. The behavioral objectives for the unit or lesson(s) within a unit. These objectives become the stepping stones to the fulfillment of the goals for a course or program.
2. Instructional materials needed by students to pursue the module of instruction.
3. Tools and equipment needed by students to do the work.
4. Materials, tools, equipment, and teaching aids needed by the teacher for each lesson within the module.
5. Drawings or sketches for projects.
6. Diagrams or sketches to be placed on transparencies or on the chalkboard before or during a lesson.
7. A list of the performance tasks or hand or machine operations identified with the module.
8. A suggestive procedure. (The steps that a student might follow in solving the problem, doing the experiment, or in planning and constructing a project.)
9. A plan for breaking the unit into a series of lessons (such as daily lessons if the class meets each day.)
10. Points to be stressed during each lesson.
11. A list of informational topics to be studied.
12. Exit test covering requirements or competencies to be demonstrated by the learner at conclusion of unit.

Planning Units That Fulfill Established Goals

The guide posts or course goals for VAE courses are concerned with such underlying factors as:

1. The degree of desired skill in job tasks.
2. Essential informational content.
3. Emphasis on educational, personal, and vocational development.
4. The development of wholesome attitudes.
5. Desired appreciations.
6. Problem-solving experiences.

The teacher needs to think of units of instruction, methods, techniques, teaching aids, and evaluation procedures that would set the stage for such student growth and development. Each of these guideposts must be examined for the type of content, the way instruction might be taught, and evaluation instruments that would result in such student accomplishments.

Degree of Desired Skill in Operations

In vocational and technical subjects the selected operations, identified through occupational analysis, become essential content to be taught. The degree of skill comes from meaningful student repetition of an identified task. The desired level of skill in VAE may range from a practical use level for the applied arts to the high degree needed in vocational technical education for occupational competence. The degree of skill to be achieved is expressed in the behavioral objectives that classify in the psychomotor domain (as discussed in Chapter 8). Such objectives will determine what the teacher writes in his/her course of study to describe the methods, techniques, teaching aids, and the instruments and devices for evaluating the progress of each student and the role of the teacher.

Informational Content

Fryklund (1970, 70-77) advocates that the selected informational content be identified through occupational analysis, with the titles for such instructional units falling under technical, general, and guidance information. In vocational education, such instructional units would be specified in the teacher's course of study under the section on **Content**. In applied arts, where essential instruction is generally tied to the project, experiment, or activity that is of interest to the student, the information ferreted out and acquired by any one student depends on how far drive and desire carry that student into what is recognized as desired and essential research as he/she plans and undertakes the job. Many students become so engrossed in a project, especially at the senior high and adult levels, that their natural interest and needs carry them to great depths. Content enrichment is, therefore, highly individualized. Some students do very little with it, especially the slow learners, while the very able are often motivated to become greatly involved in scientific technological and social principles that underlie the work. This range in the mastery of related content is completely defensible where the objective is general education, as it is in much of the applied arts programs. In contrast, vocational education, for salable skills purposes, calls for a mastery of identified informational content. What is written by the teacher for the **Content**, **Methods**, and **Evaluation** sections of a course of study should clearly spell out what has been planned pertaining to the outcomes for informational content.

Educational, Personal, and Vocational Guidance Values

The role of the teacher in the guidance program has been emphasized with the career education movement. Units of instruction need to be placed in the section for **Content** to cover such topics as occupational opportunities and schools and institutions that provide desired educational experiences. Opportunity for personal guidance also comes from the way the course is taught and the instruments for evaluation. Provision for personal development should, therefore, be found in sections of the course of study which describe **methods** and **evaluation** procedures.

Development of Wholesome Attitudes

Desired student attitudes come in large part from the way the course is taught. The content is paramount for it is essential that the student be enthusiastic about what he/she is expected to learn. It is only when a student is motivated through meaningful activity that an educational experience brings change in attitude toward safety precautions, care of equipment, honesty, integrity, responsibility, and cooperation. The **methods** section of the course of study could describe plans for student involvement in the organization and management of the class, and the provisions for having the more able students assist the teacher with the construction of teaching aids and the research and development of the course. There are instruments and devices that might be described in the **evaluation** section of a course of study to assist students in appraising their present attitudes. Such a device is described as the "Bamberger Instrument" in **Managing Multiple Activities in Industrial Education**.[5]

Desired Appreciations

The development of an appreciation of sound business practices, industrial products, craftsmanship, working relationships, industrial design, the place of the home in family life, and the work ethic are among the concomitant values that come from meaningful experience with VAE subjects. In the **content, methods,** and **evaluation sections** of a course of study, the teacher needs to spell out the specific appreciations that students are expected to derive from the outcomes of the course. The man who has forged a spoon from silver has real appreciation for articles made from this medium. One who has practiced the courtesies of salesmanship will be a discriminating user of sales talents. The desired appreciations may well appear in one or more places in a course of study.

Problem-Solving Experiences

It should be a major objective in vocational and technical education to develop research-minded students. Tomorrow's technicians and skilled craftsmen will be called upon to build and service products not even visualized. Students in VAE should, therefore, have experiences in problem solving, so that they will look with favor upon the research and continued effort needed to keep up with the technological developments that are basic and essential to a post-industrial society. Appendix O describes a program which recognizes this need and uses problem-solving activities for all phases of instruction.

[5]Silvius and Curry (1971, 334-336).

Fig. 9-7. Students planning a model community must solve numerous problems including traffic flow, population density, location of recreation areas, waste disposal, etc. (Courtesy Jacqueline Killam, Beverly Hills Unified School District, California)

Those who champion the cause for industrial arts present a strong case for the values that come from student participation in planning a project. Solving problems through the scientific method is an important aspect of one's liberal education. Industrial arts provides unique opportunity for student participation in the planning and evaluation of projects.

What is provided in VAE programs in the way of opportunity for students to get experience in doing research, being creative, and solving problems needs to be completely described in the **methods** and **evaluation** sections of the course of study.

Examples of Units of Instruction

Selected examples of units have been placed in the appendices of this book to illustrate functional plans for organizing and presenting units of instruction. The reader is encouraged to study the units listed below:
- Appendix I — Units of Instruction on Business and Office Machines
- Appendix J — Examples of Laboratory Units

- Appendix K — Examples of Units Concerned with Informational Topics
- Appendix L — Examples of Modules of Instruction Organized Around the Development and Construction of a Project
- Appendix M — Modules Designed for Individualized Instruction
- Appendix N — An Example of a Unit of Instruction in Family Life Education
- Appendix O — Individualized Instruction and Problem Solving for Design, Drafting, and Model Building.

Summary

The selection and organization of content for courses is probably the most important undertaking of the curriculum builder. The effectiveness of this step sets the stage for the entire program and determines whether the course will be rich with educational experiences which will meet the ever-changing needs of students. Some of the important points are these:

1. Do not permit units of instruction or methods of teaching to be dull and repetitious. VAE offers opportunities for almost all types of informational and operational activities.
2. Select units which fulfill the appropriate course goals.
3. This is a rapidly changing society. A teacher **cannot teach** as he/she was taught because our post-industrial society is rapidly progressing. New units must be introduced and old units revised, upgraded, or discarded.
4. Applied arts should reflect a concept of the total area under consideration just as the vocational offerings must reflect specific occupational requirements and fulfill the needs of on-the-job workers.
5. Arrange units in a logical instructional order giving consideration to the time requirements of each unit.
6. Make provisions for laboratory activities whenever the **formal/descriptive** method of organization is used.
7. Check unit titles to make certain that course goals are fulfilled. Consideration must be given to methods of instruction (delivery systems) and evaluation as this is done.

In summation, the information presented to students must be carefully selected from the vast array of available knowledge.

Many methods of outlining and arranging units can be used, but two principles should be followed. The first is plan **all** the activities for the course. These include provisions for student officers and classroom and laboratory activities. Provision must be made for student activities as well as what the teacher will do. Overplanning can be reduced or cut at any time. Underplanning cannot be corrected without considerable effort. The second principle is to select the method of arranging the instructional units which best suits the course, the method of instruction, and the needs and interest of students. This may be a combination of the modular, session, or formal/descriptive organizations (outlined in

Chapter 7 and further developed in this chapter) or it may even contain features not considered in this volume. Most often it will be one of the three forms of organization.

Regardless of the course being outlined or the method of organization selected, the teacher must make every effort to plan instruction which is challenging, stimulating, and instructional and which fits into the overall educational program of the students enrolled in the course or program.

For Self-Assessment and Discussion

1. What is the difference between a unit of instruction and a lesson?
2. What part does an occupational analysis play in building a vocational course of study?
3. In determining the number and selection of units prepared for a course of study, what consideration should be given to —
   a. Units to be scheduled near the end of a term?
   b. Provisions for more capable students?
4. What is the difference between technical, general, and guidance information, according to the Fryklund classification?
5. Give examples, in your area of specialization, for administrative units of instruction.
6. List the characteristics of an operational (manipulative) unit.
7. Illustrate what is meant by the blocks of the trade.
8. Explain why applied arts courses often have greater breadth and less depth in content than vocational or technical education courses.
9. Which has been the most popular of the three organizational patterns for developing vocational or technical education courses? Why?
10. Which organizational format is best suited to applied arts courses? Explain?
11. How can a teacher determine whether a lesson or unit should be included or excluded from a course?
12. List some of the advantages and disadvantages of preparing a daily lesson schedule for each class.
13. What is the purpose of cross-checking titles of units against goals for the course?
14. How can course content in vocational education be adapted to the rapid changes in job requirements and opportunities?
15. How is the instructional order for teaching the content of a course of study determined?
16. Why will teachers "teaching as they were taught" and "what they were taught" be likely to project a non-realistic instructional program?
17. List specific examples of problem solving which would be considered in the development of instructional units for your VAE courses.
18. Why is it often desirable to integrate content, methods, and evaluation by using the modular format for a course of study?

278 Planning and Organizing Instruction

Assignments to Demonstrate Competencies

1. Using the examples shown in this chapter prepare a list of instructional units for the VAE course you have selected as you complete the assignments described in this book. Place this list in an instructional order and prepare a time allotment chart to show the time planned for each unit, giving consideration to the following:
   a. Units which fulfill established course goals.
   b. Units of interest to students to make them cognizant of the rapid changes in technology and society.
   c. Provision for operational, informational, and administrative units within the course.
   d. Time allotment for each unit, as estimated against the abilities of the usual students in the class.
   e. Provisions for the more capable students in the class.
   Prepare a table showing how the goals for the course are being fulfilled by the units selected for the course. This may be similar to the chart shown in **Appendix H** or may be of your own design.
2. Using the examples that would be appropriate for your area of specialization, as shown in **Appendices I through O**, outline three of the units identified in assignment number one. Be thorough and complete in your outlines. To the greatest degree possible, be original. Use available resource materials as identified in Chapter 6.
3. (only for trade teachers) Using the example of the "Breakdown for the Operation: How to Knurl on a Lathe" shown in **Appendix D**, select three operations from your trade and prepare outlines for each of the operating steps. Label the new technical terms, safety precautions, quality standards, and what the learner should know — as suggested in the example.

References* and Resources

Books

Baird, Ronald J. **Contemporary Industrial Teaching**. South Holland, Illinois, The Goodheart-Willcox Co. Inc., 1972, pp. 17-62.

Friese, John F., and Williams, William A. **Course Making in Industrial Education**. 3rd edition. Peoria, Illinois: Chas. A. Bennett Co., Inc., 1966, Pp. 301.

*Fryklund, Verne C. **Occupational Analysis: Techniques and Procedures**. 5th edition. New York: The Bruce Publishing Co., 1970, Pp. vi + 213.

Good, Carter V. (Editor). **Dictionary of Education**. Third Edition. New York: McGraw-Hill Book Co., 1973, Pp. xix + 681.

Giachino, J. W., and Gallington, Ralph O. **Course Construction in Industrial Arts, Vocational and Technical Education**. 3rd edition. Chicago: American Technical Society, 1967, Pp. 314.

*Items with an asterisk have been cited in the chapter.

*Lux, Donald G.; Ray, Willis E.; and Hauenstein, A. Dean. **The World of Manufacturing: Teacher's Guide.** Fourth Edition. Bloomington, Illinois: McKnight Publishing Co., 1971, Pp. vi + 367.

Moss, Jerome, Jr., and Smith, Brandon B. "Some Steps on the Curriculum Development Process" in **Contemporary Concepts in Vocational Education** (ed.) Gordon F. Law, First Yearbook of AVA. Washington D.C., American Vocational Association, Inc., 1971, pp. 130-138.

Osborn, William C. et al. **An Instructional Program for Employability Orientation.** Alexandria, Virginia: Human Resources Organization (Hum RHO), 300 North Washington Street, February 1972, Pp. v + 303. Research performed for Manpower Administration, U.S. Department of Labor, Contract No. 51-49-70-06.

Parnell, Dale. "The Career-Cluster Approach in Secondary Education," in Goldhammer, Keith, and Taylor, Robert, **Career Education: Perspective and Promise.** Columbus, Ohio: Charles E. Merrill Publishing Co., 1972, pp. 55-61.

Silvius, G. Harold, and Curry, Estell H. **Managing Multiple Activities in Industrial Education.** Bloomington, Illinois: McKnight Publishing Co., 1971. Recommended Topics are 1, 2, 3, 4, 18, and 25.

_____. **Teaching Successfully in Industrial Education.** Bloomington, Illinois: McKnight Publishing Co., 1967. Recommended Topics are 4, 5, 6, and 7.

Singer, Edwin J. and Ramsden, John. **The Practical Approach to Skills Analyses.** New York: McGraw-Hill Publishing Co., 1967, Pp. 170. ERIC reference No. ED 040 319.

Periodicals

American Vocational Association. "Developing, Reviewing and Updating Curriculum to Meet On-the-Job Needs," in Bread and Fire series. **American Vocational Journal,** Vol. 47, No. 8 (November, 1972), pp. 89-98.

Cook, Fred S., and Lanham, Frank W. "Job Analysis Yields Individualized-Task Instruction Packets." **Business Education World** (September-October, 1971), p. 12.

Evans, Rupert N. "How to Live With Change Without Being Corrupted by Money," in Theory Into Practice (TIP). Columbus, Ohio: College of Education, The Ohio State University, Vol. 9, No. 5 (1970), pp. 280-283.

Staff of IACP. "The Industrial Arts Curriculum Project." **Journal of Industrial Arts Education,** Vol. 29, No. 2 (November-December, 1969), pp. 10-40. Reports of article (Stock No. 614-21319) @ 75¢ each from the AIAA.

Wolansky, William D. "Oregon Musters a Statewide Commitment to Clusters." **School Shop,** Vol. 29, No. 4 (May 1970), pp. 33-35, 54.

Other Published Materials

Aitman, James W. Final Report: **Research On General Vocational Capabilities — Skills and Knowledges.** Robert M. Gagné Principal Investigator. Pittsburgh, Pennsylvania: American Institute for Research in Behavioral Sciences, 1966, Pp. 159. ERIC Reference No. ED 013 870.

Barlow, Melvin L. et al. **A Guide for the Development of Curriculum in Vocational and Technical Education.** Report of National Conference on Curriculum Development, held in Dallas, Texas, March 5-7, 1969 under direction of David Allen of California and James R. D. Eddy of Texas. Los Angeles: Division of Vocational Education, UCLA, 1969.

*Cook, Wells F. (Project Director) et al. **Horizontal Articulation in Vocational Education.** A report of a project funded by Department of Education. State of Michigan. Mt. Pleasant, Michigan 48858: Central Michigan University, Summer 1968, Pp. ix + 65.

*Christal, Raymond E. "Implication of Air Force Occupational Research for Curriculum Design," in Report of Seminar on Process and Techniques of Vocational Curriculum Development. Minneapolis, Minnesota: Research Coordinating Unit for Vocational Education, University of Minnesota, April, 1970, pp. 27-61.

*Henderson, John T. Program Planning With Surveys in Occupational Education. Washington, D.C.: American Association of Junior Colleges, 1970, Pp. 28.

*Lanham, Frank W. et al. Development of Task Performance Statements for a New Office and Business Education Learnings System (NOBELS). 2nd edition. The first edition was report on Project No. 8-04-14: Grant No. OEG-0-8-080414-3733 (085) published by USOE, April, 1970, ERIC Reference No. ED 041 134. Columbus, Ohio: CVTE as Centered Related Series No. 16, September, 1972, pp. xii + 361. ERIC Reference No. for 2nd ed. is ED 068 728.

Larson, Milton E. Review and Synthesis of Research: Analysis for Curriculum Development in Vocational Education. Publication of CVTE as Research Series No. 46, October, 1969, Pp. 69, ERIC Reference No. ED 035 746.

*Minelli, Ernest L. (Chairman of Committee) et al. A Guide to Improving Instruction in Industrial Arts, revised 2nd edition. Washington D.C.: American Vocational Association, Inc., 1968, Pp. 67.

Moss, Jerome, Jr., and Pucel, David J. et al. "An Empirical Procedure for Identifying the Structure of the Technical Concepts Possessed by Selected Workers," in Process and Techniques of Vocational Curriculum Development. Minneapolis, Minnesota: Research Coordinating Unit, University of Minnesota, 1970, Pp. 71-90. Also available from ERIC Reference No. ED 042 917.

Moss, Jerome, Jr., and Smith, Brandon B. "Summary and Discussion," in Report of Seminar on Process and Techniques of Vocational Curriculum Development. Minneapolis, Minnesota 55455: Minnesota Research Coordinating Unit for Vocational Education, April 1970, pp. 1-8.

*Multanen, Monty E. "Occupational Career Clusters the Oregon Way," in Proceedings 6th Annual National Vocational Technical Teacher Education Seminar, Edited by Anna M. Gorman and Joseph F. Clark, CVTE publication, LT Series #38, March, 1973, pp. 95-102.

*Parnell, Dale, et al. Curriculum Guide for Clerical Occupations. Salem, Oregon 97310: The Oregon Board of Education, 942 Lancaster Drive NE, 1971, Pp. vii + 137.

*_____. Curriculum Guide for Health Occupations. Salem, Oregon 97310: The Oregon Board of Education, 942 Lancaster Drive NE, 1969, Pp. iv + 153.

*_____. Curriculum Guide for Metals. Salem, Oregon 97310: The Oregon Board of Education, 942 Lancaster Drive NE, 1969, Pp. iv + 152.

Schill, William J., and Arnold, Joseph J. Curriculum Content for Six Technologies. Research Study funded in part by U.S. DHEW Urbana, Illinois: Department of Vocational Technical Education, University of Illinois, 1965, Pp. vi + 118.

Unpublished Materials

Herschelmann, Kathleen M. Adopting a Retrieval System for Individualized-Task Instruction Packets (I-TIPS) Using the Basic Information Retrieval System (BIRS). In two documents. Part One, Pp. 31 and Appendices A-H; Part Two, Appendices and J (abstracts of the I-TIP Computer Bank and I-TIP Materials Bank), October, 1972. Vocational and Applied Arts Education, Wayne State University, Detroit 48202.

*Resnick, Harold S. et al. Individualized Material for Industrial Education. Based on AVA Brochure "A Guide to Improving the Instruction in Industrial Arts." In the form of modules of instruction for industrial arts education. Developed by Fellows in 1969-70 Experienced Teacher Fellowship Program. Detroit, Michigan: Department of Industrial Education, Wayne State University, 1970, Pp. 1,041. ERIC Reference No. ED 040 303.

CHAPTER 10

Methods, Aids, and Teaching Techniques [Delivery Systems]

This chapter is concerned with the teacher(s) plan for presenting any unit for a course in what is considered to be the most appropriate and effective way. With the content for a course selected and organized as teachable units or modules, the teacher(s) then needs to study each of these units, one at a time, and determine the best available methods and teaching aids that might be used to teach each unit of instruction. Much thought needs to be given to the teaching techniques (the refinement of the teacher's presentation) that could be used to make the methods and teaching aids that have been selected as functional as possible.

Pertinent Definitions

Differentiations are needed between **methods**, **aids**, or **devices** used in teaching of vocational and applied arts education (VAE) subjects, and the **teaching techniques** that make such aids and methods highly functional. This chapter covers what is needed in a specific course or program of study to describe the methods and devices selected by the teacher for each unit and the teaching techniques that make them effective.

Methods of instruction are the orderly procedures that direct learners in developing competencies such as skills and habits, acquiring specified knowledge, and in developing positive attitudes. Methods used for instruction in VAE subjects include demonstrations, lectures, discussions, simulation, directed research, visual presentations, individualized programed instruction, student-directed activity, directed references, student planning, supervised performance at the work station, experimental work, field trips, speakers, panel discussions, conferences, and testing.

Teaching aids are the specially planned devices or pieces of equipment to help students understand and learn, such as charts, films, transparencies, self-checking tool holders, and student assignment boards. They are the material aids employed as adjuncts to training or instruction and may be classified as follows:

1. Devices for the improvement of instruction.
2. Administrative devices.
3. Production aids.

Teaching techniques are the details of instruction — the personal refinements — through which the individual teacher makes learning more effective when using a method or a teaching aid. An example would be the specific directions (verbal arrowheads that are pointed out to students) regarding such issues as how to pick up and hold a tool and how one stands as he/she performs an operation. They are the things that the great teachers do that make instruction effective.

Identify Appropriate Methods for a Teaching Situation

The methods used in VAE to permit learners to acquire essential knowledge, skills, habits, appreciation, and attitudes are rather numerous. Professional judgment is needed in deciding which of these methods would be most appropriate and effective for the type of students to be scheduled for the classes. For example, time spent in lecturing to students at the junior high school level should perhaps be kept to a minimum. A possible exception would be classes consisting of selected youth with outstanding ability, such as those who would be classified with the top fifteen percent of their class. The selection of teaching methods to be brought into focus with units is, therefore, a crucial matter.

The methods currently being used by VAE teachers have been grouped in two categories in this chapter. **First** are those that are used by the teacher, or by some other designated individuals (such as an advanced student or a guest lecturer) in presenting some aspect of a unit to an individual, to a small group within a class, or to an entire class. **Second** are those methods that place the responsibility for learning and mastering some aspect of the unit squarely on the individual student. Methods in this second category are employed as the individual student, or team of students, work in a study carrel, at a work station, or a planning center. Contacts with the teacher are as needed and are instigated by the student or team as work on meaningful projects, experiments, or assignments is accomplished. The methods in the second classification become more and more significant, especially in advanced courses, as students mature and develop to the point where there is need to place more and more emphasis on individual differences.

Methods for Presenting Instruction to Others

The methods described in the following sections fit this first category and describe how instruction may be presented to others.

Student-Directed Organization

Many VAE courses are now organized to take advantage of this essential method. Course goals concerned with social efficiency have become increasingly important in recent years. Teachers in VAE, therefore, hasten to mention the values that accrue from having students participate in a student-directed organization. Through this method there is opportunity for leadership training and experience as students help direct and manage the work of others their age, assume responsibility, and deal with the human relations issues. It provides, also, for the workers to follow through on directions given by fellow students.

Demonstration

The demonstration is the method of simultaneously showing and explaining the steps in a manipulative task or operation. A demonstration may be concerned also with an explanation of some mechanism or materials.

The manipulative aspects of VAE programs are readily taught to an entire class, a small group, or an individual by this method. A demonstration might be given by the teacher, a student in the class, an expert from the field, or by a committee from a class.

Fig. 10-1. Jacqueline Killam, industrial arts teacher, demonstrates the final finishing processes on a table constructed by one of the students. (Beverly Hills Unified School District, California)

Fig. 10-2. Supervision and instruction are important as a student gains initial knowledge of the operation of a router. (Beverly Hills Unified School District, California)

Supervised Performance at Work Stations

This method provides for the practical application of what is being taught in VAE courses. **It is the method by which a student develops a desired level of skill in the manipulative work, through meaningful repetition for skill development.** It is also the method by which a student (or team of students) plans, executes, and evaluates an application of scientific and technological principles for some experiment, project, or unit.

Lecture

The lecture is a method of instruction for imparting information and stimulating critical thinking, largely by the verbal message with a minimum of class participation. The lecture method is often used with advanced groups when teaching units incorporating guidance, technical, or general information. Lectures are given by the teacher, a student presenting a report, or by an authority on the unit under study who is invited to address the class.

Review

A review consists of a re-examination of material previously presented or studied. It is usually scheduled a reasonable time after the original lesson with the teacher directing skillfully worded questions to selected members of the class. It is particularly essential as a method for checking on a knowledge of safety precautions, an understanding of identified procedures, and essential technical information.

Discussion (or Conference)

The discussion is characterized by a focus on, or adherence to, a selected objective, topic, question, or problem about which participants hope to arrive at a decision or conclusion. This method is conducted in one of three ways. An entire class (or group) may discuss a given topic under the leadership of a teacher, a conference leader, or one of its members. Another plan is to divide persons participating into groups of about equal size to discuss the specific topic or topics, with each having a chairman and a recorder; provision is made for the entire body to reassemble so the findings of each group may be reported. The third plan provides for having selected topics discussed first by a prepared and qualified panel, with the entire group invited to participate after the controversial issues have been properly introduced.

A teacher or teaching team may wish to use one or more of these discussion methods, to be referred to as (1) **discussions with entire class participating,** (2) **groupings of class for discussions,** and (3) **panel discussions.** The first type, with the entire class participating in the discussion under the leadership of a skillful teacher, is recommended as a method for applied arts, especially at the junior high school level. It is being used extensively and effectively as all members of a class work together to do such typical things as plan the steps for a class project; designate checking levels for a class project; identify safety precautions; list needed tools, utensils, and equipment for some unit; and list rough sizes or amounts of needed material.

Breaking the class into groups could be used in advanced courses for introducing issues that have social and economic implications for VAE programs.

The panel method would be useful for teaching units pertaining to guidance, especially those concerned with occupational information and placement, and institutions for furthering one's education.

Field Trip

A directed field trip is an effective method for studying modern industrial and business practices and processes. The teacher's role in this method is in the orientation of students so they are stimulated and aware of the significant elements to be observed. After the field trip, various aspects of the trip are discussed to emphasize the concepts taught by the visit.

Outside Assignment

Outside assignments may include research or any type of home study providing a learning experience.

Home reading assignments in a textbook or reference book are an excellent way of providing an increase in student accomplishment and laboratory utilization. Concepts studied and learned at home require only a minimum of class time to review, to clarify difficult information, and to answer student questions.

In addition, outside reading assignments help develop the ability to read and understand technical concepts. This is an important and valuable ability, for after the student completes formal instruction, he/she must rely, to a considerable degree, on self-study to develop an understanding of new information and solve technical problems.

Outside assignments are not limited to reading. They may include sketching, planning, and drawing or may require the student to study and integrate knowledge resulting from library or resource center study.

Televised Instruction

One of the useful methods for teaching a unit in VAE is closed circuit television. This method of instruction combines many advantages. First, instead of giving a basic demonstration to just one group, a closed circuit TV demonstration can be given to dual, or multiple groups, depending upon available monitors for classroom use. This is economical of teaching effort in larger schools where there are multiple sections of a basic course. Second, videotaped programs can be used in place of films since taped instruction of a unit can be custom-made to fit specific needs, thus eliminating much of the material now in films not directly related to the unit under study. Also, such videotaped units can easily be repeated for remedial purposes. Third, and possibly the most important, is the teaching of safety. With this method a teacher can give a confined and possibly hazardous demonstration to a class without endangering the students.

Open circuit TV has tremendous potential as a public relations medium as VAE programs are presented to the public. Through local cooperation, open or closed circuit television can bring industry, business, and home conditions into the classroom as students learn about major issues that confront society as well as technical and scientific advances. This will result in more contact and greater cooperation between education, industry, and business enterprises.

Silvius and Curry (1967, 376-377) point out that experimentation with television, as an educational medium, suggests that —

1. It is an important method for teaching and learning at all instructional levels including adult programs.
2. When used properly, television provides incentives for students to assume more responsibility for learning.
3. The use of television can improve the total instructional program.
4. Teaching with television demands more preparation and assistance from specialized personnel than does conventional instruction.

Other Audiovisual Presentations

An audiovisual presentation is a method of teaching a unit, or some phase of it, with an enlarged operating model of some mechanism, overhead transparencies, projected slides, filmstrips, or movies, accompanied by running commentary provided by a recording or by the teacher. It may be done also with a coordinated bulletin board display. This method is good for teaching or reviewing a procedure for an operation, especially when presented with a carefully prepared filmstrip. Movies provide a medium for bringing essential phases of the economy, industry, business, and the home into the classroom.

Slides are useful for teaching schematic circuit diagrams, mechanisms, and operating principles. Slides are useful also for presenting pictorial records of activity. For example, slides depicting the work and the activities of previously enrolled students are being used by VAE teachers as they introduce a course to a new class.

Carefully selected and presented bulletin board displays supplement and enrich a unit under study. It is entirely possible, too, that an entire unit for a course, such as one pertaining to pertinent occupational information, might be taught completely through a carefully planned bulletin board display.

Fig. 10-3. Media centers provide teachers with a variety of audiovisual teaching aids. (Media Center, West Valley Occupational Center, Los Angeles)

Instruction Sheets

Instruction sheets have been widely used for teaching units in VAE subjects. In an early professional book that had wide acceptance in industrial education, the late Professor Selvidge (1946, 1-263) presented a classification for instruction sheets and made recommendations that have been of great assistance to teachers in past years as they have developed materials to facilitate this method.

The greatest asset for this method is that it facilitates individualized instruction. The following descriptions characterize the types of instruction sheets advocated by the authors of this book.

Assignment sheets are usually written by the teacher or teaching team and duplicated by one of the several practical processes. They direct the activity of a student, or a team of students, pursuing a unit at a work station. This method is especially useful in assisting students who are using several different titles that make up the essential reference material for a related instruction course, such as those maintained for persons pursuing an apprenticeship in the manufacturing industries or the building trades, or a program in family life education. Assignment sheets have been written and duplicated by teachers or made available by publishers to direct the work of students performing experiments in VAE courses, and where students are studying applications of scientific and technological principles. Assignment sheets to direct the efforts of VAE students, as they study essential text and reference material or perform meaningful experiments, are often called **student study guides**.

Operation sheets are written and duplicated by teachers or published as a major section of a textbook for a course. An operation sheet may be developed for each of the operations or tasks identified for a vocational education subject through the process of occupational or task analysis, as explained in chapter 2. The objective is to discuss each of the steps in the operation or task in sufficiently complete form that it may be readily understood by the reader. Sketches and photographs are often used as illustrations to make a step even more understandable.

Information sheets are written by teachers to cover the independent informational topics for some subject identified through the process of instructional analysis. It was pointed out in Chapter 2 and Appendix D that the informational content for an occupation or activity is often classified as technical, general, or guidance. The content in these three categories, in turn, is then organized as a series of topics so that an information sheet may be written for each one. Such information sheets are often written and duplicated by a VAE teacher and his/her associates; they may have been refined and developed to the point where they have been published and incorporated with the text material now available for VAE subjects.

Planning sheets are available to aid students in developing their own plan for a project, experiment, or unit. They appear in a duplicated or printed form to facilitate having students carefully plan their work. Such planning has displaced the teacher prepared and duplicated job sheets advocated and used in many VAE programs during the first half of the twentieth century. Most educators now recognize that it is as important to involve the students in planning their job, experiment, or unit as it is to have them follow-through with the application at the work station. Planning sheets are designed, therefore, to facilitate this important educative experience. They are available as individual sheets (or bound as planning books) to be issued to students in sufficient quantity to last one student the entire term. Typical sheets provide space for such phases of planning as these:

1. Identifying the behavioral objectives.
2. Listing major steps in doing a project, experiment, or unit.
3. Making needed sketches or drawings.
4. Listing rough sizes and quantities of instructional materials.
5. Enumerating needed tools, utensils, and equipment.
6. Identifying checking levels in procedures.
7. Listing helpful references.
8. Listing the procedure to be followed when the student is assigned to the project.
9. Writing the answers for an exit or unit test.
10. Evaluating the product and learning.

An example of such planning sheets may be found in the publication by Baysinger and Silvius (1960, Pp. 65).

Role Playing

In this method students identify themselves with typical life activities as they play the part of persons who have responsibility for coping with the issues under consideration. It is a method that is

Fig. 10-4. Students role-play a job applicant and personnel director in a job interview. (Courtesy Stanley G. Lyons, Thomas Jefferson Junior High School, Pontiac, Michigan)

receiving increased attention in applied arts programs. To illustrate, role playing is used extensively in the Industrial Arts Curriculum Project (IACP), described in Chapter 2 and Appendix A. It is also used in the student-directed organization program. The student serving as shop superintendent is playing the role of a real superintendent. Through this experience, the student develops an understanding of the responsibilities and role of a shop superintendent, and experiences leadership responsibilities as he/she performs the laboratory duties related to the position. In addition, the teacher may discuss the responsibilities of plant superintendents by relating plant activities with class activities.

Simulation

This is a method that needs to be carefully considered and evaluated by those planning and organizing VAE instructional programs. Educators have observed the flawless success of simulated equipment and methods used to prepare astronauts with the needed skills to travel to and from the moon. Likewise airplane pilots have for some time received much of their basic training in specially designed ground-based equipment that simulates flight and testing conditions of an aircraft.

Model for Simulation Program

Richey (1973, 1-13) has developed a general model for using simulation that is especially helpful as curriculum builders begin to use simulation in VAE programs. This model, illustrated in Fig. 10-5, encompasses:

- The analysis of instruction to be presented to determine appropriateness of simulation as a method.
- The evaluation of prevailing simulation programs.
- The design, tryout, and evaluation of a proposed simulation.
- The operating procedures for classroom simulation.

The model focuses on simulation for instructional purposes. This delimitation was made so that the model could be applied to the usual teaching situation. The model is not applicable to research nor is it a model that employs the computer. It is a model that might be used in general VAE classroom instruction, grades K through 14, and continuing education programs.

The steps that curriculum builders follow in the flow chart (Fig. 10-5) are numbered. Here are procedures followed in the Richey model:

1. Evaluate proposed instruction to determine whether simulation is an appropriate method. This calls for a complete definition of the instructional problem. Some pertinent factors are the decisions and strategies involved, the procedural sequences, and the type of learning task.
2. Identify answer to question of **appropriateness of simulation as a method** for proposed instruction.

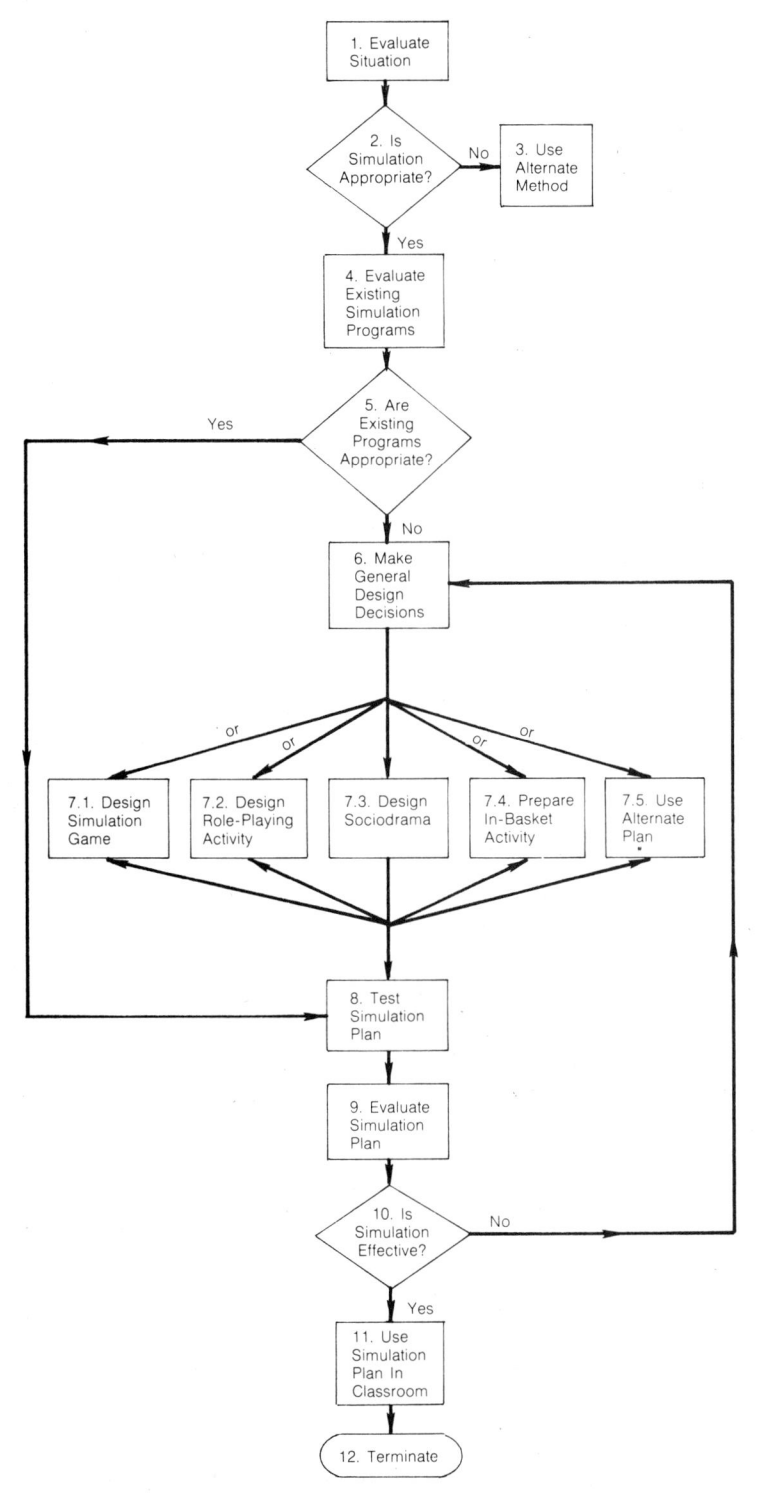

Fig. 10-5. Steps in the general application of the simulation method. (Flowchart of Richey Model, developed by Roger A. Smith, San Jose State University)

3. If unappropriate, use alternative instructional methods, this is done when the instruction to be presented does not suggest the simulation method.
4. If simulation is appropriate, review and evaluate existing applications. It is important to determine whether simulations produce real-life situations.
5. Identify answer to question of **appropriateness of existing applications as a method for proposed instruction**. If yes (appropriate), move to step 8, tryout of existing application.
6. If no existing applications are appropriate, plan the design of a new simulation program. In doing this the objectives for the simulation experience are determined, the instructional problem is described, and essential and nonessential elements identified. When design decisions are being made it is important to consider the target population, maturity of the students, and prerequisite skills. The next step is to identify the task-relevant elements of instruction and eliminate irrelevant variables. At this point, the developers of the simulation experience are ready to sequence instruction and determine the type of simulation to be employed.
7. The simulation activity to be employed is designed and developed. It might be a simulation game (7.1), role-playing activity (7.2), sociodrama (7.3), "in-basket"[1] activity (7.4), or some other simulation activity (7.5).
8. The developed simulation activity (or existing activity, from step 5), is implemented on a trial basis.
9. Evaluate the effectiveness of the simulation method. In doing this, compare the costs of the simulation method with other methods that might have been used. Determine whether student experiences were realistic and relate to real-life situations.
10. Identify answer to question of **effectiveness of the simulation** method. If ineffective (or below accepted standard), seek a new simulation procedure by returning to step 6, **making design decisions**.
11. If effective, operate the simulation in the classroom. The continued effectiveness of the simulation plan should be evaluated by repeating the questions asked in steps 2 and 10.
12. Terminate.

McClelland (1970, 23) cites a definition by Bogdanoff et al., that defines the simulation method as:

> ... the intended systematic abstraction and partial duplication of a phenomenon for the purpose of effecting (1) transfer of training from a synthetic environment to an actual environment, (2) analysis of a specific phenomenon, or (3) design of a specific system in terms of conditions, behaviors, and mechanisms.

---

[1] Where the learner reacts to various prepared situations and makes responses from a listing of choices.

McClelland states that "as educators we are most typically concerned with the transfer function of simulation — with its potential as an instruction tool."

In recent years, vocational educators have set up simulated businesses and farms to teach office and agricultural practices. The objective has been, according to Johnson (1971, 237), to provide an opportunity for students to learn and practice skills under conditions which reproduce, with some degree of realism, the actual life situation in which the skills will be eventually used. It has been rather common practice in industrial arts education to have the students study industry through a simulation experience organized to design, develop, mass produce, and merchandise a product. In describing the values of this approach, Resnick (1970, 38) states that such a simulation reinforces the student's understanding of the principles of mass production, provides opportunity to explore career opportunities in the world of manufacturing, and makes possible the application of learning from other subject-matter areas.

Games as simulation devices have been developed by VAE curriculum builders to teach selected underlying concepts associated with their areas of specialization. To illustrate, International Harvester Company has developed an interesting game that agriculture teachers use in introducing students to the process of making decisions in the production, the management, and the marketing of farm products. This game is designed to allow the student to utilize the land, labor, and capital resources commonly associated with farm production.

Zuckerman and Horn (1970, 1-323) have compiled, with the help of Twelker, a classified listing of available instructional games in eighteen categories, e.g. "Business: Industry," "Education," "Skill Development" (such as reading, spelling, and vocabulary), and "Urban Affairs." These games are further classified in each category under eleven headings, e.g. "primary," "junior high," "vocational," and "continuing education." This guide contains abstracts describing the 404 games classified under the eighteen categories and eleven headings that are used for educational purposes. Many of these are excellent simulations of conditions found in the real world of work.

In addition, **The Guide** contains a supplementary listing of 450 more games that are in development, about which the authors need more information, or have been discontinued.

Persons (1970, 35) points out that

> Games need not be commercially produced or of elaborate design to be effective classroom tools. Teachers can devise games of their own design to teach specific kinds of skills.

Simulation training is being successfully used in the preparation and upgrading of leadership personnel for vocational education. Complete simulation training packages have been developed by the staff at the CVTE at The Ohio State University on (1) **Supervision and Decision-Making Skills in Vocational Education** (1970) and (2) **Simulation Training in Planning Vocational Education Programs and Facilities** (1970).

Advantages of Simulation

These advantages are advanced by McClelland (1970, 24-25) for simulation as a method in VAE programs:

1. Students become personally involved in simulation even though they know it is not the real world in which they are operating.
2. Evaluations of the use of games in classrooms suggest that this kind of simulation is more interesting than conventional instruction.
3. It is important in such VAE areas as distribution, food service, and cosmetology for students to have the opportunity to play the role of an entrepreneur. With such an objective, simulation provides experiences patterned after conditions in the real world of work.
4. Extensive use can be made of such media as tape recordings, motion pictures, films, videotapes, and slide-audiotapes in planning simulated learning experiences.
5. In classrooms where games are used the teacher becomes more of a judge or guide than an authoritative source for content to be mastered.
6. Where classrooms are organized to produce a product as work passes from one station to another, a student may first serve as an observer, then as a trainee operator, and finally as an examiner of a

Fig. 10-6. Students playing "big builder" as they simulate the planning of a large building. (Courtesy Stanley G. Lyons, Thomas Jefferson Junior High School, Pontiac, Michigan)

subsequent trainee. In such simulated experiences trainees rotate from station to station until they have mastered all tasks.

In reviewing research to determine the effectiveness of simulation materials for application in VAE, Impellitteri and Finch (1971, 44) reported:

1. The primary concern in the development of a simulated experience is the degree that the transfer of training is actually achieved.
2. The degree to which a simulation-based training experience departs from reality is of utmost concern to vocational educators.
3. The training designer must decide (a) what equipment and functions must be simulated, (b) how precise the simulation must be, and (c) how accurately the stimulus and response situations on which training is given must simulate real life.

Testing

Testing can become an important method of teaching when it helps a student assess and understand his/her progress, growth, and development toward the fulfillment of behavioral objectives established for the units of the course.

VAE teachers employ exit or unit tests, tests to check the student's understanding of general and specific safety precautions, and examinations to determine general achievement. This may consist of a course examination administered at the end of the term to check on an understanding of technical, general, and guidance information; procedures; and sociological, scientific, or technological principles.

Methods for Individualized Instruction

The following methods describe types of individualized instruction which permit students to work on their own and to assume responsibility for their activities while the teacher(s) remains in the background to facilitate the instructional program.

Using Programed Instruction

This is a method by which a student pursues a unit for a course with a specially written program that is facilitated with a teaching machine, "scrambled" book or pamphlet, or a computer. Programed instruction is widely used by industrial firms, in government training programs, and in military training since it provides high retention and is considered to be especially effective with adults. Programed instruction has been popular with many VAE teachers. They recognize that it frees the student during the learning process from time schedules and frees teachers to enrich their subjects, as it provides greater opportunity for individual contacts and discussions with students.

Teaching machines are merely devices to facilitate programed instruction. They take many forms. Simple ones made in a school consist of folders, with viewing windows and holding slots cut to accommodate pages for the program. Business enterprises have developed a great array of programed materials and teaching machines for use in the schools; and the publishers have sponsored some excellent programed material in book or pamphlet form.

There are two basic systems used in preparing programed instruction. First, **the linear program** is a number of easy-to-follow sequential steps called "frames". The task of the learner is to construct the response with the correct words or provide the sketch to demonstrate that he/she understands the point just acquired. Before undertaking the next frame the student is given the correct response, which is either reinforcement or immediate feedback of an error. Second, **the branching system** is where the learner is confronted with several possible responses (answers). If the correct one is selected, the learner proceeds directly to the next frame of the program. If the student chooses the wrong answer, he/she is immediately apprised of the error and is given information which explains why the choice was wrong. With this explanation, the student is directed back to the frame missed for another try. The errors then set the stage for "branching" or the different routes that are followed to arrive at a correct response.

There have been a number of VAE research and curriculum projects reported in the ARM and AIM documents (described in Chapter 6) that are concerned with computerized programed instruction. Much can be accomplished by having computers operating with teaching machines. A major advantage is that the learner's abilities can be diagnosed and matched with effective methods for teaching the unit, as is done in the Personalized Educational Programs (PEP) described in Chapter 4. Stolurow (1965, 22), one of the very early pioneers in developing computer-based instruction, has said:

> The computer-based system appears to be the most efficient way of coping with the task of individualized instruction. It can store the requisite information and the various decision rules that are differently called upon to produce the program which each student requires.

Using Student Study Guides

Many VAE teachers are now developing student study guides to direct a learner's activities in pursuing a module of instruction. An example of this approach is the Learning Packets for an electronics course that are described in Chapter 3 and have been developed and tested by David L. Jelden. Other examples of such student study guides will be found in Appendix M.

The factors considered in the development of these kits or packages as modules of instruction are outlined under the topic "Instructional Packages for Individual Development," they may be found on p. 175 of Chapter 6.

Audiovisual Presentations

Many of the group audiovisual presentations may be used by students on an individual basis. Students may review and study

Fig. 10-7. Closed-loop film in a cassette is viewed by student studying graphic design. (Courtesy, Frank Mahan, Beverly Hills High School, California)

filmstrips, motion pictures and other visuals to reinforce instructions. Filmstrips are an important part of programed instruction. Viewing of filmstrips, often in conjunction with a tape recording, may serve as the core for an entire program. Students receive directions for additional activities, such as viewing a display or performing an experiment from the filmstrip and tape.

The closed-loop film, either silent or with a sound track, permits the use of the motion picture in individualized instruction. Figure 10-7 shows a student viewing a closed-loop film during class. Closed-loop films can be developed by instructors with photographic equipment or purchased commercially. Films can be used to teach (or review) demonstrations, safety, career information, or other instructional content.

Doing Research

Research to be done by a student, or team of students, before plans are made for a unit, project, experiment, or technical report often takes place at the work station in a laboratory, shop, or drafting room. Study carrels are now provided in many VAE laboratories to facilitate the use of the supporting audiovisual materials and the review of study guides and pertinent references. Many physical plants for VAE programs now have planning centers with equipment and resource materials to facilitate committee projects or individual development. It seems essential that research at the junior high school level, especially the major phases of it, be under the direct supervision of the teacher and his/her associates. As the student matures and develops, however, it becomes desirable that all the possible resources in the community be used for research to support advanced projects calling for an application of sociological, scientific, and technological principles.

It will be readily recognized that it is most essential for today's students to have experiences in doing such research. A research-minded student with some experience in solving today's problems will at least have some appreciation of what needs to be done to cope with rapid technological, scientific, and sociological developments.

Interviewing an Authority

Interviewing an authority on some (1) occupational information topic, (2) scientific or technological principle, or (3) economic or social issue could well be a most exciting and meaningful experience for an individual student or a team of students. Usually there are several persons in a community who deem it an opportunity to assist learners with such matters.

The teacher's role is to build up the contacts and set the stage for these interviews. The individual student, or a committee from a class, gains much in working under the teacher's direction and in identifying and determining the factors to be discussed in the interview with an authority.

When an entire class might benefit from the discussion that transpires from a carefully planned interview with an authority, a tape recording is easily made and edited for playback to the entire class. Some teachers have made collections of these significant recordings to augment the instructional program.

Some schools now have equipment for conducting a telephone conference with an authority. Two or more movable microphones are used as members of a class raise questions on the subject and participate in the conversation with the person being interviewed.

Planning Procedures for a Unit

In an earlier section of this chapter concerned with instruction sheets, the use of planning sheets was discussed as an essential method for presenting group instruction. Students learn to use such instruments as they cooperatively plan a class unit. As soon as students master essential phases of planning through group instruction, it is essential that this activity become highly individualized. This provides an opportunity for a student to demonstrate an application of what was taught as a group process. It is recommended, therefore, that as students advance, they be encouraged to reach the point rapidly where they assume responsibility for planning a unit such as a project or experiment. In advanced VAE courses, the objective should be to have the teacher's role become that of consultant as students do research and planning for units that call for projects or experiments.

Constructing Project or Aids for Presentation

One of the many unique contributions of VAE is that it provides for an application of fundamentals — such as sociological, scientific, and technological principles — and hand and machine tool operations. For this reason VAE has been considered basically an activity program. Many of the other subjects in the total curriculum, such as the offerings in science, are now moving to provide workshops where students may apply what is being taught. VAE has pioneered this approach by providing work stations where students may headquarter for a period of time to make an application of content that is being covered and stressed in a specific course. Some leaders in education are now suggesting that there may be need in VAE programs of the future to have some courses for advanced and carefully selected students planned with major emphasis and concern for theory and with less emphasis on application.

Another unique quality of VAE is the opportunity that it provides for individualized instruction at the work station. Demonstrations, lectures, discussions, and other methods for group instruction are usually scheduled at the beginning of a unit and presented to an entire class as efficiently as possible so that sufficient time is saved for the students to make essential application at the work station. Then when the time comes for the students to go to their work stations, they are entirely on their own (1) to work at their own rate, (2) to deal with student officers and the teacher and their associates on a one-to-one basis, (3) to use the equipment, utensils, tools, and materials in making an application, and (4) to develop the desired degree of skill.

In technical courses such as power mechanics, electricity, electronics, hydraulics, and those for medical and dental assistants, there needs to be provision for a student or a committee of students to develop and construct aids that illustrate some mechanism or application that they might use when making a presentation to illustrate and explain a scientific or technological principle. Projects of this type are needed as well as those with values for personal or home use.

Performing an Experiment

With an increased emphasis on technical education there will be more and more need in VAE programs to have students performing experiments on an individual or team basis at a work station. Planning for and carrying out an experiment needs to be highly individualized so the student can make the necessary observations to develop essential insights and understandings. An experiment in such courses as applied physics is usually directed with an assignment sheet that suggests a procedure which will adequately control conditions and/or control variations of conditions for the purpose of observing relationships or testing a hypothesis.

Writing Technical Reports

In advanced VAE courses, especially those in technical subjects, there needs to be opportunity for students to do research, organize data, and write reports on technical topics. This is an effective individualized method for dealing with general, technical, and guidance informational topics.

It is through such reports that students learn to use such indexes as **The Applied Science and Technology Index** (known as **Industrial Arts Index** prior to January, 1958), **Engineering Index, Art Index, Cumulative Book Index,** and **Architectural Index,** that are available in most good libraries. Most Americans now recognize that able persons in the technical occupations need competencies in organizing and transmitting ideas in writing. While in school, students need experiences in writing about topics that they understand and consider to be essential and meaningful. Also, technical reports written in VAE classes need, in every way, to be held to the school's standards for English composition.

Presenting the Report for a Unit

The school needs to provide optimum opportunity for students to develop skill in reporting carefully organized information. There are numerous opportunities in technical subjects for students or committees to make reports on research covering the newer developments in their area of specialization as well as on other selected topics. Articulate communication is a goal to be encouraged in all school subjects.

Evaluating a Project or Unit

To fulfill those VAE course goals that are focused on consumer values — an appreciation for good construction, industrial design in America's products, and the like — students need to participate in the evaluation of their work. The educative process is enhanced as the individual students evaluate their work and that of others against established criteria. Student involvement is as important in the evaluation of a completed unit as it is in the research, planning, and execution of the work.

Techniques for such involvement are reported by Silvius and Curry (1967, 490-504).

Feasible Methods and Specific Teaching Aids Identified with Titles for Units

The preceding major topic in this chapter has carried descriptions of the commonly used methods for presenting content and for individualizing instruction. Now that these methods are identified, it again becomes necessary to think about the teaching aids or devices that might be procured or constructed for teaching any one unit. As mentioned in the introductory section of this chapter, teaching aids are

Methods, Aids, and Teaching Techniques   **301**

classified as (1) devices for improvement of instruction, (2) administrative devices, and (3) aids to facilitate production. These are the material devices such as a chalkboard, a specific loop film, a bulletin board display, or a teacher-developed aid such as those shown in Figs. 10-8, 10-9, and 10-10.

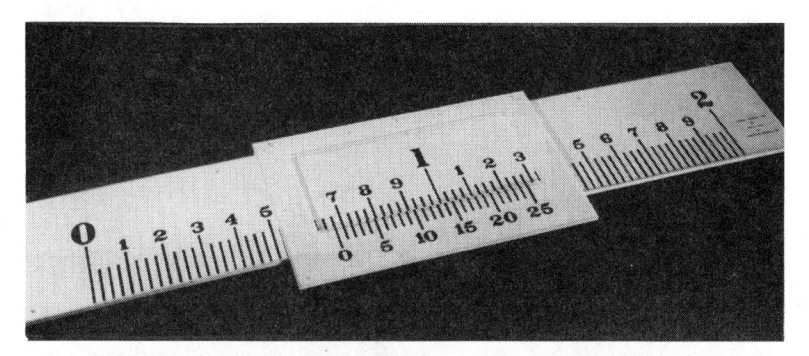

Fig. 10-8. This enlarged vernier was constructed as a teaching aid by John J. Hija.

Fig. 10-9. Ronald Richardson developed this device for teaching decimal equivalents.

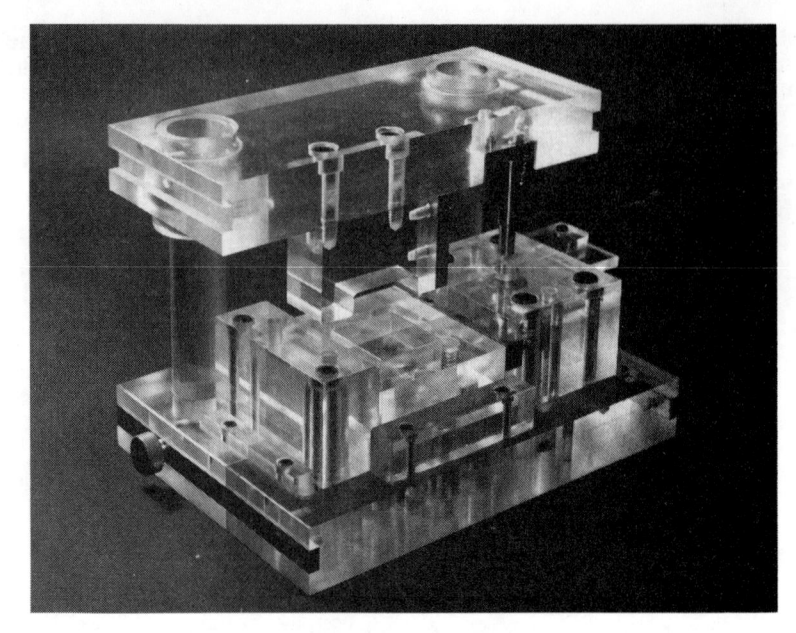

Fig. 10-10. Carl Kienle developed and constructed this aid for teaching construction and operation of a pierce, cut-off, and forming die.

The next logical step in developing a course of study is to take each of the identified units for the course, one at a time, and select the methods that the teacher or curriculum planners believe would be most appropriate and effective for teaching the unit under the prevailing learning conditions. To accomplish this, forms similar to the ones shown as Figs. 10-11 and 10-12 might be developed. At the top of Fig. 10-11, space has been provided for the teacher to list the unit number and its title. The teacher then selects suitable methods for presenting the content and for individualizing instruction by checking the appropriate items in the center columns of these two forms. Experienced teachers usually use several methods in teaching any one unit and make every effort to vary the methods selected for the different units. Inexperienced VAE teachers are likely to depend too completely, and rather exclusively, on one method like the demonstration and overlook such effective methods as a visual presentation.

It should be noted, also, that space has been provided on the two forms, shown as Figs. 10-11 and 10-12, for describing the specific teaching aids and references that might be brought into focus with each of the units.

The selection of the teaching methods and the listing of the specific teaching aids for a unit will depend on such factors as (1) the experience

UNIT NUMBER _____ TITLE OF UNIT _____

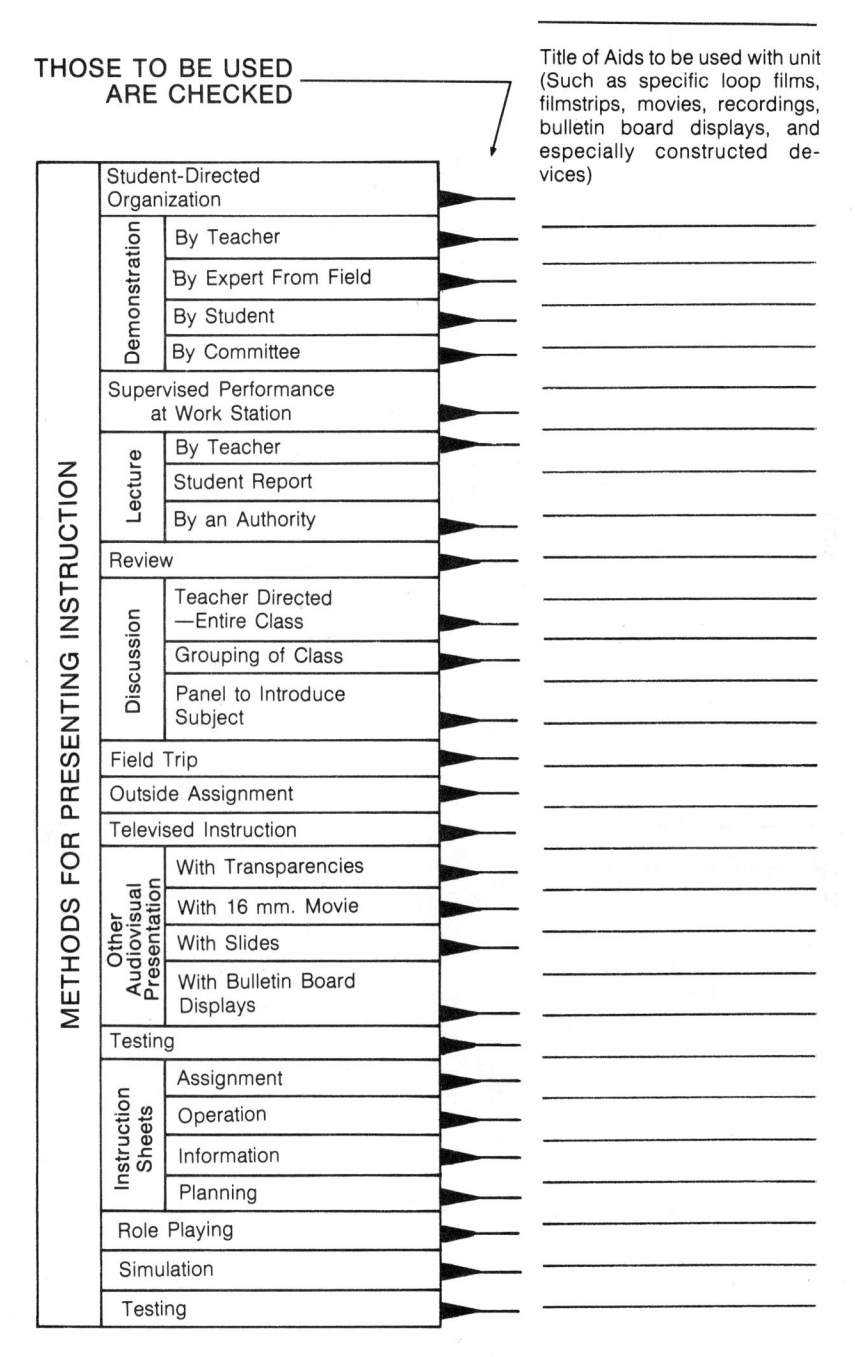

THOSE TO BE USED ARE CHECKED

Title of Aids to be used with unit (Such as specific loop films, filmstrips, movies, recordings, bulletin board displays, and especially constructed devices)

METHODS FOR PRESENTING INSTRUCTION		
	Student-Directed Organization	
Demonstration	By Teacher	
	By Expert From Field	
	By Student	
	By Committee	
Supervised Performance at Work Station		
Lecture	By Teacher	
	Student Report	
	By an Authority	
Review		
Discussion	Teacher Directed —Entire Class	
	Grouping of Class	
	Panel to Introduce Subject	
Field Trip		
Outside Assignment		
Televised Instruction		
Other Audiovisual Presentation	With Transparencies	
	With 16 mm. Movie	
	With Slides	
	With Bulletin Board Displays	
Testing		
Instruction Sheets	Assignment	
	Operation	
	Information	
	Planning	
Role Playing		
Simulation		
Testing		

Fig. 10-11. Front Side of Form for Identifying Teaching Methods and Specific Teaching Aids with the Title for a Unit

THOSE TO BE USED ARE CHECKED

Recommended References to Help Students

Methods for Individualized Instruction
- Using Programed Instruction
- Using Student Study Guides
- Reviewing a Topic
- Interviewing an Authority
- Planning Procedures for a Unit
- Constructing Project or Aids for Presentation
- Performing an Experiment
- Writing Technical Report
- Presenting Report for a Unit
- Evaluating a Project or Unit

Useful References for Teacher Competency

Description of Teaching Techniques Employed to Make Selected Methods and Teaching Aids Effective

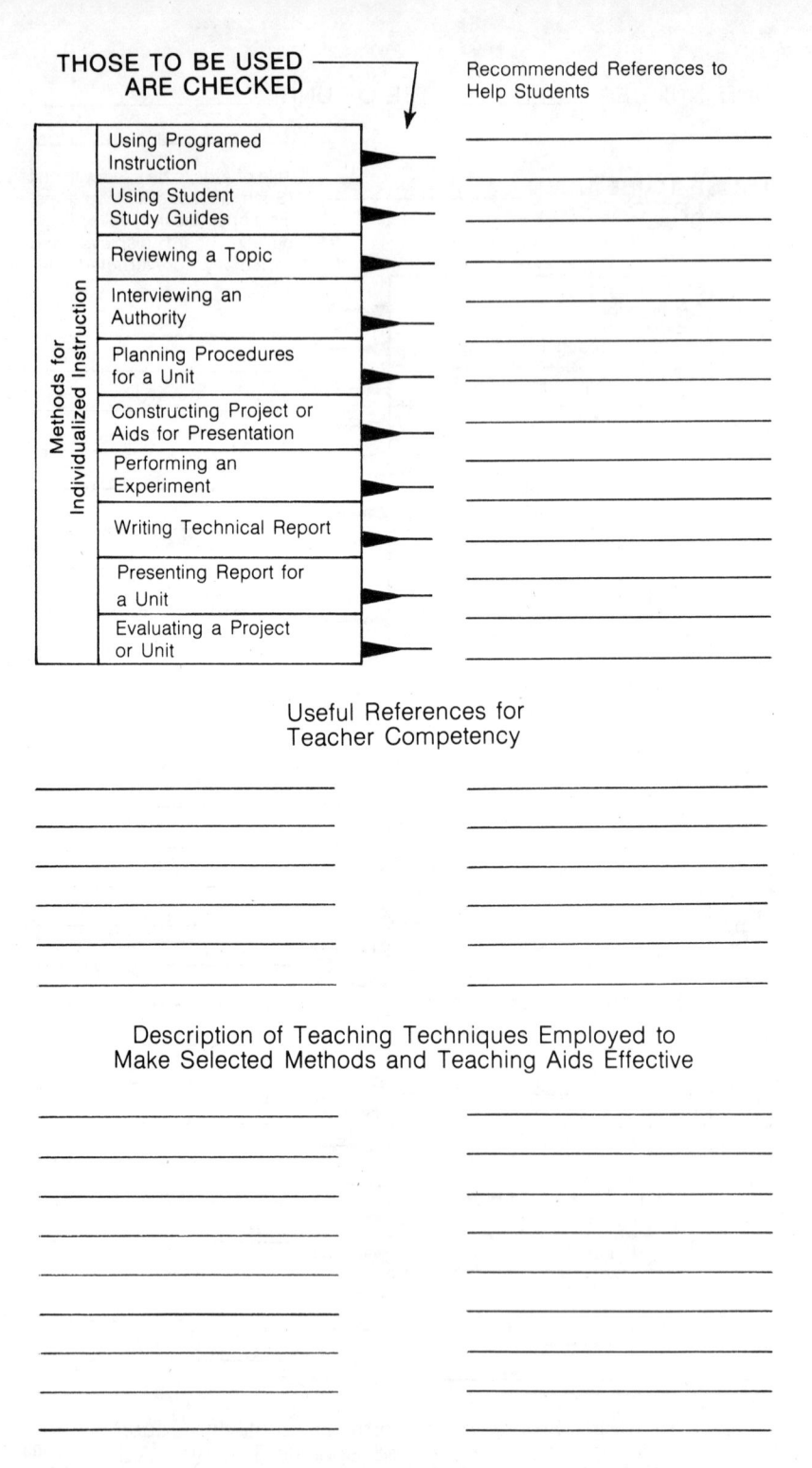

Fig. 10-12. Reverse Side of Form for Listing Individualized Method, References, and Teaching Techniques for a Unit

and competency of the teacher; (2) the previous experience, maturity, and ability of the students; and (3) the availability of the teaching aids, instructional materials, and equipment. No member of the teaching team should attempt to lecture on some topic, to direct a discussion, or to give a demonstration in an area of VAE in which he/she is not thoroughly competent. It is extremely important for a member of the teaching team to always display a high degree of technical and professional competency. Then, too, essential enthusiam is generated only through positive preparation. The decisions regarding the methods and aids to be used must be predicated on professional judgment. It becomes the teacher's responsibility to evaluate students' attitudes, abilities, and appraise what they already know and can do. These factors will greatly influence the effectiveness of chosen methods and the teaching aids that are procured or developed.

Time is often the factor that determines the methods and teaching aids that might be used when a unit of instruction is taught. A teacher might decide, for example, that it would be very effective in one of his/her courses, as a phase of the first and introductory unit, to have a visual presentation of 2" x 2" colored transparencies of previous students with their projects. Since it would take at least a term to develop these slides, he/she would need to use other methods and teaching devices until these visuals were completed.

Descriptions of Teaching Techniques for Each Unit

Teaching techniques are those details of presentation that teachers create and utilize to make the methods and useful teaching aids chosen for a unit most functional. These techniques embrace the predetermined strategy of the teacher. They are often referred to as the **tricks** of the teaching profession. Earlier in this chapter they were defined as the refinements of a teacher's presentation to make instruction more effective. **Teaching techniques make the difference between a poor and a good teacher.** To illustrate this, one could arrange to have teacher "A" present instruction to students who are known as group "C." Teacher "B" would then be asked to present exactly the same content using exactly the same methods and teaching aids, to another carefully matched and equated class to be known as group "D." The methods, teaching aids, and students (to the degree possible) would be matched to observe the effectiveness of the teaching for a specified unit. The factors, then, that would help the evaluators rate the effectiveness of teacher "A" or "B", one over the other, would rest completely with the **teaching techniques** employed with the selected methods and available teaching aids, which remain constant in each case. It is, therefore, basically the teaching **techniques** that a person needs to acquire and develop in supervised teaching while he/she is preparing for the profession.

Friendliness, confidence, timing, and showmanship are examples of characteristics that help a teacher present instruction. They are also

306   Planning and Organizing Instruction

DEVELOPED AS

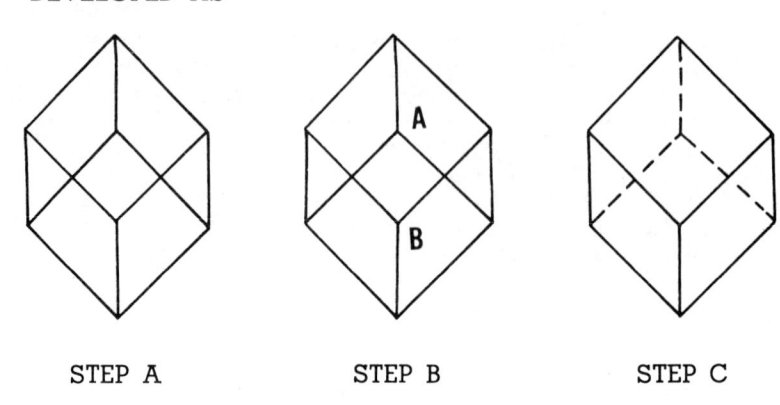

STEP A   STEP B   STEP C

Fig. 10-13. Necker's cube,[2] a visual space misconception device, consists of one square superimposed upon another so that the joined corners seem to fluctuate in spatial relations. (Courtesy John E. DeWald, Automotive Engineer, U. S. Army)

[2]Reference to "Necker's Cube" may be found in Robert S. Woodworth and Harold Schlosberg, **Experimental Psychology** (New York: Henry Holt & Co., Revised Edition, 1954), pp. 408-411.

teaching techniques which can separate the good and the poor teachers. It is easy for teachers to improve on these characteristics when they enjoy teaching and working with students in a learning situation. The teacher who enjoys his/her work and is enthusiastic about improving instruction will continually identify new and better techniques for instruction.

A good example of a teaching technique for emphasizing the (1) necessity for conventional representation, and (2) need for standard lines and symbols to accurately transmit information in drafting is one used by John E. DeWald. The illustration shown as Fig. 10-13 is developed on the chalkboard, as shown in the three steps. Students are questioned as to which of the two central corners in step "B," (A or B) is closer to them. The apparent optical illusion causes them uncertainty. However, when the three indicated lines are broken, as shown in step "C," there is immediate orientation.

Space has been provided on the reverse side of the form shown as Fig. 10-12 for describing significant **teaching techniques** that are applicable. Conceiving such teaching techniques calls for much ingenuity and an inventive approach as teachers constantly think of refinements for making their methods and teaching aids more effective. It is essential that teachers always believe that there must even be a better way to apply the methods and use the devices when teaching a unit. This is what makes teaching an exciting and challenging profession for the great teachers.

It seems appropriate to close this topic with these quotations.

> The true aim of every one who aspires to be a teacher should be, not to impart his own opinions, but to kindle minds.
> — F. W. Robertson

> The teacher who is attempting to teach without inspiring the pupils with a desire to learn is hammering on cold iron. — Horace Mann

> To waken interest and kindle enthusiasm is a sure way to teach easily and successfully. — Tryon Edwards

Adequate Forms and Records for Administration of a Program

Since VAE courses usually deal with material things and have been, to date, basically activity-type programs, a teacher finds that it is often necessary to develop and provide forms that seem essential for facilitating the teaching of administrative units of instruction (see Chapter 9) and the general management and organization of the instructional program. These forms may be needed for these purposes:

1. Attendance records.
2. Data regarding education and experience of each student.
3. Sale and/or accounting of instructional supplies.
4. Cumulative records.
5. Planning of units.
6. Safety program.
7. Student-directed organization.
8. Accounting for utensils, tools, supplies, and equipment.

It is suggested that copies of these forms be mounted in a course of study and that there be an adequate description for the use of each form.

Provisions for Substitute Teachers

It may be essential on occasion for VAE teachers to be absent from their teaching assignments for personal or family illness, professional meetings, personal business, and other important and unavoidable reasons. Providing fundamental directions to assist a substitute to take over the regular teacher's assignment poses many problems. The items presented are those that need to be written and included with the materials for the instructional program that would help other persons carry on the course of study. These include:

1. Suggestions to administration regarding student limitations for operating power machines if a substitute teacher needs to be

employed who may not be fully and legally certificated to teach a VAE course;
2. The kind of information that is needed to assist the substitute who is not fully qualified and certificated for the subject; and
3. The kind of information that would be helpful to a fully qualified substitute.

Suggestions to Administration

A policy statement needs to be formulated through the involvement of such individuals as the department head, professional teachers in the department, principal, and supervisor regarding the types of lessons that will be carried on, or other action to be taken, when it becomes necessary to employ a teacher not legally qualified for a VAE teaching assignment. The regular teacher, the department head, and the supervisor need to be especially concerned for the establishment of policies and practices that adequately cover responsibility for liability, especially where there is a possibility of having power equipment used by students where teachers do not have adequate and legal preparation to direct its use.

Plans for Lessons Where Substitute Is Not Fully Qualified

The lessons developed for a substitute not fully qualified for the teaching assignment need to be carefully planned. Such lessons might be concerned with study and discussions of selected sections of the regular text materials so that both the students and the teacher would recognize and accept them as integral phases of the course. There is much available pertinent visual material that may be secured from business and industry without cost, or for a very nominal fee, that could be used for such occasions. In VAE subjects, kits containing sufficient equipment and directions might be provided so that a substitute could teach students useful things related to the course of study. Examples of such teaching plans may be found in Silvius and Curry (1967, 104-107).

Information Needed by a Qualified Substitute

It is suggested that brief directions for substitutes be written on one or two sheets and placed in some conspicuous place, such as the very first sheets in a course of study. These will help the substitute cope with such routine matters as (1) locations of keys (2) the teacher's schedule; (3) daily order of business in each class; (4) the student-directed organization; (5) seating arrangements; (6) restrictions, if any, on use of tools and equipment; (7) names of persons teaching in adjacent rooms; and (8) marking finished work.

Examples of plans for a qualified substitute may be found in Silvius and Curry (1967, 102-104).

For Self-Assessment and Discussion

1. Explain the difference between a teaching method and a teaching technique.
2. Describe a teaching technique that might be used when teaching a specific unit in your area of specialization.
3. What factors would influence the selection of specific methods to present instruction for a unit?
4. What methods could, in your opinion, be used to a greater degree by VAE teachers? Suggest examples of units in your area of specialization that could be taught effectively by these methods.
5. How could a VAE teacher go about locating nearly every available filmstrip that might be useful when teaching identified units for his/her courses?
6. List the advantages of "simulation" as a method in VAE programs.
7. Explain the basic differences between the "linear" and "branching" systems used in the development of programed instruction. List the advantages and disadvantages of each.
8. Describe how closed-circuit television could be used in a specific VAE teaching situation.
9. What are the unique features of computer-assisted instruction?
10. Three categories were given for classifying teaching aids or devices. Cite specific examples of such aids, for your teaching situation, in each of the three classifications.
11. List kinds of lessons that might be planned for a substitute teacher not legally qualified and prepared, who has been employed to take over the teaching assignment that you are now in or for which you are preparing. What kind of information would be needed by a qualified substitute teacher?
12. In the event that a student were to be injured with power equipment during the period that an unqualified substitute teacher was in charge of a VAE class, who are the persons who might be held legally responsible for liability?
13. Name several of the methods currently advocated for facilitating individualized instruction in VAE programs.
14. What is the basic difference between a teaching technique and a teaching aid?

Assignments to Demonstrate Competencies

1. List and briefly describe methods that you would use when presenting group instruction for a selected VAE course of study. Preface this report with sufficient information about school conditions, the community, and the learners to justify the use of these methods for the specified course under consideration.
2. Name and briefly describe the selected methods for individualized instruction for the same course used to facilitate assignment one.

3. Identify methods for group and individualized instruction, teaching aids, references for students and the teacher, and teaching techniques for five selected units from any one course, with the use of the form shown in Figs. 10-11 and 10-12 or by developing a similar one.
4. Develop specific directions for a substitute teacher, considering such factors as those mentioned in this chapter under "Information Needed by a Qualified Substitute."

These assignments are to be developed to the degree that they will meet with the approval of the person directing your development to become a VAE teacher or leader.

References* and Resources

Books

Baird, Ronald J. **Contemporary Industrial Teaching.** South Holland, Illinois: The Goodheart-Willcox Co., Inc. 1972, Pp. 200.

Boocock, Sarane S., and Schild, E.O. **Simulation Games and Learning.** Beverley Hills, California: Sage Publications, Inc., 1968, Pp. 279.

Carlson, John G. H., and Misshauk, Michael J. **Introduction to Gaming: Management Decision Simulations.** New York: John Wiley & Sons, Inc., 1972 Pp. viii + 184.

Fleck, Henrietta. **Toward Better Teaching of Home Economics.** New York: The MacMillan Co., 1968, Pp. viii + 402.

Frantz, Nervin R., Jr. "Individualizing Instruction for Multi-Occupational Laboratories," in **The Individual and His Education.** Edited by Alfred H. Krebs, Washington, D.C.: American Vocational Association, Inc., 1972, pp. 175-197.

_____. **Individualized Instructional Systems for Vocational and Technical Education: A Collection of Readings.** Athens, Georgia: Vocational Instructional Systems, 1974, Pp, xxi + 192.

Hall, Olive A., and Paolucci, Beatrice. **Teaching Home Economics.** 2nd ed. New York: John Wiley & Sons, Inc., 1970, Pp. xvi + 459.

Hoover, Kenneth H. **The Professional Teacher's Handbook.** Boston, Massachusetts: Allen and Bacon, Inc., 1973, Pp. xiv + 406.

Hunkins, Francis P. **Questioning Strategies and Techniques.** Boston: Allen and Bacon, Inc., 1972, Pp. x + 146.

*Johnson, R. Gilmore. "Occupational Simulations in Career Development," in **Contemporary Concepts in Vocational Education.** Edited by Gordon F. Laws. Washington, D.C.: American Vocational Association, Inc., 1971, pp. 235-240.

Larson, Milton E. **Teaching Related Subjects in Trade and Industrial and Technical Education.** Columbus, Ohio: Charles E. Merrill Publishing Co., 1972, Pp. xvi + 366.

Lindbeck, John R. **Practical Guide to Industrial Arts Education.** New York: The Center for Applied Research in Education, Inc., 1972, Pp. 206.

Pautler, Albert J. **Teaching Shop and Laboratory Subjects.** Columbus, Ohio: Charles E. Merrill Publishing Co., 1971, Pp. vii + 185.

*Selvidge, Robert W. **Individual Instruction Sheets.** Revised edition. Peoria: Chas. A. Bennett Co., Inc., 1946, Pp. 263.

Silvius, G. Harold, and Curry, Estell H. **Managing Multiple Activities.** 2nd ed. Bloomington, Illinois: McKnight Publishing Co., 1971. Topic 5, Plan a Student Organization; Topic 6, Have a Functional Student-Directed Organization; Topic 14, Organize Instruction to Teach Principles of Manufacturing; Topic 30, Utilize Audio-

*Items with an asterisk have been cited in the chapter.

Visual Materials and Equipment; Topic 31, Develop or Procure Learning Materials for Instruction; and Topic 32, Employ Technology to Optimize Instruction.

*_____. Teaching Successfully. 2nd ed. Bloomington, Illinois: McKnight Publishing Co., 1967. Topic 7, Prepare Directions for a Substitute Teacher; Topic 18, Give Demonstration to Entire Class; Topic 19, Use Other Basic Methods for Group Instruction; Topic 20, Use Methods for Individualized and Small-Group Instruction; Topic 21, Develop and Provide Programed Instruction; Topic 22, Use and Present Televised Instruction; and Topic 27, Evaluate Student Growth and Development.

*Stolurow, Lawrence M. "Model the Master Teacher or Master the Teaching Model," in Learning and the Educational Process. Edited by J. D. Krumboltz. Chicago: Rand McNalley, 1965, p. 1239.

Twelker, Paul E. (Editor) Instructional Simulation Systems, an Annotated Bibliography. Corvallis, Oregon: Continuing Education Publication, Oregon State University, 1969, Pp. vii + 286.

*Zuckerman, David W., and Horn, Robert E. The Guide to Simulation Games for Education and Training. Cambridge, Massachusetts 02138: Information Resources, Inc., 1970, Pp. ii + 335.

Periodicals

Beck, Isabel H., and Monroe, Bruce. "Some Dimensions of Simulation." Educational Technology, Vol. 9, No. 10 (October, 1969), pp. 45-49.

Berger, Ernest G. "Simulation for Industrial Arts in a changing Society." Man/Society/Technology, Vol. 31, No. 6 (March, 1972), pp. 182-184.

Gausman, Chester H., and Vonnes, John. "The Single Concept Film-Tool for Individualized Instruction." American Vocational Journal, Vol. 44, No. 1 (January, 1969), pp. 14, 16-17.

Johnson, Richard Gilmore. "Simulation Techniques in Career Development." A description of job experience kits (based on research) that are published by Science Research Associates, 259 East Erie Street, Chicago, Illinois 60611. American Vocational Journal, Vol. 45, No. 6 (September, 1970), pp. 30-32.

Kenneke, Larry J., and Rose, Robert D. "Putting Motion in Your Overhead Transparencies." Industrial Arts and Vocational Education, Vol. 60, No. 5 (June, 1971), pp. 24-25.

Marani, Donald S., and Calder, Kenneth R. "Six Questions to Improve Reading Skills." Industrial Arts and Vocational Education, Vol. 60, No. 8 (November, 1971), pp. 30 and 54.

*McClelland, William A. "Simulation: Can It Benefit Vocational Education?" American Vocational Journal, Vol. 45, No. 6 (September, 1970), pp. 23-25.

*Meckley, Richard F. "Simulation in Leadership Training." American Vocational Journal, Vol. 45, No. 6 (September, 1970), pp. 26-27, 40.

Miller, Rex, and Culpepper, Fred W. "How to Give Effective Demonstrations." Industrial Arts and Vocational Education, Vol. 60, No. 6 (September, 1971) pp. 24-25.

*Persons, Edgar. "It's an Old Game in Vocational Agriculture." American Vocational Journal, Vol. 45, No. 6 (September, 1970), pp. 34-36.

*Resnick, Harold S. "Simulating the Corporate Structure." A learning game for industrial education. American Vocational Journal, Vol. 45, No. 6 (September, 1970), pp. 37-39.

Riley, John N. and McNeill. "Testing the Value of Silent Super 8mm Single Concept Loop Films as an Aid to the Acquisition of Manipulative Skills in the Machine Trades." Journal of Industrial Teacher Education, Vol. 11, No. 1 (Fall, 1973), pp. 80-83.

Sparks, Mavis C., and Hammond, Betty. "Crimson Company Provides the Finishing Touch." (A story of a simulated office practice course.) American Vocational Journal, Vol. 45, No. 6 (September, 1970), pp. 28-29, 32.

This, Leslie E. "What is Simulation?" **American Vocational Journal**, Vol. 45, No. 6 (September, 1970), pp. 20-21.

Twelker, Paul A. "Designing Simulation Systems." **Educational Technology**, Vol. 9, No. 10 (October, 1969), pp. 64-70.

Other Published Materials

*Baysinger, Gerald B., and Silvius, G. Harold. **The Student Planning Book.** 4th ed. New York: Litton Educational Publishing, Inc., 1960, Pp. 65. (Available also as an advanced and streamlined edition for second-term students or as packets of individual sheets.)

*Bogdanoff, E. Brooks et al. "Simulation: An Introduction to a New Technology." TM-449 Santa Monica, California: System Development Corporation (March 1960).

Cottrell, Calvin J. **Model Curricula for Vocational and Technical Teacher Education: Report No. 1, Performance Requirements for Teachers.** CVTE (RD #63) publication. ERIC Reference No. ED 059 355, December 1971, pp. 142.

Ferguson, Edward T., Jr. **Vocational Teaching in Diverse Cultural Settings.** CVTE (RD #64) publication. ERIC Reference No. ED 061 418, January 1972, Pp. 224.

*Impellitteri, Joseph H., and Finch, Curtis R. **Review and Synthesis of Research on Individualized Instruction in Vocational and Technical Education.** CVTE (IN #43) publication. ERIC Reference No. ED 058 389, December 1971, Pp. 90.

*Meckley, Richard F. et al. **Simulation Training in Planning Vocational Education Program and Facilities.** CVTE (RD #36) publication. ERIC Reference No. ED 038 501, April 1970, Pp. 203.

*Rice, Dick C., and Meckley, Richard F. **Supervision and Decision-Making Skills in Vocational Education: A Training Program Utilizing Simulation Techniques.** CVTE (RD #35) publication. ERIC Reference No. ED 038 501, January 1970, Pp. 116.

Unpublished Materials

Blankenbaker, E. Keith. **Comparative Effectiveness of Variations in Demonstration Method of Teaching a Complex Manipulative Sequence,** 1970, Pp. 123. Available from University Microfilms, Inc., Ann Arbor, Michigan 48106. Document not available from EDRS. ERIC Reference for abstract is ED 042 058.

Clements, Irene Zachry. **The Development of a Simulation Game for Teaching a Unit on the Use of Consumer Credit.** Ed D. doctoral dissertation, Oklahoma State University, 1970, Pp. 196. Available from University Microfilms, Ann Arbor, Michigan. ERIC Reference for abstract is ED 044 503. Not available from EDRS.

McCowan, Richard J., and Mongerson, M. Duane. **A Simulation Instructional Model for Educating Mentally Retarded Students for Employment in the Hotel-Motel Industry.** Project of State University of New York at Buffalo under the sponsorship of Bureau of Occupational Education Research, New York State Education Department, Albany, 1969, Pp. 37. ERIC Reference No. ED 038 532.

*Richey, Rita C. "A General Model for Simulation Processes." Detroit, Michigan 48202: Division of Teacher Education Vocational and Applied Arts Education, Wayne State University, 1973, Pp. 13.

CHAPTER 11

Evaluation Procedures

Evaluation procedures are the means by which the success of an instructional program can be determined. The main purpose of evaluation is to help teachers and program developers find the most effective instructional procedures. Numerous measurements contribute to the determination of effective instructional procedures. These include a careful appraisal of the learning achieved by each student in the course based on established objectives, comparison of the effectiveness of different instructional procedures, a comparison of the effectiveness of the teacher or teaching team in using different instructional procedures, and analysis of the cost and time effectiveness between procedures. Effective evaluation should also provide cumulative records of student growth, the development of self-evaluation abilities by the student, and a measurement of the teacher's ability to manage and present the instructional program.

Evaluation is, therefore, a continuous process, integrated into the total instructional program. Good evaluation procedures result in improved student growth and development. They help students develop a realistic appraisal of their abilities and limitations and teach them to use their strengths to overcome their shortcomings. Evaluation also provides information that will help the teacher and program developers identify units poorly taught or in need of revision.

A positive approach to evaluation is necessary to promote a classroom atmosphere in which the students look to evaluation as a means of **improving instruction, measuring their own progress, and determining where additional instruction is necessary.**

This chapter presents four major areas which must be considered when developing a complete evaluation program, integrated into the daily activities of the students. These are:

- **Rationale and principles which help structure the evaluation program:** The need to make the instructional program accountable to both students and society, the establishment of cost- and time-effective instruction, and the reporting of student growth to the student, parents, and society.

    Another principle which must be considered is the reference or standard for measurement of student progress. Is student progress

measured against an established criterion or against the norm established by the population?
- **Evaluation based on course goals and behavioral objectives:** Evaluation of the degree of fulfillment of goals and objectives is the principal measurement of program or course success.
- **Evaluation procedures:** The types of evaluation instruments and the use and development of these instruments. Teachers and program planners must be familiar with objective and subjective evaluation, student participation, development of tests and evaluation devices, and the use and interpretation of test results.
- **Teacher competency and record keeping:** A measurement of the teacher's ability to manage and provide instruction, plus the development of a system for managing the cumulative records of the students.

Evaluation is an important facet of the instructional program and must become an integral part of course and program planning. In order to adequately prepare a program of instruction, evaluation procedures must be developed in written form and appear within the framework of the course of study.

The Emphasis on Accountability

Landers (1973, 539) points out that the word "accountability" first appeared in the **Education Index** in June of 1970. He further notes that the word has many meanings and is used in a variety of ways. Despite the lack of a single definition, a Gallup Poll in 1970 revealed that two out of every three people believed that teachers and school administrators should be held more accountable for the progress of their students. Within this context "accountability" becomes a plan or procedure whereby the effectiveness of instruction is determined and appropriate personnel held responsible. Landers (1973, 540) points out three new and significant thrusts which tend to be commonly accepted and help define accountability.

> First it directs public attention to the results of the educational process rather than to its components. Second, it attempts to fix responsibility for these results. Third, it addresses itself to the consequences of no results or poor results.
> None of these ideas is entirely new. Thus parents and [others in the] community, as well as educators have always been greatly concerned with the results of education; but the focus of attention — and of praise or blame — was generally [placed on] the child rather than the institution on its individual practitioners . . . .

For this book, accountability is a plan or procedure employed by a VAE teacher or curriculum planner to determine the effectiveness of an instructional program by evaluating the extent each learner has developed the competencies specified by the behavioral objectives. A second aspect of this concept is that the plan for accountability identifies the extent the VAE course or program fulfills department or school aims, and the overall aims for education. An underlying assumption is that responsibility for success or failure rests with the teacher and curriculum planners.

New Dimensions for Evaluation

Traditionally, the evaluation of VAE educational programs has been limited to the following:
1. The grading of finished units, study assignments, projects, exercises, and experiments.
2. Testing of student ability to regurgitate content stressed by the teacher.
3. An analysis of student opinionnaires to secure reaction to the content of a course and to the methods, teaching aids, and techniques employed by the teacher.
4. Followup studies to determine the effectiveness of instruction in preparing students for employment or to continue their formal education.
5. The inspection and rating of an educational program by some outside authority or agency (such as an advisory or accreditation committee).

While these conventional approaches to evaluation are still used in VAE programs, there is currently a more coordinated and comprehensive approach to evaluation. The contemporary methods and approach to evaluation have come as educators have moved to provide for the degree of accountability demanded by the public. Figure 11-1 illustrates the Michigan plan to prepare for educational accountability.

Evaluation procedures have been refined with the application of the systems approach and the development of competency-based educational programs. The feedback loop is an integral part of the schematic plan for the models concerned with VAE curriculum development (see the Resnick model on p. 87, Chapter 3). Concepts are now discussed in terms of **input** evaluation, **process** evaluation, and **product** evaluation. Currently, administrators and curriculum builders are considering the possibility of providing for accountability in education through such contemporary approaches as these:
1. Planning, Programing, Budgeting Systems (PPBS).
2. The National Assessment of Educational Progress.
3. Performance contracts with private concerns (as described and illustrated in Chapter 4).
4. National achievement standards.
5. Program and classroom evaluation.

Input Evaluation

The administrative staff for the School of Fine and Applied Arts at Central Michigan University (1973, 11-12) define this kind of evaluation:

> Input evaluation is aimed at providing decision-making information about the appropriateness of inputs or resources for

CHART A

Preparing Children for Adolescence

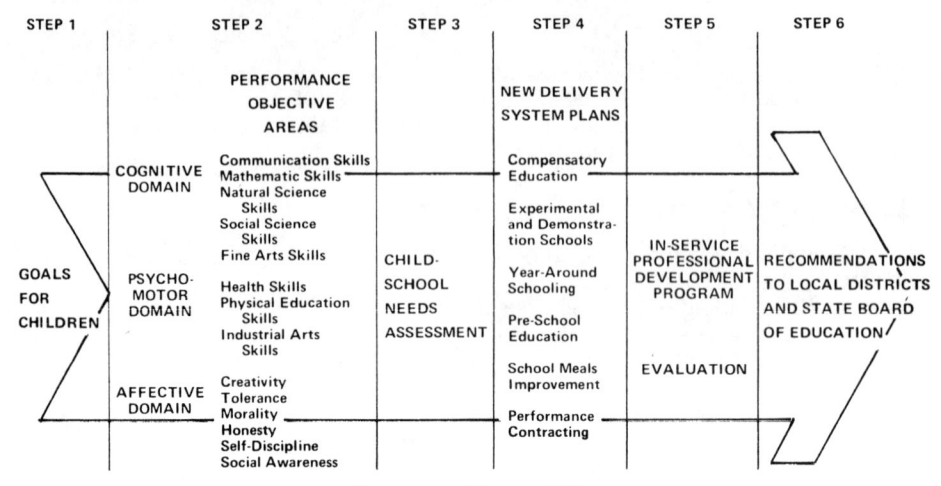

STEP 1	STEP 2	STEP 3	STEP 4	STEP 5	STEP 6
GOALS FOR CHILDREN	PERFORMANCE OBJECTIVE AREAS	CHILD-SCHOOL NEEDS ASSESSMENT	NEW DELIVERY SYSTEM PLANS	IN-SERVICE PROFESSIONAL DEVELOPMENT PROGRAM	RECOMMENDATIONS TO LOCAL DISTRICTS AND STATE BOARD OF EDUCATION
	COGNITIVE DOMAIN: Communication Skills, Mathematic Skills, Natural Science Skills, Social Science Skills, Fine Arts Skills		Compensatory Education		
	PSYCHO-MOTOR DOMAIN: Health Skills, Physical Education Skills, Industrial Arts Skills		Experimental and Demonstration Schools, Year-Around Schooling, Pre-School Education, School Meals Improvement	EVALUATION	
	AFFECTIVE DOMAIN: Creativity, Tolerance, Morality, Honesty, Self-Discipline, Social Awareness		Performance Contracting		

Ages 3 - 12

CHART B

Preparing Youth for Adulthood

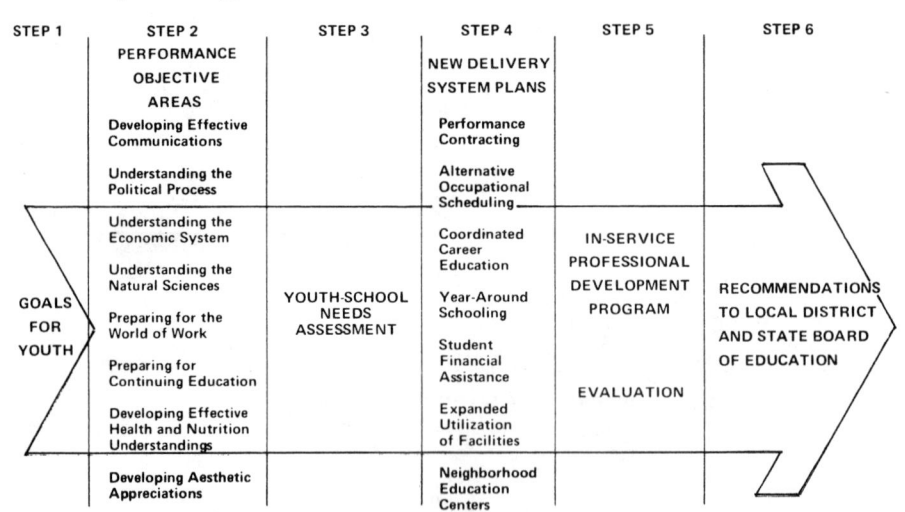

STEP 1	STEP 2	STEP 3	STEP 4	STEP 5	STEP 6
GOALS FOR YOUTH	PERFORMANCE OBJECTIVE AREAS	YOUTH-SCHOOL NEEDS ASSESSMENT	NEW DELIVERY SYSTEM PLANS	IN-SERVICE PROFESSIONAL DEVELOPMENT PROGRAM	RECOMMENDATIONS TO LOCAL DISTRICT AND STATE BOARD OF EDUCATION
	Developing Effective Communications		Performance Contracting		
	Understanding the Political Process		Alternative Occupational Scheduling		
	Understanding the Economic System		Coordinated Career Education		
	Understanding the Natural Sciences		Year-Around Schooling		
	Preparing for the World of Work		Student Financial Assistance	EVALUATION	
	Preparing for Continuing Education		Expanded Utilization of Facilities		
	Developing Effective Health and Nutrition Understandings				
	Developing Aesthetic Appreciations		Neighborhood Education Centers		

Ages 12 - 18

Fig. 11-1. Charts A and B describe the steps in Michigan's plan for educational accountability. These steps provide for the implementation of The Common Goals of Michigan Education, shown in Appendix G. (Reprinted from *A Position Statement on Educational Accountability*, Courtesy Michigan Department of Education)

the instructional program such as staff, facilities, finances, students, curriculum, strategy, and teaching methods.

In their school's five-year plan, input evaluation is planned to answer these questions:

1. What modifications can be made or alternatives developed to provide better instructional programs?
2. How can the staffing procedures be changed to make more effective use of time and resources?
3. What procedures are used to insure the most appropriate use of funds in purchasing new equipment?

The Process Approach to Evaluation

Process evaluation is planned to provide decision-making information about the educational process and a record of the events and activities occurring in this process. Medsker (1971, 9) points out that the process approach is largely concerned with how the program functions including the environmental factors that affect its success. He states that:

> This approach would evaluate such factors as curriculum and how it is developed, the use of advisory mechanisms, the equipment used for instructional purposes, the quality of the facility, the methods of teaching, the process of selecting students, and the manner in which placements are made, to name only a few. The premise is that by an evaluation of program characteristics, conclusions can be inferred.

The Product Approach to Evaluation

Product evaluation provides decision-making information relative to the outcome or products of the school's activities — the students and curriculum products. In describing this approach, Medsker (1971, 10) points out that:

> The product approach is based on concern for the student and what the training does for him. It begins with attention to program objectives and ends with an inquiry into program outcomes, both qualitative and quantitative. It is particularly concerned with how well the program fulfills its objectives, the extent to which students persist, how they find jobs appropriate to their training, and how they perform in these jobs. Naturally, there are other overall product concerns, an important one being the extent to which the training program meets local, state, and national manpower demands.

Process evaluation is descriptive while product evaluation attempts to measure performance. Both of these approaches are essential. Currently there is considerable interest in product evaluation as educators cast behavioral objectives in operational terms so data may be collected to determine how well the objectives are achieved. Traditionally, the emphasis in VAE evaluation has been on process rather than product evaluation. In too few instances has evaluation started with the appropriateness of the overall aims and then proceeded step by step through the departmental aims, course goals, behavioral objectives, content, and methods to systematically measure the competencies that can be demonstrated by the learners. This type of evaluation calls for a major focus on the product approach with some aspects of the data collected through a critical evaluation of the educational process. It also calls for an evaluation of the input factors that influence the program, such as the adequacy and qualifications of staff, suitability of facilities, and the finances for the program under consideration.

Planning, Programing, Budgeting Systems (PPBS)

PPBS, and other similar planning-budgeting systems, require the curriculum planner, often with the help of systems analyst, to first determine what the objectives and outputs are for the program, and then to ascertain what information needs to be organized and utilized to properly assess the achievement of the selected objectives. This approach now used rather extensively by governmental agencies at the national, state, and local levels is a means of allocating limited resources to programs having the greatest potential. This is in contrast to decisions that might have been made while employing more traditional budgeting techniques.

Conventional budgets have focused on projected cost for such items as personnel, supplies, and equipment with little attention given to the products produced. Traditionally budgets are usually for one or two years while PPBS (and similar plans) are projected over a longer period, e.g., five years. In the newer approaches importance is placed on quantifiable objectives and alternatives (their costs and benefits) and an adequate period of time for the implementation of the system.

McGivney (1971, 165) has observed that:

> The systems approach may seem revolutionary. Yet PPBS is not revolutionary. Its ingredients are largely not new, except in their arrangement and use. Concepts and methodologies relating to PPBS include program budgeting, benefit/cost, cost/effectiveness, cost/utility, operation research, and systems analysis.

The advantages advanced for PPBS are:

1. There is provision through the systems approach for integrating the planning, the programming, and the budgeting processes.
2. Application of PPBS often results in the consolidation, within a state, of small and inefficient educational units.
3. Application of PPBS has a desirable impact on the improvement of staffing patterns.

4. Systems analysts may encourage a wider range of resource inputs such as the use of differentiated staffing, computer-assisted instruction, performance contracting, and other yet-to-be developed approaches arising from factors associated with the age of accountability (McGivney, 1971, 169).

In summary, Salatino (1971, 78) has said:

> The PPBS approach is organized by identifiable programs rather than by objects of expenditure as used by traditional budgets. It is classified by the outputs of the program rather than by the input. It centers on resources allocation, with the object of attempting to get the greatest return on the investment of resources in education. This involves, of course, identifying objectives, alternatives in allocations of resources, and measurement of outcomes . . . .

National Assessment of Educational Progress

The National Assessment is designed to furnish information to all interested Americans regarding the educational achievement of children, youth, and young adults. Reporting is both to the general public and the educational community. The reports are designed to provide a basis for intelligent decisions regarding the allocation of resources for educational purposes (Nichols, 1971, 1).

The concept of a national assessment emerged in the summer of 1963 during discussions with Francis Keppel, the U.S. Commissioner of Education, John Gardner, Ralph Tyler, and others. In 1964, the project was funded by a Carnegie Corporation grant and plans were laid to conduct a nationwide evaluation of educational progress. The project became a responsibility of the Education Commission of the States in 1969, the year the first assessments were conducted across the nation.

Initial plans called for assessment in ten areas: science, writing, citizenship, reading, literature, music, social studies, math, art, and career and occupational development. By 1975, all areas were assessed at least once, with a number of the areas (science, writing, reading, and citizenship) assessed twice.

National Assessment represents one aspect of accountability since it "directs public attention to the results of the educational process." However, it does not fix responsibility for the results or lack of results. National Assessment has some characteristics in common with the National Census since the Assessment is designed to provide the public with factual information regarding the abilities of people within the areas assessed.

Assessments are conducted at four age levels: 9, 13, 17, and adult. Assessment items are of a variety of types including demonstration of skills, viewing motion pictures and answering questions, writing stories, and answering a variety of oral and written questions. For example, in Career and Occupational Development (COD), children at ages 9 and

13 are given a group of pictures showing a librarian, a watch repairman, a carpenter, and a telephone operator. They are asked to identify the occupation of each person. Another is a series of questions asked of 13- and 17-year-olds to identify the extent they have evaluated different occupations and professions as potential career choices.

The assessment of each area is conducted nationwide, using carefully determined sampling techniques. Individuals tested include both in and out of school people. After the test is completed and analyzed, a portion of the questions are set aside as norms for future testing. The remaining questions, with scores, are reported to the people via mass media (popular journals, radio, and television) as well as through educational journals and special reports.

No effort is made to determine the source of student knowledge nor are reports provided on individual school districts and states. The emphasis is on providing direct information on knowledge and performance by different age groups and by a limited number of selected divisions such as urban/rural, boys/girls, high and low socioeconomic status, and geographics areas — northeast, southeast, central, and west.

National Assessment is of special significance to VAE teachers since Career and Occupational Development (COD) was assessed for the first time during the 1973-74 school year. The objectives for the assessment are shown in Chapter 2, pages 55 to 58.

National Standards for Accountability

Handbook VI on Standard Terminology for Curriculum and Instruction in Local and State School Systems (National Center for Educational Statistics, x + 317) was described in Chapter 6. This Handbook is one of a series of handbooks developed by the National Center for Educational Statistics to facilitate the collection, maintenance, and reporting of educational information. The others in the series are **Handbook I, The Common Core of State Educational Information**; **Handbook II, Financial Accounting for Local and State School Systems**; **Handbook III, Property Accounting for Local and State School Systems**; **Handbook IV, Staff Accounting for Local and State School Systems**; and **Handbook V, Pupil Accounting for Local and State School Systems**. The items of information in the various handbooks are interrelated and cross referenced.

In addition to **Handbook VI**, the publication **Vocational Education and Occupations** (1969, xv + 292) is indispensable in planning and projecting occupational education programs. The use of this publication is explained in Chapter 6 in matching educational definitions and codes with the codes and titles in the **Dictionary of Occupational Titles** (DOT).

The consistent use of the terminology recommended in these publications is essential to local, state, and national audits of VAE programs. This system for educational accounting is being promulgated to help improve the quality of education by facilitating realistic planning, the efficient operation of educational programs throughout the United

States, and to facilitate meaningful evaluation. It should result in improved decision-making capabilities in such areas as administration, guidance of individual learners, curriculum improvement, and instruction. The compilers of Handbook VI (1969, 2) have indicated that:

> Wide use of the items of information in this handbook, accurately recorded at their source, will result in these advantages:
> - A sound basis for describing and evaluating administrative, organizational, and teaching practices.
> - A greater quantity of significant information to guide local, state, and national authorities in determining educational needs and policies.
> - Easier and more reliable reporting to the public on the condition and progress of education.
> - Ease in utilizing local administrative information in reports to state agencies (facilitated by the use of electronic data processing equipment).
> - Greater consistency in the kinds of information accompanying pupils who transfer from one school or school system to another or from a secondary school to a college or other institution.
> - Greater comparability of information about instructional programs within the various communities and states.
> - Greater accuracy in the summaries of information compiled by local, state, and national offices.
> - More favorable conditions for research and use of research data.

Basic Definitions

A few of the foundational definitions found in **Handbook VI** are described below:

The term **instructional program** is defined as the totality of the curriculum and its implementation through direct instruction and other means.

The **curriculum** is considered to encompass the instructional activities planned and provided for pupils by the school or school system. The curriculum, therefore, is the planned interaction of pupils with instructional **content**, instructional **resources**, and instructional **processes** for the attainment of educational objectives.

Figure 11-2 illustrates these relationships. It shows the way in which —
- Educational objectives are derived from identified needs.
- An organizational arrangement is developed or utilized for achieving these objectives.

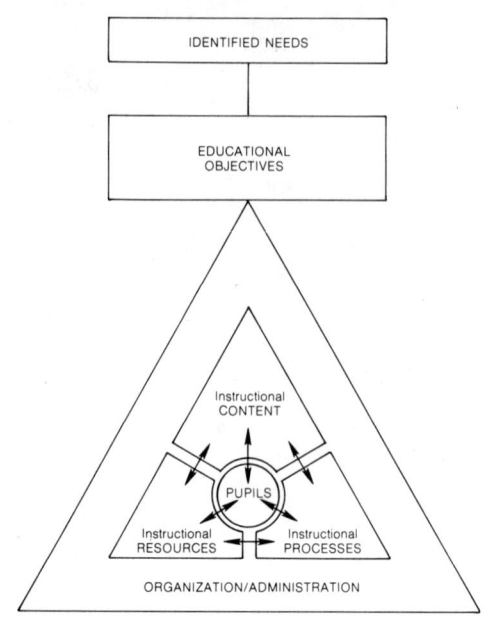

Fig. 11-2. Some Aspects of Curriculum and Instruction and Their Interrelationships (Reprinted from p. 2 of **Handbook VI** on **Standard Terminology.**)

- Pupils are brought into the environment of this organizational arrangement (usually a school) where they interact with the content, resources, and processes of instruction.

Instruction includes the activities dealing directly with the teaching of pupils and with improving the quality of teaching. **Teaching,** the major aspect of instruction, may be provided for pupils in a classroom of a school or in another location such as in a home or hospital; it may be provided by direct pupil-teacher interaction or through some other approved medium such as television, radio, telephone, and correspondence.

Learning is of greatest importance. The purpose of instruction is to enhance learning. The items of information in **Handbook VI** were however, selected to describe that which is provided for pupils in the instructional process rather than that which is acquired by pupils as learning.

In summarizing the meaning of the two terms **curriculum** and **instruction,** one might consider that the curriculum is what **is taught,** and instruction is **how it is taught.**

A **pupil** is defined as an individual for whom instruction is provided in an educational program under the jurisdiction of a school system. No distinction is made between the terms **pupil** and **student**; the term pupil is used here to include all individuals receiving instruction.

Other definitions may be located through use of the index.

Content of Handbook VI

Handbook VI provides three principal kinds of information about the standard terminology of curriculum and instruction at various levels in local and state school systems:
1. Items of information about the organization, administration, content, resources, and processes of instruction.
2. The subject matter of the curriculum.
3. Related terminology and other considerations.

Items of information about the organization, administration, content, resources, and processes of instruction are classified under curriculum areas, such as agriculture, art, health occupations, industrial arts, and technical education.

Accreditation of Occupational Programs

Much has been accomplished through the National Study for the Accreditation of Vocational/Technical Education, under the sponsorship of the American Vocational Association with funds from the U.S. Office of Education. This study was planned to produce evaluative criteria and guidelines to be applied to vocational/technical education at all levels.

Late in 1971, Lane C. Ash, study director, released a pilot-test edition of the **Instruments and Procedures for the Evaluation of Vocational/Technical Education: Institutions and Programs**. This pilot-test edition presents radical departures from other accrediting instruments. In summarizing the unique features,[1] Ash states:

1. It requires schools to account for efforts to prepare students for gainful employment. Traditional accreditation has only asked schools to account for efforts to prepare students to continue their education.
2. Product and process factors are clearly differentiated. Emphasis is on the outcomes.
3. Objectives are expected to be in measurable performance terms permitting evaluation of achievement.
4. The relationship between need, objectives, and outcomes is expressed and used as a basis for evaluation.
5. The concept of external examination as audit is introduced. Evaluation is seen as a responsibility of the institution with verification from competent external examiners.

---

[1]Extrapolated from a memorandum of transmittal sent with pilot edition of **Instruments and Procedures** (Ash et al, December 1971, Pp. 144).

6. In keeping with accrediting practices, evaluation is in terms of the stated objectives for the institution under consideration.
7. The concept of negative outcomes has been introduced. Provisions are made for institutions to account for negative as well as positive outcomes.
8. The need is emphasized for adequate resources and processes at all steps of the planning-implementing-evaluating-feedback cycle, at both institutional and program levels.

In commenting on the sterling efforts of the AVA in the development of these Instruments and Procedures for the evaluation of vocational/technical programs, Arnold (January 1972, 6) has observed:

> Now it is possible — even likely — that, ultimately, all six regional accrediting commissions will examine the criteria, standards, evaluative instruments, and procedures developed in this project with the view toward fitting them into their accrediting instruments.

Program vs. Classroom Evaluation

Strong (1972, 139-149) and other VAE leaders have recognized the advantages of making a distinction between institutional and classroom[2] objectives. Utilizing this distinction, all of the aims which describe the total program are grouped as institutional aims, and an evaluation is developed which will determine the overall success of the program. Aims which serve as the guide for program evaluation include the overall aims for education, departmental or program aims, and the specific course goals.

The classroom evaluation then consists of the measurement of student progress in terms of the behavioral objectives identified for each unit or module of instruction.

Criterion-Referenced vs. Norm-Referenced Evaluation

During recent years educators have been concerned with the need for developing techniques for criterion-referenced evaluation to supplement well-established and validated procedures for norm-referenced evaluation. The distinctions between these two approaches to measurement are:

- A criterion-referenced measure identifies an individual's competence in respect to an established standard of performance or behavior. Glaser (1971, 8) points out that this "does not necessarily refer to final, end-of-course behavior. Criterion levels can be established at any point in instruction where it is necessary to obtain information as to the adequacy of an individual's performance." It is when a learner's per-

[2]Interpreted generically to include all school and community contacts.

formance is compared with some established criterion rather than with other individuals that there is criterion-referenced evaluation.
- A norm-referenced evaluation compares the competence of a learner, on some measure, to the capabilities of others at a similar grade level. It is concerned with the relative standing of a learner along a continuum for the purpose of determining attainment in respect to others in a course or at a designated grade level. It is the traditional approach commonly used to determine achievement on the standard curve and often for the purpose of assigning grades for card-marking purposes. Norm-referenced evaluation determines that one student is more or less proficient than another, but it does not tell the proficiency of either student in respect to the subject matter task identified in a behavioral objective.

There has been a renewed emphasis on individualized VAE instruction. It is now facilitated with modules of instruction organized around specific behavioral objectives, and with the standards of performance specified (such as shown in the examples in Appendix P). It is imperative, therefore, for VAE teachers to become proficient in techniques for developing criterion-referenced evaluation.

It may be helpful to examine some of the observations of authorities in the field of measurement in respect to these two approaches to evaluation. Glaser (1971, 8-9) points out:

1. Achievement in terms of a criterion standard to be attained by a particular student is independent of reference to the performance of others.
2. Achievement examinations are often given for the purpose of grouping students based on a specific norm rather than for assessing specific curriculum attainment.
3. Emphasis on norm-referenced measures has come from the preoccupation of researchers with test theory, student aptitude, and with selection and prediction of problems.
4. Norm-referenced measures are useful for correlational analysis.
5. There is need to specify the least amount of end-of-course competence to be attained. Specifying the characteristics of maximum or optimum achievement poses more difficult problems in criterion delineation.

Popham and Husek (1971, 19-25) point out:

1. A casual inspection of a test does not reveal if it is norm-referenced or criterion-referenced. A criterion-referenced test could be used also as a norm-referenced test, but the reverse is not likely.
2. In criterion-referenced evaluation we want to know what an individual can do, not how the student stands in comparison to others.
3. These authors cite the Red-Cross Senior Lifesaving Test as an example of a criterion-referenced test, where an individual demonstrates the swimming skills needed to pass the examination, irrespective of how others perform on the test.

4. A criterion-referenced test may be given to determine whether a learner has mastered a skill considered prerequisite to commencing an educational program.
5. It is most essential that the person preparing a criterion-referenced test item be sure that the item is an accurate reflection of the criterion behavior.

A final observation may clarify a key difference between criterion-referenced evaluation and norm-referenced evaluation. Norm-referenced evaluations can be developed which sample the knowledge, performance, and attitudes being measured. A good sample provides enough information for the evaluator to identify each individual with the established norm. Criterion-referenced evaluation requires a more complete and exhaustive evaluation to determine whether the specified criteria have been met.

A Noteworthy Example of Criterion-Referenced Evaluation

The staff[3] of the Vocational Division of the Oakland Schools, Pontiac, Michigan is at work on the development of instruments to facilitate criterion-referenced evaluation for each of the 32 vocational education programs in Oakland County.

In a brochure titled *A Methodology for Program Evaluation in School Systems,* Joos (1970) points out that the PACER (Prescriptive Analysis for Curriculum Evaluation) program employed in the Oakland Schools (an intermediate school district in the Michigan educational system) utilizes a computer in a system that has these characteristics:

1. Provides analytic and prescriptive processing of testing data to facilitate the evaluation or assessment of school programs at the classroom level.
2. Makes it possible to prescribe improvements or changes in school programs.
3. Provides a methodology that is adaptable to clinical evaluation, developmental program evaluation, or special program evaluation.
4. Gives individual feedback of performance on tests.

In commenting on the PACER program and its application in vocational education, David H. Soule[4] has said:

> The strength of the PACER system lies in its being a criterion-referenced plan rather than one that provides norm-referenced measures. Another of its strengths is that it may be

---

[3]David H. Soule is the Director of the Vocational Division. Consultants who have assumed major responsibility for the development of the earlier Vocational PACER instruments include William A. Baranyai, John Cain, James Hannemann, Ruth Midjaas, and Marie Schrag. Loyal W. Joos serves as Director, Systematic Studies, Oakland Schools.

[4]Statement included in a letter to G. Harold Silvius from Dr. David H. Soule under date of July 11, 1973.

used to test in any of the domains of learning (cognitive, affective, and psychomotor) and to provide data on a student's achievement in a particular area or aspect of a vocational program.

The test booklets for each vocational program contain objective type questions (i.e., selecting the correct response from multiple choice answers, identifying false and true items in a listing of conditions, matching pictures of tools and items of equipment with their names or descriptions, and determining the correct answer to a mathematical problem) and identifies tasks, under the direction of an instructor, that a learner can now perform. The PACER pamphlet for **Medical Office Assisting** contains 129 test items. The one for **Major Appliance Repair** has 116 items and the one for **Distributive Education** carries 205 test items.

The test items in the test booklets for the vocational programs are designed to cover each performance goal that has been designated and approved for the program. The performance goals were developed by the subject matter teachers as they worked closely with the craft committee and under the leadership of the designated vocational consultants for the Oakland Schools. The test items for each program were developed by a team of persons consisting of vocationally qualified instructors (persons with extensive work experience in the subject area), and consultants who have expertise in curriculum development.

Criterion-referenced tests provide a very precise measure of the amount of learning a student has acquired in a given time. Another feature of the vocational education PACER tests is that they have been constructed in concert with people who are practitioners in the particular trade.

The tests are administered by having a student record his responses to test items on a form that can be optically-scanned. It is then processed by the computer. Feedback, covering an analysis of each student's achievement is rapid so that he may quickly be appraised of his strengths and weaknesses in respect to the behavioral objectives of the program.

In the vocational programs, the PACER instruments are first used as a pre-test to determine what a student already knows and can do. The response is analyzed by the computer to determine a student's area of strengths and weaknesses (e.g., he may be already competent in the mathematical concepts that underlie the technical area or he may be found to need instruction in the mathematical skills essential to the occupation.)

The computer analysis of the pre-test provides several bases for prescribing individualized instruction, in that all **wrong** choices are reported to students and student groups, as well as **right** answers. Specific instructional strategies may then be implemented where needed, so that learners' achievement can be assessed in specific ways. The same PACER instrument is again used as an exit test at the conclusion of instruction, to determine that the student can demonstrate the competencies specified in the performance goals for the program.

The PACER instrument is not used to compare the achievement of a student with others in his group. This approach provides a means that makes it possible for a student to assess his own achievement and readily see, and understand, what he needs to do to become competent and qualified for entry employment in his chosen area of specialization. Vocational achievement is in terms of a criterion standard to be attained by a student and is completely independent of reference to the performance of others.

Program Evaluation in Terms of Specific Course Goals

Many teachers develop excellent course goals for a course or program but fail to establish a method to determine whether the goals have been achieved. It is relatively easy to develop a norm-referenced evaluation program based on unit test (cognition), activities (psychomotor), and a final course examination. However, even if these achievement examinations are adequately prepared and graded, the teacher only has an evaluation of factual information and operational procedures that are focused on how well a learner's achievement compares with others in the class. Then too, these measurements may represent only one or two of the specific course goals. Other goals concerned with such factors as leadership development, problem-solving ability and attitudes (affective domain) toward safety precautions, industry, and society are usually not considered in this phase of grading and, if no other evaluation procedures are used, will be overlooked in the total evaluation program.

It is not necessary to consider each of the course goals as equally important in evaluating the program and student growth. Nor is it necessary to determine importance by the length of time allocated to the fulfilling of a specific course goal. It is, however, important that the place of each goal be considered and some measure of the degree to which it was fulfilled be determined in the evaluation program. The weight given to the evaluation of any one goal on the student's final accomplishment in the program must be left to the professional discretion of the teacher.

An evaluation of the fulfillment of each course goal is important when the course is being studied for possible improvement. If, for example, several students have failed to develop an understanding of one of the areas of instruction, such as general and specific safety precautions, this phase of the course must be studied to determine new and better ways of presenting this instruction to fulfill the goal related to safety.

Evaluation procedures must therefore be established that will determine the degree that the various specific course goals were reached. Such information is valuable for course, student, and teacher evaluation.

Student Evaluation in Terms of Behavioral Objectives

The determination of whether the knowledge, attitude, and/or motor skill specified in a behavioral objective has been obtained by a learner can be determined by using the **product approach** to evaluation. The degree of desired competency is specified in the behavioral objective as the conditions to be demonstrated by the learner or measured against established criteria, as illustrated in Appendix P. This is why behavioral objectives are the heart of the systems approach (as discussed in Chapter 3).

The product approach is highly individualized as the evaluation assesses each learner's capability at the conclusion of instruction. Evaluation procedures are appropriate for the behavioral objective under consideration — such as teacher-made pre- and post-tests to measure the achievement of the knowledge, attitude, and/or motor skill specified. Achievement is measured against the established criterion or standard for the measure under consideration.

There is provision in many VAE courses for the student to make an application, at the work station, of what is being stressed in group instruction while he/she is being assisted and observed by the instructional staff. Since this phase of instruction is on a highly individualized or small group basis, there is ample opportunity for the teacher and associates to observe the effectiveness of the educational **process** as well as the **product**.

Chapter 8 explains how behavioral objectives are established. They make it possible to plan for a product evaluation program by assessing a student's competence in respect to the behavioral objectives for a unit. This is accomplished through a pre-test before instruction and an exit test at the conclusion of instruction for the unit or module.

Where there are many units in a program and in turn many behavioral objectives, sometimes organized in a hierarchical order, it may be possible to develop or establish evaluation procedures or instruments that would cover more than one unit or module of instruction. In criterion-referenced evaluation it is essential that curriculum planners not lose track of the purpose of such evaluation, i.e., to measure a student's accomplishments against established criteria, for termination of instruction or practice, or to proceed to more advanced work.

There still may be need for general quizzes and mid-term and course examinations. Such teacher-developed examinations are usually samplings for norm-referenced evaluation. These teacher or staff prepared measures are often composed of objective type questions as illustrated in Appendix Q. The items in such tests are designed to discriminate between the most competent and least competent students in a class or grade level as they sample the content stressed by the teacher during a period of time. It is also possible for these tests to be part of a criterion-referenced evaluation. This occurs when the items are planned to determine the competence of **a student** in respect to an interim or end-of-program performance goal.

The classification of behavioral objectives in respect to the cognitive, affective, and psychomotor domains is discussed at some length in Chapter 8. While it is often possible to classify the learning that comes from a behavioral objective in one of the three domains, the problem is that the learning that results from many performance-based objectives readily classifies in more than one of the domains. When this occurs, evaluation procedures must consider each of the domains included by learning experiences covered by the objective.

The remainder of this topic is devoted to a discussion of procedures and techniques that might be employed in determining a student's competency, as assessed against a criterion in one of the domains. While this may be helpful, the authors suggest that teachers or curriculum builders look at each of the behavioral objectives (such as those listed in Appendix P) and deal creatively with evaluation procedures that would be most useful in determining the student competency in the objective.

Evaluating Objectives in the Cognitive Domain

Objectives in the cognitive domain include those describing course content and factual information. There are several approaches and techniques for evaluating these objectives, including:

1. Written or oral response to selected questions or issues listed in a pre-test or an exit test (an example of such questions or issues may be found in the concluding sections of each of the chapters under the heading "For Self-Assessment and Discussion").
2. The use of "Teacher-Made Tests," discussed later in this chapter. Items from such examinations are illustrated in Appendices Q and R.
3. Preparation of a short paper or essay covering standards and criteria for evaluation.
4. Having a student chair or serve as a member of a comittee, preparing and presenting a report on some aspect of a unit of instruction.
5. An evaluation of the learner's response to questions raised by a teacher in a review of group instruction. Such techniques are discussed by Carin and Sund (1971).
6. The insights that are demonstrated at the higher levels of the cognitive domain by a student making an application of fundamentals of instruction.

Evaluating Objectives in the Affective Domain

Since these objectives center around the interests, attitudes, appreciations, and adjustments of the learner, they are especially significant in VAE programs. Some educators have tended, however, to bypass such objectives since they are more difficult to measure than those classified in the cognitive and psychomotor domain. This is indeed unfortunate with career education calling for the knowledge, attitudes, and skills needed to engage in meaningful vocational, avocational, leisure, social, and personal pursuits. Also, the third edition of the **Dictionary of Occupational Titles** is based on the premise that every job requires a worker to function in relation to **data, people,** and **things.** These considerations in respect to occupational education have significant implications for behavioral objectives cast in the affective domain.

Mager (1972, 11) in his book on **Goal Analysis** has suggested techniques for identifying and describing performances and specific outcomes. If achieved, such descriptions would make it possible for the evaluator to determine whether the objective goal is attained. To illustrate, Mager (1972, 46) reports that managers from an industrial plant, concerned with improving the safety consciousness of their employees, decided that a safety conscious person would be one who —

- Reports safety hazards.
- Wears safety equipment.
- Follows safety rules (no infractions).
- Practices good housekeeping (keeps his work area free of dirt, grease, and tools).
- Encourages safe practices in others (reminds others to wear safety equipment).
- Says favorable things about safe practice.
- Suggests ways to improve safety record.

Mager (1972, 47) concludes that —

> This, [the listing of these performances], then, was the main basis for deciding whether a person was safety conscious or not. These were the performances that would cause one of the managers to pin the label of "safety consciousness" on someone. This was their meaning of the goal of safety consciousness.

It is recommended that the teacher, or curriculum builders, employ Mager's goal analysis procedures in developing criteria for evaluating behavioral objectives in the affective domain. Through group discussion with students and/or other staff members, these listings of performances or outcomes can be identified for each instructional objective. These listings would also have considerable impact on a viable instructional program and would provide the criteria and standards for the evaluation of the objective. It is further suggested that the final decision as to whether a learner exhibits such performance traits be left to the professional judgment of the teacher in charge. The associates of the teacher, such as those on the teaching team and selected student officers and assistants, might be involved in the process, but the responsibility for the final decision should rest with the professional teacher in charge. What is being suggested for the teaching profession is the same as practiced in the other professions where critical decisions having to do with human relationships are made by persons in the profession who have the training, experience, certification, and status to do so.

Evaluating Objectives in the Psychomotor Domain

As will be noted from the examples in Appendix P, behavioral objectives classified in the psychomotor domain describe the conditions for a laboratory experience that results in the development of motor abilities and the specified degree of skill. Motor skills are developed as the learner performs a manipulative task such as operating a business machine or doing a hand or machine operation. There is every opportunity, in this setting for the person in charge to be monitoring and assessing the progress of the student in respect to skill development. In many VAE activity programs students plan, design, and fabricate projects; work with apparatus in doing experiments; or do exercises for skill development purposes. Time factors, established tolerances for the completed assignments, and the quality of the finished product may be factors to consider in evaluating student competency. In many cases the product provides the vehicle for the evaluation of an objective classified in the psychomotor domain.

Fig. 11-3. Floristry requires a combination of knowledge and abilitites including design and proportion, aesthetics, and psychomotor skills. (Garfield High School, Los Angeles)

There are several approaches and techniques for evaluating objectives in the psychomotor domain, including:
1. Observation of the student as he/she demonstrates a skill or the application of knowledge.
2. Assessment of a finished product requiring the use of psychomotor skills being evaluated.
3. Use of a performance test where the student demonstrates the psychomotor ability as part of the test.
4. Written or oral information needed to develop and use a psychomotor skill. This is a secondary evaluation and should be used in conjunction with direct evaluation, such as 1-3 above.

An automatic evaluation by the student often takes place when a student is engaged in an activity. For example, a typing student will be able to quickly find typing errors; a home economics student will be able to find layout and cutting errors, especially when pieces do not fit as they should; and a woodworking student carving a bowl can immediately see a crack or chip resulting from improper use of a gouge. All of these are immediate evaluations and take place prior to the teacher viewing the work or the problem.

Objective vs. Subjective Evaluation

Good objective tests are tests that leave little or no opportunity for disagreement as to the correctness of response while subjective tests require personal judgment on the part of the evaluator. In general, true-false, multiple-choice, matching, and completion questions are used in objective tests. Their construction is time consuming but their evaluation is rapid. Essay questions and oral examinations are the two typical examples of subjective types of examinations. Such tests can be quickly prepared but the analysis of response is very time consuming.

Each method of evaluation has strengths and weaknesses. The evaluation procedures of a good course will usually combine elements of both with the final evaluation of the course being as objective as possible. In other words, if an essay test is given, it should be evaluated, a grade given, and this grade then averaged or totaled with the other grades, whether they be the results of objective tests or a subjective evaluation of projects. The averaging or totaling of the grades will result in a grade having some objectivity within the limitations imposed on the validity and reliability of the subjective evaluations used in computing the grade.

Objective Tests

Objective tests offer the following strengths and weaknesses which should be considered when this method of test construction is used.

Reliability

Results are usually quite reliable since teacher bias and opinion of the student is not a controlling factor. This is the greatest advantage of objective tests since test scoring is void of personal prejudice. Even though test scoring is reliable, selection of questions often remains as the subjective judgment of the evaluator.

Difficulty of Construction

These tests are very time consuming to devise, and clarity is often a problem. Students may not answer the questions in the same frame of reference that they were written. As a result, terms in these tests often become vague, tricky, misleading, and ambiguous (at least in the minds of students). Through item analysis techniques these problems can be eliminated to a considerable extent. See Minelli, (1959, 263-265).

Depth of Evaluation

It is often difficult to ask thought-provoking questions and determine depth of understanding with an objective question such as true-false or multiple-choice. At the same time, objective tests permit a complete review of the entire course, since time per question is kept low.

Factual Information

Objective tests are very effective in evaluating factual information. They may also be used to evaluate more complex concepts, such as technical understanding, but the questions are often difficult to phrase without developing ambiguity.

Speed of Scoring

One of the major strengths of objective tests is the ease with which they can be graded. Answer keys permit rapid grading. Many schools are now equipped with computers or machines that will evaluate test results by comparing a student-completed answer sheet with the teacher-prepared answer key. Computers also provide needed statistical data for test analysis.

Subjective Tests

Subjective tests have these advantages and disadvantages in the classroom.

Depth of Insight

Subjective testing, especially an oral examination, permits the use of thought-provoking questions. An oral examination provides insights into the depth of a student's knowledge and understanding of any phase of knowledge. This is the primary reason why graduate students in colleges and universities are often asked to submit to an oral examination.

Reliability

This factor depends on the teacher evaluating the test. Even the great teachers, however, will not be able to develop the degree of reliability obtained with an objective test. In most cases, reliability is very low. This fact must be taken into account during evaluation.

Time Consumption

While the subjective test is easy to prepare, it takes considerable time to evaluate. Often the student's handwriting is difficult to read and the sentence structure is poor. Each test consumes a large amount of the teacher's time and often overcrowds an already heavy teaching schedule.

Test Construction

While subjective tests are easy to construct, the teacher must guard against questions which the student might interpret differently than the teacher.

English Mastery

The subjective test provides a motivational force for writing and gives practice in organizing and presenting thoughts, in writing, and in spelling. These factors should be checked by every teacher to assist the students in understanding their writing weaknesses and to identify their needs for remedial study.

Teacher-Made Tests and Evaluation Devices

The primary responsibility for preparing tests and evaluation devices rests with the teacher and curriculum developers. Three aspects of development are presented in this section:

- Written tests on informational content. These examinations primarily evaluate learning from objectives in the cognitive domain.
- Safety tests. These need to assure that students can work safely in the shop or laboratory.
- Evaluation of laboratory activities. These examinations are designed to evaluate learning resulting from objectives in the psychomotor domain.

Written Tests to Cover Informational Content

Every course of study should contain plans for evaluating student accomplishment of instructional units. In general, this evaluation consists of pre-tests and end-of-unit tests plus periodic major examinations. Occasionally all examinations are arranged on a time rather than a unit system. This is especially true when the session plan of organization is used; it may also be used with the formal/descriptive plan.

Regardless of test frequency or location in the course of study, a number of principles must be followed when tests to evaluate student knowledge of instructional information are developed.

1. **Objectivity.** In general, tests should be designed to eliminate teacher bias in grading. This may be accomplished by using objective questions, such as multiple-choice, true-false, or matching, or by using simple completion items or questions requiring direct answers.
2. **Validity.** A test should measure the information it was designed to measure. If the test succeeds in evaluating the phase of instruction the teacher wants evaluated, it is valid. At first this seems like a simple concept. When studied thoroughly, it will be discovered that determining validity is the hardest part of the analysis. Such factors as misleading questions, use of terms, student vs. teacher interpretation of questions, and student vs. teacher frame of reference for answering the question may enter either test construction or utilization and result in questionable validity.
3. **Reliability.** A test should consistently provide the same results. A test is reliable when it provides a consistent evaluation of a person's knowledge or ability of the subject being tested. For example, a reliable test would yield nearly the same score if it were administered twice to the same student, provided that no learning took place during the first writing of the test or between the two administrations of the tests.
4. **Length.** A long test is not necessarily a good one even though length generally increases reliability. Many times, teachers give long tests only to find they do not have sufficient time to grade them and go over the results with the class. While examinations do provide information about knowledge gained and help both students and teachers understand accomplishment, they should also serve as a tool for reviewing instruction. To do this it is essential that provisions be made to review the results with students.
5. **Ease of Administration and Grading.** A test which is easy to administer and grade will save time and permit the accomplishment of other educational tasks. In general, an objective test of moderate length consumes minimum time and provides maximum information for the time expended.
6. **Simplicity.** Direct, simple questions provide the best written communication between student and teacher. Too often lengthy questions become so involved that students give the wrong answer or do not answer at all because they do not understand the question.

Examples that illustrate format and questions for objective tests which have been used to evaluate student knowledge of instructional information are included in Appendix Q. Only a few of the questions used in these tests have been included. Just enough questions were selected, in each case, to illustrate the type. The numbers of the questions are the same as in the complete tests.

Safety Tests

Safety tests should be designed to serve two purposes. First, they must determine whether a student has sufficient understanding of the general laboratory regulations or specific safety precautions for a particular piece of equipment to work safely. In this regard, safety tests are criterion-referenced examinations. Second, a safety test should aid the teacher in determining whether the student is developing an attitude directed toward the importance of observing the safety precautions that are so essential to the correct use of industrial, commercial, or household tools and equipment. While the first factor provides indications for the second, it does not provide complete information. A student could, for example, pass a test covering the safety precautions for a circular saw or power sewing machine and then later be involved in an injury with this equipment because of his/her attitude toward observing the safety precautions that were understood and known well. One's attitude toward safety is an essential factor. Approaches for assessing this objective from the affective domain were discussed in an earlier topic of this chapter.

Since this second concept of safety evaluation deals with attitudes, a psychological variable, simple factual tests are inadequate. Through careful observation of the student's work habits and noting whether the necessary precautions for the power machines are being observed, a teacher can determine whether a student is developing or already has safe working patterns in using business and industrial equipment. To facilitate this evaluation, it is suggested that VAE teachers record their observations on the cumulative record kept for each student covering the student's attitude concerning safety, as well as factual results of demonstrated proficiency on the general laboratory safety test and those for the specific machines. When evaluating laboratory processes, safety becomes an important part of evaluation.

In preparing tests to determine whether a student has sufficient knowledge about safety precautions (the first concept mentioned), the testing program can be divided into two phases. The first covers laboratory precautions that are concerned with (a) good personal habits, and (b) general safety in the laboratory. Those precautions in the (a) classification would cover such items as proper dress, what to do about clothing that might be caught in a machine, horseplay, illness and fatigue, and protecting long hair. General safety in the shop, items in the (b) classification, would include those precautions concerned with handling supplies and materials, storage of projects, the operation of certain machines by one person, operation safety zones, connecting electrical appliances, slippery floors, and the like. This safety instruction should be presented and discussed early in the course followed by a **before-going-to-work** test to determine whether the students understand these important general safety precautions and preventive measures.

The second phase of testing covers the specific safety precautions for individual machines or equipment. It is recommended that these tests be administered only after the students have studied the safety guides and have participated in the instruction on safety that has been presented by the teacher, such as the demonstrations on operations when the safety precautions were identified and listed.

Many teachers believe that a student should not be permitted to work in the laboratory or use a piece of equipment until he/she has scored 100 percent on the safety test. This belief stems from the possibility of the student's being injured by not observing one of the precautions not completely understood. For example, if a safety test reveals that a student does not understand the need to wear goggles when using a motor-driven wire wheel, an accident happening due to this lack of knowledge would place the burden of responsibility on the teacher. Therefore, many districts require a teacher to administer safety tests before permitting students to work on specified power equipment. Often, they further specify that the student must score 100 percent, and that all safety exams must be kept on file for the term and sometimes for the duration of the student's enrollment in school.

Because of the need for a simple, factual, quick analysis, most safety tests are objective, using either true-false statements, multiple-choice statements, or questions requiring short answers. Appendix R is made up of examples of safety tests which illustrate the types of tests which should become a permanent part of the course of study.

Evaluation of Laboratory Activities

The evaluation of student accomplishments provides a challenging situation to the teacher offering an activity program in which students individually or in groups plan, design, and construct projects or solve problems. The behavioral objectives dictate activities to be emphasized and, hence, activities that require evaluation.

In a fabrication course having, for example, a goal "to develop a degree of skill through the fabrication of a self-designed project," a simple rating scale such as shown in Fig. 11-4 could be used. This scale could be used by the student for self-evaluation prior to submitting the project and then later by the teacher. The two sets of scores could then be compared. The very simple scale guides the student or teacher through a series of subjective evaluations. The list could be lengthened to include other criteria or shortened by eliminating some of the items included, depending on the behavioral objectives for the course and professional judgment of the teacher.

In many teaching situations, problem-solving abilities could be tested through observation of laboratory activities such as bookkeeping

Evaluation Procedures   339

Student Name_____Class_____
Name of Unit _____Teacher_____
Date_____

Directions

This sheet may be used by students or the teacher. The bottom section permits the comparing of the self-evaluation made by the student with that of the teacher.
Rate each of the items on the five-point scale by circling a number on the scale.

	Best In Class	Better Than Average	Class Average	Just Below Class Average	Unsatisfactory
1. **Pre-planning.** Thoroughly planned. Activity, when necessary, included: drawings, steps, checking levels, lists of tools and supplies.	10	7	5	3	0
2. **Design.** Originality, functional, pleasant appearance, proportional, best use of materials.	10	7	5	3	0
3. **Accuracy.** Within established dimensions and tolerances.	10	7	5	3	0
4. **Finish.** Surface preparation, selection of finishing material, application of finishing material.	10	7	5	3	0
5. **Safety.** Exhibited safe attitude and practical safety precautions in all activities.	10	7	5	3	0

Student and Teacher Evaluation

List the number circled above in each of the appropriate spaces. The total number of points will be used in determining the final evaluation of the activity.

	Pre-Planning	Design	Accuracy	Finish	Safety	Total
Student						
Teacher						

Fig. 11-4. Activity Grading Sheet

340 Planning and Organizing Instruction

or computer science activities, analysis of the solutions to a problem, and/or an activity type examination, such as those shown in Fig. 11-5 and 11-6. Self-assessment checklists shown in the section on **Student**

DIRECTIONS: Match letters on the right with the numbers at left.

Fig. 11-5. This matching test on development of surfaces was devised and drawn by Chazkel Falik.

Evaluation Procedures 341

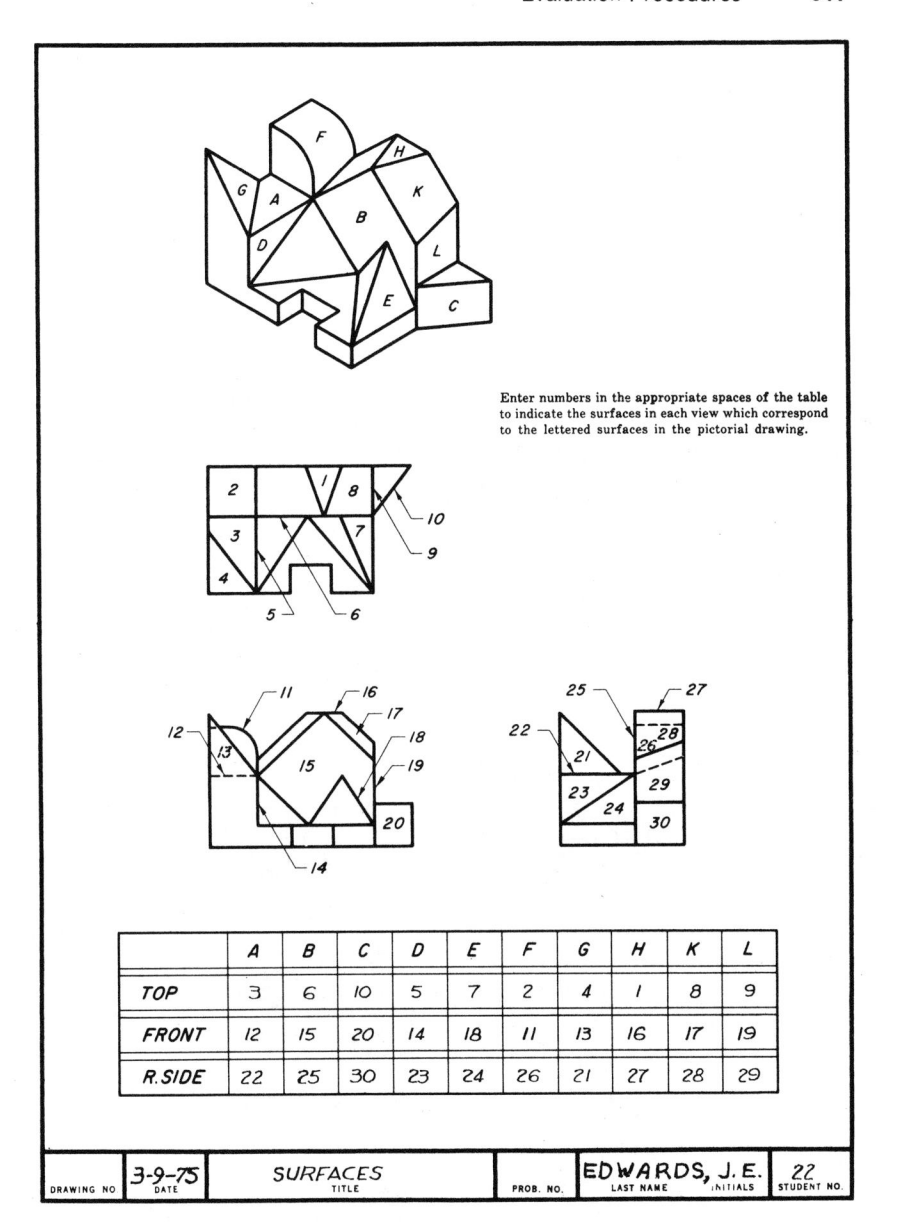

Enter numbers in the appropriate spaces of the table to indicate the surfaces in each view which correspond to the lettered surfaces in the pictorial drawing.

	A	B	C	D	E	F	G	H	K	L
TOP	3	6	10	5	7	2	4	1	8	9
FRONT	12	15	20	14	18	11	13	16	17	19
R.SIDE	22	25	30	23	24	26	21	27	28	29

DRAWING NO | DATE 3-9-75 | TITLE SURFACES | PROB. NO. | LAST NAME EDWARDS, INITIALS J.E. | STUDENT NO. 22

Fig. 11-6. Example of a Completed Examination in Orthographic Projection and Visualization Used at the Highland Park Community College, Highland Park, Michigan

Participation in Evaluation, later in this chapter, is another way of assessing problem-solving abilities.

Often laboratory activities are designed to develop an understanding of technical information and concepts that call for an application of sociological, scientific, and technological principles. As a result, evaluation may center around the informational aspect with only partial concern for an evaluation of activity performance. Evaluation might combine a check sheet of the type shown as Fig. 11-4 with a written norm-referenced examination sampling the essential informational concepts. It might also involve work sheets or drawings to be completed during the laboratory activity. The work sheets shown in Figs. 11-7 and 11-8 were designed to be completed by high school students while working on automotive components. In order to complete the assignment, a student must name and describe the function of each numbered item and submit this information on a separate sheet of paper. Upon completion of an assigned activity and work sheet, each student is either (a) questioned orally on the work accomplished, operating principle, and the specified references, or (b) given a written examination to determine the degree of understanding developed while working on the activity.

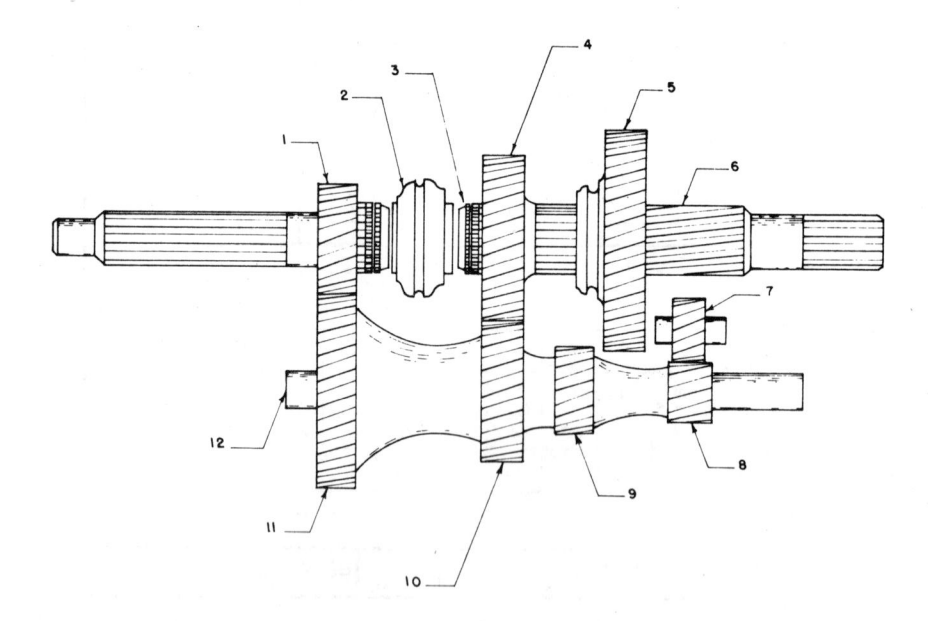

Fig. 11-7. Student Work Sheet for Three-Speed Syncromesh Transmission (Office of the Superintendent of Schools, Santa Clara County, California)

Evaluation Procedures **343**

HYDRAULIC BRAKE

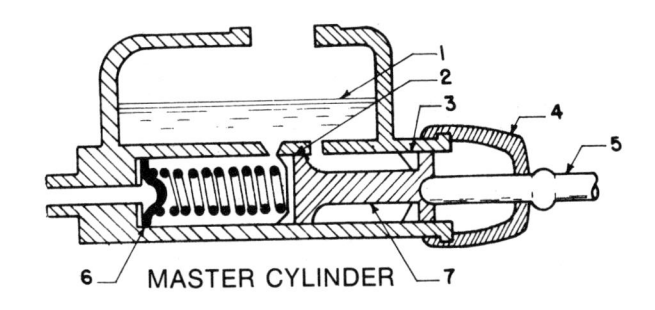

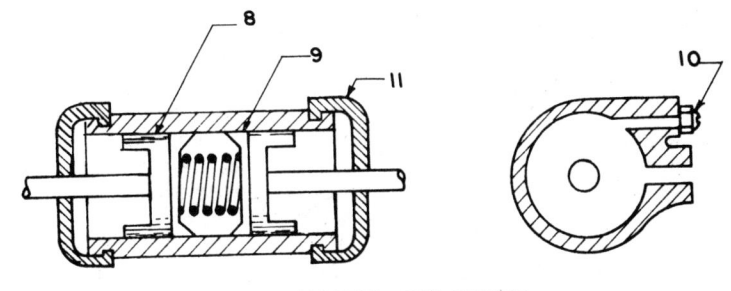

MASTER CYLINDER

WHEEL CYLINDER

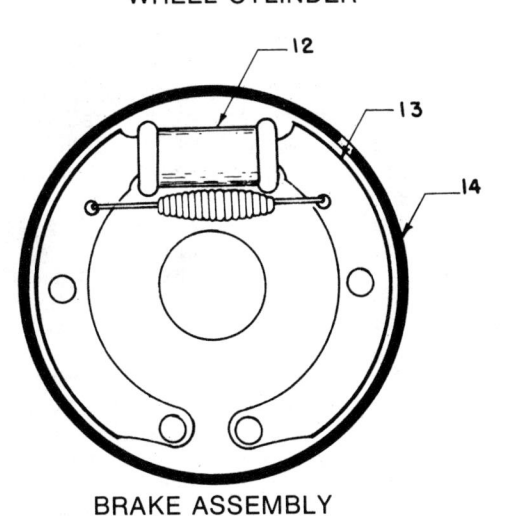

BRAKE ASSEMBLY

Fig. 11-8. Student Work Sheet for Hydraulic Brake System (Office of the Superintendent of Schools, Santa Clara County, California)

In VAE courses emphasizing a degree of skill, operation rating scales could be provided by the teacher or developed as a class project. For example, an accurate zipper installation plus a series of completed units containing common errors might be fabricated and mounted on a board. Students could then compare their work with models on the board and evaluate the units they have completed. Applications of this type of evaluation device are almost unlimited.

Interpretation and Utilization of Test Results

Norm-referenced test results should not be considered an absolute prediction of student success or a complete evaluation of the student's knowledge of the material being tested. There are many intervening variables which may make the test unreliable for a student, group, or entire class. Such factors as personal problems, a common cold or sickness, need for glasses, room temperature, lighting, or distractions in or around the classroom could result in poor performance. In addition, some students may not be motivated to learn, nor want good grades. In such cases, the end result will be performance below capability.

Another problem which arises during interpretation is the large number of questions that do not discriminate between those who understand the material being tested and those who do not. Many times tests contain large numbers of questions which are rarely answered incorrectly, or conversely, rarely answered correctly. These questions tend to force the class distribution into an undesirable pattern having a very limited spread and skewed either to the high or low end of the scale.

One method of evaluating examinations to determine whether questions are discriminating between the capable and less capable students is through an item analysis of each question on the test. Minelli (1959, 263-264) points out that the process of item analysis is invaluable for these purposes:

1. Determining and selecting test items which discriminate between good and poor students.
2. Discovering and eliminating test items that are overly easy.
3. Uncovering and excluding items that are overly difficult.

The method simply involves an analysis of each test question as to how it was answered by students making high scores and by students receiving low scores. Good questions will be answered properly by the students receiving high test scores and incorrectly by those scoring low.

A teacher must be exceptionally cautious in the evaluation of psychological factors. In general, if an undesirable personality pattern or attitudes detrimental to the class are noted, the student should be referred to the school psychologist for thorough study. The teacher should not place him- or herself in the role of analyst. In many cases, however, the school psychologist may request the classroom teacher's assistance in working with the student.

Student Participation in Evaluation

Student self-evaluation is a significant element in the VAE program. The ability to evaluate accomplishments in reference to the work of others as well as one's personal ability is invaluable in modern society. In order to make an appropriate career choice, a person must be able to assess his/her own abilities, as well as likes and dislikes. As a result, many teachers consider student self-evaluation sufficiently important to list it as a course goal and provide the necessary class and laboratory time for its accomplishment.

A good self-evaluation program can contribute to efficient class operation. As students develop the ability to evaluate their own progress realistically, teacher evaluation becomes more meaningful for it provides students the opportunity to see how others view their accomplishments. This, coupled with a personal evaluation, gives each student a better understanding of performance in the situation being evaluated.

Many types of checklists may be developed for evaluating student activities. The following one permits a simple and rapid evaluation of a completed project by an industrial arts student. It calls attention to certain phases of the project considered important and provides the student with simple choices.

In contrast to this simple, factual check sheet for evaluating a finished project, the second example is more complex and requires a more subjective evaluation on the part of the student and teacher. This sheet could be used for almost any type of class activity — construction project, experiment, group activity or individual study lesson. If a section did not apply, it could be omitted. Use of this sheet requires teacher guidance to develop an understanding of the importance and need for realistic appraisal on the part of the student.

The third example is one of a series of student self-evaluation sheets designed to assess the student's solution to an architectural drawing problem. Other sheets evaluate the living areas, sleeping areas, halls, and service and utility areas. The problem used with this self-evaluation sheet is shown in Appendix O.

EXAMPLE

STUDENT PROJECT SELF-EVALUATION FORM[5]

Name_____ Date_____

Name of Project _____

Directions:

1. As you complete your project, check it against your drawing to see whether your measurements are:
    (a) _____ exactly correct to specifications.
    (b) _____ 1/32" above or below specifications.
    (c) _____ 1/16" above or below specifications.
    (d) _____ 1/8" or more above or below specifications.
2. Are the tool marks:
    (a) _____ entirely removed?
    (b) _____ slightly visible?
    (c) _____ plainly seen?
3. To complete your project, did you need:
    (a) _____ just one issue of materials.
    (b) _____ a reissue of materials.
4. Did you finish your project:
    (a) _____ smoothly without laps and runs.
    (b) _____ with a few laps and runs.
    (c) _____ with several laps and runs.
5. Are you proud and happy with the final results?
    Yes_____ No_____

---

[5]Developed by Dr. Paul E. Powell and his graduate students at California State University, Long Beach.

Evaluation Procedures   **347**

EXAMPLE

SELF-EVALUATION SHEET[6]

Name_____Course_____ Date_____

Directions:

1. Use the numbers "4" for excellent, "3" for good, "2" for average, "1" for poor, and "0" for failure in rating your activities.
2. Your teacher will evaluate you on an identical form.
3. The teacher will compare your evaluation with his/hers. In case of too much disagreement, a private conference will be held.

Doing: What Have You Done?

    Consider only the quality and quantity of work produced during this card marking period.

    I believe my grade for the "doing" or "activity" part of the course during this period should be a _____ because_____

_____

_____

Knowing: How Well Did You Apply What You Learned?

    Consider information gained about tools, materials, the tasks performed, and the quality of your written work.

    My test average is _____. I believe my grade for the knowing phase of the course should be _____ because_____

_____

_____

Being: What Kind of Person Have You Been?

    Character traits developed are far more lasting than the knowledge gained. Effort should be made to improve in (a) acceptance of responsibilities, (b) personal appearance, (c) courtesy, (d) cooperation, (e) dependability, (f) honesty with self and others, (g) writing and speaking, (h) punctuality and attendance, (i) work effort, (j) safety practices, and (k) care of equipment.

---

[6]Developed by Floyd M. Dickey, South Bend Public Schools.

(continued on next page)

I believe my grade in these factors should be a _____ because

_____

_____

Your Total Score

Add the three numbers that you listed under **Doing, Knowing,** and **Being** and divide by 3.

Score for "Doing" _____ plus "Knowing" _____ plus "Being" _____ equals _____.

Total score _____ divided by 3 equals my score _____.

I believe my grade for this grading period should be _____.

EXAMPLE

ARCHITECTURAL DRAWING SELF-EVALUATION SHEET[7]

Architect: _____
Date: _____
Total Points in Correct Column: _____
Total Possible Points: _____

OUTSIDE AREA DESIGN ANALYSIS

Note all "not-applicable" (N.A.) items.   (Circle "0" if answer is NO and "1" if YES)

	NO	YES	N.A.

Porches, Patios, Lanais & Walkways:

1. Are porches, patios, and lanais built into the design of the house rather than appearing "tacked-on"?   0   1   X
2. Are patios located adjacent to the area of the house to which they relate?   0   1   X
3. Are barbecue pits provided in patio areas?   0   1   X
4. If your house has a wooden floor, are there porches at each door and 3 steps to get up to the correct level? (crawl space 18 inches)   0   1   X
5. Are there adequate paths, walkways, stepping stones, etc., to get around house without walking through gardens or across lawns?   0   1   X

Sub-Total _____

Plot Plan:

1. Is your house no closer than 5 feet to the side property line?   0   1   X
2. Is your garage or carport(s) no closer than 15 feet from your front property line (sidewalk)?   0   1   X
3. Is the house at least 15 feet from the front sidewalk?   0   1   X
4. Are there adequate trees, shrubbery, garden and lawn to fully show off the beauty of the house and cover up the less desirable features (blank walls, etc.)?   0   1   X

Sub-Total _____

Pool: (if applicable)

1. If there is a swimming pool, is it in the northwest and not shaded by the house?   0   1   X
2. Is there adequate decking around the pool to prevent carrying dirt into the pool (at least 4')?   0   1   X
3. Is there an area provided for pool equipment?   0   1   X
4. Is there a cabana dressing area and toilet facilities available near the pool or readily accessible in the house?   0   1   X

Total Points _____

---

[7]Developed by Frank Mahan, Beverly Hills High School, California.

When using a system for student evaluation, the teacher must guard against the following undesirable characteristics which easily creep into the program.
1. Students tend to rate themselves too low. A student may be modest or want to give the impression that he/she is a modest person. This may be controlled through careful discussion with the class or individual student. Actually this tendency and the educational opportunity it affords is one of the reasons why such an evaluation program is so desirable.
2. Students tend to rate themselves too high. This tendency is not as common as might be suspected. It does, however, become more common when course grades are based almost completely upon self-evaluation procedures.
3. Whenever a teacher considers such evaluation a waste of valuable instruction time or sees little value in the program, it should be dropped. Student participation in evaluation requires teacher supervision and assistance and completely fails when he/she does not have an appreciation of the values developed.

In many situations, it is desirable to have students' work evaluated by other class members. This may be accomplished through group action or through the student organization system. Evaluation experiences of this type can provide excellent leadership training. The ability to evaluate the accomplishments of others objectively is important to all VAE students.

Cumulative Records

Adequate and pertinent records are the end product of a good evaluation system. Cumulative records should clearly show student growth and development in all of the program goals and be helpful in detecting the strengths and weaknesses of various units of instruction. Such records need to be carefully planned so that they are easy to maintain and use. When records just accumulate as tests are administered and as laboratory activities are evaluated, they may become very difficult to use and fail to provide the teacher with needed information about the students and course.

There should be a description in the course of study of the method used to accumulate student records. This preplanning for inclusion in the course of study should result in the preparation of a record system that makes allowance for the numerous evaluations made of student progress during the term.

Teachers need to take a personal interest in the adequacy of cumulative records kept in the central office as well as those they develop and maintain for use with their classes. Cumulative records now kept in central offices often fail to provide the type of data desired by industrial, business, and governmental employment personnel. As a result, many vocational teachers maintain supplementary records with essential information about their students. These data should, of course, be placed in central records when the teacher is finished with them. An

Evaluation Procedures 351

example of a cumulative record kept by one school is shown in Figs. 11-9 and 11-10.

In summary, the teacher's cumulative record of class progress is basically concerned with units completed, test scores, and the other data suggested in the earlier sections of this chapter. The cumulative record

Trade _Stationary Steam_   Henry Ford Community College   Registered _I.D._
                                  APPRENTICE RECORD CARD
Name _____   Social Security No. _000-00-0001_

Company _Ford Motor Co. - Rough Plt._   Training Officer _____

TERM 1 Sept., 1971			TERM 2 Jan., 1972			TERM 3 May, 1972		
COURSE	Time	Grade	COURSE	Time	Grade	COURSE	Time	Grade
501C		96	1M		73	2A		100
541A		89	231A		91	232A		87
			234A		89			

TERM 4 Sept., 1972			TERM 5 Jan., 1973			TERM 6 May-'73		
233A		90	235A		87	236A		86
241A		91	242A		91	245A		75

Fig. 11-9. The Henry Ford Community College, Dearborn, Michigan keeps this cumulative record of the related training of apprentices. The vertical spaces at the bottom contain the series of courses selected by the sending company as those which will, in their opinion, give the apprentice the technical background needed to function effectively as a journeyman in their particular plant. Assignments to classes are made by the college and are entered in the proper column, by term, along with the time the class meets. The final grade for each class is entered in the percentage column. At the extreme bottom, "x's" indicate classes satisfactorily completed.

352   Planning and Organizing Instruction

TERM 7 Sept. '73			TERM 8			TERM 9		
COURSE	Time	Grade	COURSE	Time	Grade	COURSE	Time	Grade
237 A		95						
246 A		100						
272 A		80						
TERM 10			TERM 11			TERM 12		

DATE	9-11-71	12/71	4/72	9/72	2/73	9/73				
SHOP HOURS		500	1000	2000	3000	4000	5000	6000	7000	7424	8000
REQ. COURSES		1	2	5	7	10	12	15	17	19	

REMARKS: _____

Form 56-03-04

Fig. 11-10. This is the reverse side of the cumulative record card at the Henry Ford Community College. The section headed "date, shop hours, required courses" is used for entering the progress in hours on an apprenticeship. These data are sent four times each year to the company sponsoring the apprentice, making it possible to keep the apprentice's related instruction in phase with his progress on the job, thus ensuring simultaneous completion of the two parts of the training program. For example, if the apprentice has completed 4000 work process hours, he/she should have completed 16 of the required 32 classes. Please note in the example of the record for a stationary steam engineer that the student had completed 4000 work hours and 16 courses by Sept. 1973.

provides for a running record of units completed. With a place for remarks, it provides valuable information for course evaluation or review.

The individually designed and developed cumulative records kept by teachers for each student in their courses will include such pertinent items as these:

1. Name of the unit, date completed, mark, and remarks.
2. Name of the unit, points earned on unit, total points to date, classification of unit, and teacher's approval. (Such data are recorded when a point system is used).
3. Dates that safety tests covering general safety precautions and those developed for the major machines were passed with grades of 100 percent.
4. An evaluation of the student's attitude toward safety.
5. An evaluation of character traits such as willingness to accept responsibility, personal appearance, punctuality, attendance, cooperation, and dependability.
6. An appraisal of the student's ability to express himself in oral and written communication.
7. The teacher's appraisal of the student's competencies, interests, aptitudes, and potential for considering occupational placement opportunities and/or additional preparation.

Evaluation of Teacher Competency

While the evaluation of student accomplishment is a very important function of teaching, an evaluation of the teacher's own accomplishments during a term is equally important. Teachers need to evaluate their own weaknesses and make provisions to correct them. All too often teachers have not been able to identify major shortcomings which are readily noticed by staff or students.

The first (and perhaps best) evaluation may be in the performance of the students. For example, if students rate consistently below the expected standards on examinations, the teacher should immediately look at his/her instructional program to determine whether an acceptable job of instruction has been done. The teacher who describes an entire class as "stupid or subnormal because they all failed an easy test" does not realize that his/her methods of presentation need immediate attention.

Subjective evaluations indicating poor laboratory performance, unsafe attitudes, and undesirable personality traits may provide insights for teaching effectiveness. Uncooperative, restless, inefficient student officers should prompt remedial action on the part of the teacher in strengthening the plans for the student-directed organization to avoid this weakness the next time. The objective should be to correct the condition that is the cause of the situation or problem.

Another approach to the evaluation of the work of a teacher is through faculty seminars or informal meetings concerned with instructional improvement. Where the seminar is constructively directed, very frank appraisals with constructive suggestions will be made by teachers and/or administrators viewing a class in operation. Such suggestions can be most valuable when they are directed at the improvement of instruction.

A third evaluation technique — that of involving students in the evaluation of the program and teacher — is somewhat controversial. It involves the use of either a subjective or objective evaluation sheet dis-

354 Planning and Organizing Instruction

tributed to each student at the end of the term to be returned to the teacher anonymously. The following factors need to be considered as students participate in evaluating the work of their teachers:

1. Poor students may tend to evaluate their teachers too low while the good students present too high a rating. This problem can often be reduced by thorough instructions to the students.
2. When students rate a teacher higher than he should be rated, the result is increased ego on the part of the teacher. Again, as in 1., this sometimes happens. The purpose of the evaluation form should be to isolate the weaknesses which, it is hoped, will be few in number and will become a challenge for improvement to the professional teacher.
3. Teachers can tell the handwriting of the students. When this is a problem, it can be avoided by using an objective form and having them collected by a student, placed in an envelope, and left in the office for the teacher to pick up.
4. Students are not teachers and cannot judge teaching competency. This is also true. The evaluation form, however, obtains information about what the students think of the course and teacher. It must always be remembered that the course is for the students. If they feel they did not get the instruction they should have received, the teacher either failed to present adequately the course goals and the behavioral objectives for the course or to provide adequate instruction, or both.
5. Generally, it is impossible for a teacher to communicate and reach every student in each class. The best teachers have students who think they have learned little or nothing from the course. Some evaluation of this type should, therefore, be expected. The master teacher, however, is continually watching for methods of providing superior instruction for his/her students within the allotted time.

The following examples show different evaluation forms used to obtain information for course and teacher improvement. This first example is a simple open-ended request for constructive criticsm from the class after the course is complete. This approach could be expanded by providing additional leading questions if the teacher desired additional information about specific facets of the course.

EXAMPLE

CONSTRUCTIVE COMMENTS FOR THE TEACHER[8]

Dear Student,

This course, A-C Electricity 205 is terminating. For benefit of the students who will take this course in the future, and to myself, I am making a request for your constructive criticism.

Specifically I am interested in finding out, from your standpoint as a student, which topics were effectively taught and your reasons for regarding them as so. Also of interest are those topics you regard as having been ineffectively taught and your suggestions as to how they may be improved. Any additional comments you would care to make will be welcome.

Your reply below will be greatly appreciated, though totally optional. Feel free to express yourself and please do not sign your name.

Sincerely,

O. Karl Rose

---

[8] This approach for securing student reaction has worked well at the Henry Ford Community College in Dearborn, Michigan.

Planning and Organizing Instruction

This following example illustrates an upgrading check list which may be used to evaluate teacher performance. The one illustrated is for demonstrations. Others may be prepared for lectures, discussions and other methods used by VAE teachers.

EXAMPLE

UPGRADING CHART — GROUP DEMONSTRATIONS[9]

School_____Department_____Teacher_____

Title of Lesson_____Observer_____Date_____

Directions: Draw a circle around one of the five numbers following the item to indicate your evaluation. No. 1 is the lowest rating and No. 5 the highest. Add a note if you wish to clarify your observation or make suggestions. If any item does not apply specifically to the lesson, place an X opposite it in the right-hand margin.

The Good Teacher	Low		Aver.		High
1. Arranges the group so that all can see and hear clearly.	1	2	3	4	5
2. Has all required materials, utensils, tools, and equipment on hand and properly arranged.	1	2	3	4	5
3. States behavioral objective to motivate students.	1	2	3	4	5
4. Relates demonstration to projected lessons.	1	2	3	4	5
5. Explains new terms and parts of equipment.	1	2	3	4	5
6. Explains each step as performed.	1	2	3	4	5
7. Emphasizes each key step.	1	2	3	4	5
8. Checks timing; performs steps at right pace for clear understanding.	1	2	3	4	5
9. Performs demonstrations skillfully.	1	2	3	4	5
10. Uses questions to good advantage.	1	2	3	4	5
11. Uses supplemental aids to improve the demonstration.	1	2	3	4	5
12. Stresses safety precautions.	1	2	3	4	5
13. Talks directly to the students, not to the equipment or walls.	1	2	3	4	5
14. Summarizes the demonstration.	1	2	3	4	5
15. Makes the demonstration of correct length to do the job.	1	2	3	4	5
16. Maintains interest throughout demonstration.	1	2	3	4	5
17. Efficiently assigns students to work stations.	1	2	3	4	5
18. Follows up — checks individual performance.	1	2	3	4	5
19. Keeps other students constructively busy when demonstrating to part of the group.	1	2	3	4	5

[9]This form was developed by Edward C. Estabrooke of the American School, Chicago.

EXAMPLE

STUDENT OPINIONNAIRE[10]

For Appraising a Course and Its Information

Often a frank student reaction to questions relating to the teaching and the content of a course will be of great help to the teacher in improving instruction or altering and improving the course content and structure. The faculty members solicit sincere response.

This brief rating opinionnaire will give you an opportunity, as a student, to pass on information to your teacher which can be used as an aid to the improvement of teaching and the course. Only the instructor will know the results of this **opinionnaire**. Please make your responses conscientiously and individually. You, of course, will not be identified — **the opinionnaire is completely anonymous.**

Directions

Select the one completion phrase under each statement that best describes the teacher or class, and place a check mark in the appropriate space on the answer sheet provided. In case you feel that there is no response listed that correctly answers the question, or if you do not feel qualified to react to the question for some reason, check the space "N.R." which will signify "No Response," or write comments in the appropriate blank space on the answer sheet. Please read the statements and responses carefully and work rapidly. **Remember, do not consult with others and do not sign your name.** (The original opinionnaire consisted of 23 items. Seven of these were selected to illustrate the character of the instrument.)

2. Plans for the course, as it progressed from week to week, were:
   a. very well organized.
   b. evidently organized.
   c. loosely organized.
   d. vague and sketchy.
   e. not evident to students.
   f. N.R.
4. Students were drawn into class and laboratory activities in a way which:
   a. strongly stimulated thinking and problem solving.
   b. moderately stimulated thinking and problem solving.
   c. produced relatively little stimulation to thinking and problem solving.
   d. tended to discourage thinking and problem solving.
   e. discouraged thinking and problem solving.
   f. N.R.

---

[10]Developed by Robert Moore of San Jose State University, San Jose. (This opinionnaire is the result of integrating questions and ideas from numerous evaluation forms.)

7. The tests and examinations in this course:
   a. provided excellent opportunity to demonstrate possession of broad knowledge and understanding.
   b. were well balanced; sufficiently broad to cover the main objectives of the course.
   c. provided a reasonable coverage of the main objectives.
   d. tended to emphasize some parts of the course to the neglect of others.
   e. stressed minor or irrelevant points; providing little or no opportunity for students to demonstrate a broad knowledge of the subject.
   f. N.R.
9. I believe that specific information obtained from this course is, or will be:
   a. extremely useful.
   b. quite useful.
   c. of some use.
   d. of very little use.
   e. of no use at all.
   f. N.R.
12. Relative to helping students individually, in and out of class, the teacher seemed:
    a. very willing.
    b. quite willing.
    c. neither pleased nor displeased to do so.
    d. reluctant to do so.
    e. opposed and unwilling.
    f. N.R.
15. The teacher's ability and willingness to answer relevant questions in laboratory and class were:
    a. excellent; quick, to the point, and clear.
    b. good.
    c. fair.
    d. rather poor.
    e. very poor, grudging, vague, confusing.
    f. N.R.
23. In cases of honest disagreement with the teacher, I:
    a. always felt free to discuss the differences.
    b. often felt free to discuss the differences.
    c. sometimes felt free to discuss the differences.
    d. rarely felt free to discuss the differences.
    e. felt that self-expression of any difference would affect my grade adversely.
    f. N.R.

Summary

Evaluation procedures are the means by which the success of an instructional program can be determined. Information is provided which will help the teacher in these ways:
- Measure the growth of each student based on pre-established criterion and/or norms.
- Determine the effectiveness of instruction in fulfilling the behavioral objectives established for each unit or module of instruction, and in fulfilling the goals established for the course or program.
- Provide student experiences in self-evaluation which, in turn, will assist students in gaining a better understanding of their own interests, aptitudes, and abilities.
- Assess the strengths and weaknesses of instruction, and plan procedures which will improve the teacher's performance.

VAE programs now make good use of evaluation programs based on preestablished criteria. Many students in VAE programs use the instruction they receive to establish and meet their career goals. Since many careers require the possession of specific knowledge and abilities prior to entry into employment, criterion standards can be established which help students and teachers know when the specific knowledge and abilities have been attained. A good criterion-referenced evaluation program will keep the student appraised of progress toward essential and planned knowledge and competencies.

To make school boards, administrators, and teachers accountable to the public, evaluation procedures must be in operation which provide for the continuous assessment of the progress of students in meeting specific behavioral objectives and the goals of the program. Accountability requirements call for a thorough evaluation program which provides valid and reliable information regarding each student's progress through the instructional program.

For Self-Assessment and Discussion

1. How would you define "educational accountability"? Identify major thrusts for the modern concept of accountability in American education.
2. Define:
    - **Input** evaluation.
    - **Process** evaluation.
    - **Product** evaluation.
3. What is significant about the program for the National Assessment of Educational Progress?
4. What is meant by PPBS? Describe the unique features of this system.
5. How is "Product Evaluation" identified with behavioral objectives?

6. What distinctions are made between "program" and "classroom" evaluation?
7. Describe the differences between "criterion-referenced" and "norm-referenced" evaluation. Cite examples in your area of specialization that would be classified in each of these two approaches to measurement.
8. Identify behavioral objectives that would call for learning in your area of specialization that would classify in the —
   - Cognitive domain.
   - Affective domain.
   - Psychomotor domain.
9. In what ways are examinations designed to help the teacher as well as the students?
10. What is meant by reliability and validity in relation to measuring instruments?
11. In what way may the achievement of students in laboratory activities be evaluated?
12. What is the purpose of giving a "before-going-to-work test" covering the general safety precautions?
13. When should tests covering the safety precautions on the operation of power equipment be administered?
14. What is the role of the specific course goals in the evaluation program?
15. Name the reasons for having students participate in evaluation.
16. What are the advantages and disadvantages of an objective test? Of a subjective test?
17. Of what value are cumulative records?
18. How is an "item analysis" of a test made?
19. What issues need to be considered when involving students in an evaluation of the teacher's work?

Assignments to Demonstrate Competencies

1. Prepare a statement, not to exceed 200 words, describing the salient features of one of the following:
   - The Concept of Accountability.
   - Input Evaluation, Process Evaluation, and Product Evaluation.
   - Planning, Programing, Budgeting Systems (PPBS).
   - National Assessment of Educational Progress.
   - How **Handbook VI** on **Standard Terminology** and the publication **Vocational Education and Occupations** may be used in planning VAE programs.
   - The projected plan for the Accreditation of Vocational/Technical Education.
   - Program vs. classroom evaluation.
2. Prepare a proposal, not to exceed 200 words, outlining a plan for the evaluation of an educational program within your area of specializa-

tion. This statement is to explain how your plan will employ criterion-referenced as well as norm-referenced measures.
3. Prepare a statement of the method used to accumulate student records for your area of specialization. The description should include sample records and an account of how the records are used and their value to the program.
4. Prepare the unit and/or other periodic tests needed for your course. Consider the following when preparing the tests:
   a. Objective testing vs. subjective testing.
   b. Use of pre-tests and exit test for the units.
5. Develop and describe plans for student participation in the evaluation of their laboratory and/or classroom activities. Present the necessary forms, describe their use, and explain how self-evaluation enters into the periodic evaluation of the student's work.
6. Develop the needed safety tests (as suggested in Appendix R) for a course that you are, or will be, qualified to teach. Consider the following when preparing these tests:
   a. General laboratory safety precautions.
   b. Specific safety precautions related to tools or equipment.
   c. Development of wholesome attitude toward observing safety precautions.
7. Locate a number of standardized guidance, aptitude, interest, or personality tests or scales that could prove helpful for your teaching situation. The book by Gronlund (1971) identifies a large number of these standardized tests or scales. Describe these tests and show how they will be valuable to your course of study.
8. Administer a unit or course examination (such as examples in Appendix Q) and make an item analysis of the test results using the methods described by Minelli.
9. Devise and describe a means of securing student reaction to the course content, instruction, and general value of a course that you are qualified to teach.

References* and Resources

Books

Byram, Harold M. **Locally Directed Evaluation of Local Vocational Education.** 3rd ed. Danville, Illinois: The Interstate Printers and Publishers, Inc., 1971, Pp. viii + 98.
*Carin, Arthur A., and Sund, Robert B. **Developing Questioning Techniques.** Columbus, Ohio: Charles E. Merrill Publishing Co., 1971, Pp. v + 169.
Ebel, Robert L. **Essentials of Educational Measurement.** 2nd ed. Englewood Cliffs, N.J.: Prentice-Hall Inc., 1972, Pp. xiv + 622.
*Glaser, Robert. "Instructional Technology and the Measurement of Learning Outcomes," in **Criterion-Referenced Measurement: An Introduction.** Edited by W. James Popham. Englewood Cliffs, N.J.: Educational Technology Publications, 1971, Pp. 5-17.
*Gronlund, Norman E. **Measurement and Evaluation in Teaching,** 2nd ed. New York: The MacMillan Co., 1971, Pp. viii + 545.

*Entries marked with an asterisk are cited in this chapter.

Johnson, Milo P. and Grafsky, Albert J. Jr. **Accountability: Evaluation for Occupational Programs.** Chicago, Illinois: American Technical Society, 1973, Pp. v + 95.
Mackenzie, Louise, Evaluation in the Teaching of Home Economics. Danville, Illinois: Interstate Printers & Publishers, Inc., 1970, Pp. 82.
*Mager, Robert F. **Goal Analysis.** Belmont, California: Fearon Publishers, 1972, Pp. vi + 136.
*McGivney, Joseph H. "Accountability: Promise and Problems of PPBS." in **Contemporary Concepts in Vocational Education.** Edited by Gordon F. Law. Washington, D.C.: American Vocational Association, Inc., 1971, pp. 164-171.
McNeil, John D. **Toward Accountable Teachers: Their Appraisal and Improvement.** New York: Holt, Rinehart and Winston, Inc., 1971, Pp x + 176.
Plihal, Jane, and Brown, Marjorie. **Evaluation Materials: Physical Home Environment and Psychological and Social Factors.** Minneapolis, Minn. 55415: Burgess Publishing Co., 1969, Pp. iv + 198.
Popham, W. James (Editor) **Criterion-Referenced Measurement.** Englewood Cliffs, New Jersey 07632: Educational Technology Publications, 1971, Pp. xviii + 108.
──────. **Educational Criterion Measures.** New York: Van Nostrand Reinhold Co., 1971, Pp. 24.
*Popham, W. James, and Husek, T. R. "Implications of Criterion-Referenced Measurement," in **Criterion-Referenced Measurement.** Englewood Cliffs, N.J.: Educational Technology Publications, 1971, pp. 17-37.
*Silvius, G. Harold, and Curry, Estell H. **Teaching Successfully.** 2nd ed. Bloomington, Illinois: McKnight Publishing Co., 1967. The references that apply to this chapter are: Topic 8, Provide Cumulative Records; Topic 23, Plan and Maintain a Safety Program; Topic 27, Evaluate Student Growth and Development; Topic 28, Plan and Use a Marking System; and Topic 29, Evaluate Teacher Competence.
*Strong, Merle E. "Performance Objectives in Vocational Education," in **The Individual and His Education.** Edited by Alfred H. Krebs. Washington, D.C.: American Vocational Association, Inc., 1972, pp. 138-150.

Periodicals

*Arnold, Walter M. "National Study Makes Bid to Evaluate Quality of Vocational Education." **Industrial Education,** Vol. 61, No. 1 (January, 1972), pp. 6 and 8.
*Banks, Jane M. "Measuring the Immeasurables: Performance Goals for the Affective Domain." **American Vocational Journal,** Vol. 48, No. 4 (April, 1973), pp. 36-37.
Bundy, Robert F. "Accountability: A New Disneyland Fantasy.": **Phi Delta Kappan,** Vol. 56, No. 3 (November, 1974), pp. 176-180.
Byers, Edward E. Accountability's Offspring: The Case for Performance Goals." **American Vocational Journal,** Vol. 48, No. 4 (April, 1973), pp. 24-25.
Creekmore, Anna M. "The Concept Basic to Home Economics." **Journal of Home Economics,** Vol. 60, No. 2 (February, 1968), pp. 93-102.
Gallington, Ralph O. "How to Test the Accountable Vocational Teacher." **Industrial Education,** Vol. 6, No. 4 (April, 1972), pp. 26-28.
House, Ernest; Rivers, Wendell; and Stufflebeam, Daniel L. "An Assessment of the Michigan Accountability System." **Phi Delta Kappan,** Vol. 55, No. 10 (June, 1974), pp. 663-669.
Ladas, Harold. "Grades: Standardizing the Unstandardized Standard." **Phi Delta Kappan,** Vol. 56, No. 3 (November, 1974) pp. 185-188.
*Landers, Jacob. "Accountability and Progress by Nomenclature: Old Ideas In New Bottles." **Phi Delta Kappan,** Vol. 54, No. 8 (April, 1973) pp. 539-541.

Millman, Jason. "Reporting Student Progress: A Case for a Criterion-Referenced Marking System." **Phi Delta Kappan**, Vol. 52, No. 4 (December, 1970), pp. 226-230.
*Minelli, Ernest L. "On Improving Your Tests." **Industrial Arts and Vocational Education**, Vol. 48, No. 9 (November, 1959), pp. 263-265.
Morrison, Edward J. "How to Test Performance." **American Vocational Journal**, Vol. 48, No. 4 (April, 1973), pp. 38-39.
Mousley, Woodrow. "Report Cards Across The Nation." **Phi Delta Kappan**, Vol. 53, No. 7 (March, 1972), pp. 436-437.
Mulski, John H., and Levy, Mathew. "When a Computer Fills Out Student's Report Cards: A System to Personalize Individual Evaluation." **Industrial Education**, Vol. 61, No. 7 (October, 1972), pp. 57-59.
Norris, Eleanor L. "The National Assessment: Where Is It Now?" **American Education**, Vol. 5, No. 8 (October, 1969) pp. 20-23.
Page, Ellis B. "How We All Failed in Performance Contracting." **Phi Delta Kappan**, Vol. 54, No. 2 (October, 1972), pp. 115-117.
Paul, Warren I. "How Do you Rate?" **Phi Delta Kappan**, Vol. 56, No. 1 (September, 1974), p. 33.
Popham, W. James, and Husek, T. R. "Implications of Criterion-Referenced Measurement." **Journal of Educational Measurement**, Vol. 6 No. 1 (Spring, 1969), pp. 1-9.
*Porter, John W. "The Accountability Story in Michigan." **Phi Delta Kappan**. Vol. 54, No. 2 (October, 1972), pp. 98-99.
Ridenour, Harlan E. "Cultivating the Affective Domain." **American Vocational Journal**, Vol. 48, No. 4 (April, 1973), pp. 44-45.
Schaefer, Carl J. "Accountability: We Asked For It." **American Vocational Journal**, Vol. 48, No. 3 (March, 1973), pp. 24-25.
Schroeder, Allan M. "Grading Drawings with the Overhead Projection." **School Shop**, Vol. 32, No. 5 (January, 1973), p. 42.
Steagall, Paul H., Jr. "What Student Feedback Can Do For You." **American Vocational Journal**, Vol. 49, No. 8 (November, 1974), pp. 62, 64, 66, and 68.
Tyler, Ralph W. "National Assessment — Some Valuable By-Products for Schools." **The National Elementary Principal**, Vol. 48, No. 6 (May, 1969), pp. 42-48.
Wormer, Frank E. et. al. "The National Assessment of Educational Progress: Concept and Organization." **Capsule**. College of Education, University of Michigan, Ann Arbor, Vol. 3, No. 2 (Winter, 1970), pp. 1-7.

Other Published Materials

*Ash, Lane C. (Project Director et al. Instruments and Procedures for the Evaluation of Vocational/Technical Education: Institutions and Programs. Pilot Test Edition. Washington, D.C.: American Vocational Association, Inc., December, 1971, Pp. 144.
Beatty, Walcott H. (Chairman and Editor). Improving Educational Assessment and An Inventory of Measures of Affective Behavior. Washington 20036 D.C.: ASCD, NEA, 1201 16th Street N.W., 1969, Pp. viii + 164.
D'Costa, Ayres. The Development of The Ohio Vocational Interest Survey. A paper presented by D'Costa at the national convention of the American Vocational Association, Dallas, Texas, December, 1969. Washington, D.C.: American Vocational Association, Pp. 10. ERIC Reference No. ED 031 715.
Do Teachers Make a Difference? A report on research on pupil achievement. Papers by Mood, Guthrie, Leven, Hanushek, Mayeske, Michelson, Gagné, and Coleman. Washington, D.C.: Bureau of Educational Personnel Development, USOE, 1970. Supt. of Docs. Reference No. OE-58042, Pp. v + 181.
Hull, William L. (principal investigator), and Wells, Randall. **The Classification and Evaluation of Innovations in Vocational and Technical Education.** A CVTE publication (RD#71), 1972. Note: A 14-page Innovations Evaluation Guide based on this study is available from the CVTE.

*Joos, L. W. **A Methodology for Program Evaluation in School Systems** (covering the PACER system). Pontiac, Michigan: Oakland Schools, 1970, Pp. 25.

*Medsker, Leland L. "Strategies for Evaluation of Post-Secondary Occupational Programs," in **The Second Annual Pennsylvania Conference on Post-Secondary Occupational Education**. Edited by Angelo G. Gillie. University Park, Pennsylvania: Center for Study of Higher Education, The Pennsylvania State University, June 1971, pp. 7-28.

Moss, Jerome Jr. **The Evaluation of Occupational Education Programs**. Minneapolis: Research Coordinating Unit in Occupational Education, University of Minnesota, September 1968, Pp. 22.

Murphy, Patricia D. **Teaching for Employability**. Order No. 261-08414. Washington, D.C. 20036: Home Economics Education Association, NEA, 1973, pp. 24.

*National Center for Educational Statistics. **Standard Terminology for Curriculum and Instruction in Local and State School Systems: Handbook VI**. Compiled and edited by Putnam, John F. et al. Reference No. HE 5.223: 23052, U.S. HEW, 1970, Pp. x + 317.

*Nichols, Daryl G. et al. **Career and Occupational Development Objectives**. National Assessment of Educational Progress, The Education Commission of the States, 300 Lincoln Tower, 1860 Lincoln Street, Denver, Colorado, July 1970, Pp. vi + 47.

*Office of Dean, School of Fine and Applied Arts **Five-Year Plan, 1973-77**. Mt. Pleasant, Michigan: Central Michigan University, 1973, Pp. 71.

*Salatino, Anthony J. "The Accountability of Occupational Education in Society," in **The Second Annual Pennsylvania Conference on Post-Secondary Occupational Education**. Edited by Angelo C. Gillie. University Park, Pennsylvania: Center for Study of Higher Education, The Pennsylvania State University, June 1971, pp. 75-85.

Starr, Harold et al. **A System for State Evaluation of Vocational Education, Final Report**. CVTE publication (RD#39). ERIC Reference No. ED 041 121, May 1970, Pp. 196.

Strong, Merle E. (Study Director). **An Assessment of Wisconsin's Vocational and Technical Education Program**. A study conducted for the Wisconsin Advisory Council on Vocational Education. Madison, Wisconsin: Department of Educational Administration, University of Wisconsin, 1970, Pp. xxi + 194.

*U.S. Departments of HEW and Labor. **Vocational Education and Occupations**. Reference No. OE-80061. Washington, D.C.: Supt. of Docs. (Catalog No. FS 280: 80061), July 1969, Pp. xv + 292.

*Wiegman, Robert. "Strategies for Assessing Teacher Effectiveness in Post-Secondary Occupational Programs," in **The Second Annual Pennsylvania Conference on Post-Secondary Occupational Education**. Edited by Angelo C. Gillie. University Park, Pennsylvania: Center for Study of Higher Education, The Pennsylvania State University, June 1971, pp. 49-59.

CHAPTER 12

Specifying Equipment and Instructional Supplies

Since there is extensive literature now available to help a VAE teacher plan and equip laboratories and other needed facilities, this chapter is directed only at those aspects of this information that should be included with a specific program or course of study. It is concerned with what a teacher would need in writing to present the case for the needed facilities (defined as a generic term to include the hand, power, and other laboratory equipment, instructional supplies, materials, and housing) to carry out a well-planned VAE course of study.

This chapter will also help the teacher see that **the time to specify needed facilities for a course is after specific goals, behavioral objectives and units, methods, and evaluation procedures have been planned.** It is only then that minimum and essential facilities for an optimum educational experience can be identified. A capable teacher should never place professional integrity in jeopardy by recommending hand, power, and laboratory equipment, instructional supplies, and provisions for housing that are not needed for an envisioned educational experience. On the other hand, a VAE teacher needs to be prepared to explain how the equipment and the recommended instructional supplies are to be used in teaching specific units. This is the scientific approach that produces a maximum educational effort at minimum costs.

Instructional Facilities Needed for a Program

The instructional facilities must be planned to develop a learning environment which will help each student successfully complete each unit (in terms of the specified behavioral objectives) and meet the specific goals established for the course or program. A variety of facilities and materials must be considered, including equipment and machines, hand tools, utensils, instruments, supplies, textbooks, reference books, and audiovisual aids.

Specific Programs or Learning Experiences Dictate Needed Equipment and Machines

It is assumed that VAE teachers agree that it is highly desirable to have justification in writing for every tool, machine, piece of laboratory equipment, storage rack, or whatever is needed to implement a course of study. The use of such items needs to be identified with specific courses of study. Shop "A," for example, in a comprehensive high school might be planned to house a course in hydraulics, courses one and two in power mechanics, and a basic course in general metalworking. Before offering these courses in such a multipurpose laboratory, the industrial education teacher would need to consider the courses, one at a time, to determine the essential power machines and equipment that would need to be secured or constructed and placed in such a room. In undertaking this task, a careful examination of established course goals and units of instruction with behavioral objectives for each of these courses must be made to determine the type of equipment and facilities that appear to be most appropriate. The goals, for example, might well suggest that equipment for a drafting room be similar to that used in in-

Fig. 12-1. This welding laboratory has a variety of stations utilizing different types of equipment and different types of welding. (Courtesy Henry Ford Community College, Dearborn, Michigan)

dustry for modern drafting. On the other hand, equipment to facilitate instruction for drafting in industrial arts, as it is planned as a part of general education, would not, of course, necessarily call for the type of facility used in industrial drafting rooms.

For most trade and technical courses, where there is a variety of high-quality equipment available, it is suggested that the machines and equipment that are to be duplicated be purchased from different companies, especially where operating mechanisms differ. To illustrate, in a machine shop course where eight engine lathes are needed, it is recommended that several makes be considered so that students may become familiar with the differences in operating controls and in the fundamental mechanisms. If all eight lathes were to be purchased from one company, students would then be deprived of the opportunity to learn about differences in the machines used in industry.

Such variety of equipment may not be desirable nor needed in the applied arts. There is some advantage in large schools or systems in having like machines manufactured by the same company. This facilitates maintenance and the interchange of accessories. Then too, the time that students would require to learn about the different controls might be used to advantage in other work.

By examining the behavioral objectives and units of instruction for each of the courses and the methods that will be used to teach these units, qualified teachers should have no difficulty in ascertaining exactly what laboratory equipment is needed to facilitate the courses of study in any one VAE facility.

Factors That Determine Number of Needed Utensils, Instruments, Hand Tools, Machines, and Other Items of Specific Equipment

1. The first factor to consider is the number of work stations that are needed for the course.

    The work station is defined as **the bench, machine, desk, study carrel, or place where one student may work or headquarter for a period of time while the student does research, plans and constructs a project, or carries out some experiment or unit of work.** A student takes hand tools, portable machines, and materials to the work stations. The student leaves the work station to use service equipment permanently placed in the room, such as a duplicating machine, band saw, refrigerator, key-driven calculator, or squaring shear. It is essential, therefore, that the service machines and equipment never be counted as work stations.

    An engine lathe or long-carriage typewriter, as expensive permanent items of equipment, could either be a work station or a service machine, depending on the goals and organization of a course. For example, in a general metalworking course requiring students to develop a use level of skill in the basic operations of an engine lathe,

the laboratory should be equipped with several lathes which become work stations where students remain for a period of time to work on specially planned lathe exercises or projects to develop these fundamental skills. There are other general metalworking courses where the aims are to foster avocational interests and general education functions. In these courses one or two engine lathes are sufficient since they are used as service machines. Students leave their assigned work stations to use an engine lathe as there is need to fabricate some metal part. In such a course, an engine lathe is just one of the service machines, and an industrial education teacher would be in real difficulty if this condition were not understood and recognized by administration.

The number of needed work stations depends on the optimum number of students to be scheduled at any one period of time and the organizational plan for the laboratory. There are three basic systems used, according to Silvius and Curry (1971, 90-99), to organize laboratory experiences for VAE multiple activity programs: **group rotation, individual rotation,** and **individual progression.** For optimum learning conditions where **individual progression** is used, it will be necessary to have approximately 15 to 20 percent more work stations (bench, study carrel, machine, desk or place where one student may headquarter for a period of time) than the maximum number of students to be scheduled in a laboratory at any one time. This system provides for normal and individual progress since a student may start a unit, project, or experiment at any work station not assigned. Through scientific planning, the additional work stations needed for **individual progression** should be readily acceptable to educational administration and the community. Those who present the case for VAE courses should be prepared to show exactly what is needed for an optimum learning climate.

The following is a typical application of an organizational plan based on **individual progression** for a ninth grade laboratory experience in general metalworking:

EXAMPLE

A. The maximum number of students to be scheduled in the laboratory has been established with administration as 26.
B. Needed work stations: 26 X 1.20 (for individual progression) equals 31.2 or 31 for a maximum size group of 26.
C. The plan for major activities, needed work stations, and permanent machines provides for the following distribution of work stations and service equipment:

Specifying Equipment and Supplies   **369**

Major Activities	Work Stations	Service Equipment	
Sheet Metal	10	Drill Press	1
Metal Casting	2	Engine Lathe	1
Metal Spinning	2	Bench Grinder	1
Metal Forging	2	Pedestal Grinder	1
Ornamental Iron	9	Pedestal Buffer	2
Metal Enameling	2	Power Hack Saw	1
Welding			
Acetylene	2		plus 1
Electric	2		plus 1
	31		9

D. In this laboratory for general metalworking there is a need, therefore, for 9 permanently mounted machines as **service** equipment in addition to the 31 work stations. It should be noted that there are 6 welding stations; 4 to be used as work stations for basic instruction in welding, while 2 are to be used to service other units in the course.

E. Where the organizational plan provides for some students to devote their **full time** to such responsibilities as superintendent or safety engineer, the capacity of the shop, laboratory, or room is automatically increased by the number of such officers. For example, if the teacher for the general metalworking program just described had planned for 3 full-time officers — a superintendent, a general foreman, and a general service person — the largest size group that could be scheduled with the specified equipment would then be 26 (number to be accommodated by planned equipment) plus 3 (full-time officers) or 29. **The capacity for the facility is not increased where part-time student officers are used.** In this plan of organization the students leave their assigned work stations to perform their responsibilities as officers.

---

2. The second factor to consider is the number of hand tools, instruments (in health occupations), utensils, or other items of specialized equipment needed for each program. To determine the minimum number of hand tools or other items of special equipment needed by students at any one time, a teacher needs to anticipate the kinds of units, projects, experiments, or activities that will be done at the work stations. This is done by taking each of the typical projects, experiments, or activities and analyzing the manipulative tasks or operations that are involved, and in turn listing the different service tools and equipment that will be used by any one person for each of the operations or tasks (this is an application of instructional analysis as a research technique, explained in Chapter 2). When curriculum

370   Planning and Organizing Instruction

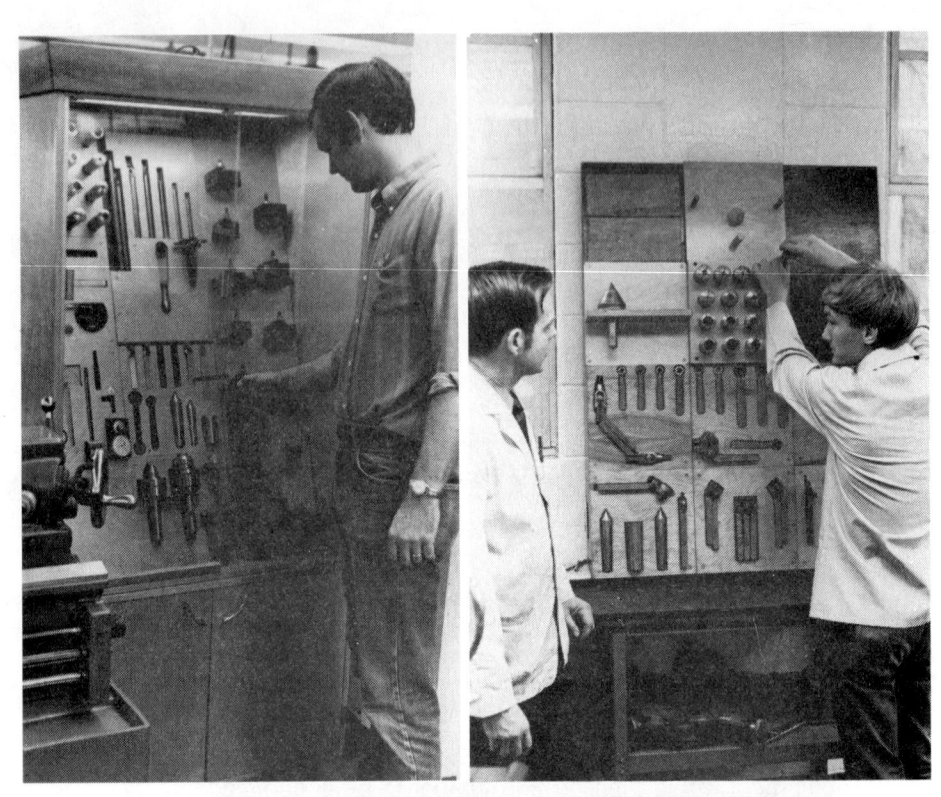

Fig. 12-2. Items of specialized equipment are carefully selected and cared for in this metals laboratory at Eastern Kentucky University. (Courtesy Tommy R. Brown and J. Homer Davis)

builders have identified the tools and equipment that will be needed by one student, they then need to consider:
A. The number of work stations where such projects, experiments, or activities are likely to be performed concurrently.
B. The degree that certain tools, instruments, or other items are used in doing an operation or task.
C. The amount of expected student cooperation in the use of any one tool, utensil, instrument or piece of service equipment.

An example should help clarify these criteria. The situation chosen is a course in woodworking technology for eighth grade students where the school has provided ten work stations for bench woodworking. In this hypothetical case, the first unit has been planned around instruction that is identified with what a student would do to design and build a wall shelf, bird house, or bird feeder. The operations and tools and equipment needed by any one of the first students to be assigned to the ten work stations for bench woodworking would be as follows:

EXAMPLE

Operation	Needed Tools or Equipment
Make Plan of Work	Drafting board, drafting tools and instruments, and reference materials.
Select and Get Out Stock	Saw horse, flexible metal tape, steel square, and crosscut and rip saw.
Shape Each of Parts	Coping saw, turning saw, jig saw, band saw, sander, try square, steel rule, marking gauge, back saw, jack plane, woodworking vise, expansive bit, auger bit, wood chisels, mallet, brace, and spoke shave.
Assemble Parts	Nail hammer, nail set, hand drill, carriage clamps, hand screw clamp, countersink, and screw driver.
Apply Appropriate Finish	Stain, shellac, paint, plastic wood and varnish brushes; spray equipment; finishing bench and rack; and containers for finishing supplies.
Service Activity	Bench brush.

Criterion "B" and "C," the degree that a tool or other item of special equipment is used in doing an operation or task and the amount of expected student cooperation in the use of any one tool or piece of equipment need to be considered at the same time. This example calls for the optimum possibility of having ten different students working on this unit since it has been planned as the very first one to be done at the ten work stations for bench woodworking. This means that from one to ten of each of these tools or items of equipment needs to be recommended. The number to be specified will need to be predicated on the professional judgment of one or more teachers. It will be recognized that such a decision might well be made by a committee. It would seem highly desirable, in this case, to equip each of the ten benches with a woodworking vise and a cleaning brush and to consider purchasing a jack plane for each of the ten stations. A try square might be shared between two stations. While some tools might be purchased for each of the work stations, it might be decided that the program could be facilitated with three marking gauges, two saw horses, two hand crosscut saws, and two hand rip saws.

In addition to the tools and special items of equipment used by students for their work in VAE programs, there is need to identify:

1. **Machines and equipment needed to prepare instructional supplies.** For example, an industrial arts teacher assigned to help elementary teachers with the career education activities in self-contained classrooms would need such machines as a circular saw and a band saw to prepare materials to be sent to these rooms to facilitate construction of three-dimensional objects by children in an elementary school situation. Another example would be the need of the teaching team for an electric typewriter and a duplicating machine to prepare directions for modules of individualized instruction (as shown in Appendix M).
2. **Equipment and machines needed for demonstrations and lessons to be presented by the teacher.** In VAE there is often need to purchase or develop equipment or machines that would be used by the teacher to demonstrate technical and scientific principles, operations or tasks, and mechanisms. The equipment that is to be housed permanently in a laboratory to facilitate audiovisual instruction, such as a recorder, an overhead transparency projector, and a filmstrip projector might well be identified and classified in this category.
3. **Tools and equipment needed for the maintenance, repair, and upkeep of other tools, equipment, and machines.** Examples of such items are sterilizers for disinfecting instruments in health care programs, wrenches for the disassembly and assembly of machines, oil stones for sharpening and honing tools, and a file card for cleaning files.
4. **Tools and equipment needed to provide for the student working on some research problem or developing a unit or project.** In most cases, this would consist of specialized tools or pieces of

equipment designed to enrich the program, such as a bearing load tester, viscosity meter, or fuel consumption analyzer for automotives, a microscope for the study and evaluation of microbes in health care programs, or microwave oven in home economics. Generally, only one of each tool or piece of equipment would be needed because of limited utilization.
5. **Tools and equipment needed to service or repair items brought into the laboratory.** In electrical and power mechanics programs, students are often permitted to bring service and maintenance problems into the laboratory. The investment in needed specialized tools and equipment to work on these devices could be almost unlimited. In general, the areas in which work will be permitted should be determined and these areas equipped with one of each necessary tool or piece of equipment. For required or common activities, the system outlined in previous sections should be used.
6. **Extra small tools needed for those misplaced.** Experienced teachers have discovered that there is need for a few extra of the commonly used small instruments, utensils, and tools that may be easily misplaced or lost. For example, if ten pair of bandage scissors are essential for instruction in a health care program, it is suggested that two extra pair be purchased so that they may be used to fill the instrument holder when a pair of scissors is misplaced. In industrial education, such common tools as nail sets, countersinks, steel rules, drills, pliers, and scribers are easily misplaced, especially where there is a high frequency of use.
7. **Extra tools, utensils, instruments, or parts needed to facilitate reconditioning.** Another practice worthy of consideration is to purchase a few additional hand tools, utensils, or instruments to provide the extra ones needed to facilitate the reconditioning and repairing of items having a high frequency of use. For example, if ten jack planes were in rather constant use, it would be expedient to maintain an inventory of twelve. This would provide two planes that could be kept out of circulation while plane irons were being sharpened or broken handles repaired or replaced. Extra plane irons are often provided to facilitate keeping the planes sharp. This practice is recommended for the common tools, utensils, or instruments that are subjected to a high frequency of use and need to be sharpened or reconditioned at regular intervals.

Determining Needed Instructional Supplies

The process of identifying needed instructional materials for a program is not too difficult nor involved. It is done through an analysis of student needs by one or more professional teachers. The first step is to anticipate the units of instruction to be expedited through projects, experiments, or other work by one typical student in the course or program. Then a list, or bill of materials with rough sizes or amounts, is made of those instructional supplies that would be needed by this student.

As mentioned, this amount of instructional supplies will represent the needs of one student. Where two or more students will be doing the same unit, the amount needed for a particular unit may then be multiplied by this number. This amount might then be increased by 25 percent to allow for instructional supplies that serve these purposes:

1. That may be reissued to a student who has ruined the original issue.
2. For experimental work being projected by the teacher.
3. For construction of teaching aids.
4. For other unforeseen activities.

Obviously this process becomes more and more involved and difficult where there is a high degree of individualized instruction in advanced VAE courses. In most extreme cases, where no two students would be doing the same basic projects, experiments, or other work, the estimates would have to be calculated for each person in the program or activity. This is really not too difficult since such classes are usually limited in size. Then too, advanced students should not be deprived of the educational experience of both specifying and procuring the instructional supplies needed for their work, especially for unique activities. While an advanced student in VAE is doing research and planning to implement units under study, there is usually sufficient time to identify and procure the highly specialized items — either through the regular ordering channels or by having the student obtain the materials directly from the source of supply. Records of amounts and kinds of instructional supplies used in any one previous course become most useful. Such information will guide a teacher as purchase orders are prepared.

Particularly in applied arts, because of the diversification of the activities, teachers need to build up a variety of materials and instructional supplies. For many items, the amounts needed will not be great; as a result, it is not too difficult to develop a variety of materials, especially in the well-established courses. A variety of kinds of wood and metal, for example, is essential in industrial arts to implement the important emphases in problem solving and industrial design. A variety of instructional supplies are needed also where students are constructing projects that provide for a practical application of scientific and technological principles.

Consideration needs to be given to the minimum and optimum quantity or amount of any one item of instructional material that can be purchased economically by a school system. For example, the expense of processing a purchase order for one dozen wood screws would probably be more than the value of one gross. A policy regarding the purchase of practical minimum quantities, therefore, needs to be ascertained. It is for this reason that regularly audited revolving petty cash funds (where they are legal) have been established for VAE programs. This is a very practical way for school systems to reduce the purchasing costs of small quantities of instructional supplies needed for advanced VAE courses.

Determine Needed Textbooks, Reference Books and Audiovisual Aids

It is the right and responsibility of professional teachers to participate in the establishment of criteria for the selection of needed texts, reference books, and audiovisual materials for the courses they will be teaching. In our democratic educational program, the selection of these items and the defense of such action should rest primarily with qualified professional teachers employed to offer the subject. The selection and defense of textbooks, reference books, and audiovisual materials are not matters to be left completely to administration or to those in supervisory capacities. Many systems appoint teacher committees to review, recommend, or select text and audiovisual materials.

To participate cooperatively in the selection of textbooks, reference books, and audiovisual materials, a teacher must first become familiar with prevailing adoption procedures that may be in effect in his/her state or school district. Silvius and Curry (1967, 153-162) have identified factors often considered by VAE teachers when establishing criteria for evaluating published text and reference books and audiovisual materials.

Each of the units in a course needs to be studied and matched with available visuals, printed materials, and recordings that might be used by the teacher when preparing for or when teaching the unit, or by students during the period that they are studying the unit. Teachers, therefore, need to be fully familiar with the available indexes for locating text, reference, and visual material. Such common library guides as **The Art Index, Cumulative Book Index, Applied Science and Technology Index, Education Index,** and **Reader's Guide to Periodical Literature** — all published by the H. W. Wilson Company of New York — may be used for this purpose. Useful periodicals, such as the trade journals, may be identified in **Ulrich's Periodicals Directory** or the **Standard Periodical Directory**. Those who teach the technical subjects should make a careful study of the **Engineering Index** published by the Engineering Society. Silvius and Curry (1971, 409-413) list the several sources available to curriculum builders for locating pertinent motion pictures, filmstrips, prepared overhead transparencies, loop films, microfilm, and other audiovisual aids.

After films, printed items, and recordings have been identified through these available indexes, they then need to be studied by the teacher and evaluated against established criteria to determine their appropriateness and usefulness when a specific unit is taught. Too few teachers have scientifically screened all available materials to select those items that would be appropriate and most useful as resource material in the preparation of instructional units or for students studying a block of instruction. The printed material used in VAE laboratories has been classified as textbooks, reference books, workbooks, handbooks, manufacturers' operator's manuals, trade catalogs, magazines, and pamphlets (Silvius and Curry, 1967, 147-149).

It is suggested that each course of study carry the titles of needed text and reference items, classified by types of material, and identified with the titles for specific units in the course. Titles and available sources for selected recordings, filmstrips, 16mm movies, and other visuals should be given for each of the units. A section of the bibliography, listing titles especially for the teacher of the course, might also be prepared.

Develop Floor Plan Showing Machines, Equipment, and Instructional Areas

As mentioned in the introduction for this chapter, there is much available literature to help VAE teachers intelligently (1) plan for the best use of floor space or (2) present a proposal for optimum physical facilities in new situations.

Procedures have been recommended, in the first topic of this chapter, for identifying the exact number and character of work stations, service equipment and machines; needed tools, instruments, and utensils; audiovisuals and recordings; and text and reference materials. Suggestions have been made for estimating the instructional supplies that need to be stored for a course.

The discussion in this chapter has been directed at determining tools, equipment, and materials that must be housed in one or more rooms for one course. Sometimes, it is necessary to show as much as an eighty percent minimum use of a school room during any one term to justify its place in the school. This suggests that VAE laboratories should be planned for multiple activities and courses. The laboratory shown as Fig. 12-3 has been planned to accommodate activities representative of careers found in the fifteen career clusters identified by the U.S. Office of Education (listed in Fig. 1-4 of Chapter 1). Ressler (1973, 73-74) reports that the following criteria were used in selecting the major activities for the elementary career education laboratory shown in Fig. 12-3:

1. Does the activity clearly describe what a person in a particular occupation does? If it does not, it should be discarded.
2. Can the activity be done in a short enough period of time to enable pupils to recall what career it represents?
3. Can pupils of various ages and abilities accomplish the task? There must be provision for differences of ability among pupils.
4. Is the activity interesting? It must be appropriate to the younger child to be really meaningful.
5. Can all children experience success in the activity? There must be a reasonable chance for success for every pupil.
6. Is the activity appropriate for either sex? Both sexes should be able to undertake the task.
7. Is the space required prohibitive? Minimal space should be consumed to enable as many "stations" as possible in the career center.
8. Is the cost prohibitive? Can materials be reused?
9. Can the activity be done elsewhere in the school, rather than consume space in a career laboratory?

Specifying Equipment and Supplies 377

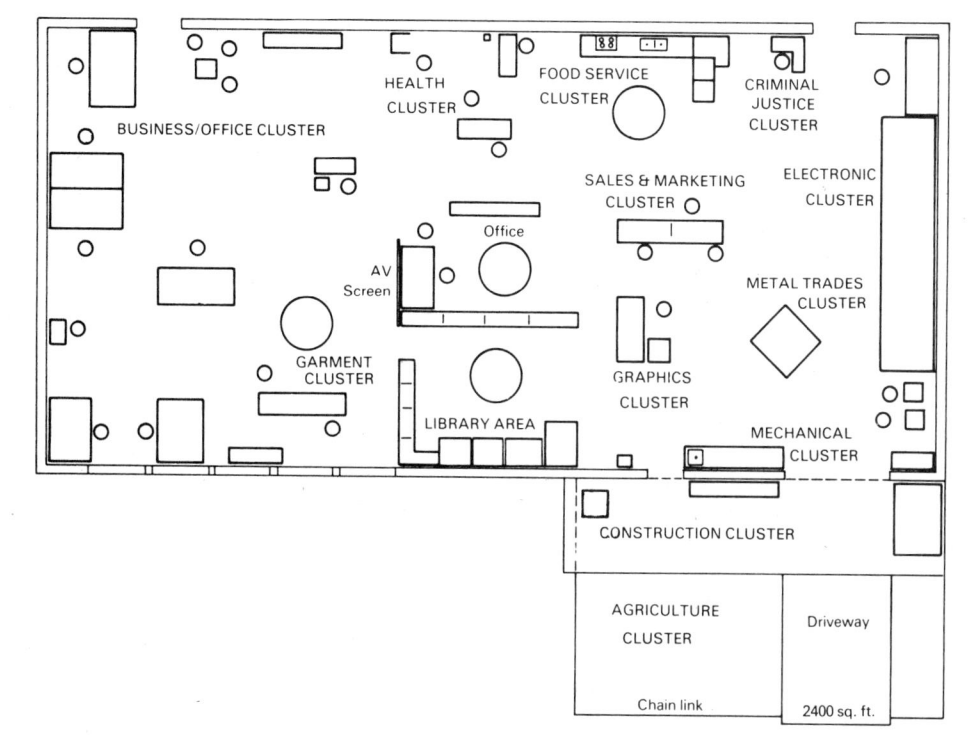

Fig. 12-3. A plan for a multi-activity laboratory for career education in an elementary school. Described in an article by Ralph Ressler[1] (1973, 73-75) and reprinted from p. 75 of April 1973 issue of **School Shop**. (Courtesy Howard Kahn, Managing Editor)

[1]Coordinator, Elementary Career Education, Office of Vocational and Adult Education, Dade County Public Schoools, Miami, Florida

10. Is it safe, assuming a reasonable amount of supervision will be provided?
11. If the activity is related to an in-school prevocational or vocational program found in upper grades, is this made known to pupils?
12. Is teacher training required for the activity? If so, what kind and how much?

To plan a VAE facility, those concerned need to identify exactly the equipment and instructional supplies to be placed and housed on the floor space under consideration for each of the major activities to be scheduled in the room.

There are other items that should not be overlooked when planning an instructional facility, such as acoustical treatment for noise control,

378 Planning and Organizing Instruction

bulletin and chalkboards, electrical outlets, first-aid cabinet, adequate lighting, planning area, space between equipment, traffic lanes, wall clock, washing facilities, and ventilation. Silvius and Curry (1971, 182-183) have identified fifty-two such items for consideration.

At this point, the procedure for scientifically identifying all items that must be placed in one room or more for use in specific courses has been considered. The final step is to arrange these items on the floor plan so that the facility will provide an optimum educational climate with safe working conditions. This can be done by shifting about within the given floor areas either two- or three-dimensional models. Space requirements — for safety purposes and optimum working conditions, to be maintained around items of industrial education equipment, by instructional areas — have been identified in a research project by Willard M. Bateson (1954, 5-42).

The actual floor plan, showing machines and other equipment in place, might well be presented in a course of study as a photograph showing three-dimensional models in place or as a floor plan drawn to scale showing a top view of machines and equipment in place, as illustrated in Figs. 12-4 through 12-9. There need, of course, to be adequate codes and descriptions so the reader of a course of study will quickly see and understand what is needed for the specific course under consideration.

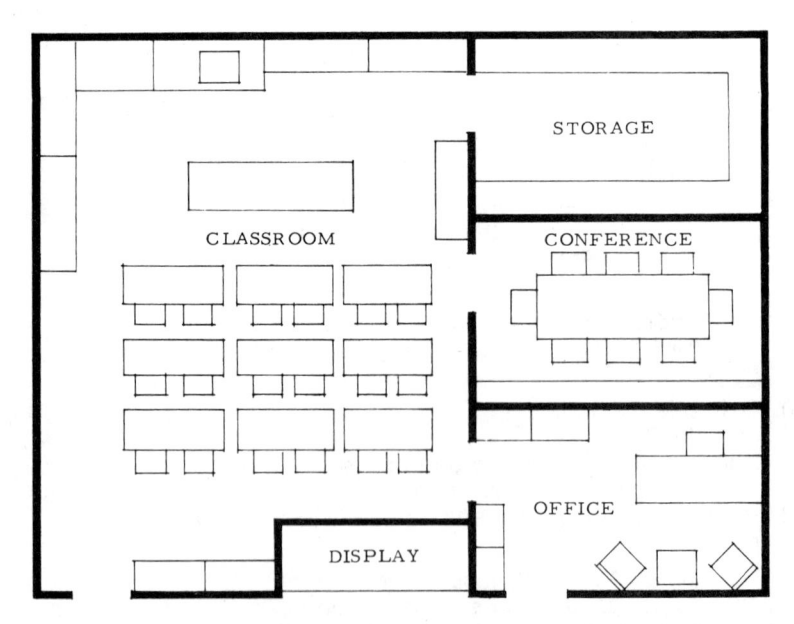

Fig. 12-4. A classroom layout for instruction in marketing. Nonload-bearing walls are utilized to provide the four areas for this facility so that they could be easily changed if an alternative plan is later desired. (Reprinted from p. B-3 of the Oregon **Occupational Cluster Guide for Marketing**, Oregon Board of Education.)

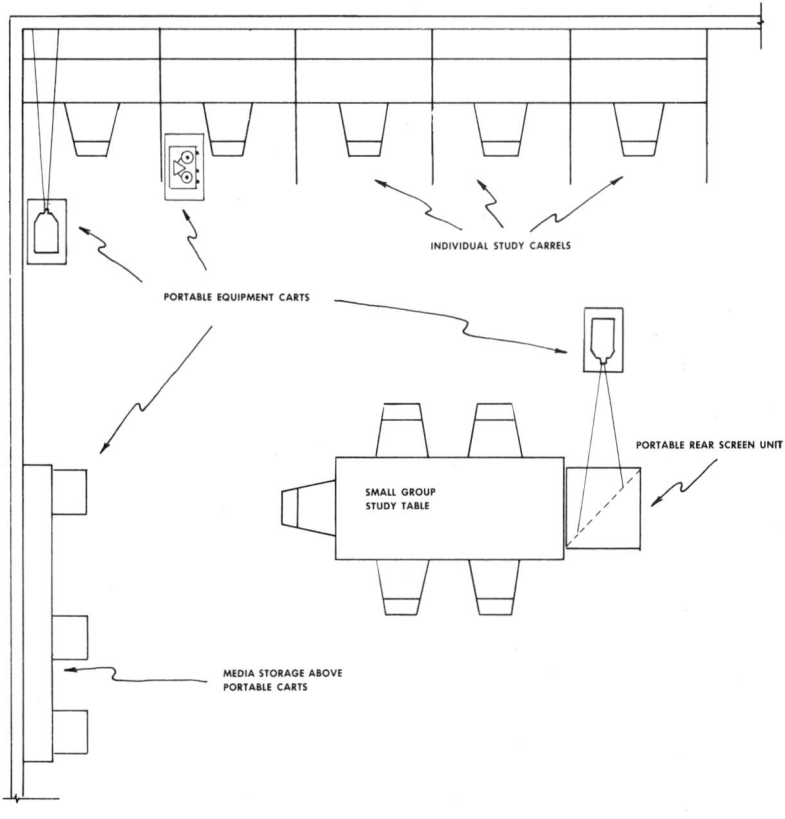

Fig. 12-5. A plan for arranging multimedia equipment for a VAE program. (Courtesy Alvin E. Rudisill, University of Northern Iowa at Cedar Falls)

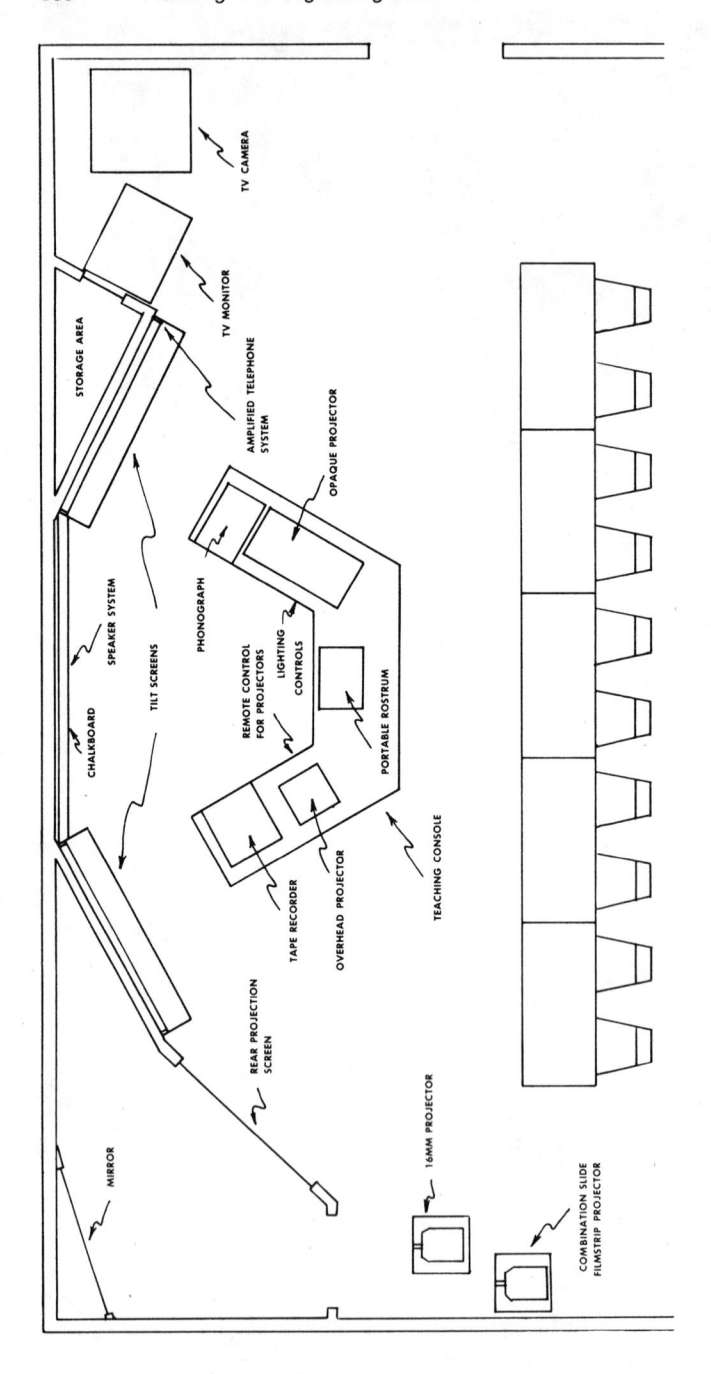

Fig. 12-6. A plan for arranging multimedia equipment in front of a console-controlled classroom for VAE instruction. (Courtesy Alvin E. Rudisill)

Specifying Equipment and Supplies   **381**

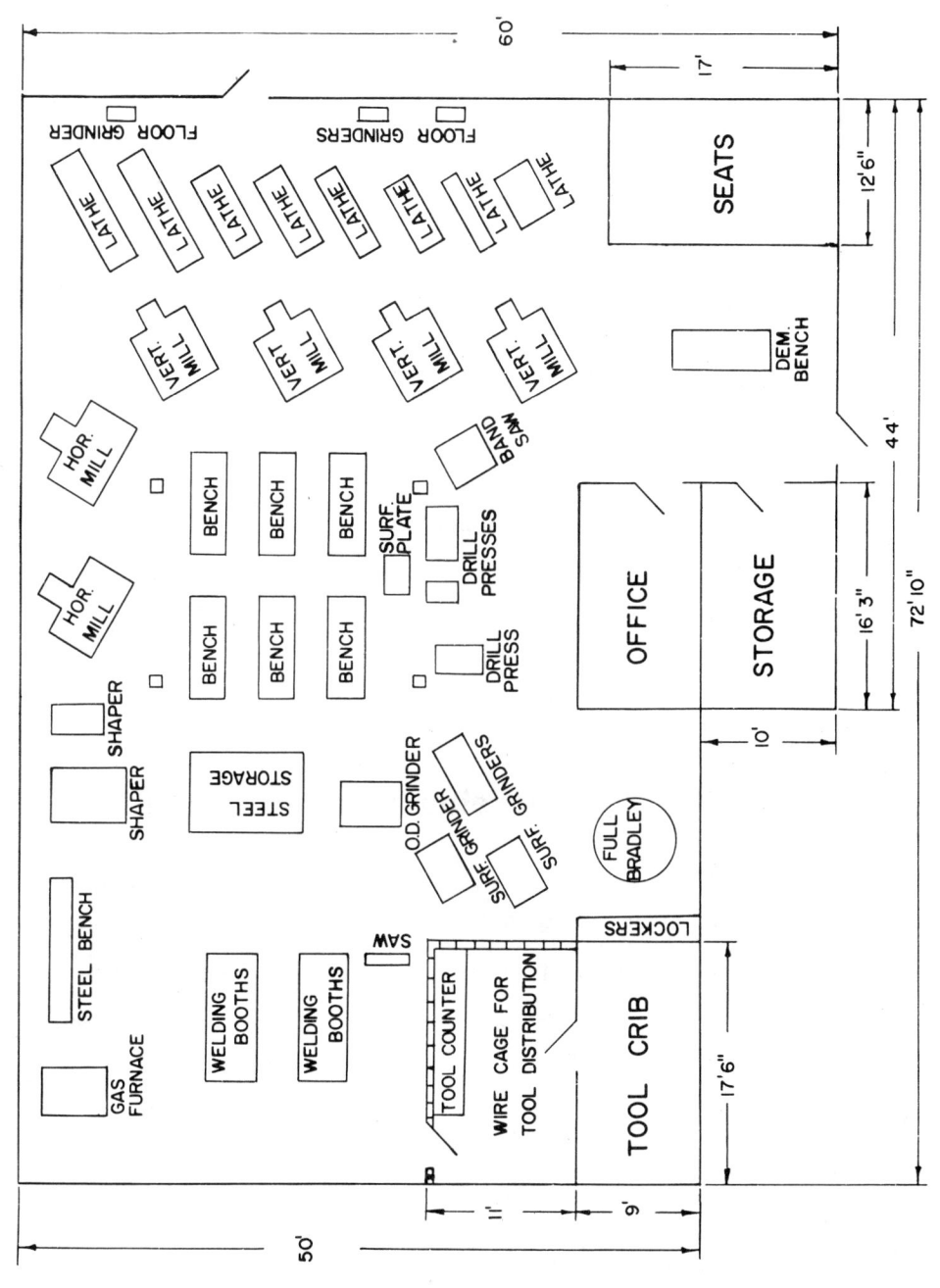

Fig. 12-7. Equipment plan as shown in course of study for metal processing at Lincoln High School, Warren, Michigan. (Courtesy Robert C. Hollister)

382 Planning and Organizing Instruction

INDIVIDUAL STUDY CARREL

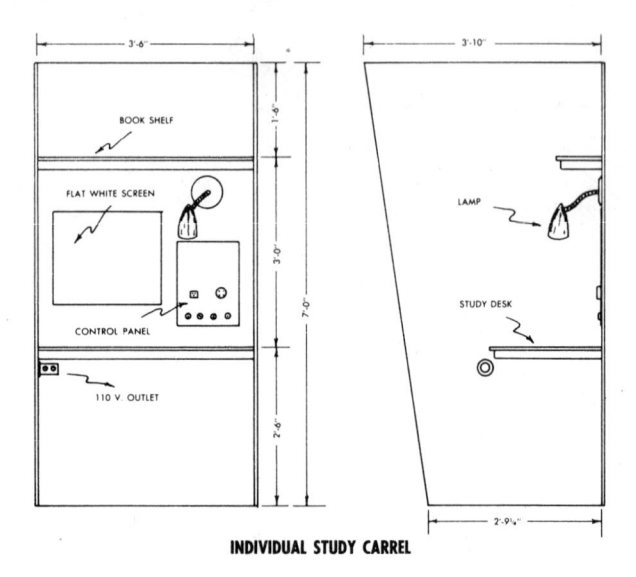

Fig. 12-8. Plan for constructing the study carrels shown in Fig. 12-5. Many VAE laboratories are now equipped with such booths for individualized instruction. This simple and functional design for a carrel was developed by Alvin E. Rudisill.

Plan Projected Development of Physical Facilities

Vocational and applied arts teachers often raise these questions:

1. "Should I plan a program that is delimited to the equipment and instructional supplies now available to me?
2. "How do I cope with an instructional program where it is only possible to get the needed equipment a little at a time?
3. "How do I secure the needed floor space to house the equipment arranged to provide optimum conditions for safety and learning?"

These are very real problems that need to be handled in the most astute manner. The following may be helpful in effectively dealing with the issues that are inherent in these questions.

There is generally opportunity to involve other teachers, a department head, the principal, the supervisor, the superintendent of schools, and the members of the advisory committee in the formulation of aims for the school system, the department, and the specific course. This is where able VAE teachers set the stage and get the support for the

Fig. 12-9. Portable screens are used at the Wadena Area Technical Institute at Wadena, Minnesota, to designate areas in laboratories used for group instruction. Such arrangements facilitate the degree of flexibility now desirable in VAE laboratory planning. (Courtesy of Stanley Heins and James B. Baymler)

needed program. It should be easy then, through **scientific procedures,** for the professional teacher to present the minimum physical facilities required to carry out an educational program to fulfill established goals. Where the physical facilities are currently below par, a well-written course of study might be transmitted officially to the principal of the school, clearly showing how the current offerings are necessarily curtailed in terms of the agreed upon aims. Such courses of study should also carry a specific section showing what needs to be purchased or provided, with a specific proposal, so that the program may be offered in an optimum manner.

It is unfortunate that **some of today's VAE teachers do not have even a minimum course of study to support requests for essential equipment and instructional supplies. It is only through sound planning and articulate description that needed items will be enthusiastically endorsed by those who control and support education.** It is important that key administrators, school board members, and people in a community fully understand what is needed. The responsibility for such an interpretation should rest with the professional teachers employed to project and teach the program. It is recognized that advisory committees can be influential in helping teachers through the supervisor, director, and principal, present the case and prepare a practical plan to secure what is needed.

Determine Responsibility for Budget and Accounting Systems

Nearly all school systems have established policies that govern budget and accounting practices, such as Planning, Programing, Budgeting Systems (PPBS) or similar plans, as discussed in Chapter 11. A VAE teacher needs, therefore, to ascertain the understandings immediately to deal with the following concerns:

The Budget

- Major divisions of the budget for the entire school system and the amounts allocated for each part.
- The management of the school's budget.
- The amount allocated for equipment and instructional materials or supplies for any one program.

Purchasing Procedures

The teacher in requisitioning and purchasing instructional supplies and equipment must consider:

- Purchasing practices of school system.
- Preparing purchasing specifications.
- When and how to submit requisitions.
- Delivery dates for supplies and equipment.
- Instructional supplies furnished to students.

- How purchases for emergencies are made.
- Policy for establishing a revolving petty cash fund.
- Policy for charging students for instructional supplies.

The Inventory

School system policy and the practice for accounting requires these specific considerations:
- Methods and forms for inventory.
- Frequency of inventory.
- Records for —
  1. Expendable instructional supplies.
  2. New equipment.
  3. Repairs and maintenance.
  4. Replacement of worn or obsolete equipment.

Source of Information

The information needed regarding school and district policies is often available in a handbook published by the school system. When not available in this form, the information can be secured through interviews with the department head, the principal, or the purchasing agent for the school system. Where this information does not appear in official publications of the school system, it is suggested that the teacher include in his/her courses of study these data covering board of education policy and practice on these matters.

Distinction Between Equipment and Supplies

It is important for school systems to establish sharp definitions for budget and accounting purposes in order to distinguish items as **instructional supplies, or equipment.**

A distinction often made is that **instructional supplies** (used interchangeably and synonymously with **instructional materials**) are those items that are changed in some way to facilitate a unit of work or in the construction of a project — usually used once or a few times by the student. They are the expendable items. **Equipment,** on the other hand, would include the tools and machines that can be used again and again over a period of time. They are not expendable. Examples would be:

Equipment	Wheelchair (for transporting patients.)
Supply	Medicine droppers.
Equipment	Cash register.
Supply	Paper.
Equipment	Machine lathe.
Supply	Tool bit.
Equipment	Refrigerator.
Supply	Flour.

Another approach is to classify items that cost less than $25 (or some appropriate amount) as **instructional supplies** and those more than $25 as **equipment**. Under this definition, small instruments, tools, and some accessories are listed with raw materials as **supplies**. This definition can be modified also by classifying "miscellaneous small tools" separately.

The advantage of the second definition is that it reduces the initial capital costs for equipment by transferring some of these costs to the budget item for instructional materials. In most communities it is usually much easier to secure money from year to year for instructional supplies than it is to have adequate funds allocated for equipment. The distinction between equipment and supplies varies between school systems. The VAE teacher must, for budget purposes, become acquainted with the classifications established by the board of education. This needs to be done before a system for purchasing and accounting for supplies and equipment is established.

Facilities Provided with Mobile Laboratories

Traveling VAE laboratories are becoming more popular as they are being used to facilitate career education programs. In a survey, Smith (April 1973, 22-24) found that sixteen states were using more than fifty different mobile units for various VAE programs. Other states reported that they planned to use mobile units in the future. Smith found that the fifty units were being used for various purposes:

> Most popular uses were for career exploration and vocational programs for disadvantaged and adults. Twelve responses indicated that they used the trailers for either career exploration or for guidance. We construed these types of programs to have a great deal in common although obviously they are not the same thing. Six units served the disadvantaged.
>
> Three types of trailers were found in use. One is the commercially available "house" type units outfitted by firms which are in the business of providing mobile classrooms. Another approach is to buy an old passenger or school bus and either build in the equipment for the program or contract for a commercial firm to do it. The third approach is where a vocational school constructs the trailer on a purchased chassis and installs the equipment.

Smith states that the reasons for using mobile units vary widely. New Jersey, which operates twelve units, hopes to promote permanent programs by demonstrating what can be accomplished with a mobile unit. Some districts use them when low enrollments do not warrant a permanent facility. Others find it feasible to share the cost of the laboratory and the instructor's salary, e.g., the facility for electronics that shuttles daily between two schools eighteen miles apart in Colorado. The units in New York City are used to enrich the elementary program with hands-on career oriented activities.

The advantages advocated for mobile units are:
- They are initially less expensive than adding a laboratory to a school.
- The cost per student is lower when the program can be shared with one or more additional districts.
- Expensive equipment is used in a more maximum way as the mobile unit moves on to another school when instruction is completed.

The disadvantages of mobile units are:
- The rather rapid depreciation of the facility.
- High maintenance costs for the tractor or power unit (gasoline, oil, tires, and repair.)
- Delicate instructional mechanisms and equipment may be damaged when transported over rough terrain.
- The safety zones and work space around machines are usually limited because of the narrow widths of the mobile units.

These disadvantages are offset by the popularity and value of the program. To illustrate, in a three-year period in Arizona, a mobile machine shop has been used at eighteen different high schools. Mobile units have been especially effective with the disadvantaged and slow learning students. Such learners are motivated by activity programs which become more readily available through the use of mobile laboratories.

Maximize the Use of Community Facilities in Development of VAE Programs

Many facilities are now available for carrying on VAE programs away from public schools. This was made possible by the provisions of the Vocational Education Act of 1963, The Amendments of 1968, and the involvement of employers in planning and offering career education programs (as discussed in Chapter 1). Through cooperative arrangements with business, industry, hospitals, and government and community agencies, it is now possible to establish training stations for vocational/technical education in the community.

Considerable space in Chapter 4 was devoted to the concept of occupational education "without walls." The topic on "Community Resources to Expand Occupational Education" considered:

- Expanding the cooperative education program.
- Procuring auxiliary facilities from companies to house expanding vocational education programs, as is done in Cleveland.
- Making use of the facilities of business and industry as training stations for the highly specialized programs, as is done in the Los Angeles Regional Occupational Programs.
- Negotiating contractual vocational programs with companies or individuals to expand the options in occupational education.

When training stations are established in business or industry, the student is generally being trained on up-to-date equipment. Most progressive companies have a plan for the amortization of their equipment and do not, therefore, have the problem that faces many public

Fig. 12-10. Students work on aircraft engines at Pacific Continental Engines, Van Nuys Airport, California. The use of industrial facilities provides up-to-date equipment for instruction. (Regional Occupational Program, Los Angeles)

schools of replacing obsolete equipment. Then too, in the years ahead it may be more and more difficult for public schools to purchase the intricate and expensive equipment, such as that now used in modern hospitals, that is needed to prepare persons for a place in productive industries and business. Finally, from the values to society, it seems most desirable that the facilities of industry and business be used for the dual purpose of training and production.

For Self-Assessment and Discussion

1. Some school systems define **equipment** in a generic way to include hand tools, instruments, utensils, power machines, furniture, teaching aids, portable power tools, visual and auditory equipment, and non-power machines. Is such a general classification satisfactory when specifying needed items for specific courses of study? For inventory purposes?
2. What names could be placed on the glass panels of the outside doors leading to shops, laboratories, or other rooms used to house

equipment for two or more major activities or different subjects in VAE programs?
3. Cite examples to show how the specific course goals would influence size and kinds of machines or equipment that would be appropriate for a VAE course.
4. What factors determine the number of any one tool, instrument, or utensil needed for a course or program?
5. What factors need to be considered when purchasing specifications are prepared for equipment needed for a VAE program?
6. Where might a VAE teacher locate three-dimensional models to plan a layout for a shop, laboratory, or drafting room?
7. Explain the steps for estimating needed instructional supplies for a VAE course or program.
8. Is it desirable to use the terms **instructional supplies** and **instructional materials** synonymously?
9. What specific indexes and sources does a VAE teacher use to locate the following useful items:
   A. Filmstrips?
   B. Commercial overhead transparencies?
   C. 16mm movies?
   D. Loop films?
   E. Recordings?
   F. Textbook, handbook, and other reference books?
   G. Pertinent service manuals?
10. What factors should prevail in determining when a power machine or piece of equipment should be discarded or replaced in VAE programs?
11. Should a course of study be planned around "what ought to be" or should the teacher limit it to those activities that can be carried on with the equipment and instructional supplies currently provided by the school system?
12. Explain techniques that might be employed by a professional teacher to transmit to administration a course of study that has been "tailored" for the teaching situation.
13. Describe the advantages of mobile laboratories. Their disadvantages.
14. List several ways that community resources are now employed to extend and expand occupational education programs.

Assignments to Demonstrate Competencies

For your specific course of study — with community, school, and student conditions specified; and the course goals, content, methods reported; and evaluation procedures identified —
1. Develop a report showing needed work stations and service machines or equipment for a maximum-size class (with number of students to be accommodated reported).
2. Make an analysis of needed hand tools, instruments, utensils, portable power equipment, and machines not included in assignment one.

3. List kinds and amounts of needed instructional supplies.
4. In complete bibliographical form, indicate needed numbers of each textbook and reference book for a selected course and grade level.
5. Prepare a bibliography, organized by units in the course, carrying titles that would assist the teacher as he/she prepares to present the units.
6. List filmstrips, 16mm movies, and other visuals and recordings, with their sources, to be used when teaching specified units.
7. Use Ulrich's **Periodical Directory** and/or the **Standard Periodical Directory** in identifying magazines that would be useful to students studying the course.
8. Present a floor plan, using two- or three-dimensional planning, showing equipment placed for optimum learning conditions.
9. Write purchasing specifications for the power machines and heavy equipment needed for a specific course of study.

References* and Resources

Books

Meckley, Richard F. **Planning Facilities for Occupational Education Programs.** Columbus, Ohio: Charles E. Merrill Publishing Co., 1972, pp. xiii + 161.

*Silvius, G. Harold, and Curry, Estell H. **Managing Multiple Activities.** 2nd ed. Bloomington, Illinois: McKnight Publishing Co., 1971. The references that apply to this chapter are: Topic 8, Provide for Students to Progress from One Activity to Another; Topic 16, Plan for Facilities and Equipment; Topic 17, Maintaining Tools and Equipment; Topic 19, Plan and Provide for Storing Material; Topic 20, Plan and Construct Suitable Tool Racks; Topic 21, Provide a Tool Checking System; Topic 22, Purchase Supplies and Equipment and Keep an Inventory; Topic 25, Encourage Wholesome Attitudes Toward Care of Tools and Equipment; and Topic 30, Utilize Audiovisual Materials and Equipment.

*_____. **Teaching Successfully.** 2nd ed. Bloomington, Illinois: McKnight Publishing Company, 1967. The references that apply to this chapter are: Topic 9, Select Text, Reference, and Visual Materials; and Topic 11, Plan for the Teacher's Professional Library.

Pamphlet

Taylor, James L., and Christian, Johnie. **Planning Functional Facilities for Home Economics Education.** Publication No. OE-83015. Washington, D.C.: Supt. of Docs., 1965, Pp. vii + 48.

Periodicals

*Bateson, Willard M. "Standards for Physical Facilities of School Shop Developed in a Research Study." **School Shop,** Vol. 13, No. 8 (April, 1954), pp. 5-14, 16-17, 20-21, 24-25, 29, 34-35, 42.

Dean, Harvey and Thuma, Ron. "Model Facilities for New Industrial Arts Programs." **School Shop.** Vol. 34, No. 5 (January, 1975), pp. 36-37.

*Items with an asterisk have been cited in the chapter.

Dean, Thomas C. "Let Your Budget Express Your Long-Range Goals." **Industrial Education,** Vol. 62, No. 4 (March, 1973), pp. 24-26.
*Ressler, Ralph. "R for K-6." **School Shop,** Vol. 32, No. 8 (April, 1973), pp. 73-75.
"Shop Planning Annual." Industrial Education. The March issue each year features exemplary plans for VAE laboratories.
*Smith, Howard. "Mobile Units — Boon or Bust in Industrial Education." **Industrial Education,** Vol. 62, No. 4 (April, 1973), pp. 22-24.

Selected CVTE Publications on Laboratory Planning

Adams, Jon P. A Guide for Planning Facilities for Occupational Preparation Programs in Automotive Service. ERIC Reference No. ED 028 280, April 1969, Pp. 89.

German, Carl Jr. A Guide for Planning Facilities for Occupational Preparation Programs in Metallurgy Technology. ERIC Reference No. ED 027 420, March 1968, Pp. 111.

Larson, Milton E. A Guide for Planning Facilities for Occupational Preparation Programs in the Machine Trades. ERIC Reference No. ED 023 926, September 1968, Pp. 74.

MacConnell, James D. et al. A Guide for Planning Facilities for Occupational Preparation Programs for Dental Assistants. ERIC Reference No. ED 029 965, May 1969, Pp. 67.

_____ et al. A Guide for Planning Facilities for Occupational Programs for Dental Laboratory Technicians. ERIC Reference No. ED 029 127, May 1969, Pp. 53.

_____ et al. A Guide for Planning Facilities for Occupational Preparation Programs for Medical Assistants. ERIC Reference No. ED 029 117, April 1969, Pp. 67.

_____ et al. A Guide for Planning Facilities for Occupational Preparation Programs for Medical Secretaries. ERIC Reference No. ED 029 120, April 1969, Pp. 59.

_____ et al. A Guide for Planning Facilities for Occupational Preparation Programs for Medical X-Ray Technicians. ERIC Reference No. ED 028 283, April 1969, Pp. 61.

McIntosh, William A. A Guide for Planning Facilities for Occupational Preparation Programs in Data Processing. ERIC Reference No. ED 023 927, November 1968, Pp. 67.

Meckley, Richard F. et al. A Guide for Planning Facilities for Home Economics Occupational Preparation Programs. ERIC Reference No. ED 022 924, July 1968, Pp. 86.

_____ et al. A General Guide for Planning Facilities for Occupational Preparation Programs. ERIC Reference No. ED 030 771, June 1969, Pp. 87.

_____ et al. A Guide to Systematic Planning for Vocational and Technical Schools. ERIC Reference No. ED 026 537, December 1968, Pp. 33.

Selden, William. A Guide for Planning Facilities for Occupational Preparation Programs in Business and Office Occupations. ERIC Reference No. ED 027 401, November 1968, Pp. 91.

Sitterlee, L. J. A Guide for Planning Facilities for Occupational Preparation Programs in Electrical Technology. ERIC Reference No. ED 028 278, April 1969, Pp. 112.

Selected Oregon Occupational Cluster Guides

Oregon Board of Education. Salem, Oregon 97310: The Division of Community Colleges and Career Education, 942 Lancaster Drive N E. References that pertain to this chapter are:

Occupational Cluster Guide for Clerical Occupations, 1971. The Appendix includes (1) plans for a model office, (2) suggested equipment, (3) bibiography, (4) audiovisual aids, and (5) state-adopted textbooks, pp. A-1-31.

Occupational Cluster Guide for Food Service Occupations, February 1970. Appendix B is on Facilities and Equipment, pp. B-1-19.

Occupational Cluster Guide for Forest Products Occupations, July 1972. Appendix B is on Suggested Tools and Equipment, pp. B-1-5; and Appendix C covers Resources, pp. C-1-15.

Occupational Cluster Guide for Health Occupations, December 1969. Appendix B is on Equipment and Supplies, pp. B-1-9; and Appendix C covers Instructional Materials, pp. C-1-9.

Occupational Cluster Guide for Marketing, February 1970. Appendix B is on Facilities and Equipment, pp. B-1-19.

Occupational Cluster Guide on Steno-Secretarial Occupations, May 1970. Appendix B on Facilities, pp. B-1-9; and Appendix C covers materials, texts, references, and audiovisual equipment, pp. C-1-16.

Appendices of Curriculum Examples

Most of the examples of curriculum materials used to illustrate the principles and procedures presented in this book have been placed in the eighteen appendices presented on the following pages. They are grouped together to permit easy reference from a number of chapters, as well as present to the reader a unified set of examples.

In addition to the curriculum examples included on the following pages, a number of examples have been placed within the manuscript. These are necessary to illustrate the principles being presented, and are an integral part of the explanation.

A listing of appendix titles and pages is included in the Table of Contents at the front of the book.

A appendix

CONTENT AND PLAN FOR ORGANIZING IACP LEARNING EXPERIENCES

Identified Content for The World of Construction

This one-year exploratory IACP course provides an opportunity to learn and apply the basic knowledges and skills of the construction industry. Titles for the units of instruction in **The World of Construction** are identified below:

Man and Technology
Construction Technology
Applying Technology to People
Managing Construction
Beginning the Project
Selecting a Site
Buying Real Estate
Surveying and Mapping
Soil Testing
Designing and Engineering Construction Projects
Identifying the Design Problem
Developing Preliminary Ideas
Refining Ideas
Engineering the Designs
Selecting the Design
Making Working Drawings
Writing Specifications
The Designing and Engineering Cycle
Selecting a Builder
Contracting
Estimating and Bidding
Scheduling
Working as a Contractor
Collective Bargaining
Hiring Construction Personnel
Training and Educating for Construction
Working Conditions
Advancing in Construction
Construction Production Technology
Getting Ready to Build
Clearing the Site
Locating the Structure
Building Superstructures
Building Mass and Masonry Superstructures
Erecting Steel Frames
Erecting Concrete Frames
Building Wood Frames
Installing Utilities
Installing Heating, Cooling and Ventilating Systems
Installing Plumbing Systems
Installing Electrical Power Systems

IACP Learning Experiences   **395**

Installing Electrical
   Communications Systems
Making Inspections
Mediating and Arbitrating
Enclosing Framed
   Superstructures
Roofing
Enclosing Exterior Walls
Striking
Insulating
Applying Wall Materials
Applying Ceiling Materials
Laying Floors
Finishing the Project
Painting and Decorating
Installing Accessories
Completing the Site
Transferring the Project
Servicing Property
Building Dams
Bridge Building
Road Building
Building Skyscrapers
Constructing in the Future
Constructing Housing
Earthmoving
Handling Grievances
Stabilizing Earth and
   Structures
Classifying Structures
Setting Foundations
Building Forms
Setting Reinforcement

Mixing Concrete
Placing and Finishing
   Concrete
Completing Foundations
Enclosing Exteriors
Roughing in Utilities
Working on the Interior
Completing the House
Landscaping Homesites
City and Regional Planning
   Factors
Planning Community
   Services
Your Dream House
Selecting and Purchasing a
   Lot
Planning the Living Space
Preparing Working Drawings
Writing Specifications
Financing and Contracting
Building the Substructure
Building Walls
Building Floors and Ceilings
Building Roofs
Housing People
Planning Business Facilities
Planning Schools and
   Recreational Facilities
The Economics of
   Community Developing
Managing Community
   Development

Organizational Plan for
The World of Construction

Course Design

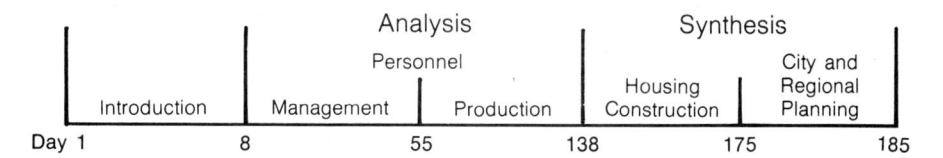

Introduction	Management	Analysis — Personnel Production	Synthesis — Housing Construction	City and Regional Planning
Day 1	8	55	138	175	185

Course Continuum

This one-year course is divided into three major sections:
1. An analysis of the managed personnel-production system of construction.
2. A synthesis of housing construction practices.
3. A synthesis of city and regional planning practices.

The analysis of the managed personnel-production system begins with an introduction to construction technology (8 assignments). Then management practices (47 assignments) and production practices (84 assignments) are described. Personnel practices are dispersed throughout the 131 assignments, wherever they are most relevant. The analysis section provides a basic understanding of the common construction system for building any structure, whether it is a dam, building, tower, tunnel, bridge, utility network, or marine project.

The housing construction section (36 assignments) is a synthesis of construction practices applied to a specific structure: a house. Each student designs and builds his or her own model dream house or commercial housing, thus reinforcing knowledge of major construction practices. The city and regional planning section (11 assignments) introduces the impact of construction upon society and the effects of large scale and long range decision making.[1]

Identified Content for
The World of Manufacturing

The IACP World of Manufacturing course is designed to help students understand the basic concepts of management, personnel, and production techniques for creating finished goods in a plant or factory. Titles for the units of instruction are identified below:

Man and Technology
The Evolution of Manufacturing
Manufacturing and the Economic System
Manufacturing Technology
Manufacturing Management Technology
Inputs to Manufacturing
Organization, Ownership, and Profit
Identifying Consumer Demands
Researching and Developing
Designing Manufactured Goods
Creating Alternate Design Solutions
Making Three-Dimensional Models
Refining the Design Solution
Obtaining Approval of Management
Engineering the Product
Designing Power Elements
Making Working Drawings
Building the Production Prototype
Technical Writing and Illustrating
Planning Production
Planning Processes

[1]Reprinted from IACP World of Construction: Teacher's Guide, p. 1.

IACP Learning Experiences

Measuring Work
Automating Processes
Estimating Cost
Tooling Up for Production
Installing Production Control Systems
Material Separating Practices
Shearing
Chip Removing
Separating by Other Processes

Making Assemblies or Finished Products
Combining Components
Mixing
Coating
Bonding
Mechanical Fastening
Operating Quality Control Systems
Designing and Engineering the Plant
Establishing Accident Prevention Programs

Supplying Equipment and Materials
Processing Data or Information
Using the Computer
Employment and Occupations in Manufacturing
Manufacturing Personnel Technology
Hiring and Training

Working, Advancing, and Retiring
Organized Labor and Collective Bargaining
Securing Reproducible Raw Materials
Extracting Raw Materials
Harnessing Energy from Nature
Manufacturing Production Technology

Converting Raw Materials to Industrial Materials
Making Industrial Materials into Standard Stock
Story of Primary Metal Products
Story of Textile Mill Products
Story of Petroleum Products
Story of Chemical Products
Making Components by Forming or Separating Standard Stock
Material Forming Practices
Casting or Molding
Compressing or Stretching
Conditioning Material

Relating People to the Corporation
Making the Sales Forecast
Obtaining Capital, Estimating Profits, and Keeping Records
Locating the Plant and Securing Inputs
Designing and Engineering the Product
Planning Production Processes
Establishing Production and Quality Control
Combining Subassemblies
Preparing for Distribution
Servicing Manufactured Products

Story of Printed Products
The Manufacturing Corporation
Forming a Corporation
Making and Combining Components and Assemblies
Arranging for Distribution and Sales
Liquidating the Corporation
Manufacturing in the Future
Story of Basic Machine Tools
Story of Rubber Products
Story of the Telephone

Organizational Plan for The World of Manufacturing

Course Design

Introduction	Analysis		Synthesis
Overview of Manufacturing Technology	MANAGEMENT AND PERSONNEL Researching, Designing, and Engineering: Products and Processes	PRODUCTION AND PERSONNEL Processing and Producing Components, Subassemblies, and Assemblies	The Manufacturing Corporation: Formation, Operation, and Liquidation
Day 1	15	77	143 185

Course Continuum

This one-year course is divided into three major sections:
1. An introduction that provides a brief history of manufacturing and an overview of the major concepts of the course.
2. An analysis of the managed personnel-production system of manufacture.
3. A synthesis of manufacturing practices applied to the corporation.

    The introduction to the managed personnel-production system begins with an overview of manufacturing technology (15 assignments). Then an analysis of the concepts of researching, designing, and engineering are cycled as they apply to products and processes (62 assignments). This is followed by an analysis of production practices (66 assignments). Personnel practices are interspersed throughout the assignments wherever they are most relevant. The analysis section will provide a basic understanding of the common system of manufacture for any product, whether it is a textile, metal, plastic, wood, chemical, leather, food, electrical, rubber, printed, or petroleum product, to name a few.[2]

Resources

[1]Lux, Donald J.; Ray, Willis E.; Hauenstein, A. Dean. **The World of Construction: Teacher's Guide.** 4th edition. Bloomington, Illinois: McKnight Publishing Co., 1970, Pp. viii + 309.

[2]_____. **The World of Manufacturing: Teacher's Guide.** 4th edition. Bloomington, Illinois: McKnight Publishing Co., 1971, Pp. vi + 367.

[2]Reprinted from IACP **World of Manufacturing: Teacher's Guide,** p. 1.

appendix **B**

Steps in Specifying the Curriculum and Content for the Oregon Career Cluster Approach

1. Available job analyses from the DOT are studied for each job title included in the occupational analysis. To illustrate, the specific tasks for a **Welder, Combination**, the second key job classification in the METALS cluster (DOT code number 812.884) are:

   EXAMPLE

   - Welds metal parts together, according to layouts, blueprints, or work orders using brazing, and any combination of arc welding processes. Performs related tasks such as flame cutting and grinding. May repair broken or cracked parts, fill holes, and increase size of metal parts. May position and clamp together components of fabricated metal products preparatory to welding.
     Instructional Code: 1.0, 2.0, 3.0, 4.0, 6.0, 8.0, 9.0[1]
   - Repairs worn or damaged machined, fabricated, castforged, or welded metal parts as specified by sketches, diagrams, or sample parts; uses arc welding equipment.
     Instructional Code: 1.0, 2.0, 9.0
   - Examines workpiece and measures dimensions for conformance to specifications. Uses tape, rule, square.
     Instructional Code: 6.0, 9.0
   - Chips or grinds out holes, bubbles, or cracks in workpiece preparatory to filling with weld.
     Instructional Code: 5.0, 8.0
   - Cleans grease or corrosion from workpiece using wire brush, grinder and solvents.
     Instructional Code: 5.0, 6.0, 8.0

[1]The "Instructional Code" is a cross-referencing plan for identifying a job task with planned instruction. See Fig. B-2.

- Clamps broken parts together in jig or vise. Uses gas or arc welding process. Selects welding process according to type and thickness of metal.

    Instructional Code: 2.0, 4.0
- Cuts defective part from assembly. Uses cutting torch. Rewelds new piece into place.

    Instructional Code: 2.0, 3.5
- Straightens bent pieces using heating torch, straightening press or jack.

    Instructional Code: 2.0, 4.0, 5.0
- Welds layers of metal onto damaged parts to obtain original dimensions.

    Instructional Code: 2.0

---

2. The on-the-job tasks for all of the job titles are then cross-checked against the key job classifications, as illustrated in Fig. B-1. "Tasks" in this context are defined as the "job components common to a number of occupations."
3. An analysis of instructional content is made by checking each of the major instructional areas and their sub-points against the key job classifications determined from the occupational analyses. All entries are assigned an instructional code number for identifying and cross-referencing the various materials developed for teachers, and needed for the implementation and development of the curriculum guides for any one of the clusters. Figure B-2, page 402, illustrates the outcome of this step for the METALS cluster.
4. Curriculum materials for each of the clusters are published and disseminated to provide qualified teachers with the "educational specifications" covering the knowledge and skills (the content) that will qualify their students for entry-level employment in the cluster occupations. In the Oregon plan, the professional teacher is called upon to organize an educational delivery system that will assure students training that will fit their individual needs and desires. The substeps in the development of these curriculum materials are:
    a. Overall objectives for each of the clusters are suggested. To illustrate, the objectives for the HEALTH OCCUPATIONS at the secondary school level are to provide experiences to enable the student to achieve these goals:

EXAMPLE

- Develop basic concepts in health-related subjects such as science, mathematics, and communications.

ON-THE-JOB TASKS	IDENTIFICATION CODE *	MACHINIST	FOUNDRY WORKER	AUTO BODY	WELDER COMB.	WELDER	SHEET METAL	PRODUCTION MACH.
Follows work order	1.0	X	X	X	X	X	X	X
Follows oral instructions	1.1	X	X	X	X	X	X	X
Uses hand tools	1.2	X	X	X	X	X	X	X
Sweeps and cleans	1.3	X	X	X	X	X	X	X
Uses vises	1.4	X	X	X	X	X	X	X
Uses portable power tools	1.5	X	X	X	X	X	X	X
Operates bench grinder to sharpen tools	1.6	X	X	X	X	X	X	X
Works to specifications	1.7	X	X	X	X	X	X	X
Interprets blueprints and sketches	1.8	X	X	X	X	X	X	X
Tends welders	1.9	X	X	X	X	X	X	X
Has knowledge of metals (identification)	2.1	X	X	X	X	X	X	X
Uses math thru geometry	2.2	X	X		X	X	X	X
Understands mathematics including geometry	2.3	X	X		X	X	X	X
Does layout	2.4	X	X		X	X	X	X
Uses measuring tools	2.5	X			X	X	X	X
Inspects assemblies according to specifications	2.6	X			X	X	X	X
Plans sequence of operations	2.7	X	X	X	X	X	X	X
Brazes	2.8							
Arc welds	2.9	X	X	X	X	X	X	X
Inspects welds	3.1	X	X	X	X	X	X	X
Grinds and finishes joints and surfaces	3.2	X	X	X	X	X	X	X
Preheats	3.3	X	X	X	X	X	X	X
Applies knowledge of metal properties	3.4	X	X	X	X	X	X	X
Uses jacks and stanchions	3.5		X	X	X	X		
Repairs broken or cracked parts	3.6	X		X	X	X	X	X
Fills holes	3.7			X	X	X		
Straightens metal	3.8			X	X	X	X	
Cuts metal	3.9	X		X	X		X	X
Uses production cutting and welding equipment	4.1	X	X		X	X	X	
Verifies dimensions and alignment with measuring instruments	4.2	X	X		X	X		X
Uses test and inspection equipment	4.3	X	X		X	X		X
Follows specified layout	4.4		X		X	X	X	
Uses fluid power operated equipment	4.5	X	X	X	X			
Uses machines (metal removal, cutting, boring)	4.6	X	X			X	X	
Increases size of metal parts	4.7	X		X	X	X		
Solves problems to specifications	4.8	X	X			X		
Shapes and forms metal (hand or power)	4.9	X	X			X		
Positions and clamps metal parts preparatory to fabrication	5.1	X		X	X			
Fabricates using jigs	5.2	X		X	X			
Uses precision measuring tools and equipment	5.3	X	X		X			
Cleans and degreases	5.4	X				X	X	
Uses gauges to select thickness of metal	5.5				X	X	X	
Fabricates, installs, assembles, repairs sheet metal	5.6					X	X	
Solders	5.7					X	X	
Estimates costs of repairs	5.8			X	X			
Layout using dimensions and reference points	5.9	X				X		
Uses abrasives	6.1	X				X		
Applies knowledge of mechanics	6.2	X						X

Fig. B-1. The Task Analysis for Determining Course Content for the METALS Cluster (This analysis appears on p. 16 of the Oregon Occupational Cluster Guide for METALS.)

[2]A number assigned to the task for identification and analysis purposes and is not to be confused with the Instructional Code shown in Fig. B-2 which relates to supporting instruction.

INSTRUCTIONAL ANALYSIS FOR ORGANIZING LEARNING EXPERIENCES	INSTRUCTIONAL CODE	SUB CODE	DIVISION CODE	MACHINIST	FOUNDRY WORKER	AUTO BODY	WELDER, COMBINATION	WELDER, ARC	SHEET METAL	PRODUCTION MACHINIST
METALLURGY	1			X	X	X	X	X	X	X
Knowledge of metals (identification)		1.1		X	X	X	X	X	X	X
Ferrous metal (alloys)			1.11	X	X	X	X	X	X	X
Nonferrous metal (alloys)			1.12	X	X	X	X	X	X	X
Metal properties			1.13	X	X	X	X	X	X	X
HOT METALS	2			X	X	X	X	X	X	X
Oxy-acetylene		2.1		X	X	X	X		X	X
Ferrous metals			2.11	X	X	X	X		X	X
Nonferrous metals			2.12	X	X	X	X		X	X
Soldering			2.13						X	
Equipment adjustment and setup			2.14	X	X	X	X		X	X
Cutting and heat treating			2.15	X	X	X	X	X	X	X
Brazing			2.16							
Arc welding		2.2		X	X	X	X	X	X	X
Ferrous metal			2.21	X	X	X	X	X	X	X
Inert gas - nonferrous metals			2.22	X		X	X	X		
Equipment adjustment and setup			2.23	X	X	X	X	X		
Spot welding			2.24	X		X	X	X	X	X
Cutting			2.25	X	X	X	X	X		X
Heat treating, furnace, foundry			2.26	X	X	X	X	X		X
Production cutting and welding equipment			2.27				X	X		
Foundry		2.3		X	X	X	X	X	X	X

(Analysis of Machining, Fabrication, Hand Tools, Layout Tools, Precision Measuring and Testing Tools, and Portable Power Tools omitted.)

COMMUNICATIONS	9			X	X	X			X	X
Drafting		9.1		X	X		X	X	X	X
Interprets blueprints and sketches (reads)			9.11	X	X		X	X	X	X
Plans sequence of operations			9.12	X	X		X	X	X	X
Does layouts to specifications			9.13	X			X	X	X	X
Makes elementary sketches using dimensions and reference points			9.14	X		X	X	X	X	X
Follows specifications			9.15	X	X		X	X	X	X
Math thru geometry			9.16	X	X		X	X	X	X
Solves problems to specifications			9.18	X	X		X	X	X	X
Follows work orders (written)		9.2		X	X	X	X	X	X	X
Follows oral instruction		9.3		X	X	X	X	X	X	X
Job application, interview		9.5		X	X	X	X	X	X	X
Communicating with public and other workers		9.6		X	X	X	X	X	X	X
Human relations		9.7		X	X	X	X	X	X	X
Read		9.8		X	X	X	X	X	X	X
Labor - apprenticeship & organization		9.9		X	X	X	X	X	X	X
Can make out work order		9.10		X	X	X	X	X	X	X
FINISHING OF SURFACES	10			X						X
Touch-up and painting			10.1			X				
Polishing, buffing, and grinding			10.2	X	X	X			X	X

Fig. B-2. The Major Instructional Areas and Their Sub-Points. Checked against the METALS Cluster. (Reprinted from the Oregon Occupational Cluster Guide for METALS, pp. 17-19)

- Function effectively as a person and as a member of health team.
- Communicate with patients, health team members, health facility administrators, and persons in the community, using appropriate methods and terminology.
- Perform personal and supportive health care tasks for patients of all ages, applying principles of prevention, therapy, and rehabilitation.
- Perform select tasks supportive of other health team members.[3]

b. Consideration is given to recommended allied and supporting courses that would be helpful in the fulfillment of the cluster objectives. Such ongoing high school courses as economics, speech, technical writing, general science, and mathematics (through trigonometry) may be supportive of the overall objectives for one of the cluster curriculums. For some of the clusters, specific allied supporting VAE courses are mentioned and described. For example, the following two courses are suggested for those in the METALS cluster curriculum:

EXAMPLE

Graphic Communications

A course designed to introduce the student to the area of graphic communications, i.e., the methods and mechanics used in modern industry by which individuals communicate ideas and concepts. Included in the course is instruction and practice in principles of visualization, oral communications, technical sketching, basic drafting, blueprint reading, shop processes, specification and tolerancing, photography, and printing. Specific technical information is correlated with laboratory experiences to provide an opportunity for students to develop a fundamental concept of methods by which human beings communicate ideas, i.e., schematic drawings, blueprints, technical service manuals, and oral communications.

Basic Electricity

A basic course in electrical fundamentals covering magnetism and electricity. Laboratory time is provided for

---

[3]These overall objectives appear on p. 14 of the **Occupational Cluster Guide** for **HEALTH OCCUPATIONS**.

demonstrations and experiments to help classify the principles of basic electricity, specifically Ohm's Law. Emphasis is placed on the use and care of electrical machinery. Stress is placed on the field analysis of electrical equipment failure and use of equipment, and electrical test devices to determine and make needed repairs on electric motors, switches, and transfer equipment.[4]

c. Occupational specialty courses for the cluster curriculum with descriptions (and suggested time allocations) have been identified for each of the 13 clusters. In addition, there are suggested guides for each major phase of instruction within the clusters covering (1) a suggested educational purpose for the section; (2) a listing of the expected outcomes (in terms of what the student can do after instruction); and (3) a listing of required knowledge, expected skill development, and suggested learning activities. These guides are for school districts and teachers and have been developed for all items in the instructional code.[5]

The content for each of the Oregon occupational specialty courses has been developed, reviewed, and validated in cooperation with the State Lay Advisory Committee made up of Oregon technicians and leaders working in the key occupations represented in the cluster. To change the specifications of knowledge and skills required for entry-level employment sequences, therefore, requires the review and approval of the designated advisory committee. This does not affect the teaching methods and the sequencing of instruction. The educational delivery system is flexible and is left entirely to the local district and the classroom teacher.

d. A curriculum plan for grades 7 through 12 is suggested for each of the occupational clusters. These curriculum plans illustrate how it is possible to schedule the required, occupational specialty, and elective courses. Each school district is encouraged, however, to organize the program in a manner that best fits the needs and requirements of the community. A suggested plan for scheduling the instructional program for the INDUSTRIAL MECHANICS curriculum is shown in Fig. B-3.

The present 13-cluster classification in Oregon is established from a consideration of all DOT job titles, employment data, and projected manpower needs. Each of the cluster programs is designed to provide:
1. Occupational exploratory experiences in grades 7 through 10.

---

[4]These course descriptions appear on pp. 26-27 of the **Occupational Cluster Guide** for **METALS**.
[5]An example of the instructional code, including the sub and division codes, for the **METALS** cluster is shown in Fig. B-2.

7TH AND 8TH GRADES	9TH GRADE	10TH GRADE	11TH GRADE	12TH GRADE
1. Social Studies	1. English I	1. English II	1. English III	1. English IV
2. Language Arts	2. Math I	2. Math II or Algebra	2. U.S. History	2. Modern Problems
3. Math	3. Health and Physical Education	3. Health and Physical Education	3. Physical Education	
4. Health and Physical Education	4. Science	4. Biology	*ALLIED SUPPORTING ELECTIVE	*ALLIED SUPPORTING ELECTIVE
5. Science, General Music	5. INDUSTRIAL ARTS (EXPLORATORY)	5. INDUSTRIAL ARTS (SPECIALITY)	SYSTEMS TECHNOLOGY	TECHNIQUES OF MECHANICAL MAINTENANCE
6. Arts, Homemaking, INDUSTRIAL ARTS			INSPECTION AND TESTING	COMMUNICATIONS

Occupational Speciality Courses   Curriculum Electives   Required Courses

Fig. B-3.
The Suggested Scheduling Plan for the Industrial Mechanics Curriculum (Reprinted from p. 18 of the Oregon Occupational Cluster Guide for INDUSTRIAL MECHANICS.)

2. Occupational guidance to help students learn more about themselves and to choose an occupational field which will offer them both challenge and self-fulfillment.
3. Occupational specialty courses in grades 11 and 12.

appendix C

Selected Tables Showing Outputs from Computer Programs of Task Analyses of Medical Laboratory Specialists for the Air Force

Tables C-1 and C-2, pages 408-410, present typical duty and task descriptions for an occupation that exists in all military services and in the civilian sector. They illustrate activities performed by journeymen medical laboratory technicians who work in hospitals and clinics throughout the Air Force.

In commenting on the data in Table C-2, Christal pointed out:

Every task performed by journeymen laboratory technicians is listed. The first task in Table C-2 reads "collect blood specimens directly from patients." In the first of the four columns of numbers, you will observe that 93.4 percent of these workers perform this task as part of their normal job. The second column indicates that the individuals who perform this task spend about 1.7 percent of their worktime on it. In the third column, we find that about 1.58 percent of the total worktime available to journeymen technicians is spent on this activity. If you were to sum the values in this third column across all tasks on this job description, the total would be 100 percent, since every task performed by any journeyman is listed. Cumulative times are shown in the fourth column, so you can see that the tasks in the top section of Table C-2 account for about 19.62 percent of the total worktime available to the group. Finally, you will notice that the tasks are listed in order of the time spent values in the third column.

The first column of values is of special concern. It reports the probability that a journeyman in this occupation will be required to perform each of the tasks listed. You will observe that the tasks appearing in the first section of Table C-2 are encountered by 78 to 93 percent of journeyman medical laboratory technicians. In the Air Force, an entry level course would include training on these tasks. Now look at the job description in the lower part of Table C-2. Here you will observe tasks which are encountered by very few journeymen. Consider for a moment task M 35, which is concerned with conducting vitamin assays. Only about one percent of the journeymen are asked to

Table C-1
Duty Description for Journeymen Medical Laboratory Specialists (N=394)

D-TSK	DUTY TITLE	CUMULATIVE SUM OF AVERAGE PERCENT TIME SPENT BY ALL MEMBERS	AVERAGE PERCENT TIME SPENT BY ALL MEMBERS	AVERAGE PERCENT TIME SPENT BY MEMBERS PERFORMING	PERCENT OF MEMBERS PERFORMING
J	Performing Hematology Procedures	92.64	20.48	18.97	18.97
M	Performing Biochemistry Procedures	87.82	16.42	14.42	33.39
N	Performing Urinalyses	90.36	13.07	11.81	45.20
F	Performing General Medical Laboratory Tasks	99.49	11.07	11.01	56.21
L	Performing Blood Banking Procedures	87.56	10.72	9.39	65.60
G	Performing Bacteriological Procedures	90.36	6.39	5.77	71.37
A	Organizing and Planning	74.62	6.56	4.89	76.26
K	Performing Serology Procedures	82.23	5.41	4.45	80.71
E	Maintaining Supplies and Records	87.31	5.04	4.40	85.11
I	Performing Parasitology Procedures	83.50	4.85	4.05	89.16
C	Inspecting and Evaluating	67.01	4.62	3.10	92.26
H	Performing Mycology Procedures	77.66	3.07	2.38	94.64
D	Training	59.14	3.56	2.11	96.75
O	Performing Histology Procedures	60.15	2.84	1.71	98.45
B	Directing and Implementing	47.21	2.90	1.37	99.82
P	Preparing Medical Illustration Materials	8.63	1.05	0.09	99.91
Q	Performing Radioactivity Detection Procedures	1.78	2.10	0.04	99.95

Table C-2
Task Job Description for Journeymen Medical Laboratory Specialists (N=394)

D-TSK		TASK TITLE	CUMULATIVE SUM OF AVERAGE PERCENT TIME SPENT BY ALL MEMBERS	AVERAGE PERCENT TIME SPENT BY ALL MEMBERS	AVERAGE PERCENT TIME SPENT BY MEMBERS PERFORMING	PERCENT OF MEMBERS PERFORMING
F	18	Collect Blood Specimens Directly from Patients	93.40	1.70	1.58	1.58
J	3	Perform Blood Count	89.09	1.56	1.39	2.98
J	17	Perform Hematology Procedures for Differential Cell Counts	88.83	1.49	1.33	4.30
J	24	Perform Hematology Procedures for Hematocrit Tests	89.09	1.45	1.30	5.60
N	2	Examine Urine Specimens Microscopically	88.07	1.43	1.26	6.85
J	5	Prepare Blood Smears	89.85	1.39	1.25	8.10
F	10	Prepare and Process Specimens	87.56	1.39	1.22	9.32
N	9	Perform Urinalyses for Glucose Tests	87.82	1.38	1.21	10.53
N	15	Perform Urinalyses for Specific Gravity Tests	87.06	1.38	1.20	11.73
N	6	Perform Urinalyses for Albumin Tests	87.06	1.36	1.19	12.92
F	3	Clean Area and Equipment Aseptically	80.96	1.46	1.18	14.10
N	1	Examine Urine Specimens Macroscopically	87.82	1.32	1.16	15.26
J	6	Separate Serum from Blood	87.31	1.30	1.14	16.40
F	11	Prepare Reagents	93.40	1.19	1.11	17.51
J	2	Identify Morphological Variations of Blood Cells	88.07	1.21	1.06	18.57
M	4	Operate Spectro-Photometer	77.66	1.34	1.04	19.62

(continued on next page)

Table C-2 (continued)

Only the first 16 and the final 11 task job descriptions are shown in this table. Two hundred seventy-one (271) tasks were omitted to reduce the length of the table.

M	35	Perform Biochemical Procedures for Vitamin Assays	1.27	0.47	0.01	99.91
M	31	Perform Biochemical Procedures for Serum Magnesium Tests	1.52	0.35	0.01	99.92
Q	8	Record and Summarize Data	0.76	0.64	0.00	99.92
B	11	Supervise the Health Physics Program	1.02	0.46	0.00	99.93
M	26	Perform Biochemical Procedures for Noradrenaline Studies	0.76	0.61	0.00	99.93
Q	4	Count Fluid Specimens	0.76	0.56	0.00	99.94
Q	12	Use Scaling Devices	0.51	0.69	0.00	99.94
Q	2	Calibrate Instruments	0.51	0.68	0.00	99.94
Q	10	Use Crystal and Liquid Scintillation Detectors	0.25	0.63	0.00	99.94
Q	9	Segregate and Prepare Radioactive Specimens for Measurement of Radioactivity	0.51	0.31	0.00	99.95
Q	11	Use Geiger-Mueller Equipment	0.25	0.58	0.00	99.95

perform this task, and even these cases spend only about one-half of one percent of their worktime on it. The question is whether one can afford to train everyone going into this field to perform a task which is so rarely encountered. In this instance, as far as the Air Force is concerned, the answer is "no."[1]

---

[1]These quotations appear on pp. 31-32 of the paper by Christal, listed with the references for Chapter 2. Raymond E. Christal is Chief, Occupational and Career Development Branch, Personnel Research Division (AFHRL), Lackland Air Force Base, San Antonio, Texas.

D appendix

Examples of Operational and Informational Topics Identified through the Process of Instructional Analysis

(This Process, as a Research Technique, Is Discussed in Chapter 2, pp. 67-74.)

List Operations for a Subject or an Activity

There are several approaches for identifying and listing titles for operations according to the eleven factors described in Chapter 2, pp. 69-72.

In a subject where students make projects, perform exercises or experiments, or do jobs, the analyst needs to think through the procedures for several of the typical projects, jobs, experiments, exercises, or blocks of a trade to see what operations are performed in doing them. By analyzing the operations that are performed by students in typical projects or blocks of a trade, the analyst is soon able to identify those that are repetitive.

Titles for operations can be listed under typical projects as illustrated in the following examples.

EXAMPLE

ALUMINUM TRAY

This is a typical project for ninth grade students in general metalworking. The operations and informational topics for the entire analysis will, therefore, be designed to survey the entire content of general metalworking. The points that are to be listed later under the operations which follow will determine whether such a goal is to be attained. This is why an analysis needs to be made by a professional teacher with a sound educational philosophy and understanding of the aims for the course and for a total program of education.

1. Develop design.
2. Plan procedure.
3. Shape metals.
4. Buff metal surfaces.
5. Design and transfer the pattern.
6. Etch the design.

EXAMPLE

FREE FORM WOODEN TRAYS

The instructional analysis, represented by the titles for the following operations, is planned for an adult course where the instruction will need to be organized to encourage the problem-solving approach. What will be listed under the breakdown of these essential operations identified for this project represents the needed and organized instruction basic for this project for an industrial arts course designed to encourage the greatest possible degree of creative application.

1. Design tray.
2. Plan procedure.
3. Select and cut stock.
4. Plane a surface.
5. Transfer design to stock.
6. Cut tray to shape on bandsaw.
7. Shape exterior.
8. Gouge interior to shape.
9. Sand.
10. Apply suitable finish.

EXAMPLE

BLOCKS OF THE TRADE

The blocks of the trade are recognized by the tradesman as the major divisions of the subject. The toolmaker will note that the work of his/her trade may be classified in such blocks as:

EXAMPLE

1. Benchworking.
2. Drilling.
3. Turning.
4. Boring.
5. Milling.
6. Grinding.
7. Sawing.
8. Shaping.
9. Heat Treating.
10. Inspecting.

The Trade of Toolmaking

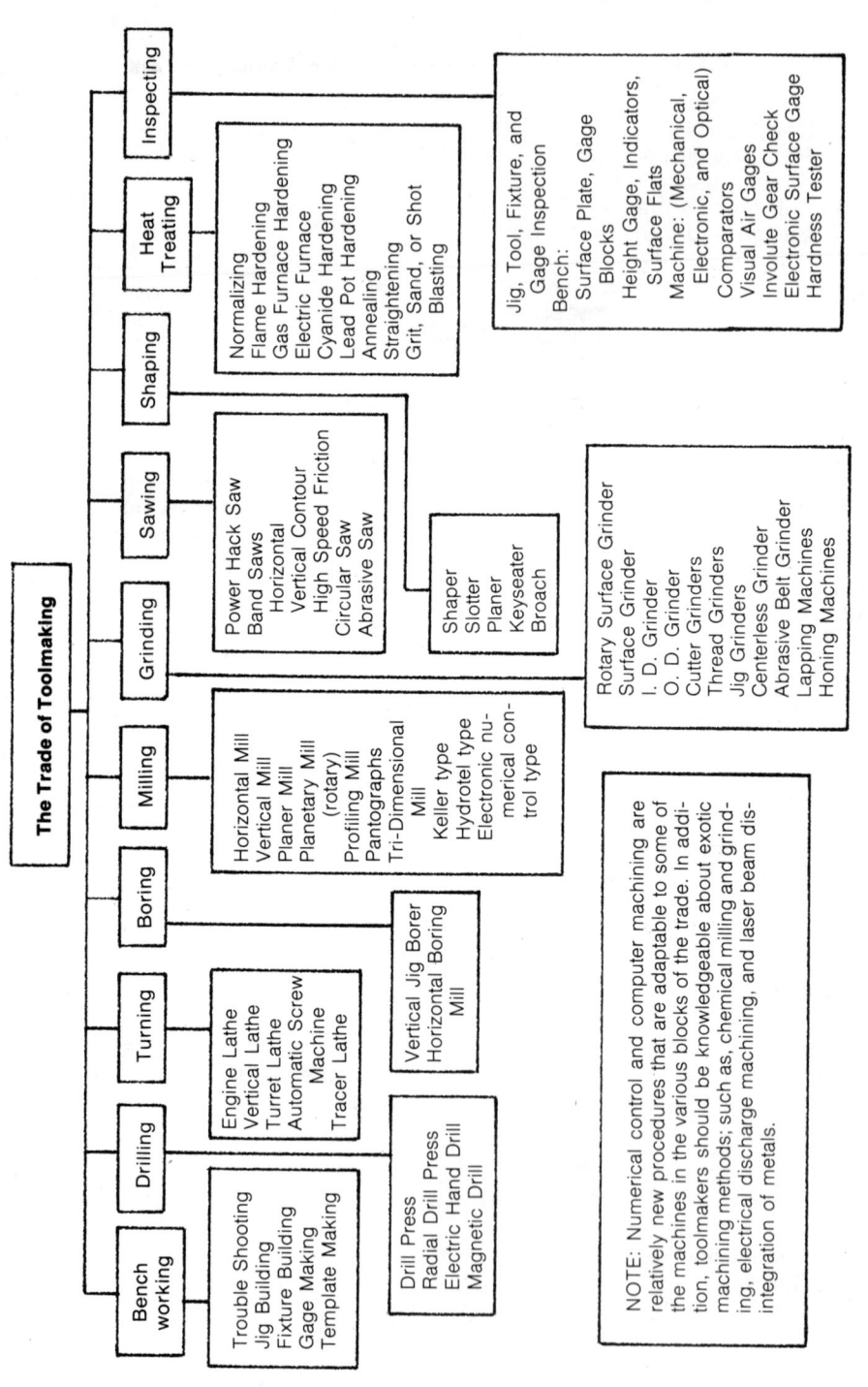

Bench working
- Trouble Shooting
- Jig Building
- Fixture Building
- Gage Making
- Template Making

Drilling
- Drill Press
- Radial Drill Press
- Electric Hand Drill
- Magnetic Drill

Turning
- Engine Lathe
- Vertical Lathe
- Turret Lathe
- Automatic Screw Machine
- Tracer Lathe

Boring
- Vertical Jig Borer
- Horizontal Boring Mill

Milling
- Horizontal Mill
- Vertical Mill
- Planer Mill
- Planetary Mill (rotary)
- Profiling Mill
- Pantographs
- Tri-Dimensional Mill
- Keller type
- Hydrotel type
- Electronic numerical control type

Grinding
- Rotary Surface Grinder
- Surface Grinder
- I. D. Grinder
- O. D. Grinder
- Cutter Grinders
- Thread Grinders
- Jig Grinders
- Centerless Grinder
- Abrasive Belt Grinder
- Lapping Machines
- Honing Machines

Sawing
- Power Hack Saw
- Band Saws
- Horizontal
- Vertical Contour
- High Speed Friction
- Circular Saw
- Abrasive Saw

Shaping
- Shaper
- Slotter
- Planer
- Keyseater
- Broach

Heat Treating
- Normalizing
- Flame Hardening
- Gas Furnace Hardening
- Electric Furnace
- Cyanide Hardening
- Lead Pot Hardening
- Annealing
- Straightening
- Grit, Sand, or Shot Blasting

Inspecting
Jig, Tool, Fixture, and Gage Inspection
Bench:
- Surface Plate, Gage Blocks
- Height Gage, Indicators, Surface Flats

Machine: (Mechanical, Electronic, and Optical)
- Comparators
- Visual Air Gages
- Involute Gear Check
- Electronic Surface Gage
- Hardness Tester

NOTE: Numerical control and computer machining are relatively new procedures that are adaptable to some of the machines in the various blocks of the trade. In addition, toolmakers should be knowledgeable about exotic machining methods; such as, chemical milling and grinding, electrical discharge machining, and laser beam disintegration of metals.

Fig. D-1. The Blocks of the Toolmaker's Trade
(Courtesy John P. Takis)

Figure D-1 was contributed by John P. Takis, Trade and Industrial Coordinator for Ferndale High School, Ferndale, Michigan, and a journeyman toolmaker. When a professional trade teacher such as Robert J. Kirchner thinks through the work involved in any one of these blocks, such as using the engine lathe, he/she is able to list from experience such operations as:

EXAMPLE

1. Start, stop, and reverse lathe.
2. Clean and oil lathe.
3. Grind lathe turning tool bits.
4. Chuck work.
5. Set lathe speeds and feeds.
6. Face stock in lathe.
7. Layout centers and center drill stock.
8. Turn stock between centers.
9. True a soft or hard center.
10. Measure outside dimensions.
11. Layout and measure lengths.
12. File cylindrical work.
13. Polish work.
14. Set compound rest for angular cuts.
15. Turn a squared shoulder.
16. Turn a radius.
17. Knurl on a lathe.
18. Turn tapers with the compound rest.
19. Turn an undercut or groove.
20. Drill in the lathe.
21. Bore in the lathe.
22. Drill with a crotch center.
23. Set a taper attachment.
24. Turn R. H. external threads.
25. Turn L. H. external threads.
26. Turn R. H. internal threads.
27. Turn L. H. internal threads.
28. Tap threads in a lathe.
29. Cut threads with a die in a lathe.
30. Ream a hole.
31. Turn work on a mandrel.
32. Test work with inside calipers.
33. Set up or use a collet chuck.
34. Fit a taper to a gauge.
35. Turn work in a center rest.
36. Turn work in a follower rest.
37. Turn multiple lead threads.
38. Turn taper threads.
39. Turn internal tapers.

Fig. D-2
Breakdown for the Operation: How to Knurl on a Lathe

Operating Step	Remarks
1. Select grade of *knurl* required (fine, medium, coarse).	*New technical term: knurl.* *What learner should know:* Select only a sharp tool for clean-cut pattern.
2. Mark limits of workpiece to be knurled.	
3. Set up work to drive between centers (or chuck).	
4. Set knurling tool square to work.	*What learner should know:* Equal pressures on knurling rolls result in a symmetrical pattern. Therefore, the knurl tool should be set to approximate center of work axis and the feed-in line of force of the cross slide (or select a self-centering knurling tool).
5. Set slowest lathe speed.	
6. Set coarse lathe feed.	
7. Set direction of feed for right to left.	
8. Start the lathe.	
9. Hand feed knurling tool into workpiece at right end of knurl area about .015".	
10. Engage automatic horizontal feed.	
11. Apply cutting oil liberally to work.	*Safety precaution:* Keep oiler and fingers away from knurls as they tend to pull in objects touching them.
12. Disengage feed at knurl limit.	*What learner should know:* Do not disengage tool from work. Recognition of satisfactory quality.
13. Feed tool in another .015".	
14. Reverse spindle rotation and feed back to right end.	
15. Stop lathe and inspect work.	
16. Repeat steps 9 through 15 as needed.	Recognition of satisfactory quality.
17. File lightly to remove sharp peaks.	*Safety precaution:* File left handed to avoid contact with face-plate (or chuck).

Equipment and Tools:

1. Face-plate, lathe dog, and centers (or chuck).
2. Tool post assembly.
3. Knurling tool.
4. Tool post wrench.
5. Lathe dog (or chuck) wrench.
6. Smooth mill file.

Figure D-2, also contributed by Kirchner, shows a breakdown for one of the operations in machine shop, as analyzed for a basic vocational course at the senior high school level. In the second column under "Remarks" will be found factors pertaining to safety precautions, essential information, new technical terms, and quality requirements that need to be included as points to be stressed with the steps in the breakdown of an operation.

In the breakdown for the example of knurling, it should be noted that the tools and equipment needed to perform this operation have been identified and listed. This practice seems desirable in vocational or technical courses where the operations are the unit of instruction. In the applied arts, however, where the instruction is usually tied to some interesting project or activity that becomes the nucleus for a unit of instruction, it is more functional for the teacher to list the tools or equipment, and materials that are needed for the activity. The project or activity that becomes the vehicle for instruction usually involves two or more operations. It may, therefore, not be too functional to have the tools or equipment and materials listed for each of the operations for an applied arts project or activity.

Examples of Informational Topics

An example of a "technical" informational topic for machine shop, prepared by John P. Takis, broken down with points to be taught is:

EXAMPLE

CUTTING SPEEDS AND FEEDS

1. Definition of speed.
    a. Expressed in revolutions per minute.
    b. Expressed in surface feet per minute.
2. Cutting speeds for tools.
    a. High-speed steel.
        1) For various SAE steels.
        2) For nonferrous metals.
        3) For cast irons.
    b. Haynes Stellite — Grade 3, J-metal, and 2400.
        1) For cast iron.
        2) For semi-steels.
        3) For nonferrous metals.
    c. Carbides — tungsten, titanium, and tantalum.
        1) For various SAE steels.
        2) For nonferrous metals.
        3) For cast iron.

3. Determining factors affecting cutting speeds.
    a. Type of tool bit.
    b. Hardness of material to be cut.
    c. Type of material to be cut.
    d. The effect of coolants.
    e. Shape of tool bit.
    f. Amount of feed.
    g. General condition of equipment.
    h. Machinability of material.
4. Formulas for cutting speeds.
    a. RPM = 4 x cutting speed ÷ diameter.
    b. RPM = SFPM x 12 ÷ diameter.
    c. SFPM = diameter x RPM ÷ 12.
5. Definition of feed.
    a. Tool advance per revolution of spindle (as on lathes, boring mills).
    b. Amount of volume of stock removal in a given amount of times (as on mills).
    c. The chip load per tooth or cutter (as on mills, broaches).
    d. Table advance per stroke of machine (as on shapers, planers, grinders).
6. Determining factors affecting the feed.
    a. Cutting speed.
    b. Depth of cut.
    c. Type of tool.
    d. Surface finish.
    e. Rigidity of work and/or machine.
    f. Number of teeth in the cutter.
    g. Shape of tool.
    h. Machinability of material.

Examples of "general" information (desirable but not essential to performance of the manipulative activity) are the following two drafting topics prepared by Chazkel Falik:

EXAMPLE

DRAFTING MEDIA

1. Tracing paper.
    a. Vellum.
    b. Bond.
2. Tracing cloth — starch coated.
   Tracing cloth — plastic coated.
    a. Pencil.
    b. Ink.
3. Coated aluminum sheets.
4. Photographic film.

EXAMPLE

REPRODUCTION OF DRAWINGS MADE BY DRAFTSMEN

1. Photochemical process — using transmitted light.
    a. Blueprints.
    b. Van Dyke.
    c. Direct process (color of line will depend on type of print paper used).
    d. Ammonia process (same as "c").
2. Photocopies (photostat).
3. Microfilming.
4. Lithoprinting.
5. Mechanical copying.
    a. Photocopier.
    b. Mimeograph.
    c. Hectograph.
    d. Copyflex Positive prints.

The guidance classification would be for those topics that contribute to vocational, educational, and personal guidance. An example of a guidance topic outline with points to be stressed which would provide occupational information for drafting is submitted by Falik:

EXAMPLE

POSITIONS IN INDUSTRIAL DRAFTING

1. Types of drafting.
    a. Manufacturing.
        1) Product or engineering.
        2) Tool, die, and machine.
    b. Building construction.
        1) Architectural.
        2. Mechanical-structural, Heating, and Air conditioning.
    c. Civil.
    d. Electrical.
    e. Aeronautical.
    f. Electronic circuitry.
    g. Plastics.
    h. Community planning.
    i. Instrumentation.
    j. Computers.
    k. Space industry.

E appendix

Curriculum Information for a Two-Year Preparatory Program in Radio-Television Service

The following curriculum information concerns a two-year radio-television service preparatory program taking place at the Northeast and Southeast Oakland Vocational Educational Centers, Oakland County, Michigan.[1]

I. TITLE
   Radio Television Service (U. S. Education Code 17.1503). Within family of Electronics Occupations (DOT codes 720.281-010, 720.281-018, and 720.281-022).

II. DESCRIPTION
   This curriculum is concerned with the theory and practice of constructing, installing, maintaining, and servicing most types of communication and entertainment equipment. Students are to be taught the techniques of diagnosing and repairing the various types of electrical-electronic and mechanical malfunctions that are common to radios, phonographs, sound recorders, high-fidelity sound systems, television receivers, antenna and sound systems, electronic organs, garage door openers, and the like.

III. LIST OF COURSES
   Radio-Television Repair I, II, III, IV.

Name of Course	Number of Minutes Per Day	Total Time per Week in Hours	Number of Weeks Scheduled	Number of Sections[2]	Students per Section[2]
R-TV I	150	12½	20	1	24
R-TV II	150	12½	20	1	24
R-TV III	150	12½	20	1	24
R-TV IV	150	12½	20	1	24

[1]Provided by Dr. David H. Soule and Dr. William A. Baranyai, Oakland Schools, Pontiac, Michigan 48054.
[2]Facilities as designed to accommodate up to 24 students; however, the number and/or course levels of the students enrolled in any section may vary from semester to semester.

IV. PREREQUISITES
   A. General Mathematics.
   B. Industrial Arts (one year or more).
   C. Drafting.
   D. Basic Electricity.

V. RECOMMENDED ELECTIVES
   A. Applied Physics.
   B. Algebra.
   C. Trigonometry.

VI. ACADEMIC SKILLS AND LEVEL REQUIRED
   A. Must have at least an average intelligence.
   B. Should understand the basic principles of mathematics and physical science.
   C. Must be proficient in the use of applied mathematics; especially as related to the understanding, application, and calculation of fundamental algebraic formulae and/or equations.
   D. Must be able to read and interpret written instructions carefully.

VII. PHYSICAL ABILITIES REQUIRED
   A. Good vision and color perception are important; however, correction is permitted.
   B. Must have good eye-hand coordination and finger dexterity.
   C. At least normal levels of hearing are essential; especially for those contemplating work on quality audio systems.
   D. Should be able to work in difficult physical positions; frequently requiring prolonged standing, stooping, and bending and the lifting of heavy components.

VIII. PERSONAL-SOCIAL SKILLS REQUIRED
   A. Should have the ability to present oneself in a favorable manner and to communicate effectively with others.
   B. Should possess or desire to develop neat and orderly work habits.
   C. Must be able to work with a minimum of assistance and/or supervision.

IX. UNIQUE SKILLS AND ABILITIES REQUIRED
   A. Should reflect a very strong interest in things of a mechanical and electronic nature.
   B. A high level of patience and the ability to "stick at the job" are very important traits of the "successful" electronics serviceman.
   C. Must be capable of learning and following methodical procedures, especially as related to "troubleshooting" malfunctions.

X. SUGGESTED TEST SCORES

TEST	SECTION (Aptitude)	SCORE RANGE
GATB	Intelligence	85-125
	Verbal	65-120
	Numerical	50-125
	Spatial	60-135
GATB	Form	65-140
	Clerical	70-135
	Motor	45-135
DAT	VR	3rd quartile
	NA	3rd quartile
	VR + NA	2nd or 3rd quartile
	MR	2nd quartile
	Space Relations	2nd quartile

XI. MAJOR INSTRUCTIONAL AREAS
 A. AM and FM radio.
 B. Audio recorders and phonographs.
 C. Television receivers.
 D. High fidelity sound equipment.
 E. Master antenna and sound systems.
 F. Electrical/electronic appliances.

In the Radio-Television Service Program, students will be taught the techniques of assembling, installing, maintaining and servicing mechanically and electronically all types of radios, television receivers, high-fidelity sound equipment, phonographs, recorders, master antenna and communication systems, and other electrical/electronic appliances such as garage door openers and electronic organs. Upon satisfactory completion of the two-year curriculum, the students will have had the appropriate amounts and types of exposure and work experience on actual communication appliances and systems to enable them to enter the world of work as electronics servicemen. The curriculum is also designed to prepare the more able students to continue their formal education beyond the secondary school level and eventually become electronic technicians and/or electrical engineers.

XII. EXPECTED STUDENT OUTCOMES
The following behavioral items are the objectives of the Radio Television Service Program:[3]

 A. AM and FM Radio
  1. Using sketches and other audio and/or visual aids, the student shall be able to describe in both written and oral form the phenomena of transferring sound waves from any given source to another point by means of a transmitter and a receiver.

[3] The time alloted and the proficiency level(s) required for the completion of each of these student outcomes will vary from course to course.

2. Given an assortment of radio-type electronic components, the student shall be able to identify each item by name and value, by graphic symbol, and describe its function(s) in a radio receiver.
3. Given an AM-FM receiver which has one or more malfunctions (or misalignments), the student shall be able to 1) locate the maladies; 2) determine the most expeditious and/or economical repair procedures; 3) assess the cost of such repair(s); 4) make the necessary repairs, if warranted economically; and 5) do all these activities in a predetermined time and at a level to assure customer satisfaction.
4. Knowing the complexity and duration of a given repair procedure, plus having the appropriate price breakdowns for materials and labor, the student shall be able to prepare an itemized bill for the parts and services rendered.

B. Audio Records and Phonographs
 1. Using sketches and/or actual components, the student shall be able to communicate an intelligible description of the audio recording processes, describing accurately the electronic and/or mechanical functions of all components of the hardware involved.
 2. Given functioning audio recorders, the student shall be able to set up all standard type units for recording and playback functions, evaluating the relative quality of reproduction being delivered by the unit being evaluated.
 3. Given a specific audio recorder, the student shall be able to correctly and efficiently perform the following routine maintenance procedure: 1) inspection and cleaning; 2) lubrication; 3) reel and roller adjustment and/or replacement; and 4) head adjustment and demagnetization.
 4. Given any standard phonograph, the student shall be able to 1) assess its relative value and general condition; 2) perform routine maintenance procedures; 3) check, adjust, service and/or replace needles and pickup cartridges; 4) check, adjust, and repair the turntable for accuracy of speed and rotation; 5) test and repair or replace motors and drive mechanisms; 6) adjust and repair change cycles and trip mechanisms; 7) determine the level of audio input being sent to the amplifier; and 8) service the amplifier to supply its optimum level of performance.
 5. Given a number of different audio recorders, the student shall be able to accurately 1) determine type, make and model; 2) locate the appropriate service manuals and schematic drawings; 3) determine the nature and extent of the malfunctions; 4) decide upon the most expeditious and/or economical repair procedures; and 5) if warranted/or desired, make the repairs necessary to make the units operational.

C. Television Receivers
   1. With the aid of drawings, schematics, and components, the student shall be able to verbally describe the physical and electronic phenomena that are utilized to pick up, transmit and reproduce audio and visual images in both black-white and color television receivers.
   2. Having a new television receiver as it is shipped from the manufacturer, the student shall be able to correctly 1) unpack it; 2) determine the antenna needs; 3) install the type of antenna warranted (and desired by the customer); and 4) adjust the receiver for the optimum levels of performance.
D. High Fidelity Equipment.
   1. The student shall be able to describe the physical, mechanical and electronic phenomena that are associated with the production, recording, transmission, receiving, and distribution of modulated and high fidelity audio signal.
   2. Given a set of malfunctioning high fidelity receiving and reproduction components, the student should be able to 1) identify the make, model, and function of each item; 2) locate and interpret the service manuals and schematics; 3) determine the nature and extent of the malfunctions; 4) make an accurate cost estimate for performing the needed service; 5) make all repairs authorized by the customer; and 6) prepare an accurate itemized bill for the parts and services rendered.
E. Master Antenna and Sound System
   1. With the aid of the appropriate test equipment, the student should be able to accurately measure the signal strength levels at a given location for a series of stated FM and video frequencies, taking such data and designing an antenna system to deliver signals of the desired type and strength.
   2. Given a set of performance specifications, installation diagrams, and all the necessary components, the student should be able to install 1) a single-outlet antenna system; 2) an antenna rotator; 3) a multi-element mast antenna; 4) a sectional antenna tower with appropriate grounding and guy wires; and 5) a multiple outlet master antenna system.
   3. Having an unbalanced master antenna system, the student shall be able to install and/or adjust the appropriate devices to achieve the types and signal strengths described in a given set of performance specifications.
F. Electrical/Electronic Appliances
   1. Given any type of used portable household electrical appliance, the student should be able to 1) identify its make and model; 2) determine its rated electrical characteristics; 3) locate the appropriate service manuals and wiring diagrams; 4) evaluate the overall electrical and mechanical condition, performance, and safety of its components; 5)

calculate the costs involved to return the item to its maximum operational level; 6) determine the degree to which the item should be repaired (or if it should be discarded); 7) make the authorized repairs and adjustments; and 8) prepare an accurate itemized bill for the parts and services rendered.

F appendix

Format for a Preface for a Course of Study

The preface for a course or program of study usually carries a description of the conditions that set the stage for the teacher's or teaching team's efforts; describes the purposes of the document; explains how the material has been brought to its present state of development; and acknowledges persons, companies, and organizations who may have assisted. It is suggested that the preface be concluded with the name of author(s). The following format illustrates the content of a preface.

EXAMPLE

A SAMPLE FORMAT

The purpose of the course of study is to describe the instructional program provided for students enrolled in the _____ course at the _____ High School. This document covers the educational justification for the course, the behavioral objectives that lead to competencies to be acquired by the students, the teaching and student activity plans for each of the modules of instruction, and a description of the physical facilities essential to support the instructional program.

It is hoped that this course of study is an accurate description of what has been planned for the course and the way the students participate and become involved in the instructional program. A major purpose of the document is to provide the administrators of the school, advisory committees from the community, and accreditation committees with an accurate description of the instructional program in _____ at _____ High School.

The author is indebted to _____, head of the department of _____; the other teachers in the department; and _____, principal; for their input, assistance, and encouragement during the development of this course of study. The writer is especially indebted to _____, city supervisor for _____, for his/her fine support and in providing many source materials for this document.

_____ (name)

appendix G

The Common Goals of Michigan Education [1]

The Three Goal Areas

I. CITIZENSHIP AND MORALITY
   Michigan education must create an educational environment which fosters the development of mature and responsible citizens. Three goals have been identified in this area:
Goal 1 — Morality
Goal 2 — Citizenship and Social Responsibility
Goal 3 — Rights and Responsibilities of Students

II. DEMOCRACY AND EQUAL OPPORTUNITY
   Michigan education must support and advance the principles of democracy by recognizing the worth of every individual and by respecting each person's right to equal educational opportunity. Six goals have been identified in this area:
Goal 1 — Equality of Educational Opportunity
Goal 2 — Education of the Non-English Speaking Person
Goal 3 — Education of the Exceptional Person
Goal 4 — Allocation of Financial Resources
Goal 5 — Parental Participation
Goal 6 — Community Participation

III. STUDENT LEARNING
   Michigan education must help each individual acquire a positive attitude toward school and the learning process so that, as a result of the educational experience, he/she is able to achieve optimum personal growth, to progress in a worthwhile and rewarding manner in the career of his/her choice, and to render valuable service to society. Thirteen goals have been identified in this area.

---

[1] Published in September 1971 by Michigan State Board of Education. Description of goals in Citizenship and Morality and in Democracy and Equal Opportunity were omitted in the interest of brevity.

Goal 1 — Basic Skills

Michigan education must assure the acquisition of basic communication, computation, and inquiry skills to the fullest extent possible for each student. These basic skills fall into four broad categories: (1) the ability to comprehend ideas through reading and listening; (2) the ability to communicate ideas through writing and speaking; (3) the ability to handle mathematical operations and concepts; and, (4) the ability to apply rational intellectual processes to the identification, consideration and solution of problems. Although the level of performance that can reasonably be expected in each of these areas will vary from person to person, the level of expectation of each individual must be accurately assessed.

Goal 2 — Preparation for a Changing Society

Michigan education must encourage and prepare the individual to become responsive to the needs created and opportunities afforded by an ever-changing social, economic, and political environment both here and throughout the world. An appreciation of the possibilities for continuing self-development, especially in light of increasing educational and leisure-time opportunities, will encourage him/her to pursue chosen goals to the limits of his/her capabilities under such changing conditions.

Goal 3 — Career Preparation

Michigan education must provide to each individual the opportunity to select and prepare for a career of his/her choice consistent to the optimum degree with the individual's capabilities, aptitudes, and desires, and the needs of society. Toward this end, the student should be afforded, on a progressive basis, the necessary evaluation of progress and aptitudes, together with effective counseling regarding alternatives available, the steps necessary to realize each of these alternatives, and the possible consequences of his/her choice. In addition, each individual should be exposed, as early and as fully as possible, to the adult working world and to such adult values as will enable more thoughtful and meaningful decisions as to career choice and preparation.

Goal 4 — Creative, Constructive, and Critical Thinking

Michigan education must foster the development of the skills of creative, constructive and critical thinking to enable the individual to deal effectively with situations and problems which are new to his/her experience in ways which encourage thinking and acting in an independent, self-fulfilling, and responsible manner.

Goal 5 — Sciences, Arts, and Humanities

Michigan education must provide on a continuing basis, to each individual, opportunity and encouragement to gain knowledge and experience in the area of the natural sciences, the social sciences, the humanities, and the creative and fine arts so that his/her personal values and approach to living may be enriched by these experiences.

Goal 6 — Physical and Mental Well-Being

Michigan education must promote the acquisition of good health and safety habits and an understanding of the conditions necessary for physical and mental well-being.

Goal 7 — Self-Worth

Michigan education must respond to each person's need to develop a positive self-image within the context of his/her own heritage and within the larger context of the total society. The development of a positive self-image will enhance the individual's ability to fruitfully determine, understand, and examine his/her own capacities, interests, and goals in terms of the needs of society.

Goal 8 — Social Skills and Understanding

Michigan education must provide for each individual an understanding of the value systems, cultures, customs, and histories of his/her own heritage as well as of others. Each student must learn to value human differences, understand and act responsibly upon current social issues, participate in society and government while seeking to improve them, and seek a society where every person has equal access to the lawful goals he seeks regardless of his/her background or group membership. Each person must learn to develop and maintain effective interpersonal relationships.

Goal 9 — Occupational Skills

Michigan education must provide for the development of the individual's marketable skills so that a student is assisted in the achievement of his/her career goals by adequate preparation in areas which require competence in occupational skills.

Goal 10 — Preparation for Family Life

Michigan education must provide an atmosphere in which each individual will grow in his/her understanding of and responsiveness to the needs and responsibilities inherent in family life. Joint efforts must be made by school, parents, and community to bring together the human resources necessary in this endeavor.

Goal 11 — Environmental Quality

Michigan education must develop within each individual the knowledge and respect necessary for the appreciation, maintenance, protection, and improvement of the physical environment.

Goal 12 — Economic Understanding

Michigan education must provide that every student will gain a critical understanding of his/her role as a producer and consumer of goods and services, and of the principles involved in the production of goods and services.

Goal 13 — Continuing Education

Michigan education must promote an eagerness for learning which encourages every individual to take advantage of the educational opportunities available beyond the formal schooling process.

H appendix

Interrelationship of Course Goals and Aims of Education for Henry Ford Community College[1]

```
┌─────────────────────────────────────────┐
│         PHILOSOPHY OF EDUCATION         │
│              OVERALL AIMS               │
│              DEPARTMENTAL               │
│              COURSE GOALS               │
│                 AIMS                    │
│                  OF                     │
│              EDUCATION                  │
└─────────────────────────────────────────┘
```

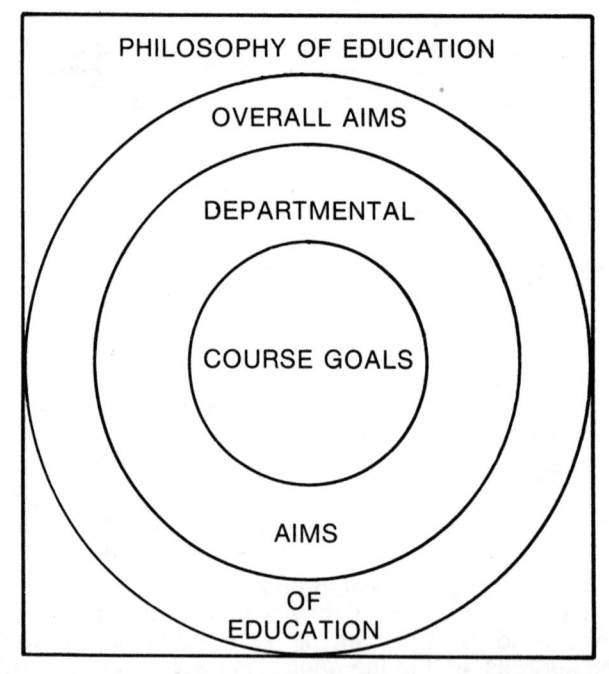

Fig. H-1. The course aims are an integral part of the departmental aims which, in turn, fall within the overall aims of education. These, in turn, are within the philosophy of education. Each is a part of the whole; removing one leaves an incomplete picture. (Courtesy Stephen R. Matt, Director of Training, Russell Burdsall & Ward, Inc., Mentor, Ohio)

[1]The goals and aims presented in this appendix were developed, with units and interrelationship, by Paul J. McElligatt, Training Specialist, Ford Motor Company and part-time staff member, Henry Ford Community College, Dearborn, Michigan.

EXAMPLE

AIMS of the Henry Ford Community College

1. To provide the first and second years of work in the Liberal Arts and Pre-Professional fields for those students who wish to transfer to higher educational institutions.
2. To provide one- or two-year technical programs of business and industrial education for those students who expect to terminate their formal education by preparing for employment at the semiprofessional level.
3. To provide a program of two additional years of general education for the social, cultural, and personal development of students wishing to continue beyond senior high school.
4. To provide for the adults of the community single courses or combinations of courses in those fields in which there are sufficient interest and demand to warrant the organization of classes. Classes may be scheduled for day or evening hours, from a single class meeting to a two-year program, on a credit or noncredit basis.
5. To provide educational services to the organizations and individuals of the community, including speakers, resource personnel or material, organization of special institutes or programs, reading lists, educational counseling and teaching, etc., as requested.
6. It is a general objective of all programs, technical, general, liberal arts and professional, to stress the importance of all students eventually becoming effective members of society and active participants in the democratic way of life.

AIMS of the Related Trade Instruction Program

1. To develop a systematic method of approach in the solving of trade connected problems.
2. To provide theoretical knowledge of the process and materials needed to supplement the job experience in the development of a craftsman.
3. To acquaint the apprentice with the nomenclature, care and safe operating practices concerning the tools and materials of his/her trade.
4. To develop an awareness of the changing demands upon the skilled craftsman in an increasingly complex industrial society, and the necessity to keep abreast of technological developments.

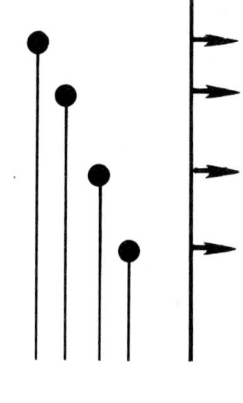

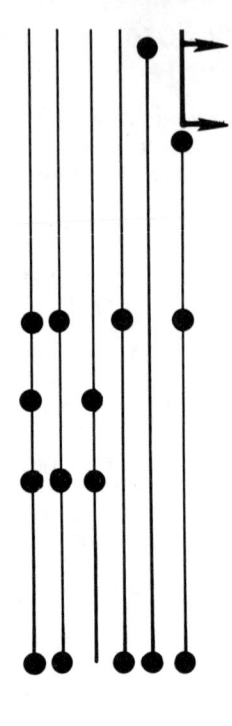

5. To develop an understanding of, and appreciation for, the skilled craftsman as an important, contributing member in an industrial society.
6. To create a sympathetic realization of limiting factors which create problems for craftsmen in trades other than his/her own.

Course Goals for Metallurgy

1. To develop an understanding of ferrous metallurgy as it affects the apprentice in the performance of his/her job.
2. To acquaint the apprentice with safe operating practices of various metal producing and working equipment.
3. To have the apprentice acquire knowledge of:
   a. The nature and behavior of metals.
   b. Crystalline structures.
   c. Theory of alloys.
   d. Principles of heat treatment.
   e. Properties of metals and alloys.
   f. Physical testing of metals.
4. To help the apprentice gain an appreciation for the necessity and value of obtaining a thorough technical background.

Fulfillment of Course Goals by Course Units

Course Goals

1. To develop an understanding of ferrous metallurgy as it affects the apprentice in the performance of his/her job.
2. To acquaint the apprentice with safe operating practices of various metal producing and working equipment.
3. To have the apprentice acquire knowledge of:
   a. The nature and behavior of metals.
   b. Crystalline structures.
   c. Theory of alloys.
   d. Principles of heat treatment.
   e. Properties of metals and alloys.
   f. Physical testing of metals.
4. To help the apprentice gain an appreciation for the necessity and value of obtaining a thorough technical background.

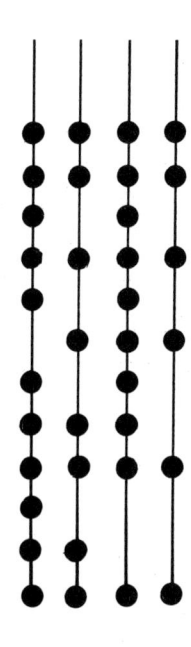

Units for Program

1. Introduction and early steelmaking processes.
2. Modern steelmaking processes.
3. Ingot types and physical properties of metal.
4. Chemical formation of metal.
5. Alloy steels.
6. Steel castings and wrought iron.
7. Cast iron and molding technology.
8. Alloyed cast iron.
9. Metal forming operations and power metallurgy.
10. Fusion welding.
11. Resistance welding.
12. Final examination.

appendix

Units of Instruction on Business and Office Machines [1]

EXAMPLE

Mission for Units on Business and Office Machines

This course is designed to prepare students to operate the types of business machines which they will most often be required to use on the job. Business machines used most commonly by clerical workers in a variety of job titles have been identified nationwide as: adding and calculating machines, duplicating machines, filing and mailing devices, transcribing machines, and, more recently, key punch machines.

Careful consideration and planning should be exercised in setting up a program to train students in the use of office and business machines. Budget pressures often restrict the purchasing of an adequate number or variety of machines, but wise planning can do much to establish an effective program, even with a limited budget.

Behavioral Objectives

The student should be able to exhibit the following behaviors:

- Operate the ten-key adding machine with speed and accuracy using the touch system.
- Perform simple to complex mathematical problems on the semi- and fully automatic rotary and listing calculators.
- Use the full-key adding-listing machine.
- Perform record and bookkeeping transactions on bookkeeping machines.

---

[1] Reprinted from the Occupational Cluster Guide For Clerical Occupations, 1971, pp. 88-93 (Courtesy of the Oregon Board of Education, 942 Lancaster Drive N.E., Salem, Oregon 97310).

- Perform various duplicating operations on both fluid and stencil duplicating machines and photocopiers.
- Dictate effectively into transcribing machines.
- Transcribe directly from transcription equipment.
- Properly care for various office machines.
- Accurately perform all activities of the office machines course.
- Use a key punch machine.

BUSINESS AND OFFICE MACHINES

(Code 1.8, 7.0)

REQUIRED KNOWLEDGE AND SKILLS	THE STUDENT CAN	SUGGESTED LEARNING ACTIVITIES
Purpose and use of the most commonly used adding and calculating machines	Operate ten-key by touch system. Calculate arithmetical problems, such as percentages, discounts, decimals, and fractions. Handle and care for adding and calculating machines properly.	Consider using block assignment work. Demonstrate, through a problem approach and a preview of business papers and procedures, the machine operations. Have carefully selected problems for each new machine technique assignment. Provide an opportunity for the student to test his knowledge and understanding of each technique. Provide opportunities for every student to improve his skill through a variety of problems involving the use of repetitive drills for mastery of techniques. Provide opportunities for the student to apply the learned technique to typical business situations. Provide for individual differences by assigning supplementary problem work which is appropriate for the student's maturity and ability level.

BUSINESS AND OFFICE MACHINES

(Code 1.1, 1.5, 2.4, 3.4)

REQUIRED KNOWLEDGE AND SKILLS	THE STUDENT CAN	SUGGESTED LEARNING ACTIVITIES
Duplicating and copying machines and equipment most commonly used in today's business office	Prepare stencils and other types of duplicating masters. Operate duplicating machines with skill and efficiency. Care for and clean duplicating machines. Proofread stencils. Make corrections on stencils and masters. Use tracing equipment. Store or file stencils and masters.	Have students: • Practice typing stencils and other forms of duplicating masters. • Prepare sketches and drawings on a mimeoscope. • Proofread masters and stencils. • Operate duplicating machines. • Practice storing or filing masters and stencils properly. • Correct errors on stencils and masters.

BUSINESS AND OFFICE MACHINES

(Code 3.8)

REQUIRED KNOWLEDGE AND SKILLS	THE STUDENT CAN	SUGGESTED LEARNING ACTIVITIES
The purpose and use of transcribing machines and equipment most commonly used in today's business office	Manipulate dictating-transcribing equipment. Ascertain length of communication to be transcribed. Detect corrections and special instructions. Arrange special tabulations needed. Use correct punctuation. Transcribe acceptable letters and communications from machine.	Give students lots of practice in transcribing from machines. Introduce them to as many types of transcribing machines as possible — by field trips or by demonstration in the classroom by firms selling such equipment. Have students dictate by machine as well as transcribe.

BUSINESS AND OFFICE MACHINES

(Code 1.7, 4.7, 12.0, 13.0)

REQUIRED KNOWLEDGE AND SKILLS	THE STUDENT CAN	SUGGESTED LEARNING ACTIVITIES
Use and importance of the key punch machine	Prepare cards for unit record process.	If possible, arrange for actual hands-on experience with key punch. If machine is not available, provide simulated exercises on the typewriter. Give exercises in handling and care of cards before and after punching.

J appendix

Examples of Laboratory Units

When instructional units are organized, the question of laboratory activities to provide experiences in the desired operational units must be considered. These activities with teaching techniques should be described accurately. The following factors cover issues to be considered in planning activities to provide operational experiences.

Projects

In fabrication activities, projects can be selected that provide experiences in the operations being demonstrated. The instructional analysis, if carried to completion, could describe typical projects which are to be used. Where projects are used as vehicles for instruction, the teacher must select them and develop the project teaching plans as modules of instruction as a part of the course of study.

Operational Drills

The use of operational drill (the meaningful repetition of operations) is very common, especially in vocational education where the degree of skill calls for occupational competency. Welding, for example, is an activity that calls for repetitious drill in welding operations. These exercises are often planned as preliminary to more advanced activities, such as building projects. Repetitious drill through exercises has been discarded by many applied arts teachers since it is believed that operations can be learned through projectmaking. While this position may be essentially true, the teacher should not discard practice drill from teaching methods. Situations may well arise where this technique would be one that would best fulfill course goals. For example, a metalworking teacher might insist on some operational practice through exercises in soldering and welding before a project calling for such skills is undertaken. This will ensure a higher quality of craftsmanship on the finished project. Also, in advanced courses where an individual, or team of students, is developing a project calling for the application of scientific and technological principles, there may be great need to perform selected operations with the highest degree of skill. In these new programs and on advanced levels, such programs as industrial arts need not be a broad and exploratory program but may seek depth and thorough understanding. Interest comes from depth and is essential in the second dimension of general education that provides for the general educational development of an individual (Chapter 8, pp. 203-205).

Finished Products

In service and technical areas such as appliance repair, many of the operations may be accomplished by working on finished products. In automotive mechanics, diagnosis, disassembly, inspection, and assembly of engines and other parts provide opportunities to experience many of the operational units.

Individual or Team Reports and Demonstrations

Occasionally, operational units cannot be performed by the student due to a shortage of time or materials, safety factors, or lack of equipment. The units for the power mechanics course (Chapter 9, p. 267) will serve as good examples. In these, several instructional presentations are to be given by the teacher, a student, or a team of students. This is satisfactory in a course where a degree of skill is considered somewhat secondary. Vocational education, concerned with salable skills, must not overload courses with individual or team reports and special demonstrations.

Regardless of the problems, it is essential that applied arts remain basically an activity program. Student activities must be considered, therefore, in the course of study. These activities and the teaching techniques which provide for student involvement in demonstrating and presenting the operations in keeping with the goals for the course must be planned and described.

Two laboratory units are listed which illustrate different methods of organizing the laboratory phase of an instructional program:

EXAMPLE

A UNIT FROM A HEALTH CARE SKILLS COURSE[1]

Objective

Upon the completion of this course the student will be able to transport patients and assist with ambulation safely and efficiently.

---

[1] Reprinted from pp. 75 & 76 of the Oregon **Occupational Cluster Guide** for **Health Occupations.**

Content
Patient transportation:
1. Importance of body mechanics and good posture.
2. Lifting and moving techniques:
   a. Move and roll patient from one side to other.
   b. Move patient up in bed.
   c. Change mattress with patient in bed.
   d. Move patient from bed to wheel chair.
   e. Move patient from bed to stretcher.
   f. Return patient to bed.
   g. Assist patient in walker.
   h. Assist patient to walk.
3. Safeguarding patient in transit.
4. Supportive equipment:
   a. Wheelchair.
   b. Walker.
   c. Hydraulic lift.

Suggested Activities to Be Shared by Teacher and Student
1. Present review of body mechanics and good posture by showing films and charts, and use of models.
2. Demonstrate correct body mechanics in lifting and moving. Have students practice and return demonstration and summarize by listing precautions to follow in avoiding muscle strain.

Evaluation
The student can:
1. Understand what is expected of him/her during the course.
2. Use results of a pretest to assess personal learning needs.

Students observe demonstrations and follow with self-critique and class evaluations of the following:
1. Safety of patient.
2. Essential equipment.
3. Support of patient.
4. Body mechanics:
   a. Uses even motions.
   b. Maintains body balance.
   c. Distributes load of work among many muscles.
   d. Uses leg and arm muscles rather than back.
   e. Kneels for low-level lifts and moves.
   f. Uses broad base.
   g. Works in same direction.
   h. Holds objects close to body.
   i. Pushes or pulls objects, rather than lifting, when possible.

AN OPERATIONAL UNIT FROM A WOODWORKING TECHNOLOGY COURSE[2]

Behavioral Objective
　　The student will demonstrate ability to select the proper rough stock and then cut it to the required sizes.

Tools and Equipment
　　Tape or rule.
　　Marking pencil.
　　Radial saw.

Materials
　　Rough stock that has not been checked for defects.

Teaching Aid
　　Display of common defects found in rough stock.

Points to Be Stressed in Teacher's Demonstration
1. Select lumber.
2. Check for defects.
3. Position Board.
4. Be sure saw is locked before it is started.
5. Move saw back and forth on wide or warped stock.
6. Turn wide board over, edge for edge.
7. Keep fingers in clear.

Questions to Be Discussed After Teacher's Demonstration
1. What defects should you look for in cutting rough stock?
2. What is the proper position of the board on the table before starting the saw?
3. When should the saw be started?

Procedure for Student
1. Select rough stock from lumber rack.
2. Check for defects: wane, wind, warp, checks, decay, knots and splits.
3. Demonstrate method of determining thickness of a long board having wind.
4. Make certain saw is locked.
5. Place board in proper position on table before turning on radial saw.
6. In cutting wide or warped stock move saw back and forth to clean saw kerf.
7. Caution: A wide board has to be cut from both outside edges toward the center.
8. Keep fingers clear of saw at all times.

---

[2] This unit was developed by James Rodriquez, August Boeger School, San Jose, California.

K appendix

Examples of Units Concerned with Informational Topics

All administrative and most independent informational units are taught exclusively in the classroom or lecture area of a VAE laboratory. Informational units need not, however, be sterile of activity. Too often, a teacher depends on the chalk-talk method of presentation, ignoring the use of teaching aids and failing to involve students in discussion and with reports.

In outlining an informational unit, topic headings in outline form should be used in preference to long sentences or written material which may be read. Lesson objectives and assignments, however, are often presented in complete sentence form for clarity. The following examples will illustrate informational units outlined for teaching purposes. The teacher may wish to use a simple instructional outline, listing teaching aids and instructional materials utilized.

EXAMPLE

A UNIT SESSION PLAN ON DIE CAST DIES[1]

Objectives
The student will demonstrate an understanding of how industry makes extensive use of **die cast dies** for producing strong and economical castings in quantity. As an apprentice tool-and-diemaker, the student should be familiar with the basic principles and terminology surrounding this phase of diemaking.

References
1. **Die Casting Dies** by Charles O. Herb.
2. **Die Casting** by H. H. Dochler.

---

[1] Reprinted from a course of study for apprentice tool and diemaking by Roger R. Carver.

Review
   Discuss and answer questions arising from the study of the inverted and return type dies.
Outline for Session Unit
A. Principles and Theory of Operation.
   1. Molten metal forced into cavity giving it shape and size.
   2. Types of metal used — see metal samples on display.
B. Terms and definitions.
   1. Sprue — location.
   2. Water channel.
   3. Cavity.
   4. Runner.
   5. Core pins, fixed and retractable.
   6. Ejector pins.
   7. Platen.
   8. Gates.
   9. Flash.
   10. Inserts.
C. Die Casting Machines.
D. Application.
   1. Automotive.
   2. Aircraft.
   3. Television.
   4. Home Appliances.

Assignments
   Read and study sheets 1 and 2 on **Die Casting Die Theory**. Answer questions on **Die Cast Die Theory**, sheet 3.

EXAMPLE

AN INFORMATIONAL UNIT FROM AN ELECTRICAL COURSE

   An excellent form for the organization of informational units of instruction involves blocking a page into various compartments, duplicating the page, and then writing the units into the duplicated page. Figure K-1 illustrates this procedure in an electrical course for apprentices. A similar form could be developed for listing operational units. In this case, the assignment section could include the student activities planned for the unit while the procedures section would include necessary demonstration and other instructional information.

Fig. K-1.
Organization of Informational Units of Instruction[2]

METHODS OF INSTRUCTION	COURSE TITLE	SESSION NO.
Review, Lecture Demonstration, Illustration, Discussion	Electricity 205	10

TOPIC Parallel Circuits - Resistive, Inductive, and Capacitive Loads

BEHAVIORAL OBJECTIVE   The student will demonstrate through an exit test that he understands the effects of resistive, inductive, and capacitive loads in determining the characteristics of parallel circuits, how to represent the circuits pictorially, and how to make the related calculations.

TOOLS, EQUIPMENT AND MATERIALS	PROCEDURE

3 - resistors
3 - coils
3 - capacitors
1 - a-c voltmeter
1 - dual beam oscilloscope
1 - wattmeter
15 - leads
	I. Preliminaries
	  A. Pass attendance sheet
	  B. Return corrected assignment
	  C. Collect assignment
	  D. Student questions
	  E. Review questions, problems
	II. Introduce Topic
	  A. Parallel circuits, problems
	    1. Current
	      a. R-L-C combinations
	      b. Impedance loads
	    2. Voltage
	    3. Impedance
	    4. Power
	    5. Power Factor
	III. Summarize Topic
	  A. Review approach to solution of parallel circuit problems
	IV. Assignment

TEACHING AIDS AND DEVICES	
White, colored chalk Chalkboard Chalkboard straight edge Chalkboard protractor	
TECHNIQUES	
1. Demonstrate characteristics of parallel circuits, how characteristics may be changed. 2. Use measurements for related calculations.	
ASSIGNMENTS	
1. Study pages 230-232 - textbook. 2. Solve problems, supplement #10. (Textbook: Basic Electricity NAVPERS 10086-B).	REFERENCE Industrial Electricity by Nadon and Gelmine; pp. 306-311.

REVIEW QUESTIONS AND PROBLEMS
1. A 50-ohm resistor and a coil having negligible resistance and 75 ohms reactance are connected in parallel across a 150 volt a-c line. Calculate the line current and the circuit impedance.

$$\text{Ans.} \quad \begin{aligned} I &= \underline{3.60} \text{ amps} \\ Z &= \underline{4.16} \text{ ohms} \end{aligned}$$

[2]O. Karl Rose prepared this lesson outline for an information unit for a course titled "Electricity 205: Single-Phase Alternating-Current Fundamentals," at the Henry Ford Community College, Dearborn, Michigan.

appendix L

Examples of Modules of Instruction Organized Around the Development and Construction of a Project

When the project method of organizing instructional materials is used, the unit of instruction (module) often involves both theory and laboratory activities. This method of organization is designed to facilitate the integration of informational and operational materials.

The project-teaching module of organization, however, does not restrict itself to just that instruction centered around some project that is being developed in a shop or laboratory. The project teaching method may be used also to facilitate the teaching of administrative and informational units.

The examples which follow illustrate two projects which integrate both informational and operational activity. It is possible to develop an integrated modular instructional program around an individual project, a production project, experiment, demonstration, or team activity.

This integrated approach is very desirable since it facilitates the organization of a course into functional modules of instruction.

Pole Supports

This project (Fig. L-1) may be used as an individual activity, group activity, or production job. When used individually, it will provide experiences in planning the design and fabrication of the template and pole support.

When used as a group activity, the individual experiences will be supplemented by group planning of the design. In addition, the advantages of the template when duplicate objects are made may be emphasized by the teacher.

When used on a production job involving part or all of the class, the project serves as an activity for the teaching of production methods and procedures. Discussions regarding the design and development of dies to replace the template and fabrication procedures are other opportunities for good teaching.

446 Planning and Organizing Instruction

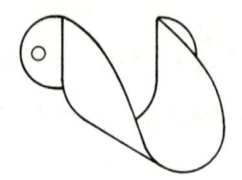

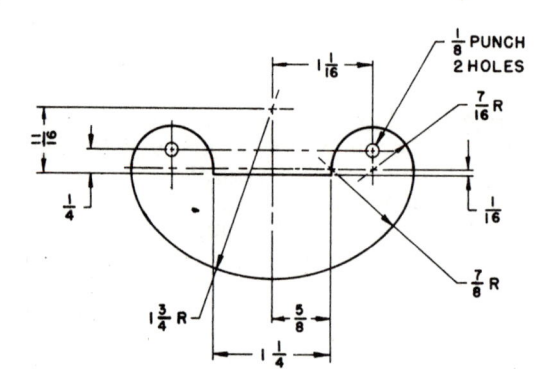

LAYOUT FOR TEMPLATE

MATERIAL REQUIRED

2 PIECES 28 GAUGE METAL

1¾ x 3¼ EACH

4 - ¾ NO. 7 R.H. WOOD SCREWS

Fig. L-1. Example of Design Developed for the Pole Supports (Drawn by Clifford Kim)

EXAMPLE

POLE SUPPORTS

Behavioral Objective
   The student will design and develop a template and fabricate two or more pole supports.

Instructional Information
   The following operational and informational topics must be taught as part of this unit or have been taught in previous instructional units.

(Techniques for identifying operations and informational topics associated with a project are explained in **Appendix D**.)

A. Operations:
1. Get out stock.
2. Cut metal with tin snips.
3. Dress metal with a file.
4. Use a template.
5. Punch holes in sheet metal.
6. Bend sheet metal.
7. Apply enamel.
8. Care for brushes.

B. Informational Topics:
1. Plan and design.
2. Kinds and sizes of sheet metal.
3. Kinds and uses of tin snips.
4. Kinds and uses of files.
5. Kinds and sizes of punches.
6. Selection and care of brushes.
7. Kinds of paint.

Description of Project to Class
A. Obtain following materials:
   1. Set of finished pole supports.
   2. Piece of galvanized iron.
B. (Following information is in script form but could also be prepared as a simple outline for teaching purposes.)

A homeowner should be able to design and build conveniences for his/her home. A few which may be designed and built to make the home a more desirable place are: a rack on which to store the garden hose during the winter, a shelf for soap in the laundry, and additional shelves for the closets. These items and others which may occur to you might require more laboratory experience than you have had. You will be able to do them after you have had more experience. The job which will be discussed today is simple, and can be successfully done by any junior high student.

These are pole supports and made of galvanized iron. (Exhibit.) They are attached to opposite walls of a closet, and support a short length of broomstick or pipe. A closet rod is very convenient and enables you to hang more clothes in your closet. Perhaps some of the closets in your home are equipped with one rod. In this case the pole supports which you are going to make, can be installed in these same closets so you will have two rods instead of the one that is now in it.

These supports also can be used for shoe racks in the lower part of the closet.

Tools and Equipment
Scratch awl
Tin snips
Rule
Solid punch
File
Hammer
Scissors

Mallet
Hardwood block
Broomstick or small pipe
Paint brush
Vise
Pencil

Materials
#28 gauge galvanized iron
Enamel
Firm paper (suitable for template)

Steps and Checking Levels (Procedure for students)
(Checking levels are actually determined by the class through group planning.)
1. Design and layout the template on paper. Have checked.
   a. By foreman _____.
   b. By teacher _____.
2. Cut the template to exact shape.
   Have checked by foreman _____.
3. Using template for layout of ___(no. you desire)___ pairs of pole supports.
   Have checked by foreman _____.
4. Punch holes in ears.
5. Cut out with tin snips.
6. Remove burrs from edges and file to exact shape.
7. Bend ears in the vise.
8. Shape the pole supports. Have checked.
   a. By foreman _____.
   b. By teacher _____.
9. Paint pole supports with enamel.

References
1. Bruce and Meyer, **Sheet Metal**, 3rd ed., pp. 272-273.
2. Feirer, **General Metals**, 3rd ed., pp. 42-43.

Exit or Unit Test
The questions should be answered on your answer sheet by placing a capital "C" if you believe the statement is correct or an "X" if you believe the statement is not true.
1. Sheet iron coated with zinc is called galvanized iron.
   Answer — C.
2. In a shop, a pattern is called a template.
   Answer — C.
3. 28 gauge galvanized iron is thicker than 24 gauge.
   Answer — X.
4. Garbage cans are commonly made of galvanized iron.
   Answer — C.
5. Remove the burr on the edges of the pole holder with sandpaper.
   Answer — X.
6. The end of a solid punch is flat.
   Answer — C.
7. Punch the holes in the metal, on the end grain of a wooden block.
   Answer — C.
8. A pencil is always used to trace round templates on sheet metal.
   Answer — X.
9. Tin snips should not be used to cut wire.
   Answer — C.
10. The size of a pair of tin snips is determined by the length of the handles.
    Answer — X.

Examples of Modules of Instruction

Scoring
All correct .... "A"
1 wrong .... "B"
2 wrong .... "C"
3 wrong .... "D"
4 or more wrong .... "Failure"

EXAMPLE

APPLICATION OF SOLAR ENERGY THROUGH THE USE OF SOLAR CELLS

This module of instruction is designed for high school students in either electricity or power mechanics. It provides them with the opportunity to develop a project which puts solar energy into practical use. A simple motor project is recommended. However, students should be encouraged to develop other ways to use solar energy.

This unit may be developed as an individual or group activity. The organization provides for group planning and dividing of responsibilities, so that the project may be completed more rapidly. It has the possible weakness, however, of not permitting each student to engage in each phase of the activity.

Fig. L-2 Angus J. MacDonald, Professor, San Jose State University, California, developed this microwatt motor using two solar cells wired in series. (Photo by Don Donatelli)

Problem

Design, plan, and develop a practical use of solar energy, using a single cell or bank of solar cells. Each student group is encouraged to use library facilities as group members plan a new or unique use of solar energy. Class activities will center around the application of solar energy to an electric motor.

Behavioral Objectives

The student will be able to exhibit the following behaviors:
- Describe how solar energy formed fossil fuels, provides the energy for hydro-electric power, and produces heat.
- Explain how solar energy (light) is able to produce an electric current.
- Explain how a solar generator is constructed, and the function of each generator component.
- Assemble a solar generator system to operate an electric motor, completing the necessary design, layout, fabrication and assembly.
- Operate and test the solar generator and motor, calculating motor torque and the amperage and current output of the solar generator.
- Explain current and future uses of solar power.

Instructions

A. Teaching Aids:
   1. Film: "Our Mister Sun" — Bell Telephone Laboratories.
   2. Solar Cells.
   3. Microwatt motor.
   4. Chart showing operation of solar cell.

B. Outline:
   1. Show introductory film — "Our Mister Sun." Precede film with description of content and important information.
   2. Discuss film content.
   3. Historical development.
      a. Solar energy and development of fossil fuels — no replacement of these fuels.
      b. Solar energy and falling water.
      c. Direct transfer of solar energy to heat.
   4. Current application — direct conversion of solar energy to electricity.
   5. Types and principles of solar cell operation.
      a. Show cells to class. Use chart.
      b. Selenium cells.
      c. Silicon cells.
      d. Voltage and amperage output.
   6. Cost and efficiency of solar cells.
   7. Some uses of solar cells.
      a. Power transistor radios.
      b. Control switching, for alarms, lights, etc.
      c. Solar tracking devices.
      d. Novelty and demonstration of cars and motors.
      e. Demonstrate operation of microwatt motor.
      f. Power for geological and meteorological instruments.

8. Future uses of solar energy.
   a. Power source for space travel.
   b. Operation of electrical equipment.

Construction of Solar Motor
A. **Tools and Equipment:**

Band saw	Pliers
Files	Layout tools
Buffing wheel	Drill press
Knife	Drill — size equal to motor housing diameter

B. **Materials:**
   Clear Plastic
   Microwatt motor
   Solar cells — either selenium or silicon. (Determine number required to run motor by experimentation.)
   Rubber cement.

C. **Construction Steps:**
   1. Plan and design base, motor mount, and solar cell mount.
   2. Layout design on paper cover of plastic. Have checked.
      a. By foreman _____.
      b. By teacher _____.
   3. Drill hole for motor (alternate method — cut motor mount in half, cut out motor area).
   4. Cut out all parts.
   5. Remove saw marks — form to correct shape.
   6. Buff and polish edges.
   7. Remove paper — assemble with plastic cement.
   8. Use rubber cement to fasten microwatt motor and solar cells.
   9. Wire cells and motor. Experiment with series and parallel arrangement of solar cells — calculating motor torque, amperage, etc.
   10. Test operation — calculate motor torque, amperage, etc.

References
A. Barrow, **Light, Photometry, and Illuminating Engineering.**
B. Sasuger, **The Use of Selenium Photocells and Sun Batteries.**
C. Zworykin and Ramberg, **Photoelectricity and Its Application.**

Exit or Unit Test
Answer the following questions on a separate sheet of paper. Be brief and specific.

1. Why is it necessary to use a microwatt motor with solar cells?
2. Would solar cells be a practical source of power for tube type radios? Why?
3. Describe how solar cells could be used in a sun tracking device.
4. Describe the difference in energy transfer between solar energy to heat and solar energy to electricity.

M appendix

Modules Designed for Individualized Instruction

Many VAE teachers are now organizing their programs as a series of instructional packages to facilitate individual development. In pursuing such a program, students move through the sequential modules of instruction as they assume personal responsibility for their learning activities. In this approach the teacher facilitates and coordinates the instructional program and works with individuals in their problems. An example of this approach is Jelden's "Learner Controlled Education" plan explained in Chapter 3.

To illustrate individualized instruction, three examples were selected from the repertoire of "Individualized Materials in Industrial Education" that were developed under the direction of Harold S. Resnick et al. Wayne State University by the Fellows in the 1969-70 Experienced Teacher Fellowship Program. The mission of the project was to develop instructional packages for the implementation of the program outlined for industrial arts education in **A Guide to Improving Instruction in Industrial Arts** (1968). Persons interested in examining the other modules in this program are referred to the microfiche for the project (see references for Chapter 9).

EXAMPLE

REPLACING A SINGLE-POLE LIGHT SWITCH
(NO H-39)
DIRECTIONS FOR STUDENT

Objective
You will be able to replace a single-pole light switch, given the following tools and materials.

1. An operable single-pole light switch.
2. A screwdriver.
3. A needle nose pliers.
4. A defective single-pole light switch complete with electrical supply box and wall cover plate.

Designing Individualized Instruction 453

Activity
1. Get the tools and materials listed above and take them to the work station.

2. **TURN OFF THE ELECTRICAL POWER** so you do not get a **SHOCK!!!**

3. Remove the wall cover plate with a screwdriver. Be careful that the screwdriver does not slip and scratch the wall plate.

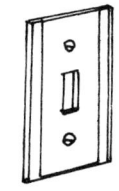

4. Loosen screws and remove the electrical wires (do not bend any more than necessary).

5. Remove screws labeled (1) and (2) and remove light switch from the electrical box.

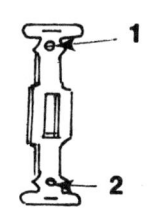

6. Using the needlenose pliers, check and shape the loops at the end of the wires to look like this.

7. Place one wire under the head of each screw and tighten them with a screwdriver. The wire loop should always be wound around the screw in a clockwise direction as shown here. The color of the wires do not matter on a single-pole switch hookup.

8. Now fasten the switch to the electrical box with the two screws as shown here.

9. Get your instructor to check your wiring — have him sign below if your work is approved.

    Instructor approval _____

10. Replace the wall cover plate, turn on the electrical power and make sure the switch works.

EXAMPLE

IDENTIFICATION OF STRIKING TOOLS
(NO I-46)
DIRECTIONS FOR STUDENTS

Objective
   Given pictures of a claw hammer, ball peen hammer, wood mallet, rawhide mallet, rubber mallet, plastic mallet and riveting hammer, you will be able to name each tool.

Activity
1. Take the set of pictures named hammers and give each tool a name. Turn the pictures over and read the correct name on the back to see whether you are correct.
2. Repeat until you can name all tools from memory.
3. Go to your tool panel and find these tools.
4. Name them for your teacher aide.

TEACHER REFERENCE INFORMATION FOR STUDENT PACKAGE
(NO. I-46)

1. For this package the student will need:
   A. Seven pieces of cardboard (8" x 6").
   B. Pictures of the following tools (5" x 7")
      1. Claw hammer
      2. Ball peen hammer
      3. Wood mallet
      4. Rawhide mallet
      5. Rubber mallet
      6. Plastic mallet
      7. Riveting hammer
   C. Folder with the following word on the front.
      1. Hammers

2. Explanation
   Pictures should be attached to cardboard with the name of each tool on the back of the cardboard. The entire card laminated and placed in the folder.

EXAMPLE

USING A DIE TO THREAD A ROD OR PIPE
(NO. I-85)
DIRECTIONS FOR STUDENT

Objective
  Given a 4" long, ¼" diameter rod or pipe, cutting oil, and a ¼-20 die, you will thread 1½" at the end of the rod.

Activity
1. View the filmstrip, "Cutting Threads with Taps and Dies."
2. Mount the rod upright in a bench vise, and file a slight bevel on the end of the rod for easier starting. See Fig. A.
3. Select the correct die and insert it in the die stock.
4. Place the die, with the beveled end down, over the rod and apply some cutting oil. See Fig. B.
5. Grasp the die stock with both hands near the die, press down firmly upon the work, and at the same time slowly screw it on the work in a clockwise direction.
   Be sure the die goes on squarely. You can check for squareness by using a solid steel square.
6. After the thread is started, turn the die forward one revolution and then back one quarter turn in order to break and clean away the chips. Continue to apply cutting oil.
7. Cut threads until they are 1½" in length.
8. When finished, clean the threads and check with a nut or thread gage. If the threads bind, close the die slightly by turning the set screw. Recut the thread.
9. When completed, take work to the teacher for checking.

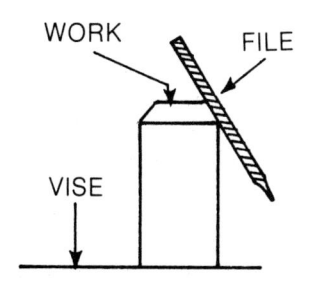

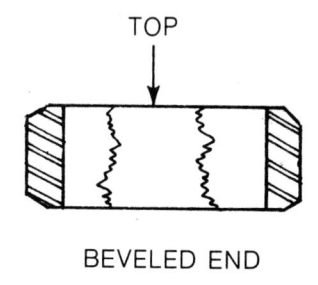

Fig. M-1. Beveling End of Work   Fig. M-2. Bevel on Threading Die

TEACHER REFERENCE INFORMATION FOR STUDENT PACKAGE (NO. I-85)

1. For this package the student will need:
   A. 1 — 4" long, ¼" diameter rod or pipe.
   B. A ¼-20 round adjustable split die.
   C. A die stock.
   D. A double-cut medium file.
   E. Can of cutting oil.
   F. A ¼" screwdriver.
2. For this package the teacher will need:
   The filmstrip, "Cutting Threads with Taps and Dies" (black and white 48 frames), shows how a hand die cut threads on a stud to fit a tapped hole. The filmstrip can be borrowed or rented from local or state film libraries listed by the U.S. Office of Education, Washington, D.C. 20225.

   A film loop, "Cutting External Threads," No. 67-1293, is available from McGraw-Hill Films, 330 West 42nd Street, New York, New York 10036. Cost is $20.00. Length 4 minutes.

appendix N

An Example of a Teacher's Plan for a Unit in a Course in Child Care and Development [1]

EXAMPLE

UNIT II — THE HOME AS A BACKGROUND FOR REARING CHILDREN

Instructional Objectives

The student:
1. Will be able to explain factors that determine personality.
2. Will gain insight and understanding of his/her own behavior through study of basic needs.
3. Will develop an awareness of the responsibilities and obligations of parents to an offspring.
4. Will show genuine concern for learning experiences through his/her attendance, attention and reading assignments.

WHAT THE STUDENT SHOULD BE ABLE TO DO AT CONCLUSION OF UNIT

1. Define health and explain how it affects the offspring.
2. List **four** basic needs and relate their importance to one's growth and development.
3. Identify hereditary traits and environmental factors that influence growth and personality development.
4. State reasons why genetic counseling is advisable for black people.
5. Define a philosophy of life.
6. Discuss the responsibilities of parenthood.
7. Identify two (or three) conditions that result in unwanted children.

---

[1] Developed by Sylvia S. Johnson, Teacher of Family Life Education, Pershing High School, Detroit, Michigan.

LEARNING EXPERIENCES TO BE DIRECTED BY THE TEACHER

Have students:
- Compile a list of the components that students think to be essential in the rearing of children. Categorize these on the chalkboard.
- View the film **From Generation to Generation** and then discuss the family and its influence in making a home for a child.
- Bring articles clipped from magazines or newspapers to share with others in the class concerning home life and the activities of people in their homes. Articles on such subjects as adoptions and child abuse are easy to find.
- If possible, invite an expectant mother to share her views with the members of the class on her desire to have children.
- View and discuss the film **Early Marriages** and then develop a checklist on the chalkboard which emphasizes points to be considered in marriage and the rearing of children.
- View the film **Heredity** and then organize a class discussion that emphasizes both hereditary traits and environmental factors.
- View the film **Worth Waiting For** and then have the class discuss the role of mature parents who are prepared to give children the love and attention they need.
- View the filmstrip **Sickle Cell Anemia** and organize a class discussion that focuses on the problem of this disease with black parents and what needs to be done to encourage black youth to secure genetic counseling.
- Study Chapters 1 and 2 in the text by Landis and Landis on **Personal Adjustment, Marriage, and Family Living,** and then organize panel discussions on "You and Your Family" and "What You Are."
- Prepare a short essay on "The Basic Needs of Individuals" (not to exceed 100 words).
- Complete the exit tests that are interspersed throughout the unit.

appendix O

Individualized Instruction and Problem Solving for Design, Drafting, and Model Building[1]

The Design, Drafting, and Model Building program at Beverly Hills High School includes instructional programs in architecture, commercial building design, engineering research and design, city planning, and technical drawing. The program considers the socioeconomic structure of the community, the abilities and interests of the students, and the individual differences between students.

While the instructional program uses many of the concepts presented in this book, two are emphasized and are the principles around which the program is structured.

- **Individual Instruction.** Each student works on his/her own problem. Assistance and cooperative effort with other students is encouraged. Small group instruction is often used to demonstrate specific operations, to critique a problem introduced by a student, to provide instruction on career opportunities or to cover information of general interest.
- **Problem Solving.** All student activities are planned to solve problems. The problem may be one presented by the teacher or one presented by the student.

Within this structure, the teacher serves more as a "facilitator of learning" rather than as the "presenter of instruction." Sometimes problems arise where needed information is not available from either the teacher or library within the laboratory. When this occurs, students leave the classroom seeking information and assistance from libraries and visiting research agencies, city and federal offices, and local businesses and industries.

To make the concept of individualized instruction and problem solving workable, the laboratory includes:

- Work areas for drafting, model making, reproduction, research, and small group meetings.
- A sound loop film library developed by the students and teacher. The sound loop films include instruction on such topics as the use of tools, rendering, and model construction.

[1]Examples and information presented in this appendix were provided by Frank Mahan, Industrial Arts Teacher, Beverly Hills High School, California.

- Information sheets, problem sheets, teacher prepared technical bulletins, and other types of information available in written form (sometimes on microfilm) and available to students as they select and work on individual problems.
- A reference library to be used by students as they seek solutions to the problems they have selected.

Fig. 0-1
Design, Drafting, and Model Building Program—Sequence of Classes

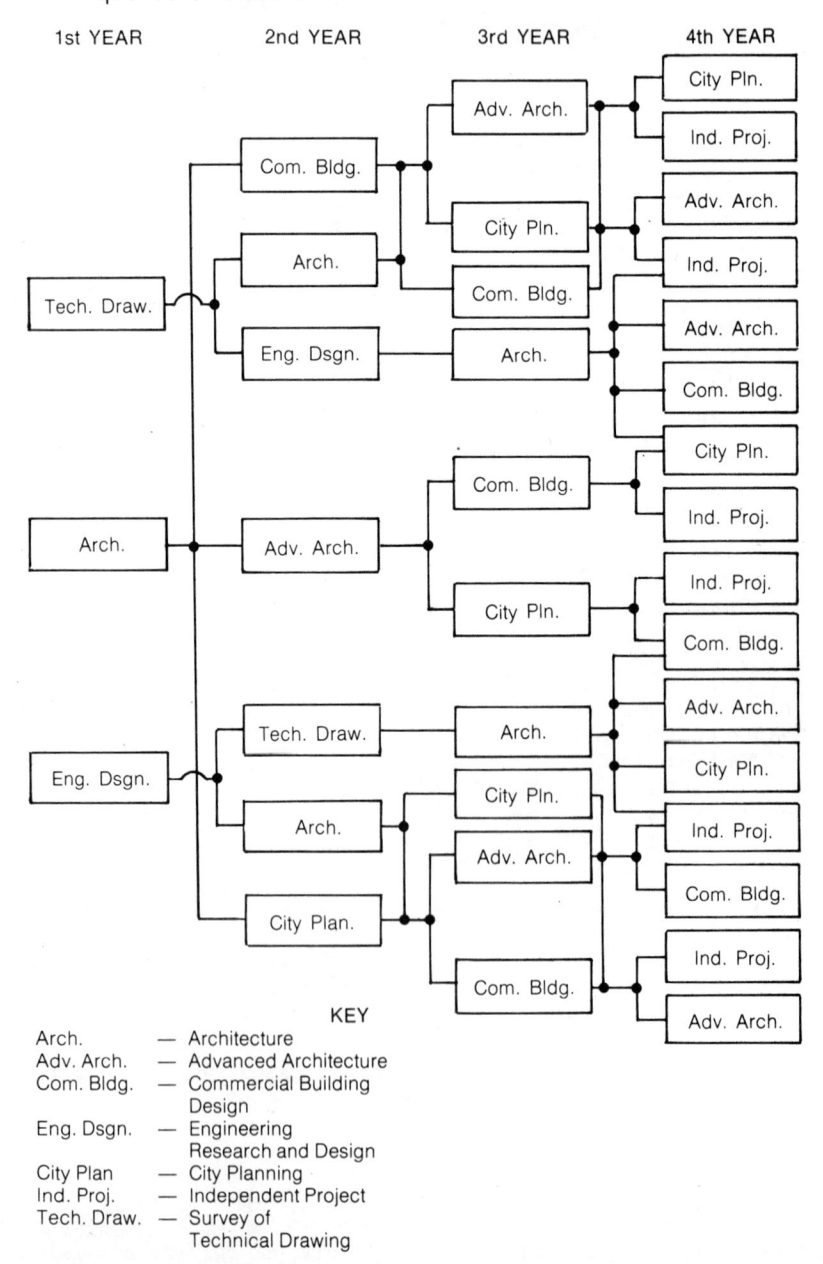

1st YEAR	2nd YEAR	3rd YEAR	4th YEAR
Tech. Draw.	Com. Bldg.	Adv. Arch.	City Pln.
			Ind. Proj.
	Arch.	City Pln.	Adv. Arch.
			Ind. Proj.
	Eng. Dsgn.	Com. Bldg.	Adv. Arch.
		Arch.	Com. Bldg.
Arch.	Adv. Arch.	Com. Bldg.	City Pln.
			Ind. Proj.
		City Pln.	Ind. Proj.
			Com. Bldg.
Eng. Dsgn.	Tech. Draw.	Arch.	Adv. Arch.
			City Pln.
	Arch.	City Pln.	Ind. Proj.
		Adv. Arch.	Com. Bldg.
	City Plan.	Com. Bldg.	Ind. Proj.
			Adv. Arch.

KEY

Arch.	— Architecture
Adv. Arch.	— Advanced Architecture
Com. Bldg.	— Commercial Building Design
Eng. Dsgn.	— Engineering Research and Design
City Plan	— City Planning
Ind. Proj.	— Independent Project
Tech. Draw.	— Survey of Technical Drawing

Since instruction is individualized, courses may be combined into a single class. However, what makes the combined classes work are the interwoven responsibilities between the classes — not only in the running of the facility, but in actual check outs on theory and practical assignments. The combining of classes also adds interest and results in many options which students can pursue during their four years in high school. Figure O-1 shows the options available to students interested in studying in the design, drafting and model building program for four years.

One of the prime parts of the program is the study twin (or design twin, model building twin, etc.) concept. All students have a study twin (coach). This student has passed as a student and a coach on all material studied with his/her twin (See checklist example, Fig. O-2). Any

Fig. O-2
Architectural Model Building Checklist (Showing checkout responsibilities by model building twin *.)

Student's Name: _____ Date Started: _____
Mods Class Meets: _____

This check sheet lists in order the actions to be done to complete your model. Have each step signed off before starting the next one. There will be cases when the teacher (+), student supervisor (advanced student) (**), your model building twin (*) or yourself (o) sign off your check list.

Check Out Code	Theory	Points	Accum. Points	Action Sign Off	Date Completed
o	1. Technical Bulletin F.M. 301 "The Purpose of Architectural Models".	10			
o	2. Film Cartridge "Model Room Materials, Tools and Equipment".	10			
*	3. Film Cartridge "Building the Base - Methods of Contouring".	10			
*	4. Film Cartridge "Building the Base - Methods of Contouring" as a coach.	10			
*	5. Film Cartridge "Assembling the Base"	10			
*	6. Film Cartridge "Assembling the Base" as a coach.	10			
+	7. Practical Finished Base without contour fill	0-60			
o	8. Have you expressed to your model building twin or someone in the class any disagreements, complaints or bad feelings you have about numbers one through seven?	20			
*	9. Theory Film Cartridge "Pools, Walkways, and Patios".	10			
*	10. Film Cartridge "Pools, Walkways, and Patios" as a coach.	10			
**	11. Practical Finished prepared areas for pools, walkways, patios, etc.	20			

(Note: This is a partial checklist. Theory may be presented by lectures, film cartridges, slides, audiotapes, films, microfilm, text-books, technical bulletins, and information sheets.)

student can be a successful coach if trained. This is an important part of the student's study which ranges from basic communication theory to training on coaching and checkouts. The training is of a general nature so that when the students begin their individual problems, they can still coach each other. The study twin concept frees the teacher so that he/she has more time to walk around and spot confusion and problems before they become mistakes.

Problems selected by students must be within the program they select, as well as within their abilities. The teacher is careful not to underestimate the abilities of the students since their enthusiasm and desire to solve selected problems encourages their maximum potential. For example, it is quite common to have students studying and using complex mathematics as they plan the orbit of a satellite, determine the proper time to launch a rocket to intercept a planet in our galaxy, or solve a mining problem through descriptive geometry.

The following examples of problems, requirement sheets, and specifications will illustrate a few of the problems available from the teacher. Each year, students develop and solve hundreds of individual problems, each contributing to their individual growth and development.

EXAMPLE

ARCHITECTURAL PROBLEM REQUIREMENTS

I. Select Site: Pick lot from given selection.
II. Select Family: Family X, Y, Z or one of student's own choice. (NOTE: If student chooses a family other than X, Y, Z, it will be necessary for him/her to write a family description (typed on 8½" by 11" sheet) using family X, Y, and Z as an example for format.)
III. Design Sketches.
    A. Circle area planning.
    B. Thumbnail sketches.
    C. Graph paper floor plan (¼" = 1' -0" or one square equals 1 sq. ft.).
       1. If more than one floor, use an overlay for each additional floor.
       2. Include on graph paper preliminary landscape plan.
       3. Use an overlay to show roof plan.
    D. All elevations (¼" = 1' -0").
IV. Presentation Drawings.
    A. Combination site and floor plan, ¼" = 1' -0".
    B. Elevations (two most interesting views), ¼" = 1' -0".
    C. Exterior rendering.
    D. Section through entire building.
    E. Interior renderings (optional).
V. Presentation Model, ¼" = 1' -0".

View A

View B

View C

Fig. 0-3
Constructing model homes as part of architectural design problem. Views A and B show students at work on their models. In View C, a student explains to her instructor the location she has selected for a tree. (Courtesy Beverly Hills High School, California)

VI. Working Drawings.
   A. Combination roof, site, plot and landscape plan.
   B. Floor plan including electrical plan.
   C. Elevations (all four views and any additional ones necessary to describe house).
   D. Foundation plan (optional).
   E. Detail sheet (optional).
VII. Specifications (Description of materials).

ARCHITECTURAL SPECIFICATIONS

(Students are given a number of specification sheets providing information such as topography, climate, costs, size limitations, and domestic help requirements. In the interest of space, only the **climate** information is provided as an example).

Climate

Summer: Generally low humidity, warm mornings tempered by afternoon breezes. Night temperature drop of 30°F. is usual. No rain during summer.

Autumn: September and October are usually the warmest months of the year. Hot days are relieved by westerly afternoon breeze. No rain until late October.

Winter: Rainy season (average about 20" per year). Wide temperature range 32° to 85°F. Occasional strong, dry winds from North — hot or cold depending on snow in the mountains to the North. Rains are heavy but infrequent.

Spring: Wide temperature variation (50° — 90°F.), westerly afternoon breeze; high morning overcast usual in May and June.

General: Cool nights preclude outside evening dining during much of the year except in areas sheltered from breeze and dew. Occasional rains until May 15.

Earthquakes of variable intensity occur from time to time in most of Southern California's coastal area. Construction regulations are severe because of this.

Building materials of all types are available but wood predominates in residential construction. Poured concrete and concrete masonry are sometimes used as principal materials, but brick and stone are rarely used except for chimneys, garden walls or patio construction. Unreinforced masonry building walls are not permitted in Southern California. Wood is plentiful and inexpensive by worldwide standards. Many varieties of roofing materials are used including wood shingles, composition and gravel, ceramic tile and synthetics. The architect should remember that labor costs in the USA are high and that building costs can be kept within reason only if standard methods and materials are used predominately.

EXAMPLE

PROBLEM — HOUSE FOR MR. AND MRS. X

(This is one of the available problems students may choose. Most students select their own architectural problem, using limitations provided in the specifications — such as size, 4500 sq. ft. Since Beverly Hills has one of the highest average per capita incomes in the United States, the following example is typical of the community.)

Doctor and Mrs. X have been married for twelve years and have four lively children ranging from 2 to 10 years of age. Three are boys and the next to the youngest is a girl.

Doctor X (age 44) is a dedicated surgeon with an excellent practice. He writes an occasional article for medical journals, enjoys reading and trout fishing, and along with the latter has developed considerable skill in the art of tying artificial flies.

His avocations demand frequent isolation from the usual noises and confusion caused by children and Dr. X has declared that his only specific requirement in a house would be a secluded and comfortable study adjacent to the master bedroom.

Mrs. X participates in community affairs to some degree, but she is more concerned with her children, house, and the preparation of interesting foods. As a consequence she feels that special emphasis should be placed on the design for her kitchen. Skilled kitchen help is scarce in the USA, and she (as many American women) spends much of her time in the actual preparation of the daily meals or in supervising her one domestic helper who has worked for the family for some years but is not a skilled cook.

Dr. and Mrs. X entertain in a simple manner and although a modest dining room is required for some occasions, they usually prefer to eat with their children. This suggests the inclusion of an attractive and informal space for eating in the kitchen area. This arrangement is often called a family room and should be accessible to terraces and a swimming pool. No bar is desired.

So far the children have developed no special interests other than outdoor fun and games; areas for their recreation should be important features of the plan.

A two-car garage or carport is required.

Dr. and Mrs. X have very little furniture of value and have no preconceived ideas as to what might be suitable in their new home, except that they desire a high degree of simple comfort. They are open to suggestions by the architect.

EXAMPLE

PROBLEM — CHARCOAL GRILL HOOD DESIGN

Du Mar's Restaurant Fireplace Hood

Remodeling Requirement: Design a charcoal grill hood to be installed in the specified odd-shaped corner of Du Mar's Restaurant.

Technical Specifications: The top edge of the hood will be fastened flush to the wall between the end limits of the hood and two feet below the ceiling level, as shown in the sketch below. The front edges of the hood are parallel to the wall and will be six feet from that wall at all points. It is necessary to support the weight of the hood from the ceiling. Design the braces and determine where they are to be fastened. Similarly, determine how the hood will be fastened to the wall and the location of the flue (12" diameter).

Construction and Presentation Information: There are 6" by 12" beams that run across the ceiling at intervals of 15' and 2" by 4" studs in the walls at intervals of 16". Draw a development of the hood including all construction specifications for the hood, such as materials to be used, bend angles, welded seams, sizes of surfaces, etc. The presentation will be on one or more size "D" sheets. Build a model and submit an engineer's report.

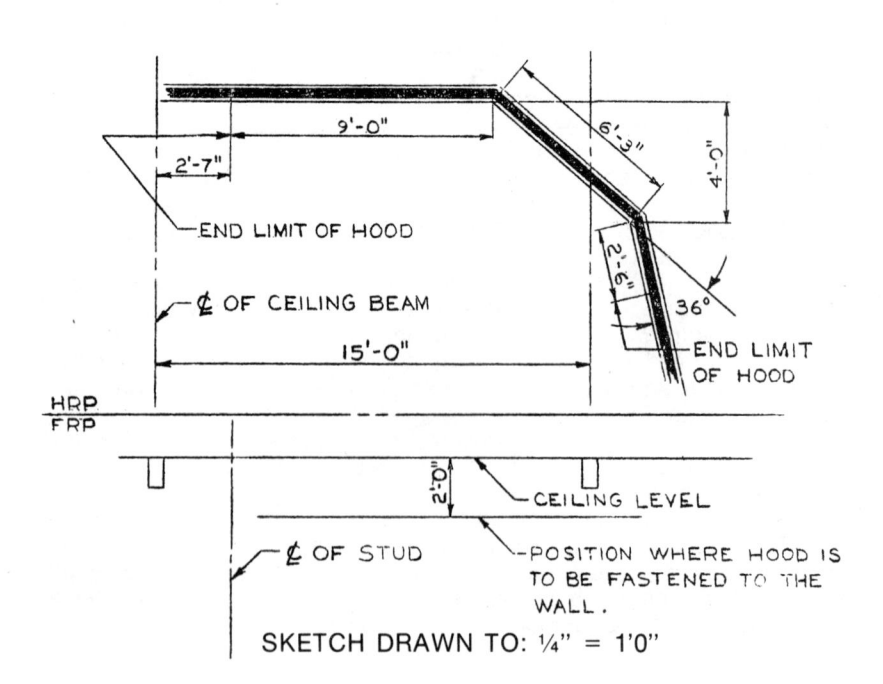

SKETCH DRAWN TO: ¼" = 1'0"

EXAMPLE

PROBLEM — BRIDGE CONSTRUCTION

It is necessary for a portion of freeway and a bridge to be constructed in Bay County to continue a freeway system. Compare two bridge styles that could be used to span the Curran Bay. Compare them as far as costs, stresses, materials, and other data are concerned. A six-lane freeway merges into a ten-lane roadway at the bridge.

Three bearings locate two borings of a substrata which is unsafe for heavy loads. The bearings are as follows:

BORING 'A': Located on the intersection of 2 bearings (1) from B.M. 320' N 75°E and (2) from B.M. 50' S 38°W.

BORING 'B' Located at sea level from B.M. 320' N 79° 30'E.

Boring 'A' is vertical and Boring 'B' is inclined at 5° (perpendicular to substrata). The thickness is found to be 14 feet.

The following is necessary to solve the problem:

A. Location of bridge
   1. Plot contours on a grid at 100' intervals.
   2. Find the strike and dip of substratum.
   3. Locate outcropping of substratum.
   4. Locate bridge and foundations for towers.

B. Freeway
   1. Plot the best curve for a six-lane freeway.
   2. No grade shall be greater than 10%.
   3. Show curve data and calculations of vertical curve elevations.
   4. Figure amount of cut and fill.
   5. Cut material is used for fill and any other material that has to be hauled in for additional fill will cost $2.00 per load. Fill is 50¢ per cubic yard and grading and surfacing is $200.00 per linear foot. At these rates, figure cost for fill and grading and surfacing of freeway.

C. Miscellaneous
   1. Show major details of both bridges.
   2. Give a stress analysis on the cables, trusses, and other vital points of the bridges.
   3. Submit a financial summary, order of operations of the construction of the bridge recommended, reports on findings and recommendations of the problem.
   4. Also submit a model and a rendering of the proposed bridge.
   5. Locate storage space for equipment.
   6. Submit any additional information pertaining to the problem.

468   Planning and Organizing Instruction

1130	800	10 ⑨ 6 7	① 1010	200	100 2 5″/32 ↓	-10 4 1/4″	1300
500	1210	800	-10	-100	-40 B.M.50′	200	900
1200	100	60	60	-220	100	300	1220
600	820	④ 100	-30	←3″SQ.→ -110 ↓	-200	-20	② 800
B.M.320′ 9″/32 410 3 3″/16	200	500 ③	-500	⑧ 10	⑤ 410	110	400
200	-200	-600	-700′	-500	-350	-250	-200

GRID — SCALE ½″ = 1000′

1. Grizzly Mt.
2. Wilson Peak
3. Rock Point
4. West Beach
5. Cerro Gordo
6. High County
7. Bay County
8. Curran Bay
9. Kelly River

Note: Total dimension of the above grid is 21″ x 15″.

appendix P

Examples of Behavioral Objectives with Criteria for Evaluation

The following examples of behavioral objectives were suggested by Robert Wiegman, Dean of the College of Education, Florida Atlantic University (1971, 55-56).

In his preface to these objectives, Dean Wiegman (1971, 54) said:

... writing performance-based objectives is difficult and time consuming, but I submit that ... we will be held more and more accountable for what we are trying to do in the classroom. The emphasis will be more and more upon the product that we are turning out. The concern is what the student is capable of doing when he finished this part of his education. Teachers will be judged more and more on the extent to which students learn to do those things that we say we are teaching them to do, and less and less emphasis will be placed upon what we do in hopes that something will result.

EXAMPLE

BEHAVIORAL OBJECTIVES

- Upon request, the student will describe the procedure for changing the oil and filter in an automobile. The description must include reference to the following steps in order: (1) raise the car on the lift; (2) position the used oil receptacle under the pan; (3) remove plug; (4) let oil drain; (5) remove filter; (6) remove used oil receptacle; (7) replace plug; (8) put oil on seal of filter; (9) replace filter; (10) lower automobile; (11) put new oil in crankcase; (12) check for leaks.
- Given a quantity of ⅜" plywood, handsaw, hammer, woodfile, sandpaper, ruler and assorted nails, the students will construct a cube with a side of 8". All measurements must be within 1/16" of the specified size. The quality of the finish of the cube will have no bearing on the successful achievement of this objective.

- Given a flat-bladed shovel and trowel, the student will dig a trench 10' long, 1' wide, and 1' deep. All measurements must be to the nearest ½". The student will have 45 minutes to complete this exercise.
- Given one gallon of latex wall paint, a roller, pan, sash tool, and 3" brush, the student will paint an interior wall 8' by 15' within one hour. Satisfactory achievement of this objective will be determined by a panel of three master painters. Ratings will be above average, satisfactory, or unsatisfactory. The student must achieve a rating of above average or satisfactory as determined by at least two of the three master painters.

A Behavioral Objective in Home Economics

The following example of a performance goal (synonymous term with behavioral objective) was reprinted from an article by Maurice E. Ryan (1973, 31-33) of Santa Barbara City College in California. Criteria for the evaluation are included also. The wording of this objective follows the format, shown in Fig. P-1, of "The Model: Ability to Adjust to Future Changes in Equipment and Machines," advocated by Harry Huffman of Colorado State University (1973, 26-30). The numbers in the wording of the objective correspond to the numbered items in the Huffman model.

Figure P-2 shows the criteria for evaluating the performance goal which follows.

EXAMPLE

LEARNING TO OPERATE A NEW MODEL OF AN ELECTRIC OVEN

Given the assignment of learning to operate a completely automated (9) electric oven (5) located at a sales representative's showroom (19) the student observes a 30-minute (64) demonstration (35) of cooking a roast (17) conducted by the teacher and a sales representative familiar with the oven (45). Learning time is limited to observation of the demonstration (24) after school hours on specified dates (26). The student is to discover similarities and differences in the cooking process as compared to an electric oven (i.e., to learn the effects of radio waves on protein) (31). The student is to note the safety features and precautions taken during the demonstration (42). The teacher will record on a printed checklist (60) the student's ability to state the advantages and disadvantages (51) of cooking by this new method. The degree of this knowledge and understanding should not be expected to exceed that of a beginner (58). The student must have completed the unit on meat preparation prior to observing the demonstration (68).

The Model[1]
Ability to Adjust to Future Changes in Equipment and Machines

CONDITIONS

A. GIVEN
( ) 1. Agriculture: sono-scope for measuring fat covering on live swine, sheep, and cattle
( ) 2. Business: word-processing system utilizing magnetic tape typewriter and voice-recording terminals
( ) 3. Distribution: cash register system with change return, perpetual inventory control, automatic order processing, and security-control components
( ) 4. Health: equipment to monitor condition of patient in an intensive care unit
( ) 5. Home economics: electronic oven for home preparation of food
( ) 6. Trade and industry: computer diagnosis or semi-automated trouble-shooting instruments for discovering malfunctions of motor vehicles
( ) 7. Technical: cybernetic systems and feedback controls using solid state components
( ) 8. Other

A1. Degree of Automation
( ) 9. Completely automated
( ) 10. Partially automated
( ) 11. Not automated
( ) 12. Other

A2. Supplemental Supplies and Materials
( ) 13. Punched cards to be used in the operation
( ) 14. Magnetic tape to be used in the operation
( ) 15. Paper tape to be used in the operation
( ) 16. No supplemental supplies and materials needed
( ) 17. Other

B. SOURCE OF GIVEN
( ) 18. Business or industry (away from school)
( ) 19. Sales representative's showroom
( ) 20. Rental
( ) 21. Other

B1. Time Availability
( ) 22. Opportunity to learn a specific application
( ) 23. Opportunity for limited practice
( ) 24. Observation of operation
( ) 25. Other

B2. Time Constraint
( ) 26. Only after school
( ) 27. Weekends
( ) 28. No constraints
( ) 29. Other

C. PURPOSES
( ) 30. Gaining skill and knowledge of operation
( ) 31. Discovering similarities and differences in operation
( ) 32. Discovering advantages and disadvantages of new machines or equipment
( ) 33. Learning terminology
( ) 34. Other

D. METHODS
( ) 35. Observation of demonstration
( ) 36. Self-instruction
( ) 37. Formal instruction
( ) 38. Coaching
( ) 39. Other

D1. Safety Measures
( ) 40. Legal age restrictions
( ) 41. Safety clothes and gear required
( ) 42. Recommended safety features
( ) 43. Other

D2. Assistance Available
( ) 44. Ample printed references
( ) 45. Experienced worker to help teacher
( ) 46. Experienced worker only
( ) 47. Teacher only
( ) 48. None
( ) 49. Other

E. OUTPUTS (OUTCOMES)
( ) 50. Ability to demonstrate machine or equipment
( ) 51. Ability to state advantages and disadvantages
( ) 52. Desire for additional knowledge and information
( ) 53. Ability to recall terminology
( ) 54. None
( ) 55. Other

E1. Degree
( ) 56. Similar to an expert
( ) 57. Similar to a novice
( ) 58. Similar to a beginner
( ) 59. Other

F. QUALITY MEASURES TO USE
( ) 60. Meets stipulated criteria on a printed checklist
( ) 61. Conforms to specified error tolerance level
( ) 62. Is judged by competent judges to meet quality measure
( ) 63. Other

G. TIME LIMITS OR PRIORITY RATINGS TO USE
( ) 64. Specified time in minutes, hours, days: _____
( ) 65. Priority rating, with time limit unspecified: _____
( ) 66. Completion date specified: _____
( ) 67. Other

H. PREREQUISITE ABILITIES TO LEARN THE TASK
( ) 68. Prerequisite instruction (specific units or courses)
( ) 69. No special background or experience required
( ) 70. Other

Fig. P-1. The Huffman Model for Describing Behavioral Objectives (Reprinted from April, 1973 issue of American Vocational Journal)

[1]This model was first published in **Writing Performance Goals: Strategy and Prototypes.** A CVTE publication (CR #15), 1971.

DIRECTIONS
(Task Sequence)

SUBSTEP 1: (Procedure of determining awareness or acquiring need) Visits a concern presently using an electronic oven.	a. Concern using the oven was telephoned for appointment. b. Manager of concern was interviewed for purpose of determining proper person to interview. c. Advantages of electronic oven over currently used electric ovens were discussed with manager.
SUBSTEP 2: (Methods of gathering resources) Interviews the person using or demonstrating the oven—an oral resource.	a. Operator was questioned concerning the benefits he felt were achieved by using the electronic oven. b. Desire to observe the oven in operation was expressed.
SUBSTEP 3: (Methods of applying the resources) Makes arrangements to observe a demonstration.	a. Permission for an hour's visit was obtained from manager. b. Oven manual was obtained and studied.
SUBSTEP 4: (Continuation steps or procedures) Observes the demonstration.	a. Oven settings were carefully noted. b. Safety features and precautions were carefully observed and noted. c. Each step in the demonstration was recorded in sequence.
SUBSTEP 5: (Revisions, evaluations, or modifications) Discovers the need to ask questions.	a. Settings and operation of the equipment were discussed. b. Additional questions concerning safety features and precautions were asked. c. Similarities and differences as compared to the electric oven were discussed. d. Reason for lack of browned appearance of meat was discussed.
SUBSTEP 6: (Final procedure or task) Discusses his knowledge and understanding of the machine or equipment.	a. Student reported to the operator his knowledge and understanding of the oven in reference to advantages and disadvantages of the oven, similarities and differences as opposed to the electric oven, and safety features and requirements. b. Any detected discrepancies were noted by operator and discussed with student.

Fig. P-2. Criteria Used for Evaluating the Performance Goal (Behavioral Objective) on Use of an Electric Oven.

References for Appendix P

Byers, Edward E. (Editor) and Huffman, Harry H. **Writing Performance Goals: Strategy and Prototypes.** A publication of CVTE (RS #15). Columbus, Ohio: CVTE, The Ohio State University, 1971, pp. ix + 101.

Huffman, Harry. "A Model for Generating Performance Goals." **American Vocational Journal,** Vol. 48, No. 4 (April, 1973), pp. 26-30.

Ryan, Maurice E. "Directions and Criteria for Performance Goals." **American Vocational Journal,** Vol. 48, No. 4 (April, 1973), pp. 31-33.

Wiegman, Robert. "Strategies for Assessing Teacher Effectiveness in Post-Secondary Occupational Programs," in **The Second Annual Pennsylvania Conference on Post-Secondary Occupational Education.** Edited by Angelo C. Gillie, University Park, Pennsylvania: Center for Study of Higher Education, The Pennsylvania State University, June, 1971, pp. 49-59.

appendix Q

Examples of Entries from Tests Developed by VAE Teachers

EXAMPLE

DIE THEORY I
APPRENTICE TOOL AND DIEMAKER PROGRAM[1]

Midcourse Examination
   Part I: Match the statements in the right-hand column with the word they describe in the left-hand column. Place the letter from the matched phrase in the provided space in front of the word in the left-hand column.

_____ 1. Die shoes.	a. is usually machined first.
_____ 2. Bushings.	b. are usually forged.
_____ 3. Die block.	c. governs the press size.
_____ 4. Composite sections.	d. must be of tool steel.
_____ 5. Punch.	e. minimum of .005.
_____ 6. Stripper.	f. has blanking clearance.
_____ 7. Shear on die.	g. standard sizes.
_____ 8. Clearance.	h. should be .015 greater than metal thickness.
_____ 9. Bolster plate.	i. made of brass and steel.
_____10. Shut height.	j. has clearance for the punch.
	k. is mounted to the bolster plate.
	l. for flat blanks.
	m. should have 10% clearance.

[1]Developed by Roger R. Carver.

Part II: Read each of the following statements. If the statement is true, place a "C" in the provided space in front of the statement; if false place an "X" in the space.

_____ 3. Trial and error is one method used to determine the size of a blank for a formed work part.

_____ 5. The Danley type automatic gage can be used on both the solid and spring stripper dies.

_____ 7. The direction the stock is fed into the die can be determined by the size and shape of the blank.

_____ 10. Clearance between a punch and die should be 5 percent of metal thickness at all points.

EXAMPLE

PRETEST ON INTERIOR DESIGN[2]

This is a pretest, given at the very beginning of the course in Interior Design, to determine what the student already knows and can do. To help each student make an assessment of her/his competencies, an answer key is provided. With this "key" each student can participate by assisting in her/his own self-assessment and in determining objectives and content to be mastered as they move ahead with the course.

(**Note:** Part I, True-False no examples shown)

Part II — Completion
Directions: Complete the following statements. More than one word may be needed in each blank to complete the answer. Each completed statement equals 1 point.

2. Two types of window decorations which are used on the tops of windows to cover the curtain rods are _____ and _____.

5. Backgrounds are done in one hue with the main difference being in _____.

20. A rule of thumb to follow when determining the amount of the total yearly house payment a family can afford is _____.

---

[2]Developed by Barbara MacDonald.

Part III — Multiple Choice

Directions: To the left of the letter, indicate by a check mark, the correct answer for each item. Each correct answer equals 1 point.

1. Two rooms in which the use of ceramic tile is a wise choice are:
   _____a. Bath.
   _____b.. Foyer.
   _____c. Basement recreation room.
   _____d. Kitchen.
7. The legal description of property and history of ownership is described in:
   _____a. Deed.
   _____b. Appraisal.
   _____c. Abstract.
   _____d. Mortgage.

Part IV — Matching

Directions: Write the letter of the correct term in Column B on the line to the left of each definition listed in Column A. Each term in Column B may be used once, more than once, or not at all. Each correct answer equals 1 point.

Column A (Definition)	Column B
_____1. An apartment found in a 2-story home occupied by two families.	A. Apartment.
_____2. An apartment complex operated like a corporation.	B. Condominium.
_____3. A series of living units with common walls.	C. Cooperative.
_____4. A type of house where two families own two houses with a common wall.	D. Duplex.
_____5. An apartment that is owned by title by the family living in it.	E. Income or flat.
	F. Mobile home.
	G. Townhouse.

Column A	Column B
_____1. Begins with first baby.	A. Founding stage.
_____2. Begins when the last child leaves home.	B. Expanding stage.
_____3. Children begin to leave home.	C. Crowded stage.
_____4. Newlywed stage	D. Teenage stage.
_____5. Children are young; need constant care and attention.	E. Launching stage.
	F. Retirement stage.

Part V — Compound Matching

Directions: On the line to the right of each statement in Column C, write the number of the term in Column A and the letter of the definition in Column B that identifies that statement. Each term in Column A and each definition in Column B may be used once, more than once, or not at all. Each correct answer equals 2 points.

Column A	Column B	Column C
1. Influenced by Madame de Pompadour.	A. Letter "N" a furniture symbol.	1. Duncan Phyfe____
2. English monarchs with Dutch ancestry during 17th century.	B. Referred to as a hodgepodge of design.	2. Empire____
3. Napoleon was emperor of France.	C. Motifs were lyre and acanthus.	3. Louis XV____
4. Considered to be the first American designer.	D. Staid, solid quality.	4. Victorian____
5. Queen Victoria came to the throne.	E. Lavish carvings, very ornate, feminine, Rococo styling.	5. William and Mary ____

Part VI — Essay

Directions: In the following two questions, list and discuss fully the items required in each problem. Underline key points. Do not use more than 5 minutes on each problem. Each **completed** and satisfactory answer equals 5 points.

1. Explain the inherent needs of every person which in turn dictate the type of home to be considered when purchasing a house. (5 points)
(Appropriate space provided)
2. Name and discuss the long-range expenditures which must be accounted for when considering home ownership. (5 points)
(Appropriate space provided)

KEY: PRETEST FOR INTERIOR DESIGN[3]

Part I True-False	Part II — Completion	Part III — Multiple Choice
1. +	2. Valance and cornice.	1. a. Bath.
4. O The answers	5. Value.	b. Kitchen.
5. + were shown	20. 25% of annual net pay equal total yearly house payments.	7. c. Abstract.
6. O in this		
7. O manner		
12. +		
20. O		

Part IV — Matching

1. E   1. B
2. C   2. F
3. G   3. E
4. D   4. A
5. B   5. C

Part V — Compound Matching

1. 4C
2. 3A
3. 1E
4. 5B
5. 2D

Part VI — Essay
1. All needs cannot be satisfied since they vary according to the ages of the family members and the stages through which the family will move. The basic needs are:
   A. Physical needs.
      (1) Work area — adequate size.
      (2) Activities area — conducive to personal interest as well as group interests.
      (3) Quiet zones — need for privacy.
   B. Emotional needs.
      An emotional climate which respects individual differences and encourages positive personal growth.
   C. Social needs.
      A setting where good social habits will be formed. Space for both individual and group activities.
   D. Aesthetic needs.
      Consider psychological effect of surroundings.
2. A. Mortgage principal.
   B. Interest charges.
   C. Taxes.
   D. Insurance premiums:
      (1) Home.
      (2) Contents.
      (3) Liability.
   E. Furnishings.
   F. Utilities.
   G. Maintenance and repair costs.
   H. Special assessments.

[3]This is a sample of the complete "Key". Only answers for the selected questions are included.

R appendix

Examples of Questions from Safety Tests

Sample questions are shown from two tests selected to serve as examples of those designed to cover the general laboratory safety precautions and those that need to be practiced for a specific machine. It is recommended that the student successfully answer all questions. Students should not undertake these tests until they have familiarized themselves with the study guides on safety, studied the shop or laboratory safety precautions, and have seen the teacher's demonstration on the use of the specific machine. These questions call for direct answers which check on the specific knowledge of the student.

EXAMPLE

SAMPLE QUESTIONS FROM A
"BEFORE-GOING-TO-WORK TEST"
Covering the
General Laboratory Safety Precautions

(Five questions have been selected for this example.)

Directions: Prepare an answer sheet for taking the test. Use a piece of plain notebook paper and write your name and the name of the test on the top line. Draw a small square in the upper right-hand corner of the sheet. Label this square NUMBER RIGHT. Number the sheet as you write the answers.

39. When bench vises are adjusted at the end of the period, should they be completely closed or slightly open?
41. In case of a fire drill, what should you do about outer garments that have been removed?
47. Give two reasons for not holding wood screws, nails, or other small objects in the mouth.
49. When you lift a heavy object, should you bend your back or your knees?

51. What power machines, usually found in school shops, were designed to be used by two students at one time?

EXAMPLE

GRINDER
(Four of the questions have been selected for this example)

General Directions: Prepare an answer sheet for taking the test. Use a piece of plain notebook paper and write your name and the name of the test on the top line. Draw a small square in the upper right-hand corner of the sheet. Label this square NUMBER RIGHT. Number the sheet as you write the answers.

3. What should be the distance between the tool rest and the wheel?
5. Where would you stand when turning on a grinder? Why?
7. Why is it dangerous to grind on the side of the wheel of a small bench grinder?
8. Should the rest be set above or below the center of the wheel?

Index of Acronyms

AIAA — American Industrial Arts Association.

AIM — Abstracts of Instructional Materials in Vocational and Technical Education (publication available from the CVTE at The Ohio State University).

ARM — Abstracts of Research Materials in Vocational and Technical Education (publication available from the CVTE at The Ohio State University).

ASCD — Association for Supervision and Curriculum Development.

AVA — American Vocational Association, Inc.

CA — Carrel Arcades (at Oakland Community College in Michigan).

COD — Career and Occupational Development (used in the National Assessment of Educational Progress for assessment of subject areas that contribute to career and occupational development).

COE — Central Office Equipment (telephone company).

CVTE — Center for Vocational and Technical Education at The Ohio State University.

CWE — Cooperative Work Education.

DAT — Differential Aptitude Test.

DHEW — See HEW.

DO — Diversified Occupations.

DS — Differentiated Staffing.

DOT — **Dictionary of Occupational Titles** (U.S. Department of Labor).

EDRS — ERIC Document Reproduction Service (P.O. Box 190, Arlington, Virginia 22210).

EPPS — Edwards Personal Preference Schedule (a test to determine personal adjustment measures).

Index of Acronyms

ERIC — Educational Resources Information Center.
FMS — Flexible Modular Scheduling.
GATB — General Aptitude Test Battery (developed by U.S. Employment Service).
HC — Hard Copy — a reproduction on paper of pages in report available from EDRS.
HEW — U.S. Department of Health, Education and Welfare.
HumRRO — Human Resources Research Organization (U.S. Department of Labor).
IACP — Industrial Arts Curriculum Project.
IPLL — Individualized Program Learning Laboratory (at Oakland Community College in Michigan).
ITIP — Individualized — Task Instructional Packet (Department of Vocational and Applied Arts Education, Wayne State University).
LCE — Learner Controlled Education (at Oakland Community College in Michigan).
MC — Microfiche — a reproduction on film of pages in report available from EDRS.
NAEP — National Assessment of Educational Progress.
NEA — National Education Association.
NIER — National Industrial Equipment Reserve (Office of Surplus Utilization, U.S. Government).
NIT — National Institute for Education.
OCC — Oakland Community College (Michigan).
PACER — Prescriptive Analysis for Curriculum Evaluation and Review (a system of evaluation used by Oakland Schools, Pontiac, MI).
PEP — Personalized Educational Programs (at Oakland Community College in Michigan).
PPBS — Planning, Programing, Budgeting Systems.
RIE — Research in Education.
ROC — Regional Occupational Center (Los Angeles Unified School District).
ROP — Regional Occupational Program (Los Angeles Unified School District).
USOE — United States Office of Education.
VAE — Vocational and Applied Arts Education.
WS — Work Study.
YTY — Youth-Tutor-Youth (at Oakland Community College in Michigan).

Index

Abstracts of instructional materials, 167
Academic vs. vocational education, 34
Accelerated progress through individual instruction, 91
Accountability, 101, 314
   national standards for, 320
Accreditation, 323
Accounting system, 384
Achievement and evaluation, 325
Acronyms, index of, 480
Action-pattern domain, 213
Activities —
   evaluating laboratory, 338
   planning concurrent, 270
Acquisition, task source, 99
Adaptation, 212
Administration —
   and substitute teacher, 308
   of tests, 336
Administrative and organizational strategies, 107-142
Administrative units of instruction, 252
Admission requirements, 169
Adults, retraining of, 16
Advisory committees, 129
   crafts, 135
Advisory groups, and content, 76
Affective domain, 205, 208
   evaluating objectives in, 330
Aids —
   methods and units, 300
   teaching, 171, 281-312
Aims —
   and accountability, 315
   developing, 222
   for education, 213, 215
   relationships of, 235
   showing goal relationship to, 236
   stability of educational, 221
   use of, 227
Air force —
   medical task analysis, 407
   task analysis, 62
Allen, Blaine W., 119
Allen, C. R., 68
Allen, David, 243
Allen, Dwight W., 121, 122, 123
Altman, James W., 55
Analog systems approach, NOBELS, 97
Analysis, 207
   and instructional units, 254
   occupational, 165
Applied arts, 203
   units for, 256
Application, 207
Appreciations —
   as goals, 274
   stating as goals, 233
Arnold, Walter M., 324
Articulation, 49
Ash, Lane C., 323
Assessment, see Evaluation
Assignments, as method, 285
Assignment sheets, 288
Attitudes —
   and evaluation, 344
   as goals, 274
   stating goals of, 231
   toward work, 58
Audiovisual materials, 171
Audiovisual presentations, 287, 296
Authority, interviewing, 298
Auto body repair, units for, 218
Avocational activities, 24
Awareness —
   career, 7, 225
   self, 225

Bamberger, George, 274
Banathy, B. H., 6, 14, 82, 83
Banks, Jane M., 208, 210
Barlow, Melvin L., 34
Bateson, Willard M., 378
Baysinger, Gerald B., 289
Behavior —
  and evaluation, 314
  and payroll tasks, 59
Behavioral domains, 205
Behavioral objectives, 84, 90, 151, 187, 188
  and evaluation, 325
  and evaluation criteria, examples, 469
  and instruction, 189
  stating, 241
  and student evaluation, 329
Bloom, Benjamin S., 109
Bogdanoff, E. Brooks, 292
Books, 173
Branching program, 296
Briggs, Paul W., 129
Budgets —
  approaches to, 318
  system, 384
Bulletin Board, 287
  materials, 171
Burt, Samuel M., 76, 127
Bush, R. N., 121
Bushnell, David S., 100, 243
Business and office machines, units of instruction, 275, 434
Byers, Edward E., 244

Campbell, Robert E., 188
Career awareness, 7
Career choice, 61
Careers curriculum, 214
Career decision-making, 56
Career development, general, 55
Career education, 5, 202, 217
  aims, 224
  in schools, 11
  interrelating school and employer programs, 15
Career Education Document Information System, 168
Career exploration, 7
  units, 268
Career guidance center, 17

Career preparation, 16
  radio-television service, 420
Careers, in elementary school, 9
Cardinal Principles of Secondary Education, 216
Carin, Arthur A., 330
Carrel, plan for, 382
Carrel arcades, 113
Catalogs, 173
Center for Vocational and Technical Education, resources of, 160
Change —
  necessary elements, 3
  producing, 2
  in seventies, 1
Characteristics, of teacher, 305
Characterizing by value, 209
Checklists —
  to evaluate teacher demonstrations, 356
  for self-evaluation, 345
Child care, teacher's unit plan, 457
Childs, John L., 203, 204
Christal, Raymond E., 62
Citizenship goals, 427
Civic education, 217
Civic responsibility, 219
Class discussion, 285
Classes —
  and individualized instruction, 110
  instruction in, 115
Class session organization, 191, 196
Clerical cluster, goals, 234
Cleveland, use of auxiliary facilities, 130
Closed-circuit television, 286
Closed-loop film, 297
Classroom evaluation, 324
Clusters, 21
  career, 10, 12
  career in elementary schools, 13
  characteristics of, 46
  as content organizers, 45
  model of Oregon development, 50
  Oregon, 52
  rationale for identity, 13
  USOE and CVTE, 13
Codes —
  DOT, 162
  matching instructional and manpower, 163
  terminology, 161
Cognitive mapping, 108, 205, 207
Cognitive domain, evaluating objectives in, 330
Collegiate education, 22
Command of fundamental processes, 217

484 Planning and Organizing Instruction

Communication, of objectives, 189
Community, teacher knowledge of, 181
Community facilities, use in VAE programs, 387
Community resources, uses, 126
Commonalities, and clusters, 47
Competence —
   assessing initial, 85
   assessing students, 329
   and evaluation, 325
Competency, teacher, 353
Completion test, 474
Comprehension, 207
Computer —
   in criterion-reference test, 327
   in education, 107
Computer-based instruction, 296
Conditions, in behavioral objectives, 241, 244
Conference —
   as teaching method, 285
   telephone, 298
Construction, 39
   information topics in IACP text, 394
   of objective tests, 334
   of subjective tests, 335
Construction cluster, Oregon, 51
Content —
   approaches to identifying, 36
   cluster commonalities, 47
   and clusters, 45
   criteria for selection, 35
   essential informational, 73
   for general vocational program, 54
   as goal, 273
   identifying and selecting, 32-81
   from instructional analysis, 67
   to meet industrial arts goals, 42
   and minority groups, 74
   Oregon cluster approach, 399
   organic curriculum guidelines, 100
   and payroll tasks, 59
   selecting, 151
   selecting applied arts, 257
   selecting to meet established goals, 41
   teachers materials for, 170
   in unit, 252
   and work tasks, 43
Continuing education, 26
Contractual VAE programs, 135
Contracts, negotiated, 165
Coordinator, of cooperative work education, 127
Cooperative work education, 127

Cooperative work-study program, aims of, 223
Correspondence courses, 21
Cost effectiveness, 313
Course, 186
   develop goals for, 227
   educational justification for, 169, 201-249
   goals and aims of education, 430
   needed instructional materials, 158-179
   students evaluate, 357
   supporting and related, 403
   unitized, 110
   units for, 170
   units for applied arts, 256
   units in vocational, 254
Course goals, 149, 188
   and program evaluation, 328
   stating, 229
Course materials —
   organization patterns, 191
   organizing for specific situation, 180-200
Course planning, first considerations, 143-157
Course of study, 144
   development chart, 230
   preface format, 426
Crafts, advisory committees, 135
Creativity, 23
Criteria, in behavioral objectives, 242, 244
Criterion-referenced evaluation, 324
   example, 326
Cumulative records, 350
Curriculum, 186, 321
   elements of, 101
   employs simulation, 290
   Oregon cluster approach, 399
   radio-television serviceman, 420
Curriculum building as process, 202
Curriculum development, goals and procedures, 34
Curriculum development model, systems approach, 86
Curriculum guide, using, 180
Curriculum plan, Oregon cluster, 404
Curriculum planning, components of, 101
Curriculum specifications, 169
Curry, Estell H., 33, 111, 121, 171, 286, 300, 308, 368, 375, 378
Cutting speeds and feeds, 417

Data, in DOT code, 163
Decision-making, career, 226

Definitions, standard terminology, 320
Delivery systems, instruction, 281-312
Democracy, goals, 427
Demonstration, 283
  evaluating, 356
  student, 439
Depth —
  of objective testing, 334
  of subjective testing, 334
Descriptive course organization, 191
Descriptive knowledge, 37
Design, 23, 276
  problem solving and individual instruction, 459
Developmental tasks, 220
Devices —
  teaching, 171, 282
  types of teaching, 301
DeWald, John E., 306
Dewey, John, 204
Diagnostic testing, 108
Die theory, units for course, 264
Differentiated staffing, 122
  roles, 125
Discrimination, and minorities, 74
Discussion, 285
Disposition, task completion action, 99
Distributive occupations, task analysis, 264
Diversified occupations, 128
DOT codes, and educational descriptions, 162
Domains, and evaluation, 330
Domains of learning, 205
  fourth, 213
Drafting, 276
  goals of, 235
  example of problem-solving plan, 459
  industrial positions, 419
Drafting media, 418
Drawings, reproduction, 419
Driver education, 204
Duration, and skill development, 210

Economic efficiency, 219
Economic order quantity, 374
Education for All American Youth, 216, 219
Education —
  aims and course goals, 430
  overall aims for, 213

  philosophy of, 227
  through life, 2
Educational aims, published, 215
Educational justification, 201-249
Educational philosophy, 146
Educational prescription, 108
Educational Sciences, The, 112
Edwards, Tryon, 307
Efficiency, 189
Elementary schools, career education, 7
Employability orientation program, 60
Employee instruction programs, 16
Employers, in career education, 14
Employment data, use in Oregon, 50
Employment stability, 62
Energy, and skill development, 210
Engineering drawing goals, and engineering department aims, 240
English, mastery and subjective tests, 335
Entry-level job skill, 12
Environment, learning, 365
  see also Facilities
Equal opportunity, goals, 427
Equipment —
  and cooperative programs, 154
  determining quantity, 367
  determining special needs for, 372
  to fit program, 366
  maintenance, 372
  planning for, 365
  service, 367
  specifying, 153, 365-392
  vs. supplies, 385
Equipment layouts, 175
Equipment lists, 174
ERIC, 159
Essay questions, examples, 476
Ethical character, 218
Evans, Rupert N., 35, 127, 128
Evaluation, 2, 207, 313-364
  and achievement, 110
  with behavioral objectives, 329
  behavioral objectives and criteria, 469
  of competence, 85
  and content, 35
  of contents, 75
  diagnostic, 108
  and domains of learning, 330
  final, 96
  and goals, 201
  input, 315
  laboratory activities, 338
  norm- and criterion-referenced, 324
  objective vs. subjective, 333
  product approach to, 317

process approach to, 317
program vs. classroom, 324
of psychological factors, 344
self, 166, 183, 345
standards for, 321
of students, 90, 189
of student work, 300
of teacher competency, 353
teacher's devices for, 335
teachers materials for, 170
of teaching, 172
and testing, 295
in unit, 252
and unit management, 253
uses of, 152
Exploration, 20
career, 7, 225, 268
stated as goal, 229
Experimentation, as method, 299

Facilities —
auxiliary, 128
and content, 35
and cooperative programs, 154
determining needed, 152
mobile, 386
planning for, 174, 365, 377
planning for future, 382
and unit, 252
use of community, 387
Facts, and objective tests, 334
Falik, Chazkel, 418
Family life education, 276
Family responsibilities, 60
Federal agencies, instructional materials from, 161
Field trip, 285
Fifties, decade of, 1
Films, 171
Film loops, 297
Filmstrips, 287
Finch, Curtis R., 295
Fine, Sidney A., 83
Fitzgerald Public Schools, basic course description, 184
Flexible modular scheduling, 115, 187
Floor plans, 175
developing, 376
Flow chart, of performance tasks, 98
Flow chart symbols, 101

Forest products cluster, goals of, 234
Form, for planning unit presentation methods, 303
Formal course organization, 191, 255
Formal knowledge, 38
Format, for course of study, 426
Forms and records, 307
teachers, 172
Fryklund, Verne C., 68, 74, 205, 256, 273
Frequency, and skill, 210

Games, in simulation, 293
Gardner, John, 319
Gayde, William F., 182
General content, 74
General education, 201
function, 203
General information topic, 418
Glaser, Robert, 324, 325
Goals —
appreciations as, 274
attitudes as, 274
compare with other courses, 228
and content, 35
course, 149, 188
develop course, 227
of education, 213
and education aims, 430
of employability orientation, 58
equipment needed to meet, 366
and evaluation, 314, 328
of industrial arts, 41
of instruction (in PEP), 110
of Michigan education, 427
planning to meet, 272
phrasing, 233
problem-solving as, 274
purposes of, 201
relate to aims, 235
role of instructional, 143
secondary school, 49
showing relationship to aims, 236
skill as, 273
stating course, 229
teaching methods to reach, 282
and units, 250, 251
and values, 273
Goals for American Education, 215
Goals of Secondary Education, 221
Goldhammer, Keith, 6, 202, 214

Goods and services, 13
Grading, of tests, 336
Green, John J., 74
Gronlund, Norman E., 206
Guidance, 20
  career, 10, 268
  as goal, 273
  stating goals of, 232
Guidance content, 74
Guide to Improving Instruction in Industrial Arts, A, 266
Guides, teacher, 167

Hampton, William, 108, 109
Handbooks, 173
Handicapped students, 25
Haroian, Henry A., 168
Havighurst, Robert J., 216, 220
Healas, Donald V., 129
Health, 216
Henry Ford Community College, course goals and education aims, 430
Herschelmann, Kathleen M., 64, 66
Hill, Joseph E., 108, 109, 111, 112
High School in a Changing World, The, 216
Hood, Paul D., 14
Home membership, 217
Home responsibilities, 60
Homework, 285
Horn, Robert E., 293
Huffman, Harry, 127, 244, 470
Human relations, teaching, 283
Human relationships, 219
Human systems, 82
Humanizing, mediated instruction, 112
Husek, J. R., 325
Hybrid systems, 82

Impellitteri, Joseph H., 295
Imperative needs of youth, 219
In-basket activity, 291
Indexes, using standard, 300
Independent study, 116, 121, 297
Individual assignment, 297
Individual instruction materials, 175
Individual study, 121

Individualized instruction, 2, 88, 276, 295
  in design and drafting, 459
  modules for, 452
Individualized Program Learning Laboratory, 113
Individual progression, 368
Individualized-task instruction packet, 64
Industrial arts —
  emphases, 19
  in VAE, 17
Industrial Arts Curriculum Project, 1, 19, 34, 37, 39, 266, 269, 394
Industrial education goals, and education goals, 239
Industrial training programs, 24
Industry —
  advisory committees, 135
  offers schools, 25
  using in VAE, 126
  using facilities of, 128
Industry-education cooperation, 77
Information —
  derived from operations analysis, 73
  as goal, 273
  stating goals for, 231
  tests of, 336
Information content, types of, 74
Information sheets, 288
Information topic, 418
  identified through instructional analysis, 412
  machine shop, 417
Information units, 255, 276
  examples, 442
Innovation, era of, 1
Input evaluation, 315
In-service education, 16
Insight, testing, 334
Instruction, 322
  adapting to situation, 181
  developing units of, 271
  emphasis in, 19
  integrating, 24
  justification of program of, 201-249
  level of, 204
  measuring, 313
  methods of, 281
  and objectives, 189
  standardization, 162
  types of, 115
Instruction modes, in systems approach, 85
Instruction sheets, 288
Instructional media, 2
Instructional area, planning, 376

488   Planning and Organizing Instruction

Instructional analysis, 54, 67, 263
  examples of, 412
  Oregon, 402
Instructional facilities, 365
Instructional materials —
  needed, 158-179, 375
  selecting applied arts, 258
  for systems approach, 85
Instructional objectives, see Behavior objectives
Instructional packages, individual, 175
Instructional program, 321
Instructional sequence, 254
Instructional supplies, uses of, 374
Instructional units, 250-280
Integration —
  in sixties, 2
  of instructional programs, 24
Interns, teacher, 122
Interview, of authority, 298
Inventory, 174
Inventory practices, 385
Item analysis, of test, 344

Job simplification, 25
Janeczko, Robert J., 241
Jelden, David L., 83, 88, 92, 96, 175, 189, 206, 296
Job analysis, 72
  use in Oregon cluster approach, 399
Job inventory plan, Air Force, 63
Job seeking, 61
Johnson, R. Gilmore, 293
Johnston, William J., 132
Joos, L. W., 326

Keppel, Francis, 319
Killam, Jacqueline, 20, 283
Kimbrell, Grady, 220
Kirchner, Robert J., 415, 417
Kirkendall, L. A., 215
Knowledge, 207
  career, 55
  classifying, 38
  domains of, 37
Knurling, operational instruction, 416

Koscierzynski, Barbara R., 148
Krathwohl, David R., 205
Kuengli, I. R., 215

Laboratories, mobile, 386
Laboratory activities, evaluating, 335, 338
Laboratory instruction, 115
  uses, 120
Laboratory units, 276
  examples, 438
Landers, Jacob, 314
Lanham, Frank W., 64, 84, 96, 100
Large group instruction, 115
  uses of, 116
Lathe —
  knurling instruction, 416
  operational analysis, 415
Leadership, teaching, 283
Learning, 322
  individual pacing of, 85
  measurement of, 313
Learning activity, types, 92
Learning Resource Center, 114
Learning skills, 187
Learning styles, 110
  and instruction, 107
Lecture, 255, 284
Leisure activities, 24
Leisure time use, 218
Length, test, 336
Lesson plans, 271
Lessons, for substitute teacher, 308
Liability, and safety tests, 338
Life skills, 187
Lifestyle goals, 9, 12
Linear program, 296
Loree, M. Ray, 213
Los Angeles, regional centers, 131
Lux, Donald G., 34, 37, 38

MacDonald, Angus J., 150
Machines —
  to fit program, 366
  operational analysis of, 415
  special needs for, 372
Machine shop, information topic, 417

Index **489**

Mager, Robert F., 208, 210, 331
Maintenance equipment, 372
Man, assumptions of nature of, 112
Management, teaching 283
Manager, teacher as, 107
Manistique, Michigan, instructional contracts, 137
Mann, Horace, 307
Manpower data, use in Oregon, 50
Manuals —
 operating, 173
 teacher, 167
Manufacturing, 39
 content of IACP text, 396
 scheduling instruction in, 270
Marketing classroom, 378
Marland, Sidney, 5, 27
Mastery, in learning, 109
Matching test, 340, 473, 475, 476
Materials —
 adapting, 181
 needed instructional, 158-179
 organizing for specific teaching situation, 180-200
McClelland, William A., 292, 294
McGivney, Joseph H., 318
Mechanism, of response, 211
Media center, 287
Mediated instruction, staff roles in, 111
Medical specialist task analysis, Air Force, 407
Medsker, Leland L., 317
Messenger, R. Terry, 147
Metal laboratory, 381
Methods —
 aids and units, 300
 and content, 35
 identifying appropriate, 282
 selecting applied arts, 257
 teachers materials for, 170
 teaching, 281-312
 as tools, 151
 in unit, 252
Methods of instruction, 281
Michigan, aims for education, 213
Michigan education goals, 427
Michigan Plan for Accountability, 315
Miller, Aaron J., 12
Minelli, Ernest L., 41, 42, 334, 344
Minority groups, and content, 74
Mobile laboratories, 386
Models, 287
 facilities, 378
 for use of simulation, 290
Model building, problem-solving plan, 459

Modular course, 255
Modular scheduling, 115
Modules, for individualized instruction, 452
Module of instruction, 191, 194, 276
 project organization, 445
 and unit, 252
Morality goals, 427
Moss, Jerome, 43, 44, 209
Motion pictures, 171
Movies, 287
Multanen, Monty E., 52
Multimedia arrangement, 379, 380
Multiple choice test, 475
Multiple activity programs, 368

National Assessment of Educational Progress, 319
National Standards for Accountability, 320
Natural systems, 82
Necker's cube, 306
Needs, and instruction, 322
Neff, Frederick C., 149
Nichols, Daryl G., 55, 319
NOBELS analysis, 266
NOBELS project, 64
NOBELS study, 96
Norm-referenced evaluation, 325
Novosad, John P., 107
Nunney, Derek N., 108, 109, 110
Nursing, aims of, 224

Oakland County curriculum program, 420
Oakland Community College, 107
 individualized program (PEP), 112
Objectives —
 affective domain, 208
 behavioral, 151
 career development, 56
 cognitive domain, 207
 and content, 35
 content and method, 322
 and evaluation, 314, 317
 evaluating affective, 330
 evaluating cognitive, 330
 evaluating psychomotor, 332
 for general capabilities, 55

in Oregon cluster approach, 400
psychomotor domain, 210
statement of, 90
stating behavioral, 241
and unit, 252
Objective evaluation, 333
Objective tests, teacher made, 473
Objectivity, of tests, 336
Occupational analysis, 52, 165
Occupational centers, 131
Occupational development, 21
general, 55
Occupational programs, accreditation, 323
Occupational specialty courses, Oregon cluster, 404
Occupational surveys, 32, 165
Office occupations —
systems approach applied, 96
task analysis, 64
Olsen, Jerry C., 47, 48
Open labs, 121
Operations —
analyzing, 72
describing, 71
identified with instructional analysis, 412
in manipulative work, 68
Operation sheets, 288
Operational drills, 438
Operational units, 255
Oregon —
content clusters, 48
goals of clerical clusters, 234
Oregon cluster approach, specifying curriculum and content, 399
Oregon clerical cluster, analysis, 263
Oregon metals cluster, 266
Oregon Plan, model, 52
Organic curriculum theory, 100
Organization —
psychomotor, 212
world of construction, 395
Organization patterns, course materials, 191
Organizational and administrative strategies, 107-142
Organizing, 209
Organizing materials, for specific course, 180-200
Orientation, career, 225
Orthographic projection test, 341
Osborn, William C., 55, 58, 59
Overt response, 211

PACER, evaluation system, 326
Panel discussion, 285
Paraprofessionals, 122, 125
Parnell, Dale, 48, 49
People, in DOT code, 163
Perception, 210
Performance —
and affective learnings, 331
levels of, 243
measuring, 317
supervised, 284
Performance objectives, **see** Behavioral objectives
Periodicals, 173
Persons, Edgar, 293
Personalized approach to education, 107
Personalized Educational Program, 108
Peterson, Robert, 14
Petrequin, Gaynor, 119
Philosophy, gives direction to education, 146
Philosophy of education, 227
Physical education, 204
Pittsburgh, cluster, concept in, 47
Plan —
course of study as, 144
example teacher's, 457
nature of instructional, 143
for term's work, 170
Planning —
instructional area, 376
materials for early, 158
programing, budgeting systems, 318
and systems approach, 154
unit instructional methods, 303
units, 271
Planning sheets, 288, 298
student, 173
Policies for Education in American Democracy, 215
Popham, W. James, 325
Post-high-school education, 16
Post-secondary career education, 16
Power Mechanics —
goals, 150
units, 267
Practical nursing, aims for, 224
Praxiological knowledge, 38
Praxiology, as basis for content selection, 37
Preparation, career, 16, 226, 250
Preplanning, materials needed for, 158
Preplanning materials, reviewing, 180
Prescription, educational, 108
Prescriptive knowledge, 37

Prevocational education, 54
Principles —
  of career education, 226
  of evaluation, 313
Problem solving, 276
  in design and drafting, 459
  evaluating, 338
Problem-solving abilities, 22
Problem-solving experiences, 274
Process, task actions, 99
Process approach to evaluation, 317
Product approach, to evaluation, 317
Product maintenance, 439
Professional development, 21
Program —
  dictates equipment and supplies, 366
  educational justification of, 201-249
  entry to training, 169
  evaluation of, 328
  instructional, 321
  planning future, 382
Program development, 1
Program evaluation, 324
Program planning, first
  considerations, 143-157
Programed instruction, 295
Programed texts, 113
Projects, 438
  evaluating, 300
  in instruction, 299
  instructional analysis of, 412
  modules of instruction for, 445
  team and individual, 439
Project evaluation form, 346
Projecturals, 171
Proprietary schools, 16, 21
  contract with public, 136
Psychomotor domain, 206
  and action-pattern domain, 213
  evaluating objectives, 332
Psychomotor objectives, 210
Pupil, 323
  see also Student
Purchasing, 384
Purposes of Education in American Democracy, 215, 218

Radio-television service curriculum, 420
Rationale, importance to learner, 90
Ray, Willis E., 37, 38

Reading assignments, 286
Receiving, 208
Record keeping, and evaluation, 314
Records and forms, 307
  teachers, 172
Reeves, F., 215
Reference materials, 173
Regional occupational centers, 131
Reliability —
  of objective tests, 334
  of subjective tests, 335
  test, 336
Repetition, meaningful, 70
Reports —
  presenting, 300
  as teaching method, 300
  team and individual, 439
Research —
  equipment for, 372
  instructional analysis as, 68
  student, 297
  use in preplanning course, 159
Resnick, Harold S., 83, 86, 116, 117, 293, 315
Responding, 208
Response —
  guided, 210
  psychomotor, 211
Ressler, Ralph, 376
Review, 284
Richey, Rita C., 290
Robertson, F. W., 307
Role, in work, 43
Role playing, 289
Rose, O. Karl, 355
Rotation systems, multiple activity programs, 368
Royster, Rosetta L., 66
Rudisill, Alvin E., 382
Rural areas, retraining adults, 17
Ryan, Maurine E., 470

Safety, 253
  materials for, 171
Safety conscious person, 331
Safety tests, 335, 337
  examples, 478
Salatino, Anthony J., 319
Sampieri, Robert A., 13
Schedule, daily, 269

Scheduling —
  instruction, 266
  Oregon cluster, 405
School —
  develops aims, 222
  teacher knowledge of, 182
Scientific method, 275
Scoring —
  of objective tests, 334
  subjective tests, 335
Screens, portable, 383
Secondary school, career education, 10
Selection, of instructional materials, 375
Self, knowledge of, 8
Self-education, 16
Self-evaluation, student, 345
Self-evaluation sheet, 347, 349
Self-realization, 218, 221
Selvidge, Robert W., 68, 288
Service equipment, 373
Service machine, 367
Services and goods, 13
Session plan, 255
Set (readiness), 210
Silvius, G. Harold, 33, 111, 121, 171, 286, 289, 300, 308, 368, 375, 378
Simms, Eugene, 136
Simplicity, of tests, 336
Simpson, Elizabeth J., 205, 206, 213
Simulation, 290
  in leadership development, 293
  types, 291
Sipes, Theodore L., 148
Sixties, change in, 2
Sjorgren, Douglass, 46
Skills —
  career, 55
  development of, 69, 206
  evaluating, 332
  as goal, 428
  of learning, 187
  stating as goal, 229
  teaching, 273
  types of career, 56, 57
Skill development, 210
Slides, 287
Small group instruction, 115
  uses of, 117
Smith, Brandon B., 43, 44, 309
Smith, Howard, 136, 386
Social effectiveness, 221
Sociodrama, 291
Soule, David H., 326
Special educational needs, 24
Specialists, in differentiated staffing, 122

Specifications, preparing, 174
Specialized education, 202
Spoilage, and supplies, 374
Staff —
  and curriculum building, 202
  for individual instruction, 110
  for individualized program, 112
  role in mediated instruction, 111
Staffing, differentiated, 122
Standards, in behavioral objectives, 244
Stern, Jacob, 37
Stolurow, Lawrence M., 296
Strategies, organizational and administrative, 107-142
Strong, Merle E., 324
Students —
  committee research, 297
  construct teaching aid, 299
  and criterion-referenced evaluation, 327
  determine needs of, 228
  educational prescription for, 108
  in evaluation, 313
  evaluation with behavioral objectives, 329
  evaluation of learning, 317
  evaluate teacher, 353
  and general education, 203
  individual instruction, 295
  learning skills of, 187
  participates in evaluation, 342
  planning instruction for, 181
  in program, 322
  role in class, 253
  roles in differentiated staffing, 125
  scheduling, 266
  self-evaluation, 345
  and self rating, 350
  teacher knowledge of, 182
  test performance of, 344
  and unscheduled time, 121
Student-directed organization, 121, 152, 170, 253, 283, 369
Student learning goals, 427
Students with special needs, 25
Student study guides, 296
Study carrels, 113
  plan, 382
Study guides, 174, 288, 296
Subject, 186
Subjective evaluation, 333
Subjective tests, 334
Substitute teacher, plan for, 172
Subsystem, 83
Sund, Robert B., 330
Supervised performance, 284

Index

Supplies —
  estimating needs, 373
  specifying, 365-392
  vs. equipment, 385
Supply lists, 174
Suprasystem, 83
Surveys —
  occupational, 32, 165
  occupational, questions, 33
Symbols, flow chart, 101
Synthesis, 207
Systems —
  for accountability, 315
  for planning aids and methods in unit, 300
  PPBS, 318
Systems approach, 82-106, 318
  and accountability, 315
  concomitants of, 101
  curriculum development model, 86
  definition, 82
  to develop program, 154
  in education, 83
  learner controlled packets, 88
  NOBELS, 96
  and units, 252

Take home project, 299
Takis, John C., 125, 415, 417
Tasks —
  clerical (Oregon cluster), 264
  in Oregon cluster approach, 400
  statements of, 100
  in work role, 44
Task analysis, 190, 264, 266
  Air Force, 62
  Air Force medical specialists, 407
  office occupations, 64
  Oregon, 401
Task-competency analysis, 52, 53
Taxonomy —
  affective domain, 208
  cognitive domain, 207
Taxonomies of objectives, 205
Taylor, Robert E., 6, 202, 214
Teacher aide, 122, 125
Teacher competency, in evaluation, 314
Teacher guides, 167
Teacher-made tests, 335
  examples, 473
Teacher rating sheet, 355, 356, 357

Teachers —
  contracts of, 165
  develop aims, 222
  competency evaluation of, 353
  notes for instruction, 272
  plan for substitute, 307
  planning information needed, 182
  role of, 107
  role in mediated instruction, 111
  role in small group, 119
Teachers cummulative record, 351
Teachers plan, example, 457
Teaching, 322
  measuring, 313
  planning the methods of, 298
Teaching aids, 171, 193, 281
  constructing, 299
Teaching machines, 295
Teaching order, 255
Teaching plans, 170
Teaching systems, 281-312
Teaching techniques, 281-312
Teaching time, 267
Technical content, 74
Technical reports, as method, 300
Techniques —
  describing teaching, 305
  teaching, 282
Technology —
  educational, 109, 111
  understanding, 23
Telephone technology, units for, 259
Televised instruction, 286
Terminology —
  for instruction, 160
  standard, 320
Text materials, 173
Test questions, validity of, 344
Testing, 295
Test —
  entry and exit, 328
  examples, 473
  examples of safety, 478
  interpreting and using results, 344
  objective, 333
  for student competency, 172
  teacher, 335
  types of, 325, 329
  qualities of, 336
  written, 336
Things, in DOT code, 163
Thiokol, 135
Time —
  and subjective tests, 335
  and teaching methods, 305

Planning and Organizing Instruction

Time effectiveness, 313
Toolmaker, instructional analysis of trade, 413
Tools —
  determining number needed, 369
  extra, 373
  and operations, 70
  system for, 253
  vs. equipment, 386
Towers, Edward R., 37
Trades —
  analysis, 165
  instructional analysis of, 413
Trailers, as facilities, 386
Traister, Leon, 212
Transfer, of simulation experience, 293
Transparencies, 2, 287
True-false test, 474
Twelker, Paul E., 293
Tyler, Ralph, 319

Unified vocational program, 1
Uniqueness, 250
Units —
  aids and methods for, 300
  business and office machines, 434
  course, 170
  developing, 271
  evaluating, 300
  examples of, 275
  examples of information, 442
  examples of laboratory, 438
  instructional, 250-280
  planned to meet goals, 272
  planning instructional procedures, 303
  planning teaching procedures for, 298
  scheduling, 266, 269
  scheduling multiple activity, 270
  sequence of, 254
  teachers, 196
  teaching time, 267
  VAE, 258
Unit of instruction, 251
  administrative, 252

VAE, 1
  accreditation, 323
  auxiliary facilities, 129
  contractual programs, 135
  cooperative programs, 127
  development, 3
  emphasis in instruction, 19
  and industrial arts, 18
  involving community resources, 126
Validity, test, 336
Values —
  and course goals, 151
  and education, 149
  as goals, 273
Valuing, 208
Videotape, 286
Vineyard, Ben S., 220
Visual materials, 171
Vocational and Applied Arts Education, see VAE
Vocational vs. academic education, 34
Vocational competency, 217
WIN Orientation Training Program, 59
Wagschal, Peter, 122, 123
Wiegman, Robert, 469
Williams, J. Earl, 25
Work attitudes, 58
Work habits, 57
Work sheet, as test, 342, 343
Work stations, determining number 367
Work Study, 128
  aims of, 223
Work Tasks, as content base, 43
World of Construction —
  content, 394
  teaching plan, 395
World of Manufacturing —
  course design, 398
  textbook content, 396
Worthington, Robert M., 7
Worthy home membership, 217

Youth, imperative needs of, 219
Youth-Tutor-Youth, 114

Zuckerman, David W., 293